Special Edition

Using

Linux, Sixth Edition

David Bandel

Robert Napier

201 W. 103rd Street
Indianapolis, Indiana 46290

TRADEMARKS

WARNING AND DISCLAIMER

Associate Publisher
Jeff Koch

Acquisitions Editor
Gretchen Ganser

Development Editor
Maureen A. McDaniel

Technical Editor
Erik Ratcliffe

Managing Editor
Thomas F. Hayes

Project Editor
Karen S. Shields

Copy Editor
Cynthia Fields

Indexer
Kelly Castell

Proofreader
Harvey Stanbrough

Team Coordinator
Vicki Harding

Interior Designer
Ruth Lewis

Cover Designers
Dan Armstrong
Ruth Lewis

Production
Lizbeth Patterson

CONTENTS

ABOUT THE AUTHORS

David Bandel earned a Master of Aviation Management from Embry-Riddle Aeronautical University in 1989 at Ft. Campbell, Kentucky. He retired from 20 years in the Army in February, 1996. While on active duty, he learned many of the basics of UNIX working on DEC 5000s running Ultrix and SUN SparcStations running SunOS 4. He has worked on a variety of systems and architectures, including Sparc Solaris, HP-UX, AIX, and SCO OpenServer. In 1993, he began dabbling with Linux, a hobby that quickly grew on him. Currently, David is semi-retired and living in the Republic of Panama where he writes, does Linux/UNIX consulting, and works on his farm. He co-authored Que's *Special Edition Using OpenLinux*. He can be reached at `david@pananix.com`.

Robert Napier has been playing in and around Linux since about 1995. His current pet project is keeping up with KDE2 development. Professionally, he has spent most of his time developing software and supporting various UNIX-like systems. Currently he spends most of his time supporting Perl and writing scripts in RTP for Cisco Systems, spending what time he can to write books on the side. Rob also co-authored *Special Edition Using Linux, Fifth Edition*. Robert can be reached at `rnapier@employees.org`.

DEDICATION

David Bandel: Dedicated to my wife, Silvia, my children, and the entire Linux community.

Robert Napier: To Janet, who kept my life in order during this distraction.

ACKNOWLEDGMENTS

David Bandel: Special thanks go to a number of folks who've made this book possible. First and foremost, to my wife, who still doesn't understand deep hack mode, but tolerates it anyway. Without her support, none of this would have been possible. Thanks also to Erik Ratcliffe at Caldera for his help and diligence in technical editing the book. Erik not only contributed his talent for technical review, but also acted as liaison with some of Caldera's engineers who like to surprise us all with changes. Thanks to the folks on the Caldera mailing list. They remind me daily how bewildering all this can be to Linux newbies. They also remind me just how small the world really is, and how diverse and widespread the Linux community has become.

Thanks to all the software programmers, particularly the kernel hackers who've made all this possible, a number of whom who have slipped out of deep hack mode long enough to respond to questions about their code, including Richard Gooch (devfs) and Rusty Russell (netfilter). Thanks also to the entire Linux community, especially the recent converts to Linux.

We are grateful also to Macmillan, particularly Gretchan Ganser and Maureen McDaniel and their team, for wanting to publish a reference like this and putting up with this author's nits.

Robert Napier: First and foremost, I would like to thank my wife, Janet. Many months ago, when we were first considering this project, I said that it would probably take over all of my "home" time. She told me to take care of the writing and she would take care of the rest. True to her word, she has, and it's meant much more to the success of this book than any of my meager writing talents.

Because this is my first time as a lead author, I would like to thank the man who got me started in this business, Steve Burnett. Steve gave me my first break by allowing me to write a couple of chapters for the fifth edition of this book. His continuing advice and assistance since then has been invaluable to my career as an author.

I would also like to thank my co-author, David Bandel. I'm really glad that at least one of us knew what we were doing.

Since my first writing assignment for Macmillan Publishing, I have worked several times with Gretchen Ganser and Maureen McDaniel. During this book in particular, they have been incredibly helpful in keeping me organized, on time, and in the right direction. At the same time, they have shown incredible flexibility and patience with me. Thank you.

Finally, I would like to acknowledge all the incredible open-source developers out there. In particular, I have had the pleasure of following the KDE2 project very closely over many months now. These guys have done a much better job of managing all the conflicting interests of features versus schedules and stability than most of the software companies I've worked with. Thanks to groups like this one and many others like it, the world is finally learning what we've known all along: open source works.

TELL US WHAT YOU THINK!

As the reader of this book, *you* are our most important critic and commentator. We value your opinion and want to know what we're doing right, what we could do better, what areas you'd like to see us publish in, and any other words of wisdom you're willing to pass our way.

As an associate publisher for Sams, I welcome your comments. You can fax, email, or write me directly to let me know what you did or didn't like about this book—as well as what we can do to make our books stronger.

Please note that I cannot help you with technical problems related to the topic of this book, and that due to the high volume of mail I receive, I might not be able to reply to every message.

When you write, please be sure to include this book's title and author as well as your name and phone or fax number. I will carefully review your comments and share them with the author and editors who worked on the book.

Fax: 317-581-4666
Email: quetechnical@macmillanusa.com
Mail: Associate Publisher
         Que
         201 West 103rd Street
         Indianapolis, IN 46290 USA

INTRODUCTION

In this introduction

LINUX TODAY

For those of you who haven't been hiding under a rock during the past few years, you almost couldn't help hearing about Linux. It has been in all the tabloids, magazines, even on TV and radio news. Several Linux companies have gone public with stocks trading on the open market, and some have even bought out other companies. One historic purchase happened when Caldera Systems bought most of the Santa Cruz Operation (SCO) that sold SCO OpenServer and SCO UnixWare.

All this is a long way for a previous guerrilla operating system to come. Introduced little by little through the back door into the Fortune 1000 companies and other places, Linux gained management attention and recognition with uptimes and reliability Microsoft could only dream of. At first these companies hid their use of Linux, often denying they used the "little OS that could." But servers sitting on the Internet are hard to hide, as are systems administrators proud that they could solve a problem the company had been struggling with for a long time unsuccessfully with Microsoft products. Little things, such as the entire network of Cisco Systems print servers running on Linux. Success stories like these can be stifled for just so long.

Now some of these Fortune 1000 companies openly support Linux. Many are eschewing other operating systems in favor of Linux for a number of specialized uses. Linux is now being used in embedded systems (Adomo), in palm-top systems (Yopy), in servers, and even in massive parallel processing systems—sometimes called Beowulf clusters—that rival some of the biggest supercomputers in the world. If you look in the list of the Top 500 Supercomputers (`http://netlib2.cs.utk.edu/benchmark/top500/top500.list.html`), you'll probably find still listed the Avalon Beowulf cluster at the Los Alamos National Laboratory. Finally, Linux can be used where a Real-Time kernel is required. Linux can handle many tasks.

Linux can also run on many different types of hardware. Almost everyone knows that Linux can run on an Intel Pentium processor. But just about anything from a 386 on up is fair game. Linux also runs on Alphas, on some SUN hardware (both 32- and 64-bit systems), on PowerPCs, and a variety of others. Developmental support is also available for the Intel 64-bit architecture (IA64). Some experimental porting has also been done to a VMS VAX. Got an old 32-bit or bigger system lying around gathering dust? Linux might be able to breathe new life into that old hardware.

But don't let this fool you. Linux isn't a do-it-all system (yet). Although it scales better than its competition and runs on more different platforms and architectures than any other OS in the world, it still isn't up to the job in a few areas. Specifically, Linux can't replace the UNIX "big-iron." It doesn't scale well enough to stand up to industrial-strength usage that might be given to some of the big UNIX boxes. One reason is that Linux hasn't incorporated support for NUMA (an architecture where the access times for different regions of memory from a processor varies according to the "distance" of the memory region from the processor). Although this support is necessary for large multiprocessor systems with gigabytes of RAM memory, it makes small systems excruciatingly slow.

But that leaves many areas where Linux can still make work and grow. The home and business desktop is one area where Linux growth is set to explode in the next few years. With every new software product that's ported to Linux, that's one less reason for users not to switch their desktops. When the few remaining holdouts do port to Linux, expect to see the desktop arena start to change dramatically.

Now, products abound for Linux, sufficient products for almost any need, in almost any category you can think of: office suites (word processing, spreadsheets, databases, personal information managers, email), games, educational software, SQL servers, you name it.

So what has held Linux back from the home and desktop market to date? For one thing, the average user will explore exactly what comes on the computer system he or she brings home from the local computer shop or Electronics World. These users know very little except that if they turn the system on and click whatever button looks likely to offer them something, they might be able to find a game or a word processor. They are unaware that choices exist.

More specifically, they are unaware that Linux is an operating system (*What's an operating system?*) that could be installed and used on their new computer (*You can do that? Put another operating system on a computer? How?*). The OEMs up to now have been no friend of Linux either. Until it became clear that Microsoft was going to lose the trial on charges of being a monopoly, even the biggest OEMs feared Microsoft enough to only offer one operating system. This too is changing, albeit slowly.

Several large OEMs (IBM and Dell to name two) now offer servers with Linux, and even desktop machines can be ordered this way (though with desktops and laptops you have to know to ask for it).

Still, Linux rates as one of the fastest growing operating systems in the world for one reason: It works. There's a lot to be said for marketing hype. It can confuse and bewilder. But after the hype is revealed for what it is, users choose what works.

A WORD ABOUT HARDWARE

Before you rush out and buy Linux to install on your system, you might want to take some time to see whether your distribution of choice will support, out of the box, the hardware that you have.

One of the most frustrating things for newcomers to Linux is that in all the excitement of trying out this great new operating system, they forget to see whether the hardware they intend to use it on is supported.

Windows NT cannot be installed on all hardware; some is just not supported. Ditto for nearly every operating system in the world. Not all hardware vendors support Linux; some disdain this operating system, so expect no support from them. Also expect either no drivers, or drivers that work only marginally well. Older hardware is more likely to have the required support. Newer hardware might or might not, depending on the particular manufacturer. So look before you buy.

ABOUT THIS BOOK

This edition of *Special Edition Using Linux* actually started life as the second edition of *Special Edition Using Caldera OpenLinux*. As such, this book is still somewhat Caldera-centric. But the authors have taken pains to see that Debian and Red Hat were included when the plans for this text changed.

That doesn't mean you need to run Caldera or Debian or Red Hat to get something out of this book. In fact, it almost doesn't matter what Linux distribution you choose. This book will provide insights into your own particular distribution choice. So whether you use SuSE, Mandrake, Corel, or even Slackware, this text has something for you. In fact, over 90% of this text is distribution non-specific, but decidedly Linux-centric. Covering specifics of all the distributions on the market would be a difficult task, and in the end, would only result in a lot of text repeating itself.

As you'll see while reading through this book, only a few things differentiate Linux distributions, installation, system administration, software package management, software package selection, system initialization, and philosphical bent. The kernel is (for all intents and purposes) the same. The major pieces are the same. Most software packages are exactly the same. So don't fret the small stuff; look to see what's different where, and see how it still all works the same.

This book is written to the not-yet-released 2.4.x kernel, and the latest unstable software snapshots available. So what you see might not be exactly what is described in the text, but should be valuable to you for a number of insights for the next few years (at least until v 2.6 or 3.0 comes out).

By the time this book is on the shelves, however, you should be able to judge how well the authors predicted the future, even though the future looked fairly stable while it was being written about.

Also for the first time, *Special Edition Using Linux* is published *sans* CD-ROMs. This decision was made so as to not do a disservice to either the book or its audience by providing something that wasn't ready for prime time. (Only Caldera's Linux Technology Preview was released with the 2.4.0test3 kernel, a kernel which is significantly different from any of the test6 and beyond kernels) or wasn't completely in step with the book (that is, a kernel version 2.2.x).

Additionally, the authors are committed to maintaining a Web site to update material in this book to make it as useful as possible throughout the life of the 2.4.x kernel.

WHO SHOULD USE THIS BOOK?

Anyone who is contemplating installing Linux for the first time should read through this book and keep it handy after their install. Any new Linux systems administrators or UNIX administrators who are not considered gurus or wizards will benefit from using this book.

This book is aimed at the beginning, intermediate, and in some cases, advanced systems administrators who need a reference to most aspects of running and administering Linux.

WHO SHOULD NOT USE THIS BOOK?

If you are a Linux kernel hacker or a UNIX guru, this book might not be up to your expectations. This book is a great resource if you want to know more about Linux and UNIX but have never been involved with either operating system as anything more than a user.

This book will not go into a fairly large number of extremely complex, but mostly "niche" topics, such as the use of iproute2 to do bandwidth limiting, ingress and egress queuing, and the like. Nor will it cover security in any great detail. Some of the topics covered in the book also have conveniently ignored aspects considered either too advanced or too detailed to be covered completely, such as network netmasks that don't correspond to the /nn designations. You will find books devoted to the subject of networking, which here has dedicated only one, albeit large, chapter, as well as to a number of other specialized areas of knowledge covered for basic and intermediate orientation and reference in this book.

However, even if you know how to install Linux and maneuver around in UNIX, you might still find this book of use, particularly if you are only a UNIX user and have never had the chance to perform system administration tasks. Several sections of the book explain the finer points of system administration and how to maintain a Linux/UNIX system. Typically, a normal UNIX user does not perform these system administration tasks, but with Linux, you are the system administrator, free to do whatever you want to do!

Now, if you don't have a clue what a computer is or what a floppy disk looks like, you might want to brush up on some computer basics before tackling Linux. Linux isn't for everyone, but there's little reason why it shouldn't be.

CONVENTIONS USED IN THIS BOOK

This book uses several special conventions that you need to become familiar with. These conventions are listed here for your reference:

- Linux is a *case-sensitive* operating system; that means when this book instructs you to type something at a command or shell prompt, you must type exactly what appears in the book, exactly as it is capitalized.

- This book uses a `monospaced typeface` for Linux commands to set them off from standard text.

- If you're instructed to type something, what you are to type also appears in `monospaced text`. For example, if the book gives the instruction "Enter `cat`," you must press the letters *c*, *a*, and *t* and then press the Enter key.

- Keys are sometimes pressed in combination; when this is the case, the keys are presented like this:

Ctrl+h

This example implies that you must press and hold the Ctrl key, press the *h* key, and then release both keys.

Note

This book uses a convention for key names that might vary from what you are accustomed to. To avoid confusion in the case-sensitive UNIX environment, this book uses lowercase letters to refer to keys when uppercase letters might be the norm. For example, this book uses the form Ctrl+c instead of the form Ctrl+C (the latter form might make some readers wonder whether they should press Ctrl and Shift and *c*).

- Some sample listings show a portion of the screen after you type a specific command. These listings show the command prompt or shell prompt—usually a dollar sign ($)—followed by what you type in **bold monospace**. Don't type the dollar sign when you follow the example on your own system. Consider this example:

```
$ lp report.txt &
3146
$
```

You should type only what appears in **bold** on the first line (that is, type lp report.txt & and then press Enter). The rest of the listing shows Linux's response to the command.

- When discussing the syntax of a Linux command, this book uses some special formatting to distinguish between the required portions and the variable portions. Consider the following example:

lp *filename*

In this syntax, the *filename* portion of the command is a variable; that is, it changes depending on what file you actually want the lp command to work with. The lp is required because it's the actual command name. Variable information is presented in *italic monospace*; information that must be typed exactly is not in italic.

- In some cases, command information is optional; that is, it's not required for the command to work. Square brackets ([]) enclose optional parts of the command syntax. Consider the following example:

lp *filename* [*device1*] [abc]

Here, lp is the command name and is neither optional nor variable. The *device1* parameter is both variable and optional (it is in italic and enclosed in square brackets); this means that you can type any device name in place of *device1* (without the brackets), or you can type nothing at all for that parameter. The abc parameter is optional (you don't have to use it if you don't want to), but it's not variable; if you use it, you must type it exactly as it appears in the book—again, without the brackets.

- Tips, Notes, and Cautions appear throughout the book in special formats to make the information they contain easy to locate. Longer discussions not integral to the flow of the chapter are set aside as sidebars with their own headings.

PART

I

INTRODUCTION TO LINUX

CHAPTER 1

WHAT IS LINUX?

In this chapter

WHAT IS LINUX?

Linux is based on the UNIX operating system. It must be made clear that Linux is not UNIX, though. It is its own operating system, with its own nuances, its own quirks, and its own special features. It was written from the ground up by hundreds of developers spanning the globe, with the majority of the development taking place over the Internet.

The original idea behind Linux germinated in the early 1990s, at the Helsinki University Technology in Finland, by a Swedish student named Linus Torvalds. What began in 1991 as a project to provide an alternative to the Minix operating system became something of a movement when the first ALPHA grade Linux systems—generally in the form of a *root* and a *boot* disk—made their way to the Internet. Back then the number of Linux users could have been counted in the dozens, but that soon changed.

Within a few years, the Linux development team, having expanded to include not only driver and kernel developers, but also software developers and enthusiasts who worked feverishly to port open-source UNIX software to Linux, had gained significant attention from the computer industry.

Soon, what was considered a typical Linux system grew to the point of being unwieldy and difficult to maintain. Eventually, groups of people started pooling their efforts to create what are known as Linux *distributions*, or predefined sets of software packaged with the Linux operating system. These were typically distributed on disks and accompanied by some sort of installation utility. Early distributions such as SLS and Slackware quickly became popular among Linux enthusiasts for their relative ease of installation and frequent updates. By coincidence, the prices of CD-ROM drives dropped at about the same time that these early distributions were gaining popularity, and CD-ROMs quickly became the preferred (almost standard) media for Linux distributions. Today, distributions that are made to be installed from disks are rare. It is notable, however, the there are still distributions of Linux that fit on one or two floppy disks. While these are generally used for recovery, or occasionally to boot a diskless workstation, it is important to recognize that the Linux kernel and the parts required to get a working system are just a small part of a distribution.

For a while it seemed that everyone wanted to make his or her own Linux distribution. For the most part, these distributions differed only in the sets of software that they included. As time passed, the various distributions diversified their offerings, sometimes adding software written for the distributions themselves (such as packaging utilities and graphic interfaces) in an effort to differentiate themselves from the rest. Some offered subscriptions, where you get quarterly updates for a set yearly fee; others added technical support and moved in a more commercial direction. In time, even commercial software packages that had been ported to Linux were included, adding to Linux's commercial viability.

Many of the original distributions still exist, but they are mostly used by hobbyists and in academic scenarios. There is currently only a handful of actual commercially produced and supported Linux distributions.

Tip

Various Web sites that contain more information on the history and development of Linux are available, such as http://www.linux.org. See Appendix B, "Finding More Information on Linux," if you want to locate other sources of Linux history.

Note

One of the most confusing—and pointless—arguments that has ensued within the Linux community involves how to pronounce Linux. However you pronounce it is fine, but the official pronunciation sounds like "lint-tux" without the Ts. To hear Linus Torvalds, the original author of Linux, pronounce "Linux," type the following on Red Hat and similar distributions:

```
$ play /usr/share/sndconfig/sample.au
```

LINUX DISTRIBUTIONS

If you end up participating in online Linux discussions through mail lists, newsgroups, or Internet relay chat (IRC) channels, or even if you just read Linux publications such as *Linux Journal*, there is one term you will undoubtedly see repeated: Linux community.

Despite the incredible evolution Linux has experienced over the last few years, there is still a very real sense of community surrounding Linux and its users. The spirit of sharing and helping others without asking for anything in return is still prevalent and has even won the Linux community awards for providing the best technical support in the computer industry. The majority of Linux users believe that by sharing with others, they will ultimately be rewarded in other ways. The same applies to commercial distributions of Linux. What goes around comes around, so supporting commercial distributions of Linux results in the production of more contributions to Linux development.

In some realms of the Linux community, the term *community* can be stretched a bit. Arguments over whose distribution is better have been elevated by some to the level of religion. This has proven to be somewhat unhealthy for Linux in general, especially when articles that are not favorable to one distribution or another are written. A rather vocal minority of Linux users have tended to respond with an unfair degree of venom, causing yet more bad press and creating a snowball effect.

Note

Although a great deal of community spirit is felt within the Linux community, this same community can be its own worst enemy when dealing with individuals who use or advocate any other operating system. The animosity displayed toward users of alternative operating systems does more harm than good to the Linux community overall. If you become a Linux advocate, please read the Linux Advocacy HOW-TO (http://www.linuxdoc.org/HOWTO/mini/Advocacy.html) before becoming embroiled in a "get a clue" debate. This same tolerance should be displayed for those using alternative distributions as well as alternative operating systems.

It is with this in mind that I say that you must not read the following as implying anything detrimental toward any particular Linux distribution. Comparisons made here are just that—comparisons. Linux users are members of the Linux community, and as members they acknowledge that part of what makes Linux so great is that there is variety, and that whatever helps one distribution will ultimately help others. The differences give users choices, and choice is what differentiates Linux from the rest of today's popular operating systems. This is something to celebrate, not something to be used to fuel fires.

CALDERA OPENLINUX

Caldera Systems sells two flavors of OpenLinux: an end-user–targeted version generally called OpenLinux eDesktop OpenLinux and a server version called OpenLinux eServer.

Special attention was made to usability and functionality in OpenLinux. For instance, the desktop environment, although not a clone of Windows95/98/NT, is probably familiar enough to make migration from Windows systems relatively painless—at least from a *graphical user interface (GUI)* standpoint. The sharp edges that plague many other Linux distributions have been smoothed down to make OpenLinux more usable, yet power users who like command prompts still have access to the guts of the system, just as they always have.

OpenLinux has perhaps the most user-friendly installer on the market, with very easy to understand dialogs and some clever features (like a video game you can play while waiting for the install to finish). It also includes a wonderful Web-based configuration utility, Webmin.

It provides fewer packages than many distributions, and the packages tend to be the older, most stable versions. This is a good and bad thing. Fewer packages means fewer ways to do the same thing (which means less confusion for new users). It also means that OpenLinux can ensure a higher level of integration and more stable software than many distributions. On the other hand, OpenLinux tends to be behind the curve in terms of cutting-edge packages. If you want a rock-solid, easy to configure distribution, then OpenLinux is a great choice. But if you want to live more on the technological edge, OpenLinux might be too tame for your tastes. As with all things in the Linux world, this seems to be changing, and the next releases of OpenLinux may very well be more aggressive.

RED HAT

In the early days of Caldera, they sold a Linux package called Caldera Network Desktop. This system was essentially Red Hat's version 2.1 distribution with some commercial enhancements that provided NetWare connectivity and a graphical drag-and-drop desktop, among other things. Some of the early development of Red Hat's RPM packaging utility and some of the graphic administration utilities were originally produced with financial help from Caldera, primarily for the release of Caldera Network Desktop (of course, Red Hat used these updated utilities in their distribution as well).

This particular system was only released once. After version 1.0 was sold for a few years, Red Hat and Caldera amiably parted ways. Since then, Red Hat has gone on to become one of the most popular Linux distributions available. Many of the utilities that were used in their early distributions (including the RPM packaging utility and some of the graphic administration utilities) have persevered and are still included in their distributions today.

Red Hat traditionally focused on the cutting-edge market, appealing to individual users, hobbyists, and hackers. In recent years, however, this has changed. Red Hat has become a very commercially savvy company, focused on business partnerships and support contracts. Red Hat is a de facto standard in many circles, and is often the distribution that commercial software vendors support first. Rational's Clearcase, a critical tool for software configuration management at leading companies such as Cisco Systems and Nortel, is now sold for Linux. Rational only supports it on Red Hat 6.2, though. Linux is no longer only for free software, as a look at Clearcase's licensing costs will assure you.

DEBIAN

Originally started as the *Free Software Foundation's (FSF)* official distribution of Linux, the Debian project has since broken off from the FSF and become an independent entity. Debian still has strong ties with the FSF, and its members are among the most diligent at protecting Open Source software.

Instead of RPM, Debian uses a package management system known as dpkg. The general idea behind dpkg is similar to that of RPM, but some extra features enhance dependency checking for package installation and removal, and some other features offer convenient package updating mechanisms.

dpkg is perhaps the most powerful packaging tool available for Linux. It is not always the most convenient, however, because it tends to ask many technical questions during installation. This is confusing for new users and annoying for advanced users. It means you can't just leave an install of Debian running and expect it to be complete when you come back because it stops installing every time it comes to a configuration question.

Recent changes to dpkg and its front-end, dselect, should greatly improve this. All configuration questions are being moved to after the installation. Questions are also now ranked by their importance, meaning that a novice user can automatically accept defaults for all but the most critical questions.

In addition to running on Intel x86 and Pentium platforms, Debian has been ported to other systems such as Sun's SPARC machines and StrongArm (currently used in systems such as Corel's NetWinder machines). There is also a port to the Alpha and the Mac 68k available.

This distribution is highly regarded as being one of the most stable and technically sound distributions of Linux. Unfortunately, it is also regarded as being one of the most unfriendly distributions for new Linux users from a usability and installability standpoint. This is understandable because technical quality was the main focus of the development team when the system was pieced together. Because of the level of technical Linux savvy required to install and use this distribution, Debian is aimed at experienced Linux users and developers.

Much like OpenLinux, Red Hat, and SuSE, fee-based technical support is available for Debian, but only in the form of corporate support contracts (the others offer lower priced end-user support as well as corporate support contracts). Free support, as usual (and as applicable to all the available Linux distributions), is available on the Internet through mail lists and newsgroups.

SuSE

SuSE has proven to be quite popular in Europe and is enjoying growing success in the United States. It uses a SysV initialization scheme, which makes it act much like distributions such as Red Hat and OpenLinux. It also uses RPM as its package management mechanism. Most of the administration centers on a utility called YaST2 (Yet Another Setup Tool), which handles package maintenance and upgrades, user administration, and a number of other essential administration tasks.

The main difference between OpenLinux and SuSE (and other distributions for that matter) is that SuSE strives to be more *voluminous*, meaning that it tends to carry more packages than most other distributions (over twice as many as OpenLinux for example). This is an advantage and a drawback. The advantage is that everything you might ever want is likely to be there. The drawback is that it is difficult to test and integrate so many packages. So many packages can also be extremely confusing to new users.

Like other distributions mentioned before, SuSE includes a graphical installation system and uses KDE as its default graphic environment. As Linux has spread to more and more users, ease of use has steadily become a core part of many distributions.

TurboLinux

Unlike most Linux distributions which focus on either the advanced user or the business server, TurboLinux focuses on the very high-end server market. TurboLinux (www.turbolinux.com) prides itself on building some of the best Linux clusters in the world, and is a leader in the fast growing Linux supercomputer field.

Mandrake

Another commercial player in the Linux market is MandrakeSoft (www.linux-mandrake.com). Originally, Mandrake was a repackaging of Red Hat Linux with a focus on KDE and Pentium optimizations. Since then, Mandrake has become a more serious competitor to Red Hat and has forged ahead with new innovations (which are often then picked up by Red Hat and others).

A software package like Mandrake really demonstrates how the Linux world is different than almost any other part of the computer industry (or almost any other industry). MandrakeSoft openly takes Red Hat Linux, makes their own modifications, and resells with without paying Red Hat and without Red Hat's permission. Though Red Hat publicly approves of Mandrake-Soft's actions (because they are fully in keeping with the Linux culture), it is very likely that Red Hat would be happier without this kind of competitor. For the Linux community, this has been a true boon, because each company has driven the other to create better and better products without either being able to lock the customer into a proprietary solution.

Recently, Mandrake has diverged more from Red Hat, pushing toward more cutting-edge packages and a faster time to market.

SLS

The first Linux distribution was the SLS distribution from Soft Landing Software in Canada. It provided convenient, pre-compiled and ready to run sets of packages that could be installed in any combination. SLS reduced the steps that were previously required to install software on Linux systems—search for the source code, download it, extract it, compile it, and hope it installs and works correctly—and saved so much time and effort that many people had no problem with its $150 price tag.

However, it was still rather unfriendly to install, especially from the standpoint of someone migrating to Linux from a DOS background.

SLACKWARE

The next major distribution answered many complaints that people had about SLS by simplifying the installation and offering a package management system called pkgtool.

For installation, instead of running a command-line program and passing the names of the package sets to be installed as in SLS, Slackware offered a full-screen, menu-driven interface. It enabled the user to browse the package sets that were available for installation, and went the extra mile by offering users the capability to select or deselect individual packages within those sets.

One of its biggest boosts to the Linux distribution world was the management of installed packages. Using plain tarred and compressed archives (.tgz files), the pkgtool program did a fair job of making the installation and removal of software packages more painless. The main problem that occurred—and still occurs because Slackware hasn't really changed much in this regard—is that some files from individual packages are inevitably left behind when packages are removed. Without a database to keep track of where all the installed files are (such as those used by Red Hat and OpenLinux's RPM package manager or Debian's dpkg), it is impossible to know how to cleanly remove files after they are installed. Regardless, Slackware's package management system does a good job, considering that it just uses ordinary archive files.

Slackware uses a BSD-style initialization scheme. The benefit of this is a simpler system for loading services at boot time. A drawback is that the user does not have very much control over the services that are being started up. For instance, in SysV initialization you can have a different set of services set to start with different *runlevels*, not unlike the runlevel menu you sometimes get when a Windows 95 system becomes corrupted (Safe Mode with Networking, Safe Mode without Networking, and so on). You cannot do this with BSD initialization such as the one used by Slackware.

Slackware is favored by many as the most traditional of the Linux distributions. Nostalgia and inertia (keeping what is familiar on one's system) seem to be doing a good job of keeping this distribution alive, not to mention the fact that it is typically quite current with its software versions and technical fortitude. It provides its user base with consistency and an unflinchingly familiar installation system from version to version.

YES, THERE ARE OTHERS

Just when you think all the distributions have been made, another one pops up. These distributions all have their own focuses, each one being created to fill a perceived gap.

For instance, there is Stampede that is optimized from top to bottom to run on Pentium-based systems. There are also distributions targeted at non-Intel platforms such as Yellow Dog for PPC, distributions targeted specifically at Microsoft Windows users such as DragonLinux, and distributions targeted for inexperienced users such as easyLinux.

For a comprehensive list of Linux distributions, including over 120 different distributions, see the Linux Weekly News Distributions page at www.lwn.net.

THE LINUX STANDARD BASE PROJECT (LSB)

One of the biggest complaints that software vendors have about Linux is that it appears to be a "moving target." If you wanted to do so, you could update your systems to the latest version of the C library, the latest alpha-grade kernel, or the latest beta test versions of software on a weekly (sometimes even daily) basis. Some people actually do this, and it is those people who, innocently enough, have given Linux this moving target stigma.

> **Note**   There is absolutely nothing wrong with updating a Linux system in this manner. An explanation of how Linux got this image was warranted, however.

This can be fun for a hobbyist or a casual tinkerer, but business users and developers tend to shy away from systems that change weekly. This fear tends to bleed over into the corporate IT world—the same world that has to use the software that vendors are trying to keep working under Linux.

For instance, say a developer ported a software package to one Linux distribution that uses the latest version of the GNU C library (glibc 2.1). The application might work great on that Linux distribution, but when moved to another distribution that uses an older C library (glibc 2.0, or the very old libc version 5), some essential pieces of the library are missing that might prevent the software from running. This implies that a whole slice of Linux users will probably not purchase that software package, or will ring up significant hours of technical support trying to get the software vendor to help with installation.

All in all, it is not a situation in which many vendors want to find themselves. It is situations like this that can prevent a company from porting their software to Linux.

To address this concern, a group was assembled under the umbrella of the Linux Standard Base project to discuss how to develop a solid, stable platform with known, established binaries and libraries with which software developers can reliably port their software. This group is not centered around any particular Linux distribution—far from it, actually. There is representation from at least seven of the top Linux distributions (Slackware being a major exception), some Linux hardware vendors, and volunteers who are driven by the idea of slowing down the moving target syndrome described earlier.

The LSB project will address compatibility issues between the various Linux distributions by settling on a common set of binaries, libraries, and directory layouts that have been the source of many cross-distribution problems in the past. Hopefully, in the end, software developed or packaged for one Linux distribution will simply plug into another distribution with a minimum of hassles, if any at all.

Anyone who wants to contribute time to this project is encouraged to participate. There are mailing lists and Web pages that cater to the LSB project and that are open to the general public. Observers are encouraged to lurk (read without posting) on the mail lists in an effort to keep the signal to noise ratio high-low. For this reason, ideas and concerns need to be submitted to committee members instead of the mail lists. Everyone is encouraged to follow the discussion and consider becoming an official part of the effort, though. Be sure to check the LSB Web page (`www.linuxbase.org`) for more information on this project.

THE LINUX PROFESSIONAL INSTITUTE AND LINUX CERTIFICATION

The Linux Professional Institute (LPI) was created by a group of volunteers who perceived the need for an accepted certification process that would recognize and certify the talent and hard work of Linux users everywhere. Since its inception, the effort has taken on a life of its own and has now involved some of the Linux movement's best and brightest in a fully open process aimed at providing certification for all.

The LPI isn't the only organization offering Linux certification. Others exist. However, LPI is the only one with an open process for developing certification exams. These exams are being developed by the Linux community for the Linux community. Exams are kept to the absolute minimums as far as number and price, but they strive for the highest quality. For more information about the Linux Professional Institute, see their Web page at `www.lpi.org`.

HOW DOES LINUX FIT IN WITH OTHER NETWORKED ENVIRONMENTS?

Many people within the Linux community want to establish Linux as a viable alternative to other graphical desktop operating systems. This is a good cause to support. Linux has proven itself as a highly stable end-user operating system, and with graphical interfaces such as the one provided by the K Desktop Environment and GNOME, which are covered in Chapters 3 and 4, migration from other operating systems is becoming easier and easier. In addition, commercial software companies such as Loki Entertainment Software and Oracle have targeted Linux as the plate on which their bread and butter (games and databases respectively) can be served, and so far their porting efforts have gone over quite well with the Linux community in general.

Note

Loki Entertainment Software is particularly interesting for the Linux community because of their focus on a very under-served market: games. Loki began by porting *Civilization: Call to Power,* and have since then ported at least 10 other commercial games to Linux, including Quake III Arena and SimCity 3000. If you are interested in commercial games for Linux, visit their web site at www.lokigames.com.

However, to simply look at Linux as a replacement for other graphical operating systems is like looking at a fire truck and considering using it to pick up your sister at the airport. There are many, many other features of Linux that go well beyond simple desktop interaction, and many people think that this is where Linux shows its true colors. To ignore these features is to ignore the size and functionality (not to mention the misuse) of the fire truck mentioned earlier.

Networking is where the most power resides within Linux. No other operating system to date has offered the connectivity features that Linux offers at the price tag that Linux holds. Similar functionality might cost you literally a few thousand U.S. dollars with other variants of the UNIX operating system. With Linux, it is all included "in the box."

TCP/IP NETWORKS

Regardless of whether it is a simple dial-up PPP connection to an Internet provider or a server that sits at the center of your company and serves up Web pages, FTP downloads, and peripheral pools, Linux is a hands-down winner over the current alternatives. It offers full IPv4 support (even IPv6), including the capability to do the following:

- **Forward network packets**—Can make it a nice gateway system to the Internet
- **Masquerade network packets**—Provides the capability to use only one valid IP address to give access to networks, such as the Internet, to an entire company
- **Tunnel network packets**—Creates a pipeline using IP that permits other IP packets, or even non-IP packets such as IPX packets from NetWare, to pass across the connection in encapsulated form
- **Alias IP addresses**—Hosts multiple addresses on one network interface, which is useful when providing virtual hosting services
- **Filter network packets**—Packet filtering firewall capabilities are contained within the Linux kernel, just waiting to be configured

Also, special things you can do with TCP/IP—such as remote configuration via DHCP and bootp—are possible with OpenLinux. FTP services, Web services, NFS file system sharing, mail (POP, SMTP), USENET news, and even video conferencing can be done either with software that is included with OpenLinux or with a few items that are freely downloadable from the Internet.

Basically, if it can be done with TCP/IP, it can be done with OpenLinux. See Part IV, "Networking with Linux," to address these features in more detail.

INTRANETS

Intranets—small versions of the Internet available solely within a closed network such as one found within a company—are quite popular today. The capability to use one set of tools to access both intra- and extra-company network services such as mail and document distribution is smart from an administration standpoint. Also, services that are popular on the Internet typically offer, in one form or another, inexpensive or free client software; this makes the choice economical as well. Web browsers, news readers, mail readers, and other client software can be used for Internet access as well as for accessing intra-company network services.

All you need to create an intranet complete with the major services that everyone has come to depend on from the Internet is included with most distributions of Linux. There is the Apache Web server, sendmail for mail transportation, and POP3 for mail downloading (as well as IMAP for those who want to leave all mail on central mail servers). There is also INN for news servers, BIND for name resolution services, and even IP masquerading features to help your company/group get the internal systems on the intranet out to the Internet. These are all the same tools that are used as the backbone of the Internet.

TCP/IP services are not the only network services offered by Linux, though. Linux fits in well with heterogeneous networking scenarios, combining different protocols for file and print sharing services into one cooperative system; each networking system is capable of sharing the services of another, as you will soon see.

NetWare Networks

Yes, Linux can connect to NetWare networks. This includes NDS as well as bindery services. Starting with the Linux NetWare client (originally developed with the Caldera Network Desktop system), Caldera Systems has continued its NetWare line with the addition of NetWare Cross Platform Services (NCPS) for Linux. With this package, Linux jumped into the Novell server business with the capability to offer Novell file and print services.

The right to port such items to Linux was obtained primarily because of Caldera Systems' early close relationship with Novell (www.novell.com). Novell now also works closely with other Linux distributors to ensure that NetWare is well supported for Linux users.

Complete information on the NetWare for Linux client is available later in this book in Chapter 28, "Using NetWare."

Microsoft Windows Networks

With the popularity of Microsoft Windows systems comes the popularity of Windows networking through the *Session Message Block (SMB)* protocol. This networking scheme allows connections to be browsed, established, and then dropped using simple graphic interfaces on the Windows system. The networks themselves are dynamically built and updated through a series of "elections" between computers on the network, with a new election being held every time another computer signs on.

In most Windows networks, a machine running Windows NT sits at the center of the network, acting as a source for passwords and home directories for client machines on the network. These central machines are known as *Domain Controllers*. Domain Controllers are quite powerful, and their pivotal role as the centerpiece of the network makes them appealing to administrators. It is much easier to maintain one computer (the Domain Controller) than to maintain password files and such on each individual client machine on the network.

This type of networking is thankfully not limited to machines running Windows. A number of years ago, a protocol suite called Samba was developed by a gentleman named Andrew Tridgell that offered simple file sharing based on the SMB protocol. The project has taken on a life of its own, adding support for the *Common Internet File System (CIFS)*, and recently taking on features that enable it to emulate Domain Controllers to a certain extent. Samba has been given support by major hardware vendors (for instance, DEC, Silicon Graphics, IBM), has outperformed other SMB implementations using Ziff-Davis's NetBench benchmark, and is now capable of being a domain client (obtaining authentication from a Domain Controller running on Windows NT). There are many more features of Samba that make it a worthy (if not superior) addition to any Windows network, but those are best left to the Samba Web pages (www.samba.com) and Chapter 29, "Sharing Resources with Samba."

CHAPTER **2**

Introduction to the Desktop

In this chapter

WHAT IS A DESKTOP?

In 1981, Xerox created the first computer to be sold with a graphical user interface (GUI), the $16,000 XeroxStar. By this time, research into GUIs had been going on for nearly 40 years, with a few working systems, but all too expensive or experimental to sell. With such a high price tag, though, the XeroxStar was a commercial failure. Soon after, in 1983, Apple released the Lisa. At nearly $10,000, it quickly suffered the same fate.

Finally, in 1984 Apple released the first commercially viable GUI for a personal computer—MacOS for the Macintosh. This system introduced the world to the desktop, and included many of the features of today's desktops. Most importantly, the desktop provided metaphors: files were kept in folders; you deleted things by putting them in the trash; text could be cut out and pasted elsewhere. This provided a new way of thinking about how to use computers, and helped people with a less technical background to understand them.

About the same time, the Laboratory for Computer Science at the Massachusetts Institute of Technology was working on the Athena project with DEC. From the Athena project grew a windowing system for UNIX called X, based on an earlier windowing system called W.

Also released in 1984, X is very different from MacOS. Although the MacOS GUI is tied directly to the operating system and provides the only user interface generally available, X is loosely tied to the operating system and the user can bypass it using the command-line interface. Although MacOS programs are almost exclusively graphical, many UNIX programs are still text based.

X specifies a protocol for applications to display graphical components, or *widgets*, such as windows, buttons, and icons. It does not specify how these widgets should behave, or how the interface responds to user input. Window managers handle this. X also provides protocols for networking (particularly to provide remote display), but we will focus on the graphical capabilities here.

WINDOW MANAGERS

Because X does not specify a particular window manager, many have grown up over the years. Some of the more popular for Linux are fvwm2, Window Maker, blackbox, and AfterStep. Many window managers are either based on Tom's Window Manger (twm), a very simple, lightweight window manager, or NeXTSTEP, a highly configurable, full-featured window manager developed for the NeXT computer.

Window managers are generally more lightweight than desktops, and are more targeted at expert users who are more comfortable with a command-line interface.

Desktops include the capability to place files and directories directly on the background. They also include drag-and-drop, which allows icons representing files to be dragged with the mouse and dropped onto an icon representing an application. The application will then be launched using the file. Desktops can also provide an interface allowing programs to communicate with the desktop and with other applications. In general, desktops are targeted at more novice users (though advanced users often still find them incredibly useful). Often, a desktop user can do all her work without ever invoking a command line.

CDE

Several UNIX producers, including Hewlett-Packard, IBM, Novell, and Sun Microsystems, have worked together to produce *CDE*, the *Common Desktop Environment*. This environment is based on earlier UNIX desktops such as HP-VUE. Although CDE provides a very configurable interface, including drag-and-drop, session management, and a powerful panel, it lacks several features that other desktops provide:

- Files and shortcuts cannot be placed directly on the desktop.

- Much of the configuration must be handled through complex configuration files instead of graphical dialogs.

- Whereas CDE has been ported to Linux, it is not Open Source software, nor is it free.

KDE

In 1996, Matthias Ettrich began work on KDE, which is shown in Figure 2.1. Built on top of the Qt toolkit from Trolltech, KDE provided a friendly, powerful, and highly configurable environment targeted at the novice user. Billed as "UNIX for the Desktop," KDE represented one of the first major steps toward Linux for the mass market.

Figure 2.1
The KDE desktop provides a friendly interface similar to the Macintosh, Windows 98, and BeOS interfaces.

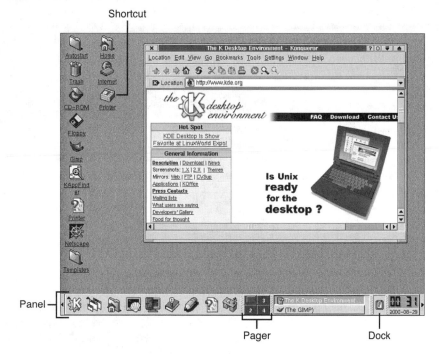

Shortcut

Panel

Pager

Dock

PART

I

CH

2

> **Tip** The "K" in KDE doesn't stand for anything. KDE is simply the K Desktop Environment.

KDE provides many features, some of which will be covered later in "Common Desktop Features," and still more of which will be covered in Chapter 3, "KDE." The most significant, however, is a consistent desktop metaphor, similar to the one first introduced by MacOS. Also like MacOS, KDE applications follow a consistent style guide, which means that all KDE applications tend to work similarly. For example, nearly all KDE applications have a File menu as the first entry on their menu bar and a Help menu as the last entry.

GNOME

The KDE project's basis on the Qt toolkit caused much controversy in its early days. The original Qt license was not Open Source (as defined by the Open Source Initiative, or OSI), and there was some concern that Trolltech might someday go out of business or modify its license in such a way that KDE could no longer be free. This concern was generally alleviated with the creation of the KDE Free Qt Foundation, which ensures that if Trolltech ever stops developing Qt Free Edition, it will be released under the BSD Open Source license. Furthermore, should Trolltech (or their successors) ever want to change Qt Free Edition's license, it must be approved by the Foundation, of which KDE developers have a majority voting interest. Trolltech went even further, first by releasing Qt Free Edition under the Qt Public License (QPL), which was certified as an Open Source license by the OSI, and finally by releasing Qt under the GPL.

These historical concerns led to the creation of the GNOME project. The GNOME project set out to create a desktop, which is shown in Figure 2.2, and which was fully under the GPL license.

Figure 2.2
GNOME is the first fully Open Source desktop for UNIX.

Where KDE has a fairly strict style guide, ensuring that its applications conform to a consistent look and feel, GNOME thrives on individuality. Although this has allowed GNOME to often leap ahead in configurability and features, it has also generally reduced the integration of its parts. This has changed greatly recently as GNOME has moved towards Bonobo, an interface for exchanging information between applications (similar to KParts in KDE or COM in Microsoft Windows).

Today, several commercial and non-profit organizations have arisen to help support GNOME. One of the most interesting is the GNOME Foundation. Founded in 2000, the GNOME Foundation is an advisory board that helps direct the development of GNOME. It is made up of the many volunteers who work on GNOME, but also includes numerous companies such as Compaq and Sun Microsystems.

PART
I
CH
2

Other corporate interests in GNOME include Helix Code and Eazel. Helix Code (www.helixcode.com) has put together a distribution of GNOME that is incredibly easy to install. This will be discussed more in Chapter 4, "GNOME." Eazel (www.eazel.com) is working with GNOME and Helix Code to develop a very user-friendly desktop. Founded by some of the original Macintosh team, their goal is to bring Linux to the masses. Nautilus, their file and desktop manager, is expected to be the default desktop in GNOME 2.0.

As KDE and GNOME evolve, they begin to resemble each other more and more. Some of this is simply good ideas being passed back and forth, but some of this is very active. Efforts are underway currently to provide greater interoperability between the two desktops, allowing applications written for one to work more seamlessly with the other. Although it is unlikely that the two groups will ever merge, it seems very likely that users in the future will be freer to pick and choose the desktop and applications that suit them best.

XFCE

GNOME and KDE are both very powerful desktops, but they also use a lot of memory and other system resources. XFce offers much of the friendliness and configurability of the larger desktops at a fraction of the resources. Based on the same libraries as GNOME (gtk+) and offering an interface similar to CDE, XFce works especially well with GNOME-based programs, but it also handles KDE applications without difficulty.

XFce is ideal for those users who want a friendly interface on an underpowered machine, or simply for those users who prefer to save their resources for their applications instead of all the extra features of KDE or GNOME.

COMMON DESKTOP FEATURES

Although every desktop has its own special features, most desktops have many things in common. This is especially true in the Linux world as KDE and GNOME converge more and more. In this section we will cover the features that are common to most desktops and are more important to the user's experience. For specific examples of these features, see Chapter 3, "KDE," and Chapter 4, "GNOME."

DESKTOP

The most noticeable difference between a desktop environment and a window manager is the active nature of the desktop background. Whereas most window managers treat their background as simply area that does not include a window, desktop environments allow you to use the background as if it were a globally available directory (in fact, it is usually implemented as a directory).

In a desktop environment, you can copy files, directories, shortcuts, and other objects directly to the desktop for quick access. These elements are available regardless of which virtual desktop you're viewing (see the following section, "Pager," for more information on virtual desktops). This is incredibly useful for providing quick access to your most used files and directories.

SHORTCUTS

In an environment such as MacOS, where all applications know how to interact with the desktop, shortcuts are little more than symbolic links. In environments with a command-line heritage, such as Microsoft Windows and any UNIX desktop, shortcuts need much more information to be useful.

In KDE and GNOME, shortcuts are files that reference other files, applications, directories, or even desktop-specific features such as services or MIME types. They provide information about which icon to use, what application is used for this file, how to mount or unmount a device, the name of the application in numerous languages, and much more. Shortcuts can be placed on the desktop, the panel, a menu, or in other locations that the desktop uses for configuration.

FILE ASSOCIATION

If you have ever clicked a file's icon in MacOS or Microsoft Windows and had your machine automatically launch the correct application, you've used file associations. In Linux desktops, file associations match files to applications by their filenames or by fingerprints within the file. This allows files to display the correct icon and automatically launch the correct application.

PANEL

Linux desktops generally have a panel that includes shortcut buttons, menus, and *applets* (small, embedded applications). Generally the panel is a bar across the bottom of your screen, but it can almost always be moved to one of the other edges of the screen.

The panel is one of the most useful parts of the desktop environment because it provides quick access to your most needed functions. Shortcuts quickly launch your most used applications, menus give access to lesser-used applications, applets such as a pager (see the following section), battery monitor, or clock provide extra functionality or monitoring. Panel is usually extremely configurable to your preferences and work style.

PAGER

Unlike MacOS and Microsoft Window, most UNIX window managers and desktops include a *pager*. A pager gives you access to multiple virtual desktops for displaying applications. Although the icons directly on the background and the panel are shared between all the virtual desktops, individual applications run on one or more of them. This allows you to spread out more, placing related applications on separate desktops. For example, I run a word processor on one, a mail client and Web browser on another, and several terminal windows on a third. Using the pager, I can move quickly between my virtual desktops.

DOCK

The dock provides a place for applications to provide quick access and user feedback while using a minimum of screen real estate. The dock often occupies a small area of the panel, with individual icons representing each of the applications running there. For example, a battery monitor might display a small gauge in the dock to show you how charged your batteries are. Clicking on the gauge could launch the battery monitor configuration dialog or provide access to the power management system. Applications are usually written specifically for a particular desktop's dock.

THEMES

One great way to personalize your desktop is to choose a good *theme*. Themes modify the appearance and behavior of the desktop and all theme-aware applications. For example, a theme can include a color scheme, backdrop, and sound effects. Even more interesting, a theme can change the appearance and behavior of the application windows and window buttons themselves. For example, Figures 2.3 and Figure 2.4 show the same dialog under the default KDE theme (Figure 2.3) as well as the KDE-Sgi theme (Figure 2.4). Notice how the check boxes and other features are modified.

Figure 2.3
The default theme is
very clean.

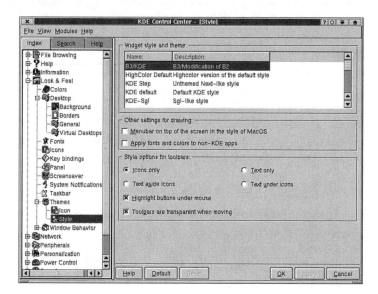

Figure 2.4
Some users prefer more pronounced buttons.

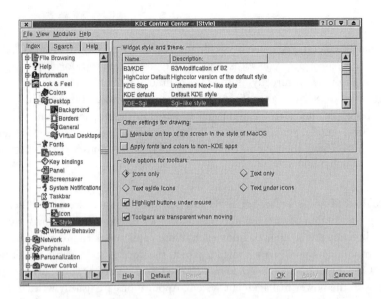

> **Tip**
>
> If you like themes, take a look at www.themes.org. Here you will find hundreds of themes for many desktops and window managers.

USER-FRIENDLY CONFIGURATION

Linux applications and environments have historically required modifying somewhat arcane configuration files scattered all over the filesystem. This represents a very large learning curve for the average user. Linux desktops have moved to centralized configuration through easy-to-use dialogs. Instead of entering Color1=#356390 in desktop0rc, the user can simply select light blue from the color dialog in the Desktop Background dialog.

PROGRAMMING API

One of the things that separates a desktop from a window manager is an *Application Program Interface*, or *API*. An API allows software written for the desktop to interact with the desktop and other applications. This allows data from one application to be embedded in another. For example, the KDE Web browser, konqueror, can display text files by embedding kwrite in one of its panels. In fact, this is how konqueror displays everything, including Web pages. It simply passes information off to components that can render them (khtml in the case of Web pages) and displays the output. Because everything is modular, any KDE application can display Web pages by embedding the khtml component.

Another important application of an API is *session management*. Session management allows the desktop to save the state of applications when you log out, and then resume that state when you log back in. For example, suppose you log out in the middle of typing a paper in a session management-aware application. When you log back in, the desktop should be able not only to restart the application, but also to load the file you were working on and place your cursor right where you stopped.

INTERNATIONAL SUPPORT

For the majority of the world's population, English is not the primary language. Linux desktops, therefore, speak many other languages as well. KDE and GNOME each support dozens of languages, including those with non-Latin alphabets such as Japanese and Russian, right-to-left alphabets such as Hebrew, and alphabets that change in different parts of the word such as Arabic. Both projects have many contributors (in fact, probably most of their contributors) from outside of the United States, so they are well aware of international issues.

As of version 2, KDE handles nearly all of its text using Unicode. GNOME is also rapidly integrating Unicode with the Pango project ("Pan" is Greek for "all," and "go" is Japanese for "language"). Unicode is a single encoding standard for all of the world's languages (and even some not-of-this-world languages such as Klingon). Although neither desktop can render every language (dozens of alphabets are in the Unicode standard), they are making rapid progress toward a more language-neutral environment. For more information on Unicode, see Roman Czyborra's excellent Web pages at www.czyborra.com.

PART

I

CH

2

Tip

Internationalization is usually abbreviated i18n, because there are 18 characters between the *i* and the *n*. Similarly, localization is usually abbreviated l10n.

CASE STUDY: KDE VERSUS GNOME

As recently as 1999 there were large differences between KDE and GNOME. GNOME was more customizable; KDE was more integrated. GNOME was Open Source through and through; the Qt license caused great debates over whether KDE could be considered Open Source. KDE had a very Microsoft Windows look and feel; GNOME was pushing the envelope on user interface with the Enlightenment window manager.

Today, with KDE 2.0 and Helix GNOME, there is less and less difference between the two environments. Which you use has become more a matter of taste. Here are some things to consider when making your choice:

- KDE is still much more integrated than GNOME. Although GNOME is improving its interoperability with the Bonobo component framework and other technologies, KDE already heavily uses KParts to manage its components.

- KDE has a more consistent look and feel than GNOME because it has a more rigorous style guide.

- GNOME is more dynamic than KDE. Its components are generally upgraded more often, and individual components are easier to upgrade. On the other hand, the core KDE packages tend to be tested more thoroughly with each other.

■ With the help of Helix code, GNOME is incredibly easy to install on a wide range of Linux distributions, including non-Intel architectures like Yellow Dog Linux and even non-Linux operating systems like Solaris. Helix Setup Tools has made updating GNOME incredibly easy, and in the future they should make configuring GNOME and Linux very easy. Even with its 90+ packages, GNOME is easier to install than KDE's dozen or so, especially on systems that don't use RPM.

KDE

In this chapter

WHAT IS KDE?

KDE stands for the *K Desktop Environment*. The *K* doesn't stand for anything in particular. KDE provides some of the same functionality for a graphical environment that is found in other popular operating environments, such as Macintosh OS or Windows 98. However, it also provides some unique features of its own to enhance your graphical work environment.

KDE is a complete desktop environment, as opposed to being just a window manager or program launcher. Several capable window managers exist for Linux, including olwm, fvwm, afterstep, and others. However, KDE provides much more functionality than a simple window manager provides. For more information on the differences between desktops and window managers, see Chapter 2, "Introduction to the Desktop."

KDE IS A GRAPHICAL DESKTOP

KDE provides all the capabilities of a desktop. For example, KDE enables you to do the following:

- Put icons on the desktop to mount and unmount removable disks, such as floppies.
- Browse the filesystem graphically.
- Associate applications with files of a particular type so that when you click a file, it automatically loads the correct application.
- Create a desktop printer icon, to which you can drag files to print them.

None of these are features of a window manager or program launcher by itself. The value of KDE is that it simplifies many tasks that a user must perform by providing a graphical environment that simulates something more familiar to the user. In other words, KDE provides a desktop metaphor, which is a way of displaying and manipulating documents, directories, and programs in a manner that is more intuitive and appealing than typing commands at a shell prompt.

KDE APPLICATIONS

The KDE system includes not only the desktop, but also a whole host of applications and utilities to go along with it. In the default distribution of KDE, there are more than 100 programs, ranging from games to system utilities to a full-blown office suite. Each of these programs is useful in its own right; in addition, however, the KDE applications can interoperate with each other to make certain operations easier. For example, you can drag a package file from the file manager to the package manager to view the contents of the package and install it.

KDE IS A PROJECT

In addition to being a graphical desktop, KDE is also a huge project. The KDE project provides a complete applications development framework and many guidelines and resources for the development and use of KDE programs.

Thousands of developers around the world work on various aspects of the KDE system, including programming, documentation, translation, all kinds of testing, and packaging. The KDE Web site is located at http://www.kde.org.

This Web site contains many resources for both users and developers of KDE. For example, the Web site provides online documentation in many languages. Also, users can participate in mailing lists to receive or give assistance in working with KDE. For developers, application style guides, automated tools for constructing KDE applications, bug and feature wish lists, and more can be found here.

The KDE project is devoted to a philosophy of ease-of-use, consistency, and quality for graphical applications in the Linux world.

INSTALLING KDE

PART
I

CH
3

Most major Linux distributions include KDE automatically when you install them. Debian is a major exception because of disagreements over licensing (though this may change in the next release). If you run Debian or another distribution that does not include KDE by default, or if you simply want to upgrade to a later version, installing the latest version is fairly easy. All the files you need are available at ftp://ftp.kde.org/pub/kde.

KDE is made up of various packages, which are listed in Table 3.1. This list of packages is consistent throughout the various distribution systems (such as RPM, deb, or tar).

TABLE 3.1   KDE PACKAGES

Package	Use
qt	(required) The Qt toolkit from Trolltech. All of KDE is based on this windows toolkit.
kdesupport	(highly recommended) Non-KDE libraries that KDE relies on.
kdelibs	(required) KDE shared libraries.
kdebase	(required) Core KDE applications, such as the window manager, control center, terminal, and Web browser.
kdeadmin	(optional) System administration tools, such as the package manager, kpackage.
kdegames	(optional) Various games for KDE.
kdegraphics	(optional) Graphic viewers and manipulation programs.
kdemultimedia	(optional) Multimedia applications, such as the CD player.
kdenetwork	(optional) Network applications, such as the mail client and new reader.
kdetoys	(optional) Miscellaneous fun applications, such as kmoon, which shows you the current phase of the moon.
kdeutils	(optional) More useful utilities, such as the calculator and text editor.
koffice	(optional) The K Office Suite includes a powerful word processor, spreadsheet, and more.

For any distribution, you will need to install the recommended and required packages in the order listed in Table 3.1. The optional packages can be installed in any order.

RPM-BASED DISTRIBUTIONS

For RPM-based distributions, such as Red Hat, Caldera OpenLinux, SuSE, Yellow Dog, and many others, you simply need to download the RPMs and install them. Go to either `ftp://ftp.kde.org/pub/kde/stable/latest/distribution` or `ftp://ftp.kde.org/pub/kde/unstable/distribution` and select the distribution closest to your own. The stable tree contains the officially released version of KDE, whereas the unstable tree contains pre-release betas and day-to-day snapshots of the development tree. Pick the version most suitable to you.

➔ **See** Chapter 32, "File Transfer Protocol (FTP)," for more information on downloading files with FTP.

After you have downloaded all the packages you want to a directory, you can install them with RPM:

```
$ su
Password: <password>
# rpm -i k*.rpm
#
```

➔ **See** Chapter 16, "Software Package Management," for more information on using RPM.

After you have installed KDE, see "Selecting KDE" later in this chapter for more information on getting KDE up and running.

DEBIAN

KDE is not directly supported by Debian, and KDE packages are not currently available at the main Debian site, as previously stated, because of disagreements over licensing. For more information on the Debian/KDE debate, see `http://www.uk.debian.org/~phil/KDE-FAQ.html`. Note that this FAQ is from the Debian point of view and claims that distributing KDE binary packages is a violation of the GPL (because of linking with the non-GPL Qt). The KDE developers have not posted an official statement, but their general agreement is that they are within their license, and that Debian is free to distribute or not distribute KDE as they see fit. This can change soon (in fact it will likely have changed by the time this book is published) because Qt 2.2.0 will be released under the GPL, which should remove Debian's objection to KDE.

Some Debian developers maintain semi-official packages. To install them, add the following to your `/etc/apt/sources.list`:

`deb http://kde.tdyc.com potato kde2`

This is accurate at the time of writing, but because KDE2 is in final beta at this time, you should check `http://kde.tdyc.com/Debian` for the most up-to-date information.

After you have updated `/etc/apt/sources.list`, do the following:

1. Run dselect.
2. Select Update to download the package list from the KDE mirror site.

3. Select Select and choose kdebase by pressing the Plus key. dselect will automatically select the other packages you need. Press Enter to accept the suggested packages or add additional packages from the list using the Plus key, and press Enter when complete.

4. If you want additional packages, select them with the Plus key.

5. Press Enter when complete.

6. Select Install to download the packages and install them.

After you have installed KDE, see the following section, "Selecting KDE," for more information on getting KDE up and running.

Note

Depending on which version of Debian you are running, you might need to install the libasound1 package as well. This is available at http://www.debian.org/Packages/unstable/sound/libasound1.html. Download the package and install it:

```
# dpkg -i libasound1_0.5.9-1.deb
```

Your file might be named slightly differently.

PART

I

CH

3

SELECTING KDE

Many distributions allow you to select whether to use KDE, GNOME, or some other desktop during installation. Switching desktops is usually fairly simple after installation, however. The only complicated part is determining how your particular distribution starts the desktop.

USING THE DISPLAY MANAGER

If you're using either gdm (the GNOME display manager), or kdm (the KDE display manager) you can select your desktop during login using the Session (or Session type) menu.

After you have selected your desktop once, the display manager will remember it when you log in again. Just leave the setting as Default.

USING SWITCHDESK

Red Hat includes a utility called switchdesk that enables you to easily change between GNOME, KDE, and twm (a simple window manager). From the command line, enter

```
$ switchdesk-kde
```

then select the desktop you want (KDE in this case), and press OK.

The option Change Only Applies to Current Display enables you to have different desktops for different displays. Generally changing displays indicates that you are logging in from a different machine. For example, you might have an NCD X terminal (a machine that displays X, but doesn't do any computations of its own and has no operating system). If your X terminal is across a slow network link, you might prefer to use a lightweight desktop like twm instead of KDE.

> **Tip**
>
> You can use another utility called switchdesk-gnome instead of switchdesk-kde. The difference between these tools is in the toolkits used for displaying the dialogs. Either tool can be used to select either desktop.

SELECTING KDE MANUALLY

If you want to select KDE by hand, you can modify the configuration files directly. This can be useful if you have a very customized start-up sequence or if you are running Debian (which has no built-in support for KDE).

To modify the default desktop for all users under Red Hat and similar distributions, edit `/etc/sysconfig/desktop` and enter KDE as a single line. This will automatically set the desktop for all users who haven't selected their own already.

If you want to set the default desktop for a single user under Red Hat, edit `${HOME}/.Xclients` to read `exec startkde`.

Under Debian, there is no easy way to set the default desktop, though you could modify `/usr/bin/x-window-manager` if you understand shell scripting. To modify the desktop for a given user, edit `${HOME}/.xsession` to read `exec startkde`. Then verify that `/etc/X11/Xsession.options` includes a line reading `allow-user-xsession`.

OpenLinux has no native support for anything but KDE, so there's no need to modify anything to use KDE as default.

> **Tip**
>
> `${HOME}/.Xclients` or `${HOME}/.xsession` is the last file run by the window manager start-up sequence, so this is the place for anything you want run before your window manager. Running your window manager should always be the last line of this file, and should always be preceded with `exec` (as in `exec startkde`). The `exec` tells the shell to completely replace itself with the window manager. Otherwise, an unnecessary copy of your shell will be left in memory. See "SHELL BUILT-IN COMMANDS" in the bash man page for more information on `exec`.

`${HOME}/.Xclients` or `${HOME}/.xsession` should be executable. You can make them executable by running the following:

```
$ chmod u+x ${HOME}/.Xclients
```

If you are using `.xsession`, of course, replace `.Xclients` in the preceding command.

> **Tip**
>
> If you have set environment variables in your `${HOME}/.bash_profile` (Red Hat/OpenLinux) or `${HOME}/.profile` (Debian), KDE might not know about them. This will affect things such as your PATH setting when using the Run Commands dialog. If this is a problem, you can use the following `.Xclients` (or `.xsession`) to fix it:
>
> ```
> if [ -e ${HOME}/.bash_profile ]; then
>     . ${HOME}/.bash_profile
> ```

```
elsif [ -e ${HOME}/.profile ]; then
    . ${HOME}/.profile
fi
exec startkde
```

BASIC DESKTOP ELEMENTS

When KDE first appears, it displays the desktop in the default configuration, shown in Figure 3.1. There are two basic screen components to be it aware of—the Desktop and the Panel.

Figure 3.1
The default KDE desktop configuration.

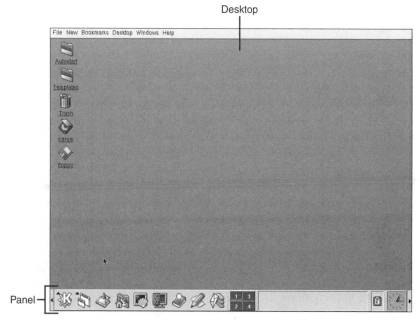

THE DESKTOP

The Desktop is the main working area of the KDE environment. This is the background behind all the other components that run on the screen. In the Desktop area, you place icons for programs, documents, and devices that you work with frequently. This makes these items readily available for access and manipulation. Think of the Desktop area in the same way that you think of an actual desktop, where you keep documents and tools handy to accomplish whatever tasks you are currently working on.

In addition to what you see onscreen, KDE actually provides more desktop space in which to run programs. Four virtual desktop areas are provided by default. A virtual desktop is another screen to which you can switch to run applications or to perform work. You can easily move programs and windows between virtual desktops. The extra space provided by virtual desktops gives you more room for your running programs, which enables you to leave application windows open and spaced apart, and therefore ready to use, instead of minimized or overlapped. Virtual desktops also enable you to organize the tasks that you are currently working on by placing related program windows on the same virtual desktop.

THE PANEL

The Panel (kicker) has icons for important KDE functions, as well as for frequently used programs. One particularly important item on the Panel is the Application Starter button, which is located (by default) on the left side of the Panel. It is the icon with a large K over a gear. From this button, you can access a menu that lists all the KDE applications installed on your system. Furthermore, this menu provides access to several other aspects of the KDE system, including the online help system and the KDE Control Panel. Figure 3.2 shows the contents of the default applications menu for KDE.

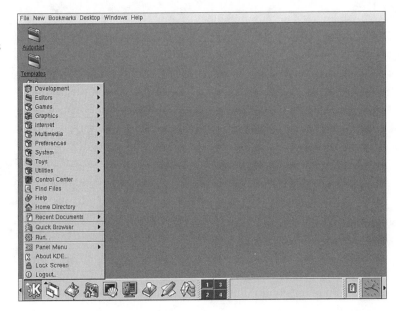

Figure 3.2
The Application Starter menu provides access to programs and KDE options.

The Panel also includes the virtual desktop Pager, the Taskbar, and the Clock. The Taskbar shows the windows that are open on the current desktop. Clicking a program in the Taskbar takes you immediately to that program.

RUNNING PROGRAMS

Probably the first thing you want to do after you've started KDE is run some applications. KDE's philosophy is that you can directly manipulate all the objects in the system, whether they are files containing documents to work on, programs that you run, or devices that you control.

LAUNCHING AN APPLICATION

To launch a program, you can do any of the following:

- **Single-click a button on the Panel**—Several useful programs are provided by default on the Panel. For example, the default Panel includes icons for a virtual terminal emulator, the Control Center, the Help Center, and a text editor.

- **Single-click an item on the Desktop**—By default, only two items are on the Desktop (the Trashcan and a link to your home directory), but after you've used KDE for a while, you will probably have placed your favorite programs here, ready to use. Your distribution might also have placed many other links on the desktop, such as links to useful programs or to their Web site.

- **Select a program from the Application Starter menu**—Click the large K and follow the menus to the program you want to run.

- **Click an item in the File Manager**—Inside a file manager window, click an item to launch it.

You can also run a program the old way, by opening a terminal window and typing its name at the shell prompt, or by using the Run Command window by pressing Alt+F2 and entering the program's name there.

PART

I

CH

3

ESSENTIAL PROGRAMS

A few oft-used programs are described here to get you started.

First, the terminal program, konsole, enables you to open a window and access a regular command-line shell environment. A button for konsole is provided on the Panel, with a small monitor and a shell in the icon.

Online help is available by clicking the icon of a book and lightbulb on the Panel. The online help includes a getting started guide, as well as an index for accessing help for all the KDE applications on your system.

You can browse the filesystem or access the World Wide Web using a file manager window. To start a file manager window showing the contents of your home directory, click the folder with the little house on it on the Panel.

STOPPING KDE

To stop KDE, open the Application Starter menu and select the Logout menu item. By default, this will return you to the KDM login dialog.

When KDE exits, it closes all the applications that are currently running. Many KDE applications remember their current positions, contents, and other attributes from one session to the next. When you restart KDE later, these applications are restored to their former state, enabling you to continue where you stopped. For non-KDE applications, or for applications in which saving the state is not possible, you are warned before KDE exits that you might lose your work, and you are shown a list of the applications. This enables you to save your work and exit those applications cleanly before ending your KDE session.

Tip   You can also log out by pressing Alt+F2 and typing `logout`.

KDE CAPABILITIES

As stated previously, KDE provides much more than just a graphical window manager or launch environment. It provides many integrated features that are designed to make it easier to work in a graphical environment.

First and foremost, KDE provides an object-oriented environment in which to work. Instead of composing and typing commands at a shell prompt, you manipulate the objects on your system using the desktop or file manager windows. In KDE, you treat things as objects that can be accessed, manipulated, or combined by directly touching or moving them (clicking or dragging them). For example, to work on a document, click the document and it opens the correct application. To print a document, drag the document and drop it onto a printer icon. To examine the contents of a floppy, click the floppy device on your desktop.

This object orientation is provided by a sophisticated file-typing system, as well as by rigorous adherence (on the part of application authors) to standards that enable KDE applications to interact in intelligent ways.

KDE enables you to control a whole range of options to customize the appearance and functionality of the desktop. You can change the appearance of many things—the desktop backgrounds, the title bar buttons, or the icons—for the individual filesystem items themselves. You can also change the behavior of KDE to suit your tastes by adjusting such things as the focus policy (which determines how windows become selected) or the default application for certain types of files. Finally, you can alter the contents of the Desktop itself—or the Panel or applications menu—to match the set of programs or files that you use on a day-to-day basis.

KDE allows for completely graphical configuration of all these aspects. This is in stark contrast to many other window managers in Linux, where you often have to edit text files by hand and restart the window manager to accomplish the same thing.

Another important aspect of KDE is that it provides a single framework for application development. All KDE applications share a highly consistent look and feel because they use the Qt graphical library to provide similar looking and functioning buttons, menus, controls, and other window items. Nevertheless, the KDE team has put together application style guidelines as well to help make sure that KDE applications look and behave consistently. For example, all KDE applications have a menu item located on the right side of the main application menu for accessing the program's online help. All the online help follows a consistent layout and style. Similar icons are used across all the KDE applications for buttons with similar functionality. Although these might seem like small things, when taken in the aggregate, this uniformity contributes to your ability to easily use KDE applications because you don't have to re-learn interface details from one application to the next.

> **Note**
>
> If you are familiar with object-oriented programming (OOP), you might be interested to know that nearly all KDE applications derive from a single C++ class: KApplication. By adhering to good OOP practices, KDE has made it fairly easy to develop a program that follows the KDE standards, and automatically inherits many of the configuration, interoperability, and internationalization features.

Another—often overlooked—facet of the KDE project is the complete support for internationalization of all KDE programs. Support for multiple languages is built right into KDE from the ground up, with documentation and online help files available in many languages.

Finally, because of the massive effort that has gone into KDE, numerous applications are already available for it. The KDE and Qt libraries provide a foundation for rapid development of new applications that conform to KDE requirements. KDE applications are rich in functionality, there are many of them available, and more are being developed every day.

PART

I

CH

3

CONFIGURING KDE WITH THE CONTROL CENTER

Configuring KDE could easily fill several chapters (in fact, it does in *Special Edition Using KDE*, from Que Publishing). This section will try to cover the most important configuration issues and introduce you to the rich KDE documentation. After you become used to how KDE does things, you'll discover that finding most basic configuration options is easy.

The Control Center, shown in Figure 3.3, is at the heart of configuring KDE. It is a highly modular configuration system that encapsulates the configuration panels for numerous desktop components and even some KDE applications.

Figure 3.3
The Control Center provides "one-stop shopping" for KDE configuration.

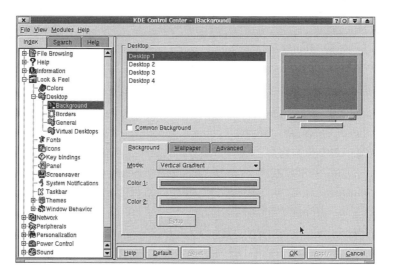

Because of its modular nature, you might notice the same dialogs appearing in more than one place. For example, Figure 3.3 shows the Control Center dialog under Look & Feel, Desktop, Background. Figure 3.4 shows the dialog from right-clicking the background and selecting Configure Background. Notice that the interiors of these two dialogs are identical, although the widgets (the buttons along the top of the window frame) are slightly different. This is because the interiors for both of these windows are provided by the same module (libkcm_background.so), using the kparts protocol. The window frames (and therefore the widgets) are drawn by the individual applications, such as the Control Center (kcontrol) or the desktop (kdesktop) .

Figure 3.4
You can also access the same configuration dialogs from Application's local menus.

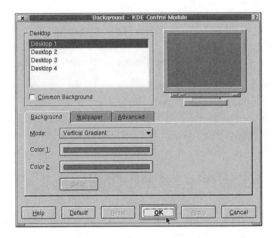

The Control Center is laid out in categories, similar to a directory tree. By clicking the plus sign beside a category, you can see its components. By pressing the minus sign beside a category, you can hide its components. If you prefer a more straightforward icon view, shown in Figure 3.5, rather than a tree, you can select View, Mode, Icon View. You can access all the dialogs with a cascading menu tree by using the Modules menu (which is identical to the Preferences menu on the Application Starter).

Most Control Center dialogs include extensive help. The easiest form of help is usually quicktips. To access quicktips, click the question mark on the window frame. The cursor will change to an arrow with a large question mark beside it. Click the item that you're interested in and a yellow box will appear explaining that option. Click anywhere to make the tip go away. For more extensive help, you can click the Help tab on the left panel. Finally, if you are having trouble finding the dialog you want, try the Search tab on the left panel. Enter the keyword you're looking for, and it should help you find the right dialog.

Some configuration dialogs require root access to make modifications. These dialogs will include a button at the bottom labeled "Run as root". Click this button and enter your root password to make modifications to these options.

The rest of this section will cover some of the more useful categories. For a more complete description of all the KDE configuration options, see Que's *Special Edition Using KDE*.

Figure 3.5
The Control Center's icon view can be less intimidating for some users.

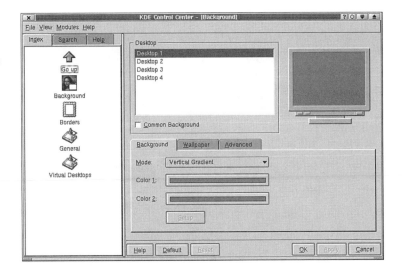

INFORMATION

This category isn't actually used to configure anything. Instead, it provides useful information about your system. Some of the options, such as DMA-Channels or Interrupts, give you direct access to the information stored in the /proc filesystem (see the section "The /proc Directory" in Chapter 10, "Understanding the Linux Filesystem," for more information). Other options, such as X-Server, provide nicely formatted information about various devices. Still other options, such as Memory, give continual feedback about information such as available free memory and swap usage. For intermediate to advanced users who don't want to search all over the filesystem for this information, this category is extremely useful.

LOOK & FEEL

One of the nice things about KDE is the vast number of items that are configurable. KDE enables you to configure many different aspects of the desktop and window appearance, including background images, icon appearance, fonts, and so on. Also, you can control in minute detail how the desktop and windows behave, such as how they respond to the mouse, how windows are loaded and activated, and what screen saver is used when your Desktop is inactive. These options and more are described in the sections that follow.

To configure the appearance and behavior of the desktop and windows, select one of the configuration dialog boxes underneath the Look & Feel category in the Control Center tree list.

CHANGING THE WINDOWS COLOR SCHEME

The Colors dialog box is used to change the color scheme for the windows of KDE and other graphical applications that you run.

A color scheme consists of 18 color selections for different parts of a program window and a contrast setting. The window preview area shows all the different parts of windows that are affected by the color scheme. As you make selections or adjust settings, the preview area changes to reflect the settings so that you can see how your new colors will look. Figure 3.6 shows the Colors dialog box of the Control Center.

Figure 3.6
Customize window and text colors using the Colors dialog box.

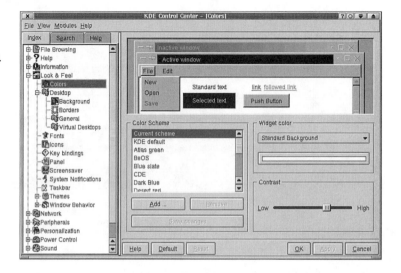

To pick a predefined collection of color settings, pick a scheme from the Color Scheme list.

To change one of the color settings, either choose the name of the window part from the drop-down list in the Widget color area or click the window part in the preview area.

After you have selected a window part, change the color for that part by clicking the color button and selecting a color from the dialog box that appears.

After making your selections, choose a contrast setting by dragging the Contrast slider bar between Low and High. The Contrast setting adjusts the colors used for the highlight and shadow of the three-dimensional frames around KDE interface elements. You can see the effect of the Contrast setting in the window preview area when you drag the Contrast slider.

After all your selections are made, click OK or Apply to save your settings. If you switch between color schemes frequently, you might want to manipulate the color scheme list. To add the current collection of color settings to the list, click the Add button and type a name for your color scheme. To remove a color scheme, highlight a scheme in the list and click Remove. You can only remove color schemes that you have created, not any system color schemes.

CHANGING THE DESKTOP BACKGROUND

To change the background color or image of the Desktop, select Look & Feel, Desktop, Background in the Control Center tree list. The dialog box that appears has three main areas:

■ A list of (virtual) desktop names

■ A preview monitor

■ A multitab selection area

Each virtual desktop in KDE can have its own background settings. This enables you to easily identify the virtual desktop you are on from its appearance. The first thing you need to do to change the background is select the virtual desktop that you want to change from the Desktop list.

For each desktop, you can choose a background consisting of either a single color, a two-color pattern, or a background image. If you choose a background image, you can configure how the image is displayed, or you can choose several images and cycle between them automatically. More advanced options, including blending between colors and images, and dynamic backgrounds are also available.

As you make modifications to your selections, the preview monitor displays the background that results from your settings .

VIRTUAL DESKTOPS

The Look & Feel, Desktop, Number & Name dialog allows you to configure the virtual desktop feature of KDE. For more information on virtual desktops, see the section "Pager" in Chapter 2, "Introduction to the Desktop."

The Number of Desktops slider determines the total number of virtual desktops available. This can be any number between one and sixteen. Each of the Desktop entries allows to to set the name of the desktop, which appears on the Window List or on the panel in certain configurations.

CHOOSING A SCREENSAVER

The Screensaver dialog box of the Control Center enables you to select a screensaver for your system and customize its settings. You can configure global options, such as the time before the screensaver kicks in, as well as options specific to the individual screensaver that you choose. The Screensaver dialog box is divided into three major areas (see Figure 3.7):

■ A preview monitor

■ A screensaver list

■ Some general screensaver settings

To choose a screensaver, select the screensaver from the Screen Saver list. To customize the screensaver you have chosen, click the Setup button and edit the entries in the dialog box that appears. Each setup dialog box includes a preview window so that you can see the effect of your settings before you accept them.

Figure 3.7
The Screensaver dialog box enables you to pick a screen saver and adjust its settings.

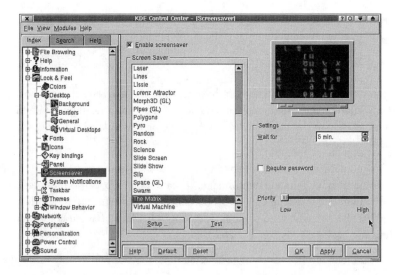

To configure the amount of time before the screensaver starts, enter the number of minutes in the Wait for field of the dialog box. If you want the screensaver to lock the screen when it is activated so that a password is required to regain access to your machine, select the Require password option. You can also select whether you want KDE to echo password characters as stars as they are typed by selecting the Show password as stars option. If this option is not selected, the characters of the password are not echoed at all when the password is typed. To allow the use of the root password as well as your regular user password to unlock the screen, select the Accept root password to unlock option .

The Priority setting controls how much processor time is devoted to the screensaver when it is active. This corresponds to the Linux nice value of the screensaver process. If you want the screensaver to run at a higher priority than other processes on your machine (so that the animation is smooth, for example), drag the slider to High. If you want other processes to have priority, slide it to Low.

To test the screensaver settings on the full screen, click the Test button. After adjusting the screensaver settings, click OK or Apply to save your changes.

CONFIGURING SYSTEM NOTIFICATIONS

The Look & Feel, System Notifications dialog box enables you to specify how you would like to be notified when various events happen. To associate a notification with a particular event, select the event from the nested menus in the Application/Events list. Then select one or more notification types:

- **Log to file**—KDE will append a message to the file you specify in the Filename text box.
- **Play sound**—KDE will play the sound file you specify in the Filename text box. Click the button beside the Filename text box to test the sound.

- **Show messagebox**—KDE will open a message box.

- **Standard error output**—KDE will output a message to standard error (stderr). This generally will go to your text console. Generally this is only useful for debugging purposes.

After you have made your changes, click OK or Apply to save them.

SETTING WINDOW MANAGER POLICIES

Settings in the Look & Feel, Window Behavior, Actions dialog box of the Control Center enable you to adjust window manager policies. These policies affect the appearance of windows when they are moved and resized, as well as how windows are maximized, placed, and selected (receive focus) by the window manager. The options in the top part of this dialog box determine how windows look while they are being moved or resized, and how the Maximize operation works on a window. During a resize or move operation, you can choose to have windows appear with their contents intact, or as transparent rectangles. When windows are drawn with their contents during these operations, it requires more time to update the display during the move or resize operation. If you are on a slow machine, this can result in the operation appearing choppy or jerky.

To display the contents of windows during move or resize operations, select the appropriate options on this dialog box. However, if you want faster (smoother) performance for move or resize operations, deselect these options.

If you choose to display contents in resizing windows, you can also choose to have windows update their contents while they are being resized, using the Resize animation setting. Use the slider to specify a speed. If you select a value other than None, when you resize a window its contents are redrawn while it is being resized. This gives you a visual indication of how the program will lay out the window contents at various window sizes, so you can select the best size. However, it also makes the resize operation slower, and it can be choppy looking.

The Placement policy drop-down menu allows you to configure where windows are placed on the desktop. The following policies are supported:

- **Smart**—Minimizes overlap between windows.

- **Cascade**—The first window is displayed in the upper left. The next window is placed slightly to the lower right so it mostly overlaps, and so on. The result is similar to how you might lay down a hand of playing cards.

- **Random**—Windows are placed on the screen randomly.

Focus policy is perhaps one of the most personal decisions in configuring KDE. Focus policy is how KDE determines which window is currently active, and what to do when a window becomes active. The policies are as follows:

- **Click to focus**—Windows gain focus only when you click on them. The window is automatically *raised*, or put on top of any other desktop windows. This is the default and is the focus policy of Microsoft Windows.

- **Focus follows mouse**—Windows gain focus when you move into them (using the mouse pointer or using Alt+Tab or otherwise). This might or might not raise the window. Moving the mouse pointer onto the desktop does not cause the currently active window to lose focus. If Auto Raise is selected, the window will be raised after the mouse pointer is in it for the number of milliseconds set by the Delay slider. If Click Raise is selected, clicking anywhere in the window will raise it. Otherwise, only clicking on the border will raise it. This is an incredibly useful focus policy, because it enables you to type in one window while reading another window that might obscure it.

- **Focus under mouse**—Windows gain focus whenever the mouse pointer moves into them. Keyboard shortcuts like Alt+Tab will probably not work correctly. This focus policy is really only provided for true purists.

- **Focus strictly under mouse**—Windows gain focus only while the mouse pointer is within them. If the mouse points to the desktop, no window will have focus. This is generally not useful and is only provided for nearly masochistic old-time purists.

> **Tip**
>
> If you have experience in other operating systems, you might be most comfortable using Click to focus, which is the default. But you should try Focus follows mouse. It really separates UNIX-based desktops from less feature-rich ones.

PERSONALIZING KDE

The Personalization menu includes many features for making KDE more tailored to you. This section is also fairly confusing, because there is not a clear connection between all the modules placed here. This layout will likely be redesigned in KDE 2.1.

SELECTING COUNTRY AND LANGUAGE SETTINGS FOR THE DESKTOP

The Personalization, Country & Language dialog box enables you to customize how numbers, dates, and currency are displayed, as well as your preferred language.

LOCALE   This tab allows you to set the most general information, country, language, and character set.

The Country pull-down sets your country to one of the more that 60 pre-set countries that KDE knows about. This information is generally used to set the defaults, so if your country is not listed, simply select either a country with a similar culture, or select Default (C) and configure the settings yourself. No matter what you select in this pull-down, you can always reconfigure any of the options in this dialog.

The Language pull-down sets your preferred language to one of the nearly 50 languages that have KDE message translations. It is possible (even likely) that not all applications have been translated to your preferred language. Because each message in KDE must be individually translated, it is even possible that only some of the messages in a given application have been translated. If KDE cannot find a translation for a given message, it will display U.S. English.

Tip

> If you are fluent in a non-English language and can also read English, the KDE Internationalization project can probably use you. Translation is a great field for non-programmers (and also for programmers)! Just visit i18n.kde.org to get started. *i18n* is the abbreviation for *internationalization* because there are 18 characters between the *i* and the *n*. Similarly, the abbreviation for *localization* is *l0n*.

The Charset pull-down sets your preferred *character set*. A character set is a way of mapping integers (which computers understand) to letters (which humans understand). They generally have obscure sounding names such as iso8859-1, which is the character set for Western European languages. These names generally come from the International Standards Organization, or ISO, specification 8859. These superseded the previous "code page" standard, which is currently being replaced by the Unicode (ISO 10646) standard. Unicode should eventually unite all of the world's alphabets into a single character set, removing the ambiguity in the current system. KDE already includes a great deal of Unicode support, and is now using it as its preferred internal format. As the world moves to Unicode, KDE will be prepared, while still providing compatibility with the many current and historical formats you are likely to encounter.

PART

I

CH

3

NUMBERS   This tab allows you to configure how numbers are displayed and entered in KDE applications. Note that not all KDE applications are well-behaved about accepting localized input. For instance, at the time of this writing, if your decimal symbol is set to comma (as it is in many parts of the world), KOffice will still not accept "0,5" as one-half. You must enter "0.5", which KOffice will then display as "0,5".

MONEY   This tab allows you to configure how money is displayed in KDE applications. These settings are generally independent of the settings from the Numbers tab, except for the positive and negative signs.

Tip

> If you are confused with the Number and Money tabs, just look at the bottom of the dialog to see a preview of your selection.

TIME & DATES   This tab allows you to configure one of the most ambiguous display formats available: time and date.

The Time, Date, and Short date formats are all based on the format specifiers in Table 3.2.

Characters without a leading percent sign are treated as literals. For example, to display the time as 21:34:55, the format would be %H:%M:%S. At the time of this writing, there is no way to put a percent sign in the format itself.

The Start Week on Monday option determines whether the week starts on Monday versus Sunday.

TABLE 3.2 FORMAT SPECIFIERS FOR DATE AND TIME

Specifier	Meaning
%H	Hour in 24-hour format with leading zero (00–23)
%k	Hour in 24-hour format without leading zero (0–23)
%I	Hour in 12-hour format with leading zero (01–12)
%l	Hour in 12-hour format without leading zero (1–12)
%M	Minute with leading zero (00–59)
%S	Second with leading zero (00–59)
%p	"am" or "pm" as needed
%Y	Year with century
%y	Year without century (00–99)
%m	Month with leading zero (01–12)
%n	Month without leading zero (1–12)
%b	Three letter abbreviation for month
%B	Full name of month
%d	Day of month with leading zero (01–31)
%e	Day of month without leading zero (1–31)
%a	Three-letter abbreviation for day of week
%A	Full name of day of week

CONFIGURING EMAIL

This dialog allows you to configure your email address and server for mail clients (like kmail) and other programs that can send mail (such as the bug-reporting facility in most KDE applications).

Most of the information in this dialog is incredibly straightforward. Full Name and Organization are free-form identification fields. Email Address is your sending email address, whereas Reply Address is the email address you want replies sent to (leave this blank if you want them sent back to the sending address).

The server information box configures your connection to your mail server (if you have one). Username and Password refer to your information on your mail server, not necessarily your local machine. Incoming host is your IMAP or POP server. Leave this blank if you receive mail directly to your local machine (or do not receive mail to this machine at all). Outgoing host is your mail relay. Leave this blank if your machine is running postfix or sendmail itself.

KDE understands IMAP, POP3, and Local mailbox delivery schemes. Use the latter if you receive mail directly to your machine. See Chapter 25, "Email Clients and Servers," for full information on mail delivery.

If you prefer a mail client other than kmail, enter this in the Preferred email client box. If your mail client is text-based (mutt for example), click Run in terminal .

CONFIGURING THE PANEL

You can change the location, size, and other options of the Panel using the Panel configuration dialog box. Also, you can adjust the positions of the items on the panel or remove and add items on the Panel by accessing individual item context menus.

PANEL CONFIGURATION DIALOG BOX

The Panel configuration dialog box is available on the Application Starter menu, under Panel Menu, Configure, Settings or on the Panel context menu, under Configure, Settings. Right-click an empty area of the Panel to access the Panel context menu. Finally, this menu is also available on the Control Center under Look & Feel, Panel.

The Panel Configuration dialog box, shown in Figure 3.8, enables you to select the location of the Panel, as well as the size of the icons in the Panel. Other options are available as well. This dialog box has five pages, which can be accessed using the General, Look & Feel, Menus, Buttons, and Applets tabs.

Figure 3.8
The Panel is at the core of the desktop and is highly configurable.

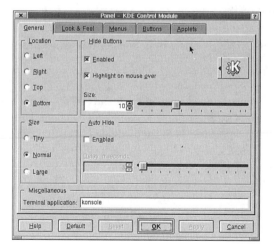

PART

I

CH

3

GENERAL

The General tab allows you to select the Location and Size of the Panel. The Tiny option uses small icons and shrinks the height of the Panel. The Normal and Large options use large icons, but with different Panel heights.

By enabling Auto-hide Panel, the panel will disappear whenever it is not in use. This is handy for gaining a little more screen real estate. To bring the panel back, move the mouse to the panel's edge. The Delay in Seconds determines how long the panel waits before disappearing.

The two hide buttons on either side of the panel are used to quickly move the panel off-screen. This is basically the manual version of Auto-hide Panel. If you are using Auto-hide Panel, you probably don't need the hide buttons, so you can uncheck the Enabled check box in the Hide Buttons section. If you do choose to have the hide buttons, they can be highlighted whenever the mouse is over them by selecting Highlight on mouse over. You can also change their relative size using the Size slider.

The Miscellaneous section allows you to set the Terminal application. This is the program that is used whenever KDE needs a terminal, such as when you select Run in Terminal from the Run Command menu.

LOOK & FEEL

The Look & Feel tab generally makes selections from the General tab fancier. Enabling Hide Animation will cause the panel to "slide" off the screen when using the hide buttons (otherwise it just disappears). The sliding speed is controllable with the Speed slider.

Similarly, enabling Auto-hide Animation will cause the panel to slide off the screen when using Auto-hide Panel. Once again, the sliding speed is controllable with the Speed slider. Note that there is no problem with having both Auto-hide Panel and the hide buttons available simultaneously, though there is seldom a reason to do this.

In the Miscellaneous section, you can select Fade Out Applet Handles. This causes the handles (the two sets of vertical dots) to the left of each applet to disappear except when you place the mouse pointer over them. This gives you a smoother-looking panel that some people prefer.

MENUS

The Menus tab enables you to control the various menus on the panel, including the K menu (Application Starter). The first option, Clear Menu Cache, allows you to determine whether (and by using the Clear After N Seconds slider, how often) the menus are re-read from disk. All panel menus are stored on disk as directory trees (for example, the K Menu is stored in `${KDEDIR}/share/applnk`). To improve performance, these directories are read into memory the first time they are needed and cached. If you change the directory after it's been read, the panel will not reflect this unless the cache is cleared. Setting this option indicates how often this should happen. You can always manually clear the cache by restarting the panel (right-click the panel and select Restart).

Browser Menus configures quick browsers, which are cascading menus that give quick access to your directory (for example, the Quick Browser link on the Application Starter). The Show hidden files entry determines whether files beginning with a period are displayed. These files are usually considered "hidden." The Maximum Browser Menu Entries slider ensures that you do not overwhelm the browser by entering a directory with an excessive number of files.

The K Menu selections configure the Application Starter. The Merge Different Menu Locations option determines whether the personal and system menus are merged into one, or listed separately. The Show Recent Documents Submenu determines whether Recent Documents entry is available. Similarly, the Show Quickbrowser Submenu determines whether the Quick Browser is available on the Application Starter.

BUTTONS

The Buttons tab configures the appearance of individual buttons on the panel. If you turn on background tiles, then each type of tile can be colored differently. For each type of tile, select whether it should be specially colored by clicking the Enabled check box. Then select the color from the drop-down list.

APPLETS

The Applets tab determines what applets are available for embedding in the panel and how they run. Applets are applications such as the taskbar, pager, and dock.

Applets can either run internally or externally. To the end user, there is little difference, except that internal applets run faster. The problem with internal applets is that if they are unstable or insecure, the entire panel can crash or be compromised. The panel is protected from external applets by a wrapper script. That way, if the applet crashes, the panel is unaffected.

You can choose one of the following security levels:

- **Load only trusted applets internal**—Applets listed in the Trusted Applets list will be loaded internally. All other applets will be loaded externally. You can move applets between the Trusted and Available lists using the arrow buttons between the two lists.

- **Load startup config applets internal**—Applets that are configured to run on startup are loaded internally. Applets started later are loaded externally. This is usually a good selection.

- **Load all applets internal**—Trusts all applets. This will improve performance, but can decrease stability.

ADJUSTING ITEMS ON THE PANEL

To move an item on the Panel, or to remove an item from the Panel, use the options on the context menu for that item. Right-click an item and the context menu appears (see Figure 3.9). To move an item, select the Move option on this menu, and drag the item to the desired position on the Panel. Other buttons on the panel shift to make room for the item when you drop it. You can also move an item by clicking it and dragging with the middle mouse button. To remove an item, select Remove from the context menu.

ADDING ITEMS TO THE PANEL

Adding items to the panel is fairly simple. Just select Panel Menu, Add from the Application Starter. This will provide several classes of items to add:

- **Application**—This provides a list of all the applications on the Application Starter. Selecting one will add a short-cut button to that application.

- **Applet**—This provides a list of known applets. Applets include the taskbar, the pager, the clock, and the dock. Things in the dock such as klipper are not applets. The list of available applets is determined by the desktop files in `${KDEDIR}/share/apps/kicker/applets`.

- **K Menu**—This adds an Application Starter. You can have multiple Application Starters if you like. For example, you might put one on each side of the panel for easier access. You can also remove the Application Starter altogether if you would rather have the panel space. As with most things in KDE, everything on the Application Starter is available through other means.

- **Windowlist**—This adds a button that provides quick access to all applications running on all desktops.

- **Desktop Access**—This adds a button that, when pressed, temporarily hides all the windows on the desktop. This makes it easy to get to icons on your desktop (such as the Trash). Pressing this button again restores all your windows.

- **Quick Browser**—This adds a Quick Browser, after asking you for the directory you would like to view. Quick Browsers give easy access to directories by making all of the directory entries appear as menu entries.

- **Legacy Application**—This adds a non-KDE application shortcut. KDE applications will automatically add themselves to the Application Starter, so you can just select them from the Application list, but non-KDE applications don't do this. Selecting Legacy Application allows you to add these applications easily.

Figure 3.9
The Panel item context menu pops up when you right-click an item on the Panel.

USING THE MENU EDITOR

The menu editor, kmenuedit, modifies the main Application Starter menu. To open the menu editor, select System, Menu Editor on the Application Starter menu. Figure 3.10 shows the menu editor window.

To open or close submenus, click the box beside a name. To move a menu item from one location to another, drag it using the mouse.

To create a new menu item, select the submenu you want to add it to and select File, New Item (or click the New item button on the toolbar). On the General tab, the fields are as follows:

- **Name**—Language-specific name of application. This is the name that appears in the menu.

- **Comment**—Longer comment for application. This appears in the quick-tip for the application.

- **Command**—Command to run.

- **Type**—Generally this should be Application.

- **Work Path**—Directory to change to before running application.

- **Run in terminal**—If selected, application will be run in a terminal. The terminal will be started with the options listed in the Terminal Options textbox.

- **Run as different user**—If selected, application will be run as user specified in the Username textbox. You will have to enter the password for that user whenever you execute this command.

- **Icon**—The button beside Work Path allows you to select an icon for this application.

Figure 3.10
The Menu Editor for the Application Starter menu.

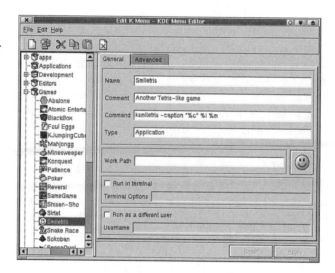

The Advanced tab allows you to set a short-cut key for this application. Click Change, select Custom Key, select your modifiers, and finally click the box to the right of Alt and then press the key you would like to use. Whenever you press that key, this application will be executed. To add a new submenu, select File, New Submenu, and enter the name.

Tip

Unlike older versions of KDE, you no longer have to worry very much about whether a particular desktop file is in the system directory or in your personal directory. If you try to edit a system entry, kmenuedit will automatically make a copy to your local directory. The two locations are merged in the Application Starter menu, so it all works transparently.

RESTART OPTION

After making adjustments to the Panel or Application Starter menu contents, it might be necessary to restart the Panel program in order for the changes to take effect. To restart the Panel, select Panel Menu, Restart on the Starter menu, or choose Restart from the Panel context menu. Few changes, however, require restarting the panel.

MANIPULATING FILES AND DIRECTORIES

The file manager, konqueror, is such an integral part of KDE that it deserves special discussion. This section covers how to use konqueror to manipulate files and directories, as well as to navigate remote filesystems and view World Wide Web pages.

INTRODUCTION TO THE FILE MANAGER

konqueror is different from other file managers that you might have encountered because it treats all the objects that it browses in a very consistent manner. konqueror is really a generic browser, capable of viewing not only file and directory listings, but many other things as well. The way konqueror achieves this is by using Uniform Resource Locators (URLs) for all the paths that it browses and by using plug-in modules to display various types of information. Thus, in addition to being a filesystem browser and manager, konqueror is also an FTP client, a World Wide Web browser, an archive file viewer, an image viewer, and much more.

LOCATION TRANSPARENCY

Because all the separate things that konqueror can browse are treated the same, it enables you to perform operations conveniently, with little regard for the location of the item you are manipulating. For example, you can drag links from a World Wide Web page onto your Desktop, where you can click them at any time to call them up. You can do the same thing for FTP directories, placing them on your Desktop just like folders. When you click a file on a remote FTP site, konqueror launches it or opens it as if it were a local file. The only difference is that it might take longer as konqueror downloads the file to your system to operate on it.

In another example, you can drag files directly from a remote FTP site (in a folder in konqueror) directly to another KDE application running on your Desktop. You can drag a package file on an FTP site directly to the package manager program to view the package information and install it on your system.

This kind of seamless interaction between remote and local objects makes it easier to access and manage the things you work with on a day-to-day basis.

> **Tip**
>
> Not all KDE applications are as location transparent as konqueror. Just because you can click an FTP site's text file and automatically pull up a text editor doesn't mean that saving from the editor will automatically upload the file back to the FTP site. Unfortunately, you might find that when you save the file, you are simply updating the temporary file, which will be deleted when you close the text editor. Hopefully this will be improved in future versions of KDE.

ACTIVE MANIPULATION

konqueror is not just a viewer. It is also a manager that can be used to adjust and actively manipulate the objects it is browsing. For example, it uses the KDE file typing system to determine how to launch programs and documents. It recognizes file types on both local and remote files, so it knows what icons to display and what context menus to present to manipulate the items. When you launch a remote file, KDE downloads the file and starts the correct application. You can drag an item from one file manager window to another to make a copy of the item or to make a link to the item. Finally, on your local filesystem, konqueror enables you to manipulate the filesystem attributes of the item (such as the owner and the permissions) with an easy, graphical dialog box.

To get started with the file manager, some user interface elements are described first. The subsequent sections cover specific tasks you can perform with konqueror.

NAVIGATING THE FILESYSTEM WITH KONQUEROR

To start the file manager, click any directory folder or the Home Directory button on the Panel. The file manager is started and displays the contents of the directory you selected in its main window. This is referred to as the browser area of the window. Usually, this is the only area in the main window. However, there is also a directory tree view, which shares the space in the main window with the browser area when it is exposed. Finally there is terminal emulation window area. Figure 3.11 shows the file manager with all three areas exposed.

PART

I

CH

3

Figure 3.11
Use the file manager to browse files and directories on your system and remote sites on the Internet.

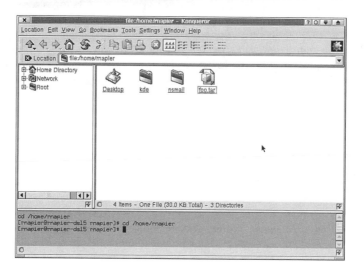

THE BROWSER AREA

The browser area is usually filled with the contents of the current directory. The items in the directory have icons identifying their file type. You can change the view of the directory contents using options on the View, View Mode menu. The five display types (corresponding to options on the View menu) are as follows:

- **Icon View**—Shows the directory contents as large icons in a grid.
- **Text View**—Shows a detailed listing of files and directories, as well as their filesystem attributes.
- **MuliColumn View**—Shows just the filename and mini-icon in a multicolumn view.
- **Detailed List View**—Shows the same file details at the Text View, but also includes mini-icons to indicate the file type.
- **Tree View**—Similar to Detailed List View, but each icon can be expanded into a tree of subdirectories.

Normally, hidden files (those that start with a dot) are not shown in the listing. To see these files in the listing, select View, Show Dot Files from the menu. Other options to control the view of the browser area are also available, and will be described. There are a number of ways to navigate to other directories in the file manager. To move to a subdirectory, click the folder or directory name in the browser window. To move to the parent directory, click the up arrow in the file manager button bar. To switch between directories that you have already visited, use the forward and back arrows on the button bar. Each of these buttons also has a small down arrow under it. This is to indicate that if you hold down the button, you will see a list of places to go. For the up arrow, this will be a list of parents, grandparents, and so forth of this directory (or URL). For the left and right buttons, this will be backward and forward in the history the cache.

To switch to an item in the bookmark list, select it in the Bookmarks menu.

Finally, you can type the location to which you want to jump to in the location bar at the top of the file manager window, or in a pop-up Open Location dialog box. You can access this dialog box by selecting the Location, Open Location menu item, or by using the keyboard shortcut Ctrl+O. When you type in the location, you can specify it as either a regular directory path or as a URL. Use the file prefix for locations within your local filesystem.

THE DIRECTORY TREE

The left pane of the file manager window area is generally the Tree View. By default it is hidden, but you can show it by selecting Window, Show Directory Tree in the file manager menu. The Tree View has three top-level directories corresponding to different places to begin browsing the filesystem:

- **The Home Directory folder**—Corresponds to your home directory.
- **The Network folder**—This folder has three sub-folders: FTP Archives for FTP sites that you frequent; Web Sites, which contains your bookmarks; and Windows Shares, which provides access to SMB shares.
- **The Root folder**—Corresponds to the root of the entire filesystem.

The Tree view only shows directories, not individual files or links. To expand or collapse a directory, click the box with a plus or minus sign to the left of the directory name. When a directory is collapsed, the box has a plus in it; when it is expanded the box has a minus sign. To make the browser window jump to a directory in the Tree view, click the directory name (provided the browser window is linked; see "Linking Windows" in the following text.)

THE TERMINAL EMULATOR WINDOW

You can display a terminal emulator window (similar to konsole) in the bottom of the file manager by selecting Window, Show Terminal emulator window. This will give you access to a shell prompt, where you can enter normal UNIX commands. As you change directories using the browser or directory tree, this window will automatically change directories as well (provided they are linked; see "Linking Windows" in the following section). Changing directories in the terminal emulator using the cd command will not change the views of the browser or directory tree.

PART

I

CH

3

LINKING WINDOWS

When you change directories using the browser or directory tree, other windows can change as well. By default, all windows are locked together so they select the same directory. Sometimes it can be convenient to unlink an individual window, however, so that it will always view the same directory.

To link or unlink windows, select the Link box. All windows with the link box selected are linked together and will always point to the same directory. The one exception is the terminal emulator. If you use the cd command, it will be out of sync with the other windows.

ADDING MORE WINDOWS

The three default windows are just the start of your layout options. You can create multiple copies of the browser and terminal emulator windows, and each copy can view a different directory or Web site.

To create a new window, select an existing window of the type you would like to create. Then select one of the following menu options:

- **Window, Split View Left/Right**—Splits the current window vertically into two windows of the same kind. The shortcut for this is Ctrl+Shift+L.
- **Window, Split View Top/Bottom**—Splits the current window horizontally into two windows of the same kind. The shortcut for this is Ctrl+Shift+T.
- **Window, New View on Right**—Creates a new window of the same kind on the far right.
- **Window, New View on Bottom**—Creates a new window of the same kind at the bottom.

Newly created windows will be unlinked by default, making it easier to view other locations. You can change the location they view by clicking them (the small green light in the lower-left corner will indicate which window is active), and then entering a new location in the Location bar at the top of konqueror.

To remove an existing browser or terminal emulator window, click it and then select Window, Remove Active View or Ctrl+Shift+R. To resize a window, click and drag the border between two windows.

Saving a Layout

When you've created a particularly useful layout, you can save it by selecting Window, Save/Remove View Profile.

First, choose a name for your profile, or select an existing profile name. Then select whether to Save URLs in profile. If you select this, then whenever you load this profile, it will visit the same URLs.

Select whether to Save window size in profile, which will save the overall size of the konqueror window. Otherwise, just the relative sizes of the windows will be remembered.

Finally click Save to save the profile, or click Delete Selected Profile to delete it.

Performing Management Tasks

This section describes all the different management tasks you can perform with the file manager. This includes such things as getting information about a file; moving, copying, and removing files; and changing various attributes of a file, such as its name, ownership, and permissions.

Getting Information About a File

The most basic management task is simply finding out information about a file. Information can be obtained in a number of different ways.

First, the status bar shows the size and type of the item that is currently under the mouse pointer. To see this information, move the mouse over the items in which you are interested.

You can also see detailed file information by selecting either Text View or Detailed List View from the View menu. This shows the type, name, size, modification time, permissions, owner, group, and link target for each item in columns across the screen. The icons in the browser window indicate the type of each item, as recognized by KDE. KDE provides a large set of different icons to identify files of different types. By convention, a directory has a folder as its icon, a documents file often has a piece of paper in its icon, and a program often has a gear. Over time, you will learn these conventions and begin to identify easily, by the icon, the types of files you are looking at.

Selecting Items

Certain management actions can be performed by directly manipulating the items in the browser window. There are multiple ways to select more than one item to manipulate.

To select an item without launching it, hold down the Ctrl key and click the item. The item is shaded to indicate that it is selected. To add items to the selection, or to remove items that are already selected, use Ctrl+Click as well. You can also select a group of items by dragging a rectangle around them.

If you have a large number of items and it is awkward—or impossible—to select them with a rectangle, you can select them using a name and wildcard specification. To do this, choose Edit, Select from the menu, or use the Ctrl+Plus (on the number pad) keyboard shortcut. Then type a filename or wildcard specification into the Select files dialog box. Click OK, and files matching your specification are selected. Similarly, you can unselect files using the Edit, Unselect or Ctrl+Minus (on the number pad). Edit, Unselect All (Ctrl+U) will unselect all files, and Edit, Invert selection (Ctrl+*) will invert your selection.

MOVING AND COPYING FILES

The easiest way to move or copy files from one part of your filesystem to another, or to make links to a file, is to select and drag them. You can drag files between two open file manager windows, between the file manager window and the Desktop, or from the file manager window to a folder icon (either on the Desktop or in another file manager window). When you drop the item, you are presented with a menu with three options: Copy, Move, and Link. Select one of these options, and the operation is completed. For operations that can take a long time, a status window opens to inform you of the progress of the operation.

You can also copy files (but not move or link them) by selecting them and then choosing the Copy option from either the Edit menu or the context menu for the files. This marks the items for copying. Now browse to the location where you want to copy the files, and select Paste from either the Edit menu or the context menu of the directory in which you want to copy the files.

> **Note**
>
> Using the Copy and Paste menu options requires only one file manager window to be open. If your screen is cluttered, or if there is some other reason why it might be awkward or time consuming to have two file manager windows open, this method of copying files can be very useful. Similarly, you could open multiple browse windows within the file manager window and drag files between them.

Sometimes it is hard to decide which of the possible actions (Copy, Move, or Link) is the most appropriate. This is especially true when you start working with special KDE files and directories, such as the Desktop itself. Some of the following suggestions might seem obvious, but here are some rules of thumb to help you decide:

- **Only select Copy if you really want to create another copy of the item**—This is rarely what you want to do with executable programs and scripts. It might or might not be what you want with documents and other files, depending on the circumstances. Remember that having multiple copies means that modifications to one copy won't affect the other. Although it is possible to put real documents on the Desktop, most people just put links there, or put files there only temporarily.

■ **Only select Move if you want to change the location of the original item**—This is rarely what you want to do with a program or script. Programs are usually located in bin directories on the path, and moving them makes them inaccessible for command-line use.

■ **For a desktop configuration file, you usually copy it or link it**—Sometimes, moving a desktop file from its original location results in it no longer working correctly. For example, MimeType desktop files only have meaning in a `mimelnk` directory. Don't move desktop files out of special directories unless you know what you are doing.

REMOVING FILES

To remove a file from your system, you have three options: move it to the Trash can, delete it, or shred it. Moving it to the Trash moves the file to the `Trash` directory, which means that it still takes up space in your filesystem, but that you can recover it if you need it in the future. Deleting the file completely erases it from your system. There is no way to recover the file. Shredding the file goes an extra step by first overwriting the file with a complex series of data before deleting it. This should ensure that even advanced data recovery techniques won't be able to restore all or part of the file.

To move a file to the Trashcan, choose the Move to Trash option from either the Edit menu or the local context menu, or drag the item from the file manager window to the Trash icon on the Desktop. TSimilarly, to delete it, select the file (or files), and then choose the Delete option from either of these menus. Finally, to shred it, select the file (or files), and choose the Shred option.

LAUNCHING FILES

Launching a file from the file manager is exactly the same as launching it from the Desktop window. You can either click the item, drag the item on top of a program, select Open With from the context menu of the item, or select one of the programs listed in the context menu.

If you single-click the item, KDE determines an appropriate course of action, depending on the file type. If KDE cannot determine a default program for the file, KDE prompts you for a program with which to open the file.

MODIFYING FILES AND DIRECTORIES

KDE makes it very easy to manipulate the attributes of an item in the filesystem by providing a simple graphical dialog box to manipulate an object's properties. To access this dialog box, select Properties from the item's context menu. The dialog box has different tab pages, depending on the item type. But the first two tab pages of the dialog box, General and Permissions, are common to all types.

RENAMING A FILE   To rename a file, select Properties from the file's context menu. When the dialog box opens, you are on the General page of the dialog box. Edit the Name field, and click the OK button.

CHANGING OWNERSHIP AND PERMISSIONS To change ownership and permissions on a file, access the Properties dialog box, and select the Permissions tab (see Figure 3.12).

Figure 3.12
Click the check boxes
to change permissions.

To modify the permissions of an item, click the check boxes in the Access permissions section of the dialog box. To change the owner or group of the file, use the controls under Ownership.

NAVIGATING THE WEB

The file manager operates not just on local files. It is also a generic World Wide Web browser. To go to a Web page, click a URL item, or enter the URL for the page in the location bar of the file manager.

To navigate, use the same techniques as you do with a normal Web browser. Click links and use the forward and back buttons in the button bar. Reload a page using the reload button. Access the history list from the Go menu.

To go to a bookmarked site, click the item in the Bookmarks menu. To add the current page to the bookmarks, select Bookmarks, Add Bookmark. If you have sub-menus in your book-mark list, you can select Add Bookmark for the menu on which you want the site to be placed.

You can edit bookmarks by selecting Bookmarks, Edit Bookmarks. This will open another konqueror window viewing your bookmark directory. By dragging links here, or using the local menu's Create new dialog, you can create new bookmarks. By creating directories here, you can categorize your bookmarks into whatever classifications you would like.

To save a link in a Web page on the Desktop, drag the link from the file manager window to the Desktop. To save the current page to the Desktop, back up one page and drag the link from the previous page to the Desktop. If you don't have a link to drag (for example, you got to a site by typing it in instead of following a link), you can make an entry on the Desktop by following these steps:

1. Select Bookmarks, Add Bookmark to add the page to the bookmark list.
2. Now select Bookmarks, Edit Bookmarks to show the Bookmarks folder.
3. Drag the item from the Bookmarks folder to the Desktop.

LOOKING INSIDE ARCHIVES

To view the contents of an archive (tar, tgz, zip, and so forth) file, click the file. You can operate on individual files and directories inside the archive, just like you do in a normal directory. You can also right-click the archive and select Archiver, which provides a more archive-specific view, including the ability to easily extract and add items to the archive.

SPECIAL FEATURES OR TIPS

The file manager has a couple of other features that serve as handy shortcuts for common operations.

MISCELLANEOUS HANDY SHORTCUTS

To open a terminal window with the current directory the same as the file manager, select Tools, Open Terminal, or use the keyboard shortcut Ctrl+T. This is handy when you get to a directory and discover that you need to perform some complex action there. Instead of opening a terminal window and navigating there manually, just type Ctrl+T. Of course you can always use the integrated terminal emulator by selecting Window, Show Terminal emulator window.

To open a folder in a new file manager window instead of the current file manager window, click it with the middle mouse button.

To open a new file manager window with the same current directory as the current window, click the gear icon in the toolbar (located on the right of the toolbar).

Sometimes, you need to perform a file manipulation for which you just don't have permissions. In this case it is possible to start a terminal window, su to root, and execute the commands by hand. However, to make it more convenient to overcome this situation, and to enable you to continue operating using a graphical file manager, KDE provides a way to launch a file manager with superuser (root) privileges.

To do this, select System, File Manager (Super User Mode) from the Application Starter menu. A special terminal window starts up and prompts you for the root password for your machine. Enter it, and a file manager with root privileges starts. To remind you that you are operating with special privileges, the handle of the menu bar in the file manager window is shown in bright red. You can use this file manager window to perform operations that require root privileges. When you drag files between file manager windows of both types (root and regular user) onscreen, the window that performs the copy, move, or link operation is the destination window (the window being dropped on). This means, for example, that you cannot drag a file to which you don't have permissions from a root file manager window to a non-root file manager window. You can, however, perform this drag the other way around.

To view a window in full-screen mode, select Window, Fullscreen Mode (Ctrl+Shift+F). This will expand the current window to fill the entire screen, including the normal panel and menu areas. It will also get rid of the konqueror menu bar and status bar, leaving just the toolbars. This will give you the most screen real estate for viewing. To exit full screen mode, click the icon with four arrows pointing toward the center of a screen.

PROJECT: SETTING UP A DEVELOPMENT ENVIRONMENT

konqueror's capability to display many panes simultaneously is useful for much more than just Web browsing. It can also enable you to make very efficient use of your desktop. When I want to make quick modifications to my Web pages, I often need two terminal windows (one for vi and one to run commands) and a browser. Working on a laptop where screen real estate is very valuable, three separate windows use up far too much space with all their frames, menu bars, and widgets. Luckily, konqueror lets me make the most efficient use of my available space, as shown in Figure 3.13.

Figure 3.13
konqueror can pack a lot of work space into a small screen.

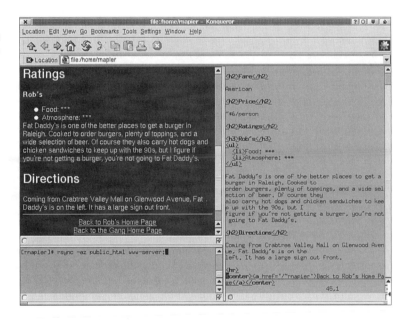

Setting up this environment is easy. Here are the steps I use:

1. Open a konqueror window by clicking the Home button on the panel.
2. Maximize the window.
3. Click Window, Show Terminal Emulator.
4. Click Window, New View on Right.
5. Get rid of the Button bar and Location bar by clicking their handles (on the far left of each bar).
6. Resize the panels as desired using the sizing bars between the windows.
7. Run vi (or emacs -nw if you prefer), in the right panel.

8. In the left browser panel, press Ctrl+O to open the location of your applet.

9. In the lower panel, use your compiler and other simple command-line tools.

10. Click Window, Save/Remove View Profile to save this profile.

11. Enter a profile name, and select Save window size in profile. Then click Save.

Now, whenever you want to get back to this profile, simply bring up a konqueror window and select Window, Load View Profile, and your profile's name. Note that I've saved even more space by hiding the panel at the bottom (by clicking the hide button on the right), and getting rid of the desktop menu (Control Center, Look & Feel, Desktop, General).

## CHAPTER 4

GNOME

In this chapter

WHAT IS GNOME?

GNOME stands for the *GNU Network Object Model Environment*. GNU itself is an acronym, meaning *GNU's Not UNIX*. As with many acronyms in the UNIX world, GNU is recursive. GNOME was developed primarily in reaction to concerns with KDE's reliance on Qt. Qt did not originally have a fully Open Source license, though that has changed. Today Qt is licensed under the GPL, which is the same license used for KDE and GNOME. For more information on KDE and its history, see Chapter 3, "KDE."

Like KDE, GNOME is a full desktop, as described in Chapter 2, "Introduction to the Desktop." It provides much of the same functionality for a graphical environment that is found in other popular operating environments such as Macintosh OS or Windows 98.

GNOME IS A GRAPHICAL DESKTOP

GNOME provides all the capabilities of a desktop. For example, GNOME enables you to do the following:

- Put icons on the desktop to mount and unmount removable disks, such as floppies.
- Browse the filesystem graphically.
- Associate applications with files of a particular type so that when you click a file, it automatically loads the correct application.
- Create a desktop printer icon, to which you can drag files to print them.

None of these are features of a window manager or program launcher by itself. The value of GNOME is that it simplifies many tasks that a user must perform by providing a graphical environment that simulates something more familiar to the user. In other words, GNOME provides a desktop metaphor, which is a way of displaying and manipulating documents, directories, and programs in a manner that is more intuitive and appealing than typing commands at a shell prompt.

You might notice that this list is very similar to the list from Chapter 3. This is because GNOME and KDE are very similar in their features. See "GNOME Is a Philosophy" in the following text for more information on the relationship between KDE and GNOME.

GNOME APPLICATIONS AND GTK+

The GNOME system includes not only the desktop, but also a whole host of applications and utilities to go along with it. In the default distribution of GNOME, there are more than 50 programs, ranging from games to system utilities to office applications. Most of these applications share a common look and feel because they are based on a single toolkit: gtk+.

gtk+ is the GIMP toolkit. The GIMP is the *GNU Image Manipulation Program* and is now part of GNOME. Peter Mattis and Spencer Kimball originally wrote the GIMP as an Adobe Photoshop work-alike for Linux, but it has grown to much more than that. First, the GIMP has become an image-manipulation program in its own right, not just in the shadow of Photoshop. More importantly for GNOME, however, is that when the authors of the GIMP needed an easy way to display buttons, windows, dialog boxes, and other graphical elements, they chose to write a generic toolkit that could be used by other programs. That toolkit became gtk+.

gtk+ helps GNOME applications have a similar appearance, and lets them honor themes (see "Themes" in Chapter 2 for more information on themes). Note, however, that gtk+ is mostly just a toolkit for drawing widgets (such as buttons, windows, scrollbars, and other visual elements). Nothing in gtk+ makes GNOME applications *behave* similarly. And because GNOME does not have a strong style guide, different GNOME programs often do behave very differently. This is part of the individualistic nature of GNOME .

GNOME IS A PHILOSOPHY

In Chapter 3 I described KDE as a project. GNOME is more of a philosophy, or at least it was (we'll get to that in a moment).

When KDE first came on the scene, its goal was to join the Macintosh and Windows' ease of use with the power of UNIX. To do this, KDE needed a toolkit to display widgets. The usual X toolkits, such as Athena, were too primitive to provide the advanced GUI features that KDE developers wanted. More importantly, the KDE developers wanted to develop a totally object-oriented environment in C++. The usual X toolkits were all C based. So they turned to Qt from Troll Tech, which was (and is) one of the best object-oriented GUI toolkits available for UNIX.

The problem was that Qt wasn't free software. KDE was allowed to use it without paying any license fees, but the developers couldn't modify the Qt sources and redistribute them. In open source terms, this is the "free speech versus free beer" problem. When open source developers say "free," they mean liberty, not price.

To address this problem, the GNOME project started. Based on gtk+, it quickly became a serious rival for KDE in terms of functionality. With no licensing issues, groups who wouldn't use KDE (such as the Debian distribution), were happy to use GNOME.

The GNOME philosophy was best summed up in the GNOME Manifesto (see the following sidebar). I say *was* because the GNOME Manifesto is no longer referenced on the main GNOME site, though at the time of this writing it was still available through the old GNOME site at http://www.gnome.org:65348/about/manifesto.shtml.

PART
I
CH
4

The GNOME Manifesto
What is GNOME

GNOME is an Open Source desktop environment built from components that meet the Open Source guidelines in full.

No Compromises

GNOME is open in the full sense of the word. It seeks to impose only that order necessary for consistency.

Window Manager

GNOME defines a set of "hints" for window managers. If you use a GNOME aware window manager it will cooperate nicely with GNOME. If you don't then GNOME works just fine. The "hint" interface is published in full for anyone to use

No religion—pick any window manager

Commercial Use

GNOME is the key to the desktop. Its authors recognize that it is not appropriate to "control" that interface or require that a commercial vendor pays some third party for the ability to write GNOME compliant applications. All the core GNOME software is distributed under the GNU Library Public License, a license which permits the software to be used so long as it is dynamically linked or the user can relink it to new versions of the libraries. This is the same license used by the Linux C libraries.

You need to purchase no expensive software licenses to make your commercial application GNOME compliant.

Vendor Neutral

No component of the interface is controlled solely by one company, or restricted from modification. Any organisation or person however large or small can contribute to GNOME. Furthermore if you don't happen to agree with a decision the license enshrines rights to distribute modified versions.

Truly open. No core component is non Open Source

Language Bindings

GNOME enforces no programming language restrictions on a developer. The core libraries are written in C so are fast and efficient.

The external interface is currently available in C, C++, Objective C, TOM, Guile.

If you want to add bindings for another language we will be delighted to help.

Themes

The low level GNOME/GTK interface is currently being extended to support themes. A mechanism already used in Enlightenment and Windowmaker window managers to allow a user to freely control the look and feel of the base interface components without forcing the original program author to do the work.

User driven look and feel

Portability

The toolkit and libraries used in GNOME are intended to be portable to all Unixlike platforms, and if people contribute code beyond.

GNOME seeks to avoid ties with any platform specific interfaces where possible, and when not possible to provide code for all platforms.

Multiple operating systems

Today, those working on the GNOME project are a less militant group. In some ways, this is because they have won the central ideological arguments. First, Troll Tech released an open source version of Qt and recently has released a completely GPL version, which is what the GNOME supporters demanded in the first place. Second, they have proven that they could build a world-class desktop based purely on open source components from the start.

To a greater sense, however, the place of GNOME has changed. GNOME is no longer the only totally GPL desktop, and although they still have much of the moral high ground, social arguments against KDE are now very weak or non-existent. GNOME must now compete for users with its features and ease of use. Luckily, GNOME is prepared to do just that.

INSTALLING GNOME

Most major Linux distributions include GNOME automatically when you install them. If you use a distribution that does not include GNOME by default, or if you simply want to upgrade to a later version, installing the latest version is incredibly easy, thanks to Helix Code (`www.helixcode.com`).

Helix Code is a for-profit company focused on improving GNOME and providing fee-based support and development. The company has built a very easy-to-use installer, and is currently hard at work on the Evolution (email/calendaring) and Gnumeric (spreadsheet) open-source projects.

To install Helix GNOME, visit `http://www.helixcode.com/desktop/download.php3`, select your distribution, and follow the instructions. At the time of this writing, the instructions for every distribution of Linux were exactly the same:

```
$ su
Password: password
# lynx -source http://go-gnome.com/ | sh
```

Lynx is a text-based Web browser. The `-source` option instructs lynx to output the source of the Web page to stdout and exit. The Web page at `go-gnome.com` is actually a shell script. So this is then run through sh (the bash shell interpreter). The shell script will then take you through the rest of the installation process.

Tip

Helix GNOME is also available for Solaris, but the process is slightly different (though almost as easy). Select Solaris from the download page and follow the instructions.

Also note that at the time of this writing, the default Helix GNOME installation on Caldera OpenLinux had some problems. Instructions for installing Helix GNOME on OpenLinux are available on the OpenLinux support site at `support.calderasystems.com`. Search for "GNOME Helix."

The first question you will be asked is where to download GNOME from. Unless you happen to be close to one of the main mirrors in Palo Alto, California, or Cambridge, Massachusetts, select the Helix Code, Inc. Ubiquitous (Akamaized) link. See the following sidebar "How to Be Everywhere" for more information on Akamai.

How to Be Everywhere: Akamai

You will hopefully see the phrase "Ubiquitous (Akamaized)" showing up more and more in mirror lists. Akamai (`www.akamai.com`) is a company that effectively provides mirroring on demand, but it's much more than that. When you connect to an Akamai server, the network links you with the server that can serve the data you want fastest. This means the server closest to you and with the least load. If too many people want the same piece of information, Akamai automatically generates new mirrors in the areas of the network that need it most. All of this is done transparently.

I've been downloading software from the Internet for years now. I've spent many nights hunting for a mirror of the information I wanted that wasn't overloaded (in Virginia, sometimes it was faster to download from Germany than from Massachusetts). I have yet to find the Akamai system overloaded. You get your data faster, with less hassle, and with less strain on the network. As a user, I highly recommend using this service when it's available, unless you happen to be very close to a primary mirror.

After you select your mirror, the main graphical installer will download. This file is approximately 2MB, so it can take a little while unless you have a fast link. A small bar graph will show you how much has been downloaded. When it completes, the graphical installer shown in Figure 4.1 will automatically launch.

Figure 4.1
The Helix GNOME graphical installer is extremely easy to use.

Next, you will be asked to select where to pull the rest of Helix GNOME from. Usually you will select Helix Code Mirror Site, which will download from one of the many Helix Code mirrors. If you are installing from a Helix Code CD, however, you might choose Local Media. Finally, if you have the packages somewhere on your local network, you might choose Other Network Site.

Because the Helix Code installer can use HTTP, you might need to configure a proxy on the next page if your network needs one.

Then select a mirror. These are general GNOME mirrors, which is why there are many more than when you chose the installer mirror. Once again, look for a city near you. If there isn't one, select Helix Code Inc. Ubiquitous (Akamaized). You should prefer an HTTP proxy over an FTP proxy, because HTTP tends to be much easier for sites to load-balance. Obviously you should not pick any of the testing mirrors (which are labeled DO NOT USE!).

Finally, start choosing packages, as shown in Figure 4.2. If this is your first time installing GNOME, you should probably at least look through what's available, even if you're going to accept the default. It will give you a good sense of what comes with GNOME. If you have a lot of disk space (and a fast network link), you can select Install Everything, which is nice because you won't have to worry about missing anything.

When you click Next, Helix GNOME will install. You can watch the progress on the bar graphs, but you will probably want to just leave it alone. No more interaction is required until it's finished installing. It will then ask whether you want to use the gdm login manager, which you probably do if you're going to use GNOME primarily. Finally, it will restart X (make sure you've quit all other X applications!) and you can start using GNOME.

Figure 4.2
There are a lot of packages, but at least a quick look will give you a good overview of what's available.

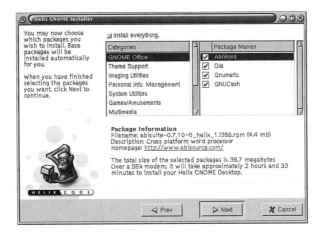

SELECTING GNOME

Many distributions allow you to select whether to use KDE, GNOME, or some other desktop during installation. Switching desktops is usually fairly simple after installation, however. The only complicated part is determining how your particular distribution starts the desktop.

USING THE DISPLAY MANAGER

If you're using either gdm (the GNOME display manager) or kdm (the KDE display manager), you can select your desktop during login using the Session (or Session type) menu.

After you have selected your desktop once, the display manager will remember it when you log in again. Just leave the setting as Default.

USING SWITCHDESK

Red Hat includes a utility called switchdesk, which allows you to easily change among GNOME, KDE, and twm (a simple window manager). From the command line, enter the following:

```
$ switchdesk-gnome
```

Then select the desktop you want (GNOME in this case), and press OK.

The option Change Only Applies to Current Display allows you to have different desktops for different displays. Generally changing displays indicates that you are logging in from a different machine. For example, you can have an NCD X terminal (a machine that displays X, but doesn't do any computations of its own and has no operating system). If your X terminal is across a slow network link, you might prefer to use a lightweight desktop like twm instead of GNOME.

PART

I

CH

4

Tip

switchdesk-kde is another utility that you can use instead of switchdesk-gnome. The difference between these tools is in the toolkits used for displaying the dialog boxes. Either tool can be used to select either desktop.

SELECTING GNOME MANUALLY

If you want to select GNOME by hand, you can modify the configuration files directly. This can be useful if you have a very customized start-up sequence.

To modify the default desktop for all users under Red Hat and similar distributions, simply edit /etc/sysconfig/desktop and enter GNOME as a single line. This will automatically set the desktop for all users who haven't selected their own already.

If you want to set the default desktop for a single user under Red Hat, edit ${HOME}/.Xclients to read exec gnome-session.

Under Debian, at least with the current state of woody, there's no automatic way to select GNOME for all users. On a per-user basis, you can add the following to ${HOME}/.xsession:

```
# Load default window-manager
/usr/bin/x-window-manager&
# Start GNOME
exec /usr/bin/gnome-session
```

You may also want to make sawfish your default window manager:

```
# update-alternatives --config x-window-manager
```

```
There are 4 programs which provide 'x-window-manager'.

    Selection    Command
        1        /usr/bin/sawfish
        2        /usr/bin/X11/twm
        3        /usr/bin/kde2
  *+    4        /usr/X11R6/bin/wmaker

Enter to keep the default[*], or type selection number: 1
Using '/usr/bin/sawfish' to provide x-window-manager'.
```

OpenLinux has no native support for GNOME, and although it has some hooks similar to Red Hat's /etc/sysconfig/desktop, it appears to be moving away from this strategy with OpenLinux 2.4. Currently, the best way to make GNOME your desktop is to edit ${HOME}/.xsession to read exec gnome-session (as in Debian).

Tip

${HOME}/.Xclients or ${HOME}/.xsession is the last file run by the window manager start-up sequence, so this is the place for anything you want run before your window manager. Running your window manager should always be the last line of this file, and should always be preceded with exec (as in exec startkde). The exec tells the shell to completely replace itself with the window manager. Otherwise, an unnecessary copy of your shell will be left in memory. See "SHELL BUILTIN COMMANDS" in the bash man page for more information on exec.

.Xclients or .xsession should be executable. You can make them executable by running the following:

```
$ chmod u+x ${HOME}/.Xclients
```

If you are using .xsession, of course, replace .Xclients in the above command.

BASIC DESKTOP ELEMENTS

When GNOME first appears, it displays the desktop in the default configuration, shown in Figure 4.3. There are two basic screen components to be aware of—the Desktop and the Panel. A menu is also at the top of the screen, but this is technically a panel.

Figure 4.3
The default GNOME
desktop configuration.

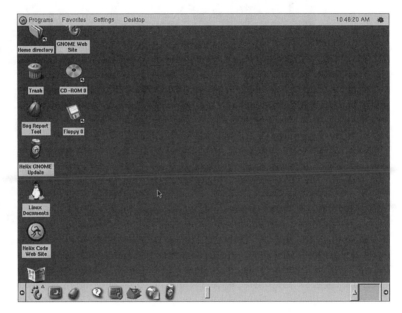

PART

I

CH

4

THE DESKTOP

The Desktop is the main working area of the GNOME environment. This is the background behind all the other components that run on the screen. In the Desktop area, you place icons for programs, documents, and devices that you work with frequently. This makes these items readily available for access and manipulation. Think of the Desktop area in the same way that you think of an actual desktop, where you keep documents and tools handy to accomplish whatever tasks you are currently working on.

In addition to what you see onscreen, GNOME actually provides additional desktop space in which to run programs, called *workspaces*. A workspace is a collection of viewports, or virtual desktops, as described in "Pager" in Chapter 2. In GNOME, you can have multiple workspaces, each of which can have multiple viewports.

THE PANEL

The Panel has icons for important GNOME functions, as well as for frequently used programs. One particularly important item on the Panel is the Main Menu button, which is located (by default) on the left side of the Panel. It is the icon of a foot, which is the GNOME logo. From this button, you can access a menu that lists all the GNOME applications installed on your system, as well as panel configuration. Figure 4.4 shows the contents of the default main menu.

Figure 4.4
The main menu provides access to programs and panel options.

The Panel also includes the Tasklist, and the Desk Guide (viewport pager). The Tasklist shows the windows that are open on the current desktop. Clicking a program in the Tasklist takes you immediately to that program.

RUNNING PROGRAMS

GNOME allows you to directly manipulate all the objects in the system, whether they are files containing documents to work on, programs that you run, or devices that you control. Probably the first thing you will want to do after you've started GNOME is run some applications.

LAUNCHING AN APPLICATION

To launch a program, you can do any of the following:

- **Single-click a button on the Panel**—Several useful programs are provided by default on the Panel. For example, the default Panel includes icons for the Help Browser, a virtual terminal emulator, the Control Center, Netscape, and a system updater, among other things.

- **Double-click an item on the Desktop**—After you've used GNOME for a while, you will probably have placed your favorite programs here, ready to use. Your distribution might also have placed many other links on the desktop, such as links to useful programs or their Web site.

- **Select a program from the Main Menu**—Click the GNOME foot and follow the menus to the program you want to run.

- **Double-click an item in the File Manager**—Inside a file manager window, click an item to launch it.

You can also run a program the old way, by opening a terminal window and typing its name at the shell prompt, or by using the Run Program option from the main menu.

ESSENTIAL PROGRAMS

A few oft-used programs are described here to get you started.

First, the terminal program, gnome-terminal, enables you to open a window and access a regular command-line shell environment. A button for gnome-terminal is provided on the Panel, with a small monitor and a GNOME foot in the icon.

Online help is available by clicking the icon of a question mark on the Panel. The online help includes a general GNOME user's manual, as well as an index for accessing help for all the GNOME applications on your system.

You can browse the filesystem using the file manager, Midnight Commander. To start the file manager, from the Main Menu, select Programs, File Manager.

LOGGING OUT OF GNOME

To log out of GNOME, click the icon of a monitor with a moon in it on the Panel. By default, this will return you to the gdm login dialog box. Currently, GNOME has very limited session management, mostly because of a lack of application support. As with most things in GNOME, this should improve as more applications integrate GNOME features.

GNOME CAPABILITIES

As stated previously, GNOME provides much more than just a graphical window manager or launch environment. It provides many integrated features that are designed to make it easier to work in a graphical environment.

First and foremost, GNOME, like KDE, provides an object-oriented environment in which to work. Instead of composing and typing commands at a shell prompt, you manipulate the objects on your system using the desktop or file manager windows. In GNOME, you treat things as objects that can be accessed, manipulated, or combined by directly touching or moving them (clicking or dragging them). For example, to work on a document, click the document and it opens the correct application. To print a document, drag the document and drop it onto a printer icon. To examine the contents of a floppy, click the floppy device on your desktop.

GNOME enables you to control a whole range of options to customize the appearance and functionality of the desktop. You can change the appearance of many things—the desktop backgrounds, the title bar buttons, or the icons for the individual filesystem items themselves. You can also change the behavior of GNOME to suit your tastes by adjusting such things as the focus policy (which determines how windows become selected) or the default application for certain types of files. Finally, you can alter the contents of the Desktop itself—or the Panel or Main Menu—to match the set of programs or files that you use on a day-to-day basis.

GNOME allows for completely graphical configuration of all these aspects. This is in stark contrast to many other window managers in Linux, where you often have to edit text files by hand and restart the window manager to accomplish the same thing.

GNOME includes a component framework called *Bonobo* to allow applications to communicate with each other, and to a larger extent to allow applications to be embedded within other applications. This is similar to kparts in KDE and OLE in Microsoft Windows. Although Bonobo has a lot of promise, it is not heavily used by GNOME applications yet, so few GNOME applications can handle advanced embedding.

Finally, GNOME has begun to include Unicode support through Pango (as described in "International Support" in Chapter 2). As with Bonobo, Pango is an emerging part of GNOME. Although there was a great deal of work being done on Pango in the early part of 2000, its main Web site had not been updated in several months at the time of this writing.

Generally, GNOME's main strengths are in its individualistic nature. Each application is free to be the best it can be, without having to bend to style guides or a pre-defined object model. At this time, GNOME lacks many of the core features of KDE and is currently playing catch-up. With the addition of corporate help from Helix Code and other companies that have joined the GNOME Foundation, it is likely to rapidly develop in the coming months. This kind of competition continues to improve the state of the art in the open source world.

Configuring GNOME with the Control Center

Configuring GNOME could easily fill several chapters, so in this section we will try to cover the most important configuration issues and introduce you to the layout of the GNOME Control Center. When you become used to how GNOME does things, you'll discover that finding most basic configuration options is easy.

The Control Center, shown in Figure 4.5, is at the heart of configuring GNOME. It is a highly modular configuration system that encapsulates the configuration panels for numerous desktop components.

Figure 4.5
The Control Center provides "one-stop shopping" for GNOME configuration.

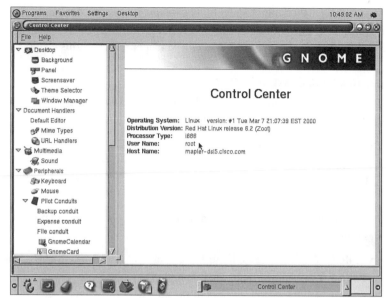

The Control Center is laid out in categories, similar to a directory tree. By clicking the small triangle beside a category, you can see or hide its components.

Most Control Center dialog boxes include extensive help. Select the Help menu and then either select Help on Control-Center for general help with the Control Center, or select Help With *Component* Settings for help with the *component* dialog box (a component would be Panel or Background, for instance).

If you make changes to a dialog box and then switch dialog boxes without applying your changes (by clicking OK or Try), the name of that dialog boxwill turn red in the Control Center's list. This indicates uncommitted changes. If you try to exit the Control Center with uncommitted changes, it will give you the opportunity to discard these changes or apply them.

The rest of this section will cover some of the more useful categories.

DESKTOP

The Desktop category covers most visual issues, except those handled by the window manager. GNOME draws a fairly strict line between itself and its window manager (unlike KDE, which treats its window manager as a more integral part of the system). The advantage of this scheme is that it makes it easy to change window managers. For instance, GNOME used to ship with Enlightenment as its window manager. Enlightenment was not completely "GNOME-compliant" (whether this term means anything, or whether it would be better to say that GNOME was not "Enlightenment-compliant" is a subject of much debate). Because Enlightenment had its own extensive configuration options, it had to be configured separately from GNOME. When GNOME and Enlightenment chose to go their separate ways, it was fairly easy to integrate the new Sawfish window manager.

PART

I

CH

4

Sawfish (originally named Sawmill) is a relatively new window manager. In the GNOME tradition, it continues to be only loosely coupled to the desktop. For more information on Sawfish, see "Configuring the Window Manager," later in this chapter.

CHANGING THE DESKTOP BACKGROUND

To change the background color or image of the Desktop, select Desktop, Background, in the Control Center tree list. The dialog box that appears has three main areas:

- A wallpaper selection
- A color selection
- A preview monitor

For wallpaper, you can select any graphic image to display, and either display it once or tile it as follows:

- **Tiled**—Display repeatedly to fill the screen. This is usually how wallpaper is used unless it is a single image (such as a photograph or other scene).
- **Centered**—Display one copy in the center of the screen.
- **Scaled (keep aspect)**—Display one copy, scaled to fill the screen as much as possible without distortion.
- **Scaled**—Display one copy, scaled to fill the entire screen regardless of distortion.

For a single color or gradient, you can select the color (or colors) using the GNOME color picker by clicking the colored buttons. Then select Solid, Vertical Gradient, or Horizontal Gradient to determine how the colors are blended.

As you modify your selections, the preview monitor displays the background that results from your settings.

You can also completely turn off the GNOME background by unselecting Use GNOME to Set Background. This is useful if you set your background using another tool, such as xsetbg.

CHOOSING A SCREENSAVER

The Screen Saver dialog box of the Control Center enables you to select a screensaver for your system and customize its settings. You can configure global options, such as the time before the screensaver kicks in, as well as options specific to the individual screensaver that you choose.

The Screen Saver dialog box is divided into three major areas (see Figure 4.6):

- A preview monitor
- A screensaver list
- Some general screensaver settings

Figure 4.6
The Screen Saver dialog box enables you to pick a screen-saver and adjust its settings.

To choose a screensaver, select the screensaver from the Screen Saver list. To customize the screensaver you have chosen, click the Settings button and edit the entries in the dialog box that appears. Each setup dialog box includes a preview window so that you can see the effect of your settings before you accept them.

To configure the amount of time before the screensaver starts, enter the number of minutes in the Start After field of the dialog box. If you want the screensaver to lock the screen when it is activated so that a password is required to regain access to your machine, select the Require Password option.

The Priority setting controls how much processor time is devoted to the screensaver when it is active. This corresponds to the Linux nice value of the screensaver process. If you want the screensaver to run at a higher priority than other processes on your machine (so that the animation is smooth, for example), drag the slider toward Normal. If you want other processes to have priority, slide it toward Low.

Finally, you can have GNOME use the power management features of your monitor (if it has any) to shut the monitor off after a specified length of time. To do this, select Use Power Management and enter the number of minutes to wait.

After adjusting the screensaver settings, click OK or Try to save your changes.

CONFIGURING THE WINDOW MANAGER

GNOME is only loosely coupled with its window manager, and it's very easy to use almost any window manager you want. In contrast, KDE is fairly tightly coupled with its window manager, though it is possible to change it to other KDE-aware managers.

PART

I

CH

4

GNOME used to ship with Enlightenment, but has recently switched to Sawfish, which is much lighter weight. It is also somewhat less configurable than Enlightenment, but then *everything* is less configurable than Enlightenment. In this section, we will discuss Sawfish. If you want more information on Enlightenment, see www.enlightenment.org.

Sawfish was developed in an effort to create an extremely configurable window manager (in the tradition of Enlightenment) with a small footprint. It has been fairly successful in this regard, though some Sawfish configuration still requires diving into its LISP-like configuration language. This section will focus on the majority of things that you can configure within the Control Center.

SETTING FOCUS POLICY

Focus policy is how GNOME determines which window is currently active, and what to do when a window becomes active. The policies are as follows:

- **Click**—Windows only gain focus when you click them.
- **Enter-only**—Windows gain focus when you move into them (using the mouse pointer or using Alt+Tab or otherwise). Moving the mouse pointer onto the desktop does not cause the currently active window to lose focus. This is an incredibly useful focus policy because it allows you to type in one window while reading another window that might obscure it.
- **Enter-exit**—Windows gain focus only while the mouse pointer is within them. If the mouse points to the desktop, no window will have focus. This is generally not useful and is only provided for historical reasons.

The Focus Windows When They Are First Displayed setting determines whether new windows automatically get focus. Sometimes having new windows stealing focus can be very annoying, because you suddenly wind up typing in a different window. This is particularly frustrating when informational boxes steal focus. On the other hand, many people prefer not to have to explicitly give focus to every new window.

The Dialog Windows Inherit the Focus From Their Parent setting is very useful if you've turned off Focus Windows When They Are First Displayed. This means that if the window you are working in displays a dialog box, that dialog box automatically gains focus, even if new windows usually don't. This is usually what you want.

Users accustomed to MacOS or Microsoft Windows sometimes have difficulty adjusting to the idea that window focus and window raising are separate. A window gains focus when keyboard input is directed to it. A window is raised when it appears on top of all other windows on the desktop. In the MacOS and Windows worlds, these two things are tied together, but not in GNOME (or UNIX in general). By turning off automatic raising, you can type in windows that are not on top. This is incredibly useful if you are reading in one small window and typing in a larger one.

Another problem with always raising the windows as they gain focus is that if you have Enter-Only or Enter-Exit focus policies and you move the mouse across the screen to select a new window, you might inadvertently raise other windows on the way. To avoid that, even if you do like automatically raising windows when they gain focus, you can set a delay between when the window gains focus and when it is raised. The default is 500ms.

WORKSPACES AND VIEWPORTS

By selecting Control Center, Sawfish window manager, Workspaces, you can configure the virtual desktop feature of Sawfish (and GNOME). For more information on virtual desktops, see "Pager" in Chapter 2.

Enter the total number of workspaces in the Workspaces text box. This is the number of viewport collections you want. For many users, it's easiest to have just one workspace and multiple viewports. Think of a viewport as one piece of your desktop. You could keep your mail in the upper left of your desktop, while you kept your editor in the lower right. The total desktop is much larger than your actual screen. Workspaces are completely separate desktops, with their own viewports.

In the Columns and Rows text boxes, enter the number of columns and rows of viewports that you want. The total number of viewports will be the product of these numbers (times the number of workspaces if you have set that).

CONFIGURING THE PANEL

You can change the location, size, and other options of the Panel using the Panel Configuration dialog box. You can also adjust the positions of the items on the panel, or remove and add items on the Panel, by accessing individual items' context menus.

GNOME also allows you to have multiple panels, which can be in various places around the screen depending on their type. The panel types are described in "Configuring a Panel," later in this chapter.

GLOBAL PANEL CONFIGURATION

Global Panel options apply to all panels. These generally impact look and feel for special features such as animations or special button appearances. To access the global panel configuration dialog box, click Main Menu, Panel, Global Preferences.

ANIMATION

The Animation tab configures how the panel will animate the following events:

- **Auto hide**—If the panel is configured to hide automatically whenever it does not have focus, this configures how fast it will appear to slide off the screen.
- **Explicit hide**—If you click either of the hide buttons on the far sides of the panel, this configures how fast it will appear to slide off the screen in that direction.
- **Drawer sliding**—If you have placed a drawer (sub-menu) on the panel, this is how fast the drawer will appear to open or close.

The Enable Animations selection determines whether anything will animate. If you turn this off, hiding and drawer sliding will be instantaneous.

If you turn off Constant Speed Animations, the panel will start moving slowly and then accelerate.

The Delay and Size settings impact auto-hiding panels. Delay is how long to wait after the mouse has left the panel before hiding it. The size setting determines how many pixel rows remain on the screen in the area that the panel would occupy. This helps you know where your hidden panels are, and is the area that you need to put the mouse in to redisplay the panel.

BUTTONS

The Buttons tab configures the appearance of the buttons on panels. For each type of button, you can select a tile, or background image, to display behind it. This helps you distinguish between buttons of different types, and provides a little more "flash" when you click them. Separate tiles can be selected for clicked and unclicked button states.

The Border Width setting determines how much padding to place between the icon in the button and the edge of the button. Selecting Make Buttons Flush With Panel Edge will override this setting in the direction of the panel edge.

The Depth setting determines how far the button appears to move when you click it. This gives the impression of a real button.

By selecting Show Button Tiles Only When Cursor Is Over the Button, you can easily see which button you're about to click. For a subtler effect, try Prelight Buttons On Mouseover.

PANEL OBJECTS

The Panel Objects tab mostly deals with button movement. You can move any item on the button bar by clicking the middle mouse button and dragging. The Default movement mode dialog box simply determines the movement behavior when you do this. The three options are as follows:

- **Switched**—As your button moves along the panel, other buttons switch places with it. This is the default behavior.
- **Free**—No other buttons are moved. This is useful if you basically like the layout of your panel. It prevents accidentally moving buttons you don't want to move.
- **Push**—Other items are pushed along with the one you are moving. This is handy if you want to pack your buttons together after you have rearranged them.

No matter the default, you can always select any of the modes by holding down a modifier key. Control selects Switched, Alt selects Free, and Shift selects Push.

On this panel, you can also set the panel object padding. This is the amount of space put between panel objects. If you have a very full panel, you can reduce this to get a little space back. Conversely, if you have a very high-resolution monitor, you might want to increase this to spread things out a little more.

MENU

The Menu tab determines the appearance of panel menus, particularly the Main Menu.

If you have a high-resolution display (1280×1024 or higher), the default icon size in menus might be too small for you. If so, you can choose Use Large Icons to select a more visible icon size.

A terminal menu item is any item other than a sub-menu. All terminal menu items have a pop-up menu, accessible by right-clicking the item. Generally, these menus allow you to automatically add the item to your panel or favorites list. Some users prefer a button they can left-click to get this same functionality. The Show Buttons selection displays a small "…" (ellipsis) button beside any menu item with a local menu.

Small screens can sometimes become too cluttered if the pop-up menus appear too close to the main menu. If this becomes a problem for you, you might try the Show Pop-Up Menus Outside of Panels option, although I have found very little difference while using this option.

The Keep Menus In Memory option caches the menu information in memory. This speeds up access considerably in some cases. It can cause GNOME to fail to automatically pick up new menu items if they are put in the menu directory tree. Unless you plan to modify the GNOME configuration directories by hand, I recommend turning on this option.

The Global menu is the menu you see when right-clicking the panel itself. This menu is the same for all panels (which is why it's called the Global menu). It is also highly configurable. For each of the elements listed, you can remove them entirely from the menu (Off), make them a submenu (In a Submenu), or integrate them directly into the Global menu (In the Menu). Unless you find yourself using particular items from particular menus very often, it's usually best to just leave these all set to their defaults (which are generally In a Submenu).

MISCELLANEOUS

The Miscellaneous tab is a catch-all for some general panel configuration options.

All panels provide tooltips, shown in Figure 4.7. These are small, helpful boxes that appear when the mouse hovers over a button. If you would prefer not to receive this pop-up help, deselect Tooltips Enabled.

Figure 4.7
Tooltips provide instant help about desktop features.

Panels can also have drawers, which provide sub-menus of buttons (including other drawers). When you select a launcher in a drawer, the drawer can close or remain open,

PART

I

CH

4

depending on your configuration. This is determined by the Close Drawer If a Launcher Inside It Is Pressed option.

With a GNOME-compliant window manager, such as Sawmill, panels get special treatment. They can automatically float over all other windows so they're always within reach. If you have a small screen, this can be a problem, so you can select Keep Panel Below Windows to have the panel stay under all other windows.

Without a GNOME-compliant window manager, your panels will be treated like any other window. To get them to automatically show up over other windows (at least when the mouse crosses them), you can select Raise Panels on Mouse-Over.

Finally, for safety, you almost certainly want to select Confirm Removal of Panels with a Dialog. Otherwise there will be no confirmation if you request to remove a panel (which is right between Create Panel and Panel Properties on the Panel menu). Because there is no way to recover a menu removed in this way, it's worth having a confirmation dialog box.

ADJUSTING ITEMS ON A PANEL

To move or remove an item on the Panel, use the options on the context menu for that item. Right-click an item, and the context menu appears (see Figure 4.8). To move an item, select the Move option on this menu, and drag the item to the desired position on the Panel. The behavior of other buttons on the panel will be determined by the Default Movement Mode option on the Panel Objects tab of the Global Panel Preferences dialog box (refer to "Panel Objects," earlier in this chapter). You can also move an item by clicking and dragging it with the middle mouse button, with or without modifier keys (also as described in "Panel Objects"). To remove an item, select Remove From Panel on the context menu.

Figure 4.8
The Panel item con-
text menu pops up
when you right-click
an item on the Panel.

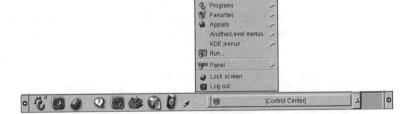

ADDING ITEMS TO THE PANEL

Adding items to the panel is fairly simple. Just click Main Menu, Panel, Add to Panel. This will provide several classes of items to add:

- **Applet**—This provides a list of installed applets. Applets include the Desk Guide, the tasklist, the clock, and many, many more. The list of available applets is determined by the desktop files in /usr/share/applets (your actual directory can vary).

- **Menu**—Three types of menus are in GNOME: Main Menu, which is the "GNOME foot" menu on the main panel; Programs Menu, which is a shortcut to the Programs sub-menu of the Main Menu; and Favorites Menu, which is a shortcut to the Favorites sub-menu of the Main Menu.

■ **Launcher**—This allows you to create a new launcher for your panel. Selecting this option will display the Create Launcher Applet shown in Figure 4.9.

Figure 4.9
Creating new laun-chers is straight-forward with the Create Launcher Applet.

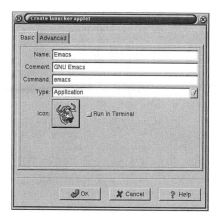

In the Name field, enter the name of this application in your native language. In the Comment field, enter a more descriptive comment for this application (this is what the tooltip displays). In the Command field, enter the command to run for this application. In the Type field, select Application. You can then select an icon by clicking the Icon button, and if the application needs a terminal, you can select that option.

The Advanced options tab is generally only useful for people who are building GNOME distributions. The Try Before Using field is a command to look for before displaying this launcher (in case the target is not installed). The Documentation field is not currently used. Finally, the Language box allows you to define names and comments for various languages (not usually useful for a single-user machine) .

■ **Drawer**—This creates a drawer that can hold other buttons (including other drawers). Clicking the drawer opens or closes it.

■ **Log out button**—This creates a quick log out button.

■ **Lock button**—This creates a button that will lock your screen (using your screensaver).

■ **Run button**—This creates a button that will provide a run dialog box. A run dialog box allows you to type in an application's name to quickly launch it.

■ **Swallowed app**—A swallowed app is an application that runs directly on your panel. This is similar to an applet, but is not as efficient, because the swallowed app is not specially written to run in the panel.

• To create a swallowed app, you need a program that can handle being run in a very small window with no frame or widgets. Applications such as xbiff (a mailbox watcher) or xclock (a clock) usually work well, though both of these have better applet versions already.

PART
I

CH
4

- The Title of Application to Swallow field is the window title of the application. This is usually the title displayed at the top of the window, but if you don't know it, you can use xwininfo to find out. Run xwininfo from a terminal window and click on the window in question. The title is in the first line of output.

- The Command field is the command to run to start this program. If you leave it blank, no command will be run, but as soon as a window with the given title appears (should you run it at start-up for instance), it will be swallowed.

- Finally, the width and height fields are how large to make the swallowed app.

- Before creating a swallowed app, you should probably look at the applets list to see whether there is already an applet that does what you want. Applets are more efficient and often provide more features.

■ **Status dock**—The Status dock holds Status docklets. These are identical to the Dock applets for KDE (such as the CD player and klipper). There are currently no GNOME Status docklets, but the Status dock is compatible with the KDE dock, so you can run KDE Dock applets here.

USING THE MENU EDITOR

The menu editor modifies the Main Menu. To open the menu editor, click in the main menu, Programs, Settings, Menu Editor. Figure 4.10 shows the Menu Editor window.

Figure 4.10
The menu editor for the main menu.

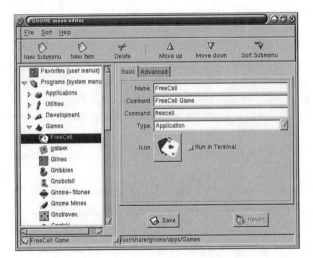

Note that some menus are marked User Menus and others are marked System Menus. You can only modify user menus unless you are root.

To open or close a submenu, click the arrow beside its name. To move a menu item from one sub-menu to another, drag it using the mouse. To move it within a sub-menu, right-click and select Move Up or Move Down.

To create a new menu item, select the submenu you want to add it to and select File, New Item (or click the New Item button on the toolbar). On the Basic tab, the fields are as follows:

- **Name**—Language-specific name of application. This is the name that appears in the menu.
- **Comment**—Longer comment for application. This appears in the quick tip for the application.
- **Command**—Command to run.
- **Type**—Generally this should be Application.
- **Run in terminal**—If selected, application will be run in a terminal.
- **Icon**—Allows you to select an icon for this application.

The Advanced options tab is generally only useful for people who are building GNOME distributions. The Try Before Using field is a command to look for before displaying this launcher (in case the target is not installed). The Documentation field is not currently used. Finally, the Language box allows you to define names and comments for various languages (not usually useful for a single-user machine).

To add a new submenu, select File, New Submenu and enter the name. You can also use the New Submenu button on the toolbar.

Configuring a Panel

GNOME panels are highly configurable; even more than KDE panels. For instance, there are a wide variety of panel types:

- **Edge**—These panels extend all the way across an edge of the screen, regardless of how many buttons are in them. The default panel is an edge panel.
- **Aligned**—These panels are fixed to a corner of the screen and grow to accommodate whatever buttons are in them.
- **Sliding**—These panels are also only as large as they need to be to hold their buttons, but they can be placed anywhere along a screen edge.
- **Floating**—These panels can be placed anywhere on the screen.
- **Menu**—This is a special panel across the top of the screen. It is the pull-down menu you see by default. There can be only one of these panels, and it must be at the top of the screen.

All these panel types, except Menu, can be configured individually by right-clicking them and selecting Panel, Properties, All Properties. All these options are also available under the Properties menu as their own sub-menus. The Edge Panel configuration dialog box is shown in Figure 4.11.

PART

I

CH

4

Figure 4.11
All the panel dialog boxes are similar to the Edge Panel dialog box.

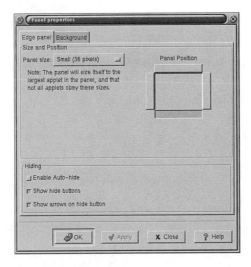

The main options are as follows:

- **Panel size**—All panels can range from Tiny (24 pixels) to Huge (80 pixels). On particularly large or small displays, changing the size of the panel can really help.

- **Panel position**—This easy-to-use selector allows you to place the panel in any of the locations it is allowed. Push the button corresponding to the area of the screen you want.

- **Enable Auto-hide**—If Auto-hide is selected, the panel will disappear whenever the mouse leaves it. To make the panel reappear, move the mouse to the panel's edge of the screen.

- **Show hide buttons**—If Auto-hide is not selected, you might want to provide the two hide buttons on either side of the panel. Clicking either of these buttons slides the panel off the screen in the direction indicated. Clicking the other button (which will still be visible) brings the panel back. If Auto-hide is selected, there is generally no reason to show these buttons.

- **Show arrows on hide button**—If you prefer a simpler hide button, you can choose not to display the small arrow on it.

The Background tab allows you to modify the appearance of the panel. There are three background types:

- **Standard**—The panel will conform to the current gtk+ theme.
- **Color**—The panel will be the chosen color.
- **Pixmap**—The panel will use the chosen pixmap as a background. The pixmap can be scaled in three different ways:
    - **Unscaled**—The image will be tiled along the panel, but will not be scaled (so it might be clipped or there might be blank space around it).

- **Scaled**—The image will be scaled without distortion so that it fills the smallest dimension of the panel. It will then be tiled along the panel.
- **Stretched**—The image will be stretched so that a single copy of it fills the panel.
- **Rotate image for vertical panels**—If this option is selected, the image will automatically be rotated 90 degrees if the panel is vertical.

All the other panel types have exactly the same options, except for floating panels. For floating panels, there is no edge selector. Instead there is a Top Left Corner Position text box. There are also Orient Panel Horizontally and Orient Panel Vertically radio buttons so you can set the orientation. For other panel types, the orientation is set by the edge they are on.

> **Tip**
>
> You can move any panel (except the Menu panel) by dragging it with the middle mouse button.

Any of the panel types (except Menu) can be easily converted to any of the other types by right-clicking the panel and selecting Panel, Properties, Type.

CREATING AND REMOVING PANELS

Now that you understand how to configure panels (as described in "Configuring a Panel"), adding and removing them is easy. To create one, just right-click any panel and select Panel, Create Panel, and the panel type you would like. To remove a panel, right-click it and select Remove This Panel and then click Yes to confirm. Note that removing a panel is permanent, so be careful before removing one that you have carefully configured.

PART

I

CH

4

> **Note**
>
> Because you need a panel to create more panels, you would be stuck if you deleted your last panel. Luckily, GNOME will not allow you to delete all of your panels.

UPDATING HELIX GNOME

One of the best things about Helix GNOME is how easy it is to keep it up-to-date. GNOME's design is a big part of this. Whereas KDE is primarily made up of a small number of very large packages, GNOME is made up of a large number of fairly small packages. This means that as each package is updated, it's easy to drop it into your system with a minimum of trouble.

Helix Code made this even easier with Helix Code Update. To access Helix Code Update, click the soda can on the panel (or on the desktop, or click Main Menu, Programs, System, Helix Code Update) and enter your root password. After selecting a mirror, you will be shown a screen like that in Figure 4.12.

Figure 4.12
Helix Code Update
takes the pain out
of maintaining the
numerous GNOME
packages.

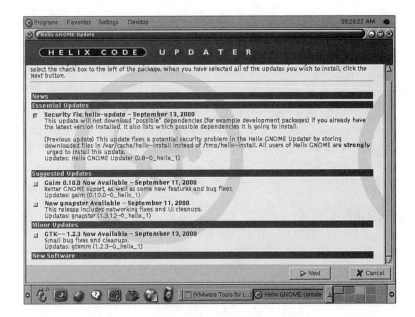

Note that Helix Code Update separates the available updates into News (which just provides information, not packages), Essential Updates, Suggested Updates, Minor Updates, and New Software. It also provides helpful information about why you would want this update (something lacking from most update utilities).

Choose the packages you want, and click Next. Helix Code Update will automatically download and install the packages you selected. There's nothing else you need to do.

PROJECT: INSTALLING ENLIGHTENMENT

Sawfish is a very nice window manager, but for some people there's nothing like Enlightenment. E, as it often called, is possibly the most configurable window manager ever developed. It is huge (the RPM is about 10MB), slow on old hardware, and can sometimes fight with GNOME. It can also be a lot of fun and is one of the prettiest (or at least flashiest) window managers around. It's also one of the few window managers that is Xinerama-aware (see "The ServerLayout Section" in Chapter 5, "Configuring X," for more information on Xinerama) .

One of the great things about GNOME is that it is very easy to drop in another window manager, which is exactly what we will do in this section.

First, go to www.enlightenment.org and look at some of the information and screen shots to see whether you think E might be for you. If so, go to http://www.enlightenment.org/download and download the latest version. You might also need to download some of the supplemental libraries in the libs directory if you don't have the cutting-edge versions of the packages listed there. At the time of this writing, the latest version is 0.16.4. The leading zero is to indicate that E is considered experimental software and should not be considered stable. There is no evidence that an Enlightenment v1.0 will be available anytime soon.

When you have downloaded the appropriate packages for your distribution, install them. On RPM-based systems, for example:

```
# rpm -i enlightenment-0.16.4-1.i386.rpm
```

On Debian, add the following line to `/etc/apt/sources.list` and run dselect normally:

```
deb http://www.debian.org/~ljlane/downloads enlightenment/
```

Next, open the Control Panel and select Desktop, Window Manager. Enlightenment should show up automatically in the list. If it doesn't, add it by clicking Add and entering the following information:

- Name: Enlightenment
- Command: enlightenment
- Configuration Command: e-conf
- Select Window Manager is Session Managed.

Select Enlightenment, click OK, and hold on. When Enlightenment finishes initializing, your desktop will resemble Figure 4.13.

Figure 4.13
Your first introduction to Enlightenment.

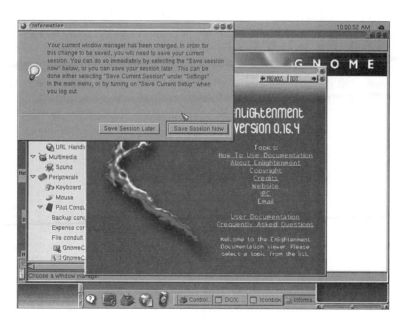

PART

I

CH

4

As suggested, save your session, and then begin investigating the documentation. You also might just try poking around. If you get lost, don't worry, Enlightenment has extensive tooltips. Just leave your mouse sitting almost anywhere, and a tooltip, such as the one shown in Figure 4.14, will appear.

Figure 4.14
Enlightenment's tooltips are extensive and pervasive.

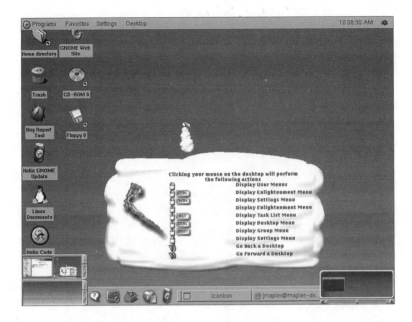

E has a much more advanced pager, shown in Figure 4.15, than most window mangers. Not only does it show a small image of your desktop in the pager, but if you hover your mouse over a particular window within the pager, it will magnify so you can get a better look. Also notice that there are two pagers. Each represents a separate workspace. You can, of course, have more or fewer workspaces if you prefer.

Figure 4.15
Enlightenment's pager has some unique features.

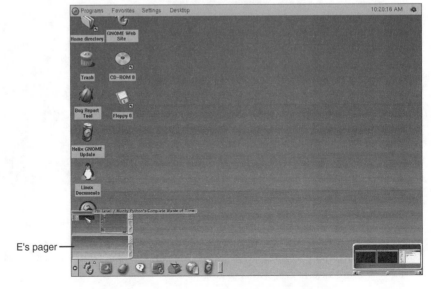

E's pager —

E uses an icon box, shown in Figure 4.16, to manage minimized applications. All minimized applications go into this box, making it easy to see what applications are hiding. Instead of just a title, you can see a miniature version of the whole window.

Figure 4.16
Enlightenment's icon box lets you see what's minimized.

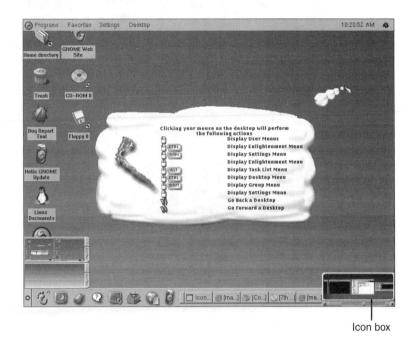

Icon box

Finally, (for here), Enlightenment almost defines the idea of themes. Figure 4.17 shows the Blue Steel theme that comes with Enlightenment, but over 200 more are at e.themes.org. To switch themes, middle-click the desktop and select Themes. Note that these themes are for the window manager and are separate from GNOME's themes. To select GNOME's themes, use the Control Center, Theme Selector.

There is so much to say about Enlightenment that I can't possibly cover it all here. Many people don't like E because it's huge, slow, and unstable (very sensible reasons!), but if you like a flashy desktop and a fast machine, you might just give Enlightenment a try.

Figure 4.17
E's Blue Steel theme goes nicely with GNOME's Blue Steel theme.

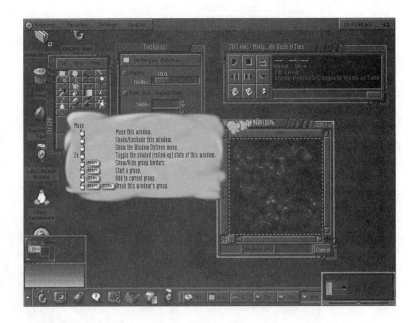

PART II

SIGHT AND SOUND

CONFIGURING X

In this chapter

WHAT IS THE X WINDOW SYSTEM?

Linux provides the capability to run windowed applications across a heterogeneous network by incorporating the XFree86 implementation of the X11 standard of the X Window System created at the Massachusetts Institute of Technology (MIT). This system is much more than a graphical interface used to run applications; it's a powerful client/server system that allows applications to be run and shared across a network. Although XFree86 is meant to run in a networked environment, it runs fine on a single machine. You don't need a network to run XFree86 or X applications.

Historically, XFree86 has been one of the most complex parts of Linux to install and configure. This is no longer the case for most standard hardware configurations because the most popular Linux distributions now install and configure it automatically. Additionally, with XFree86 v4, some of the most complex parts of configuration are handled automatically.

Like most parts of Linux, XFree86 also has a HOW-TO document. The XFree86 HOW-TO is maintained by Eric S. Raymond (esr@thyrsus.com) and can be found on the World Wide Web at http://www.linuxdoc.org.

Caution

Typically, you don't have to worry about software damaging your hardware. However, because XFree86 deals directly with your video card and monitor, it can cause physical damage, especially if you try to use XFree86 with an unsupported video card. Make sure that you have the necessary hardware before trying to run XFree86.

I strongly suggest that you read the documentation that comes with the XFree86 system. Always refer to the documentation that comes with your installed version of XFree86 because older or newer documentation might not be accurate for your installation. For many distributions, the documentation can be found at /usr/X11R6/lib/X11/doc. In particular, read the README file, and the XFree86 HOW-TO by Eric S. Raymond. The most up-to-date version of XFree86 is available at http://www.xfree86.org, so you should look there before trying to work with an unlisted video board or chipset.

UNDERSTANDING THE X WINDOW SYSTEM

The X Window System is a powerful graphical operating environment that supports many applications across a network, and it can be freely distributed. The version of the X Window System discussed in this chapter is X11R6.4. However, Linux and XFree86 are constantly evolving, and a newer version of X may be available on the Net. In fact, at the time of this printing, work is under way to incorporate X11R6.5 into XFree86.

XFree86, the X server commonly used by Linux, is the X11R6.4 standard ported to Intel-based systems. XFree86 supports a wide range of standard PC hardware. The version of XFree86 discussed in this chapter is 4.0.1. Many distributions ship both 4.0.1 and 3.3.6 (at the time of this writing, Debian only ships 3.3.6).

The X Window System originally grew from a cooperative effort between two sections at MIT: the section responsible for a networking program called *Project Athena* and a section called the

Laboratory for Computer Science. Both used many UNIX workstations and soon realized they were each re-inventing the wheel when it came to programming graphical user interfaces (GUIs) for UNIX workstations. To cut down on the amount of code both groups were writing, they decided to create one robust, extensible windowing system—the X Window System.

> **Note**
>
> The original window manager that the X Window System is based on was called W. So many improvements were made to W that the authors decided to rename it X.
>
> You might also hear the terms *X* and X *Windows* used in reference to the X Window System. Although terms like X Protocol, X Server, and X Client are correct, the correct name of the entire system is the X Window System.

In 1987, several vendors—in hopes of creating a single windowing system for UNIX workstations—formed an organization called the *X Consortium* to promote and standardize the X Window System. Thanks to this effort, open computing became a reality. The X Consortium is composed of entities such as IBM, Digital Equipment, and MIT. This group of large organizations oversees the construction and release of new versions of X11.

XFree86 is a trademark of the XFree86 Project, Inc. The original programmers who ported the X Window System to the 80386 platform decided to found the project so that they could gain membership in the X Consortium. By becoming a member of the X Consortium, the XFree86 Project gained access to works-in-progress and could thus port the new features to XFree86 while the features were being implemented for the X Window System, rather than wait until after the official release to make the port. As of January 1, 1997, the X Consortium turned the X Window System over to the Open Group.

The X Window System is actually a series of pieces working together to present users with a GUI. These pieces include

- The base window system, a program providing services to the X Window System.
- The next piece, a protocol for communicating across the network—the X Network Protocol.
- On top of the program and implementing the X Network Protocol, the low-level interface *Xlib*, between the network/base system and higher-level programs. Application programs typically use functions in Xlib instead of the lower-level functions.
- Tying these pieces together is a window manager. The window manager is an X application whose purpose is to control how windows are presented to users.
- Many modern distributions of Linux also include a desktop. Although the desktop is not technically part of the X Window System, it does provide an integral part to the user's graphical environment and works very closely with the window manager. Desktops generally handle features such as customizable window styles (*themes*), session management, and inter-program communications. They often provide a simpler environment for application developers. The two most popular Linux desktops are GNOME and KDE. They are discussed in detail in Chapter 3, "KDE," and Chapter 4, "GNOME."

PART

II

CH

5

Unlike most other window systems, the base window system of the X Window System doesn't provide user interface objects such as scrollbars, command buttons, or menus. The user interface items are left to the higher-layer components and the window manager. Therefore, users have much greater flexibility in how things appear and what interface they prefer.

X applications include not only window managers, but also games, graphics utilities, programming tools, office applications, and many other tidbits. Just about any application that you need has either been written for or ported to the X Window System.

The X Window System implements a window manager to handle the task of creating and controlling the interface that makes up the visual portion of the X Window System. It isn't to be confused with the OS/2 Presentation Manager or the old Microsoft Windows Program Manager. Both of them are closer to the idea of a desktop than a window manager.

For the not-so-faint-of-heart, XFree86 also includes programming libraries and files for programmers who want to develop their own applications under XFree86 or compile X applications available on the Internet. Although the topic of creating X applications is beyond the scope of this book, ample documentation is available on any number of Internet distribution sites, such as www.xfree86.org, and on many CD-ROM distributions to help you gain the foothold necessary to create applications for XFree86. Today many programmers, however, prefer to write applications targeted at GNOME or KDE rather than pure X applications. These environments provide helpful abstraction layers for programmers; these greatly simplify writing graphical applications.

WHAT IS A CLIENT/SERVER SYSTEM?

The X Window System is a client/server system controlled by two individual pieces of software. One piece runs on the client and the other runs on the server. The client and server pieces of this puzzle can be on different systems or, as is the case with most personal computers, both pieces can reside on the same machine.

Client/server is one of the major buzzwords used in the computer industry today. Like most basic concepts in the industry, client/server has been overplayed and overused to the point of confusing the average computer user. In the traditional sense, a *server* is a machine that just provides resources—disk drive space, printers, modems, and so on—to other computers over a network. A *client* is the consumer of these services; in other words, a client uses the disk space, printer, or modems provided by a server.

In the X Window System, the relationship of client and server is quite different, and might appear backward to many users. Under the X Window System, the server displays the output of the client. This concept might seem a bit confusing at first, but it will make sense when you become more familiar with the X Window System.

An X client is made up of the programs and resources necessary to run an application. The resources reside on the client's system (remember that the client and server systems can be on the same machine), whereas the application is displayed and interacted with on the server system.

For example, if you run xcalc on your Linux system using XFree86, then XFree86 (specifically a program such as /usr/X11R6/bin/X) is the *X server*, and xcalc is the *X client*. The X server must be running on your local machine (so that it can display your information), but the X client can be on any machine that you can connect to.

The capability of an X application, which is the client, to run under a server located on either the same computer or on another computer is called *network transparency*. Thus, it doesn't matter whether an X application runs on a local or remote machine. This capability can be used to run time-consuming tasks on another machine, leaving the local machine unencumbered to perform other tasks. It can also be used to run applications on other operating systems. Using a non-UNIX X server such as WRQ's Reflection X (http://www.wrq.com/products/reflection/rxinfo.html), you can run your favorite X clients on your Linux workstation but display them on a connected machine running Microsoft NT. The reverse is not true, however, because NT does not know how to run X clients and cannot easily display its own clients on remote servers.

> **Tip**
>
> It is possible to display applications running on a Microsoft Windows machine to your Linux workstation using VNC (http://www.uk.research.att.com/vnc), a free product currently maintained by AT&T. VNC includes many remote display features for Windows, Macintosh, Linux, and other systems.

Output Capabilities

The base window system provides the X Window System with plenty of bit-mapped graphical operations. The X Window System and X applications use these operations to present information graphically to the users. XFree86 offers overlapping windows, immediate graphics drawings, high-resolution bit-mapped graphics and images, and high-quality text. Whereas early implementations of the X Window System were mostly monochrome-based, modern implementations like XFree86 support a wide range of color systems.

The X Window System also supports the multiprocessing capabilities of Linux. Each window displayed under the X Window System can be a separate task running under Linux.

Part
II
Ch
5

User Interface Capabilities

The X Consortium did not define standards for user interfaces. At the time very little research had been done on user interface technology, so no clear interface was considered the best. In fact, even today, unilaterally declaring one interface the best can alienate many people. The preferred look and feel presented by the user interface is a very personal decision.

The X Consortium wanted to make the X Window System a standard across UNIX and UNIX-like workstations, which is one reason it is available freely on the Internet. Making the X Window System freely available fosters interoperability, which is the cornerstone of open systems. Had the X Consortium dictated a user interface, the X Window System might not have gained its current level of popularity.

INPUT CAPABILITIES

Systems running the X Window System typically have some form of pointing device, usually a mouse. XFree86 requires a mouse or a device such as a trackball that emulates a mouse. If you don't have such a device, you can't use the XFree86 system with Linux. The X Window System converts signals from the pointing device and from the keyboard into events. The X Window System then responds to these events, performing appropriate actions.

INSTALLING THE XFREE86 SYSTEM

You probably installed the XFree86 system while installing the entire Linux package from your particular distribution's CD-ROM. An implementation of the X Window System is contained in the XFree86-* RPMs or deb packages. If you didn't install XFree86 at that time, you can use RPM or deselect to install it later. First, however, you must verify that you have the appropriate hardware for XFree86.

CHOOSING A VERSION OF XFREE86

Before installing XFree86, you should decide which version to use. Two versions are currently available: 4.0.1 and 3.3.6. Some distributions even allow you to choose which one you would like during install.

Version 4 represents a major re-design in XFree86. It provides several new features and much simpler configuration (ModeLines are no longer needed for normal setups). Because of the massive re-design, however, the version 4 line is not nearly as well tested as the venerable 3.X line.

If you have fairly standard hardware and are unfamiliar with configuring XFree86, you should probably choose 4.0.1.

If, however, you have a working 3.3.X XF86Config, or you have a card that is not supported well under 4.X (see http://www.xfree86.org/4.0.1/Status.html), then you should probably stay with 3.3.6.

Because most development will go into the 4.X line, this book will focus on 4.0.1.

Note

Other implementations of the X Window System are available for Linux, such as the commercial Metro-X (http://www.metrolink.com/metrox/ess.html) and Accelerated-X (http://www.xig.com). Commercial solutions are worth considering if you have hardware that XFree86 doesn't support, are interested in some of its special features, or if you need better performance than XFree86 can provide.

ENSURING HARDWARE SUPPORT FOR XFREE86

You must make sure that you have the proper hardware to run X Window System, the proper amount of memory, and the necessary disk space.

You need about 50–65MB of disk space to install the XFree86 system and the X applications provided (depending on distribution and how many optional components you install). You need at least 16MB of virtual memory to run XFree86. *Virtual memory* is the combination of the physical RAM on your system and the amount of swap space you've allocated for Linux. You must have at least 4MB of physical RAM to run XFree86 under Linux, thus requiring a 12MB swap file. The more physical RAM you have the better the performance of your XFree86 system will be.

Next, you need a video card containing a video-driver chipset supported by XFree86. See `http://www.xfree86.org/4.0.1/Status.html` for an up-to-date list of all the supported chipsets. Table 5.1 lists a summary of chipset support in XFree86 4.0.1. Note that although many vendors are unsupported in 4.0.1, the most common chipsets generally are supported. Also, if you see a comment such as "most are supported," you should look at the previously listed Web page for a detailed explanation.

TABLE 5.1   CHIPSET SUPPORT IN XFREE86 4.0.1

Manufacturer	Comments
3Dfx	Support for Voodoo 1 and Voodoo 2 though glide driver. Accelerated support for Voodoo Banshee and Voodoo 3 through tdfx driver.
3Dlabs	Accelerated support through glint driver.
Alliance	Support for the AT24, AT25 and AT3D through apm driver. Only incomplete support for the AP6422.
ARK Logic	No support in 4.0.1. Use 3.3.6.
ATI	Accelerated support for the Rage 128 chips through the r128 driver. Accelerated support for the Mach64 Rage variants through the ati driver. Unaccelerated support for all of the others except the Mach8 and some early Mach32 chips through the ati driver.
Avance Logic	No support in 4.0.1. Use 3.3.6.
Chips & Tech	Accelerated support through the chips driver.
Cirrus Logic	Accelerated support for the Alpine, and Laguna through the cirrus driver. For other chips, you will need to use 3.3.6.
Compaq	No support, use 3.3.6.
Cyrix	Spotty support. Use 3.3.6 unless you want to help test the 4.0.1 drivers.
DEC	Accelerated support through the tga driver.
Epson	No support, use 3.3.6.
Genoa	No support, use 3.3.6.
IBM	Support for the standard IBM VGA chip (and compatibles) through the vga driver. No support for IBM 8514/A or XGA-2. Use 3.3.6.
IIT	No support, use 3.3.6.
Intel	Accelerated support for the Intel i740 through the i740 driver. Support for the Intel i810 through the i810 driver.

PART

II

CH

5

TABLE 5.1 CONTINUED

Manufacturer	Comments
Matrox	Accelerated support through the mga driver. Matrox is somewhat of a standard in the XFree86 world, and these cards tend to be very well tested and supported.
MX	No support, use 3.3.6.
NCR	No support, use 3.3.6.
NeoMagic	Accelerated support through the neomagic driver.
NVIDIA	Accelerated support through the nv driver.
Number Nine	No support, use 3.3.6.
Oak	No support, use 3.3.6.
Paradise	No support, use 3.3.6.
RealTek	No support, use 3.3.6.
Rendition	Support through the rendition driver.
S3	Support for the ViRGE and Trio3D chipsets through the s3virge driver. Other chipsets are only supported in 3.3.6.
SiS	Accelerated support for most chips through the sis driver. Some chips support is still experimental.
Silicon Motion	No support, use 3.3.6.
Trident	Accelerated (if applicable) support for most chips through the trident driver.
Tseng Labs	Support through the tseng driver.
Video 7	No support. Use 3.3.6.
Weitek	No support. Use 3.3.6.

INSTALLING FROM RPMs

On RPM-based systems, XFree86 is split into a large number of RPMs; some are required whereas others are optional. If you installed XFree86 when you installed Red Hat or OpenLinux, everything was probably done for you. If you didn't install XFree86 at that time, or if you're trying to upgrade XFree86, then you need to decide what packages to install. See Table 5.2 for the list of recommended packages and Table 5.3 for the optional packages that ship with OpenLinux eDesktop. Red Hat RPMs have very similar names for the most common packages.

TABLE 5.2 RECOMMENDED XFREE86 RPMS

RPM	Description
XFree86	Base XFree86 system.
XFree86-config	XFree86 configuration files.

TABLE 5.2   CONTINUED

RPM	Description
XFree86-contrib	Many useful X applications.
XFree86-fonts	Standard X fonts.
XFree86-libs	Shared libraries for most X applications.
XFree86-programs	Core X11 applications.
XFree86-server	XFree86 server (including all modules).
XFree86-setup	Configuration utility. On Red Hat, you should install Xconfigurator instead.

TABLE 5.3   OPTIONAL XFREE86 RPMs

RPM	Description
XFree86-addons	Miscellaneous demos, converters, and minor utilities.
XFree86-config-eg	Example configuration files for XFree86.
XFree86-devel-*	Development package. It is required if you plan to develop or compile X applications or servers. -prof and -static versions of this RPM are available for profiling and static linking, respectively.
XFree86-fonts-*	Various additional fonts.
XFree86-fontserver	Font server for XFree86. It is used to provide the fonts on your machine to other machines on the network.
XFree86-imake	Imake tools required if you want to compile X11 from sources.
XFree86-misc	Even more miscellaneous programs.
XFree86-twm	Basic window manager.
XFree86-xdm	Basic login manager (usually kdm or gdm is used instead).
XFree86-Xnest	A nested X server. This X server can run in a window under another X server, generally for testing purposes.
XFree86-Xprt	Print extensions to support output to hardcopy devices using X drawing request.
XFree86-xsm	Basic session manager (this will usually be handled by KDE or GNOME).
XFree86-xterm	Terminal emulator. If you install KDE or GNOME, you won't need this one.
XFree86-Xvfb	X server that does not require display hardware. It is very useful for development and can also be useful to rendering engines, but generally not used by end users.

Part

II

Ch

5

Font packages often come in several flavors. The base version (as listed in Table 5.3) is generally terminal fonts and keyboard re-maps for the languages in question. The 75dpi fonts version contains 75dpi (dots per inch) fonts, which can be used by most monitors. The 100dpi fonts version contains 100dpi fonts, which are good for high-end (usually large) monitors that can handle 100dpi. Finally, some fonts come in a scale version, which are Type 1 scalable fonts. Installing at least the base, 75dpi, and scale versions is highly recommended. If your monitor can support the 100dpi versions, having them can be quite nice as well.

Remember that you have to install the appropriate programs from each package. Although not all packages are required, if you install XFree86 after installing Linux, you should review the full details on the packages to install. If you have the 65MB needed for a full installation, you may want to simply install all of the packages.

You can get the RPMs you want to install either from your distribution's media or from their Web site. Because various distributions often configure XFree86 in different ways, it is recommended that you choose RPMs specific to your distribution. In particular, your initialization scripts can expect the X server and login manager to be in specific locations. Although most distributions agree that this is /etc/X11, many subtle differences exist in exactly where things are located under that tree.

After you have the RPMs, you can generally install them easily using rpm:

```
# rpm -i XFree86-*.rpm
```

In most cases, this should handle everything, but if you have trouble, consult Chapter 16, "Software Package Management."

INSTALLING FROM deb PACKAGES

Debian does not have supported XFree86 4.0.1 packages at the time of this writing. However, test packages are available. Add the following to your /etc/apt/sources.list, and run dselect normally:

```
deb http://samosa.debian.org/~branden/ woody/i386/
```

Select the xfree86-common package. This should automatically select most of the other packages you need. Table 5.4 lists the recommended deb packages, and Table 5.5 lists the optional packages.

TABLE 5.4   RECOMMENDED XFREE86 deb PACKAGES

Package	Description
xfree86-common	Base XFree86 system. Get this first.
xbase-clients	Basic applications.
xf86setup	XFree86 configuration utility.
xfonts-75dpi	75dpi fonts.
xfonts-base	Basic fonts.
xfonts-scalable	Type 1 scalable fonts.
xfree86-server	Xfree86 X server.
xfree86-server-common	XFree86 server infrastructure.
xlib6g	Xlib libraries (needed by all X11 applications).

TABLE 5.5   OPTIONAL XFREE86 deb PACKAGES

Package	Description
xdm	Basic login manager (usually kdm or gdm is used instead).
xfonts-100dpi	100 dpi fonts for high-resolution monitors.
xlib6g-dev	Headers and other support files for compiling X applications.
xterm	Basic terminal emulator. Generally KDE or GNOME users won't need this one.

INSTALLING FROM tgz PACKAGES

If you are running a distribution that does not have pre-built packages available, you can get XFree86 directly from that Web site and install it manually. First, go to ftp://ftp.xfree86.org/pub/XFree86/4.0.1/binaries/Common and look at Install. These are the complete installation instructions. Then download Xinstall.sh. After you have downloaded Xinstall.sh, run it to determine the correct version of XFree86 to download:

```
$ sh Xinstall.sh –check
```

The final line of output will tell you which distribution to download. Go to that directory under binaries (for example, ftp://ftp.xfree86.org/pub/XFree86/4.0.1/binaries/Linux-ix86-glibc21) and download the required tarballs (see Table 5.6) and as many of the optional tarballs as you would like (see Table 5.7) to a temporary directory.

TABLE 5.6   RECOMMENDED XFREE86 tarball PACKAGES

Package	Description
Xbin.tgz	X clients/utilities and run-time libraries
Xlib.tgz	Some data files required at runtime
Xman.tgz	Manual pages
Xdoc.tgz	XFree86 documentation
Xfnts.tgz	Base set of fonts
Xfenc.tgz	Base set of font encoding data
Xetc.tgz	Runtime configuration files
Xvar.tgz	Runtime data
Xxserv.tgz	XFree86 X server
Xmod.tgz	XFree86 X server modules

TABLE 5.7   OPTIONAL XFREE86 tarball PACKAGES

Package	Description
Xfsrv.tgz	Font server
Xnest.tgz	Nested X server

PART

II

CH

5

TABLE 5.7	CONTINUED
Package	**Description**
Xprog.tgz	X header files, config files and compile-time libs
Xprt.tgz	X Print server
Xvfb.tgz	Virtual framebuffer X server
Xf100.tgz	100dpi fonts
Xfcyr.tgz	Cyrillic fonts
Xflat2.tgz	Latin-2 fonts
Xfnon.tgz	Some large bitmap fonts
Xfscl.tgz	Scalable fonts (Speedo and Type1)
Xhtml.tgz	HTML version of the documentation
Xps.tgz	PostScript version of the documentation
Xjdoc.tgz	Documentation in Japanese

After you have placed all the tarballs and the Xinstall.sh script in a temporary directory, run Xinstall.sh as root:

```
$ su
Password: <password>
# sh ./Xinstall.sh
```

This script will ask various questions. In general, the defaults should be fine. If you have questions, consult the Install file.

When you have installed XFree86, you can configure it using xf86config, XF86Setup, or any other utility that your distribution offers.

Although it is possible to download the XFree86 source and compile it yourself, this is not recommended. XFree86 is based on the Imake system (instead of the more modern autoconf/configure system). Compiling XFree86 is extremely complex and requires a lot of hand-modification of makefiles, as well as a fairly deep understanding of the operating system.

CONFIGURING XFREE86

XFree86 has historically been one of the most complex parts of Linux to configure. This is no longer the case for most common hardware. Still, there are two cases where installation can still be difficult.

First, cutting edge hardware may or may not be supported by XFree86 at all. When XFree86 does support it, you might have to use beta versions of XFree86 or even hacks on XFree86. These will not be supported by the new configuration tools.

Second, some vendors do not publish the specifications for their boards. In order for XFree86 to support these boards, developers must reverse engineer them, which takes a lot of time and effort. Unless the board is extremely popular (for example, the S3 ViRGE), there might not be XFree86 support for a very long time. Getting unsupported boards to work can be difficult or impossible if you are unable to write the drivers yourself.

These are just the worst cases. For most popular hardware you can just use Xconfigurator, XF86Setup, or lizardx, and it should work without any trouble.

USING XCONFIGURATOR

Xconfigurator is written by Red Hat. It is a text-based, menu-driven program that walks you through setting up your X server. It provides defaults for a wide variety of hardware and is much easier to use than the configuration tools that historically came with XFree86.

After you install XFree86, you can log in as root and run Xconfigurator. If your video card and monitor are listed, select the appropriate entries, and with luck, you will be done. Then you can check out your configuration by running startx.

> **Note**
>
> If something does go wrong (and your monitor doesn't explode), pressing Ctrl+Alt+Backspace should terminate the X server and return you to a shell prompt.

If you don't find your hardware listed, you can check the information in the `/usr/X11R6/lib/X11/doc` directory. In particular, check out the files named `README.Config` and `README.Linux`, as well any of the `README` files that refer to your hardware.

If you find enough information here to get you through Xconfigurator, then you're done. Otherwise, it's time to use some other tools.

USING XF86SETUP

XF86Setup can handle some cards that Xconfigurator doesn't know about. It is also the only configurator available for Debian. After you read the files in `/usr/X11R6/lib/X11/doc`, try running it. Then select your card and monitor specifications and run startx. If that still doesn't work, it's time to start digging into XF86Config.

> **Caution**
>
> You should never use an XF86Config file from someone else, or even one verbatim from this book or any other source, without looking over the file for improper values. For example, driving your monitor at unsupported frequencies can damage your equipment.

USING LIZARDX

Configuring X has come a long way in recent years, and OpenLinux has probably the best free X configuration utilities available: lizardx. Unlike the last generation of X configuration utilities, lizardx is a fully graphical, highly automated utility. Most settings will be automatically detected for you.

> **Note**
>
> At the time of this writing, lizardx has not been ported to XFree86 version 4. It should be ported by the time Caldera releases its next version of eDesktop, however.

lizardx is run automatically during the installation of OpenLinux, but you can use it at any time by becoming root and running the following:

```
# lizardx
```

You will then see the mouse configuration screen. Select your mouse from the radio buttons and drop-down list, and then test your selection by clicking the image of the mouse in the lower-right corner. Each of the three buttons should light up in response to your mouse clicks, and if your mouse includes a wheel, the image of the wheel should move in response to turning it.

If you have a two-button mouse, select Emulate Third Button. This option will emulate the middle mouse button whenever you click the left and right mouse buttons at the same time.

When you have selected and tested your mouse, click Next to select your keyboard. OpenLinux supports a wide variety of keyboard models and layouts, in over 20 languages.

When you have selected your keyboard, click Next to select your video card. Selecting your video card has never been easier. For most of the cards available today, select your card and click Probe. With very old cards, it is possible to hang your system by probing, but this is exceedingly rare today. If your machine does hang, simply reboot and re-run lizardx. Consult your card's documentation to find its clock frequencies and video RAM size, and enter them manually. Then click Next to select your monitor.

lizardx knows about a huge number of monitors. If yours is listed, select it. Otherwise, you can choose from the Typical Monitors list. If you have exact specifications on your monitor, you can enter them in the monitor details section.

> **Caution**
>
> Selecting a frequency beyond your monitor's capabilities can seriously damage your monitor. You should only enter frequencies that you are certain that your monitor can handle. If you are uncertain, be conservative.
>
> If you ever hear a high-pitched whine coming from the back of your monitor, shut down your monitor immediately. This is the sound the transformer makes when it is over-driven. Do not rely on this sound to tell you whether you are over-driving your monitor, however. By the time you hear it, it is very likely too late.

Finally, click Next to select your video mode. Select your resolution from the list provided, and then the number of colors from the drop-down list. Selecting a higher resolution can reduce the number of colors available. For most applications, 16 bit (64k colors) is sufficient. If you are interested in computer graphics, or simply like having high-color desktops, you might be interested in 24 bit (16 million colors) or even 32 bit (4 billion colors). 32 bit color has not been very worthwhile so far, because few images are actually provided this way and many video cards that support it simply display it as 24 bit color anyway (though some are able to display 32 bit color faster than 24 bit color). 8 bit color is usually only acceptable if you never display pictures, or if you need the highest resolution possible.

Finally, select OK to save your changes. When you next log in, they will take effect.

RUNNING THE SUPERPROBE PROGRAM

If the preceding installation procedures don't work, you can run a program to configure your system. XFree86 provides a program called xf86config to help you configure your XFree86 system, but this program requires you to answer several questions. These questions deal with the type of hardware you have on your system, and incorrect information can cause X to damage that hardware.

You should read these document files located in the `/usr/X11R6/lib/X11/doc` directory: `QuickStart.doc` and `README.Config`. You can use the following command to read the files:

```
less filename
```

You should also gather any manufacturer's manuals for your video card and monitor.

Next, run the SuperProbe utility:

```
/usr/X11R6/bin/SuperProbe
```

This utility scans your system, trying to identify the installed video hardware. You should write down the information reported for later use with xf86config. You should also double-check the information generated by SuperProbe with your hardware's documentation. The SuperProbe program generates information that will be placed in the various sections of the XF86Config file, explained in the section, "Dissecting the XF86Config File."

USING XF86CONFIG

An alternative method of configuring your X Server is through the use of xf86config. This command-line program walks you through the same basic steps as XF86Setup. This program requires much more knowledge of your hardware than XF86Setup, however.

When xf86config starts, a startup screen containing information that is important to running this program is displayed. The program can be aborted at any time using the Ctrl+C sequence.

The second screen requests that you select your mouse protocol type by number from the list presented on the screen.

Some supplemental questions might appear regarding `ChordMiddle`, `Emulate3Buttons`, or `ClearDTR/RTS`, depending on the mouse protocol you selected. Read the instructions given and answer these questions.

Finally, you are asked which device the mouse is connected to. Most commonly this is `/dev/mouse` if you have a symlink set up. Otherwise it is `/dev/psaux` for PS/2 mice, or either `/dev/ttyS0` or `/dev/ttyS1` for mouse devices that are connected to the first or second serial (COM) port.

The keyboard section follows. This is probably the easiest section in the entire setup. Enter your keyboard type and language.

The monitor section follows, first with an informational screen, and then with a list of common monitor horizontal sync rates—or you can enter your own. Recall the previous cautions about selecting monitor refresh rates that are higher than your monitor is capable of.

The vertical sync range comes next, with common choices or an option to enter your own.

Three optional free-form questions ask for the monitor definition identifier, vendor name, and monitor model.

Upon completion, enter the video card selection. If you answer Yes, you are presented with over 550 separate cards from which to choose. After your card is chosen, xf86config displays the information that it intends to write to the X Server configuration file.

The amount of video RAM on the card is the next question, with standard answers available as well as a fill-in-the-blank.

The three free-form card definition, vendor, and model questions follow.

Finally, enter your default color-depth. Generally xf86config will be able to handle the rest and will enable you to save the configuration file.

USING XVIDTUNE

After you have a working X server, you might find that you need to tune the sync frequencies slightly to prevent the screen from appearing stretched, squashed, shifted, or wrapped. Note that xvidtune does not help a mode that is out of sync—that is, you can't see a picture because the image is a series of (two or more) bars, or it appears as diagonal lines on the screen. If the server comes up this way, you can use the Ctrl+Alt+Plus (numeric keypad plus) key sequence to try to find a mode that does work.

If it is run from a command line, xvidtune provides some limited information on the command line regarding what it believes to be valid horizontal and vertical sync ranges (hsync and vsync, respectively). It then shows you a standard disclaimer regarding use of the program and the developers' liability for damage (none) resulting from the use of the program.

Figure 5.1 shows you how the xvidtune program looks when it is running. You can make adjustments to the various horizontal and vertical bars if you use the buttons (such as Left, Right, and Taller), and then test or apply them. You can also see each adjustment as you make it by selecting Auto first.

The Show button only works when xvidtune is called from an xterm because that's where the output will go. In your case here, a modeline is shown:

```
"1152x864"      92.00    1152 1208 1368 1474    864  865  875  895
```

As you can see, all the numbers come directly from the xvidtune display. Modelines like this one are for your XF86Config file, explained in "Dissecting the XF86Config File." Generally, with XFree86 version 4, you should never need to generate modelines.

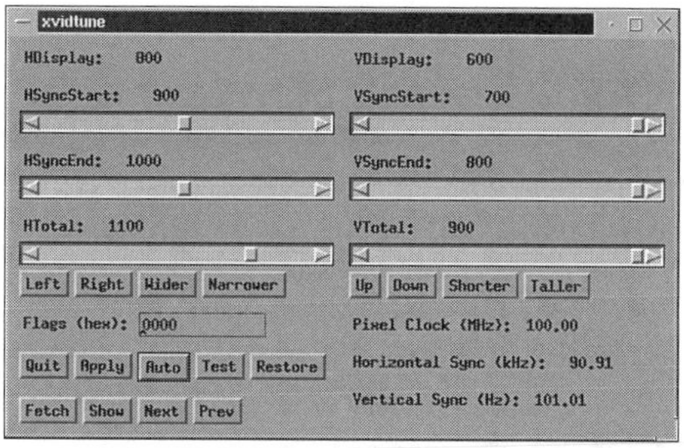

Figure 5.1
Main xvidtune screen.

Leave xvidtune running and cycle through each mode that is available for your current color depth. You can repeat this process for each color depth by starting the server in the different color depths and cycling through the modes using the Ctrl+Alt+Plus key sequence.

The easiest way to start the X server from a command line other than the default mode is to pass the color depth on the command line. However, for a script such as startx, a special syntax is required—startx -- -bpp 16, where you substitute valid values for the 16, such as 8, 15, 16, 24, or 32. The X server only starts up if a good combination of display modes, color depths, and RAM can be found for your video card and monitor.

DISSECTING THE XF86Config FILE

XFree86 v4.0 has greatly simplified configuration over the previous versions by generally handling the most complicated step (ModeLines) automatically. If you have unusual hardware, however, you might still need to do some manual configuring of XFree86.

XFree86 has one configuration file, /etc/X11/XF86Config (or /etc/XF86Config). This file is laid out in sections in the following format:

```
Section "SectionName"
   Command1 "Option"
   Command2 "Option"
   Subsection "Subsection Name"
         Command3 "Option"
   EndSubSection
EndSection
```

THE Modules SECTION

The Modules section marks one of the biggest changes to XFree86 from version 3.3 to version 4.0. In older versions of XFree86, monolithic servers provided services such as XF86_SVGA, which provided support for SVGA devices and XF86_S3, which provided support for S3 devices. The new model provides a single server called XFree86. Support for various services is now provided through dynamically loaded modules. This provides much more flexibility in how services are provided and what services users choose to actually use.

This also provides a more general mechanism for providing services like TrueType support that previously were provided by external programs.

Modules can be loaded using the Load command or using a SubSection. Using a SubSection enables options to be passed to the module:

```
# This loads the DBE extension module.
    Load        "dbe"   # Double buffer extension
# This loads the miscellaneous extensions module, and disables
# initialisation of the XFree86-DGA extension within that module.
    SubSection  "extmod"
      Option    "omit xfree86-dga"   # don't initialise the DGA extension
    EndSubSection
```

> **Tip**
>
> The omit xfree86-dga line turns off DGA extensions to XFree86. These are the extensions used by VMWare (www.vmware.com) to improve performance. If you use this product (or other products that require DGA), then you should comment out this option line.

THE Files SECTION

This section defines important files and directories for XFree86. The paths to the color (RGB) database, font definitions, and module libraries are all defined here.

THE ServerFlags SECTION

This section defines various XFree86 option flags. The defaults for these flags are good in almost all situations and should seldom need to be modified. If you do need to investigate these options, the comments in this section are very good, so just consult the configuration file.

THE InputDevice SECTIONS

InputDevice is one of the many sections that can be repeated in the configuration file. Each device (mouse, keyboard, touch screen, trackball, and so forth) has its own InputDevice section. For example, this is the beginning of the first mouse section:

```
Section "InputDevice"
# Identifier and driver
    Identifier  "Mouse1"
    Driver  "mouse"
    Option "Protocol"    "PS/2"
    Option "Device"      "/dev/mouse"
```

This section simply defines an available input device. It does not imply that this device is actually used. The ServerLayout section will associate this device with a layout. See the ServerLayout section for more information on layouts and how they are used.

THE Monitor SECTION

This section defines a monitor that is available for use. Like the InputDevice section, it does not imply that this monitor is actually used. It also does not associate the monitor with a video card. This is done in the Screen section later in this chapter. Each Monitor section has an Identifier command to name it.

All this indirection can seem confusing, but it makes XFree86 extremely flexible. By defining a monitor independently from a video card, it is much easier to define multiscreen layouts.

THE Device SECTION

This section defines a video card (or on-board video chip). As with many of the other sections, it does not imply that this device is used, just that it is available. As with most sections, the Device section uses an Identifier command to name this device.

The Driver command tells XFree86 which loadable module to use for this device. For up-to-date information on available drivers and supported hardware, see /usr/X11R6/lib/X11/doc/Status or http://www.xfree86.org/4.0.1/Status.html.

Device drivers often take a wide variety of options. For example, many devices provide hardware support to draw the mouse pointer. Sometimes this support isn't available or doesn't work correctly, so you need to turn this off and handle the mouse cursor in software. To do this, you would uncomment the following line in this section:

```
Option     "sw_cursor"
```

For information on the options available and what options are needed for various hardware configurations, see the README file for your hardware in /usr/X11R6/lib/X11/doc.

THE Screen SECTION

This section combines a Monitor and Device defined in the earlier sections to create a logical screen. It also defines a default color depth, or number of color bits per pixel.

Within this section are one or more Display subsections. These subsections define color depth/resolution combinations for this screen. They also provide view port, or virtual screen, sizes. After a screen is selected using a layout or the --screen command-line option, the current color depth will determine which display is used. The color depth can be set using the --depth command-line option, or the default color depth for the screen will be used.

THE ServerLayout SECTION

This section defines a layout of screens and input devices. One or more screens can be defined. If multiple screens are defined, options will tell XFree86 where they physically are in relation to one another. For example:

```
Section "ServerLayout"
        Identifier "Main Layout"
        Screen     "Screen 1" 0
        Screen     "Screen 2" 1 RightOf "Screen 1"
        Screen     "Screen 3" Relative "Screen 1" 2048 0
EndSection
```

In this example, Screen 1 is in the upper-left, Screen 2 is immediately to the right of Screen 1, and Screen 3 is 2048 pixels to the right of Screen 1. This enables you to distribute your

PART

II

CH

5

windows to multiple monitors and move easily between them. By default, however, you cannot have windows that overlap monitors.

By using a new module called Xinerama, you can treat multiple monitors as if they were one large workspace, moving windows around them seamlessly. Xinerama requires support from your window manager, and most window managers do not yet support Xinerama. Enlightenment (www.enlightenment.org) does (by using a special version for now), and others are likely to follow in the future.

X WINDOW SYSTEM STARTUP

The startup sequence for X is fairly complex, but understanding it can be very helpful if things go wrong. First, we will walk through an example startup (OpenLinux). In the section that follows, we'll explore how to wind your way through any startup sequence.

EXAMPLE: X WINDOW SYSTEM STARTUP ON OPENLINUX

OpenLinux is a good distribution to investigate because its startup sequence is relatively simple, but still has enough levels to be interesting.

INIT

X is started initially by the init process. For basic information about init, see Chapter 13, "System Initialization." In OpenLinux's /etc/inittab, X is started by the following line:

```
gu:5:respawn:/bin/sh -c 'C=/etc/rc.d/rc.gui;[ -x $C ]&&exec $C;init 3'
```

This line only executes if you are in runlevel 5. It runs /etc/rc.d/rc.gui if that file exists. Otherwise it switches to runlevel 3. This helps prevent your system from locking up if the GUI startup script doesn't exist or has any problems.

rc.gui

/etc/rc.d/rc.gui does one thing for OpenLinux: it starts kdm. In the process, though, it also redirects output to /var/log/gui.log. This is good to know if you're having any GUI-related problems because this is one of the log files you should check.

KDM

kdm is the K Display Manager. It is a complete replacement for the older xdm. In reality, it is just a wrapper around old xdm code, which is why many of the configuration files are the same.

After a user logs in, kdm calls /etc/X11/kdm/Xsession, which runs /etc/X11/xinit/ kdeinitrc, which calls /opt/kde/bin/startkde.

kdm is configured by /etc/X11/kdm/xdm-config. Note that this is xdm config, not kdm-config.

```
startkde
```

`/opt/kde/bin/startkde` runs the various applications required to provide the KDE environment.

EXPLORING STARTUP OF THE X WINDOW SYSTEM

Each distribution has a slightly different startup sequence, and your startup sequence will also be different if you use gdm, GNOME, or another window manager. These sequences also tend to change from version to version of a distribution. Obviously trying to document all of the possible startup sequences would take us quite a while and make for rather boring reading.

Understanding why all these scripts are run will help you understand the startup sequence for any distribution. Learning a little shell scripting won't hurt either. Let's go through the startup sequence from an explorer's point of view.

```
inittab
```

Startup of the X Window System will almost always start with `/etc/inittab`, if you've configured a graphical login. `inittab` is init's configuration file, and init is about the first thing to run during Linux startup. It is process number one and is the ultimate parent of every other process in the system.

One of the few things that is standardized among Linux startup sequences is the definition of run levels. Runlevel 5 is a graphical login. So if you want the X Window System to automatically start on boot-up, you need to set your default runlevel to 5.

Starting at the beginning of our exploration, we should verify the default runlevel by looking for the following line in `/etc/inittab`:

```
id:5:initdefault:
```

This tells us that the default runlevel is in fact 5. The other likely setting is 3, which is full multiuser mode.

Now that we know the starting runlevel, let's determine what processes init will run (this example happens to be a Red Hat system):

```
$ grep 5 /etc/inittab
#   5 - X11
id:5:initdefault:
l5:5:wait:/etc/rc.d/rc 5
pr:12345:powerokwait:/sbin/shutdown -c "Power Restored; Shutdown Cancelled"
1:2345:respawn:/sbin/mingetty tty1
2:2345:respawn:/sbin/mingetty tty2
3:2345:respawn:/sbin/mingetty tty3
4:2345:respawn:/sbin/mingetty tty4
5:2345:respawn:/sbin/mingetty tty5
6:2345:respawn:/sbin/mingetty tty6
# Run xdm in runlevel 5
x:5:respawn:/etc/X11/prefdm -nodaemon
```

The `id` line indicates the default runlevel. The `l5` line is what kicks off all the `/etc/rc.d/rc5.d` scripts. We'll get back to these in a moment. The `pr` line is for when power is restored

PART

II

CH

5

after a power failure, so we don't really care about that. All those `mingetty` lines represent the virtual consoles you get when pressing Ctrl+Alt+F#, so we're not interested in those, either.

Finally, that x line is exactly what we're looking for. Don't assume the x itself means anything. Remember that in OpenLinux, this line was labeled gu. The first field is just a name that the distribution gave to this rule. What we're looking for, generally, is something that kicks off a display manager (xdm, gdm, kdm). This version of Red Hat uses /etc/X11/prefdm. We'll investigate prefdm in a moment, but for now, notice that this rule is fired when we enter run-level five, and that if prefdm ever dies, init will restart it (that's what `respawn` means). The `-nodaemon` parameter indicates that prefdm should not put itself into the background. This is how programs run by init should work, because init will handle backgrounding them.

Sometimes its not as easy as looking for `dm` in the name. OpenLinux runs a script called `rc.gui`, which then runs kdm. Generally the line we're interested in is near the bottom, though, and should be fairly obvious (once you know what you're looking for).

You may discover that nothing in `inittab` seems to start a display manager. In this case, you should look at the *rc scripts*. rc scripts are usually stored in /etc/rc.d/rc#.d or /etc/rc#.d, where # is the run level. In the case of Debian, you'll find an rc script called xdm. This is the script that starts the display manager. A quick look inside this script will show us the line:

```
DAEMON=/usr/bin/X11/xdm
```

This is the display manager that Debian will start.

THE DISPLAY MANAGER

init's ultimate goal with run level five is to get a display manager started. Whether it does it directly (by calling xdm for instance) or through a script (like `rc.gui`), eventually a display manager should be started.

In the preceding example, we saw that Red Hat uses prefdm. In older versions of Red Hat, this was a symbolic link to the desired display manager. In newer versions of Red Hat, this is a script (similar to OpenLinux's `rc.gui`).

There are three common display managers.

XDM

xdm is the oldest display manager. Most distributions store the xdm configuration files in /etc/X11/xdm. If, for some reason, the configuration files aren't here, try the following:

```
locate xdm-config
```

As an explorer, our next way point is `xdm-config` (if we've determined that this system uses xdm). There is a lot of interesting information in this file, but the here are the most important lines:

```
DisplayManager.errorLogFile:    /var/log/xdm-error.log
DisplayManager._0.setup:        /etc/X11/xdm/Xsetup_0
DisplayManager*session:         /etc/X11/xdm/Xsession
```

The first line, `errorLogFile`, determines where xdm will output error messages. This is very important when trying to troubleshoot problems with xdm. Most distributions seem to be standardizing on `/var/log/xdm-error.log`.

The second line, `_0.setup`, determines what script xdm will run before providing a login prompt. This script generally does things such as provide an attractive background and perhaps a console window. The `_0` indicates that this configuration entry is for the primary display. On machines with multiple displays, you might have a `_1.setup` line as well, but this is very rare. Unless you are debugging problems with xdm itself, it is unlikely that you will need to investigate this script.

The third line, `session`, is probably the most important. This is the script that is run once a user logs in. This is also where different distributions most start to diverge. We'll investigate `Xsession` more in following text.

KDM

kdm is the KDE Display Manager and is almost identical to xdm in configuration. In fact, kdm is based directly on xdm's source code. kdm provides some nice features such as faces (which show available user IDs on the system), multilingual support, and a more configurable appearance. All of these advanced configurations are managed by the Control Center. The dialog's name is Login Manager, but its exact location seems to change with every minor update to KDE. Generally it should be found under Applications, System, or just System.

Because kdm uses xdm's configuration files, it will also call `/etc/X11/xdm/Xsession` when a user logs in.

GDM

gdm is the GNOME display manager, and is a complete rewrite of xdm, though it generally implements the same functions (as well as the added features of kdm).

The primary gdm configuration file is `/etc/X11/gdm/gdm.conf`. This location is fairly standard, but if you cannot find `gdm.conf` here, try this:

```
$ locate gdm.conf
```

gdm configuration is actually somewhat complicated, but the following lines from `gdm.conf` should point you in the right directions in understanding the startup sequence:

```
LogDir=/var/gdm
DisplayInitDir=/etc/X11/gdm/Init
PreSessionScriptDir=/etc/X11/gdm/PreSession
SessionDir=/etc/X11/gdm/Sessions/
PostSessionScriptDir=/etc/X11/gdm/PostSession/
```

Notice that most of the variables end with `Dir` and point to directories rather than files. This is because gdm allows extremely configurable *session* types. A session is the sequence of events between when a user logs in and logs out. Each session type has a name and is selected with the Session menu on the login screen of gdm. If no session type is selected, then Default is used (this is also what is used if no special rules exist for a particular session type). So, for

PART

II

CH

5

example, if you have chosen the GNOME session, gdm will first look for the file /etc/X11/gdm/PreSession/GNOME and then /etc/X11/gdm/PreSession/Default.

The LogDir directory is where gdm will store all of its logs. This is very important if you are debugging a problem with gdm.

The DisplayInitDir variable indicates where to look for scripts to run before presenting the user a login prompt. This is the same function as the Xsetup_0 file for xdm. In fact, /etc/X11/gdm/Init/Default is often symbolically linked to /etc/X11/xdm/Xsetup_0. Although gdm is incredibly flexible in what it allows to be done, you will find that most distributions just have it point back to what xdm does.

The PreSessionScriptDir variable indicates where to look for scripts to run after the user has logged in, but while the system is still running as root. This generally points back to /etc/X11/xdm/GiveConsole, and is where the user is generally given ownership of the console.

The SessionDir variable indicates where to look for scripts to run as the user. This generally points back to /etc/X11/xdm/Xsession. Almost all display manager configurations eventually get back to Xsession, which we'll cover next.

The PostSessionScriptDir variable indicates where to look for scripts to run after the user has logged out and after gdm is running as root again. This generally points back to /etc/X11/xdm/TakeConsole, which gives the console back to root.

Xsession

Most distributions, after the user has logged in, will run /etc/X11/xdm/Xsession. Although most distributions call this file the same thing, they tend to differ wildly about what it does. The only way to know is to actually read it.

In general, Xsession is going to do the following things:

- **Redirect output to ${HOME}/.xsession-errors**—Most distributions agree on this location, and it is an important source of information for debugging all kinds of problems. This file will catch the output of any application that doesn't have a controlling terminal, so it is a good place to look for output from applications you launch through the panel or in other ways that don't use a terminal.

- **Load resources**—Many older applications in the X Window System are configured with *resources*. Resources are explained in detail in "X Resources" (see Chapter 6, "Customizing X and Controlling X Resources"), but generally they are configuration options stored in memory by the X Window System and queried by various applications. Xsession generally includes a mechanism for loading user-specific resources from a file such as ${HOME}/.Xresources. To verify the actual name, look for parts of Xsession that call xrdb.

- **Run user-defined script**—Generally, the user is allowed to create her own startup scripts. Some distributions will run ${HOME}/.xsession if it is found. If not, they might try ${HOME}/.Xclients. Which user-defined scripts Xsession will honor is somewhat distribution specific, and you should check Xsession itself to be sure. Some distributions will also skip this step if the user requested a specific session through kdm or gdm. In that case, Xsession might just run the desktop or window manager directly.

- **Run Xclients**—The final fallback is almost always /etc/X11/xinit/Xclients. This script generally figures out what desktop or window manager the user wants (sometimes by querying distribution-specific configuration files), and starts it.

DESKTOP OR WINDOW MANAGER STARTUP

The final startup step is generally an "exec" command that starts a desktop (KDE or GNOME for example) or a window manager (fvwm2 or Blackbox for example). The exec instructs the script to remove itself from memory before launching the desired environment. This not only saves memory, but also ensures that the rest of the script won't be accidentally executed when the user logs out.

KDE starts with a script called startkde. This script launches the various servers that KDE needs for inter-process communication. It also starts the window manager, panel, and other useful applications.

GNOME starts with a script called gnome-session. This script does essentially the same things as startkde.

Window managers are generally started by simply running the window manager's executable.

VARIATION: startx

Your system does not have to be in runlevel 5 to start the X Window System. If XFree86 is not running, you can start it at any time using startx.

startx has a much simpler startup sequence than the display managers, but it is basically very similar.

After starting XFree86 itself, startx runs /etc/X11/xinit/xinitrc. This script is very similar to Xsession, except that it will generally never start a desktop or window manager itself. It generally does not honor the user's $HOME/.xsession script, but will generally honor $HOME/.Xclients. If the user does not have a .Xclients, then xinitrc will almost always run /etc/X11/xinit/Xclients, which will start a desktop or window manager.

TROUBLESHOOTING

When XFree86 starts up, text flashes on the screen, the monitor clicks and then repeats too fast to stop it.

In almost all cases, this indicates an error in your XF86Config file when your system is at runlevel 5.

Runlevel 5 means that XFree86 automatically starts up in nearly all distributions. This is because of an entry such as the following in your /etc/inittab:

```
x:5:respawn:/etc/X11/prefdm -nodaemon
```

The respawn flag tells init to restart this program if it ever dies. So when XFree86 starts up, it reads its configuration file, terminates with an error, and then init immediately restarts it. Because XFree86 switches your monitor's video mode when it starts up, you won't be able to type any commands at the console while this is happening.

You can get control of your machine by rebooting into single user mode. Press Ctrl+Alt+Delete to reboot your machine. At the boot: prompt, type linux -s and press Enter. The system will boot into single-user mode, and you will be logged in as root. Switch to runlevel 3 by typing the following:

```
# telinit 3
```

This will bring your system up without XFree86 so you can work on the configuration file. In order to test your configuration file, run startx. This will show you where the errors are so you can fix them.

> **Tip**
>
> If your problem machine is on a network, you can avoid rebooting. Just go to another machine and telnet in as a normal user (you can't telnet as root). Then su to root (type su, press Enter, and type the root password). Finally, type telinit 3 and your machine will be okay again.

XFree86 displays the wrong resolution.

XF86Config probably lists video modes that you didn't intend.

You need to edit your XF86Config file. Before doing this, you need to switch to runlevel 3. If you don't and you make any errors in this file, it will be difficult to get control of your machine again. To switch to runlevel 3, become root and type telinit 3 at the command prompt.

Now edit /etc/X11/XF86Config (or /etc/XF86Config) and look for the Screen sections. They will look something like this:

```
Section "Screen"
    Identifier    "Screen0"
    Device        "Card0"
    Monitor           "Generic Monitor"
    DefaultDepth 8
    Subsection "Display"
        Depth   24
        Modes   "320x200" "800x600"
        Virtual 0 0
    EndSubSection
EndSection
```

There might be several Screen sections. Make sure you are using the one for your device.

Notice the 320×200 in the Modes line. XFree86 will start with the first resolution it finds in the Modes line. Unless you really need to switch video modes (it is usually less useful than it would seem), just list one mode here. Run startx and make sure it works. Then switch back to runlevel 5 with telinit 5 at the command prompt.

XFree86 doesn't start when Linux boots.

You are in runlevel 3 instead of runlevel 5. Edit your /etc/inittab and change the id line to this:

```
id:5:initdefault:
```

When you restart your machine, XFree86 will start automatically.

CASE STUDY: THE X WINDOW SYSTEM ACROSS A NETWORK

The X Window System is an incredibly flexible, portable system. Because it is network transparent, it is easy to run applications on remote machines and display them on your desktop. Figure 5.2 shows my personal desktop.

Figure 5.2
The X Window System makes remote machines seem local.

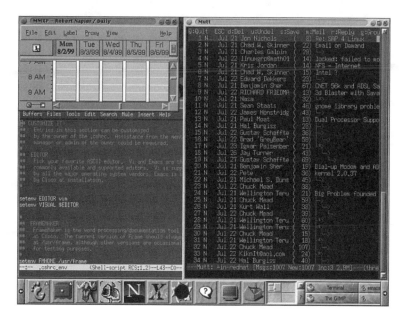

This desktop is noteworthy because of how complex it really is. The X Window System hides so much of that complexity that it is easy to take it for granted. Here are some facts to consider:

- Mutt (the mail program) is running on a remote Solaris machine through an ISDN line. All the text data is encrypted and compressed as it is sent between the two machines (this is done with a program called ssh). The graphical part of the xterm, however, is actually running on my local Linux machine, so the ISDN line only has to handle the text.

- Emacs (the editor) is also running on the local Linux machine. But the file being edited is actually on the same remote machine that Mutt is running on.

- Meeting Maker (the calendar program) is running completely on the remote Solaris machine, sending all of its graphics information back to my Linux machine (once again compressed and encrypted). This allows me to run Meeting Maker even though it isn't ported to Linux.

- The buttons at the bottom will launch these remote applications automatically. After this is set up, I can generally ignore which machine is running what application. They all display on the same machine, and I can treat them all the same.

- What isn't obvious from the screen shot is that I'm actually sitting at a Windows 98 machine running Reflection X. The Linux machine and Windows 98 machine are connected with a fast local network. The Linux machine displays my desktop on the Windows machine. I still get all the advantages of Linux, but I can run Windows applications without leaving my chair. Besides that, another user (my wife) can log in to the Linux console and use Netscape there while I'm reading mail, running my own copy of Netscape, and so forth. It's all transparent.

I've used many different operating systems and graphical user interfaces and have yet to find one that can offer the incredible flexibility and power of the X Window System.

## CHAPTER 6

CUSTOMIZING X AND CONTROLLING X RESOURCES

In this chapter

NAVIGATING THE X WINDOW SYSTEM

The X Window System presents several windows to the user, and each shows the output of an X application called a *client*. The client can be running on the user's PC, which is more than likely with Linux, or on another workstation on the network.

How you move around in the X Window System very much depends on your window manager. Most window managers use an onscreen pointer called a *cursor* to indicate where you're working. The cursor can take on many shapes, depending on what you're doing and what window manager you're running.

The X Window System, like most graphical user interfaces (GUIs), allows input from the keyboard and a pointing device, which is usually a mouse. Typically, for a window to accept input, it must be the active window. An active window normally has a different appearance (for example, a highlighted border) than an inactive window. When a window is selected, it is said to have gained *focus*.

Most of this chapter will focus on window managers such as fvwm2, Blackbox, and Enlightenment. Desktops such as GNOME, KDE, and XFCE, often do things quite differently. KDE and GNOME are covered in detail in Chapter 3, "KDE" and Chapter 4, "GNOME."

GETTING FOCUS

Making a window active depends on how you've configured your window manager. Some configurations allow the window to become active when you merely move the cursor into the window; others require you to click the window with the mouse, as you do in Microsoft Windows. Table 6.1 lists the most common focus schemes (particular window manager may have different names for these schemes).

TABLE 6.1 COMMON FOCUS SCHEMES

Name	Description
Click	You must click a window for it to receive focus. Microsoft Windows uses this focus scheme.
Mouse	Whatever window the pointer is currently in has focus. If the pointer is not currently in a window, then no window has focus.
Sloppy	This scheme is very similar to Mouse, except that a window does not give up focus until the pointer moves into a new window. Using this scheme is often much more convenient than using Mouse focus.

Mouse and Sloppy focus can take some getting used to if you are familiar with GUIs that allow only Click focus. When you get used to them, though, these types of focus let you do things you couldn't do with Click focus. For example, if you are reading one window and typing in another, you can have the window you're reading appear on top, even partially obscuring the active window, while the window you are typing in retains focus.

USING MENUS

Many GUIs on PCs today provide drop-down and pop-up menus. Again, the availability of such items depends on the window manager, including the types of menu choices provided. Most X window managers don't have a main menu bar across the top or bottom of the monitor; instead, they use a floating menu. You typically invoke this floating menu by clicking over an empty area of the desktop. You hold down the mouse button and drag the cursor through the various menu selections. When you find the desired menu choice, you simply release the button, which is very much like how you navigate menus on a Macintosh and very unlike how you navigate menus under Microsoft Windows.

USING VIRTUAL TERMINALS IN XFREE86

Your X server runs on a virtual terminal assigned by Linux. This terminal is assigned to the seventh virtual terminal, which you can reach by pressing Ctrl+Alt+F7 from a character terminal. From XFree86, you can reach the other terminals by pressing the Ctrl+Alt+Fx key combination, where x represents the number of the virtual terminal you want to access. Although accessing the other virtual terminals can be handy, XFree86 also allows you to start character terminal emulators, called *xterm sessions*.

> **Note**
>
> If your X server is running, you must use the Ctrl+Alt+Fx combination to move from the X server to a virtual terminal. You can still use the Alt+Fx combination to move among the virtual terminals.

USING WINDOW MANAGERS FOR LINUX

As stated earlier, the X Window System doesn't specify a window manager. The look and feel of the X Window System is left up to the user—completely up to the user. Almost every aspect of the behavior of the GUI is in your control. In this spirit, Linux doesn't provide just one window manager for XFree86. Table 6.2 lists some of the various window managers available for Linux.

TABLE 6.2 SOME WINDOW MANAGERS AVAILABLE FOR LINUX

Name	Description
twm	Tab Window Manager (sometimes called *Tom's Window Manager*). It is the ancestor of many other window managers, such as vtwm, ctwm, tvtwm, piewm, fvwm (and its descendants), and was the first ICCCM window manager. (ICCCM is a standard for how programs communicate with each other.) twm is still in use today as a common default window manager because it is very small and many people know how to use it (though not as many people use it as their day-to-day window manager).
fvwm2	F Virtual window manager (no one remembers what the F actually stands for, including Rob Nation, the author). It is one of the most popular window managers for Linux (and elsewhere). Note that some Linux systems have an fvwm

TABLE 6.2   CONTINUED

Name	Description
	and an fvwm2 executable. fvwm is usually version 1.24r, whereas fvwm2 is some 2.x version. You almost always want fvwm2. Many of the more modern distributions have stopped shipping the original fvwm.
fvwm95	Hack of fvwm2 that looks a lot like Microsoft's Windows 95.
AfterStep	Emulation of the NeXT interface written on top of fvwm2.
Window Maker	Window Maker emulates the NeXT interface. It is very popular and has a lot of extensions available. It is now somewhat integrated with GNOME and KDE.
Blackbox	Blackbox is also based on the NeXT interface, but it is designed to be small and fast, without lots of fancy features.
Enlightenment	Enlightenment, or E as it is often called, is quite large but very pretty. It used to be the default GNOME window manager, but it has since been replaced with Sawfish. E still works well with GNOME, however, as well as with KDE to some extent. Enlightenment is perhaps the most configurable window manager ever developed.
Sawfish	Originally named Sawmill, Sawfish is rapidly becoming one of the more popular window managers. Highly configurable, but much lighter weight than Enlightenment, Sawfish is now the default window manager for GNOME.
kwin	The primary window manager for KDE. kwm is almost never run without KDE.

TWM

Although few new users use twm, studying this window manager is very valuable because it sets the groundwork for many of the most popular window managers today. In particular, the very popular fvwm2 is based on twm code, and many other window managers are based on fvwm2.

The twm window manager for the X Window System provides title bars, shaped windows, several forms of icon management, user-defined macro functions, click-to-type and pointer-driven keyboard focus, and user-specified key and mouse button bindings. This program is usually started by the user's session manager or startup script. When used from xdm or xinit without a session manager, twm is frequently executed in the foreground as the last client. When it is run this way, exiting twm causes the session to be terminated (that is, logged out).

By default, an application window is surrounded by a frame with a title bar at the top and a special border around the window. The title bar contains the window's name, a rectangle that's lit when the window is receiving keyboard input, and function boxes known as title buttons at the left and right edges of the title bar. Clicking Button1 (usually the leftmost mouse button, unless it has been changed with xmodmap) on a title button invokes the function associated with the button. In the default interface, windows are *iconified* (minimized to an icon) when you click the left title button, which looks like a dot. Conversely, windows are *deiconified*, or restored, when you click the associated icon or entry in the icon manager.

You can resize windows by clicking the right title button (which resembles a group of nested squares), dragging the pointer over the edge that's to be moved, and releasing the pointer when the outline of the window is the size you want. Similarly, you can move windows by clicking the title bar, dragging a window outline to the new location, and then releasing when the outline is in the position you want. Just clicking the title bar raises the window without moving it.

When you create new windows, twm honors any size and location information you request. Otherwise, you see an outline of the window's default size, its title bar, and lines dividing the window into a three-by-three grid that track the pointer. Each mouse button performs a different operation:

- Clicking Button1 positions the window at the current position and gives it the default size.
- Clicking Button2 (usually the middle mouse button) and dragging the outline gives the window its current position but allows you to resize the sides as described previously.
- Clicking Button3 (usually the right mouse button) gives the window its current position but attempts to make it long enough to touch the bottom of the screen.

FVWM2

The fvwm2 window manager is a derivative of twm, redesigned to minimize memory consumption, provide a three-dimensional look to window frames, and provide a simple virtual desktop. Memory consumption is estimated at about a half to a third the memory consumption of twm, primarily because of a redesign of twm's inefficient method of storing mouse bindings (associating commands to mouse buttons). Also, many configurable options of twm have been removed.

XFree86 provides a virtual screen whose operation can be confusing when used with the fvwm2 virtual window manager. With XFree86, windows that appear on the virtual screen actually get drawn into video memory, so the virtual screen size is limited by available video memory.

With fvwm2's virtual desktop, windows that don't appear onscreen don't actually get drawn into video RAM. The size of the virtual desktop is limited to 32,000×32,000 pixels. Using a virtual desktop of more than five times the size of the visible screen in each direction is impractical.

Note

Memory usage with the virtual desktop is a function of the number of windows that exist. The size of the desktop makes little difference.

When you're becoming familiar with fvwm2, disabling XFree86's virtual screen by setting the virtual screen size to the physical screen size is recommended. When you become familiar with fvwm2, you might want to re-enable XFree86's virtual screen.

PART

II

CH

6

fvwm2 provides multiple virtual desktops for users who want to use them. The screen is a viewport onto a desktop that's larger than (or the same size as) the screen. Several distinct desktops can be accessed. The basic concept is one desktop for each project or one desktop for each application. Because each desktop can be larger than the physical screen, windows that are larger than the screen or large groups of related windows can be viewed easily.

The size of each virtual desktop must be specified at startup; the default is three times the physical size of the screen. All virtual desktops must be the same size. The total number of distinct desktops doesn't need to be specified but is limited to approximately 4 billion total. All windows on the current desktop can be displayed in a pager, miniature view, or the current desktop. Windows that aren't on the current desktop can be listed, with their geometries, in a window list, accessible as a pop-up menu. (The term *geometries* specifies the coordinates and number of pixels needed for the window under an X window manager.)

Sticky windows are windows that float above the virtual desktop by "sticking to the screen's glass." They always stay put onscreen. Using this type of window is convenient for clocks and xbiff, for example, so you need to run only one such utility, and it always stays with you.

Note The xbiff application notifies you when new mail arrives.

Window geometries are specified relative to the current viewport; that is, *xterm-geometry +0+0* always appears in the upper-left corner of the visible portion of the screen. You can specify geometries that place windows on the virtual desktop but off-screen. For example, if the visible screen is 1,000×1,000 pixels, the desktop size is three-by-three, and the current viewport is at the upper-left corner of the desktop, invoking *xterm-geometry +1000+1000* places the window just off the lower-right corner of the screen. You can find it by moving the mouse to the lower-right corner of the screen and waiting for it to scroll into view. Keep in mind that you can map a window only onto the active desktop, not an inactive desktop.

A geometry specified as *xterm-geometry −5−5* generally places the window's lower-right corner five pixels from the lower-right corner of the visible portion of the screen. Not all applications support window geometries with negative offsets.

On some versions of Linux, you can find either fvwm or fvwm95. fvwm is from the 1.X line (versus fvwm2, which is version 2.X). You will seldom want to use the original fvwm. fvwm95 is a hack on top of fvwm2 to make it act more like Microsoft Windows 95. At one time, this was the default window manager for Red Hat, but this hack hasn't been worked on in years and is not commonly used anymore.

AFTERSTEP

AfterStep started life as a package for fvwm called BowMan. BowMan gave fvwm a NeXT look and feel. It was renamed AfterStep when it started picking up new features beyond simple emulation. The most notable of AfterStep's features is the *wharf*. It is based on NeXT's *dock* but was renamed to avoid copyright problems.

The wharf holds buttons that can launch applications or can be applications themselves. This concept is what eventually led to KDE and GNOME's *panels*.

WINDOW MAKER

Window Maker is another window manager based on the NeXT interface. It is original code, however, and is not based on fvwm. Several of the AfterStep developers have moved over to the Window Maker project. This window manager, which includes some integration into KDE and GNOME, also provides themes.

BLACKBOX

In the words of its author, "from the time the first line of code was written, Blackbox has evolved around one premise, minimalism." It is also based on the NeXT interface but is not as flashy as Window Maker. For that reason, it is also much faster and requires less memory. Blackbox is a very good choice for users looking for a clean, fast window manager, with nice features but little flash.

ENLIGHTENMENT

Enlightenment provides more bells and whistles than perhaps any other window manager. It is also one of the larger window managers and requires a significant amount of memory and CPU speed to operate properly. Enlightenment is covered in more detail in Chapter 4, "GNOME."

SAWFISH

Sawfish is a relative newcomer. Somewhat in the shadow of Enlightenment, it aims to be one of the most configurable window managers available while remaining as small and fast as possible. All its configuration is managed in a lightweight LISP dialect called rep. Luckily, most of Sawfish can be configured using graphical dialogs.

Sawfish recently became the default window manager for Helix GNOME. It is likely to become a very popular window manager in coming years.

KWIN

The K Desktop Environment (KDE) is a large open source project that was designed to create an integrated desktop environment and released entirely under the GNU General Public License (GPL).

The primary window manager for KDE is kwin. For more information on KDE and kwin, see Chapter 3, "KDE."

PART
II
CH
6

CHOOSING A WINDOW MANAGER

Each distribution has a slightly different way to determine the default window manager. One of the most common ways is to place exec `window-manager` as the last line in `${HOME}/`.Xclients, where `window-manager` is the window manager's executable. If this doesn't work, see "X Window System Start-Up" in Chapter 5."

THEMES

Using themes is perhaps one of the most fun parts of using window managers. Themes allow you to define the look and feel of the window manager in a central, consistent way (see Figures 6.1 and 6.2).

Figure 6.1
KDE using the B3/KDE theme.

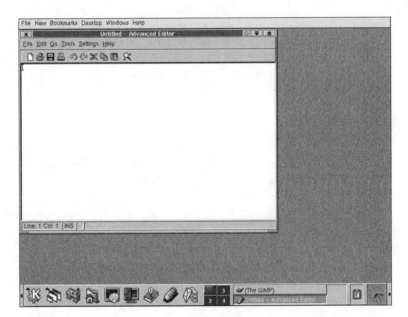

The only difference between the two desktops in Figure 6.1 and Figure 6.2 is the theme. The first desktop uses the default KDE theme, B3/KDE, whereas the second desktop uses the Aquatica theme by Zeljko Vukman. Switching between themes does not require shutting down the currently running applications.

Exactly what a theme can do and how to install it are dependent on the window manager. Many window managers now support themes in various ways. Check out the site http:// themes.org, which has become the definitive repository for themes, including themes for AfterStep, Blackbox, Enlightenment, GTK+, IceWM, KDE, Sawfish, and Window Maker.

Figure 6.2
KDE using the
Aquatica theme.

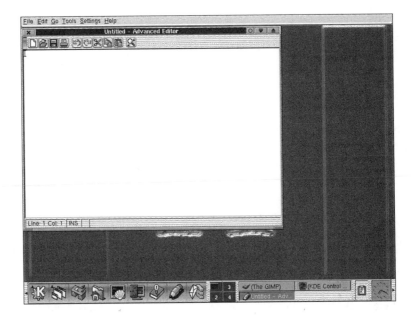

X RESOURCES

Many older X applications rely on *resources* for configuration. Resources are key-value data
that are stored centrally by the X server. Resources are stored in a hierarchy of classes and
instances. Each instance has a value. This is easiest to describe by way of some examples.
Listing 6.1 shows typical resource entries. These would generally be found in a file called
`${HOME}/.Xdefaults`. Note that the numbers in italics indicate line numbers and are not
actually in the file.

LISTING 6.1   TYPICAL X RESOURCES

```
emacs*Background: DarkSlateGray    (1)
emacs*Foreground: Wheat            (2)
emacs*pointerColor: Orchid         (3)
emacs*cursorColor: Orchid          (4)
emacs.geometry: 80x25                     (5)

XTerm*highlightSelection: true     (6)
XTerm*VT100*colorBDMode: on               (7)
XTerm.VT100.titeInhibit: true             (8)

!XTerm.VT100*colorMode: off               (9)

*visualBell: true                  (10)
Scrollbar.JumpCursor: True         (11)

*VT100.Translations: #override \   (12)
<Key>BackSpace: string(0x7F)\n\    (13)
<Key>Delete: string("\033[3~")\n\  (14)
<Key>Home: string("\033[1~")\n\    (15)
```

LISTING 6.1 CONTINUED	
`<Key>End: string("\033[4~")`	*(16)*
`Vim*background: black`	*(17)*
`Vim*foreground: lightyellow`	*(18)*

NODES AND VALUES

In all the preceding entries, the text to the left of the colon is a node address, whereas the text to the right of the colon is a value. Notice that node addresses are made up of various parts separated by asterisks or dots. These are based on the hierarchies of nodes. For example, line 5 refers to the node `emacs.geometry`. This references the node `geometry`, which is a child of the node `emacs`. When emacs starts up and requests the value for its geometry (the size and location of its window), this is guaranteed to be the node that the X Resource Manager will return. The dot *binds* the node `emacs` directly to the node `geometry`.

LOOSE BINDING

Line 3 is similar to line 5, but instead of binding with a dot, it binds with an asterisk. This is called *loose binding* and tells the X Resource Manager that any number of nodes can come between `emacs` and `pointerColor`. For example, `XTerm.VT100.titeInhibit` listed in line 8 would also match the address `XTerm*titeInhibit`. If two addresses match the same node, the X Resource Manager will select the most specific address (in this case `Xterm.VT100.titeInhibit`). Most people use the asterisk even when fully specifying a node. This way they don't have to remember the exact node hierarchy.

Notice that line 10 has a leading asterisk. This means that any application that requests a `visualBell` node and doesn't have a more specific definition listed will match this address.

CLASSES

Line 2 includes an example of a *class* address. `Foreground` is a class that includes various other nodes such as `foreground`, `borderColor`, and `cursorColor`. Note that `Foreground` is a class, while `foreground` is an instance. By convention, classes begin with a capital letter while instances begin with a lowercase letter. When emacs requests its foreground color, it will request the node `emacs.foreground`, which will match the `emacs*Foreground` definition. On the other hand, when emacs requests the node `emacs.cursorColor`, it will match the `emacs*cursorColor` definition, even though `cursorColor` is a member of the `Foreground` class. This is because `emacs*cursorColor` is more specific. If `emacs.cursorColor` were defined, that one would be returned instead.

By convention, an application's name is its instance node and it is generally the only member of a class with the same name but a leading capital letter. For example, the program Emacs uses the node `emacs`, which is a member of the class `Emacs`.

To find out what classes and instances exist for a particular application, consult its man page.

OTHER RESOURCE FILE ISSUES

Line 9 demonstrates a comment in a resource file (such as `.Xdefaults`). A line beginning with an exclamation point will be ignored by the X Resource Manager. Note that this is in contrast to most other Linux configuration files, which generally use # to denote a comment.

Lines 12–16 demonstrate a multiline entry. Note the trailing backslashes on each line. These indicate the entry continues to the next line. No other characters (including spaces) can come after the backslash.

FONT DEFINITIONS

Often resource files are used to define font use, as in the following example:

```
Vim*font: -misc-fixed-medium-r-normal--20-200-75-75-c-100-iso8859-15
```

This font definition is called an *X Logical Font Description* (*XLFD*) and is made up of 14 parts:

- **Foundry**—This is the provider of the font. These providers are registered with the X Consortium and include groups and companies like Adobe and Bitstream.
- **Family Name**—This identifies the family of typeface such as Helvetica or Times Roman.
- **Weight Name**—This identifies the typographic weight such as bold or demibold. Note that bold for one font family could be very similar to demibold for another family, so these entries should only be taken as a rough guide.
- **Slant**—This indicates the slant of the font as follows:

R	Roman (upright)
I	Italic
O	Oblique
RI	Reverse Italic
RO	Reverse Oblique
OT	Other

- **Set Width Name**—This indicates the nominal width of the font in the foundry's judgment. Examples are normal, condensed, narrow, or double-wide.
- **Add Style Name**—This indicates additional style information such as serif, sans serif, informal, or decorated.
- **Pixel Size**—This indicates the size of the font in pixels for a nominal point size and Resolution Y.
- **Point Size**—This indicates the designed point size of the font, or 0 for a scalable font.
- **Resolution X and Resolution Y**—These indicate the resolution that the font was designed for. By giving both X and Y resolutions, the font server can determine the aspect ratio of the font, and by comparing these with the pixel size and point size, can determine what font will be the appropriate size for your particular display. Generally users want a particular point size or dots per inch. To determine whether a 10-point font will appear as 10 point on your screen, the server needs to match your resolution

PART II
CH 6

and aspect ratio to a font that was designed with similar values. Otherwise, it might need to select an applicable scalable font to get the desired effect.

- **Spacing**—This indicates the spacing class of the font as follows:

  P   Proportional
  M   Monospaced
  C   Char Cell (every character fits in a rectangle)

- **Average Width**—This is the arithmetic mean of the widths of all the characters in the font. If it begins with a tilde (~), the font is dominantly right to left.

- **Character Set Registry and Character Set Encoding**—These fields indicate the character set used to encode the font. Often these are ISO-registered tables such as ISO8859-1 for Latin-1.

Note that none of these values are case sensitive. Font definitions always start with a leading hyphen and each field is separated by a hyphen.

REQUESTING A FONT

Fonts are always defined with all 14 fields. These definitions are made in the `font.dir` files in the font libraries. These font libraries are generally found in `/usr/X11R6/lib/X11/fonts`, but other directories can be defined through XF86Config by using the `FontPath` command in the `Files` section.

When using a font, however, you do not have to specify all 14 fields. In fact, it is often easiest not to define all the fields. The Font Server will then pick a font that most closely matches your request. To skip a field, use an asterisk instead of a value. Consider, for example, the following font definition:

```
-misc-fixed-medium-r-normal--20-200-75-75-c-100-iso8859-1
```

You probably don't care about most of these entries. You probably just want a fixed, medium-weight, Roman font of an appropriate size for your current resolution. You can probably get this with the following:

```
-*-fixed-medium-r-normal-*-*-*-*-*-*-*-*-*
```

I say *probably* because it can depend on the order of your font definitions. The font server will select the first font that matches your request, so if you had a font with a non-Latin encoding early in your search, you might have to include iso8859-1 in this definition to get the font you want.

Using wildcards can be especially helpful when using the same resource files between different machines, especially machines running different distributions of Linux or non-Linux machines altogether. Not all flavors of Linux have the same fonts installed by default. If you are too specific in your font definition, you might discover that the machine you are on doesn't have that font at all, in which case the font server will guess what font you want (unfortunately the font server is not always a good guesser). If you provide some leeway by specifying only the fields you really care about, you are much more likely to get an acceptable font.

On the other hand, the advantage of specifying exactly the font you want is that you will always get exactly that font. This will save you some grief if you ever install new fonts that can come earlier in the search path.

XFONTSEL

Selecting a font purely by name and metrics can be fine for publishing professionals, but it's not a minor task for most of the world. For the rest of us, we have xfontsel. xfontsel provides a GUI interface for selecting just the font you want (see Figure 6.3).

Figure 6.3
xfontsel helps you find the font you want.

After running xfontsel from the command line, click each of the fields (such as `fndry` or `fmly`) to select available options. The second line will show the font selector you can use to choose the font displayed in the lower box. When you get the font you want, you can click the Select button and paste the selector into another application.

xfontsel has several handy command-line options, shown in Table 6.3.

TABLE 6.3 XFONTSEL COMMAND-LINE OPTIONS

Option	Description
`-pattern fontname`	Limits listed fonts. This is an XFLD pattern.
`-print`	If this option is selected, the font selector will be printed to the terminal when you click the Quit button.
`-sample text`	Usually, xfontsel uses an alphabet sample to test the font. This option lets you choose specific sample text for linear addressed fonts. Most fonts are linearly addressed, so this is usually the option you want.
`-sample16 text16`	This option provides sample text for 16-bit matrix-encoded fonts. These are generally glyph-fonts. See the xfontsel man page for more information.
`-sampleucs textUCS`	This option provides sample text for UTF-8 encoded text. See the xfontsel man page for more information.
`-scaled`	This option allows you to choose arbitrary point-sizes for scalable fonts.

CONNECTING TO A FONT SERVER

Generally, your own workstation will provide your fonts, but in some environments it can be convenient to centralize your fonts onto a single server. Although there is seldom a need to set font servers up, your network might already have one that you would like to use.

PART

II

CH

6

To select a font server, add entries in the following form to the `FontPath` entry in the `Files` section:

```
transport/hostname:port
```

Generally this will be something like the following:

```
tcp/myserver:7100
```

In this example, `tcp` is the protocol, which is the usual protocol for fonts. `myserver` is your font server, and `7100` is the port. This is the normal font server port.

For more information on setting up a font server, see the xfs man page.

LOADING AND QUERYING RESOURCES

Generally, resource definitions are put in a file called ~/.Xresources. If you want to update your resources after you've logged in, update this file and run the following:

```
$ xrdb -merge ~/.Xresources
```

If you want to see what resources are currently in use, run this:

```
$ xrdb -query
```

PROJECT: AUTO-SHRINKING XTERM

Most people just use X resources to make simple modifications to colors or fonts. Even then, they generally just copy the X resources from another user without ever really understanding what the resources are doing. In this short project, we'll investigate an interesting set of resources in xterm: Translations.

Translations in xterm enable you to execute certain actions in response to events. Often these events are key presses or mouse clicks (a good way to build macros), but there are other events such as when the mouse enters or leaves the window.

Say you want the xterm to shrink whenever the mouse leaves it and then grow when the mouse enters. This way, you could have many xterms on the screen and could somewhat watch what they were doing without having them take over your entire desktop. This can be very handy when you have a lot of compilations going on. You might want to watch them all to see when one completes, but you don't really care what the output looks like most of the time.

To get this effect, you can instruct xterm to change its font in response to mouse actions. The following X resource would do this:

```
shrinkterm*VT100.Translations: <EnterWindow>: set-vt-font(d) \n\
                               <LeaveWindow>: set-vt-font(1) \n
```

Let's look at this in detail:

- **shrinkterm**—This indicates that this resource only applies to windows with the name shrinkterm. We did this so that it wouldn't automatically impact all xterm windows. To create an xterm window with the name shrinkterm, type the following:
```
xterm -name shrinkterm
```
- ***VT100.Translations:**—This is the rest of the binding. The asterisk indicates that any number of nodes can come between shrinkterm and VT100. The VT100 node indicates that this only applies to xterms in VT100 emulation (as opposed to Tek emulation). The Translations node is the node we're configuring.
- **<EnterWindow>**—This event occurs whenever the mouse enters the window. It does not occur when the window simply gains focus, only when the mouse enters.
- **set-vt-font(d)**—This is an *action*. Actions are how the xterm can respond to events. In this case, it sets the VT100 font to the default. For a list of available actions, see the xterm man page.
- **\n**—This can be one of the trickier parts to remember. Translations can have multiple actions per event. For example, to have the bell ring whenever the mouse enters the window (as well as the font-changing action) you would use this resource:
```
shrinkterm*VT100.Translations: <EnterWindow>: set-vt-font(d) bell() \n\
                               <LeaveWindow>: set-vt-font(1) \n
```

  The \n terminates a series of actions, so the next item must be an event (in this case <LeaveWindow>). The final \ actually has nothing to do with Translations itself, but is rather a line continuation character, indicating that the next line is still part of this resource. Note that the final line does not end in a backslash.

- **<LeaveWindow>: set-vt-font(1) \n**—This line is almost identical to the last line. It instructs the xterm to set the VT100 font to the first font in its font list. This font is the "Unreadable" font, which is quite small. To see the list, Ctrl+right-click in the xterm window. If you would like another font (for example, the "Tiny" font), you could change the number in parenthesis .

This example is based very closely on the shrinkterm resource file written by Stephen Martin. If you're interested in the subject, you should see x.themes.org, which includes this and several other useful resource files (as well as many other things to make your desktop more interesting).

CHAPTER 7

MULTIMEDIA

In this chapter

OPEN SOUND SYSTEM FOR LINUX

Linux was once a rather serious infant when it came to multimedia. Now, however, many of the same multimedia features that are found with other operating systems are available to Linux as well. The ones that have garnered the most enthusiasm have been the applications that operate over networks such as the Internet. Streaming audio and video and multimedia documentation distribution have almost become standard in today's Internet.

Linux kernels use two versions of the sound driver system. One is free (included with the kernel source code) and must be compiled manually and linked into the Linux kernel itself (this is done for you by most distributions). The other is a commercial product that offers more functionality, sound card auto-detection (including PnP sound cards), and a much simpler configuration, all at a slight cost.

For many people with common sound cards, the free sound driver package that is included in kernel source code works fine. Even people with PnP sound cards can often get them working using a utility package called isapnptools, which is included with most distributions. This is just fine for those who are adventurous, but many people simply do not want to bother with all the work that is involved in getting such a small (but important) thing working on their systems. Then there are those who have sound cards that are simply not supported with the free drivers; there are not many that fall into this category, but they do exist.

As luck would have it, the developers of the free version of the sound driver package offer a commercial version as well: Open Sound System for Linux. Actually, the Open Sound System by 4Front Technologies is available for various UNIX and UNIX-based operating systems. With Open Sound System, 4Front Technologies is trying to establish a unified sound driver interface for UNIX developers. They are also bringing the kind of sound support available on Windows systems to UNIX. Previously, only the most basic sound support was offered on any flavor of UNIX. Now, with Open Sound System, MIDI and other advanced sound features are available.

Note   4Front Technologies supports Open Sound System. Also, a product called OSS/Free comes with the Linux kernel. Although OSS/Free was originally supported by 4Front, it has been supported by Alan Cox since 1998.

This is not, however, why so many Linux users decide to spend the money on a copy of this sound driver package. The main reason they buy it is because they can literally put the files on their system, run an installation script, and within minutes (sometimes within seconds) they have sound support. Compare this to the hours of tinkering that some people go through to get their kernels compiled with correct settings, and you will start to see why the meager cost of the driver package is well worth it.

GETTING AND INSTALLING OPEN SOUND SYSTEM FOR LINUX

The best way to start is to download the demo version and try it yourself. You can download the demo of Open Sound System for Linux (known as OSS/Linux) from the main distribution site at http://www.opensound.com, or from the Commercial Packages CD that comes with Caldera eDesktop.

Go to the Web page for Linux-x86, and then click the Download button on the left. You are asked for some information about who you are and what kind of system you are running; then you are allowed to download the demo. This demo times out after seven days, but it is sufficient for testing whether the commercial sound driver works with your hardware. Unless your hardware is very unusual, it will work fine. The demo version is the same as the licensed version, but with a timeout. Applying a license file to the OSS/Linux installation (which is covered later) removes the seven-day demo timeout. At the time of this writing, licenses for individual systems are quite inexpensive (starting at $20 U.S.). They also come with free technical support for one year and free upgrades for two years or until the next major OSS revision is released (such as a version 3.x to 4.x upgrade).

> **Note**
>
> Be sure to download the version of OSS that matches the version of your Linux kernel! If you are in doubt, execute uname -v at a command prompt to see which Linux kernel version you are running.

RUNNING THE INSTALLATION

Installing OSS/Linux is quite simple. What you download from the Open Sound site is a .tar.gz file that contains the driver package. Create a directory for the files (for example, oss in your home directory), copy the .tar.gz file you downloaded into the directory, and then run the following command to extract the contents:

```
$ tar zxvf oss??????.tar.gz
```

The question marks represent the various versions for OSS. For example, at the time of this writing, the version is 393i-2214. The results resemble the file list that is shown in Table 7.1.

TABLE 7.1   FILES CONTAINED WITHIN THE OSS/LINUX DEMO

File	Description
INSTALL	Installation instructions
LICENSE	Demo license
oss-install	Installation script
oss.pkg	An archive containing the binaries that make up the OSS/Linux package

PART

II

CH

7

Be sure that there is no sound driver support compiled into your Linux kernel or inserted as modules. Most distributions use module-based sound drivers by default. The following steps will remove them:

1. Remove sound from `/etc/modules/default` for OpenLinux or `/etc/modules` for Debian (most other distributions do not use this file).

2. Remove any sound-driver lines from `/etc/modules.conf` or `/etc/conf.modules` (depending on your distribution). These will include words such as `sound` or `soundcore`.

When you are sure that no sound support is currently loaded, run the `install` script as root:

```
$ su
Password: <root password>
# ./oss-install
```

You will see a screen that contains the license for the package. Use the Tab key to move to the Accept option, and press Enter; the release notes appear. Read through these to see whether you need to keep in mind any caveats, and then click the OK option at the bottom of the screen.

You will see a location to which to install OSS. The default (`/usr/lib/oss`) is fine; if it is highlighted, press Enter to select it. After you select the destination, the installation program verifies that the version of OSS/Linux matches the version of your Linux kernel. If it matches, the files are installed to the destination directory that you specified.

You are then asked whether you want to have OSS probe for the sound card. This is one of the main selling features of this software. Auto-probing for PnP cards does not work in the free version of OSS, but it works beautifully in the commercial version. In most cases, OSS/Linux can find your sound card and set it up for you automatically in a matter of seconds. It is highly recommended that you allow OSS to probe for your sound card.

When a card is found, you are shown the name of the card and prompted to save the configuration. Other options on the menu might be worth exploring, though, to verify that the card was indeed found and that the hardware settings were detected correctly. Verify the configuration first using the Verify configuration menu option; if everything looks okay, save your changes and exit. From there, the sound driver is configured and ready to go.

Before the sound driver can be used it needs to be loaded. A program called soundon that ships with OSS/Linux does this for you. Manually execute this command to see that it works; if everything goes well and you have sound support, add the `soundon` command to `/etc/rc.d/rc.local` (for distributions with this file), somewhere near the end of the file. That way it is started every time the computer starts.

Debian is a special case. The good news is that there is no catch-all `rc.local` file to get cluttered up with things people are too lazy to write scripts for. The bad news is that you must write scripts to do even these simple things. Listing 7.1 is an appropriate `/etc/init.d/oss` script for Debian.

LISTING 7.1   DEBIAN OSS CONTROL SCRIPT

```
#!/bin/sh
PATH=/usr/local/sbin:/usr/local/bin:/sbin:/bin:/usr/sbin:/usr/bin
SOUNDON=<path to your soundon>
SOUNDOFF=<path to your soundoff>
AUMIX=<path to your aumix> # remove if you don't use aumix
NAME=oss
DESC="OSS/Linux"

test -f $SOUNDON || exit 0
test -f $SOUNDOFF || exit 0

set -e

case "$1" in
  start)
        echo -n "Starting $DESC: "
   $SOUNDON
   $AUMIX  # remove if you don't use aumix
        echo "$NAME."
   ;;
   stop)
   echo -n "Stopping $DESC: "
   $SOUNDOFF
   echo "$NAME."
   ;;
   restart|force-reload)
   $0 stop
   $0 start
   ;;
   *)
   N=/etc/init.d/$NAME
   echo "Usage: $N {start|stop}"
   exit 1
   ;;
esac

exit 0
```

Save this script as /etc/init.d/oss, and then run the following as root:

```
# chmod +x /etc/init.d/oss
# update-rc.d oss defaults 99
```

Note that the lines including AUMIX assume that you are also using aumix, described later in this chapter. If you don't use aumix, remove them.

If you ever need to unload the driver while the system is running, a companion program to soundon called soundoff takes care of this. Note that this does not need to be run before you shut your system down.

CHANGING THE DEFAULT SOUND SETTINGS

One thing that is still bothersome about sound support on Linux is that it tends to default to rather loud settings. One method that people have employed to remedy this is to save settings in the aumix program and restore them when the sound driver is loaded. You must first establish that you have the aumix program installed, though. Running the following tells you whether you have it installed on RPM-based distributions:

```
$ rpm -q aumix
```

On Debian, use the following:

```
$ dpkg -s aumix
```

Check the status line for `installed` or `not-installed`. If it is not installed, install it.

After aumix is installed (and you are logged in as root), start it and set the controls as you want them to be every time you start your system. Then exit aumix and execute the following command:

```
aumix -S
```

This writes a file called `.aumixrc` in root's home directory (`/root`). Copy this file to `/etc/aumixrc`. There must not be a period at the beginning of this file when it is copied to `/etc`. Then, in `/etc/rc.d/rc.local` add the following command after `soundon`:

```
aumix -L
```

This loads the settings in `/etc/aumixrc` non-interactively, causing your sound system to initialize with settings that are much more reasonable than the defaults.

RealPlayer

When it comes to streaming audio and video over networks such as the Internet, one company—RealNetworks—seems to have established the standard to which all others are compared. This is especially true on the Linux platform, where RealNetworks is currently the main show in town. Everything you need for streaming networked audio and video clients, servers, and encoders is offered for Linux.

The main attraction from RealNetworks is the RealPlayer client software. Using this, anyone with a Linux system that is connected to a network such as the Internet can receive and play audio and video served from a RealNetworks server. News, entertainment, radio broadcasts, education, and many other services are available. Best of all, it is currently available free of charge from RealNetworks.

Note To get a feel for what this technology can offer, browse some of the audio/video Web sites listed on the RealNetworks home Web page (`http://www.real.com`), or check the Live Concerts Web site (`http://www.liveconcerts.com`). There is bound to be something at one of these sites that interests you.

Getting and Installing RealPlayer

You can get RealPlayer at the following location:

```
http://www.real.com
```

At the time of this writing, only the regular RealPlayer 7 Basic package is available for Linux. There is also currently no commercial (that is, one that costs money) version of RealPlayer for Linux.

It can be tricky to find the download page for RealPlayer 7 Basic. Most of the links will steer you toward their commercial product, RealPlayer 8 Plus. When you first arrive at the RealNetworks Web page, select the Download RealPlayer link at the top of the page, and then select RealPlayer 8 Basic near the bottom of the page. Finally, select Download RealPlayer for UNIX near the bottom of the screen. Fill out the presented form, selecting Linux 2.x (libc6 i386) RPM for RPM-based distributions, or Linux 2.x (libc6 i386) Self-Extracting for Debian. The Red Hat RPM will work fine for OpenLinux.

After downloading the RealPlayer package, install it with one of the following code snippets:

```
# rpm -i rp7_linux20_libc6_i386_cs1_rpmRealPlayer-8.0-1.i386.rpm

# chmod u+x rp7_linux20_libc6_i386_cs1.bin

# ./rp7_linux20_libc6_i386_cs1.bin
```

Finally, fill out the short configuration dialogs presented, and RealPlayer will start up (as well as Netscape, taking you to their home page). Note that prompting for user input and automatically starting the application are unusual (and, many would say, inappropriate) for RPM packages.

> **Note**
>
> The name of the file you download might be different from this. Just replace `linux20_libc6_i386_cs1_rpm` with the name of the file downloaded. Note also that instead of dots, these files have underscores in their names.
>
> It is possible that you will need to add the option `-nodeps` or `--force` to install this RPM. RealPlayer sometimes builds its RPMs based too strongly on Red Hat systems. It should still work fine on eDesktop or other RPM-based systems.

USING REALPLAYER

To launch RealPlayer, select RealPlayer 7 from the Application Launcher menu in KDE. If you are not using KDE, you can start RealPlayer by running /usr/X11R6/bin/realplay. The RealPlayer main screen is shown in Figure 7.1.

Figure 7.1
Main RealPlayer window—audio and video.

PART

II

CH

7

THE FILE MENU

The File menu in RealPlayer offers options that are similar to those on the file menus of Web browsers. Because most people start RealPlayer from a Web browser, this menu does not get very much traffic. But sometimes it is easier to open a RealPlayer URL manually than it is to browse to it. This is especially true when there is a RealPlayer audio/video file that you want to play sitting on your hard drive. For these situations, a File menu is available in the player software.

The following sections detail the options that are offered on this menu.

OPEN LOCATION   When you open an audio/video stream over a network, what is being opened is a location, not a file, even though the address to which you are pointing leads to a file on a remote site. You open an address that is similar to that of a Web page, and it is assumed that at the other end a RealPlayer stream is waiting to be transferred to your player. For this reason, remote audio streams must be opened with the Open Location option from the File menu.

If you choose this option, a window that is similar to Figure 7.2 appears.

Figure 7.2
The Open Location window.

Only RealPlayer URLs are to be entered in this page (these are typically preceded with `rtsp` instead of `http`). Web browsers are not required for opening RealPlayer URLs.

OPEN FILE   Contrary to what was described for the Open Location menu option, if you have a RealPlayer audio/video file that is actually sitting on your local machine and that you want to play, you open the file using the `Open File` option from the File menu. You do this because you are not accessing an audio/video stream residing on a remote site; the location is assumed to be your own personal machine, so only the filename needs to be specified, or you can use the directory browser.

PAST LOCATIONS   The Past Locations numbered list contains links to your last four locations or files. This is very useful for quickly returning to a recently visited stream.

EXIT   This option terminates the RealPlayer session and exits.

THE PLAY MENU

This menu manages the normal playback functions of RealPlayer. These functions are similar to what you would use on a CD player or VCR:

- **Play**—Starts playing the stream. Before the stream actually begins playing, though, a few seconds are read and buffered. This provides some protection from short-term network lags and is very similar to a CD player's anti-skip feature.

- **Stop**—Stops playing the stream and clears the buffer. If you start the stream again, it will resume from the beginning after refilling the buffer.

- **Mute**—This mutes the output, but the stream continues to play.

- **Playlist**—In a multiclip stream, this will display the current playlist, or table of contents. Selecting an entry here will skip to that clip if skipping is allowed. Because some streams include commercials, skipping is sometimes prevented to stop you from avoiding them.

- **Next Clip**—Fast forwards to the next clip if skipping is allowed.

- **Previous Clip**—Rewinds to the beginning of the previous clip if skipping is allowed.

- **Continuous Play**—Repeats the stream continuously whenever it is completed.

- **Shuffle**—Randomizes the order of clips in a multiclip stream. You can combine this feature with Continues Play.

THE VIEW MENU

The default window for viewing RealPlayer video streams is somewhat small. On a screen that is operating with a low resolution (for example, 640×480 or 800×600), the default window might be a manageable size. But today's monitors can handle much higher resolutions, and at these high resolutions the window can become almost too small to be useful. Changing the size of the view window is the primary function of RealPlayer's View menu.

The following sections describe the options that are offered on this menu.

NORMAL AND COMPACT

The first few options on this menu control the viewport size. RealPlayer starts with Normal by default (refer to Figure 7.1). If you select Compact from this menu, however, the video section and some of the controls are removed to reduce the size of the display. This is particularly useful for audio streams.

ZOOM

This menu contains two options, Original Size and Double Size. By selecting Double Size, you can increase the size of a video stream. Note, however, that this will quarter the resolution of the video stream and can make a very blocky picture.

PREFERENCES

In addition to viewport controls, the View menu contains the preference settings. If you select Preferences on this menu (you cannot be playing any audio or video streams when you do this), the window that is shown in Figure 7.3 appears.

The tabs at the top of the screen—General, Performance, Transport, Proxy, Connection, and Support—take you to different areas of the configuration. On the General screen you see that there is only one option: Recent Clips. This determines how many recent clips are stored in the File menu. The next tab takes you to the Performance screen (see Figure 7.4).

PART

II

CH

7

Figure 7.3
The main Preferences
window.

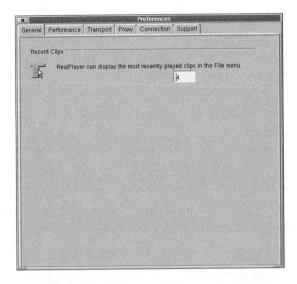

Figure 7.4
Performance
preferences.

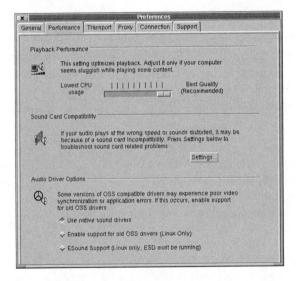

This screen contains several options. Playback Performance lets you determine how much CPU time you are willing to give to RealPlayer. Unless you find streaming media to significantly impact your machine's performance, you probably want to leave this at Best Quality.

If you are having difficulty with your sound card, you may want to experiment with the options under Sound Card. For most sound cards you shouldn't need to change these defaults. Similarly, if you have an unusual sound driver, you might need to modify the Audio Driver Options.

The Transport tab offers configuration options that control how the routing and protocols that are involved with the network connection are to be handled (see Figure 7.5).

Figure 7.5
Transport preferences.

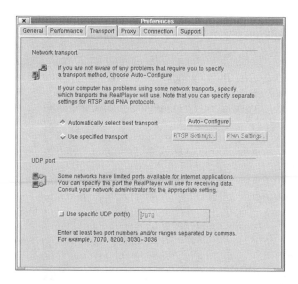

Most people are fine with the default setting, which automatically selects the most efficient transport for you. If the system administrator on your network has configured the Internet gateway system with a specific UDP port for RealPlayer usage, the UDP port can be specified at the bottom of the window.

Some proxy servers (such as Squid) allow RealPlayer streams through, but only if they use HTTP as the transport. If you are using a system that sits behind one of these proxy servers and you are having problems receiving audio/video streams, this is probably the cause. The Use Specified Transports buttons (RTSP Settings and PNA Settings) in the middle of this window take you to additional windows that allow more specific transport configuration (see Figure 7.6).

Figure 7.6
Specific transport
preferences.

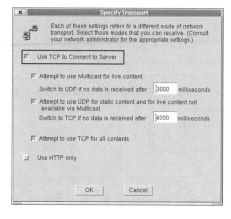

The Use HTTP Only option at the bottom of each of these windows needs to be checked if that is the only transport that is allowed through your proxy server. If this is not required, the defaults for the rest of the settings are fine.

Speaking of proxy servers, the Proxy window is where they are configured (see Figure 7.7).

Figure 7.7
Proxy server
preferences.

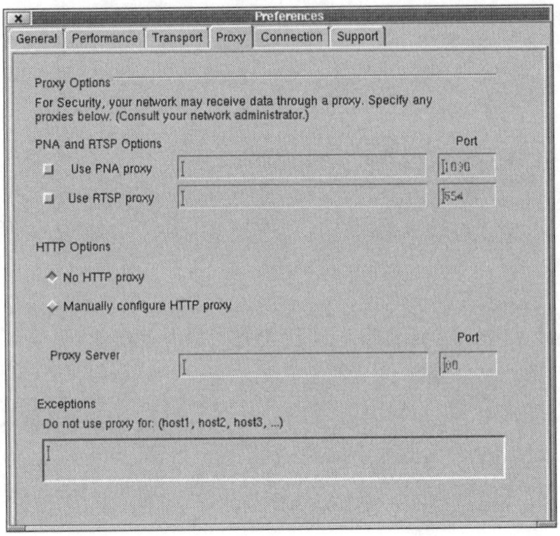

Select the Use PNA Proxy and the Use RTSP Proxy check boxes, and then enter the configuration information to point to your proxy server(s). The information that needs to be entered is fairly clear; if not, get the proxy server address and port number from the system administrator.

Next is the Connection tab (see Figure 7.8). Three sections are offered: Bandwidth, Buffered Play, and Network Time-Out.

For Bandwidth, make your Normal and Maximum selections based on your connection type. If your connection type is not listed, choose the closest bandwidth available. Generally your Normal and Maximum selections will be the same, but if you use a laptop, you can normally connect at dial-up speeds but sometimes connect at higher LAN speeds. In this case, setting your Maximum to the higher connection speed will allow RealPlayer to "up shift" to higher speeds if the connection seems faster than usual.

The Buffered Play options determine how much of the stream should be buffered before play begins. By buffering the stream, you will be less impacted by variances in network throughput. The default selection, Buffer Entire Clip Up To Available Memory, is fine in many cases, but can make RealPlayer a memory hog. If RealPlayer is using too much memory, limit its use by selecting Buffer At Least X Seconds Before Playing.

The last item, Network Time-Out, merely gives a timeout, in seconds, to wait for a server to accept a connection from your client.

Figure 7.8
Connection
preferences.

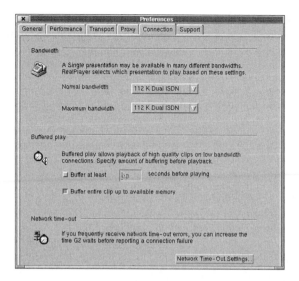

The last of the Preference tabs takes you to the Support window (see Figure 7.9).

Figure 7.9
Support preferences.

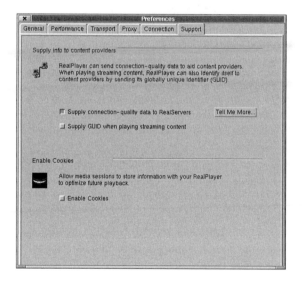

The Supply Connection-Quality Data To RealServers check box tells your RealPlayer client to send statistical information back to the person who maintains the audio/video servers to which your client connects. Server maintainers can use this information to monitor the quality of their transmissions and make improvements if required. Some people might not like the idea that information about their system is being sent to remote sites, so this box can be checked to disable this feature.

PART
II

CH

7

The Supply GUID When Playing Steaming Content check box tells your RealPlayer client to send your *GUID* to servers that provide you content. Your GUID is a unique key that identifies your instance of RealPlayer. For privacy reasons, this option is turned off by default. Some providers, generally for pay-per-view or other fee-based streams, require that you provide a GUID to receive their content. If your content provider requires this, you will need to turn on this option. Unfortunately, no way to set this on a per-site basis is available.

Finally, sites can store information about your connection in your Web browser using cookies. This is helpful, because it will tend to improve your next session because the server will already know everything it learned this time about your connection. Unfortunately, some sites use cookies to track visitors more than many users would prefer. To avoid the tracking (at the possible expense of losing some quality at the beginning of your connections), you can unselect the Enable Cookies option. RealNetworks has disabled this option by default, which is a nice move, from a privacy point of view.

STATISTICS   Another item on the View menu is a Statistics window. This gives you a method of monitoring your connection to remote sites. The most interesting tab is Bandwidth (see Figure 7.10). This window shows you how much bandwidth your stream is actually getting. This is your best indication of whether there are problems with your connection or the server.

Figure 7.10
The Bandwidth window.

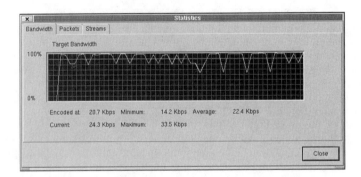

The next tab, Packets, provides statistical information about your playback. If any errors occur or network latencies prevent 100% of what is sent to be displayed or played, the problems will definitely show in this window. Unless you like to watch numbers tick by, this is not a very interesting screen to look at.

The final tab, Streams, gives you detailed information about the stream you are playing. Except for curiosity's sake, there is little that you need from this tab.

THE CONTENT MENU

The Content menu offers some of the more common RealPlayer-capable audio/video Web sites. The items on this menu are not editable in the free version of RealPlayer. Most of these options will open a Web browser.

THE HELP MENU

The Help menu offers the typical array of help items, all of which are displayed through an already-running copy of a Netscape browser.

One extra feature is Mime Type/Plugin Install. This option will automatically set up Netscape and other applications that use MIME (a standard for determining what kind of information is in a file). Select this option and then select /usr/X11R6/bin for the Helper Plugin Soft Link Directory. Click Finished, and Netscape will automatically load RealPlayer when you select streaming audio or video.

ADOBE ACROBAT READER

The Adobe Acrobat Reader is a navigator for platform-independent Portable Document Format (PDF) files. PDF files are PostScript files that are compiled in such a way that they are navigable almost like Web pages. Audio and video can be embedded within PDF files, making them multimedia as well. Numerous programs can output PDF files from their documents (programs from Adobe in particular, such as FrameMaker and PageMaker), but the main source of these multimedia documents is Adobe Acrobat itself.

The main Adobe Acrobat software is not free, nor is it currently available for Linux. The reader software, however, is available for Linux free of charge from Adobe's Web site:

```
http://www.adobe.com/prodindex/acrobat/readstep.html
```

This page allows you to select the type of reader you want to download (select the free one). You can then specify the client you want to download (operating system, type of Acrobat Reader—the Linux version does not offer search capabilities—and language).

When you have downloaded the archive, extract the contents using tar (version 4.05 is used for this example):

```
tar zxvf linux-ar-405.tar.gz
```

All the contents are extracted into an ILINXR.install directory. Table 7.2 lists the contents of that directory.

TABLE 7.2   FILES CONTAINED WITHIN THE ACROBAT READER ARCHIVE

File	Description
ILINXR.TAR	The main installation archive (binaries, libraries) for Acrobat Reader for Linux
INSTALL	Installation script
INSTGUID.TXT	Installation instructions
LICREAD.TXT	License for Acrobat Reader
READ.TAR	Fonts and documentation for Acrobat Reader
ReadMe	Release notes

PART

II

CH

7

Change to that directory, log in as root, and run the installation script:

```
cd ILINXR.install
./INSTALL
```

A license agreement is presented, which you must read and agree to (by responding Accept when you are asked) before installation can begin.

The default location for the installation is /usr/local/Acrobat4. This will be fine unless you want to install it elsewhere. After the installation directory is specified—and, if necessary, created—the software is installed.

To install Acrobat Reader as a Netscape plug-in, a few simple steps need to be taken:

1. Link /usr/local/Acrobat4/Browsers/intellinux/nppdf.so to your Netscape plug-ins directory (/usr/lib/netscape/plugins in this example). You can also do this on a per-user basis by linking to ${HOME}/.netscape/plugins:

   ```
   # ln -s /usr/local/Acrobat4/Browsers/intellinux/nppdf.so /usr/lib/netscape/plugins
   ```

2. Add /usr/local/Acrobat4/bin to your PATH with the following line:

   ```
   PATH=${PATH}:/usr/local/Acrobat4/bin
   ```

   There are several places you can add this line:

   - Add it to your per-user PATH in ${HOME}/.bash_profile (or ${HOME}/.profile).
   - Add it to your system PATH in /etc/profile.
   - On systems with an /etc/profile.d, add a new file with this line called acrobat.sh. Be sure to make it executable by running the following:

     ```
     # chmod +x /etc/profile.d/acrobat.sh
     ```

Simply adding the path to the executable files in an environment variable is not enough; the variable must be loaded before the path is recognized, and the best way to ensure that this has happened is to completely exit your login session and log back in.

USING ACROBAT READER

With the path set correctly and the plug-in in its proper place, Netscape is ready to use the Acrobat Reader plug-in. Pulling up a PDF file from a remote site looks similar to Figure 7.11.

Netscape completely swallows the plug-in, running Acrobat within itself. All the controls that are available within the regular standalone application minus the drop-down menus are available within the Netscape plug-in. The plug-in version is most commonly used when viewing PDF files. Don't worry that you can't read the text in Figure 7.11. That's just because the document is zoomed too far out.

The file /usr/local/Acrobat4/Reader/help/reader.pdf contains the online documentation. This file can be accessed from the Help menu on the standalone version of Acrobat Reader, or it can be opened as a file in Netscape.

Figure 7.11
Acrobat running as a
Netscape plug-in.

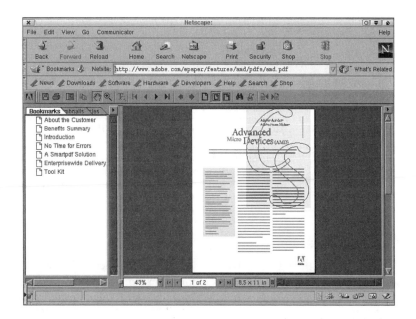

The documentation for Acrobat Reader is a bit much to read just to get hints on the functions of the toolbar buttons, so Table 7.3 gives a brief overview of them. Note that some of these buttons only exist in the plug-in version of Acrobat Reader on the Linux platform.

TABLE 7.3   BUTTONS AVAILABLE IN THE ACROBAT READER PLUG-IN FOR NETSCAPE

Buttons	Descriptions
	Takes you to Adobe's Web site. When you use this button for the first time, you will be prompted to set up your Weblink preferences. The most important of these preferences is your Web Browser Application. Set this to `/usr/bin/netscape`.
	Saves the current document.
	Prints the current document.
	Toggles display of the *palettes*. Palettes are the tabs to the left of the displayed document that show your bookmarks, thumbnails, and articles. In general, all you will need is the bookmark list to quickly get to important places in the document.
	Copies a selection from the document into the temporary clipboard for pasting into other applications.
	Controls for movement, zoom, and text selection. The first button selects the hand tool (used to drag the document around the viewport); the next selects the zoom tool (click to zoom in, Ctrl+click to zoom out); and the third allows text selection for use with the Copy button.

PART

II

CH

7

TABLE 7.3	CONTINUED
Buttons	**Descriptions**
	Page navigation. The first button jumps to page one, the second and third move forward and backward by individual pages, and the last button jumps to the last page.
	Moves to the previous view or goes to the next view, respectively.
	Controls how the page is fit into the window. The first button fits the image, including space around the image, into the viewport; the second fits the page to the upper and lower edges of the viewport; and the third expands the page to 100% of the width of the viewport.

CREATING PDF FILES

The ghostscript program that comes with eDesktop can create PDF files from any Postscript output. Because this is the normal way for Linux print drivers to work, many programs generate Postscript. For example, to turn a text file into a Postscript file, simply use `enscript`:

```
enscript -o MyFile.ps Myfile.txt
```

In this case, `Myfile.txt` is the text file you want to convert, and `Myfile.ps` is the output Postscript file. `enscript` has many options, all available on its man page.

After you have a Postscript file, creating a PDF file is easy:

```
ps2pdf Myfile.ps
```

As before, `Myfile.ps` is the Postscript file that you created. The output file will be called `Myfile.pdf`. For more information on ps2pdf and ghostscript, see each of their man pages.

TROUBLESHOOTING

RealPlayer complains that someone else is using the sound device when running under KDE.

KDE uses a sound engine called aRts (Analog Realtime Synthesizer), which takes control of all the sound devices and acts as a traffic cop to allow various applications to access them. Unfortunately, this blocks out applications that don't know how to work with aRts. Because RealPlayer does not have aRts support, you generally won't be able to run it at the same time as the aRts server. To shut down the aRts server, enter the following:

```
$ su
Password: <root password>
# kill `pidof artsd`
```

When you want to start aRts back up, enter the following:

```
# artsd -F 7 -S 1024
```

RealPlayer starts, but no sounds play.

A number of factors can cause sounds not to play. First, verify that sound works outside of RealPlayer:

```
$ play /opt/kde/share/sounds/startup.wav
```

If no sounds play, first wait one minute without playing any sounds. This will allow the `artsd` sound daemon to unload. Then try again. If it still doesn't work, check the hardware volume control and then the software volume control using `kmix`. If `kmix` complains about permissions, make sure the sound devices are world writable:

```
$ su
Password: <root password>
# chmod 666 /dev/audio* /dev/dsp* /dev/mixer*
```

Finally, make sure that you have sound support compiled into the kernel (and sound modules compile and installed), and check `/var/log/messages` to see whether you're having any driver-related problems.

I'm trying to run RealPlayer through a firewall, but I'm having trouble.

If you are behind a firewall, RealPlayer might not work unless reconfigured. Your firewall might not be configured to allow through the ports RealPlayer requires. Luckily, RealPlayer can generally work around these issues if your administrators are not specifically trying to block media streams.

To have RealPlayer determine how to best cope with the firewall, select View, Preferences, Transport, Automatically select best transport. Then click the Auto-Configure button. If this does not resolve the problem, consult `http://service.real.com/firewall/configRP7.html` for more information.

PART III

LINUX SYSTEM ADMINISTRATION

CHAPTER **8**

SYSTEM ADMINISTRATION TOOLS

In this chapter

DIFFERENCES IN LINUX DISTRIBUTIONS

Some of you are likely puzzled by the various flavors of Linux distributions. If you've been on a Linux mailing list, you know that the choice of distribution can cause as big or bigger a flame war as can the vi versus emacs debate, and so on. The flames take on a religious tone. And that's exactly what happens, because Linux is Linux. Anything else is just a religious debate and should be avoided.

Three major differences (and one minor difference) exist among the numerous flavors of Linux (if you don't count Slackware's use of BSD versus System V initialization). This book discusses three of those flavors. But at the heart is the same kernel.

The first difference that you will see almost as soon as you boot up the install disk or CD is the installation tool. No matter what this tool is called, it performs essentially the same thing: It installs the distribution and an assortment of programs on your system and sets up and configures the basic system. Every single distribution has its own installation tools and methods.

The second difference you will learn about here is in system administration. To make Linux easier to administer, most distributions have written some kind of centralized system administration tool, or included a generic administration tool much as the various UNIX flavors have centralized administration tools. This chapter will discuss some of the system administration tools you'll see on Caldera, Debian, and Red Hat. Most of the rest of the book will be devoted to providing a basic understanding of the different tools available with nearly every Linux distribution, how they work, and how to manage them. Some of what you will learn in the book can be done with the distribution-included system administration tools. But like everything else that's made easy, some of the power and flexibility inevitably suffers. If you have advanced needs, you won't want to use these generic tools, or you won't be able to use them to accomplish your objective. You'll need to learn how each distribution you want to use is set up and work within that framework (or change it to your liking).

The third difference is in the number and type of software packages available, including commercial software in some cases. Some distributions believe in providing everything including the kitchen sink. Although this is rarely necessary or even desirable (it would take weeks just to go through and see what all the packages are), it gives those who know exactly what they want a better chance of having that particular package.

One similarity is in system initialization. Currently all distributions except Slackware use System V initialization. Slackware prefers to use the BSD-style initialization. I say this is a similarity because it uses exactly the same init binary, just a modified inittab (but each distribution modifies, if only slightly, the inittab, the initialization scripts, and the location and name of initialization configuration files). If this discussion makes no sense to you, return to it after having read this book and loaded and tried each of the distributions provided.

The minor difference among the distributions is their philosophy. Both Caldera and Red Hat target the commercial market and have different products to entice certain business sectors.

Red Hat appears targeted at Enterprise servers, whereas Caldera is targeted at the Enterprise Desktop and e-Commerce. They both also have a low-end product line for home users. Debian, on the other hand, subscribes to the GNU philosophy. They go to the fanatical extreme of mislabeling it GNU/Linux as if GNU owned Linux, even discarding Linux Torvalds' response—that it is definitely not GNU/Linux—as irrelevant or incorrect. Debian has the kitchen sink (but only the GPL'd model). It is an outstanding distribution from a system administrator's standpoint for its sheer ease of upgrade/maintenance and number/type of tools, particularly networking tools that are available, but the initial install is the most difficult of all distributions.

CALDERA OPENLINUX/COAS

Caldera's centralized system administration tool is called COAS (Caldera Open Administration System). COAS is composed of various modules and includes a generalized wrapper that can be used to call the various modules.

You can invoke COAS from within KDE where it will appear as a menu selection, or type coastool from a terminal window. If invoked in an environment where the DISPLAY environment variable is set, COAS will attempt to run in graphical mode. If the DISPLAY environment variable is not set, either because it was unset or because you invoked coastool from a TTY, it will appear in a curses format, so you can even invoke COAS remotely.

The first window allows you to choose from a grouping of COAS modules. The main window selection includes the following:

- Kernel Modules
- Peripherals Administration
- Network Administration
- System Administration
- Install/Remove software packages

Each main selection is discussed in the following sections.

KERNEL MODULES

Selecting Kernel Modules results in COAS probing the system for new hardware. If new hardware is found, it will be listed with a check box. If you don't want to load the module immediately, uncheck the box. Selecting OK takes you to the next screen.

If you have no new hardware, you'll come directly to this second screen. On the left is the list of all available modules, over 400 of them. On the right is the list of those that are loaded. You can select a module and use the appropriate button to load, unload, or view information about the module. Selecting OK will take you back to the main screen.

PERIPHERALS ADMINISTRATION

The peripherals administration menu allows you to select from three sub-areas:

- **Keyboard Layout**—Allows you to change the keyboard map, key repeat rate, and key repeat delay.

- **Text Mode Mouse Configuration**—Allows you to change the GPM mouse model, driver, protocol, device file, emulation, and boot-time activation (yes or no). Unless you work on a VT (VC) a lot, you probably won't be interested in this too much. The mouse under X is changed with a different tool you'll learn about in a following section.

- **Printer Configuration**—Allows you to see what printer is configured on your system. This module lacks some functionality, though that is expected to change.

NETWORK ADMINISTRATION

The Network Administration subsystem is composed of five individual components:

- Common Network Functions
- Network Information Service
- TCP/IP Network Options
- Hostname Resolution
- Mail Transport Configuration

COMMON NETWORK FUNCTIONS

The common network functions selection allows you to configure any known interface on your system. If you have a module loaded for it, you can configure it. You can also configure an alias here.

Any changes made to this particular interface will be made as soon as OK is selected.

NETWORK INFORMATION SERVICE

This text does not delve into NIS. This text selection box would make it seem easy to set up NIS just by choosing a Domain Name (a NIS Domain Name, not your Internet Domain Name, although that could be used), the NIS Servers, and whether or not to start NIS at boot time.

Setting up a NIS server is just a little more complex than this simple Client Setup box would have you believe, and no server setup exists at the moment. If you feel you have a need to run a NIS server because your network is large and administration would be easier, read `/usr/doc/nis-server-2.0/README.server`. Then go to `/etc/nis/` and follow the six-step instructions carefully.

TCP/IP NETWORK OPTIONS

Under this particular selection only two options exist:

- **Networking**—Enabled or disabled. If networking is disabled, the network script and all scripts dependent on it will not run. This is probably not desirable because some processes use the localhost (a local network).

- **IP Forwarding**—Enabled or disabled. This option turns on the ability to pass traffic between two different interfaces. If you want traffic to pass from one interface on your system, through your system and out the other interface, you'll need to turn on this feature.

HOSTNAME RESOLUTION

When selected, the Hostname Resolution selection brings you to the Name Resolver Setup. The first line, Information Source, allows you to change the order of the listed values, host, nis, and dns. Your resolver library can't and won't take care of starting or configuring these services; this is merely the order in which they will be checked. More advanced configuration of the /etc/nsswitch file (which this selection affects) must be performed by hand.

The Try to Prevent Spoofing check box will enable or disable entries that turn on or off the kernel's spoofing code. Specifically, this puts a zero (off) or one (on) in the various /proc/sys/net/ipv4/conf//rp filter files. When turned on, the kernel rejects packets that have come in on an impossible interface, such as traffic claiming to be from localhost (127.x.x.x) coming in on eth0 or ppp0. Normally you'll want this on, but some software, like the FreeS/WAN software, will not function with this feature enabled.

The Report Spoof Attempts just logs dropped packets from spoofing.

The DNS servers allow you to enter up to three IP addresses of DNS servers for Domain Name lookups. If your local system is a DNS server, the entry 127.0.0.1 must be the first one.

MAIL TRANSPORT CONFIGURATION

Selecting the MTA configuration will allow you to make some small but significant changes to your sendmail configuration. The first option you can change is the Visible Domain. This is what will be seen after the @ in your email address. Suppose your hostname is volcan.pananix.com, but you want your email to come from you@pananix.com. Change the visible domain to just pananix.com. That way, when someone responds to your message, they'll respond to your domain's mail exchanger rather than your specific system (whose mail you might only rarely check).

If you use a particular host that is your mail relay, this host should be listed as the Mail Relay Host. This host is the one you pick up all messages from, so you want all messages to you to go to this mail server. It should have a DNS MX address.

Choose your transport method from one of SMTP (Simple Mail Transfer Protocol) or UUCP (UNIX-to-UNIX Copy Protocol). Normally, this will be SMTP. If your relay hub is on the Internet, check the next box. If your relay hub is the machine you're working from, check the last box. Both boxes can be checked at the same time if both are true.

SYSTEM ADMINISTRATION

The System Administration submenu contains seven entries:

- Account Administration
- Enable/Disable System Services
- Filesystem Administration
- System Hostname
- Bootloader Setup
- System Resource Information
- System Clock

ACCOUNT ADMINISTRATION

The account administration interface is a User Account administrator. Unfortunately, the interface is not as intuitive as others such as the Webmin user account interface. To work on an existing account, highlight that account. In the curses screen you can use the F10 key to move to the menu bar. Use the arrow keys to select the menu choice you want and the Enter key to open the selection. To move the focus to another menu item, press the Esc key. This will put you back down in the user list where you can use F10 again. Using this particular menu is much easier in an X environment.

ENABLE/DISABLE SYSTEM SERVICES

Selecting this option will provide a list of all installed services that can be run at bootup. If a service isn't listed, it either hasn't been installed or was installed from a non-Caldera RPM. Select the services you want. The ones with an X (or in the case of an X screen, a check mark) will start at bootup.

FILESYSTEM ADMINISTRATION

This selection permits you to see and mount or unmount filesystems. Selecting F10 highlights the Action menu where you can choose to mount NFS filesystems.

SYSTEM HOSTNAME

This selection permits you to change the hostname of your system. It updates all appropriate files for subsequent bootups as well as making the change immediately.

BOOTLOADER SETUP

This option allows you to modify the GRUB bootloader setup. If you decide to use LILO, you won't be able to use this particular utility. As with other menus, choosing F10 allows you to enter the menus at the top to modify (add and delete) or make system or global changes.

SYSTEM RESOURCE INFORMATION

This selection provides exactly what it says, information about the system. Selecting F10 to highlight Info in the menu bar allows you to choose among other resources to view. Note that the resources shown are those that are used. You can have a card that is not active because its module is not loaded, so will not show up.

SYSTEM CLOCK

This allows you to change your time zone and the system time. It does not have an option to allow you to change from system clock on local time to system clock on UTC. For that, you'll need to use the LIZARD timezone utility discussed later in this chapter.

INSTALL/REMOVE SOFTWARE PACKAGES

This selection allows you to install and uninstall software from your system. The main menu is a hierarchical listing of packages starting from the left and moving to the right from overall to software major groups, then software minor groups, and finally specific packages.

Selecting F10, activating the Installation drop-down list, and then selecting Source will allow you to change the directory location of RPM archives.

AUTONOMOUS LIZARD MODULES

A better alternative to COAS can be found on your system as the same modules you might or might not have seen during the Installation. To use these modules, you'll need to be root and use an X interface.

Each of the following commands will open certain configuration screens. The first of these is the modem setup screen:

```
lizard_modem
```

From this screen you can select from any of over 65 modems, specify the device it uses, select the connection speed, flow control, and enter any required commands and initialization strings.

After you have this set up, you might want to run the ISP setup:

```
lizard_isp
```

If you want to use dial-up networking as your primary means of connecting to the Internet, you can do so here. Some Internet providers have been configured for you for those countries (and states) listed. The list of providers is not an all-inclusive list, and if you choose to use another, select the User-Defined option and enter the details. If you save the authentication information (Login and Password), anyone using the system will be able to connect to the Internet.

Note

As of this writing, Caldera was considering dropping the LIZARD ISP module in lieu of a KDE Control Panel module, so you might not find this in future editions of OpenLinux.

Perhaps the simplest way to manage your Ethernet interface, albeit only the first one, is with the LIZARD network setup interface:

```
lizard_network
```

At this stage of the installation, a screen that offers the following three networking options is displayed:

- No Ethernet
- Ethernet Configured Using DHCP
- Ethernet Configured Statically

Select the No Ethernet option if you do not plan to connect this machine to a network using a Network Interface Card (NIC), usually Ethernet, or if you don't happen to have the network information that is required to complete the network setup. You can configure an Ethernet or other NIC later if desired.

Select the Ethernet Configured Using DHCP option if you want this machine to automatically configure networking at bootup by acquiring an IP address from a DHCP server.

Select the Ethernet Configured Statically option if your system is to be assigned its own static IP address, and if it will be part of a local area network. This option requires several pieces of information, including IP addresses for the following items:

- Netmask
- Gateway
- Name Server

If the system is connected to a network when this option is selected, network information is automatically determined by the contents of network traffic packets. If network traffic is not present, you might need to enter this information.

Regardless of what setup option you choose, you'll want your host to have a hostname. Most network administrators choose a theme and use names from that theme, although using movie characters as a theme and giving your hosts names such as Bob, Carol, Ted, and Alice might be frowned upon in some circles.

If you need to change your time zone or hardware clock reference (local time versus GMT), you'll find this the easiest way—the way you did during installation:

```
lizard_timezone
```

Unfortunately, you can't change the time from here; you'll either need to do it from a command line or from COAS. Assuming you have a connection to the Internet, the next two commands will set your system clock, and then reset your hardware clock to the system clock (this assumes your hardware clock is set to GMT):

```
ntpdate <ntpserver>
hwclock -u --systohc
```

Substitute the name of an NTP server on the Internet. A list is in the NTP documentation in /usr/doc.

Finally, if you want to change any of your X server settings, mouse, keyboard, X server, or video mode, you can do this with the following:

```
lizardx
```

DEBIAN SYSTEM ADMINISTRATION TOOLS

Having looked at the Caldera system administration tools and perhaps the tools available for Red Hat or even other systems, you're probably expecting something similar for Debian. If you are, I'm afraid this particular section will be a disappointment to you.

The Debian system has only one official tool for administering the distribution in the form of dpkg. This tool is principally a package manager. But dpkg, although powerful, is incredibly difficult for neophytes to the system. So Debian has a couple of front ends available to help out in the form of dselect and apt. You can do nearly everything you need using one of these two tools.

If you still want a centralized system administration tool, use apt to install the Linuxconf package and then read about Linuxconf in a section later in this chapter.

Debian decided early on that the best and easiest way to administer a system was to have configuration scripts that run when a package that requires configuration is installed. These configuration scripts are also installed on the system so that you can run them later. They're not pretty and they use a basic command-line interface, but they are functional. A partial list includes the following:

```
apt-config
esd-config
dpkg-preconfigure
dpkg-reconfigure
fdutilsconfig
ispellconfig
kdbconfig
liloconfig
paperconfig
pppconfig
sendmailconfig
shadowconfig
tzconfig
```

These configuration files are all shell scripts and can be run at any time, but these scripts are the same scripts that ran during package installation asking you questions about a particular package. Other packages might not include configuration scripts depending on whether the author decided they were needed.

The dpkg utility itself is best accessed through apt or dselect. For those who want or need the power of direct access, dpkg can be run from a command line. If you want to see all that can be accomplished with dpkg, use the dpkg --help command. The dpkg utility itself is a topic for an installation chapter, so will not be detailed here.

RED HAT SYSTEM ADMINISTRATION TOOLS

System administration in Red Hat is generally centered around Linuxconf. Linuxconf, shown in Figure 8.1, has come a long way in recent years, and now is a good competitor for other products, such as Caldera's COAS and Webmin.

Note

This section discusses version 1.21r7, which is more up-to-date than the version shipped with Red Hat 7.0, but will likely be part of future versions of Red Hat (because it includes some very nice features such as cluster management). If you want a more up-to-date version of Linuxconf, check Red Hat's Web site, or the Linuxconf homepage at http:// www.solucorp.qc.ca/linuxconf.

Figure 8.1
Linuxconf provides access to your most common configuration needs.

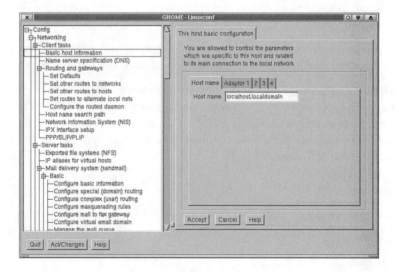

The left panel is a tree of configuration sections. As you select items from the tree, configuration dialogs appear on the right. Figure 8.1 displays the Basic Host Information dialog.

Linuxconf allows you to open multiple dialogs at a time. In Figure 8.2, two more dialogs have been selected: Name Server Specification (DNS) and Set Defaults (which is under

Routing and Gateways). Notice the tabs at the top of the right panel that read Resolver Configuration and Defaults. These correspond to the tree items you selected. Unfortunately, the name of a dialog in the tree and the name in the tab list generally do not match. This can make it very easy to lose track of where you are. Furthermore, Linuxconf creates these tabs whenever you click another item in the tree. The way to close them is to click the Accept or Cancel (sometimes labeled Quit) buttons in the dialog. I recommend that you do this before moving between dialogs, because the tab scheme can become very confusing. Despite this, Linuxconf can be a very helpful tool.

PART

III

CH

8

Figure 8.2
Linuxconf provides a very consistent interface, but it's easy to get lost.

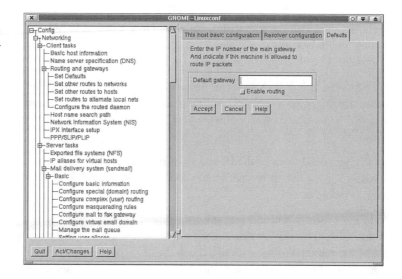

Linuxconf's main tree is broken into two main sections: Config and Control. The Config section handles the actual configuration of your system. The Control section manages Linuxconf itself.

CONFIG

The Config menu manages all the various parts of your Linux system that are configurable by Linuxconf. Changes made here won't impact your system until you quit Linuxconf and apply the changes, and you will have the opportunity at that time to discard your changes. See "Quitting and Applying Your Changes" later in the chapter for more information.

Configuration is separated into six categories:

- Networking
- User Accounts
- Filesystems
- Miscellaneous Services
- Boot Mode
- Cluster Administration

NETWORKING

Most Linux machines are connected to a network, so most users will need to configure their network connection. This is handled through the Config, Networking menus. Two basic kinds of machines are on the network, clients and servers. The Networking section is separated into tasks for each (though servers will also need to fill in the client configuration sections), as well as boot services, firewall configuration, and a miscellaneous section.

CLIENT TASKS   These tasks enable you to configure how your machine connects to the network and with which servers and gateways it communicates for basic information.

You should start with Basic Host Information. Here, enter your hostname (including your domain), and then select the Adaptor 1 tab. Linuxconf can configure up to four network adaptors for TCP/IP, which should be enough for most users.

Most networks include a DNS server for *name resolution*. Name resolution changes www.yahoo. com into 216.32.74.53 so routers can find it. In Name server specification (DNS), you can tell Linux which machine should do this for you. This is not how to make your machine into a DNS server.

Basically, you need to enter the IP addresses of the local DNS servers for your network. Obviously you cannot enter their names, because you need a DNS server to turn a name into an IP address.

Finally, most users will need to set at least a default gateway on the Routing and Gateways, Set defaults dialog. This is where packets should be sent when no other routing is available (the route of last resort). For most clients, this is the only routing they need. For servers, however, you might need to configure your routing tables in the Routing and gateways section.

For dial-up users, you should configure your dial-up connection through the PPP/SLIP/ PLIP dialog. In most cases you can simply add a new connection, select its type, and enter the phone number, your username, and password.

The Hostname search path dialog allows you to determine which name resolution sources are used, and in what order. Name resolution sources include your /etc/hosts file, NIS and DNS.

For users with NIS, you can configure this under Network Information System (NIS). NIS is a system similar to DNS, except that it manages not just hostnames, but also user ID, groups, and other information.

If you are on an IPX network (instead of IP), you can configure this in the IPX interface setup dialog. This is fairly rare, and usually applies to NetWare users.

Finally, you can configure fetchmail, which allows you to easily download your mail from remote servers for local reading.

SERVER TASKS   Linux machines are commonly used as servers, and even desktop machines can act as servers in some ways. For instance, you might share filesystems with other users through NFS, or run a local Web server. The Server tasks menus manage these various services.

Explanation of the various configuration options is given in other sections of this book, but the primary areas that can be configured here are NFS, IP aliasing, mail delivery (sendmail), Samba (Windows NT file sharing), Apache (Web server), DNS server, Squid (Web proxy and caching), and FTP server (wu-ftpd).

Note   In case you're wondering, Squid (www.squid-cache.org) got its name because, as Harris' lament points out, "All the good ones are taken."

BOOT SERVICES   Boot services have nothing to do with your machine booting. Instead, boot services provide assistance in other machines booting by configuring DHCP, BOOTP, and RARP services. Clients use these services to determine their IP address at boot time.

FIREWALLING   Linux makes a reasonably full-featured, low-cost firewall solution. Although generally not in the same league as dedicated firewall hardware, you can use Linux to build a firewall for a small company or your home network. This section enables you to configure the various firewall components.

MISC   Every category needs a "catch-all" group. The Misc menus manage /etc/hosts, /etc/networks, and Linuxconf's network access. See "Accessing Linuxconf Remotely" for more information on network access.

USER ACCOUNTS

Linuxconf is very handy for maintaining user accounts. This is probably one of the things Linuxconf handles best. Click Add and enter the information for the new user and then click Accept. The nice thing about this dialog is that you can set up various policies, like account expiration, password aging, or special permissions (like Apache administration), all without having to dive into the underlying configuration files. For full information on user accounts, see Chapter 11, "Users, Groups, and Permissions."

GROUP DEFINITIONS   The Group definitions dialog allows you to create and manage user groups. See Chapter 11 for more information.

CHANGE ROOT PASSWORD   This option is self-evident. As always, be careful with how you set your password. In particular, if you are connecting to Linuxconf remotely, note that your password can be going across the network unencrypted.

SPECIAL ACCOUNTS   Linuxconf can easily handle various kinds of special accounts. The following special types of accounts are supported automatically:

- **PPP/SLIP/UUCP**—These are users who can dial in to your system. This assumes, of course, that your system has a modem. PPP is much more common today than SLIP.

UUCP is actually a protocol for copying files across modems rather than actually getting a prompt. It is very uncommon today.

- **POP**—You can set up POP-only users who cannot log in to your machine, but can receive and download mail.

EMAIL ALIASES   Email aliases are "fake" users who can receive mail, but only forward it on to other users or programs. Email aliases are a good way to set up very simple mailing lists if you don't want to use a full package like majordomo or listproc.

POLICIES   If you are running a multiuser server, you will probably want some password and account policies. These include rules for password creation and aging, available shells, and the message of the day (a message that is shown to users when they log in).

MISCELLANEOUS SERVICES

Miscellaneous services covers only a few topics. First, you can set the default *run level*. Your default run level determines what services are started at boot time. Generally this is either 3, which is normal multiuser without X, or 5, which is multiuser with X.

Miscellaneous services also includes defining your modem connection. On Intel-based machines, you can select from one of four COM ports (or /dev/ttyS0 through /dev/ttyS3).

BOOT MODE

Linuxconf allows you to configure LILO, which is the most common Linux boot loader. GRUB is rapidly overtaking the venerable LILO, but Linuxconf does not yet support GRUB.

The Boot mode section allows you to configure the available kernels to boot with, and other basic LILO configuration. For more information on LILO, see Chapter 18, "Building a Custom Kernel."

CLUSTER ADMINISTRATION

This cluster isn't like Beowulf or other load-sharing clustering solutions for Linux. In Linuxconf parlance, a cluster is a group of machines that share common configuration files. Using Linuxconf, you can automatically keep them synchronized. This makes managing a large number of workstations much easier.

To put machines into groups, you can select Admin groups definitions and create a new group. An admin group is a collection of machines that share *subsystems*. A subsystem is a collection of configuration options. A configuration option could be an entire configuration file, or it can only be part of one (for example, specific entries in /etc/passwd, or only the NFS entries in /etc/fstab). Breaking up configuration into subsystems is generally much clearer than focusing on the specific files that implement those subsystems.

After you have selected your subsystems, you will want to put your group into an *administration tree*. An administration tree is a collection of unique subsystems. For example, one administration tree could have a `netaccess` subsystem and an `httpd` subsystem. But the same administration tree could not have two different `httpd` subsystems. However, a particular instance of Linuxconf could have multiple trees, which have different versions of the same subsystems. This allows you to maintain different configurations for different groups of machines all within one instance of Linuxconf.

> **Note**
>
> The / administration tree contains the Linuxconf server's own configuration files. Only modify this tree if you want to modify the Linuxconf server itself. Other groups can use the / administration tree as well.

After you have set up administration groups and trees, you can configure the groups using Linuxconf itself. The dialogs are identical, although only the subsystems that are part of the group will be available. When you are done, you can *publish* the configuration so that client machines will be updated. No updates will happen until you publish the configuration.

CONTROL

Although the Config section manages machine configuration, the Control section manages immediate actions and Linuxconf itself. It provides several submenus of its own:

- Control Panel
- Control Files and Systems
- Date & Time
- Features
- Status
- Logs

CONTROL PANEL

The control panel covers a wide variety of tasks, but generally handles immediate actions such as turning on or off subsystems.

ACTIVATE CONFIGURATION   None of the changes you make in Linuxconf take effect immediately. They only modify your configuration. To actually make the changes, activate the configuration by selecting Activate configuration or by quitting and requesting the configuration be activated then.

SHUTDOWN/REBOOT   Linuxconf gives access to most of the common system administration tasks, including shutting down your machines. Obviously this should be used with caution.

CONTROL SERVICE ACTIVITY   Linux machines tend to run a wide variety of services all the time, from telnet and ftp to font servers. You might not want all these services running all the time. This dialog allows you to turn each of them on or off, and determine whether they are started at boot time. Services listed as Automatic are started at boot time, whereas Manual services must be started by hand (or through Linuxconf).

MOUNT/UNMOUNT FILESYSTEMS   This dialog allows you to mount or unmount both local and remote filesystems and determine which filesystems are available at boot time.

CONFIGURE SUPERUSER SCHEDULED TASKS   The root account often runs a wide variety of automated tasks on a periodic basis. For example, once a day various logs are aged, and once a week the whatis database is updated. Generally these are handled through files in the /etc/cron.* directories (and this is becoming standard across Linux distributions), but sometimes you might like to add additional jobs without putting scripts in these directories. For example, if you want a periodic task to run at a specific time (instead of just "daily") or want one that runs more often than once an hour, you'll need to set it up yourself. This dialog simplifies setting this up. In general, however, it is better to use the /etc/cron.* directories if at all possible.

ARCHIVE CONFIGURATIONS/SWITCH SYSTEM PROFILE   Linuxconf can store entire configurations in named sets. Creating a named configuration is called archiving it. The Switch system profile dialog allows you to select one of your archived configurations. This is especially useful for laptop users who might move their machine between networks, or for machines that switch between standby and production modes quickly.

ACTIVATE/TERMINATE PPP LINKS   This is a fast way to activate and deactivate the configurations you set up in Config, Networking, Client tasks, PPP/SLIP/PLIP. This allows you to easily go on- and offline.

TURN OFF FIREWALLING   This option does exactly as it says, shutting down the firewall services.

RESTART LINUXCONF   Generally there is no need to restart Linuxconf, but sometimes it can be useful if configurations have changed outside of its scope.

CONTROL FILES AND SYSTEMS

This menu manages Linuxconf's behavior at a very low level. For example, you can modify which configuration files Linuxconf manages, paths to daemons, and file permissions. In general, unless you really know what you are doing, you shouldn't modify the entries here.

There is one exception, however. The Configure Linuxconf modules menu allows you to turn on and off various Linuxconf modules. You might want to turn on some of the additional modules provided here if they apply to your environment.

DATE & TIME

This section is fairly straightforward. You can set the current date and time, including updating your CMOS.

FEATURES

The final section allows you to configure the Linuxconf interface somewhat. There is seldom reason to modify this section.

QUITTING AND APPLYING YOUR CHANGES

None of the changes you make in the Config section take effect immediately. You must apply them. When you choose to quit, Linuxconf will give you the option of applying your changes, seeing what changes need to be made before applying them, or just discarding your changes.

ACCESSING LINUXCONF REMOTELY

Linuxconf has a very nice Web interface. It doesn't use a lot of fancy graphics, but it does give a very fast, clean interface to configuring your system. In many ways, it is a much nicer interface than the GNOME interface.

To connect to the Web interface on your own machine, open `http://localhost:98`. You might have to turn on the Web interface in Config, Networking, Linuxconf Network Access if it isn't turned on already. already. You should then log in as root, or as another user who has permission to use Linuxconf. You can grant Linuxconf permission to a user in the User accounts configuration dialogs.

You can also connect to Linuxconf servers running on other machines. For example, to manage the server `www.example.com`, you could connect to `http://www.example.com:98`. This allows you to easily manage servers anywhere on the network.

> **Caution**
>
> Connecting to Linuxconf across the network is not secure. In fact, your root password will be sent in plain text across the network. This is a problem if anyone is *sniffing*, or intercepting packets between you and your server. Note that this is true of many protocols other than Linuxconf's. For example, telnet suffers this same problem.
>
> Linuxconf does not include any security features because of U.S. restrictions on the export of cryptography, but there is a HOWTO on setting up Linuxconf with SSL. If you plan to administer machines across the Internet, this is highly recommended. See `http://www.terminator.net/linuxconf/linuxconf-ssl.html` for more information.

PROJECT: FAMILIARIZE YOURSELF

Depending on which of the particular distributions highlighted in this book you've chosen to install, familiarize yourself with them. Your system will remain unharmed is if you don't make and save changes.

You might also want to install a distribution not specifically mentioned in this book, such as SuSE or another, and look at their particular system administration tool (SuSE's installation and administration tool is called YAST, Yet Another System Administration Tool).

After you've seen how these handle the system, take a look at the chapters in this book on DHCP (Chapter 23, "Using DHCP,") or DNS (Chapter 26, "DNS and BIND,") or any of the other services and note how they're all the same. That is, you have a `/etc/dhcpd.conf` file and a `/etc/named.conf` file regardless of which distribution you've installed. If provided, the contents of the default files will likely be similar as well.

CHAPTER 9

DISK DRIVES AND FILESYSTEMS

In this chapter

HARD DRIVE INSTALLATION

Four basic steps are required to add and replace hard drives:

1. Physically connect the new drive.
2. Partition the drive.
3. Create a new filesystem on the new partitions.
4. Mount the new filesystem.

Although installing new hard drives into a PC goes beyond the scope of this book, a few general rules might be worth reviewing. The two most common types of hard drives are IDE drives and SCSI drives. The key to installing an IDE drive is to make sure that jumpers are set correctly as either a master/only drive or slave device. Each IDE controller (many systems today have two IDE controllers directly embedded on the motherboard) can support two drives. One drive must be jumpered as the master device and the other as the slave device (unless it is connected to the second controller, and then it would be the master).

SCSI drives must be connected to a SCSI adapter (typically a separate card), and there must be a terminating device on the SCSI chain. If you're adding a new hard drive to an existing SCSI environment, there is already a terminated device; make sure that the new hard drive is not terminated. Only one device on the SCSI chain will be terminated—this must be the last device on the SCSI chain. Also ensure that each SCSI device has a unique ID number. See your SCSI's manual for information on terminating devices and setting IDs.

Note The Linux kernel automatically probes for new devices as they are added to the system.

After the new hard drive is installed, it is detected when Linux is booted—that is, of course, as long as it is installed correctly and there are no conflicts with other hardware components. However, if you are installing a new SCSI controller, you have to manually install the module for it. Module management is covered in detail in Chapter 22, "Kernel Modules." The presence of the new hard drive is displayed by the boot messages as they scroll by.

Note You can review the boot messages at any time by running dmesg.

Also, in Caldera OpenLinux the `sysinfo` command displays system information, including detailed information on each hard disk installed. For example, the following is taken from the output of the `sysinfo` command:

```
# sysinfo

Hard disk 1  : /dev/hdb
   Model     : Maxtor 7850 AV
   Serial No : J502E2KS
   Capacity  : 814 MB
```

```
Cache     : 64 KB
CHS (log) : 827 cylinders, 32 heads, 63 sectors
CHS (phy) : 1654 cylinders, 16 heads, 63 sectors
```

Each installed hard drive will have a section similar to the one listed previously. As you can see, very detailed information about the hard drive is listed with sysinfo, including the hard drive make and model. If your newly installed hard drive is not detected, it is most likely a cabling or configuration issue. The key to detecting SCSI devices is to make sure that the SCSI controller is detected. After the SCSI controller is detected, all SCSI devices need to be found. If not, the problem is most likely one of incorrect termination, conflicting SCSI ID settings, or faulty cabling.

PART

III

CH

9

PARTITIONING THE HARD DRIVE

Partitioning the hard drive is done with the fdisk utility, which is very similar to the utility used on other operating systems such as DOS. A new partition can be created on the newly added hard drive by running fdisk and supplying the name of the device to be partitioned. For example, if the newly added drive is /dev/hdb, it can be partitioned as follows:

```
# fdisk /dev/hdb
```

After fdisk starts, the following directions will show you how to create and delete partitions, and how to change the partition type. After a partition is created, it becomes known to Linux by a unique device name and partition number. In the preceding example, the first partition on the drive hdb is referenced as /dev/hdb1 in Linux.

Note

> The drive devices used in this chapter follow the old naming convention. As of this writing, it is impossible to say which device names will be used with OpenLinux and the new 2.4.x kernel. The new devfs filesystem, if used, allows for only new names, mixed old and new names, and other variations. Eventually, the new device file naming convention will be used, which puts devices below their own /dev/ide/host#/bus#/target#/lun# scheme, with a parallel scheme for /dev/scsi/.../lun# (substituting numbers for the #). This change is coming to allow for the new USB and IR devices that must be accomodated.

To partition the new drive, you must know what the correct device name is in Linux. The system boot messages, as well as sysinfo, display the new device name. The device naming scheme for IDE drives is listed in Table 9.1. The naming scheme for SCSI drives is listed in Table 9.2.

TABLE 9.1   IDE DEVICE NAMES

Device Scheme	IDE Controller	Jumpering
/dev/hda	Primary	Master
/dev/hdb	Primary	Slave
/dev/hdc	Secondary	Master
/dev/hdd	Secondary	Slave

TABLE 9.2   SCSI DRIVE DEVICE NAMES

Device	Description
/dev/sda	First SCSI drive
/dev/sdb	Second SCSI drive
/dev/sdc	Third SCSI drive

Note
Some drives might be removable devices, such as Jaz and Zip drives.

When the drive is accessible as a device under Linux it can be partitioned in preparation for creating a filesystem. Like DOS, the utility for partitioning a hard drive is fdisk; however, the Linux version is much more powerful. The options available with the Linux version of fdisk are displayed in the Help menu as follows:

```
# fdisk /dev/hda

Command (m for help): m
Command action
   a   toggle a bootable flag
   b   edit bsd disklabel
   c   toggle the dos compatibility flag
   d   delete a partition
   l   list known partition types
   m   print this menu
   n   add a new partition
   o   create a new empty DOS partition table
   p   print the partition table
   q   quit without saving changes
   t   change a partition's system id
   u   change display/entry units
   v   verify the partition table
   w   write table to disk and exit
   x   extra functionality (experts only)

Command (m for help):
```

The steps for creating a new Linux partition are as follows:

1. Run fdisk on the new hard drive.

2. Examine any existing partitioning.

3. Create a new partition.

4. Select the partition type (primary, extended, or logical).

5. Select the partition number.

6. Select the beginning cylinder.

7. Select the ending cylinder or size.

8. Set the partition system ID.

9. Set the boot partition.

10. Write the new partition table.

11. Reboot the computer to update the partition table.

If you choose to use the Debian-distributed cfdisk, follow these steps:

1. Run cfdisk on the new hard drive.

2. Examine any existing partitions and delete if desired.

3. Select free space to use with the up and down arrows.

4. Select New using the left and right arrows.

5. Select Primary, Logical, or Cancel.

6. Select size of partition in Mb (max size is shown).

7. Set the boot partition (if necessary).

8. Write the new partition table.

9. Reboot the computer to update the partition table.

The following sections provide a closer look at each of these steps under fdisk. (The cfdisk utility will not be covered in detail, but is similar, as a comparison with the previous steps shows.)

STEP 1

Run the fdisk utility and specify which hard drive (by device name) you want to partition. The following is displayed on the screen:

```
# fdisk /dev/hda
Command (m for help): m
```

STEP 2

The letter p is used to display the current partition table, if any exists. If no partitions are present, the following is displayed onscreen:

```
Command (m for help): p

Disk /dev/hda: 32 heads, 63 sectors, 827 cylinders
Units = cylinders of 2016 * 512 bytes

   Device Boot    Start     End    Blocks   Id  System
```

If the partitions are already configured, the following is displayed:

```
Command (m for help): p

Disk /dev/hda: 32 heads, 63 sectors, 827 cylinders
Units = cylinders of 2016 * 512 bytes

   Device Boot    Start     End    Blocks   Id  System
/dev/hda1             1      17    17104+   82  Linux Swap
/dev/hda2   *        18     827   816480    83  Linux Native
```

STEP 3

Create a new partition as follows:

```
Command (m for help): n
Command action
    e   extended
    p   primary partition (1-4)
```

STEP 4

Select a partition type. Unlike DOS, where only one primary partition is allowed, Linux supports a hard drive of all primary partitions, or any combination of primary or extended partitions, with logical partitions inside the extended partitions. Each disk can have up to four primary partitions. If you need more partitions, you must give up one primary partition to create an extended partition. Although a primary partition is formatted for use with an operating system, an extended partition is not handled like this. Within an extended partition, you create logical partitions, which are formatted. You must plan your use of partitions with some care, because although Linux will boot from a logical partition inside an extended partition, some operating systems require a primary partition from which to boot.

```
Command (m for help): n
Command action
    e   extended
    p   primary partition (1-4)
p
Partition number (1-4):
```

STEP 5

Select the partition number. If this is to be the first partition on this drive, select 1:

```
Command (m for help): n
Command action
    e   extended
    p   primary partition (1-4)
p
Partition number (1-4): 1
```

STEP 6

Select the first cylinder number:

```
Command (m for help): n
Command action
    e   extended
    p   primary partition (1-4)
p
Partition number (1-4): 1
First cylinder (1-827): 1
```

STEP 7

Select the last desired cylinder number, or select the partition size in cylinders, megabytes, or kilobytes:

```
Command (m for help): n
Command action
   e   extended
   p   primary partition (1-4)
p
Partition number (1-4): 1
First cylinder (1-827): 1
Last cylinder or +size or +sizeM or +sizeK ([1]-17): 17
```

After the partition type, partition number, first cylinder, and last cylinder are set, the main fdisk prompt is displayed as follows:

```
Command (m for help):
```

STEP 8

Set the partition system ID. For a Linux filesystem, this is always type 83, Linux native:

```
Command (m for help): t
Partition number: 1
Hex code (type L to list codes): L
```

```
0 Empty          b   Win95 FAT32      75  PC/IX          a7  NEXTSTEP
1 DOS 12-bit FATc Win95 FAT32 (LB     80  Old MINIX      a9  NetBSD
2 XENIX root     e   Win95 FAT16 (LB  81  Linux/MINIX    b7  BSDI fs
3 XENIX usr      f   Win95 Extended   82  Linux Swap     b8  BSDI swap
4 DOS 16-bit <32M 40 Venix 80286      83  Linux Native   c7  Syrinx
5 Extended       51  Novell?          85  Linux extended db  CP/M
6 DOS 16-bit >=32M 52 Microport       93  Amoeba         e1  DOS access
7 OS/2  HPFS     63  GNU HURD         94  Amoeba BBT     e3  DOS R/O
8 AIX            64  Novell Netware   a5  BSD/386        f2  DOS secondary
9 AIX bootable   65  Novell Netware   a6  OpenBSD        ff  BBT
a  OS/2 Boot Manag
```

```
Hex code (type L to list codes):
```

Enter type 83 for a Linux native, second extended (ext2) filesystem:

```
Hex code (type L to list codes): 83
```

```
Command (m for help):
```

Tip

Repeat steps 3–8 for each additional partition. Be sure to make at least one partition a type 82, Linux swap.

STEP 9

Write out new partition table information to the hard drive as follows:

```
Command (m for help): w
The partition table has been altered!

Calling ioctl() to re-read partition table.
Syncing disks.
```

After the new partition table is written to disk, reboot your system to ensure that the partition table is updated. The newly created partitions are now ready for a Linux filesystem.

Note

You can examine the existing partition of any drive by running fdisk with the option -1. For example, fdisk -1 /dev/hda displays the existing partitions on the first IDE drive on the primary controller. You can display the partitions for all hard drives by just supplying the -1 option without specifying any particular hard drive.

LINUX FILESYSTEMS

Even though the newly added drive is now recognized by the operating system, it's not usable until it is partitioned and a filesystem is created on it. The default filesystem for Linux is the extended type-2 filesystem (ext2). Characteristics of an ext2 filesystem are listed in Table 9.3.

TABLE 9.3   SECOND EXTENDED (ext2) FILESYSTEM CHARACTERISTICS

Characteristic	Limit
Maximum filesystem size	4 terabytes
Maximum file size	2 gigabytes
Maximum filename length	255 characters
Minimum block size	1,024 bytes
Default inode allocation	1 per 4,096 bytes of partition space

The filesystem structure is built when the *make filesystem* utility (mkfs) is run. This utility is actually just a front-end program that calls subordinate routines for filesystem creation. When making an ext2 filesystem, the mkfs utility actually calls mke2fs to create the correct filesystem structure. After the filesystem structure is created, it cannot be modified without reformatting the partition, or—in other words—remaking a new filesystem with the mkfs utility.

Caution

The mkfs utility completely erases all data. You are not prompted to continue. It runs without any user interaction. Use it with caution.

The mkfs utility builds an `ext2` type filesystem by default. The results of running mkfs are reported as follows:

```
#  mkfs /dev/hdb2
mke2fs 1.10, 24-Apr-97 for EXT2 FS 0.5b, 95/08/09
Linux ext2 filesystem format
Filesystem label=
3024 inodes, 12096 blocks
604 blocks (4.99%) reserved for the super user
First data block=1
Block size=1024 (log=0)
Fragment size=1024 (log=0)
2 block groups
8192 blocks per group, 8192 fragments per group
1512 inodes per group
Superblock backups stored on blocks:
    8193 ....
Writing inode tables:  done
Writing superblocks and filesystem accounting information:  done
```

If you are installing an older hard drive, I strongly recommend that you use the `-c` option to check for bad blocks, as in the following example:

```
#  mkfs –c /dev/hdb2
mke2fs 1.10, 24-Apr-97 for EXT2 FS 0.5b, 95/08/09
Linux ext2 filesystem format
Filesystem label=
3024 inodes, 12096 blocks
604 blocks (4.99%) reserved for the super user
First data block=1
Block size=1024 (log=0)
Fragment size=1024 (log=0)
2 block groups
8192 blocks per group, 8192 fragments per group
1512 inodes per group
Superblock backups stored on blocks:
    8193 ....

Checking for bad blocks (read-only test):  done
Writing inode tables:  done
Writing superblocks and filesystem accounting information:  done
```

When an `ext2` filesystem is created, it builds a set of areas on the hard drive partition. These areas are commonly referred to as *block groups*. Each block group is segmented into several smaller sections. Figure 9.1 depicts the block group layout, and Table 9.4 describes each of the sections of a block group.

PART
III

CH
9

TABLE 9.4 BLOCK GROUP DESCRIPTION

Block Group Section	Description
Superblock	Information about the entire filesystem is stored in the superblock. Each block group contains a superblock, but it is only a backup copy of the superblock in the first block group.

TABLE 9.4 CONTINUED

Block Group Section	Description
Group descriptor	Information on each block group is stored here. Each block group contains a group descriptor, but they are all duplicates of the group descriptor block in the first block group. Pointers to the table of inodes reside here.
Block bitmap	This is a map of bits indicating which blocks are in use.
Inode bitmap	This is a map of bits indicating which inodes are in use.
Inode table	This is a table of inodes actually allocated to this block group.
Data blocks	This is where the actual data is stored.

Figure 9.1
A second extended (ext2) filesystem diagram.

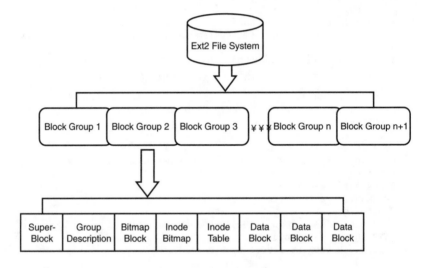

An *inode* is basically a pointer to a file; however, it contains pertinent information about the file. It stores information such as file permissions, ownership, date of last modification, and pointers to actual data blocks. An inode does not contain any file data. There is exactly one inode per file. An ext2 filesystem is built with a fixed set of inodes at creation time. By default, one inode is allocated for every 4096 bytes. This is not a literal mapping—it is only used as a general rule of thumb when establishing the block groups.

If a file is small enough, it fits entirely within the directly accessible blocks of a given block group. If not, an indirect method of linking blocks together is used to store all the data of a given file. This scheme allows a file to be as large as 2GB in size.

Note   The majority of files on a Linux system are small enough to be directly accessible.

You can change the number of inodes created on the filesystem by passing the -i <number> option to mkfs. This number should be a multiple of 512 and is commonly 512, 1024, 2048,

2096, 8192, and so on. If you have a very small filesystem with a lot of very small files, you might want to make this number 512. If you have a very large filesystem with very large files (database chunks for example), you might want to make this number larger.

> **Caution**
>
> Choosing a number unsuited to the size of the filesystem and the files you will have on it can cause you to either run out of inodes to use despite having a lot of free disk space, or to apparently run out of disk space (although you'll actually have a lot of only partially used inodes).

PART

III

CH

9

Each inode will use a block. The superblock will use one or more blocks depending on the number of inodes. Ideally, when your filesystem is full, you'll have only small percentage of unused inodes. If you are uncertain, use the default; it is best for the average filesystem.

MOUNTING FILESYSTEMS

For a newly created filesystem to be accessible in Linux, it must be mounted. Mounting filesystems dates back to the days when files were maintained on tape reels that had to be mounted before the filesystem could access them. This method of dealing with partitions makes filesystem maintenance easier, as you'll see later in the chapter.

Although the requirement to mount a filesystem seems to not be very user-friendly, it actually offers some powerful flexibility. Unlike a DOS environment, where in most cases a drive letter represents a separate partition, Linux filesystems can be logically grouped together so that they appear to be on one filesystem when in reality they aren't. This multipartition filesystem appears to the user as one directory hierarchy. For example, I can partition my hard drive into four primary partitions. Each partition can then be mapped to a specific mount point that is part of the overall directory structure, as is outlined in Table 9.5.

TABLE 9.5   SAMPLE MOUNT POINTS WITH SEPARATE PARTITIONS

Directory (Mount Point)	Physical Partition
/	/dev/hda1
/var	/dev/hda2
/home	/dev/hda3
/usr	/dev/hda4

Take the example of the /var directory. This is the directory in which incoming mail is located. With the /var directory on a separate partition, a system administrator does not have to be overly concerned about the incoming mail directory filling up and causing the system to halt because of the lack of disk space. In this scenario, the /dev/hda2 partition can completely fill up with incoming email, but the system continues to run because the /dev/hda1 filesystem is not full. Of course the mail will begin to bounce, but the system won't come to a halt. If, however, the /var directory is a part of the /dev/hda1 filesystem, the root filesystem can become filled with incoming mail and cause the system to halt due to a lack of disk space.

MANUALLY MOUNTING FILESYSTEMS

Filesystems can be manually mounted by using the mount command. The mount command uses the following syntax:

```
mount -t filesystem [-o option1,option2,...] device-name mount-directory
```

The command for manually mounting the CD-ROM is as follows:

```
mount -t -t iso9660 -o ro /dev/cdrom /mnt/cdrom
```

The actual CD-ROM device is referenced by the symbolic link /dev/cdrom.

The mount directory is similar in logic to a drive letter in an operating system such as DOS: It's a place to reference and access a drive. With Linux, however, the place of reference and access to a drive device is a directory no different from any other directory on the Linux filesystem. (In other words, you can change directories with the cd command to go to a mount directory to access the drive device mounted to it. With DOS, you type the letter of the drive with a colon to access the drive device.) For example, CD-ROM drives are often mounted to a /mnt/cdrom directory.

You can find a list of currently mounted filesystems by executing the mount command without any options. You can generate a similar list by running the cat command on the /proc/mounts file. Although df also provides you a listing of mounted filesystems under normal conditions, this command reads from /etc/mtab. The mtab file cannot be created if the root filesystem is mounted read-only, such as during filesystem maintenance and repair, and therefore, it can give misleading information.

Note

When you mount a device to a mount directory, anything that was in that directory is no longer accessible until you unmount the drive using the umount command. When you unmount the directory, the previous contents are once again intact in the directory.

Tip

Ordinary users can only mount and unmount filesystems listed in /etc/fstab that contain the user or users option, and then only as the mount is listed. Otherwise only root can mount and unmount filesystems. See the later section "Automating the Mounting Process."

UNMOUNTING FILESYSTEMS

The umount command is used to detach previously mounted filesystems from their mount directories. The syntax used is similar to the mount command, but a typical command line can be much simpler. For instance, the following command unmounts a CD-ROM drive that was mounted using the example given earlier:

```
umount /mnt/cdrom
```

> **Note**
>
> If the unmounting procedure is to succeed, no one can be using the mount directory when you unmount a device or a mount directory. If anyone is accessing the mount directory, you get a busy device error, and the unmounting procedure fails. Be sure to back out of a mount directory before unmounting the device attached to it..

AUTOMATING THE MOUNTING PROCESS

The mounting process can be automated by configuring the filesystem table file (/etc/fstab). You can do this by adding the drive device in question to the automount filesystem table contained in the /etc/fstab file.

When you start the system, Linux mounts certain devices automatically. The /etc/fstab file contains information about these devices that is necessary to have them mounted without interaction from the system administrator.

The /etc/fstab file offers two kinds of functionality. Entries in the fstab file can be configured to have specific filesystems mounted automatically each time the system boots. Furthermore, by defining an entry in the /etc/fstab file, you don't have to supply the entire mount command when mounting a filesystem manually. For example, if your CD-ROM drive has its own entry in /etc/fstab that contains all the information necessary for it to mount, the following command can be used to mount the drive:

```
mount /mnt/cdrom
```

Each filesystem is described on a separate line in the /etc/fstab file. Each entry contains all the information that you type at the command prompt, as well as a few other options that change the way the drive is mounted.

The entry in the /etc/fstab file for an ATAPI-IDE CD-ROM looks similar to the following:

```
/dev/hdc /mnt/cdrom iso9660 ro,noauto, 0 0
```

Each line entry has six space-delimited fields. The description of these fields is outlined in Table 9.6.

TABLE 9.6   FIELD DESCRIPTIONS OF THE /etc/fstab FILE

Field	Description
/dev/hdc	The actual device name or partition to be mounted.
/mnt/cdrom	The mount point. When mounted, data on this filesystem is accessible via this directory name.

TABLE 9.6	CONTINUED
Field	**Description**
iso9660	The filesystem type. Hard drive partitions are of type ext2.
ro,noauto	Mount options: ro = read-only user. noauto = do not automount this filesystem.

Note

Options must not have any whitespace (spaces) between the options, only commas. White-space separates arguments, so if whitespace is used within the option argument, the mount command will become confused. See the man page for more options.

0	Used by the dump command. 0 = don't back up this filesystem.
0	Sets the order by which filesystem checks are done at reboot. 0 = don't run a check on this filesystem.

Tip

Some options change defaults. For example, user changes the default exec to noexec. If you want the user to be able to run a program from that mount point, you must also put exec on the option line. The exec option must come after the user option because options are read in the order they occur and change the defaults as they are read. Order is important.

Note

For further information on valid values for each of the entries in the /etc/fstab configu-ration file, see the man page for fstab and mount.

After the filesystem is mounted, it can be accessed through the mount point. In other words, the newly mounted filesystem appears to the user as just another directory in the filesystem hierarchy.

TROUBLESHOOTING

When I installed OpenLinux, I already had a /home partition which I didn't tell LIZARD about (I was afraid LIZARD might accidentally format the partition). After the install, I added the fstab entry and mounted the partition. During install I added a user that I wanted to use for testing. Now that user doesn't have a home directory (I also can't find the httpd or ftp directories).

The new user directory you created (and the ftp and httpd directories) still exist, but you mounted /home on top of them. Here's one way to proceed:

1. Change to single user mode and log in as root.

2. Enter the command umount /home.

3. `cd` to `/` and then run `tar czvf home.tar.gz home`. This will create the file `home.tar.gz`, which will be the contents of the new home directory.

4. Run the following command:

   `rm -Rf /home/* ; mount /home`

5. Enter the following:

   `tar xzvf home.tar.gz ; rm home.tar.gz`

6. Return to runlevel 5.

I've been trying to unmount a directory, but it keeps giving me an `in use` error. I've tried everything I can think of.

First, make sure you're not in the directory (and no other users are in the directory) by entering the following:

`cd /`

If unmounting still fails, as root, run the `fuser` command on the mount:

`fuser /mountpoint/*`

The `fuser` command will return all PIDs (most likely with a c suffix) of all processes using files in those directories. Kill all those PIDs and you should be able to unmount the directory.

I'm trying to mount a directory, but I get an error about too many filesystems mounted or the superblock is corrupt.

If you're trying to mount the filesystem as a user, the filesystem you're trying to mount is probably a different one from that specified in `/etc/fstab`. That is, if the `/etc/fstab` says that `/mnt/floppy` is an `ext2` type partition, you won't be able to mount a DOS formatted diskette as a normal user. You'll have to become root and specify the filesystem type, overriding `/etc/fstab`.

If you're already root and getting this error, you'll need to ensure you have support for that filesystem type by entering `modprobe msdos`.

If you still can't mount the disk, it might not be formatted. Linux cannot mount a disk that's not formatted. To format the disk, put it in the drive, decide what format you want on the disk, and issue the appropriate format command: `mkdosfs /dev/fd0`. After it is formatted, you should be able to mount it. Note that formatting the disk will destroy any data you might have on that disk.

I have a CD-ROM from which I installed OpenLinux, but now I can't seem to mount it. There's no entry in `fstab` for the CD-ROM.

First, you need to determine which device your CD-ROM is. Many manufacturers put an IDE CD-ROM on `/dev/hdc` rather than `/dev/hdb`. Use dmesg to try to determine which device Linux sees your CD-ROM as. If you have SCSI, look for `/dev/sr#`. Proprietary CD-ROMs have their own device, some of which include `/dev/sonycd`, `/dev/sjcd`, `/dev/hitcd`, and `/dev/sbpcd`. Parallel port CD-ROMs will normally be either `/dev/pcd#` or `/dev/icd_bdm#`.

(The # or hash symbol is a place holder for numbers.) After you determine which device Linux knows your CD-ROM to be, create a link to it as cdrom: `ln -s /dev/hdc /dev/cdrom` (substituting your CD-ROM device for hdc).

Try to mount /dev/cdrom on the mount point. The iso9660 module should load automatically. If you get an error, try loading the module manually and try again. If you have a proprietary CD-ROM (not identified as IDE ATAPI or SCSI), ensure the module for that CD-ROM is also loaded or load it manually. You should now be able to mount your CD-ROM.

I just installed a new SCSI device, but I can't see it. What's going on?

Ensure that the new SCSI device has a unique LUN (Logical Unit Number). If the LUN conflicts with another device, you might not see either device. Also, you can often use your SCSI boot utilities to verify that the device is seen or recognized.

CHAPTER **10**

UNDERSTANDING THE LINUX FILESYSTEM

In this chapter

THE LINUX FILESYSTEM STRUCTURE

The Linux filesystem is very similar to the standard UNIX filesystem layout, but of course there are some minor differences. The key to understanding the Linux filesystem is to first understand the underlying structure. A more in-depth discussion on the internal workings of the Linux filesystem and the methodology used in handling files is covered in Chapter 9, "Disk Drives and Filesystems." The Linux directory structure, which is very similar to UNIX or DOS, is designed as a tree hierarchy. At the top level is the main directory, often referred to as the *root directory* (or the *system root directory*). It is the only directory at this level. All other directories are referenced in relation to the root directory. The root directory is denoted as the / (forward slash) directory. Microsoft mistakenly uses terms such as *documents* and *folders* to refer to files and directories, but everyone knows that documents and folders are found in file cabinets, whereas files and directories are found in filesystems.

> **Note**
>
> Don't confuse the top-level root directory (/) with the /root directory. The /root directory is a subdirectory of the / directory.

The root directory contains a small set of subdirectories and files. Remember that the /root directory is a sub directory of the / directory, and is the home directory of the root user. The root user, or *superuser*, is described in more detail in Chapter 11, "Users, Groups, and Permissions."

> **Note**
>
> In Linux, the forward slash is used in denoting paths to specific directories. DOS uses the backslash (\).

One important thing to keep in mind when examining the inner workings of a Linux filesystem is the fact that the entire Linux system is addressed under one large directory tree spanning one or more hard drives, disks, CD-ROM drives, and so on. This means different hard drives or partitions are not accessed as separate drive letters as they are with DOS or Windows. Instead, all partitions are *mounted* to subdirectories that reside under the root filesystem directory (/). To access files on a secondary hard drive or partition, simply change to the directory to which the partition is mounted. Mounting and unmounting of partitions is discussed in detail in Chapter 9.

Essentially, every part of your Linux system—including the hardware in your computer—resides on your filesystem in the form of files. Even the hardware devices are accessed as files. Of course, these aren't typical files and they can't normally be accessed like a simple text file, but as files, things such as modifying access to a specific device become a much simpler task. Devices are one of the more unique file types in Linux. They are discussed in more detail later in this chapter.

Caution

As with regular files, not all device files can be treated equally. You can "cat" an ASCII file with no problems, but a binary file will almost certainly put your terminal window in an unusable state. The same applies for device files. Some, like `sndstat`, will provide meaningful information, but most will just put your terminal in an unusable mode. And unless you're very sure of what you're doing, never try to echo to a device—if that device is your hard drive, you run the risk of destroying data on it.

THE LINUX FILESYSTEM STANDARD (FHS)

In the Fall of 1993, an effort began to restructure the file and directory layout of Linux. This project began as the *Filesystem Standards*, or *FSSTND*, project. After several iterations as the FSSTND project, the scope was widened to include issues that were general to other UNIX-like operating systems. In view of this expanded focus, the project was renamed the Filesystem Hierarchy Standard (FHS).

Many people have contributed to this effort, but the primary person behind it is Daniel Quinlan. As of this writing, the most current version of the FHS documentation was version 2.0, dated October 26, 1997. It can be obtained from `ftp://tsx-11.mit.edu/pub/linux/docs/linux-standards/fsstnd`. Dan also currently serves as the chairman of the steering committee for the Linux Standard Base Organization (`www.linuxbase.org`). It is the goal of the Linux Standard Base group to develop and promote a set of standards that increase the compatibility between Linux distributions. This enables independent software vendors to port and develop applications to a common Linux environment without worrying about compatibility issues between Linux distributions.

FHS OVERVIEW

Whereas the Filesystem Hierarchy Standard contains a great level of detail concerning what the Linux filesystem should and shouldn't be, its primary objective is to provide a consistent and standardized filesystem. This standardized filesystem can be defined into two orthogonal categories:

- **Shareable versus non-shareable files**—This category consists of files that can be shared among several hosts and files that are specific to just one particular host. For example, data from a specific database application can be shared among hosts, whereas device lock files are not shared.

- **Static versus variable files**—This category includes static files such as documentation, application binaries, and libraries that do not change without system administrator intervention. Any files that change without system administrator intervention are considered variable data files. The `/var/log/messages` file is an example of a data file that changes without any system administrator intervention.

Shareable data files need to be located in a directory structure that can be mounted as a read-only filesystem. An example of how these two categories might be summarized is depicted in Table 10.1. This table is a generalized example and does not necessarily apply to all possible implementations of a FHS-compliant system.

TABLE 10.1 GENERALIZED EXAMPLE OF FHS-COMPLIANT DIRECTORY LAYOUT

	Shared	Non-Shared
Static	/usr /opt	/etc /boot
Variable	/var/mail /var/spool/news	/var/run /var/lock

FHS SPECIFICATIONS FOR THE ROOT DIRECTORY

As was outlined in the first section of this chapter, the root directory is the first and only directory at the top level of the tree hierarchy. As such, special considerations are warranted for the root directory. The FHS document states, "The contents of the root filesystem should be adequate to boot, restore, recover, and/or repair the system." In order to accomplish that goal, the root filesystem must contain the essential components to boot the system, the essential tools to repair the system, and the essential utilities to back up or restore the system while still keeping the root filesystem as small as possible. A small root filesystem is less prone to filesystem errors and lends itself to easier maintenance if something goes wrong.

DEFAULT DIRECTORY LAYOUT

A typical installation of OpenLinux creates the root directory with the following files and directories:

```
[root@redrock /]# ls -CF
NetWare/      bru/        initrd/         mnt/        sbin/
auto/         dev/        install@        opt/        tmp/
bin/          etc/        lib/            proc/       usr/
boot/         home/       lost+found/     root/       var/
```

Directories are denoted with a trailing forward slash, and symbolic links have a trailing @ symbol when files are listed with the F option. Following is a closer look at each of these directories.

Note You might not have all the directories listed and might even have one or two others. Directories are generally created by programs as they are needed, either during program installation or when a program runs for the first time.

/NetWare

This directory is used as an automatic mount point for NetWare volumes as part of the NetWare client. The automatic mounting of NetWare volumes and NDS trees is discussed at length in Chapter 28, "Using NetWare."

/auto

This directory is used to configure devices to automatically detect and mount removable media when loaded. For example, the CD-ROM drive can be configured to be automatically mounted after a CD-ROM is detected in the drive. This differs slightly from configuring the /etc/fstab file. The /etc/fstab file is used to predefine and, with the proper option, automatically mount a given device—at boot time—but it does not detect changes when a removable medium has changed.

/bin

The /bin directory contains system and user utilities. This directory contains utilities that are mostly compiled code and are referred to as *binaries*, hence the directory name, bin. Some utilities in /bin are actually shell scripts. You can determine which are which by using the file command.

PART
III

CH
10

/boot

This directory contains crucial components for the boot process, including a grub subdirectory. If you make changes that affect bootup, like adding a new kernel you want to boot from, you may have to make changes to your boot loaders. See Chapter 12, "Boot Loaders," for more details on the boot loaders and the use of files contained in this directory.

/bru

The /bru directory contains the components of a commercial add-on program for tape backups and restores. This directory is not defined as a part of the Filesystem Hierarchy Standard, but it meets the criteria of what is required for backup and restore capability. You will only have the /bru directory if you purchased BRU commercially. Other commercial programs will create their own directories, but normally do so below /opt or /usr/local.

/dev

The /dev directory is where all the device definitions reside. The drivers themselves are in the /lib/modules/[kernel version]/ directory, but the definition of a specific device is in this directory. Devices are discussed in detail at the end of this chapter. A number of subdirectories exist under /dev for device groupings.

Additionally, the new 2.4.x kernel series introduced the devfs virtual filesystem. Distributions might opt not to use this new filesystem in the first distribution or two under the new kernel, but it will certainly figure in over time. The devfs filesystem functions similarly to the /proc filesystem (covered elsewhere in this chapter) in that it doesn't exist until the system boots.

The reason for the development of such a system is that with the advent of IR and USB, the number of devices requiring a device file is exploding. With each static device file taking some hard disk space, the root filesystem would soon need to be extremely large to hold all the possible devices.

With `devfs`, as a device is plugged in, a driver is loaded and `devfs` creates an entry for it in `/dev` dynamically and virtually. You will be able to work with it just as any real device node; it will just exist only in memory and not permanently on the disk.

The `/devfs` filesystem uses `devfsd` to create devices on-the-fly. Your system will not show any devices in `/dev` that do not exist, so you will have gone from some 1200 or so entries to just a few hundred. Additionally, `devfsd` uses `/etc/devfsd.conf` to configure what types of devices show up. You can have the old `/dev/hda` devices (for example) or only the newer device names (the old names will be `symlinks` to the new ones).

Caution

Be careful making changes to `/etc/devfsd.conf`. This file must remain in sync with the names found in your `/etc/fstab` or you risk having an unbootable system until one or the other is fixed.

/etc

The `/etc` directory might have been more aptly named the `config` directory because it contains configuration files and subordinate directories of system configuration data. It is important to be familiar with and understand the files in this directory. These files are crucial in the day-to-day operation and maintenance of your system. Whether it is a simple task, such as adding a user, or a more complicated task, such as configuring domain name resolution service, configuration files in `/etc` must be modified.

/home

This is the directory that is used for user data. For example, each new user has a directory in the home directory when his or her account is activated. Upon logging in, a user is located in his or her home directory. If someone named Natalie were a newly added user, her home directory might be aptly named `/home/natalie`.

/initrd

This directory is used in association with the requirement of initial RAM disk for some system configurations. For example, initial `ramdisk` (`initrd`) support is often used to circumvent a chicken-and-egg scenario created when the driver for a SCSI hard disk is on the SCSI hard disk which can't be mounted to access the driver until the driver is loaded. Loadable modules are discussed in detail in the chapter on system initialization.

install@

This is a symbolic link to the directory in which install scripts and files are located, `/var/lib/LST`.

/lib

Common libraries are stored in this directory. Different applications can make use of the same shared library. For example, the C programming code library set is stored in this directory. With a name like `libc-2.1.3.so`, this library contains functions common to all C programs on the system. This enables programs to be smaller because they all refer to common functions in this library. Smaller programs save disk space, save RAM, and improve speed. This C library is essential; without it, the entire system (except the kernel) would stop running.

/lost+found

Filesystem utilities to correct system errors store data (lost inodes) in this directory when attempts to fix the errors are unsuccessful or when files become truncated. You should find a `lost+found` directory at the top level of each mounted `ext2` partition.

/mnt

This directory is used for the default mount points for other filesystems. For example, by default the CD-ROM device mounts to `/mnt/cdrom`. The floppy disk drive mounts to `/mnt/_floppy`. You are not required to use this directory for mount points, but it is provided for your convenience. If you are using the `automount` daemon, you can see filesystems mounted to `/auto`. But this is just for the automounter's use. You should not use `/auto` for your mounts or you will confuse the automounter.

You are free to create and use (or just mount over) any directory you want, but beware of the possible consequences: If you mount over an existing filesystem, that filesystem becomes inaccessible.

/opt

The `/opt` (options) directory is the directory in which add-on applications are installed. For example, the Netscape Communicator and Navigator packages are installed in the `/opt` directory. To comply with the Filesystem Hierarchy Standard, all third-party applications install to this directory.

/proc

The `/proc` directory is actually a special filesystem. It contains detailed information about processes that are currently running, as well as specific information about hardware configurations. It's commonly referred to as a process information pseudo-filesystem. It acts as an interface to kernel data structures. For example, the `/proc/interrupts` file contains information about which interrupts are being used. This is covered in more detail in the section, "Examining Key Directories."

/root

This directory is the home directory of the root user. By default, the root user logs in to this directory. Only files specific to the root user are stored in this directory. As noted earlier, this directory is not to be confused with the `/` directory, which is commonly referred to as the root directory.

/sbin

The /sbin directory contains system and administration utilities or binaries. Utilities for partitioning a hard drive, checking the integrity of a filesystem, creating a new filesystem, and shutting down or rebooting the system are all stored in this directory.

/tmp

Temporary files are stored in this directory. Often, applications need to use temporary files with certain functions or when installing. These temporary files are stored in the /tmp directory.

/usr

The /usr directory is intended for shareable, read-only data. It is the major section of the filesystem, but it can be configured to reside on a secondary machine. The majority of documentation is located in the /usr/doc directory. The complete source tree for the Linux kernel is located in the /usr/src directory.

/var

The /var directory is set up to hold variable data. It contains spool directories for mail, news, print jobs, and other files, as well as other administrative files. All data logged by specific processes are stored in the /var directory.

/dev/shm

Before moving on, one filesystem that mounts to the /dev directory by default (but can be mounted anywhere, including in the root directory) is the shm directory. This directory should never be used for anything. The kernel makes use of this filesystem for shared memory access. You can occasionally see a file or two written here that later disappear. The amount of shared memory available is calculated by the kernel at bootup, when the shared memory filesystem is mounted. It will be a portion of the entire virtual filesystem available to the kernel. Its size can be varied through /proc/sys/kernel/shmmax, but if you are not familiar with this filesystem, it is best to leave the value as-is.

Caution

If you are splitting your filesystem across multiple disks or partitions, the following directories must be in the root filesystem:

- /bin, /dev (unless using the new devfs in lieu of /dev), /etc, /lib, /root
- /tmp, /var (but some subdirectories of /var, such as the spool/mail subdirectory, are often NFS mounted from a central mailhost)
- Also, some filesystems cannot be NFS-mounted (unless you are using a totally diskless client)

You can determine what is mounted on your filesystem in one of several ways. The first way is to use df. This command shows you how much disk space is free for use on each mounted filesystem; however, not all filesystems will be shown.

The second way is to use `cat /etc/mtab`. This is a table in `/etc` that will show you mounted filesystems. This will only show you filesystems mounted when the following occurs:

- The root filesystem is mounted read-write. (If the root filesystem is mounted read-only, this file will be in error.)
- The filesystem was not mounted with the `-n` option. (Don't write to `mtab`.)

The third way is to use the mount command with no options. Both the mount command and df use the `/etc/mtab` file to get lists of mounted filesystems, so both suffer from the same problem `mtab` suffers from, as discussed previously.

Finally, you can use `cat /proc/mounts`, which will show all mounted filesystems. This works as long as the `/proc` directory is mounted. If `/proc` is not mounted (which it will not be during parts of the boot sequence), this method cannot be used. Only `/proc/mounts` will show the `devfs` filesystem because it isn't of general interest.

DISTRIBUTION DIFFERENCES

As with a number of chapters in this book, some small differences will be encountered between distributions. This does not mean any particular distribution does not follow the FHS, only that some latitude exists for such differences. These differences are generally small and not significant.

This book uses examples from Caldera OpenLinux, because it is the easiest for most Linux neophytes to install. But most of the information applies across the board. This text will attempt to point out significant differences where they exist. Also remember that with directories like `/etc`, much of what you see on your system depends on what packages you've installed. If a listed file doesn't exist on your system, or you have more or other files on your system, don't worry. This is normal.

In some cases, files exist, but in a slightly different structure. For example, both Caldera and Red Hat have `/etc/XF86Config`, but Debian uses `/etc/X11/XF86Config`. Both are perfectly legitimate. You'll also find that Caldera and Red Hat collect system initialization files under `/etc/rc.d/`. Debian chose to have the directories found in `/etc/rc.d/` under Caldera directly in `/etc`, and included an `rc.boot` directory which contains files such as those files found directly in `/etc/rc.d` on other systems. When in doubt, or when you can't find a particular file, try using the `locate` command to find the file:

```
locate myfile
```

EXAMINING KEY DIRECTORIES

Whereas all the directories serve a purpose, a few are worth a closer look. The `/etc` directory contains several directories and files that are crucial to the successful operation of the system. Almost all configuration files reside in the `/etc` directory. Understanding devices, what they are, and how they work is best accomplished by exploring the `/dev` directory. As was mentioned previously, the `/proc` directory is actually a special type of filesystem.

THE /etc DIRECTORY

A listing of files and directories in the /etc directory follows:

```
AppleVolumes.default        ftpusers             man.conf             rmt@
AppleVolumes.system         gettytab             mediaprm             rpc
HOSTNAME                     gpm-root.conf        mgetty+sendfax/      rpm/
X11/                         group                midi/                samba.d/
XF86Config                  grub.conf            mime.types           sane.d/
adjtime                     host.conf            minicom.users        screenrc
afpd.conf                   hosts                modemaccess.conf     securetty
aliases                     hosts.allow          modules/             security/
aliases.db                  hosts.deny           modules.conf         sendmail/
am.d/                       httpd/               motd                 sendmail.cf
at.deny                     inbind.conf          mta/                 sendmail.ct
atalkd.conf                 inetd.conf           mtab                 sendmail.cw
autoconf/                   inetd.conf.orig      mtools.conf          services
chatscripts/                inittab              my.cnf               shadow
coas/                       ioctl.save           ndsadmin.sample      shells
config.d/                   ipx_ticks            news/                skel/
cron.d/                     irda/                nis/                 skel.d/
crontab                     isapnp.conf          nis.conf             slip/
csh.cshrc                   isdn/                nls/                 ssh/
dhcpd.conf                  issue                nsswitch.conf        std.o3
diald/                      issue.net            ntp.conf             std.sb
diald.conf                  ksh.kshrc            nwdsmgr@             sysconfig/
dosemu.conf@                ld.so.cache          nwdsmgr.english/     syslog.conf
dosemu.conf-drdos703.eval   ld.so.conf           pam.d/               system.cnf
dosemu.conf.sample          ldap/                papd.conf            termcap
dosemu.users                ldap.conf            passwd               tin.defaults
drums.o3                    lilo.conf            pcmcia/              uucp/
drums.sb                    localtime@           porttime             vga/
dumpdates                   login.defs           ppp/                 webalizer.conf
enscript.cfg                logrotate.d/         printcap             webmin/
exports                     lpd.conf             printcap.old         wgetrc
fdprm                       lpd.perms            printcap.orig        wine.d/
filesystems                 lst.cnf              profile              ytalkrc
fstab                       magic                profile.ksh          zlogin
ftpaccess                   mail.rc              protocols            zlogout
ftpconversions              mailcap              pwdb.conf            zshenv
ftpgroups                   majordomo.cf         rc.d/                zshrc
ftphosts                    makedev.d/           resolv.conf
```

The /etc directory contains both directories and configuration files. Each of the directories contains configuration files for a specific area. Table 10.2 lists the subdirectories of the /etc directory and a description of each. Your /etc directory can vary from the listing above depending on what you have installed.

TABLE 10.2   SUBDIRECTORIES OF THE /etc DIRECTORY

Subdirectory	Description
X11	Contains configuration data for the X Window server as well as several window managers.
am.d	Contains configuration files for the automounter daemon.

TABLE 10.2 CONTINUED

Subdirectory	Description
coas	Contains information files for COAS.
config.d	The main directory contains a `logrotate` configuration file and an Internationalization configuration file. It also contains a print subdirectory, with printer configuration files, and a shells subdirectory with global default shell startup configurations.
cron.d	Details on when to automatically run specific routines are outlined in this directory.
httpd	Configuration files for the setup and operation of the Apache Web server.
irda	Configuration files for IR devices.
isdn	Configuration files for the operation of an ISDN interface.
ldap	Configuration files, which must be edited, for the Lightweight Directory Access Protocol (LDAP).
logrotate.d	Configuration files for how and when to rotate log files.
makedev.d	Contains makefiles for the creation of devices. Each file has the parameters for the creation of a specific type of device such as hard drives, serial ports, or CD-ROMs.
mgetty+sendfax	Configuration files for the use of `mgetty` as the interface on a serial port. The `mgetty` routine has special features for handling things such as dial-up connections and fax transmissions.
midi	Configuration files for Midi, but principally for the Timidity player.
modules	The list of modules to be automatically loaded is maintained in this directory.
mta	This directory contains information on what is being used as the mail transfer agent and how it is configured.
nis	This directory contains the files you'll need if you want to make a NIS master or slave server.
nwdsmgr.english	NetWare directory services manager, English version.
pam.d	Files for authentication methods used for restricted services.
pcmcia	Configuration files for the operation of PCMCIA devices.
ppp	Configuration files for the setup and operation of a PPP interface.
rc.d	This directory, the run-time configuration directory, contains system initialization scripts. These routines are categorized by runlevel.
rpm	This directory is intended to contain local configurations for rpm. Principally, this will contain an `rpmrc` file that deviates from the one in `/usr/lib/rpm-3.0.3/`.
samba.d	Configuration files for the setup and operation of Samba are stored here. Samba is the network protocol (SMB) that enables the interface of Linux to a Windows network.

PART

III

CH

10

TABLE 10.2 CONTINUED

Subdirectory	Description
security	Security features for things such as user limits are maintained in configuration files in this directory.
sendmail	Specific items regarding the operation of sendmail can be fine-tuned by modifying the configuration files stored in this directory.
skel	The default files for each new user are stored in this directory. Each time a new user is added, these skeleton files are copied into their home directory.
skel.d	The skel.d replaces the skel directory as a repository for files used to populate new user directories. The directories are created as different shells are installed, so depending on what you've installed on your system, you might not have a subdirectory or all the different shells (bash, csh, sh, tcsh, ksh).
slip	Configuration files for the setup and operation of the SLIP (serial line IP) interface.
sysconfig	This directory contains configuration files and subdirectories for the setup of system configuration specifics. For example, the Ethernet configuration files are stored in the network-scripts subdirectory.
vga	The configuration file for the svgalib is stored in this directory.
webmin	This directory contains the configuration files for webmin, such as miniserv.conf, which tells the webmin webserver how to run (port, with/without ssl, and so forth).

Besides the subdirectories listed in Table 10.2, many other configuration files are in the /etc directory. Some of the most commonly modified configuration files and some of the more important ones to be aware of are listed in Table 10.3.

TABLE 10.3 COMMONLY MODIFIED CONFIGURATION FILES

Configuration File	Description
HOSTNAME	This file contains the fully qualified domain name (FQDN) of your system. The FQDN is the machine name plus the domain name. For example, if your machine name is hook and your company domain is fish.net, your FQDN is hook.fish.net.
XF86Config	This file contains all the necessary configurations to enable the X Server to function. It is described in detail in Chapter 6, "Customizing X and Controlling X Resources."
aliases	All email aliases are maintained in this file. An aliases database file (aliases.db) is built from the entries in the aliases file by the newaliases utility.
crontab	This file is the cron table set up for the automatic running of system routines. A cron table can also be established for individual users.
devfsd.conf	This file (if installed) configures devfsd and tells it which device scheme it should use when creating devices in /dev.

TABLE 10.3   CONTINUED

Configuration File	Description
dosemu.conf	This is the configuration file for the DOS emulator.
exports	This file acts as the control list for clients who want to access the system via NFS.
fstab	This is the filesystem table. Entries in this file are made to predefine specific devices, filesystems, mount points, and mount options.
ftpaccess	Controlling access to the FTP server is configured in this file.
ftpusers	This file contains the names of those not authorized to access the system using ftp. Use of this file is governed by /etc/pam.d/ftpd using the pam_listfile.so line.
group	The definition of groups and users that belong to these groups is determined by the configuration of this file. The primary purpose of a group is for access control to a set of files and directories. For example, a development group can be established and permission set in such a way that only members of this group can access files and directories belonging to this group. See Chapter 11 for more details.
grub.conf	This file contains the GRUB configuration. GRUB and LILO are mutually exclusive. One or the other will be used, though both can be present on your system if both utilities are installed.
hosts	This file is used to define a system name and domain in combination with a specific IP address. This file needs to always contain an entry for the local loopback device (127.0.0.1). It might also contain an entry for an IP address, if the machine is connected to a network.
hosts.allow	This file defines which other machines (hosts) are allowed to access this machine. This single file can function as both an ALLOW and DENY file. See Chapter 34, "TCP Wrappers."
hosts.deny	This file defines which other machines (hosts) are not allowed to access this machine. While installed, this file is not necessary if the process options of hosts.allow are used.
inetd.conf	This is a configuration of services that are started by the INETD TCP/IP super server.
inittab	This is the table that contains definitions for init processes.
issue	This file contains the text that is displayed before logging in, in other words, the message shown right above a login prompt.
lilo.conf	This file contains configuration information for the LILO boot manager. It is covered in detail in Chapter 12.
motd	This is the *message of the day* file. The system administrator can put any text in this file that is to be shown to all users upon logging in to the system.
passwd	This file contains crucial user information for individual login accounts. At one time the password was stored in this file—hence the file name passwd. However, passwords are now encrypted and stored in the /etc/shadow file.

PART

III

CH

10

TABLE 10.3 CONTINUED

Configuration File	Description
printcap	The definition for all system printers, whether local or remote, is stored in this file.
profile	This file contains systemwide environment and startup scripts. This includes such things as the default setting for the $PATH environment variable as well as other environment settings.
resolv.conf	Configuration of how domain name resolution is to occur is defined in this file.
securetty	This file contains a list of ports (tty devices) that are allowed to log in to the system as the root user. By default, only the system virtual consoles are predefined.
sendmail.cf	This is the sendmail configuration file. Do not modify it unless modification is absolutely necessary and you make a backup copy beforehand.
sendmail.cw	Machine name aliases are entered in this file. For example, if your machine name is hook.fish.net, adding an entry for just fish.net enables sendmail to recognize your email as user@fish.net as opposed to user@hook.fish.net.
services	This is a definition of the networks, services, and the associated port for each protocol that are available on this system. For example, Web services (http) are assigned to port 80 by default.
shadow	Encrypted passwords for user accounts are stored in this file.
shells	This file contains a list of shells that are available with OpenLinux.
syslog.conf	This file contains the definition of how logging is to take place on this machine. For example, all mail messages are logged in /var/log/mail by default.
system.cnf	This is an OpenLinux-specific configuration file. It is maintained by external scripts and is not normally modified directly.

Many of these configuration files can be modified and maintained by graphical utilities. However, it's important to note that these utilities are merely that—utilities to make it easier to maintain these files. The best understanding of these files will come when you are comfortable editing them directly. Of course, this requires an understanding of the purpose and syntactical layout of each configuration file. Some configuration files are self-documenting, that is, they contain comments throughout the file that describe syntax and purpose. The /etc/dosemu.conf file is an example of this type of configuration file. Other configuration files require referencing an online manual page or other documentation file. For example, the man page for the /etc/passwd file is the best reference for a succinct description of how this file layout works.

THE /dev DIRECTORY

The /dev directory is the directory in which all device definitions are stored. The majority of the devices are either block devices or character devices; however, other types of devices can be created. As a general rule of thumb, block devices can be thought of as devices that store or hold data, and character devices can be thought of as devices that transmit or transfer data. For example, devices for the diskette drive, hard drive, and CD-ROM are all block devices, whereas the devices for serial ports, mice, and modems are all character devices. What the block and character designations actually tell you is how the data is moved: Block is in 8-or 32-bit (1 or 4 byte) chunks in parallel; serial is transferred bit by bit, serially. There is some sort of naming scheme for devices, but you pretty much have to know or look up device names in order to reference them correctly. The common block devices are listed in Table 10.4, and the common character devices are listed in Table 10.5.

Note CD-ROM drives that are neither IDE nor SCSI have a proprietary device name. This type of CD-ROM has its own interface card and a unique device name.

TABLE 10.4 COMMON BLOCK DEVICES

Device Type	Device Name	Description
Disk drive	/dev/fd0	This is the floppy disk drive. The DOS equivalent is drive letter A:.
IDE	/dev/hda	An IDE device configured as the master device on the primary controller.
	/dev/hdb	An IDE device jumpered as a slave device on the primary controller.
	/dev/hdc	An IDE device jumpered as a master device on the secondary controller.
	/dev/hdd	An IDE device jumpered as a slave device on the secondary controller.
SCSI	/dev/sda	The first SCSI hard drive.
	/dev/sdb	The second SCSI hard drive.
	/dev/sdc	The third SCSI hard drive.
	/dev/scd0	The first SCSI CD-ROM drive.
	/dev/scd1	The second SCSI CD-ROM drive.
CD-ROM	/dev/gscd	A GoldStar CD-ROM drive.
	/dev/sonycd	A Sony CD-ROM drive.

TABLE 10.5 COMMON CHARACTER DEVICES

Device Type	Device Name	Description
Mouse	/dev/psaux	PS/2 style bus mouse
Serial ports	/dev/ttyS0	The first serial port

TABLE 10.5   CONTINUED

Device Type	Device Name	Description
	/dev/ttyS1	The second serial port
	/dev/ttyS2	The third serial port

Define a device by specifying a type, such as block or character, and a major and minor number. The major number is used to categorize a device and the minor number is used to identify a specific device type. For example, all IDE devices connected to the primary controller have a major number of 3. Master and slave devices, as well as individual partitions, are further defined by the use of a minor number. Listing the IDE hard drive devices displays the major and minor numbers. These are the two numbers preceding the date in the following display:

```
# ls -l /dev/hd*
brw-r-----  1 root     operator   3,   1 Aug 19 02:22 hda1
brw-r-----  1 root     operator   3,  10 Aug 19 02:22 hda10
brw-r-----  1 root     operator   3,  11 Aug 19 02:22 hda11
brw-r-----  1 root     operator   3,  12 Aug 19 02:22 hda12
brw-r-----  1 root     operator   3,  13 Aug 19 02:22 hda13
brw-r-----  1 root     operator   3,  14 Aug 19 02:22 hda14
brw-r-----  1 root     operator   3,  15 Aug 19 02:22 hda15
brw-r-----  1 root     operator   3,   2 Aug 19 02:22 hda2
brw-r-----  1 root     operator   3,   3 Aug 19 02:22 hda3
brw-r-----  1 root     operator   3,   4 Aug 19 02:22 hda4
brw-r-----  1 root     operator   3,   5 Aug 19 02:22 hda5
brw-r-----  1 root     operator   3,   6 Aug 19 02:22 hda6
brw-r-----  1 root     operator   3,   7 Aug 19 02:22 hda7
brw-r-----  1 root     operator   3,   8 Aug 19 02:22 hda8
brw-r-----  1 root     operator   3,   9 Aug 19 02:22 hda9
brw-r-----  1 root     operator   3,  64 Aug 19 02:22 hdb
brw-r-----  1 root     operator   3,  65 Aug 19 02:22 hdb1
brw-r-----  1 root     operator   3,  74 Aug 19 02:22 hdb10
brw-r-----  1 root     operator   3,  75 Aug 19 02:22 hdb11
brw-r-----  1 root     operator   3,  76 Aug 19 02:22 hdb12
brw-r-----  1 root     operator   3,  77 Aug 19 02:22 hdb13
```

The major number for both hda and hdb devices is 3. Of course, the minor number changes for each specific partition. The definition of each major number category can be examined by looking at the contents of the /usr/src/linux/include/linux/major.h file. The /usr/src/linux/Documentation/devices.txt file also documents major and minor numbers. This file defines the major numbers (outlined in Table 10.6).

Note

The same major number can be used for different device types. For example, a block device can use the same major number as a character device. Major numbers can be used in this manner because the device type is the distinguishing factor. In other words, devices are categorized by device type first, and then by major numbers, and finally by minor numbers.

TABLE 10.6   MAJOR NUMBER ASSIGNMENT

Major Number	Device Type	Description
0	Unnamed Devices	Reserved as null device number
1	Character	Memory devices
1	Block	RAM disk
2	Character	Pseudo TTY masters
2	Block	Floppy disks
3	Character	Pseudo TTY slaves
3	Block	The primary IDE, MFM, and RLL interface
4	Character	TTY devices
5	Character	Alternative TTY devices
6	Character	Parallel printer devices
7	Character	Virtual console capture devices
7	Block	Loopback devices
8	Block	SCSI disk devices
9	Character	SCSI tape devices
9	Block	Metadisk (RAID) devices
10	Character	Non-serial mouse devices, and an assortment of miscellaneous items (rtc, watchdog devices, and so forth)
11	Character	Raw keyboard device
11	Block	SCSI CD-ROM devices
12	Character	QIC-02 tape devices
12	Block	MSCDEX CD-ROM callback support
13	Character	PC speaker
13	Block	8-bit IDE/MFM/RLL controller
14	Character	Sound card devices
14	Block	BIOS hard drive callback support
15	Character	Joystick
15	Block	Sony CDU-31A/CDU-33A CD-ROM
16	Character	Non-SCSI scanners
16	Block	GoldStar CD-ROM
17	Character	Chase serial card
17	Block	Optics Storage CD-ROM
18	Character	Chase serial card—alternative devices

TABLE 10.6 CONTINUED

Major Number	Device Type	Description
18	Block	Sanyo CD-ROM
19	Character	Cyclades serial card
19	Block	Double compressed disk
20	Character	Cylcades serial card (alternative devices)
20	Block	Hitachi CD-ROM
21	Character	Generic SCSI access
22	Character	Digiboard serial card
22	Block	Secondary IDE hard disk/CD-ROM controller
23	Character	Digiboard serial card—alternative devices
23	Block	Mitsumi proprietary CD-ROM
24	Character	Stallion serial card
24	Block	Sony CDU-535 CD-ROM
25	Character	Stallion serial card—alternative devices
25	Block	First Matsushita (Panasonic/Soundblaster) CD-ROM
26	Character	Quanta WinVision frame grabber
26	Block	Second Matsushita (Panasonic/Soundblaster) CD-ROM
27	Character	QIC-117 Tape devices
27	Block	Third Matsushita
28	Character	Stallion serial card (card programming)
28	Block	Fourth Matsushita
29	Character	Frame Buffer
29	Block	Aztech/Orchid/Okano/Wearnes CD-ROM
30	Character	iBCS-2 compatibility devices
30	Block	Phillips LMS CM-205 CD-ROM
31	Character	MPU-401 MIDI
31	Block	ROM/flash memory card
32	Character	Specialix serial card
32	Block	Phillips LMS CM-206 CD-ROM
33	Character	Specialix serial card (alternative devices)
33	Block	Third IDE hard disk/CD-ROM controller
...		...

TABLE 10.6   CONTINUED

Major Number	Device Type	Description
34–119 and 128–194		Allocated: see `/usr/src/` `linux/Docuentation/` `devices.txt` for details
120–127		Local/Experimental Use
195–239		Unallocated
240–254		Local/Experimental Use
255		Reserved

Almost all devices are created by default at installation time. However, you can always create a device, if need be, by using the `mknod` command. Devices are created with this utility by supplying the device to be created, the device type (block or character), and the major and minor numbers. For example, the entry for the first serial port, COM1 in DOS, displays as follows:

```
# ls -l /dev/ttyS0
crw-rw----   1 root       uucp     4,  64 Aug 19 02:22 ttyS0
```

If this file is accidentally deleted, it can be easily re-created. Notice that the first letter in the preceding display indicates the file type. In this case, it is a character device. This device can be re-created as follows:

```
# mknod ttyS0 c 4 64
```

For the most part, you rarely have to re-create devices, but if you use Linux long enough you'll have to re-create a device at some point. A complete set of scripts is installed in the `/etc/makedev.d` directory for the easy rebuilding of any or all devices. Running `/sbin/makedev` rebuilds the entire set of devices. You can test this by setting the environment variable `$DESTDIR` to the destination at which you want the devices to be created. For example, if you want the devices to be created in the `/test-devices` directory, do the following:

```
# mkdir /test-devices
# cd /test-devices
# mkdir dev
# mkdir etc
# cd etc
# mkdir makedev.d
# cd makedev.d
# cp /etc/makedev.d/* .
# export DESTDIR=/test-devices
# makedev
```

The `/test-devices/dev` directory now contains the newly created devices.

If you need to create a nonstandard or new device that the `makedev` script doesn't know about, look for the device name, type, and major and minor numbers in `/usr/src/linux/documentation/devices.txt`.

You can also create unbuffered character devices and pipes with `mknod`. The `devices.txt` file listed previously will tell you when you need to use u in place of c with `mknod`. Named pipes, created with the p, are usually created by programs (and do not take major and minor numbers), but you can create one and use it with scripts. However, that is beyond the scope of this text.

THE /devfs DIRECTORY

Now that you've learned all about the historical devices in /dev, when you look there you might see something totally different (or not). Assuming Caldera OpenLinux uses /devfs, it might implement it using the old names. It might choose instead to use either the kernel names or the even newer (and changing) devfs names.

When you start to understand the /dev naming scheme, you'll see that it matters little what devices are called, because the kernel knows them by their major and minor numbers. After you find out what a particular device is called, you can have a program reference and use it. If you create a block device in your home directory called foo1 with major number 3 and minor number 1 and look at it (you can do this with the command: `less -f foo1`), you will be looking at your IDE 0 (drive C:) hard drive's first partition. This is why ordinary users cannot create device files—this would nullify any permissions you might have.

THE /proc DIRECTORY

As was previously mentioned, the /proc directory is actually a unique filesystem. Listing the files is this directory doesn't really give you any clues that there is anything unusual about this directory—until you take a closer look at the file sizes. All the files and directories have a file size of 0, with two exceptions: kcore and self. A directory listing looks similar to the following:

```
dr-xr-xr-x   3 root      root          0 Dec  6 01:13 1
dr-xr-xr-x   3 root      root          0 Dec  6 01:13 2
dr-xr-xr-x   3 root      root          0 Dec  6 01:13 21
dr-xr-xr-x   3 root      root          0 Dec  6 01:13 22
dr-xr-xr-x   3 root      root          0 Dec  6 01:13 23
dr-xr-xr-x   3 root      root          0 Dec  6 01:13 24
dr-xr-xr-x   3 root      root          0 Dec  6 01:13 3
dr-xr-xr-x   3 root      root          0 Dec  6 01:13 360
dr-xr-xr-x   3 bin       root          0 Dec  6 01:13 362
dr-xr-xr-x   3 root      root          0 Dec  6 01:13 373
dr-xr-xr-x   3 root      root          0 Dec  6 01:13 376
dr-xr-xr-x   3 root      root          0 Dec  6 01:13 387
dr-xr-xr-x   3 root      root          0 Dec  6 01:13 4
dr-xr-xr-x   3 daemon    root          0 Dec  6 01:13 425
dr-xr-xr-x   3 nobody    65535         0 Dec  6 01:13 465
dr-xr-xr-x   3 root      root          0 Dec  6 01:13 5
dr-xr-xr-x   3 root      root          0 Dec  6 01:13 525
dr-xr-xr-x   3 root      root          0 Dec  6 01:13 56
dr-xr-xr-x   3 root      root          0 Dec  6 01:48 860
dr-xr-xr-x   3 col       users         0 Dec  6 01:48 861
dr-xr-xr-x   3 col       users         0 Dec  6 01:48 862
-r--r--r--   1 root      root          0 Dec  6 01:13 cmdline
-r--r--r--   1 root      root          0 Dec  6 01:13 cpuinfo
-r--r--r--   1 root      root          0 Dec  6 01:13 devices
-r--r--r--   1 root      root          0 Dec  6 01:13 dma
-r--r--r--   1 root      root          0 Dec  6 01:13 filesystems
```

```
-r--r--r--    1 root      root               0 Dec  6 01:13 interrupts
-r--r--r--    1 root      root               0 Dec  6 01:13 ioports
-r--------    1 root      root        33558528 Dec  6 01:13 kcore
-r--------    1 root      root               0 Dec  3 18:12 kmsg
-r--r--r--    1 root      root               0 Dec  6 01:13 ksyms
-r--r--r--    1 root      root               0 Dec  6 01:13 loadavg
-r--r--r--    1 root      root               0 Dec  6 01:13 locks
-r--r--r--    1 root      root               0 Dec  6 01:13 mdstat
-r--r--r--    1 root      root               0 Dec  6 01:13 meminfo
-r--r--r--    1 root      root               0 Dec  6 01:13 modules
-r--r--r--    1 root      root               0 Dec  6 01:13 mounts
dr-xr-xr-x    2 root      root               0 Dec  6 01:13 net
-r--r--r--    1 root      root               0 Dec  6 01:13 pci
dr-xr-xr-x    2 root      root               0 Dec  6 01:13 scsi
lrwxrwxrwx    1 root      root              64 Dec  6 01:13 self -> 889
-r--r--r--    1 root      root               0 Dec  6 01:13 stat
dr-xr-xr-x    5 root      root               0 Dec  6 01:13 sys
-r--r--r--    1 root      root               0 Dec  6 01:13 uptime
-r--r--r--    1 root      root               0 Dec  6 01:13 version
```

Each of the numbered directories corresponds to an actual process ID. Looking at the process table, you can match processes with the associated process ID. For example, the process table might indicate the following for the Web server:

```
# ps ax | grep httpd
460    ?    S    0:00 httpd -f /etc/httpd/apache/conf/httpd.conf
```

Details of this process can be examined by looking at the associated files in the directory for this process, /proc/460. You might wonder how you can see details of a process that has a file size of 0. It makes more sense if you think of it as a window into the kernel. The file doesn't actually contain any data; it just acts as a pointer to where the actual process information resides. A listing of the files in the /proc/460 directory looks similar to the following:

```
-r--r--r--    1 root      root               0 Dec  6 21:21 cmdline
lrwx------    1 root      root              64 Dec  6 21:21 cwd -> [0303]:2
-r--------    1 root      root               0 Dec  6 21:21 environ
lrwx------    1 root      root              64 Dec  6 21:21 exe -> [0303]:43066
dr-x------    1 root      root               0 Dec  6 21:21 fd
pr--r--r--    1 root      root               0 Dec  6 21:21 maps
-rw-------    1 root      root               0 Dec  6 21:21 mem
lrwx------    1 root      root              64 Dec  6 21:21 root -> [0303]:2
-r--r--r--    1 root      root               0 Dec  6 21:21 stat
-r--r--r--    1 root      root               0 Dec  6 21:21 statm
-r--r--r--    1 root      root               0 Dec  6 21:21 status
```

Even though the files appear to be of size 0, examining their contents reveals otherwise:

```
# cat status
Name:    httpd.apache
State:   S (sleeping)
Pid:     460
PPid:    1
Uid:     0        0        0        0
Gid:     0        0        0        0
VmSize:     1332 kB
VmLck:         0 kB
VmRSS:       688 kB
```

```
VmData:       300 kB
VmStk:         20 kB
VmExe:        376 kB
VmLib:        592 kB
SigPnd: 00000000
SigBlk: 00000000
SigIgn: 80000000
SigCgt: 0000466b
```

The man page for proc describes each of the files associated with a running process ID in detail.

The files in the /proc directory act very similar to the process ID subdirectory files. For example, examining the contents of the /proc/interrupts file displays something like the following:

```
# cat interrupts
  0:    27222899    timer
  1:        3152    keyboard
  2:           0    cascade
  9:      450448    eth0
 12:        4477    PS/2 Mouse
 13:           1    math error
 14:       15198 +  ide0
 15:           0 +  ide1
```

Each number down the left-hand column represents an interrupt that is in use. Examining the contents of the file dynamically gathers the associated data and displays it to the screen. Most of the /proc filesystem is read-only; however, some files enable kernel variables to be changed. This provides a mechanism to actually tune the kernel without recompiling and rebooting.

The procinfo utility (which may not be included with OpenLinux) summarizes /proc filesystem information into a display similar to the following:

```
# /usr/bin/procinfo

Linux 2.0.35 (root@buildmeister.caldera.com) (gcc 2.7.2.3) #1 [train2]

Memory:      Total       Used        Free      Shared     Buffers      Cached
Mem:         30884       20332       10552      10840        8900        5292
Swap:        66492           0       66492

Bootup: Thu Dec 03 18:12:23 1998    Load average: 0.00 0.00 0.00 3/38 895

user   :      0:00:19.69   0.0%  page in :   10886  disk 1:   6791r  3742w
nice   :      0:00:00.00   0.0%  page out:    6089
system:      0:00:34.14   0.0%  swap in :       1
idle   :  2d 7:42:19.82 100.0%  swap out:       0
uptime:  2d 7:43:13.61         context :  1083993

irq  0:  20059365 timer             irq  8:         0
irq  1:         4 keyboard          irq  9:    326636 eth0
irq  2:         0 cascade [4]       irq 10:         0
irq  3:         0                   irq 11:         0
irq  4:         0                   irq 12:         0
irq  5:         0                   irq 13:         1 math error
irq  6:         2                   irq 14:     10515 ide0+
irq  7:         0                   irq 15:         0 ide1++
```

In general, you cannot (nor should you want to try to) alter any files under /proc. However, the /proc/sys tree contains a number of files designed to change the behavior of the kernel while it is running. For example, if you have two NICs in your host and you want to forward between them, you must make the following change:

```
echo 1 > /proc/sys/net/ipv4/ip_forward
```

By default, forwarding is turned off. Other parameters, such as those for khttpd and the kernel HTTP daemon, are set here. You can also tune your kernel. Hints for kernel tuning can be found in /usr/src/linux/documentation/sysctl/ in various files.

> **Caution**
>
> There are some things to be aware of. Be careful experimenting with kernel tuning, particularly in the vm subdirectory, because some settings might cause your system to become unstable. Also, backing up the /proc filesystem is a waste of time and tape and not recommended. Restoring the /proc filesystem should not be done under any circumstances. Attempting to do so might cause the system to become unstable or crash.

PART

III

CH

10

CHECKING FILESYSTEMS

The Linux ext2 filesystem is fairly robust. However, if you try hard enough, you can corrupt it. The easiest way to do this is to simply turn the system off without performing a proper shutdown. (Kicking the plug out of the wall accomplishes the same goal if you don't have a UPS.)

Why is this bad? Because Linux, like most UNIX systems, maintains information about files it has accessed in memory (buffers). When these buffers change, they aren't immediately written to disk. These changed buffers are said to be *dirty*. The system occasionally flushes the buffers to the disk to bring the memory and disk into sync, which is called *syncing the disk*. You can do this manually by typing sync. Custom dictates doing this several (usually three) times to ensure all the buffers were properly flushed to disk. When Linux performs a shutdown, the buffers are flushed to disk (synced) and then unmounted. When you unmount a disk, the umount command performs a sync first.

If you lose power to your system without a proper shutdown, on power-up the boot scripts check to see whether the disk was properly synced and unmounted. It knows whether this is the case because when a disk is mounted read-write, a bit (the dirty bit) is set. If this bit is still set during bootup, the system knows the filesystem could be corrupt. It then runs an fsck (filesystem check) before continuing the mounting process. This fsck also occurs after the system has been rebooted 20 times since the last fsck. This value can be changed using the tune2fs utility. You can also force a check by invoking fsck with the -f option.

Normally, fsck encounters a few 0-dtime inodes. This is nothing to worry about. These are remnants of pipes (such as those syslog uses to write to the log files) and other insignificant things and will be deleted automatically. If you have more extensive damage that appears out of the ordinary, the boot script drops you into a prompt (on OpenLinux you are asked for the root password to enter maintenance or single user mode) with instructions to run fsck manually.

This is often the most frightening thing a user who is new to Linux will encounter, but it is nothing to be feared. In most cases, you can simply run `fsck  -y  /dev/<harddrive>`, which tells `fsck` to go ahead and take care of things without intervention. Manually repairing a filesystem is beyond the scope of this book and requires extensive knowledge of how the `ext2` filesystem works. At any rate, the worst that could happen is that you will need to reinstall everything. The question "You do have a backup, don't you?" comes to mind at this point.

If worse comes to worst, you can still boot from a Linux boot floppy and save your data files before reinstalling the files on the corrupt partition. This, by the way, is the reason most seasoned systems administrators prefer to put the `/home` directory on a separate partition—to help isolate and protect it somewhat and to make running `fsck` manually easier.

The Linux community is working on a successor to the `ext2` filesystem that will be a journaling filesystem. If you are familiar with SQL databases, this is like the transaction logging that enables unfinished transactions to be rolled back and finished transactions that have been committed to be ignored. Running `fsck` on `ext2` can take a long time on a large partition. With a journaling filesystem, this would take a very short time (typically less than 10 percent of the time it takes to check a nonjournaling filesystem).

To run `fsck` manually as a preventive measure (monthly, if you never shut your system down), perform the following steps:

1. Enter maintenance (single user mode) by typing the following from a command prompt:
   ```
   init 1
   ```

2. When the system reaches runlevel 1, it prompts you for root's password; enter it to log in.

3. You need to unmount mounted filesystems you want to check. The root filesystem cannot be unmounted, so it needs to be mounted read-only. Assuming you have `/home` mounted as `/dev/hda2` and the root filesystem as `/dev/hda1`, issue the following command:
   ```
   umount /home
   ```
   Alternatively, `umount  -a` unmounts all filesystems except root:
   ```
   mount -n -o remount,ro /
   ```
   If you get the error message `cannot umount <filesystem>`, `<filesystem> in use`, you need to identify the process running on that filesystem or the user (root) that `cd`'d into that filesystem, and kill the process or `cd` out of the filesystem.

4. Run `fsck` on the two partitions:
   ```
   fsck -f /dev/hda2
   fsck -f /dev/hda1
   ```

5. When the filesystem checks finish, remount the filesystems:
   ```
   mount -n -o remount,rw /
   mount /home
   ```
   Alternatively, `mount  -a` mounts all filesystems designated to be automatically mounted at bootup.

6. Return to the default runlevel. Normally, this just requires root to log out of mainte-nance mode. However, if the system does not change to the default runlevel (normally runlevel 5), log back in as root and issue the following command:

```
init 5
```

PROJECTS

To help you get better acquainted with your Linux filesystem, this section will walk you through two quick projects. The first one is designed to show you how you can create a small filesystem on your host, the second to acquaint you with a tool to inspect files and show you how to deal with some common files you might encounter.

CREATING A SWAP FILE

Assume you need more swap, either because you created an insufficiently large swap file to begin with, or because you find a particular program temporarily needs more swap. The commands in this section will be run as root, because most of them require root privileges.

First, you need to create a file the size of the swap space you want to add. For the purposes of this text, it will be small, but you can make it any size you want as long as it fits in the free space you have on the partition. You'll use the dd command to create the file (see man dd for more information):

```
dd if=/dev/zero of=foo.swap bs=1024 count=100
```

This command reads from the device file /dev/zero (which will give you a stream of zeros) and writes that to a file called foo.swap (the name is unimportant). It reads and writes blocks of 1024 bytes (convenient because that is 1KB, so you know exactly how big this file will be in kilobytes), and writes 100 of them. When the command is finished you will have a 100KB file full of zeros (this is not the number zero, which has an ASCII code of 48, but instead an ASCII code 0, which has no printable value). The act of creating this file full of NULL characters is similar to what happens when you run fdisk and create a partition.

Next, you'll need to format the file. Because you're creating a swap file, you're going to use the mkswap utility. The mkswap utility will format the file so that it can be used as swap. You could just as easily use one of the other format utilities, such as mkdosfs, mke2fs, or mkfs.minix to put a DOS, ext2, or minix filesystem (respectively) in the file:

```
mkswap foo.swap
```

The only thing left to do now is to put this swap space to use. To do this, you need to use the swapon command:

```
swapon foo.swap
```

You can get a warning about insecure file permissions. If you are concerned, you can change them using the chmod command (chmod 600 foo.swap).

PART III
CH 10

How can you tell if this worked? Very easy, let proc tell you. Just cat the contents of /proc/swaps:

```
# cat /proc/swaps
Filename                         Type         Size     Used    Priority
/dev/hda4                        partition    176704   28      -1
/root/foo.swap                   file         96       0       -2
```

The proc file tells all. If you create any other filesystem, you can mount it using the loop-back device. For example, if you create a file and put an ext2 filesystem on it, you can mount it like this:

```
mount -oloop foo.ext2 /mnt/loop
```

This will mount the file foo.ext2 (created much as above, but formatted with the mke2fs command) on /mnt/loop.

USING THE file COMMAND

Explore your system using the file command. This command will return a number of responses, depending on the kind of file it sees.

The following are some typical responses you'll get:

```
/dev/zero: character special (1/5)
/bin/bzip2: ELF 32-bit LSB executable, Intel 80386, version 1, dynamically linked
    (uses shared libs), stripped
/dev/log: socket
/dev/initctl: fifo (named pipe)
/etc/modules/default: English text
/etc/rc.d/rc5.d/S16inet: symbolic link to .../init.d/inet
/etc/rc.d/init.d/inet: Bourne-Again shell script text
/etc: directory
whois-2.5a.tgz: empty
nmap-2.50-1.i386.rpm: RPM v3 bin i386 nmap-2.50-1
yahtzee-1.0-1.src.rpm: RPM v3 src i386 yahtzee-1.0-1
mod_ssl-2.6.4-1.3.12.tar.gz: gzip compressed data, deflated, last modified: Mon
    May  1 10:00:11 2000, max compression, os: Unix
iptables-1.0.0.tar.bz2: bzip2 compressed data, block size = 900k
2.3.99-pre5.lvm.patch: 'diff' output text
devfsd-v1.3.7.tar: GNU tar archive
```

Try to find as many different filetypes as you can. The list above is by no means exhaustive—far from it. The file command uses /usr/share/misc/magic to determine what kind of file it is working with, and it is almost 200k.

Any file that has the term text you can cat. Shell and ELF executable files can be run (permissions allowing).

If you've downloaded any files, they'll most likely be in one of three different forms:

- <filename>.tgz
- <filename>.tar.gz
- <filename>.tar.bz2

To open the first two files, you can use the following command:

```
tar xzvf <filename>.[tgz|tar.gz]
```

If you don't want to open it, but just want to see what's inside, substitute t for x above.

A simple `<filename>.tar` file opens the same way, but does not require the z option.

If you have a `<filename>.tar.bz2` file, it requires a little more work to open. You'll uncompress it and pass it using a pipe to the `tar` command as follows:

```
bzcat <filename>.tar.bz2 | tar xv
```

Again, you can substitute t for x in the previous `tar` command to see what's in the file without actually opening it.

PART
III

CH
10

## CHAPTER 11

USERS, GROUPS, AND PERMISSIONS

In this chapter

USER ACCOUNTS

Because Linux is a multiuser system, the task of adding and maintaining user accounts is common in Linux system administration. Upon a successful installation of a Linux distribution, two user accounts are configured: the root user and a normal user. These two user accounts represent the two basic types of users that are configurable with Linux.

Note   The concept of users, groups, and permissions is probably very familiar to those of you who are accustomed to multiuser environments, including NT systems.

The first type, the *root user*, is unique for several reasons. First and foremost, it is the only user account with systemwide privileges. Other accounts can be set up as an exact clone of the root user account, but it is strongly discouraged. For the most part, the root user account needs to be one of a kind.

This having been said, the root user account is not the only special account that is set up. In your Linux distribution, you will see a number of accounts set up, like bin, daemon, adm, lp, sync, shutdown, mail, operator, and others. These accounts are also special. They are called "system accounts" and are used for varying purposes, some self-explanatory, some not. They do not have the privileges afforded root, so certain applications will run as these users rather than root to protect your system from potential vulnerabilities. These accounts do not have passwords because they are not designed for login. They need to be in your password file—do not delete them or some programs will not run. These special-purpose accounts are also called *non-login* accounts.

The second type, a *normal user* account, is the type of account that is set up for each individual user. This type of account differs only in respect to access privileges and home directories. You'll examine this more closely in the subsequent sections of this chapter, which discuss groups and permissions.

Logging in to a Linux system is done in one of three ways: at the console, via a serial connection such as a terminal, or via a network connection. For some, the term *logging in* is a foreign term. If you fall into that category, think of it as authenticating a user to the server. The primary purpose for logging in, or authenticating yourself, is to establish access rights to a given set of files, directories, or services.

ROOT USER/SUPERUSER

The root user, often called the *superuser*, is the user that has the rights and privileges to perform any task or view any file on the system. He or she is, in essence, the all-powerful system administrator. There is nothing that the superuser can't do. The name *superuser* actually comes from a command called su or substitute user. This command is normally used to become the root user, and many folks still think *su* stands for superuser.

That being the case, it's very important that the root user account is closely guarded. Obviously, the password to the root user account is of primary importance when considering system security. The root password will only be given to those authorized to log in as root, and it needs to be changed periodically. The root user account is only used when performing system administration tasks, or when performing a task that can only be done as the superuser. In other words, it's best to perform as many tasks as possible as an individual user and only use the superuser account when it is absolutely necessary.

System administration tasks are performed from the superuser account. For example, the following list summarizes some of the duties and privileges of a system administrator:

- Has complete access to all files and directories regardless of owner and permissions
- Controls user account administration
- Performs system maintenance tasks such as file housekeeping
- Halts the system when necessary
- Sets up initial user passwords
- Changes passwords when necessary.
- Installs software on the system

NORMAL USERS

Normal user accounts are accounts that are set up for individual users. Each user has his or her own account and a corresponding home directory. This does not mean that system utilities and server application software can't be shared; it means that it's easier to maintain and administer a system in which each individual user has an account. This also permits each user to personalize his or her work environment because all applications will save user preferences to the user's home directory.

> **Note**
>
> It is good system practice to have a separate account for each individual user. Avoid accounts that are shared, if possible.

VIRTUAL CONSOLES

By default, six virtual consoles (often called *virtual terminals*, *VTs*) are available. Each virtual console is accessed via the function keys at the console keyboard. After the system boots, the login prompt that is presented is on console one. Five additional consoles—that is, login prompts—are available by pressing the Alt key in conjunction with function keys F2–F5. Table 11.1 describes the virtual console configuration.

TABLE 11.1 VIRTUAL CONSOLE CONFIGURATION

Key Sequence	Description
Alt+F1	First Virtual Console (Default)
Alt+F2	Second Virtual Console

PART

III

CH

11

TABLE 11.1 CONTINUED	
Key Sequence	**Description**
Alt+F3	Third Virtual Console
Alt+F4	Fourth Virtual Console
Alt+F5	Fifth Virtual Console
Alt+F6	Sixth Virtual Console

Toggling from one console screen to another is just a matter of pressing the Alt key and the desired function key.

Note

If you are working in X Windows (including KDE) and want to go to one of the VCs, you'll need to use the key sequence Ctrl+Alt+F[1–6]. In Caldera and Red Hat, the default is to boot into a graphical environment. Debian allows you to choose between console or graphical startup during installation. Use Alt+F7 or Alt+F8 to return to X (varies depending on the first free VC encountered at X startup).

Wherever any kind of login exists, be it on a VC, a graphical screen, or a serial connection, this login is put there by init. For more details on how this works, see Chapter 13, "System Initialization."

SERIAL CONNECTIONS

Login sessions are also available via a serial port. For example, dumb terminals can be connected via an RS-232 interface. This can be one or two serial ports (COM1 and COM2 in DOS) typically found on PC systems or via an add-on multiport card. Many multiport cards are supported in Linux, including Cyclades, Digiboard, and Stallion. Modifying the /etc/inittab file with the appropriate entries allows logins via any available serial connection.

NETWORK LOGINS

A very common method of logging in to a Linux server is through a network connection. In fact, a Linux server functions quite nicely as a standalone, monitorless box for specific services. For example, it is quite common to find a Domain Name Server (DNS) running on an appliance-like, Linux-based machine. Servers like this, without a monitor and keyboard (called *headless systems*), need only an occasional check via a remote login session. The most common way of connecting to a Linux server using a network link is with the telnet utility. A network connection can also be made with utilities such as rlogin, slogin, or openssh.

ACCOUNT SETUP

Adding and deleting users is simple, but understanding the files involved with user account management is a bit more complex. Many utilities have been written to manage the data files associated with user accounts, including the default useradd utility, but the key to managing user accounts is to understand the underlying configuration files.

KEY CONFIGURATION FILE

The key file used in user account setup and configuration is the /etc/passwd file. This file is a simple ASCII text file, but it's crucial to the multiuser concept of Linux. Upon a successful installation, the contents of the /etc/passwd file resemble the following:

```
root:x:0:0:root:/root:/bin/bash
bin:x:1:1:bin:/bin:
daemon:x:2:2:daemon:/sbin:
adm:x:3:4:adm:/var/adm:
lp:x:4:7:lp:/var/spool/lpd:
sync:x:5:0:sync:/sbin:/bin/sync
shutdown:x:6:11:shutdown:/sbin:/sbin/shutdown
halt:x:7:0:halt:/sbin:/sbin/halt
mail:x:8:12:mail:/var/spool/mail:
news:x:9:13:news:/var/spool/news:
uucp:x:10:14:uucp:/var/spool/uucp:
operator:x:11:0:operator:/root:
games:x:12:100:games:/usr/games:
gopher:x:13:30:gopher:/usr/lib/gopher-data:
ftp:x:14:50:FTP User:/home/ftp:
man:x:15:15:Manuals Owner:/:
majordom:x:16:16:Majordomo:/:/bin/false
postgres:x:17:17:Postgres User:/home/postgres:/bin/bash
nobody:x:65534:65534:Nobody:/:/bin/false
col:x:100:100:COL User:/home/col:/bin/bash
natalie:x:101:100:OpenLinux User:/home/natalie:/bin/bash
ryan:x:102:100:OpenLinux User:/home/ryan:/bin/bash
brittany:x:103:100:OpenLinux User:/home/brittany:/bin/bash
kelsey:x:104:100:OpenLinux User:/home/kelsey:/bin/bash
```

Each line represents one user. The information for each user is separated into seven colon-delimited fields. The description of each of these fields is listed in Table 11.2.

PART

III

CH

11

TABLE 11.2   FIELD DESCRIPTIONS OF THE /etc/passwd FILE

Field	Description
1	The first field is the username or login ID. This must be unique.
2	The second field is the password field. A lowercase x in this field indicates that shadow passwords are in use. The actual encrypted passwords are stored in a separate file for security reasons.
3	The number in this field is the User ID number. This is used to identify a unique user account. This number should be unique.
4	This field is the Group ID (GID) field number. This number is used to create logical user groups. The one listed is the login group, but users can belong to more than one group.
5	This field is a comment field. It commonly contains the user's full name. Its original (and sometimes still used) name is GECOS (GE Consolidated Operating System) field.
6	The sixth field is used to identify where in the file system hierarchy a user is to be placed upon logging in to the system. User accounts are typically configured to use the /home directory.
7	This field is used for the configuration of the default shell. The default shell is the bash shell.

New user accounts can be added by directly editing the /etc/passwd file, but passwords must be created using the /usr/bin/passwd utility. This utility is required because it creates the proper encryption.

PASSWORDS

Access to any account is controlled with a password. Shadow passwords are used by default with most Linux distributions.

> **Note**
>
> Shadow passwords are passwords that are stored in a separate file. This file, the /etc/ shadow file, adds an additional level of security.

Before the advent of shadow passwords, the password—albeit encrypted—was stored in the /etc/passwd file. The /etc/passwd file is readable by any user on the system, but it can only be modified by the root user. It has to be readable by all users for certain applications. However, this presents a problem because it means that anyone can see the encrypted (hashed) password. With the powerful machines of today, it has become easier to crack the encryption of even well-chosen passwords. To combat this potential threat, the concept of shadow passwords was defined. By storing the password in a separate file, the /etc/shadow file, it became possible to keep the /etc/passwd file readable to all accounts but make the encrypted passwords themselves only readable to the root user. You'll take a closer look at this in the "Permissions" section later in this chapter.

> **Caution**
>
> Use the pwconv and pwunconv utilities to convert the /etc/passwd file to or from shadow enabling.

The /etc/shadow password file looks similar to the following:

```
root:Rb3mAtGdwFMDE:10568:0:-1:7:7:-1:1073897392
bin:*:10542:0::7:7::
daemon:*:10542:0::7:7::
adm:*:10542:0::7:7::
lp:*:10542:0::7:7::
sync:*:10542:0::7:7::
shutdown:*:10542:0::7:7::
halt:*:10542:0::7:7::
mail:*:10542:0::7:7::
news:*:10542:0::7:7::
uucp:*:10542:0::7:7::
operator:*:10542:0::7:7::
games:*:10542:0::7:7::
gopher:*:10542:0::7:7::
ftp:*:10542:0::7:7::
man:*:10542:0::7:7::
majordom:*:10542:0::7:7::
postgres:*:10542:0::7:7::
nobody:*:10542:0::7:7::
```

```
col:pbHeht8NUW842:10573:0:-1:7:7:-1:1073897392
natalie:jEFpY1Zqm18E.:10576:0:-1:9:-1:-1:1073897392
ryan:hBcIkjWnhFk/o:10576:0:-1:7:-1:-1:1073897392
brittany:oCtbTK7DjDye2:10576:0:-1:9:-1:-1:1073897392
kelsey:dDJLXtAbiJVaM:10576:0:-1:7:-1:-1:1073897392
```

Much like the /etc/passwd file, the /etc/shadow file consists of single-line entries with colon-delimited fields. Some of these fields will contain seemingly bizarre numbers, too large to be correct. These fields have as their reference the "computing age epoch" date of Jan 1, 1970.

Field	Description
1	User account name
2	Encrypted password field
3	Days elapsed since beginning of the epoch that password was last changed
4	Number of days that must elapse before password can be changed again
5	Number of days after which password must be changed (-1 means never)
6	Days before password expiration that user will receive warning when logging in
7	Days after password expires that the account is disabled if the password is not successfully changed
8	Days elapsed since epoch on which account will be disabled (regardless of password changes)
9	A reserved field

You'll use change, the change-aging utility, to change these values from the defaults, which are found in /etc/login.defs (see the following text).

MD5 Hashed Passwords

Most distributions are also offering the use of an MD5 hash rather than the older DES hash. This text will not delve into the details of the MD5 hash other than to mention that it allows longer passwords than the DES encryption. Longer passwords only mean that the theoretical time to break the password is lengthened, but this only applies to good passwords. Bad passwords (those based on dictionary words or other common data) will be broken just as fast as they are with DES.

Part

III

Ch

11

> **Caution**
>
> If you are using NIS, you cannot use MD5. As of this writing, NIS cannot understand MD5 hashed passwords. This also applies to mixing systems using restricted services that use different password schemes. Ensure all your network programs work with MD5-hashed passwords before moving to them.

ADDING USERS

User accounts can be added by directly editing the /etc/passwd file or by using a utility such as useradd, available in all Linux distributions. Default characteristics for each user account are defined by the settings in the /etc/login.defs file, as follows:

```
###
# Password aging controls: (used by useradd and pwconv)
#
# Maximum number of days a password may be used:
# (-1 = no password changes are necessary)
PASS_MAX_DAYS -1

# Minimum number of days allowed between password
# changes:
PASS_MIN_DAYS 0

# Number of days warning given before a password expires:
PASS_WARN_AGE 7

# Number of days till account is closed after password
# has expired:
PASS_INACTIVE -1

# Force expiry at given day: (in days after 70/1/1,
# -1 = don't force)
PASS_EXPIRE -1

###
# Default values for useradd
#

# default group:
GROUP 100

# user«s home directory: (%s = name of user)
HOME /home/%s

# default user shell:
SHELL /bin/bash

# directory where the home directory skeleton is located:
SKEL /etc/skel

###
# Min/max values for automatic gid selection in groupadd
#
GID_MIN 100
GID_MAX 60000
```

The useradd utility does not create the /home directory of the new user by default, but given the correct parameter, the home directory is created. For example, using useradd to create an account for someone named natalie, with the following parameters, creates the /etc/passwd and /etc/shadow entries and the /home directory:

```
# useradd -m /home/natalie natalie
```

A new directory, /home/natalie, is created and populated with copies of the default files in the /etc/skel and /etc/skel.d directories (in that order). The /etc/skel directory contains the following files:

```
.bash_logout
.bashrc
.cshrc
.emacs
.gnupg/
.inputrc
.kshrc
.login
.logout
.profile
.profile.ksh
.tcshrc
Desktop/

.gnupg:
./
../
options

Desktop:
./
../
OpenStore.kdelnk
Register Now!.kdelnk
```

The /etc/skel.d directory contains the following:

```
.config
bash/
common/
csh/
sh/
tcsh/

bash:
.bash_logout
.bashrc

common:
.inputrc

csh:
.cshrc
.login
.logout

sh:
.profile

tcsh:
.tcshrc
```

Some files in the /etc/skel.d/ are duplicates of files found in /etc/skel/. In this case, the files in /etc/skel.d/ will overwrite those copied from /etc/skel.

Running useradd with the -D option displays the default characteristics of user accounts:

```
# useradd -D
GROUP=100
HOME=/home/%s
SHELL=/bin/bash
SKEL=/etc/skel
PASS_MIN_DAYS=0
PASS_MAX_DAYS=-1
PASS_WARN_DAYS=7
PASS_INACTIVE=-1
PASS_EXPIRE=-1
```

These are the parameters that you saw previously, as defined in the /etc/login.defs file. They can be easily changed by merely modifying the entries in the /etc/login.defs file.

DELETING OR DISABLING USERS

A user account can be disabled by simply modifying the entry for a given user in the /etc/passwd file. For example, you can disable the account for the user natalie by changing the password field as follows:

```
natalie:x123:100:100:OpenLinux User:/home/natalie:/bin/bash
```

When anything is added after the x (in this case 123), the shadow utilities will no longer look at the /etc/shadow file for the password, but will try to use this field in the password file as the password. Because nothing will ever encrypt to match this password, the account cannot be used. Changing the field back to the lone x again will enable access.

Completely removing the entry from the /etc/passwd file disables the user account as well, but it's a bit more difficult to restore the account if the need presents itself.

Note
Disabling or deleting a user account does not remove any data in the user's home directory. If you want to remove the contents of the /home/directory, you must specifically use the rm command.

If you want to prevent natalie from logging in locally but not from picking up mail from the system, you can change natalie's shell to /bin/false. You'll have to ensure that /bin/false is listed in /etc/shells.

Caution
If a user account is deleted and any files from that user remain on the system, then a new user added with the deleted user's UID will have complete access to the deleted user's files (a security risk with privacy implications). Ensure all traces of a deleted user have been removed from the system before reusing that UID. Running the following command

```
find / -nouser -exec rm -Rf {} \;
```

will remove all files and directories not owned by anyone in /etc/passwd. (Read the find man page for details.)

GROUPS

The purpose of a *Group Identifier* (*GID*) is to logically group resources or files to members of a given group. For example, source code files might need to be shared between users in the engineering department. By creating an engineering group and adding the appropriate members to this group, the files can be shared among the members of the engineering department, but secure from others accessing files that they can't see. It is the same with other departments or groups: files can be shared in the accounting, sales, or service departments without the risk of unauthorized users accessing the data.

CREATING A GROUP

Groups are created by adding an entry to the /etc/group file. A default listing of this file is as follows:

```
root::0:
wheel::10:
bin::1:bin,daemon
daemon::2:bin,daemon
sys::3:bin,adm
adm::4:adm,daemon
tty::5:
disk::6:
lp::7:daemon,lp
mem::8:
kmem::9:
operator::11:
mail::12:mail
news::13:news
uucp::14:uucp
man::15:
majordom::16:
database::17:
games::20:
gopher::30:
dip::40:
ftp::50:
users::100:
nobody::65534:
```

Each line of the /etc/group file indicates one group. You'll notice that many of the predefined groups correspond directly to a specific service. For example, the lp group is for printer services. A description of the format of the /etc/group file is listed in Table 11.3.

TABLE 11.3   FIELD DESCRIPTIONS OF THE /etc/group FILE

Field	Description
1	The first field is the name of the group. For example, this might be eng for the engineering group or acct for the accounting group.
2	This is the password for the group. It is typically not used, but it can be set.

TABLE 11.3	CONTINUED
Field	**Description**
3	This is the Group ID (GID) number. User accounts that are default members of this group have this number in their /etc/passwd entry.
4	The last field is the list of user accounts associated with this group.

Each user account must belong to at least one group. The default group in OpenLinux is users. The associated group identification number (GID) is 100. Other distributions will vary.

Note

Inclusion in the default group occurs by the group ID number (GID) being present in the /etc/passwd entry for each user. The user account names do not have to be present in the /etc/group file to be included in the default group.

ADDING USER ACCOUNTS TO A GROUP

There is no limit to the number of groups to which a user can belong. However, inclusion in groups beyond the initial default group is only accomplished by adding the user account name to the list of user account names in the /etc/group file. A user account can be added to a specific group by simply adding their username to the last field of the group entry in the /etc/group file. After the user account is added, access to shared files in that group is granted. An entry in the /etc/group file with several members (user accounts) is similar to the following:

```
eng::100:kelsey, brittany, ryan, natalie
```

All of the user accounts listed in the last field of the preceding example are members of the eng group.

The groupadd command can be used to add new groups to the /etc/group file. The general syntax is straightforward:

```
groupadd -g GID groupname
```

The -g GID parameter assigns the group ID to the new group. For instance, the following command creates a new group called eng and assigns it group ID 201:

```
groupadd -g 201 eng
```

REMOVING USER ACCOUNTS FROM A GROUP

Removing a user from a specific group is accomplished by removing the username from the list in the /etc/group file. Doing this does not remove data or change permissions—it only excludes a specific user account from accessing files that are inclusive to a specific group.

OTHER UTILITIES

To obtain a listing of all the groups to which you are assigned, use the groups command: To obtain a listing on yourself, simply execute groups with no parameters; to obtain a listing on someone else, execute groups with a user's name as a parameter.

The shadow password suite that comes with Linux includes a useful utility called gpasswd. This utility helps to manage the /etc/group and /etc/gshadow files.

The syntax for adding a user to a group is as follows:

```
gpasswd -a username group
```

To remove a user from a group, the following syntax is used:

```
gpasswd -d username group
```

> **Caution**
>
> In general, adding passwords to groups is a bad idea from a security standpoint. Group passwords are not closely guarded secrets because groups of people know them. If a group has a password, anyone who knows the password can use the newgrp command to become part of the group. As long as the group does not have a password, only those listed as members in the /etc/group file belong; no one else can join.

PERMISSIONS

There are three levels of permissions to files and directories in Linux. These levels correspond to the following three categories:

- User (the owner)
- Group
- Other

Each level, or category, has associated privileges. These privileges come in the form of three permissions: read permissions, write permissions, and execute permissions.

All three levels—Owner, Group, and Other—have read, write, and execute permissions.

In order for the set of permissions for the owner and group to work, the file must have an indicator as to who is the owner and to which group the file belongs. Each file or directory has an *owner property* (sometimes referred to as the *user property*) and a *group property*. The owner, or user, property is set to the user account name of the person who owns the file. The group property works in a similar fashion: The group property contains the group name to which the file belongs. Examining the following long listing of the /etc/passwd file makes more sense of this:

```
#ls -l /etc/passwd
-rw-r--r--  1  root  root    695  Dec 7 12:48 passwd
```

Here's a closer look at what this information means. The key elements are depicted in Figure 11.1. In the listing of the /etc/passwd file, you can see that the owner is root, and that the group is set to root as well. This can be a little confusing because the owner and the group are set to the same value. This happens often with system files. Just remember that the owner setting corresponds to the /etc/passwd file and the group setting corresponds to the /etc/group file.

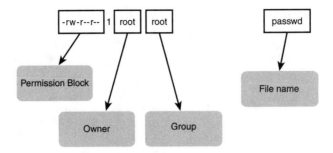

Figure 11.1
The specific characteristics of the /etc/passwd file are shown here.

The first set of dashes and letters represent the file type and permissions for this file. They are broken down into four logical groups. The first character indicates the file type. The file type will be one of the following::

Character	File Type
-	Regular file (usually either a binary or ASCII text file)
d	Directory
l	Symbolic link
c	Character device (character special file)
b	Block device (block special file)
s	Socket (a network listener)
p	Named pipe (like a pipe (|), but with a name)

Some of these will probably be foreign to you. The ones you're most concerned with are the first three (-, d, l).

The next nine placeholders represent the permissions of each of the three levels: owner, group, and other. Each level uses three places to set permissions. For example, if you want to allow read, write, and execute privileges to the owner of a file, the letters *rwx* are present in positions 2–4. Figure 11.2 depicts the permission options for owner, group, and others.

CHANGING PERMISSIONS

The access rights for any given file can be modified by using the change mode (chmod) command. To change the access rights, you must specify the following three elements:

- The level (owner level, group level, or other level) to modify
- The permission (read, write, or execute) to modify
- The file or files to modify

Table 11.4 lists the level options that can be used with the chmod command. The access rights or permissions that can be modified at each level are summarized in Table 11.5.

Figure 11.2
Detailed description
of file permissions.

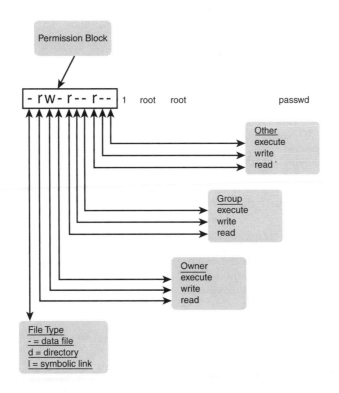

TABLE 11.4   OPTIONS WITH chmod COMMAND

Option	Level	Description
u	Owner	Owner of a file
g	Group	Group to which the user belongs
o	Other	All other users
a	All	Can replace u, g, or o

TABLE 11.5   PERMISSIONS WITH chmod COMMAND

Permission	Description
r	Sets read permission
x	Sets execute permission on files. On directories, permits users to cd into the directory.
w	Sets write permission
s	Sets group or user ID to the owner of the file while the file is being executed; on directories, specifies that the directory owner or group will be the owner or group of the file rather than the user creating the file.
t	The sticky bit. Used only with other to set a directory bit. When set, only the owner of a file can delete the file—commonly used on the /tmp directory.

The level and permission to modify are combined with a plus sign (+) or minus sign (-) to enable or disable a bit. Multiple levels and permissions can be listed as a comma-separated group.

For example, adding write privileges for the group can be done by running chmod as follows:

```
# chmod g+w /etc/passwd
```

Examining the permissions of the /etc/passwd file after the modifications shows the following::

```
# ls -l /etc/passwd
-rw-rw-r-- 1 root root     695  Dec 7 12:48 passwd
```

If the permissions to the /etc/passwd file are set for read, write, and execute for everyone (owner, group, and other), the file looks like the following:

```
#ls -l /etc/passwd
-rwxrwxrwx 1 root root     695  Dec 7 12:48 passwd
```

To remove the write bit from the group, you could use the following:

```
chmod g-w /etc/passwd
```

To ensure the /etc/shadow file cannot be read by the group or others, you could issue one of the following commands:

```
chmod g-r,o-r /etc/shadow
```

```
chmod go-r /etc/shadow
```

The following are the three symbols you can use between the level and permissions:

- **+** Add the following permissions (does not affect other permissions)
- **-** Remove the following permissions (does not affect other permissions)
- **=** Make these the only permissions (affects all permissions for the file)

The chmod utility can also use numbers to change a file's mode. The numbers range from 0–7 (octal) in a set of four (except that a zero in the first position can be omitted). In the final three positions, the numbers stand for owner, group, and others:

Level	Permissions
0	No privileges
1	Execute
2	Write
3	Write and execute
4	Read
5	Read and execute
6	Read and write
7	Read, write, and execute

An alternate way to visualize this would be the following:

```
        r w x      r - x      - - x
    =   4+2+1      4+0+1      0+0+1
    =     7          5          1
        "chmod 751 <filename>"
```

Numbers in the first position (when using all four numbers) indicate the following::

Value	Significance
0	No special permissions (default)
1	Set the sticky bit (t)
2	Group suid bit (s)
3	Group suid bit and sticky bit
4	Owner suid bit
5	Owner suid bit and sticky bit
6	Owner and group suid bits
7	Owner and group suid bits and sticky bit

If you want to make a file read, write, and execute for the owner; read and execute for the group; and execute only for all others, the command would look like the following:

```
chmod 751 <filename>
```

If you want the preceding file to execute as the group ID <sgid> of the owning group, the command would be as follows:

```
chmod 2751 <filename>
```

Note

A user, in his/her own home directory, has some special privileges. If a file is owned by root, and only root has read/write permissions on that file, that user can read, write, and delete that file in his own home directory. He cannot, however, change ownership or permissions on that file.

SUID/SGID AND THE STICKY BIT

You've seen how to set the SUID, SGID, and Sticky bit. What exactly is it? With an executable file, setting the owner SUID (set UID) bit forces the binary (which will not work with script or nonbinary files) to run as the user shown as the owner. Normally, SUID binaries are owned by root, so anyone who can execute the program is executing it as root. When a program is SUID or SGID, an "s" replaces the "x" corresponding to the user or group execute bit. This is dangerous, but necessary for some programs. For example, an ordinary user cannot read or write to /etc/shadow. For this ordinary (non-privileged) user to be able to change his password, the passwd executable must be SUID root. The SGID (set GID, or group ID) bit works the same way.

PART

III

CH

11

When the SUID or SGID bits are applied to directories, files that are saved within those directories take on the owner or group of the directory rather than belonging to the user that created the file (the usual case).

The sticky bit, shown as a "t" in place of the execute bit for "others," is normally used on directories such as the /tmp directory. This particular attribute permits only the file owner to delete the file. Others can read it, but only the owner can delete it.

CHANGING USER OR GROUP OWNERSHIP

As you learned earlier in this chapter, the key to the concept of permissions is the fact that a file has both an owner indicator and a group indicator. The chown utility changes the owner indicator, and the group indicator is changed by the chgrp utility. Only the superuser can change the ownership of a file.

> **Caution**
>
> Never change the owner indicator or the group indicator of any system file such as the /etc/passwd file. Only data files to be shared as part of a logical group are to be modified in this way. Modifying system files might render certain services unusable.

The owner indicator of a file can be modified as follows:

```
# chown natalie /tmp/testfile
# ls -l
-rwxr--r--  1 natalie     users         11 Dec 26 04:14 testfile
```

The group indicator of a file can be modified as follows:

```
# chgrp eng /tmp/testfile
# ls -l
-rwxr--r--  1 natalie     eng           11 Dec 26 04:14 testfile
```

> **Tip**
>
> The chown command can be used to modify both the owner indicator and the group indicator by specifying both and separating them with a period or a colon:
> chown natalie.eng testfile.

OTHER PERMISSIONS

Some other file permissions exist that you should be aware of. These permissions are specific to the ext2 filesystem rather than the file itself. These permissions, when set, mean the following:

Level	Permissions
A	atime modification disabled
a	Append only
c	Compressed
d	Dump disabled
i	Immutable (file cannot be changed or deleted)

Level	Permissions
s	Secure deletion set
S	Synchronous updates
u	Undelete set (file saved for possible undeletion)

Note

The c and u are currently not honored and are not expected to be honored in the future. (A new journaling filesystem has higher priority.)

These attributes can be set and unset using the chattr (change attributes) program and can be checked using the lsattr (list attributes) program.

One attribute not mentioned here is the versioning attribute. With this attribute, you can put a version number on a file. All files are created as version 1. Caldera OpenLinux, during installation, marks all files on the filesystem with a unique versioning number. Only files installed by or on the system when LIZARD finishes will have a unique version number. Most other distributions do not change this attribute.

Caution

The versioning number should not be used as an indication of a security breach. Although it can provide you a good positive indication a file has been replaced if you suddenly see a version 1 in place of a version 418900262, for example, it can also provide you a false negative. If a file is copied onto an existing file, the version number will not change. Also, an intruder can note the version number and replace it.

PART

III

CH

11

Use the chattr -v <version#> filename to write a version number or lsattr -v to read a version number. These version numbers are independent of the software. You determine the number on the file.

TROUBLESHOOTING

I want to change the password aging for one user, but not the defaults as shown earlier in the chapter. How can I do this?

Use the change (change-aging) program. The change man page provides the information you need.

I tried to use COAS to add a new user, but the program said the passwd file was locked.

If COAS exits abnormally while you are adding users, it will not properly clean up after itself. You need to remove the following files in /etc: pwtmp, passwd-, and shadow-. You should not have any further problems.

I have a shell script I want to let other people run. I set the execute bit on the file with chmod 711, but they can't run it.

Binary files can be made execute-only and will run. For shell scripts to run, both the read and execute bits must be set, so you'll need to chmod 755 the file.

When I try to execute a file, I get permission denied. *It's a shell script, and I can read the file, so why can't I execute it?*

The shell script you're trying to run probably does not have the execute bit set for you. If you own the file, you must set the owner execute bit (chmod u+x). If you are in the group, you must set the group execute bit (chmod g+s). Otherwise, you must set the world execute bit (chmod o+x). If this still doesn't fix your problem, your filesystem is not mounted exec—see next question.

I have a CD-ROM with a file install.sh. *The CD-ROM is mounted, but I can't execute the file with* ./install.sh. *I get an error message:* permission denied. *I can read the file okay, and the file has the execute bit set. What's wrong?*

In /etc/fstab, you have the mount line with user in it, but you don't have exec after the user listing (it must follow user). If you can't change this line and remount the CD-ROM, run the file this way: sh ./install.sh.

As root, I try to delete a file, but I can't. Instead, I get an error message.

More than likely, either the ext2 immutable bit or the append bit has been set on this file. Try chattr -ia <filename>, which will turn off the immutable and append bits. You should then be able to delete the file.

CHAPTER **12**

BOOT LOADERS

In this chapter

WHAT IS LILO?

LILO is a general-purpose boot loader package used on most modern Linux systems. With it, you can specify any number of installed operating systems to boot. You can also pass behavior-altering parameters to the Linux kernel. When you first start a system with LILO installed, you can enter such parameters or options and specify an operating system to load. You also can specify different partitions from which you want to boot your system.

The term *LILO* is derived from the first two letters of the words Linux Loader (LInux LOader).

LILO, in simple terms, is a boot loader program. In reality, it's a collection of several programs and files. The two primary programs are the map installer and the boot. The map installer is the Linux program that places the necessary files in the proper location and records the location in a map file. This map file is then used at boot time to determine where to find the operating system. The map installer is located in the /sbin directory and is named lilo; therefore, it is often referred to as running /sbin/lilo, or just running lilo.

The boot loader program is the program, installed by the map installer that facilitates the loading of the operating system. It is run when the BIOS initiates it.

The boot loader is executed at an interim stage when the system BIOS is determining how to pass control to the operating system.

LILO is configured and installed as part of the initial installation of most Linux distributions. However, LILO, like every other component of Linux, is packaged in RPM or .deb format. The files included in the LILO RPM/.deb are described in Table 12.1.

TABLE 12.1   THE LILO RPM FILES

Files	Description
/boot/boot.b	Installed as the default boot sector.
/boot/chain.b	Used to boot a non-Linux operating system.
/boot/os2_d.b	Used to boot an OS/2 system.
/sbin/activate	Used to change the active flag of a given partition.
/sbin/lilo	The map installer program. It installs the boot loader to the place designated in the /etc/lilo.conf file.
/usr/doc/lilo-0.20/COPYING	Contains the copying policy for LILO.

Of the several files that LILO uses, the /etc/lilo.conf file is the most crucial file to maintain. The other files are, for the most part, self-maintaining.

Extensive documentation for LILO is included on the CD in one of three RPMs: `_lilo-doc-0.21-7.i386.rpm`, `lilo-doc-dvi-0.21-7.i386.rpm`, or `lilo-doc-ps-0.21-7.i386.rpm`. The only difference is the format of the documentation. The first is plain text, the second is in `dvi` format, and the last contains the documentation in `postscript` format. Werner Almesberger is the author of LILO as well as the included documentation.

> **Note**
>
> The version number of your LILO documentation RPM might be different from that referenced here. Use `rpm -qa | grep lilo` to see what you have installed.

Operating systems have now evolved to the point where much of what they do is transparent to the user. However, transparent as the boot process is today, the boot strapping process still involves the same kind of steps that were required in the early days of computer development. The manual steps of flipping switches to boot a computer of yesterday have been replaced with the automated method of using the system BIOS and a boot loader to complete the boot process. To understand what LILO is and how it works, it is important to first know and understand what the CMOS and BIOS of a PC is, and how the boot sequence works.

BOOT STAGES

All x86-type computers boot in a similar manner. When a system is powered on, a chain of events that is referred to as *booting the computer* takes place. The term comes from an old saying, "to pull yourself up by your bootstraps." After receiving power initially, most (but not all) computers receive a "power good" signal from the power supply. The system then begins a self-check process known as the *POST* (power on self-test). This test looks for any system problems that might make the computer nonfunctional, such as bad memory. An acceptable POST normally terminates in one "beep" from the built-in speaker. Two or more (and usually a maximum of eight) beeps indicate a specific problem and give an indication of where to look for the problem. It is at this point that the boot process actually begins.

The first stage of the boot process then begins with the loading of a program called the *basic input/output system* (BIOS). This program uses settings that reside in the *Complementary Metal Oxide Semiconductor* (CMOS) to determine how to initialize hardware components and complete the first stage of the boot process. The system BIOS and the CMOS are included as part of your PC hardware.

The next stage of the boot process is begun as the BIOS passes control to the operating system. In essence, the BIOS is an operating system, but, as its name describes, it is only a very basic one. The CMOS contains several parameters based on the system hardware components and desired preferences, including a setting for the desired boot sequence. For example, a typical CMOS setting for the boot sequence might be A, C (usually configurable in the System Setup, accessible immediately following the POST). This means that the BIOS first tries to pass control to the boot sector of the floppy drive (A:); if no boot sector is found there, it then tries to locate a valid boot sector on the hard drive (C:). In simple terms, the boot sequence on a PC is as follows (see Figure 12.1):

Figure 12.1
BIOS boot sequence.

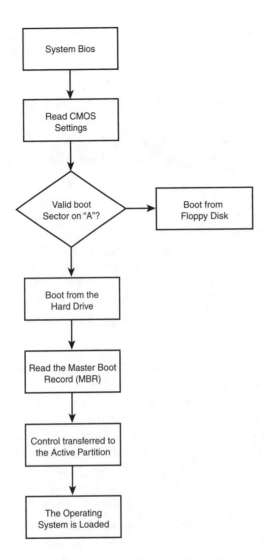

1. The power is turned on.
2. The power-good signal triggers POST.
3. The system BIOS loads.
4. The BIOS, based on CMOS settings, determines where to look for a valid boot sector.
5. Control is passed to the master boot record (MBR).
6. The MBR passes control to the boot sector of the active partition.
7. The boot sector loads the operating system.

Each step of the boot sequence initializes a minimal set of devices and builds on the previous step.

How Does LILO Work?

LILO acts as an interim agent between the system BIOS and the operating system. It is a customizable program that enables the system BIOS to pass control to the Linux kernel. It is also quite good at managing the boot processes of operating systems other than Linux. After control is passed to the boot loader program, it begins a sequence of steps to determine where to find the operating system.

LILO does not depend on any specific filesystem. It uses a map file that contains information about the physical location of a given boot sector. This map file is normally stored as /boot/map. It is rebuilt each time you run the map installer.

> **Note** LILO can be configured to boot up to 16 different images or operating systems.

After LILO is installed, the boot loader portion must be capable of accessing certain areas of the system in order to work properly. These areas are listed in Table 12.2.

TABLE 12.2   System Areas Accessed by LILO

System Area	Description
The root file	The data files LILO needs to complete a successful boot are typically located in the /boot directory.
The boot sector	The boot sector contains the first part of the LILO boot loader. It, in turn, loads the second-stage loader. Both parts of the loader are typically stored in the file /boot/boot.b.
The kernel	The kernel is located and initiated by the second-stage loader. The default kernel is /boot/vmlinuz-pc97-{kernel-version}-modular.

LILO is not designed to know how to work with a given filesystem such as the second extended filesystem (ext2). Rather, it uses the physical location (cylinders, heads, and sectors) of the required files to know how to proceed. This enables LILO to work with most of the filesystems supported by Linux.

Disk Organization

To get a better picture of how this process works, it's helpful to understand the basic organization of a disk. The simplest case is that of the floppy disk. It is basically divided into two sections—the boot sector and the data area. The boot sector itself is 512 bytes and is divided into several parts. A DOS boot sector is depicted in Figure 12.2.

LILO uses a similar boot sector, but it does not contain the disk parameters.

Figure 12.2
DOS boot sector.

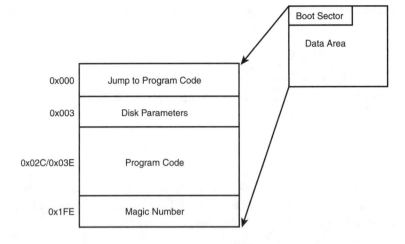

0x000	Jump to Program Code
0x003	Disk Parameters
0x02C/0x03E	Program Code
0x1FE	Magic Number

Boot Sector

Data Area

Caution

Installing LILO to the boot sector of a DOS filesystem makes the DOS data files inaccessible. This is because disk parameters are stored as part of a DOS boot sector, and a LILO boot sector does not contain disk parameters. Without the disk parameters, a DOS filesystem becomes inaccessible.

The disk organization of a hard disk differs from that of a floppy because of partitioning. Figure 12.3 shows how a typical hard disk might look if partitioned using primary and extended partitions. Because of BIOS limitations, a hard disk can be divided only into four primary partitions. If more than four partitions are required, extended partitions must be used. The partition information for a given disk is contained in the partition boot sector. The partition boot sector is commonly called the *master boot record (MBR)*.

Figure 12.3
Typical partitioned
hard disk.

Master Boot Record (MBR)-Partition Boot Sector
Partition 1 - Primary
Partition 2 - Primary
Extended Partition
Partition 3 - Extended
Partition 4 - Extended

The MBR or partition boot sector is structured as outlined in Table 12.3.

TABLE 12.3   MASTER BOOT RECORD STRUCTURE

Location	Description
0x000	Program code
0x1BE	Partition table
0x1FE	Magic number

LILO LOCATIONS

The LILO boot sector can be stored in the following locations:

- The boot sector of a floppy disk
- The MBR of the first hard disk
- The boot sector of a Linux filesystem on a primary partition on the first hard disk (recommended location)
- The boot sector of an extended partition on the first hard drive

Although many possibilities for how you can configure LILO exist, and though it often depends on your hardware, the third option is the recommended location for LILO. Installing LILO in the boot sector of the primary Linux filesystem partition on the first hard drive enables you to keep the MBR at the factory default setting.

Note   A common misconception is that you must install LILO to the MBR in order to boot LINUX or to enable the system to boot multiple operating systems.

PART

III

CH

12

BOOTING BASICS

With LILO installed to one of the four possible locations, your Linux system is ready to be recognized. As a point of reference, it might be helpful to compare the booting sequence for Linux with that of a traditional DOS system. A DOS boot sequence is depicted in Table 12.4.

TABLE 12.4   DOS BOOT SEQUENCE

Master Boot Record	Boot Sector Type	Operating System
DOS-MBR	DOS	io.sys->msdos.sys->COMMAND.COM

Probably the most common method of configuring LILO is to place the boot loader in the boot sector, sometimes referred to as the *superblock*. Such a configuration is depicted in Table 12.5.

TABLE 12.5   LINUX BOOT SEQUENCE

Master Boot Record	Boot Sector	Operating System
DOS-MBR	LILO (boot loader)	Linux kernel (`vmlinuz`)

NOTE: *In order for the MBR to pass control to LILO, the partition on which the Linux root filesystem resides must be marked as active.*

LILO depends on the BIOS of the PC to load the following items:

- `/boot/boot.b`
- `/boot/map`
- `/boot/`(kernel)
- boot sectors of all other boot images
- startup message

Because of limitations in mapping methods of the system BIOS, large IDE drives typically require something such as *logical block addressing* (LBA) mode. This is a means of mapping a large drive with many physical cylinders to a logical set of fewer than 1023 cylinders.

Note

The system BIOS cannot access cylinders beyond 1024. This is because of an addressing limitation of the original algorithm used to manage access to hard drives. A newer algorithm, sometimes referred to as *enhanced-BIOS* uses uses logical block addressing to overcome this limitation. Both LILO and GRUB overcome this limitation, LILO capable of accessing a kernel image as far out as the last cylinder on a 2 terabyte filesystem.

A map is built based on where the Linux kernel resides. LILO uses this to determine where the kernel is located on the physical disk. You might have to use the linear option (see below) with larger disk drives if LILO doesn't install successfully otherwise.

The LILO boot loader program consists of several stages, including the primary loader and secondary loader.

As each phase of the LILO boot process completes, a letter in the word *LILO* is displayed on the screen until the LILO boot process completes. If the boot loader fails, the last letter of the word LILO can be used to debug what might have caused the problem. This is covered in detail later in this chapter in the section "Troubleshooting."

As the LILO boot loader program runs, it displays data contained in the `/boot/message` file as a boot banner. Although this file is normally a simple text file and can be edited, the OpenLinux message file has embedded control characters for block characters making changes to that file a little more difficult.

BASIC CONFIGURATION

A simple installation of LILO requires the configuration of the basic pieces of the /etc/lilo.conf file and running the map installer. A sample configuration of the /etc/lilo.conf file is shown here:

```
# /etc/lilo.conf - generated by Lizard
#

# target

boot = /dev/hda1
install = /boot/boot.b

# options

prompt
delay = 50
timeout = 50
message = /boot/message

default = linux

image = /boot/vmlinuz-pc97-2.2.14-modular
        label  = linux
        root   = /dev/hda1
        vga    = 274
        read-only
        append = "debug=2 noapic nosmp"
```

The lilo.conf file is quite simple. As is typical with most configuration files, lines beginning with a hash mark (#) are comment lines. The lilo.conf configuration file consists of three primary sections: the general section (sometimes referred to as the *global* section), the Linux image section, and the section for non-Linux entries. These sections are organized in this manner for readability only. The first image entry is the default system if no option is selected at the LILO boot prompt. This is discussed further in the section "Dual Booting," later in the chapter.

Table 12.6 describes what each line in the sample lilo.conf file does.

PART
III

CH
12

TABLE 12.6   SAMPLE /etc/lilo.conf FILE

lilo.conf File Entry	Description
boot = /dev/hda1	The boot loader is installed to the boot sector, sometimes referred to as the superblock, of the first IDE drive.
install = /boot/boot.b	Installs the specified file as the new boot sector.
prompt	Forces the boot prompt to be displayed.
delay = 50	The time delay, in tenths of seconds, before the default image boots.
timeout = 50	The boot loader pauses 5 seconds waiting for operator input.

TABLE 12.6   CONTINUED

`lilo.conf` File Entry	Description
`message = /boot/message`	Contains the information that is to be displayed to the screen after LILO is run.
`default = name`	Image specified here is the default boot image. The first image listed in `/etc/lilo.conf` is the default if this option is omitted.
`image = /vmlinuz-pc97-2.2.14-modular`	The name of the Linux kernel.
`label = linux`	This label (name) is displayed at the boot prompt if the Tab key is pressed. It is used to distinguish between options if more than one OS is available to boot.
`root = /dev/hda1`	The root filesystem resides on the first partition of the first IDE drive.
`vga = 274`	Selects the display mode to be used when booting.
`read-only`	The root filesystem is mounted as read-only initially. It is remounted during the boot process as read-write.
`append = "debug=2 noapic nosmp"`	Appends options specified here to the string that is passed to the kernel—typically used for hardware parameters such as a hard disk geometry.

The options available for the `/etc/lilo.conf` file correspond with the three major sections—general, Linux images, and other images. In fact, the options for other images actually apply to any bootable image. A comprehensive list of options for each of the three sections of the `/etc/lilo.conf` file is shown in Tables 12.7, 12.8, and 12.9.

TABLE 12.7   GLOBAL OPTIONS (GENERAL)

Option	Description
`backup = filename`	Copies the original boot sector to the specified file.
`boot = boot_device`	Uses the boot sector from the specified device.
`change-rules`	Defines partition type numbers.
`compact`	Reads several adjacent sectors in a single read request.
`disk = device_name`	Sets non-standard parameters for the specified disk.
`fix-table`	Allows LILO to adjust 3D addresses in partition tables.
`force-backup = filename`	Same as the `backup` option, except an existing backup file is over-written with this option.
`ignore-table`	Ignores partition tables that appear to be corrupt and allows LILO to install a boot sector.
`install = boot_sector`	Specified file is installed as the new boot sector.
`keytable = table_file`	The keyboard is remapped based on the settings in the specified file.

TABLE 12.7   CONTINUED

Option	Description
`linear`	Generates linear sector addresses instead of addresses using cylinders, heads, and sectors.
`map = map_file`	Uses the map file specified here—if not specified, `/boot/map` is used as the default.
`message = message_file`	The contents of this file are displayed as part of the LILO boot prompt. The map installer must be rerun if this file is modified.
`nowarn`	Warning errors are ignored and not displayed.
`prompt`	Forces the display of the boot prompt—without this, you usually won't see the prompt, although you can force it by holding down the left <Shift> key while the system is booting.
`serial = parameters`	Enables console control from a configured serial port.
`timeout = tenths_seconds`	The amount of time, in tenths of seconds, that the user is allowed to press a key before the default boot image is loaded.
`verbose = level`	Different levels of progress diagnostics can be selected.

TABLE 12.8   LINUX IMAGE OPTIONS

Option	Description
`initrd = name`	The file specified here is used as the initial RAM disk.
`literal = string`	Similar to the `append` option, but the specified string replaces any previous options that are to be passed to the kernel.
`ramdisk = size`	Sets the size of the RAM disk.
`read-only`	The root filesystem is initially mounted as read-only.
`read-write`	Sets the root filesystem to mount as read/write.
`root = root_device`	Selects the device specified here as the root device.

TABLE 12.9   GENERAL PER-IMAGE OPTIONS

Option	Description
`alias = name`	Indicates a second name for this image.
`fallback = command_line`	The command line specified here is used if this image is selected to boot on a subsequent attempt to boot this image.
`label = name`	Assigns a name to the boot image for easy reference.
`lock`	Any command-line options added are recorded and used for subsequent boots until manually overridden.
`optional`	Omit this image when running the map installer if the main file is missing—typically used with test kernels.

PART

III

CH

12

TABLE 12.9   CONTINUED

Option	Description
password = password	The password set here must be entered at the boot prompt for this image to boot.
restricted	Only works with the password option set—the password is only required if boot line options are added.
single-key	Allows an image to be booted by pressing a single key.

HOW TO INSTALL LILO

Installing LILO is really quite simple. The key to a successful installation is to create the configuration file correctly. After the configuration file is created, it's just a matter of running the map installer program. Modifications to the configuration file (/etc/lilo.conf) can be made at any time, but the map installer (/sbin/lilo) must be run each time changes are made in order for the changes to take effect.

INSTALLING LILO

LILO is installed by logging in as the root user and running the map installer (/sbin/lilo). The map installer reads the configuration contained in the /etc/lilo.conf file and configures the boot loader based on directives contained therein. If the map installer is run using the sample /etc/lilo.conf file described in the previous section, the output is as follows:

```
# /sbin/lilo
 Added linux *
```

The word linux refers to the specified label. For example, if the label entry is

```
# default entry

image = /vmlinuz
label = linux2.0
root = /dev/hda2
read-only
```

the map installer, when run, reports the following:

```
Added linux2.0 *
```

The asterisk (*) indicates that this image is the default operating system. This image is booted if no other option is selected at the LILO boot prompt. The map installer has several options, most of which can be implemented by configuring the /etc/lilo.conf file. See the man page on LILO for further details.

Note   If the kernel is rebuilt, the boot loader must be reinstalled in order to have the map rebuilt. This enables LILO to find the location of the newly built kernel.

The reason is simple: The kind of information written to the boot loader includes items such as a map of where the Linux kernel is located on your hard drive, and none of it is updated if you don't run the map installer.

UNINSTALLING LILO

The process by which LILO is uninstalled is completely dependent on how LILO was installed. If LILO was installed in the default location (the boot sector, or superblock, of the Linux partition), it can be uninstalled by deleting, disabling, or overwriting the partition in which it resides.

If LILO was installed to the MBR, it takes a little bit more to disable it. The MBR of the hard drive is unaffected by changes to any partitions. As such, simply deleting or overwriting a partition has no effect on LILO.

In most cases, LILO can be uninstalled by running the map installer with the uninstall option as follows:

```
# lilo -u
```

When the map installer is run, a backup copy of the original boot sector is made. The uninstall option tries to restore the boot sector to its original state by removing the boot sector that was previously installed and replacing it with the original boot sector. This might not always work. It is completely dependent on being capable of reading the filesystem in which the backup boot sector is stored. A factory-default MBR can be restored by running the DOS version of `fdisk` with the appropriate parameter, as follows:

```
fdisk /MBR
```

Tip

OpenLinux includes the latest version of DR DOS, which can be used to configure the MBR. To do so, you need to create a DR DOS boot disk and copy fdisk to it, then boot the system with that boot disk to use the DR DOS fdisk.

Yet another way to prepare an MBR is by using the file `/boot/virgin.mbr` provided by Caldera. In Openlinux, use the following line to write a new MBR:

```
dd if=/boot/virgin.mbr of=/dev/hda bs=512 count=1
```

If you want to use an MS OS, you'll still need to use the MS supplied `fdisk.exe` because only it writes some information to the MBR required to boot most MS operating systems. This information is not included in the `virgin.mbr` file included with OpenLinux.

DUAL BOOTING

In addition to providing the means for booting a Linux kernel, LILO offers the added bonus of being capable of managing the booting of other, non-Linux operating systems and of booting multiple versions of the same operating system. You might find yourself in a position in which you need to compile a customized version of the Linux kernel; using LILO, you can set up your old kernel to be booted in case the new one doesn't work for some reason.

It's actually quite easy to configure LILO to manage the boot process of other images. The most common occurrence of a dual booting situation is that of Linux and an operating system that comes preloaded on a PC. The steps for preparing such a system for Linux are as follows:

1. Run a defragmenting program.
2. Split the existing partition into two partitions.
3. Delete the second partition.
4. Create two new partitions from the existing free space.
5. Set one partition as Linux swap and the other as Linux native.
6. Install Linux.

The last phase of the installation process enables you to configure LILO to boot all available operating systems. However, it is quite easy to modify the LILO configuration at any time to enable booting of other operating systems or other Linux kernel images. It takes only two simple steps: First, modify the /etc/lilo.conf file and add an entry for each additional operating system or image. Second, rerun the map installer. An example of a /etc/lilo.conf file with two Linux kernels and one non-Linux image is shown here:

```
# general section

boot = /dev/hda
install = /boot/boot.b
message = /boot/message
prompt

# wait 20 seconds for user to select the entry to load
timeout = 200

# default entry

image = /vmlinuz
label = linux
root = /dev/hda2
read-only

image = /vmlinuz.new
label  = linux.new
root = /dev/hda3
read-only

# additional entries
other = /dev/hda4
label = dos
table = /dev/hda
```

Reinstalling the boot loader by rerunning the map installer produces the following:

```
# /sbin/lilo

 Added linux *
Added linux.new
Added dos
```

The newly configured system is depicted in Table 12.10.

TABLE 12.10	LINUX BOOT SEQUENCE	
Master Boot Record	**Boot Sector**	**Operating System**
DOS-MBR	LILO (boot loader)	Linux kernel (`vmlinuz`) Linux (`vmlinuz.new`) DOS

PARAMETERS

By default, LILO is configured to pause at a boot prompt. This is done for two basic reasons. First, because LILO offers the capability to manage the booting of several operating systems, it must pause long enough to offer the user a choice of which operating system to boot. If you press the Tab key at the boot prompt, a selection list of available boot images is displayed (you might need to press the Shift key first). The name displayed is the label name entered in the `/etc/lilo.conf` file for each available boot image.

Second, kernel parameters can be entered at the boot prompt. These command-line options are entered at the boot prompt, and multiple entries are delineated by spaces.

Note Boot prompt options apply to kernel drivers only. The behavior of loadable modules is not altered by any boot prompt parameter.

Although several options can be entered at the boot prompt, only a few are presented here. A comprehensive list of all the options is contained in the BootPrompt HOWTO document. This document, written and maintained by Paul Gortmaker, can be found in most Linux installations as well as in many other archive locations, as discussed in Appendix B, "Finding More Information on Linux."

The boot prompt options are categorized into non–device-specific arguments and several hardware-specific ones. The hardware-specific categories include SCSI devices, hard disks, CD-ROMs, and miscellaneous devices such as Ethernet adapters and sound cards.

Most boot prompt options have the following syntax:

```
name[=value1][,value2]...[,valueN]
```

The common non–device-specific boot prompt options are listed in Table 12.11.

PART
III

CH
12

TABLE 12.11	NON–DEVICE-SPECIFIC BOOT PROMPT OPTIONS
Boot Prompt Options	**Description**
`root=device`	Specifies an alternative root device—most commonly used when the boot loader on the hard disk fails.
`single`	Boots the selected image into single-user mode.
`reserve=base,size...`	Used to reserve specified IO ports—this prevents auto-probing of these addresses.
`debug`	Logs more verbose status messages.

> **Note**
>
> You can use the installation floppy to boot to the hard disk, if necessary, by entering `boot root=/dev/hda1` at the boot prompt.

DEBUGGING LILO

Although LILO is easily installed, it's really quite a complex set of programs and routines. Fortunately, most of the process is transparent to the user. However, because of the level of complexity, it sometimes fails when trying to determine disk geometry or the location of key files. This section describes the types of error messages that LILO produces and how they can be used in debugging LILO failures. Both the map installer and boot loader produce helpful messages for debugging purposes.

MAP INSTALLER

Two types of errors are reported by LILO—fatal errors and warning errors. As the name suggests, *fatal* errors are unrecoverable. *Warning* errors are just that, a warning that everything is not completely correct but that the map installer will still run. However, often a warning error is followed by a fatal error and the map installer fails. Using the `nowarn` option suppresses all warning errors. A comprehensive list of error messages is included in the LILO documentation RPM.

Fatal errors are typically caused by problems with the interpretation of disk geometry. One main objective of the map installer is to create the map of where the required components reside for it to work. If you recall, this is done by identifying the physical location on the hard drive rather than by relying on a given filesystem.

BOOT LOADER MESSAGES

The following three types of messages can be generated by the boot loader:

- Messages resulting from invalid boot prompt options
- Disk access error messages
- Progress or error messages

The first type is basically self-explanatory. The second type, disk access errors, is described in detail in the LILO documentation RPM. They are most often the result of some sort of media problem. For example, a 0×10 error commonly occurs when the boot loader cannot be read from the floppy disk. This is almost always corrected with a new disk.

The third type of message is either a progress status report as the boot loader proceeds and completes or an identification of an error if it stops at some point. As the boot loader proceeds, the word *LILO* is printed to the screen, one letter at a time. If, for some reason, LILO fails, the last letter displayed to the screen can be used as a clue as to why it might have failed. The letter L is displayed when LILO begins to run. If the letter L does not appear, it means that LILO was not found. If LILO is completely spelled out, the boot loader completed successfully. Table 12.12 lists the descriptions of what failed if the boot loader stops before spelling out the word LILO.

TABLE 12.12   TROUBLESHOOTING THE LILO BOOT PROMPT

LILO Prompt Display	Description
L	The first stage boot loader started, but it was unable to load the second stage. This usually indicates a media failure.
LI	The first and second stages of the boot loader have successfully run. This typically means that LILO cannot find the kernel. Often, adding the option linear will fix this.
LIL	Can't read the data from the map file. Usually caused by a media error.
LIL?	The second stage boot loader was loaded but at an incorrect address.
LIL-	The descriptor table is corrupt.
LILO	LILO has successfully completed.

OTHER BOOT LOADER OPTIONS

An alternative boot loader is LOADLIN. LOADLIN is a DOS-based boot loader program that boots Linux. Because it is DOS-based, your system must be configured to first boot to DOS and then run LOADLIN.EXE to switch to Linux. LOADLIN works well in situations in which a certain hardware component depends on a DOS driver to set a few proprietary registers before it is recognized by another operating system. Table 12.13 depicts the steps of the boot sequence using LOADLIN.

TABLE 12.13   LOADLIN BOOT SEQUENCE

Master Boot Record	Boot Sector Type	Operating System
DOS-MBR	DOS	io.sys->msdos.sys->COMMAND.COM
LOADLIN.EXE	Linux kernel	

GRUB

Starting with OpenLinux eDesktop 2.4, Caldera has been using GRUB. While both LILO and GRUB continue to be installed, GRUB is the preferred boot loader by OpenLinux.

You can easily tell whether your system is using GRUB instead of LILO, because during bootup, you'll see the telltale "stage 1 stage 2" printed on your screen just before the graphical boot process starts.

This section of the chapter will not fill you in on all the details of GRUB, because as of this writing, a number of things are changing. The basics are expected to remain, but you may see differences in the various files and particularly in GRUB capabilities as this boot loader evolves.

GRUB works in a slightly different way from LILO. When LILO boots, the LILO boot image contains information about where a particular boot image is located, not by name, but by placement on the disk. It then points at that place and begins loading the image. GRUB, on the other hand, actually reads files on the partition, which means that GRUB has to be able to read at least one of the partition where its files are contained to boot different kernels.

Currently, GRUB can read and boot Linux, GNU/Hurd, FreeBSD, NetBSD, and OpenBSD partitions. Using a technique call chainloading, GRUB can also boot unsupported OS's like Windows 9x and others, but you must have one of the supported operating systems to do this. The supported OS list is expected to grow, so check the man pages for more information.

GRUB offers some advantages over LILO, but carries some disadvantages. The advantages include not having to remember to rerun the loader (LILO) just because you change kernels. If you overwrite the old kernel with a new one, and then reboot the system, GRUB will find the new kernel. The disadvantage is that the simple command line has been replaced with a more complex command line you have to edit, then boot. If you find yourself changing boot options often, you'll quickly tire GRUB. Both LILO and GRUB offer the advantage of overcoming the old 1024 cylinder limit.

USING GRUB

GRUB has a number of files you'll get to know. The first one is /etc/grub.conf. This file isn't required, but will save you setting up grub by putting in every command from an interactive prompt. Listing 12.1 shows a typical /etc/grub.conf file generated by Lizard during install.

LISTING 12.1   A TYPICAL grub.conf FILE

```
####################
#   /etc/grub.conf
#
root (hd0,2)
install /boot/grub/stage1 (hd0,2) /boot/grub/stage2 0x8000 (hd0,2)
/boot/grub/menu.1st
quit
#####################

###########################
#   /boot/grub/device.amp
#
(fd0)    /dev/fd0
(hd0)    /dev/hda
######################

#####################
#       /boot/grub/menu.1st      - generated by lizard
#
```

LISTING 12.1   CONTINUED

```
#        options
timeout=5
splashscreen = (hd0,1)/boot/messages.col24
default=0
title=Linux
root=(hd0,2)
kernel=/boot/vmlinuz-pc97-2.2.14-modular vga=normal noapic nosmp root=/dev/hda3

title=Win95
chainloader=(hd0,0)+1
```

Near the top of Listing 12.1 is the line root (hd0,2). GRUB uses (unfortunately), nomenclature for hard disk drives and partitions in the BSD format. Those of you familiar with FreeBSD will be comfortable with this particular method of device listing, but if you're not familiar with FreeBSD, it may take some getting used to. The drives are numbered starting at 0, so the first hard drive will be hd0. The partitions also are numbered starting with 0, so the partition above is actually the third partition.

The install line given previously performs the task of installing GRUB and telling it where the stage1 and stage2 files it needs will be located. The next line tells GRUB where to find its menu file.

Farther down is a listing of devices. You can see the hd0 and fd0 equivalents on the Linux system. If you are using the new devfs, you might see much longer name equivalents.

Finally, the last section contains what is written as the GRUB menu.1st file. This file is the rough equivalent to the lilo.conf file.

/boot/grub

All of the files GRUB needs are installed by default into /boot/grub. This location is not mandatory and can be on any partition with a filesystem GRUB can read.

The /boot/grub directory will contain the following files:

```
device.map
e2fs_stage1_5
fat_stage1_5
ffs_stage1_5
menu.1st
minix_stage1_5
stage1
stage2
```

The device.map file will contain a mapping of the BSD equivalent device nomenclature to that of Linux. Under BSD, no distinction is made between IDE and SCSI hard drives—they are all hard drives. So a mapping is needed for GRUB. This map will also help you know what GRUB thinks each of your disks is called. This will be created during installation from what Lizard knows to be your devices, and forms part of the /etc/grub.conf file, specifically the section called device.amp.

The various `<fs>_stage1_5` files are for each of the various filesystems GRUB can use.

The `menu.lst` is the most important file and the one you will change if you add a second or third kernel or change the name of a kernel. Your initial `menu.lst` file will look exactly like the `menu.lst` portion of your `/etc/grub.conf` file.

Looking at the `menu.lst` section of Listing 12.1 above, you see a number of items that should be familiar from the discussions of `lilo.conf`. Going through the various items you first have `timeout=5`. This variable is different from the `lilo.conf` variable in that this is actually in seconds rather than LILO's 10ths of a second.

The splashscreen line is the equivalent of LILO's message line screen. This file can be an ASCII file, or in the case of OpenLinux, a binary file designed to show graphics on the screen.

The `default=` line is akin to the default line in LILO and tells GRUB which kernel to boot after the timeout. Unlike LILO, which uses names for each image, GRUB uses numbers beginning with 0 to specify which kernel is the default of those listed.

The `title=` line in GRUB equates to LILO's `label=` line, so that each kernel carries a meaningful name on the screen. This title will be listed on the screen during boot, one title to a line so that the appropriate line may be chosen for booting.

The `root=` line tells grub where the root filesystem for that particular system can be found. While equivalent to LILO's `root=` line, it uses the BSD version of device and partition naming. Specifically, `root=(hd0,2)` tells GRUB that the root partition is on the first hard disk, third partition. The parentheses around the device are mandatory.

The `kernel=` line used by GRUB will be much longer than that used by LILO to simply identify the kernel image, since the kernel line contains a number of other lines from `lilo.conf` combined into one. First comes the actual kernel image by name that you will boot. Because GRUB will actually read this file, not just be pointed to the image by location, all you need to do is change this name, save the `menu.lst` file, and reboot. The rest of the kernel line contains other parameters that are found either on the `append=` line or other lines in `lilo.conf`. Note the `root=/dev/hda3` as part of the kernel line. Although GRUB uses `(hd0,2)`, Linux has no clue what that device and partition is, so you must include a `root=` option understandable to Linux.

When the system boots, you can change command-line parameters with GRUB by highlighting (in this case) the Linux line and pressing e. A second screen will come up with the `kernel=` line shown. Highlight that line, press e, and you can append any additional arguments you need for this boot to the line (or remove any argument you don't want). Press <Enter> to save it, and then press b to boot that kernel with those parameters.

To make permanent changes to the kernel line, just make the change in the `menu.lst` file.

The last two files in the `/boot/grub` directory are the binary files `stage1` and `stage2`. These files actually perform the kernel boot. As each is loaded and executed, you'll see the name printed on the screen. When `stage2` finishes, you'll see the message screen, in the case of OpenLinux, a graphical screen with the kernel image name.

AUTHOR RECOMMENDATIONS

When you build a new kernel, leave the old one in place. If the new one is a different version, you won't have any problems with modules. If it is the same version, you might receive some error messages regarding modules, but they won't be fatal.

Follow these steps:

1. Copy your new kernel to `/boot` as `bzImage-<kernel-version>` with this command:

   `cp /usr/src/linux/arch/i386/boot/bzImage /boot/bzImage-`uname -r``

2. Next, copy your System map similarly:

   `cp /usr/src/linux/System.map /boot/System.map-`uname -r``

3. Edit your `/etc/lilo.conf`. Copy the current Linux stanza so that you have two identical stanzas that start `image =` and end `append =`.

4. Modify the `image =` in the first stanza to point to your new kernel (`/boot/bzImage-<kernel-version>`).

5. Modify the second stanza `label =` line and change the name (`oldlinux` is a suitable name).

6. Run LILO (if you get errors, correct them and rerun LILO) and reboot (you might need to modify `/etc/modules/default` first).

Now, if you have a problem booting to your new kernel, you always have the option of booting the old kernel instead. This will allow you into the system so you can repair it by rebuilding the kernel properly and replacing it.

TROUBLESHOOTING

I added a password option to `/etc/lilo.conf`, but I don't want anyone to read it. What are my options?

You have two options here, the best one being to just `chmod 600 lilo.conf` so only root can read it. The other option is to remove it (or move it to a floppy disk for safekeeping). The `/etc/lilo.conf` is required only when you need to run LILO so LILO knows how (and where) to build the map file. But neither `/etc/lilo.conf` nor `/sbin/lilo` are actually used during the boot process.

I get a 0x×10 error during loading, and bootup stops.

This is a fatal error most often caused by a bad boot floppy. Some old floppy controllers will also give you this error. Replace the floppy. If the error continues, you might need to find another way to boot the system.

I get LI and the system stops loading. I am trying to boot from SCSI drives.

Here, you have one of two problems, each addressed in the two paragraphs below. You'll need to read both and decide which one applies.

This is a common SCSI error (though not restricted to SCSI drives). You'll need to use the linear option to overcome the disk geometry translation LILO is incapable of handling.

If you had another distribution of Linux installed and the LILO boot loader was loaded to the MBR, that copy is seen first. OpenLinux installs by default to the OpenLinux partition. So the stale copy of LILO is looking for a kernel that no longer exists. Boot using the CD-ROM or boot floppy, and at the LILO prompt enter

```
boot root=/dev/hda
```

When in OpenLinux, use the `dd if=/boot/virgin.mbr of=/dev/hda bs=512 count=1` described in the previous text and your reboots should find OpenLinux again.

I rebuilt my kernel, replaced the old one with the new one of the same name, but then forgot to run LILO before rebooting. Now the system won't reboot.

You'll need to boot from either the install floppy or the CD-ROM and do the following:

1. When you get the LILO boot prompt, press the Shift and then Tab keys in succession. Enter the following (substituting the correct location of your root drive for `/dev/hda1`):
   ```
   boot root=/dev/hda1
   ```
2. Ensure your `/etc/lilo.conf` is correct and run LILO.
3. Reboot so you can boot into your new kernel.

I want to see the kernel messages during bootup, but I get a Caldera screen instead that obscures the messages. How can I get rid of it?

Change the `vga = 274` line to `vga = normal` and remove the `debug=2` from the `append = ` line. Also comment out the `message = ` above the boot stanzas. Then rerun LILO. On your next bootup, you should see all the kernel boot-time messages.

I want to boot into [single user mode | runlevel 3 | ...] instead of runlevel 5. How can I do this?

When you see the LILO boot prompt, press the Shift key then the Tab key. Type in the kernel name, a space, and the runlevel you want (single, 1, 2, 3, or 4). See the next chapter for more information.

When I boot, I get stage1, but I never get stage2.

The `stage1` prints just before GRUB goes looking for the file. The GRUB that is booting cannot find the `stage1` file. If you created a boot disk during install, use that to boot into the system and run the GRUB command line to reinstall GRUB. If you didn't create a boot disk, you can use the CD-ROM to boot, changing the command line by editing it and specifying the root disk and partition.

CHAPTER 13

SYSTEM INITIALIZATION

In this chapter

PART
III

CH
13

ABOUT INITIALIZATION

Linux can use either System V (SysV) style system initialization or BSD style initialization. These are the two primary methods of performing system initialization in the UNIX and Linux worlds. BSD uses a few large scripts to handle all system initialization. The BSD initialization is used only by the Slackware distribution. SysV makes use of runlevels and a group of initialization scripts. The initialization scripts are run to start and stop *daemons* (background processes) depending on the *runlevel* (also referred to as the *system state*). One script per daemon or process subsystem is kept in a centralized directory (to be examined in detail later). System V runlevels range from 0–6 by custom, with each runlevel corresponding to a different mode of operation, and often even these runlevels are not all used. Although SysV initialization seems more complex, particularly to those coming from the world of DOS and Windows, this appearance belies a flexibility not seen with BSD style initialization.

Windows users might think about comparing the initial screen they see during bootup if they press F8 with Linux' SysV runlevels. The Windows "runlevels" include DOS, Safe Mode, Safe Mode with Networking, and so forth. Comparing this to runlevels in Linux is like comparing an old bi-plane that you had to land, get out the wrench, remove the climb prop and put on the cruise prop, get in, and take off again, to a modern turbo-charged Mooney with a variable pitch prop and an automatic waste-gate controller. No comparison, really.

`init`: WHERE IT ALL BEGINS

Figure 13.1 shows default boot, assuming `initrd` is not used. This boot procedure can be short-circuited or changed in different ways, but this figure will give you a good idea of how a vanilla installation boots.

Figure 13.1
A default boot sequence.

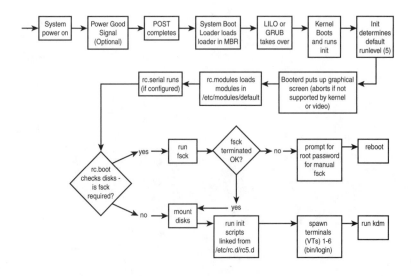

After the kernel loads into memory (refer to Chapter 12, " Boot Loaders"), you have a running Linux system—but it isn't very usable because the kernel doesn't interact directly with the user or user space (see Chapter 14, "Customizing Your Shell Environment," for more details). The kernel runs one program: init. This program is responsible for everything else, and is referred to as the parent of all processes. The kernel then retires to its position as system manager, handling kernel space and all requests for resource access.

When init starts, it reads its configuration from a file called inittab, which stands for initialization table, located in the /etc directory. Any defaults in inittab are discarded if they've been overridden on the command line. The inittab file describes how init sets up the system. See Listing 13.1 for the default OpenLinux inittab. Later, you'll see how to override inittab defaults, why you might want or need to, and the specific effects of doing so.

> **Tip**
>
> The tab ending (as in inittab, fstab, mtab, and so on) indicates that the file is a table—usually a configuration table. In the case of inittab, it tells init how to initialize the system, much like config.sys in DOS.

LISTING 13.1 THE /etc/inittab FILE

```
#
# inittab       This file describes how the INIT process should set up
#               the system in a certain run-level.
#
# Author:       Miquel van Smoorenburg, <miquels@drinkel.nl.mugnet.org>
#               Modified for RHS Linux by Marc Ewing and Donnie Barnes
#               Modified for COL by Raymund Will
#

# The runlevels used by COL are:
#   0 - halt (Do NOT set initdefault to this)
#   1 - Single user mode (including initialisation of network interfaces,
#       if you do have networking)
#   2 - Multiuser, (without NFS-Server und some such)
#       (basically the same as 3, if you do not have networking)
#   3 - Full multiuser mode
#   4 - unused
#       (should be equal to 3, for now)
#   5 - X11
#   6 - reboot (Do NOT set initdefault to this)

#
# Default runlevel.
id:5:initdefault:

# System initialization.
s0::sysinit:/bin/bash -c 'C=/sbin/booterd; [ -x $C ] && $C'
si::sysinit:/bin/bash -c 'C=/etc/rc.d/rc.modules; [ -x $C ] && $C default'
s2::sysinit:/bin/bash -c 'C=/etc/rc.d/rc.serial; [ -x $C ] && $C'
bw::bootwait:/etc/rc.d/rc.boot

# What to do in single-user mode.
```

PART

III

CH

13

LISTING 13.1   CONTINUED

```
~1:S:wait:/etc/rc.d/rc 1
~~:S:wait:/sbin/sulogin

l0:0:wait:/etc/rc.d/rc 0
l1:1:wait:/etc/rc.d/rc 1
l2:2:wait:/etc/rc.d/rc 2
l3:3:wait:/etc/rc.d/rc 3
l4:4:wait:/etc/rc.d/rc 4
l5:5:wait:/etc/rc.d/rc 5
l6:6:wait:/etc/rc.d/rc 6
# Normally not reached, but fallthrough in case of emergency.
z6:6:respawn:/sbin/sulogin

# Trap CTRL-ALT-DELETE
ca:12345:ctrlaltdel:/sbin/shutdown -t3 -r now

# Action on special keypress (ALT-UpArrow).
kb::kbrequest:/bin/echo "Keyboard Request --edit /etc/inittab to let this work."

# When our UPS tells us power has failed, assume we have a few minutes
# of power left.  Schedule a shutdown for 2 minutes from now.
# This does, of course, assume you have powerd installed and your
# UPS connected and working correctly.
pf::powerfail:/sbin/shutdown -h +5 "Power Failure; System Shutting Down"

# If battery is fading fast -- we hurry...
p1::powerfailnow:/sbin/shutdown -c 2> /dev/null
p2::powerfailnow:/sbin/shutdown -h now "Battery Low..."

# If power was restored before the shutdown kicked in, cancel it.
po:12345:powerokwait:/sbin/shutdown -c "Power Restored; Shutdown Cancelled"


# Run gettys in standard runlevels
1:12345:respawn:/sbin/getty tty1 VC linux
2:2345:respawn:/sbin/getty tty2 VC linux
3:2345:respawn:/sbin/getty tty3 VC linux
4:2345:respawn:/sbin/getty tty4 VC linux
5:2345:respawn:/sbin/getty tty5 VC linux
6:2345:respawn:/sbin/getty tty6 VC linux

# Run kdm in runlevel 5
gu:5:respawn:/bin/sh -c 'C=/etc/rc.d/rc.gui;[ -x $C ]&&exec $C;init 3'
```

Note

Runlevels are just a convenient way to group together process packages using software. They hold no special significance to the kernel. All Linux kernels start the boot process the same way. It's only after init starts that you begin to use runlevels.

inittab SPECIFICS

Note

This text uses the Caldera OpenLinux `inittab` as illustration. Your `inittab` might be different, but it works the same way. After reading this section, you should be able to understand most any Linux `inittab`.

Reading `inittab`, you'll be skipping any lines that begin with a # because these are ignored by init as comments. The rest of the lines can be easily read as many other typical UNIX-like configuration tables; that is, each column is separated by a colon (:) and can be read as follows:

- **`id`**—This first column is a unique identifier for the line. This can be up to four alphanumerics long but is typically limited to two. Older systems had a two alphanumeric limitation, and most distributions haven't changed that custom.

- **`runlevel`**—The second column indicates for which runlevel(s) this row is valid. This column can be null or can contain any number of valid runlevels. If null, it is valid for all runlevels.

- **`action`**—This can be any number of things; the most common is `respawn`, but it can also be any one of the following: `once`, `sysinit`, `boot`, `bootwait`, `wait`, `off`, `ondemand`, `initdefault`, `powerwait`, `powerfail`, `powerokwait`, `ctrlaltdel`, `kbrequest`.

- **`process`**—The specific process or program to be run.

Each row in `inittab` has a unique identifier. Normally, this is something that is easily associated with the specific action performed. For example, a line that spawns a `getty` on the first serial port might use the identifier `S0` for `/dev/ttyS0`.

The runlevels are identified as 0–6 and A–C by default. Runlevels 0, 1, and 6 are special—do not change them carelessly. These correspond to system halt, maintenance mode, and system reboot, respectively. Changing runlevel 1, for example, can have far-reaching consequences. Note that to enter maintenance mode (runlevel 1), you can pass init the argument 1 (using `telinit`). As an alternative, you can use `S` or `s`. If you change what transpires for runlevel 1, the same changes apply when `S` or `s` is passed. Runlevels 2–5, though, can be customized as desired. (See the Troubleshooting section for booting to a runlevel other than the default.)

PART
III

CH
13

Note

Using `telinit` is the preferred method for passing commands to init, but it is not unusual to call init directly.

Most Linux distributions include the command `runlevel` (found in `/sbin`), which can be used to give you information about the current and previous runlevels. Executing this command outputs the previous runlevel and the present runlevel, for example, N 3. The N indicates that there is no previous runlevel, as might occur following a reboot, and the 3 indicates the current runlevel. If you make a change to runlevel 2 and then reissue the `runlevel` command, you'll see 3 2.

HANDS-ON INIT

Because doing illustrates better than just reading about it, try this on your system: As root (only root can tell init to change runlevels), issue the `init` command. You receive a usage message telling you to pass init an argument consisting of a number from 0–6, the letters A–C, S, or Q. Lowercase letters are syntactically equivalent to their uppercase counterparts. If you pass init anything other than legal values, you receive a usage message to that effect; therefore, if you do not receive it, you know that it is a legitimate value (as far as init is concerned).

> **Caution**
>
> Only attempt the following if you are certain that you can `telnet` into your system over the network.

If the system you are using is connected to a network and you can `telnet` to it from another machine, you might want to try to pass init the argument 8, as in `init 8` (or `telinit 8` if you want). You may see some messages about sending the `TERM` and `KILL` signals to programs, and then your virtual terminal will stop responding. Go to the other system, `telnet` into your system, and type `runlevel` again; you will see 3 8. After you have confirmed that you actually did change to runlevel 8, change back to your previous runlevel. Your logins reappear on the screen.

> **Note**
>
> Depending on the specifics of system scripts, your distribution might act differently when atempting this experiment. You might retain a login until it is used for the first time and you log out, at which time it will not respawn a login.

The preceding exercise showed that although runlevels 7–9 are undocumented, they actually are available for use if needed. (What happened when you changed to runlevel 8 will become clear later in the chapter.) These runlevels aren't used simply because it's not customary to use them. The customizable runlevels for SysV Linux systems (2–5) are generally more than sufficient for anyone, and neither Red Hat nor Caldera, by default, use runlevel 4, so it is available for your use. Debian uses only runlevel 2 for both graphical and non-graphical logins, so runlevels 3–5 are available for your customization.

INIT OBSCURITIES

Here's a look at the other letter arguments you can pass to init. The letters A–C are used when you want to spawn a daemon listed in `inittab`, but only on demand. Telling init to change to runlevel C doesn't change the runlevel per se; it just performs the action listed on the line at which the runlevel is C.

Suppose that you want to put a getty on a port to receive a call, but only after receiving a voice call first (and not all the time). Further suppose that you want to be ready to receive either a data call or a fax call, and that when you get the voice message you'll know which you want. You insert two new lines in `inittab`, each with its own ID, and each with a runlevel such as A for data and B for fax. When you know which you need, you simply spawn the appropriate one from one of the following command lines:

```
telinit A
```

```
telinit B
```

The appropriate getty is put on the line until the first call is received. When the caller terminates the connection, the getty drops because, by definition, on demand will not respawn.

> **Note**   The previous example is just a contrived example. For fax and data capability, use mgetty.

The other two letters, S and Q, are special. As noted earlier, S brings your system to maintenance mode and is the same as changing runlevel to runlevel 1. The Q is used to tell init to reread inittab. The inittab file can be changed as often as required, but will only be read under certain circumstances:

- One of its processes dies. (Do you need to respawn another?)
- On a powerfail signal from a power daemon (or the command line)
- When told to change runlevel by telinit

The Q argument tells init, "I've changed something, please reread the inittab."

THE inittab FILE FROM TOP TO BOTTOM

Within the actual inittab, lines beginning with a # sign are disabled and left as examples or explanatory remarks, or as examples for possible future use. Be sure to read the comments throughout. These comments might give you a hint as to how to effectively customize inittab. Most programs, such as mgetty or efax, which were meant to run from inittab come with examples in their documentation showing how to implement them.

Because you already know how to read a line (id:runlevel:action:process), here's a look at what each line does:

- `id:5:initdefault:`

  The first line of interest is the default runlevel line. As you'll see later, this is what determines whether you boot into a graphical screen or a command-line terminal. This must never be set to 0 or 6.

- `s0::sysinit:/bin/bash -c 'C=/sbin/booterd; [ -x $C ] && $C'`
  `si::sysinit:/bin/bash -c 'C=/etc/rc.d/rc.modules; [ -x $C ] && $C default'`
  `s2::sysinit:/bin/bash -c 'C=/etc/rc.d/rc.serial; [ -x $C ] && $C'`
  `bw::bootwait:/etc/rc.d/rc.boot`

  Just below the default runlevel line, you'll see the system initialization script calls. Line ID s0, which calls booterd, is one of two programs that handles the Lizard boot screen (as long as the vga = 274 has not been removed from /etc/grub/menu.lst or /etc/lilo.conf). Line ID si loads the default modules listed in /etc/modules/defaults via the /etc/rc.d/rd.modules script. Line ID s2 configures the serial ports, but only if you've enabled the /etc/rc.d/rc.serial script (disabled by default). These three lines execute at the same time, line s0 displaying on the screen the status of the modules as the si script loads them. The line ID bw is one you'll not notice until your system shuts down abnormally. This line calls rc.boot, which handles checking the status of the disk drives to ensure that they were properly unmounted, and if not, runs fsck or continues with mounting the disks. This script drops you into a shell at runlevel 1 if fsck is not able to repair the disks without assistance. Because the system cannot continue until this script completes, the action column is bootwait.

- ~1:S:wait:/etc/rc.d/rc 1
  ~~:S:wait:/sbin/sulogin

These two lines are two scripts that run whenever you enter maintenance (single-user) mode. You'll look at the rc script later. The sulogin program is a special program to make your system a little more secure by preventing anyone who has physical access to the machine from rebooting into single-user mode and gaining access to the system without knowing the root password. Without this line, booting into single-user mode presents a root shell to the user without prompting for a password. However, this does not prevent a sophisticated user from breaking into the system if he has physical access to the machine. In fact, one of the ways to bypass sulogin is discussed at the end of this chapter in the "Emergencies" section, as well as the significance of the tilde (~) as the first character in the ID.

- l0:0:wait:/etc/rc.d/rc 0
  l1:1:wait:/etc/rc.d/rc 1
  l2:2:wait:/etc/rc.d/rc 2
  l3:3:wait:/etc/rc.d/rc 3
  l4:4:wait:/etc/rc.d/rc 4
  l5:5:wait:/etc/rc.d/rc 5
  l6:6:wait:/etc/rc.d/rc 6

The lines with IDs l0–l6 are run when you change to the particular runlevel. Each runlevel change runs the rc script with an argument for the particular runlevel that is being entered. Remember that runlevels 7–9 are legitimate runlevels that can be used if necessary. If you want to make use of any of these nonstandard runlevels, you need to add lines to accommodate those runlevels because you almost certainly want to run the rc script if you are going to use any of these runlevels.

- z6:6:respawn:/sbin/sulogin

Line ID z6 is designed to present a root password prompt in case a machine doesn't properly reboot when it enters runlevel 6. This is only precautionary. At the time of this writing, I am unaware of any machine that doesn't correctly respond to a reboot command.

- ca:12345:ctrlaltdel:/sbin/shutdown -t3 -r now

Line ID ca traps the keyboard sequence Ctrl+Alt+Delete and performs a shutdown and reboot. If desired, this line can be modified to change the -r to -h to halt the system, or you can just remove the -r to bring the system into single-user mode with a root prompt.

> From an X server, this key sequence is not available to you. The X server traps the Ctrl+Alt+Delete. You need to switch to a virtual terminal to use this key sequence.

- `kb::kbrequest:/bin/echo "Keyboard Request--edit /etc/inittab to let this work."`

Line ID `kb` traps the keyboard sequence Alt+Up arrow. Currently, it echoes the notice that this needs to be configured before use. On most default setups with bash, this particular command sequence is ignored. First, the key mappings need to be changed so that bash passes the sequence. When that is finished, simply change the process portion of the line, substituting the command that you want to run for the `echo` command.

- `pf::powerfail:/sbin/shutdown -h +5 "Power Failure; System Shutting Down"`
  `p1::powerfailnow:/sbin/shutdown -c 2> /dev/null`
  `p2::powerfailnow:/sbin/shutdown -h now "Battery Low..."`
  `po:12345:powerokwait:/sbin/shutdown -c "Power Restored; Shutdown Cancelled"`

Line IDs `pf`, `p1`, `p2`, and `po` will be of interest if you have a UPS compatible with `powerd`, the power daemon. The power daemon can monitor the serial port and perform the actions as documented in `inittab`. The `inittab` is sufficiently coherent, so I'll not belabor it here.

- `1:12345:respawn:/sbin/getty tty1 VC linux`
  `2:2345:respawn:/sbin/getty tty2 VC linux`
  `3:2345:respawn:/sbin/getty tty3 VC linux`
  `4:2345:respawn:/sbin/getty tty4 VC linux`
  `5:2345:respawn:/sbin/getty tty5 VC linux`
  `6:2345:respawn:/sbin/getty tty6 VC linux`

Line IDs 1–6 spawn gettys to the virtual terminals (VTs). Note that in single-user mode, only one VT is available. If you want to save some memory, you can run fewer VTs (you must run at least one) in runlevel 5. If you decide to make use of unlisted runlevels, you need to add those levels to the ones listed. You can increase the number of VTs simply by adding more lines (with unique IDs, of course). Examining the previous entries, you see VC on the line as the `gettytab` entry type. VC stands for Virtual Console, which is sufficiently equivalent to VT for the purposes of this text. If you'd rather have VT, you'll need to change the VC line in `/etc/gettytab` appropriately.

> If you use VTs while an X server is running, if you change the number of VTs spawned at boot, you will find that your X server will be on a different VT. By default, the first available terminal is 8 (unless you have eliminated the graphical startup–then it is 7). If you reduce the number of VTs, the X server drops to a lower numbered terminal accordingly.

Notice that `kb`, `pf`, `p1`, and `p2` run regardless of the runlevel. When the runlevel column is null, the process is run in every runlevel.

PART

III

CH

13

■ `gu:5:respawn:/bin/sh -c 'C=/etc/rc.d/rc.gui;[ -x $C ]&&$C;[ -x $C ]||init 3'`

Finally, you see in line ID `gu` that runlevel 5 spawns a script, `/etc/rc.d/rc.gui`, which, if X is installed and configured, and KDM is installed, KDM (K Display Manager). If you want to use XDM(the X Display Manager), assuming you installed XDM, simply change the line to read

`x:5:respawn:/usr/X11R6/bin/xdm -nodaemon`

If you read through the `rc.gui` script and the original `gu` line in `inittab`, the process syntax might not be familiar to you, but it basically prevents the X server from continually resetting if it fails. This syntax forces the system back to runlevel 3 and a command-line interface so that the problem can be fixed. With the previous substitute line, no such checks are incorporated (although you could simply make the change in `rc.gui` to spawn XDM), so you are responsible for installing XDM, configuring XDM, and ensuring it has what it needs to run (a properly configured X server).

If your system has a default runlevel other than 1 but your system boots into maintenance mode, the `rc.boot` script has detected a problem with a hard disk that requires you to manually run `fsck`. When finished, the system reboots and tries to enter multi-user mode again.

THE `rc` SCRIPTS

Under OpenLinux and Red Hat, you'll find all the system initialization scripts in `/etc/rc.d`. This subdirectory has more subdirectories, one for each runlevel: `rc0.d–rc6.d` and `init.d`. Within the `/etc/rc.d/rc#.d` subdirectories (where the # is replaced by a single-digit number) are symbolic links to the master scripts stored in `/etc/rc.d/init.d`. (See Listing 13.2 for a partial listing of files and subdirectories under `/etc/rc.d`.) The scripts in `init.d` take an argument of `start` or `stop`, and occasionally of `reload` or `restart`.

LISTING 13.2   PARTIAL DIRECTORY LISTING OF `/etc/rc.d`, `/etc/rc.d/init.d`, **AND** `/etc/rc.d/rcf2.d`

```
/etc/rc.d/

drwxr-xr-x  10 root     root        1024 Jan 14 17:24 ./
drwxr-xr-x  41 root     root        4096 Feb 29 11:14 ../
drwxr-xr-x   2 root     root        1024 Feb 27 22:39 init.d/
-rwxr-xr-x   1 root     root        5270 Jul 14  1999 rc*
-rwxr-xr-x   1 root     root        8930 Jul  7  1999 rc.boot*
-rwxr-xr-x   1 root     root         636 Nov 12 07:12 rc.gui*
-rwxr-xr-x   1 root     root         400 Oct  2  1997 rc.local*
-rwxr-xr-x   1 root     root        2816 Jul 19  1999 rc.modules*
-rwxr-xr-x   1 root     root       10903 Mar 12  1999 rc.serial*
drwxr-xr-x   2 root     root        1024 Feb 27 22:39 rc0.d/
drwxr-xr-x   2 root     root        1024 Feb 27 22:39 rc1.d/
drwxr-xr-x   2 root     root        1024 Feb 27 22:39 rc2.d/
drwxr-xr-x   2 root     root        1024 Feb 27 22:39 rc3.d/
drwxr-xr-x   2 root     root        1024 Feb 27 22:39 rc4.d/
drwxr-xr-x   2 root     root        1024 Feb 28 14:52 rc5.d/
```

LISTING 13.2   CONTINUED

```
drwxr-xr-x    2 root      root         1024 Feb 28 14:52 rc6.d/
-rwxr-xr-x    1 root      root          846 Jun 29  1999 unconfigured.sh*

/etc/rc.d/init.d
drwxr-xr-x    2 root      root         1024 Feb 27 22:39 ./
drwxr-xr-x   10 root      root         1024 Jan 14 17:24 ../
-rwxr-xr-x    1 root      root         2144 Jul 14  1999 bigfs*
-rwxr-xr-x    1 root      root          864 Aug 26  1999 cron*
-rwxr-xr-x    1 root      root          861 Jan 13 18:53 dhcpd*
-rwxr-xr-x    1 root      root         6948 Jul 20  1999 functions*
-rwxr-xr-x    1 root      root          833 Jan 13 19:00 gpm*
-rwxr-xr-x    1 root      root         1296 Apr  9  1998 halt*
-rwxr-xr-x    1 root      root          974 Feb  5 20:07 httpd.rpmsave*
-rwxr-xr-x    1 root      root         4044 Jan 14 17:24 hylafax*
-rwxr-xr-x    1 root      root         1092 Jan 13 18:13 inet*
-rwxr-xr-x    1 root      root        10089 Feb 10 16:19 ipsec*
-rwxr-xr-x    1 root      root         2466 Apr 17  1998 ipx*
-rwxr-xr-x    1 root      root          889 Jan 13 18:15 irda*
-rwxr-xr-x    1 root      root          978 Jul  7  1999 keytable*
-rwxr-xr-x    1 root      root         1087 Jan 13 21:05 ldap*
lrwxrwxrwx    1 root      root           11 Feb  9 19:30 local -> ../rc.local*
-rwxr-xr-x    1 root      root          804 Jan 13 19:35 logoutd*
-rwxr-xr-x    1 root      root          931 Nov  4  1998 lpd*
-rwxr-xr-x    1 root      root         1720 Aug 10  1999 mta*
-rwxr-xr-x    1 root      root         1306 Jan 14 00:10 named*
-rwxr-xr-x    1 root      root         2260 Jul 14  1999 netmount*
-rwxr-xr-x    1 root      root         2072 Jul 14  1999 network*
-r-xr-xr-x    1 root      root         1940 Dec 13 09:34 nfs*
-rwxr-xr-x    1 root      root         1350 Jan  7  1998 nis-client*
-rwxr-xr-x    1 root      root          831 Jan  8  1998 nis-server*
-rwxr-xr-x    1 root      root         1489 Apr  3  1999 ntp*
-r-xr-xr-x    1 root      root         4199 Feb 18 15:15 pcmcia*
-r-xr-xr-x    1 root      root         3157 Feb  4 21:28 pcmcia.rpmsave*
-rwxr-xr-x    1 root      root         1377 Jan 13 18:11 portmap*
-rwxr-xr-x    1 root      root          649 May 26  1998 ppp*
lrwxrwxrwx    1 root      root            4 Feb  9 19:30 reboot -> halt*
-rwxr-xr-x    1 root      root          238 Oct  2  1997 rmnologin*
-rwxr-xr-x    1 root      root          780 Oct  2  1997 rstatd*
-r-xr-xr-x    1 root      root         1130 Jan 13 18:10 rusersd*
-r-xr-xr-x    1 root      root         1130 Jan 13 18:09 rwalld*
-r-xr-xr-x    1 root      root         1130 Jan 13 18:10 rwhod*
-rwxr-xr-x    1 root      root         1180 Jul 20  1999 samba*
-rwxr-xr-x    1 root      root          969 Nov 25  1997 single*
-rwxr-xr-x    1 root      root         1212 Jul 19  1999 skeleton*
-rwxr-xr-x    1 root      root          625 Jul 19  1999 skipped*
-rwxr-xr-x    1 root      root          915 Dec 23 17:22 snmpd*
-rwxr-xr-x    1 root      root         1147 Aug 25  1999 syslog*
-rwxr-xr-x    1 root      root         1060 Mar 16  1999 urandom*
-r-xr-xr-x    1 root      root        22723 Feb 18 14:12 vmware*
-rwxr-xr-x    1 root      root          160 Feb 26 18:28 webmin*

/etc/rc.d/rc2.d
lrwxrwxrwx    1 root      root           15 Feb  9 19:43 K09samba -> ../init.d/samba*
lrwxrwxrwx    1 root      root           13 Feb  9 19:37 K25gpm -> ../init.d/gpm*
lrwxrwxrwx    1 root      root           17 Feb  9 19:31 K30logoutd -> ../init.d/logoutd*
lrwxrwxrwx    1 root      root           16 Feb  9 21:06 K39rwalld -> ../init.d/rwalld*
```

LISTING 13.2   CONTINUED

```
lrwxrwxrwx   1 root     root     16 Feb  4 16:17 K40rstatd -> ../init.d/rstatd*
lrwxrwxrwx   1 root     root     15 Feb 15 14:11 K44dhcpd -> ../init.d/dhcpd*
lrwxrwxrwx   1 root     root     17 Feb  9 19:32 K47rusersd -> ../init.d/rusersd*
lrwxrwxrwx   1 root     root     15 Feb  9 19:32 K48rwhod -> ../init.d/rwhod*
lrwxrwxrwx   1 root     root     13 Feb  4 16:17 K50mta -> ../init.d/mta*
lrwxrwxrwx   1 root     root     14 Feb  9 21:54 K55ldap -> ../init.d/ldap*
lrwxrwxrwx   1 root     root     15 Feb  9 20:46 K55snmpd -> ../init.d/snmpd*
lrwxrwxrwx   1 root     root     13 Feb  9 19:42 K60nfs -> ../init.d/nfs*
lrwxrwxrwx   1 root     root     13 Feb  9 19:47 K70ntp -> ../init.d/ntp*
lrwxrwxrwx   1 root     root     17 Feb  4 16:17 K73ipxripd -> ../init.d/ipxripd*
lrwxrwxrwx   1 root     root     20 Feb 15 13:46 K79nis-client -> ../init.d/
➥nis-client*
lrwxrwxrwx   1 root     root     20 Feb 15 13:46 K80nis-server -> ../init.d/
➥nis-server*
lrwxrwxrwx   1 root     root     14 Feb  9 19:32 K84inet -> ../init.d/inet*
lrwxrwxrwx   1 root     root     17 Feb  9 19:42 K85portmap -> ../init.d/portmap*
lrwxrwxrwx   1 root     root     15 Feb  9 21:53 K90named -> ../init.d/named*
lrwxrwxrwx   1 root     root     20 Feb  9 21:17 K96irda-utils -> ../init.d/
➥irda-utils
lrwxrwxrwx   1 root     root     17 Feb  9 19:30 S01network -> ../init.d/network*
lrwxrwxrwx   1 root     root     16 Feb  9 19:30 S05syslog -> ../init.d/syslog*
lrwxrwxrwx   1 root     root     17 Feb  9 19:30 S05urandom -> ../init.d/urandom*
lrwxrwxrwx   1 root     root     16 Feb  9 19:32 S06pcmcia -> ../init.d/pcmcia*
lrwxrwxrwx   1 root     root     18 Feb  9 19:30 S20netmount -> ../init.d/netmount*
lrwxrwxrwx   1 root     root     13 Feb  9 19:37 S26ipx -> ../init.d/ipx*
lrwxrwxrwx   1 root     root     15 Feb  9 20:04 S35ipsec -> ../init.d/ipsec*
lrwxrwxrwx   1 root     root     13 Feb  4 16:16 S35lpd -> ../init.d/lpd*
lrwxrwxrwx   1 root     root     14 Feb  9 19:46 S40cron -> ../init.d/cron*
lrwxrwxrwx   1 root     root     18 Feb  9 19:37 S75keytable -> ../init.d/keytable*
lrwxrwxrwx   1 root     root     15 Feb  9 19:30 S98local -> ../init.d/local*
lrwxrwxrwx   1 root     root     15 Feb  9 19:30 S99bigfs -> ../init.d/bigfs*
lrwxrwxrwx   1 root     root     19 Feb  9 19:30 S99rmnologin -> ../init.d/
➥rmnologin*
lrwxrwxrwx   1 root     root     17 Feb  9 19:30 S99skipped -> ../init.d/skipped*
lrwxrwxrwx   1 root     root     16 Feb  9 20:49 S99webmin -> ../init.d/webmin*
```

The files in the /etc/rc.d/rc#.d directories all begin with either an S or a K for start or kill, respectively, a number that indicates a relative order for the scripts, and the script name—commonly the same name as the master script to which it is linked (found in init.d). For example, you might see S35lpd. This is a symbolic link to /init.d/lpd and is used by rc to run the lpd script in init.d with the argument start, which starts up the line printer daemon. The scripts can also be called from the following command line:

/etc/rc.d/init.d/lpd start.

The nice part about SysV initialization is that it is easy for root to start, stop, and, in many cases, restart or reload a daemon or process subsystem from the command line simply by calling the script in init.d with the appropriate argument.

When not called from a command line with an argument, the /etc/rc.d/rc script determines what to run, and how, based on the previous and current runlevel. For example, if you are in runlevel 3 and change to runlevel 2, the /etc/rc.d/rc script uses the runlevel command as you did earlier, and looks at the differences in the two directories corresponding to the two runlevels to determine what to do. Any process subsystems that are running and that need to be stopped are stopped by calling the appropriate `kill` script; any that are not running that need to be started are started by executing the corresponding `start` scripts as explained previously. The `rc` script always runs the `Knn` scripts from lowest to highest, and then the `Snn` scripts (also in ascending order). This ensures that the correct daemons are running in each runlevel and that they are stopped and started in the correct order. For example, don't start sendmail (`mta`) or the Apache Web server (`httpd`) before you start networking. By the same token, you'll want to stop sendmail and Apache before you stop networking.

Remember when you changed to runlevel 8? Well, because there is no subdirectory `rc8.d`, and therefore there are no scripts, when you changed runlevels, no init scripts were started, and the consoles awaiting login were all stopped. Had you come from boot directly to runlevel 8, you would have had a problem. Only the kernel, init, and those daemons started using the `sysinit`, `boot`, or `bootwait` commands in the `inittab` would have been running.

The Debian distribution chose not to implement the `/etc/rc.d` subirectory, but instead puts the `rc#.d` and `init.d` directories directly in `/etc`. Scripts that would appear in `/etc/rc.d` appear instead in `/etc/rc.boot/`. You can follow the trail to these scripts from `/etc/inittab`.

THE STARTUP SCRIPTS

Here's a look at what some of the startup scripts do. This is an executive summary only. The first startup script overview you'll look at is `/etc/rc.d/rc`.

The script logic goes like this:

1. Initialize some variables.
2. If the file `/etc/isapnp.conf` exists, run `isapnp` to set up any PNP devices; otherwise, skip this step.
3. Read the module options file; the first file to be found is used. Look in this order: `/etc/modules/<kernel-version>/options/`, `/etc/modules/options/`.
4. Read the module file and insert the modules using `modprobe`. The first file found is used. The search is conducted in this order: `/etc/modules/<kernel-version>/`
`<kernel-revision>.default`, `/etc/modules/<kernel-version>/default`, `/etc/`
`modules/default`. Add any options from step 3 for any module requiring an option.
5. While loading modules, send all messages to `VT10`.

The next script of interest is the `/etc/rc.d/rc` script, run each time you change runlevels. This script takes as an argument the runlevel that it is entering. The program logic goes something like this:

1. Declare some variables, including sending all messages to TTY12.
2. Find out what the current (runlevel going to) and previous runlevels are.
3. If a directory exists for the current runlevel and the previous runlevel isn't `N`, compare the directories so you don't stop then restart processes that are already running.

4. If step 3's previous runlevel wasn't N, go through the necessary kill scripts first and stop processes that don't apply to this runlevel; otherwise, continue on to step 5.

5. Start any processes that aren't running that you need in this new runlevel.

6. Put a message on TTY7 to switch consoles for login (just in case the user is left here).

One script of great interest is the rc.local file. This file is called from /etc/rc.d/init.d/local. You can use this script to run just about anything you want to during system startup.

Caution

Use care when adding commands to rc.local. Remember that root will run commands in this file, but has no way to receive input. Probably the most common error is to forget to put the command in the background by adding the & to the end of the line if the command doesn't have a daemon mode.

The next script you'll look at is a typical shell script that is found in /etc/rc.d/init.d and is used to start a daemon or process subsystem. These scripts are linked from the various runlevel directories (as discussed previously). The program logic for this script is similar to other distribution-supplied init scripts. Some minor differences you might find are the specific arguments they take. All take start and stop. Some also take restart and/or reload.

Looking at the program logic of the mta script, which starts the Caldera-supplied mail transport agent (in this case, sendmail), the flow looks like this:

1. Initialize some variables by reading /etc/sysconfig/network and /etc/rc.d/init.d/functions. The network file sets the NETWORKING variable (yes or no).

2. The functions file checks /etc/sysconfig/daemons/mta (or whatever daemon file corresponds to the init script being called) and sets the variables inside that file. One of the first things checked is whether this daemon is allowed to start (determined by the variable ONBOOT= and a value of yes or no). Any options are also contained in this daemon file.

3. The script now looks at the argument used to call it. If the argument is invalid or nonexistent, a usage message prints, and the script exits.

4. If the script was called with a valid argument, such as start or stop, actions are taken to perform the argument's function, substituting values that the functions file learned about from the daemons file (step 2).

Although the scripts are slightly more difficult to read than the preceding steps indicate, they are not unfathomable. If specific configurations are required, particularly for options that need to be passed to the daemon as it is started, these are all located in the /etc/sysconfig/daeamons/<daemon-file> and can be modified there. If you modify the init script directly, any upgrades overwrite those modifications.

EMERGENCIES

Editing inittab or any of the rc scripts requires some degree of caution. But even the best tests cannot simulate a complete system reboot, and a script that might appear to function properly after a system has initialized might fail to execute, or worse, hang during system initialization. The reasons are diverse, but usually involve getting things out of order.

For example, in Caldera's Network Desktop (which ran on a 1.2.13 kernel and used modules), I created a script to start the `kerneld` process early in the boot sequence. When I upgraded the system to Caldera's OpenLinux v1.0 (which ran a 2.0.25 kernel), I used the same script, tested it, and—when I was satisfied that all was well—rebooted the system. Much to my dismay, the boot process hung loading `kerneld`. I found out that with the newer `kerneld`, `kerneld` needed to know the hostname of the computer, which the system did not yet know. This has since been compensated for by putting the hostname discovery process early in the initialization sequence (in `/etc/rc.d/rc.boot`), but such things can happen to anyone. Something as simple as fat-fingering a key or forgetting to full-path something without declaring a `PATH` variable in a script can leave you in a lurch.

> **Note**
>
> Before you decide that a boot process is hung, you might want to wait a full two minutes. Some daemons, especially amd, appear to hang if they try to perform DNS lookup before the system is connected to the Internet. The timeout is two minutes for an IP connection before the daemon gives up waiting for an answer.

Fortunately, you can pass boot-time parameters to init. When the system boots and you see `LILO:`, you can press the Shift key and then the Tab key to see the kernel labels that are available for booting. You can then add a kernel label and follow it by any required parameters to boot the system. Any parameters the kernel needs are used and discarded; for example, if you are using the `devfs` filesystem, you'll need to have `devfs=mount` to activate it during boot. If you pass the `-b` switch, the kernel doesn't use this but passes it on to init. The same goes for any single digit number or the letters `s` or `q` in either upper- or lowercase.

> **Tip**
>
> Use the `-b` option to boot into maintenance mode without running any scripts—for use when scripts might hang the system.

By passing any of the numbers or letters to init, you are overriding the defaults in `inittab`, as was stated earlier. Most of these numbers or letters do exactly what they might do if passed from a command line on a running system. But the `-b` argument is special. It is the emergency boot parameter. This parameter tells init to read the `inittab`. Except for some special exceptions, don't execute any of the commands, just drop into maintenance mode so no `rc` scripts will be executed. You can mount the system read-write and fix it. One exception to not executing any `inittab` commands is any process ID starting with ~, for example ~~ and ~1. If you add or change any script with an ID beginning with ~, it is a good idea to check it as another ID first. You'll not find this feature in the man pages because it's undocumented.

After you've entered the root password (a security feature enabled by the ~~ line in `inittab`), you can run `fsck` if that's what's needed or modify the broken boot file(s).

But before you can modify any files, you'll need to remount the root filesystem read-write with the following command:

```
mount -n -o remount,rw /
```

This command must be entered as above or you'll get errors from the filesystem if you try to write to it. The `-n` tells mount not to try to write to the `/etc/mtab` file, the `-o` is for miscellaneous options, in this case remount, `rw` to remount the root filesystem (`/`) read-write. Do not run `fsck` on a filesystem that is mounted read-write because the kernel will periodically sync memory to the disk. You do not want this to occur while `fsck` is writing to the disk because `fsck` bypasses the kernel and writes directly to the disk. With both `fsck` and `sync` writing to the disk, you could corrupt the disk further.

Caution
The next paragraph discusses booting directly to a shell, which can cause irreparable corruption to the filesystem. This is a last-resort option only!

If, however, despite your best efforts, you find that the boot process still hangs even with the `-b` option to LILO, or if you've forgotten the root password, don't despair. At the LILO prompt, you can pass the parameter `init=/bin/sh`. This argument will be used by the kernel itself. Remember that the kernel runs one and only one program before it goes into the background: init. By passing the preceding argument to LILO, the kernel runs a shell as its only program. This is very dangerous, but it enables you to mount the root filesystem (mount `-n -o remount,rw /`), change `/etc/inittab` or `/etc/shadow`, and then `sync` and reboot. In this case I recommend calling `sync` twice and then remounting the root filesystem read-only and rebooting. Use this as a last resort before a reinstall because it can corrupt your disk, making a reinstall inevitable.

TROUBLESHOOTING

My system is prompting me for my root password at boot up. (I was not asked for a username.) What's going on?

The system has found some corruption in the filesystem that it is unable to cope with. You should read and follow the instructions on the screen. They will say something to the effect of `File system corruption, run fsck manually`. Assuming the corruption was found on disk partition `/dev/hda3`, you need to run the following:

```
fsck -f /dev/hda3
```

You can add the `-y` option to the line if you are unfamiliar with repairing a filesystem manually. When `fsck` has finished, just log out, and the system reboots.

During boot, the process stops (at loading amd or some other daemon). What should I do?

Wait. Make sure a full two minutes has passed. If five minutes passes and nothing has happened, your system is probably frozen. When you reboot, specify the `-b` option at the LILO prompt:

```
boot: linux -b
```

If you are using GRUB, pressing E will show you what GRUB wants to boot. Highlight the appropriate entry (you might have only one) and press E again to edit the line. Add the `-b` parameter to the end of the line, exit, and with the line again highlighted (with the new `-b` entry at the end), press B to boot.

After you log in as root, you'll need to mount your root filesystem read-write:

```
mount -n -o remount,rw /
```

Now edit `/etc/sysconfig/daemons/amd` (this should be the daemon that is hanging) and change the variable `ONBOOT=` from `yes` to `no`. Save the file. Then exit and if the system presents you with a prompt for the root password, press Ctrl+Alt+Delete to reboot.

I logged out of KDE, and on the KDM screen selected the drop-down box to go to console mode. The screen turned black and the system froze.

Your system didn't freeze. When you exited the graphical screen, your system remained on the VT that would have been spawned on F8, had you had an entry to do so. To fix the situation

Press <Alt>+<F1> and then press <Enter>.

You should be greeted with a login prompt.

I don't want to boot into a graphical screen. How can I change this?

If your system is shut down, when you boot, at the LILO prompt, enter the following:

```
LILO: linux 3
```

Or with GRUB, press E, highlight the boot line, add 3 to the end, exit, and with the line highlighted, press B to boot.

This boots the system into runlevel 3. To make this permanent, edit the `/etc/inittab` file and change the following line:

```
id:5:initdefault:
```

to the following:

```
id:3:initdefault:
```

I recompiled my kernel, and now when I'm booting, the screen looks bizarre when bootup ends (and my graphical boot is completely wasted).

The graphical boot requires a patch to the kernel. If you don't want to do this, you have two options:

- Get the new kernel SRPM from Caldera, and then build and install that kernel.
- In either `/etc/lilo.conf` or `/boot/grub/menu.lst` remove the `vga=274` line (or change it to `vga=normal`) and remove the `message=` line. If you're using LILO, don't forget to rerun `lilo`.

My boot-up stopped with L, LI, LIL. What should I do?

See Chapter 12.

CHAPTER **14**

CUSTOMIZING YOUR SHELL ENVIRONMENT

In this chapter

BEYOND THE LOGIN PROMPT

After the system boots and init (or, more accurately, kdm on a standard OpenLinux install, and gdm on Red Hat and Debian, subject to the vagaries of what you've installed and configured) displays a login, what exactly happens? The short answer is, quite a lot. You'll look at the login process as a whole, but certain portions will be specific to the shell (this text will discuss only Bash, the Bourne Again shell), and other portions will deal with graphical versus non-graphical logins.

In the previous chapter, "System Initialization," you saw that init put a getty (short for get TTY) on a terminal. The getty program calls login to put a login prompt on the screen and handle the login itself.

The sequence of events goes something like this:

1. You enter a username and press Enter.
2. The login program prompts for a password and, at the same time, turns off the echo to the screen so your password does not show up.
3. The login program calls crypt to hash your password with the same salt used in the password and compares the hashed passwords.
4. If the username password pair does not match, login resets the screen after giving you an error message. If the username and password pair does match, login continues with step 5.
5. The login program sets up certain environment variables such as USER, UID, and EUID. These variables are set to read-only.
6. The login program continues to parse the /etc/passwd and /etc/shadow files, setting and changing directories to the $HOME directory and setting the shell and invoking it.
7. The default shell spawns as a login shell. This shell will read its startup file. Bourne-based login shells start by reading /etc/profile and then $HOME/.profile.
8. Then bash reads $HOME/.bashrc. This file is parsed by all bash shells spawned by the user, whether or not they are login shells. The OpenLinux .bashrc file also reads .bashrc-private. Other distributions might or might not do this.
9. If the login is a graphical login, the window manager will run and display the graphical environment. The login shell runs the graphical window. If the login is in a command-line environment, a prompt is displayed and the user will work in the login shell.

Note

In a graphical environment, shells (prompts displayed in xterms, kterms, and so on) are not login shells. This distinction is generally not important, but warrants noting, because changes to /etc/profile will not show up in subsequently spawned shells during the current login, but changes to $HOME/.bashrc will.

10. When the user logs out, $HOME/.bash_logout is executed.

Some differences exist if a C shell is used, principally in the files parsed when the shell spawns.

WHAT IS A SHELL?

To understand a shell, you need to understand a few terms; you also need to understand how you interact with the system (both hardware and other software) as a whole. Previously, you learned that Linux sees everything as nothing more than files (see Chapter 10, "Understanding the Linux Filesystem"). Whether that file is ASCII text, binary instructions, a directory, or a special file that acts as a conduit to pass data to and from a piece of hardware, it is seen by the kernel as a file.

Looking at Figure 14.1, if you imagine that all the files on a disk go in the center circle—regardless of whether or not they represent hardware—it will be a little easier to understand what happens. After the kernel boots, it is in charge of everything in the center circle; all hardware and files are accessed through the Linux kernel. The area defined by the middle ring where the kernel lives is often referred to as *kernel space*. The outer ring is *user space*; the shell, all programs spawned by the shell, and the daemons operate in the user space. These programs access hardware and other files (*resources*) only by way of the kernel—this determination is made based on permissions. (Although the preceding is oversimplified and not completely technically accurate, it is sufficient for the purposes of this chapter.)

Figure 14.1
A simplified Linux system diagram depicting user, kernel, and resource space.

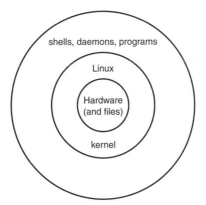

shells, daemons, programs

Linux

Hardware
(and files)

kernel

Relationship of the Linux kernel to hardware and programs

Step through this process slowly to ensure that you understand exactly how the system works. When the kernel boots, it sets up residence in a protected area of memory. The only way to access this memory, and the hardware beneath it, is through special *hooks* that facilitate that access. Some hooks are automatically built in, whereas others can be specified when you configure the kernel (see Chapter 18, "Building a Custom Kernel"). You do not (normally) want, for example, to build the kernel without the hooks that it requires to interact with a console display and keyboard. Modules and programs grab onto the hooks that are designed for them and communicate with the kernel through them. Based on *permissions*—a combination of ownership and mode—the kernel decides whether to allow access to or communication with the file. (See the "File Permissions" section in Chapter 11, "Users, Groups, and Permissions.") A binary file doesn't become a program until the kernel permits it to be loaded into memory and executed. All normal programs run in user space (again, simplified for the purposes of this chapter).

So a shell is nothing more than a program running in user space that provides you with an interactive interface to the system (a *command prompt*) to input data or specify programs to run. As stated earlier, the default shell on most Linux installations is bash (Bourne Again Shell).

The first configuration file called by a Bourne login shell is /etc/profile. Some of the other configuration files called are determined by whether the bash login shell was called as bash or via a symbolic link (sh). In Linux, the default in /etc/passwd is usually /bin/bash; therefore, the files .bash_profile, .bash_login, .bashrc, and .profile, all located in the user's home directory, are called if they exist.

When a login shell exits it calls .bash_logout, if it exists. When an interactive shell that is not a login shell is started, it reads .bashrc, if that file exists, inheriting the environment (discussed as follows). Command-line options can be used to modify this behavior and cause bash to ignore its rc file or read a different one.

Note	The environment variable SHLVL indicates whether a shell is a login shell. SHLVL=1 indicates a login shell, whereas higher numbers indicate a non-login shell, and the level of depth of that shell. See the "Variables" section that follows to learn how to read environment variables.

When you enter input at the shell prompt and press Enter, several things happen. The line is parsed, and each entry separated by white space (and not grouped by quotes) is read by the shell, interpreted if it's a shell special character, expanded if it's an alias, assigned a value in relation to its position on the command line, and executed. The shell first checks to see whether what you typed is a shell built-in command. If not, it checks to see whether it is an alias, and then a function. If it is none of these, the shell searches a predefined set of directories (PATH) for an executable file to run. (There is more on command-line processing, special characters, and aliases later in this chapter.)

TYPES OF SHELLS

Before you continue to a discussion of shell environments, it might interest you to know that a number of shells exist for Linux. Each of these shells has certain characteristics, but each is classified under one of two trees: the Bourne shell or the C shell family.

THE BOURNE SHELL

The Bourne shell is the oldest of the modern shells. It was designed for ease of use and to facilitate scripts. By default, most scripts you see on a Linux system use s, a successor to the Bourne shell. For the purpose of this text, the environment and scripts are discussed in terms of bash. Some shells available for Linux systems that fall under the Bourne shell family include another Bourne successor, ksh, the Korn shell (implemented in most distributions as pdksh); ash, a shell similar to bash but with a smaller footprint, ideal for boot floppies; kiss, another simple shell interpreter (but with only rudimentary built-in commands), which is also ideal for boot or rescue disks; and zsh, a shell that more closely resembles the Korn shell.

The C Shell

The C shell was originally created to overcome the Bourne shell's limitations (such as support for numeric computations). It appealed to advanced users, and to users more familiar with C programming language syntax. The C shell provides a friendly interface but is considered more difficult to script for, particularly for those who are not comfortable with C syntax. Environment variable syntax varies significantly, and scripts written for the Bourne shell family do not normally run on a C shell, and vice versa. C shell (csh) successors include tcsh, which is recommended over csh for those who want to use this type of interface.

For those who enjoy exploring shells and shell programming, a number of other interfaces also exist for Linux, some with built-in support for languages. These include, which has support for Scheme; flin, an interface that uses color and simple syntax; and lsh, which boasts DOS-compatible commands. Some half-dozen other shells are also available.

INTERACTIVE SHELL USE

Most people use their chosen shell interactively. You'll decide what you want to do (start a word processor, list the directory, perform system administration tasks, and so on) and perform it from a shell. bash does have some nice features that you'll want to explore before you go much further.

I've been accused of being lazy, and to a degree that's true. I don't like typing long command sequences or directory paths into the command line. If I want to traverse six subdirectory levels, I don't want to type every character. I want to type cd and just go there. But the next best thing to a single keystroke is having the shell read my mind (or more accurately, choose intelligently among alternatives)—and it can, in a shell sort of way. If you start to type a path or filename, and that path or filename is unique among the choices available, you can press the Tab key, and the shell fills out the rest of the unique portion of that name. If the choices are not unique—that is, if a range of choices is available—you hear a beep (if your speaker is working), which indicates that ambiguous choices are present. If you press the Tab key a second time, you are presented with the possible options from which to choose— unless there is a large number, in which case you can choose whether you want to see all the options. Often, just one more character makes the selection unique again.

Another feature of interest is the command history. This is saved in a file called .bash_history and shows each command you've typed in. The file grows to a predetermined size, and then discards older command lines as newer ones are added. The default is 500 lines. Typing history shows all the commands that bash remembers. (This might exceed the maximum allowable history file size, and will be truncated when the shell exits.) You also can use fc -l, which, by default, shows you the last 17 commands. The most common use of the fc command is in the form fc -s xx, where xx (any number of letters can be used) searches backward in the history for the first command starting with *xx* and executes it. When saved to disk (when the shell exits), this command history makes shell scripting easy. Just cut and paste commands that worked properly into the script.

bash makes cut and paste simple, particularly for those in the X Window environment, because this technique works between application boxes on the screen. Text can be highlighted using the mouse: Just place the cursor at the beginning of the area to be highlighted, press and hold the left mouse button, and drag. In some applications text also can be highlighted using the keyboard: Position the cursor and press and hold the Shift key while using the up and down arrow keys to highlight text. Then, use the middle mouse button—or both the left and right mouse buttons simultaneously on a two-button mouse—to paste the highlighted text.

Most commonly, the up arrow is used to scroll backward through the history buffer until the desired command is found—which can then be changed if necessary—and executed by pressing Enter.

A number of other bash shortcuts exist as well. Prefixing a command with an exclamation point (!) will tell bash to execute the last command by the name that it finds in its history.

DEFAULT SHELL ENVIRONMENT

As mentioned previously, when you log in and get a shell, a number of things happen: Certain files are read, some variables are set, and perhaps even a program or two are run. Most of what happens sets up your *default environment*. This environment is set via the previously mentioned files. A few, however, such as $HOME (a notation indicating a user's home directory—under bash, this can also be abbreviated as a tilde [~])—and $SHELL (which is the shell login called) are obtained from /etc/passwd, as is the UID.

VARIABLES

Listing 14.1 shows a sample /etc/profile. As you can see, one of the first things set is PATH. Custom dictates that environment variables are always uppercase. You can always see how a particular environment variable has been set by using echo, which tells the shell to echo whatever follows to the screen. Any variable can be referenced by prefixing it with a $. Therefore, you can type echo $PATH to find out what your PATH environment variable is set to.

LISTING 14.1   A SAMPLE MASTER PROFILE

```
# /etc/profile
# $Id$
# Minimum system wide initialization of "login"-bourne shells
# Functions and aliases go in $HOME/.bashrc
#[ -e /etc/config.d/D ] && echo "/etc/profile: \$-='$-'" 1>&2
_ETC_PROFILE=1

PATH="/bin:/usr/bin"

umask 022
if [ ! -x /usr/bin/id ]&&[ -z "$USER" -o -z "$UID" ]; then
```

LISTING 14.1   CONTINUED

```
    echo "/usr/bin/id: no such file!" 1>&2
    echo "  As this program is essential for OpenLinux shell-initialization" 1>&2
    echo "  you'll experience problems later!  Please install 'sh-utils'..." 1>&2
    [ -z "$USER" ] && USER=unknown
    [ -z "$UID" ] && UID=-1
else
    [ -z "$USER" ] && USER=`/usr/bin/id -un`
    [ -z "$UID" ] && UID=`/usr/bin/id -u`
fi

[ -z "$HOST" ] && HOST=`/bin/hostname -f`
[ -z "$HOSTNAME" ] && HOSTNAME=`/bin/hostname -s`
[ -z "$LOGNAME" ] && LOGNAME=$USER

export _ETC_PROFILE PATH USER HOST HOSTNAME LOGNAME
```

The /etc/profile file should be maintained by the system administrator, and any changes that apply to all users should be set in this file.

All bash shells then run the $HOME/.bashrc file. The Caldera-provided .bashrc is shown in Listing 14.2.

LISTING 14.2   DEFAULT .bashrc FILE

```
# ~/.bashrc--
# $Id: .bashrc,v 1.2 1999/02/12 13:32:54 ray Exp ray $
# The individual per-interactive-shell startup file for bash
#[ -e /etc/config.d/D ] && echo "~$USER/.bashrc: \$-='$-'" 1>&2

# load maintained system-defaults...  (NB: $HOME/.profile, i.e.
# /etc/config.d/shells/profile) depend on this one!!!)
[ -r /etc/config.d/shells/bashrc ] && . /etc/config.d/shells/bashrc

# load user-defaults
[ -r $HOME/.bashrc-private ] && . $HOME/.bashrc-private

# personal additions should preferably be placed in the above file,
# but may nevertheless be appended below...
```

Notice the line referencing /etc/config.d/shells/bashrc. This line instructs bash to check to see whether the file /etc/config.d/shells/bashrc exists and is readable by the user, and if so, execute it. This is a bash-specific configuration file for global use similar to /etc/profile. The difference between them is that /etc/profile is for all Bourne shells, whereas the commands in bashrc are specific (or should be) to bash. Listing 14.3 shows what the default global bashrc file looks like.

LISTING 14.3   DEFAULT /etc/config.d/shells/bashrc FILE

```
# /etc/config.d/shells/bashrc
# $Id: bashrc,v 1.3 1999/02/12 15:11:02 ray Exp ray $
# Full fledged, system-wide initialization of "interactive"-shells
# (source-able by $HOME/.bashrc)
```

LISTING 14.3   CONTINUED

```
#[ -e /etc/config.d/D ] && echo "/etc/config.d/shells/bashrc: \$-='$-'" 1>&2

# if we haven't read /etc/profile (e.g. rsh or su) read it now...
[ -z "$_ETC_PROFILE" ] && . /etc/profile

# fiddle with umask
umask 022
[ -n "$USER" ]&&[ "$USER" = `id -gn` ]&&[ "$UID" != 0 ]&& umask 002

# set up "HOME" variables for certain packages...
[ -z "$KDEDIR" ]&&[ -d /opt/kde ] &&    export KDEDIR=/opt/kde
[ -z "$OPENWINHOME" ]&&[ -d /usr/openwin ] && export OPENWINHOME=/usr/openwin
[ -z "$JAVA_HOME" ]&&[ -d /usr/java ] && {
  export JAVA_HOME=/usr/java
  [ -r $JAVA_HOME/lib/classes.zip ] &&
    export CLASSPATH=$JAVA_HOME/lib/classes.zip
}

# try to generate an elaborate PATH ...
_p="$HOME/bin"
[ "$UID" = 0 ]  && _p="$_p /usr/local/sbin /sbin /usr/sbin"

_q=`echo " $PATH " | sed -e 's/:/ /g' -e 's/ \.[. ]* / /g'`
_q="$_q /usr/local/bin  /usr/X11R6/bin /opt/bin /opt/teTeX/bin"
_q="$_q $KDEDIR/bin $OPENWINHOME/bin $JAVA_HOME/bin"

_P=""
for _i in $_p $_q; do
  case ":$_P:" in
   *:$_i:*) : $_i;;
   *) [ -d $_i ] && _P="$_P:$_i" ;;
  esac
done
while [ $_P != ${_P#:} ]; do _P=${_P#:}; done

# if you have relaxed security concerns you may uncomment the following...
#[ -n "$UID" ]&&[ "$UID" != 0 ]&& _P="${_P}:."

export PATH=$_P
unset _p _q _i _P


# try to solve this tedious 'Backspace vs. Delete' problem...
case $- in
 *i*)
  if [ -z "$TERM" ]; then
    echo ".bashrc: TERM empty: this shouldn't happen!" 1>&2
    echo "   Please contact 'support@caldera.com'" 1>&2
  else
    case $TERM in
    dumb)
      :
      ;;
    linux*)
      stty erase '^?'
```

LISTING 14.3   CONTINUED

```
      ;;
    *)
      stty erase '^H'
      ;;
    esac
  fi
  ;;
esac

# general environment settings
export MAIL="/var/spool/mail/$USER"
#export GROFF_TYPESETTER=latin1
#export LC_CTYPE=iso-8859-1
export LESSCHARSET=latin1
export PAGER=less
#export METAMAIL_PAGER=$PAGER

# bash-specific settings
PS1="[\u@\h \W]\\$ "
HISTSIZE=100

alias which='type -path'
alias h='history'
alias j='jobs -l'
alias l='ls -Fax'
alias ll='ls -Alg'
alias pd='pushd'
alias z='suspend'
```

Looking at Listings 14.1–14.3, you no longer see the PATH variable being set a second time by listing PATH=$PATH:/another/path:/yet/another/path because the programmers have opted for a method to discover available paths using a sed statement. However, you might want to use the old method, so it is explained here. To avoid replacing the entire contents of the old variable PATH with the new value, or to avoid retyping a possibly long value to insert another directory into the PATH, you can use the following shortcut:

```
# PATH=/bin:/usr/bin
# PATH=$PATH:/usr/X11R6/bin
# echo $PATH
PATH=/bin:/usr/bin:/usr/X11R6/bin
#
```

As illustrated, this gives you the same result as typing PATH=/bin:/usr/bin:/usr/X11R6/bin. If PATH=$PATH:/usr/X11R6/bin is rewritten as only PATH=/usr/X11R6/bin, you will lose the /bin:/usr/bin part. This is true for any variable substitution, not just PATH.

One other thing I want to explain at this time is the export line. This line is designed to ensure that the variables it references are available to all the subshells and programs that the current shell runs. When you type in a line to run a program, for example vi, your shell searches all the directories in the order in which they are listed in the $PATH variable and runs the first executable it finds called vi. Whenever a program is called, it normally performs a fork() and then an exec(). This detaches the program from the current shell and

PART
III

CH
14

runs it in its own shell with its own environment. When this happens, the subsequent program inherits certain characteristics from the calling shell (its parent). What it inherits are exported environment variables. So, if the program you start is another shell and you have not exported an environment variable (such as PATH), it is not available to the new (child) shell. Although this gives a great deal of power and flexibility to the shell, what ensues can be a frustrating experience for new Linux users as the new shell returns the message command not found for commands that the parent shell had no problem finding. An example of two equivalent export lines is the following:

```
VAR=foo; export VAR
export VAR=foo
```

If you want to see all the environment variables available, bash has a built-in command to help you: set. By itself, set displays your environment. (See Listing 14.4 for a sample output.) If you run a shell other than bash, the external command env might be the only way to see your environment. set also can be used to set an environment variable, as in set VAR=kludge—but why type four characters (three letters and a space) unnecessarily? Thus, common usage is to not use it. But it does suggest a complement: unset. You can use unset if you want to eliminate a variable rather than just setting it to a null value. For example, if you have an environment variable DISPLAY=:0.0, and you change from an X Window running on F7 to a non-graphic virtual terminal on F1 (by pressing Ctrl+Alt+F1), you might need to get rid of this variable. Some programs, when they start, look for the environment variable DISPLAY and use its value to determine whether or where to run a graphic- instead of non-graphic-version. If the DISPLAY environment variable is present, the program fails with an ugly error message. This might even happen if DISPLAY is set to null (that is, set DISPLAY). To avoid this, you can simply type unset DISPLAY, and the variable will no longer exist.

LISTING 14.4   SAMPLE OUTPUT FROM set

```
BASH=/bin/bash
BASH_VERSINFO=([0]="2" [1]="01" [2]="1" [3]="1" [4]="release" [5]="i486-pc-linux")
BASH_VERSION='2.01.1(1)-release'
COLUMNS=79
DIRSTACK=()
DISPLAY=LOCALHOST:0.0
EUID=1000
GROUPS=()
HISTFILE=/home/dab/.bash_history
HISTFILESIZE=500
HISTSIZE=500
HOME=/home/dab
HOSTDISPLAY=LOCALHOST:0.0
HOSTNAME=lnb1
HOSTTYPE=i486
IFS='
"
LINES=56
LOGNAME=dab
MACHTYPE=i486-pc-linux
MAILCHECK=60
OLDPWD=/home/dab/docs
OPTERR=1
```

LISTING 14.4   CONTINUED

```
OPTIND=1
OSTYPE=linux-gnu
PATH=/usr/local/bin:/usr/bin:/bin:/usr/bin/X11:/usr/games:
➥/usr/local/jdk116_v5/bin:/opt/root/bin:/usr/local/vnc
PIPESTATUS=([0]="0")
PPID=233
PS1='\s-\v\$ "
PS2='> "
PS4='+ "
PWD=/home/dab
ROOTSYS=/opt/root
SHELL=/bin/bash
SHELLOPTS=braceexpand:hashall:histexpand:monitor:history:
➥interactive-comments:emacs
SHLVL=2
TERM=xterm
UID=1000
USER=dab
WABIDIR=/home/wabi
WINDOWID=25165844
XFCE_LANG=en
_=set
```

Another important variable that you might want to know about but won't see using set is umask. This term stands for *user mask*, and is used to determine what permissions are applied to new files. The umask command by itself returns a three-digit octal number. This number is the inverse of the octal number used by chmod to set a file's mode (for more on chmod, see the "File Permissions" section of Chapter 11). The most common umasks are 002 and 022. A umask of 022 sets the mode of newly created directories and executable files to 755 (777-022), and other files to 644 (666-022). Assuming that the file kludge doesn't exist in your current directory, and that you have rights to write in that directory, typing touch kludge creates a regular file kludge with mode 644 (assuming a umask of 022).

You might notice some differences with the preceding descriptions of file layout between Caldera, Red Hat, and Debian. This is to be expected. But the filenames and how the process works are the same. You can make changes as well to customize the initialization process somewhat. Part of what Linux is about is freedom to choose how you want to do things.

ALIASES AND FUNCTIONS

Beyond variables, two other important things that affect your environment and can be set up automatically in your configuration files are aliases and functions. Aliases known to your system can be seen by typing the word alias at the command prompt. Some common aliases are which, z, h, and j (see Listing 14.5). Aliases are declared by using the alias command. For example, if you want your directory listings to show up in color, you might want the following included in your .bashrc file:

```
alias ls="ls --color=auto"
```

Now, any time you enter the `ls` command, it will be as if you typed `ls --color=auto`. Some people, to be safe, alias `rm="rm -i"` to prevent them from accidentally deleting something that they don't mean to delete. Unfortunately, if they ever log on to a system without this alias, they almost always unintentionally delete something. Therefore, an alias can be a double-edged sword. Of course, if you don't want this crutch, you can always remove it with `unalias`. An alias always takes precedence over an executable unless the executable is called via its full path (that is, `/bin/ls`). Aliases are not exported, but this is not a problem because they are usually only useful in a shell. Normally, aliases are declared in your `.bashrc` file and are available for each subshell spawned.

LISTING 14.5   SAMPLE OUTPUT FROM `alias`

```
alias h='history'
alias j='jobs -l'
alias l='ls -Fax'
alias ll='ls -Alg'
alias ls='ls --color=auto -aF'
alias pd='pushd'
alias which='type -path'
alias z='suspend'
```

Whereas an alias is generally a short command substitution, a function can be a single command or an entire multiline program. Listing 14.6 shows an example of a file called `.functions`. This file is called from the `.bashrc-private` file by the following line:

```
. ./.functions
```

As you can see, its syntax is similar to that of a shell script (discussed in a later section), and has the following form:

```
name () {statements ; }
```

Any functions can be seen from the current shell by using `typeset` or `declare`. This shows your entire environment, including functions. To see functions only, use the `-f` option with either command. See Listing 14.7 for a sample output (notice that the output shows the alias expanded `ls` call). Functions exist in the current shell, and are an exception to the rule that commands are executed with `fork()` and `exec()`.

LISTING 14.6   EXAMPLE OF `.functions`

```
# This is a file with a function

 cdd ()
{
    if [ $# = 1 ]; then
        cd $1;
        ls -aF;
    else
        echo "function requires an argument";
    fi
}
```

Functions always execute in the current shell. Functions can supposedly be exported by using declare -x name, but I've had poor results with this method. As with aliases, though, if the .functions file is called from the .bashrc-private file (as in Listing 14.7), the functions will be available each time a new shell is spawned.

LISTING 14.7 SAMPLE OUTPUT FROM declare OR typeset

```
declare -f cdd ()
{
    if [ $# = 1 ]; then
        cd $1;
        ls --color=auto -aF -aF;
    else
        echo "function requires an argument";
    fi
}
```

One thing you might have noticed is the way that the .function file is called. The command is preceded by a solitary period (.). This is a synonym for source (which can be substituted for . but rarely is) and tells the shell to run the command or file in the current shell—that is, to *source* the file. This causes exec() to run without a fork(), in a manner similar to functions.

CUSTOMIZING YOUR ENVIRONMENT

By using what you've learned previously, you can see that it is a fairly simple task to customize your environment. From within your own home directory, just change or add those things that you want, export them if necessary, and you're off. Additions and changes can be made from a command line as well as from .bashrc-private. Just type the command at a command prompt as you list it in the rc file. This is a great way to experiment.

Take a look at your environment by typing set (or declare if you're also using functions). If you look down the list, you'll see something interesting: a UID. This is how the system knows who you are, and what your permissions are. Great! If you change this, you can become root. Sound too easy? A few environment variables have been set with the -r option—they're read-only. You can't set them, and you can't unset them. They're permanent when declared, and the system has also exported them. Your system administrator can also set environment variables as read-only in files in /etc. In certain circumstances, this might be necessary.

If you decide to set a variable from scratch, such as PATH, and it is very long, breaking it up into several lines might be desirable. But how do you do that, when pressing the Enter key executes the line? If the last character in the line is a backslash (\), the shell does not execute the line, but waits for more input until you enter a line not terminated by a backslash. You also might notice that your command prompt has changed. This is a signal to you that the shell is awaiting further input. You can see the continuation prompt as the environment variable PS2. PS1 is your primary command prompt, and it can also be customized. You can change your prompt as follows:

```
export PS1="$USERNAME@$HOSTNAME \$ "
```

This gives you the prompt me@myhost $. You also can change this to always show your present directory (pwd) by using the following:

```
export PS1='`pwd` '
```

This brings up the next point. You have four sets of punctuation with which to work. Until this last example, I deliberately stayed with examples that needed only double quotes (" "); but there are also single quotes (' ') and grave quotes (` `). The grave quotes are the quote marks normally found on a 102-key keyboard in the upper-left corner below the Esc key, and to the left of the 1/! key. A shifted grave quote gives you a tilde (~). So when do you use which? The rules are as follows:

- **Use double quotes to pass what's inside the quotes to the command, but allow variable substitution**—That is, echo "$HOME" gives you /home/username. You need to use double quotes whenever you have a single argument that contains white space (as defined by your IFS environment variable, usually Space+Tab+Newline). For example, cd /etc/modules/`uname -r`/`uname -v` gives you the error bash cd: /etc/modules/ 2.0.35/#1: No such file or directory. Note that the entire name of the directory is #1 Thu Jul 23 12:41:51 PDT 1998, but cd stopped reading when it reached the first space—between the 1 and the T. So, for this to work properly, you need to surround the argument to cd with quotes:
  ```
  "/etc/modules/`uname -r`/`uname -v`".
  ```

- **Use single quotes to pass what's inside the quotes to the command, but do not allow variable substitution**—That is, echo '$HOME' gives you $HOME. This is handy if you need to pass $HOME to the next command through a pipe without it being expanded first. You'll need to use this technique in your last command prompt example (shown previously).

- **Use grave quotes to pass what's inside the quotes to the command, after executing (with variable substitution) the command inside the quotes**—That is, echo `pwd` gives you /home/username.

Note

> Currently accepted practice is to use $(command) instead of `command`. This is often easier for new users to grasp, but most scripts written by experienced users still use the grave quotes. Do not confuse $(command) with ${variable}; they are not interchangeable.

So, the command line required in the previous paragraph, export PS1='`pwd` ', is a single quote, then pwd surrounded by grave quotes, a space (for aesthetics), and the closing single quote. By doing this, when you read the environment variable PS1, you'll see `pwd`. Each time you get a command prompt, it executes pwd and displays it. If you use double quotes instead of single quotes around the argument, you see something such as PS1=/home/_username, and the variable does not update each time you change directories. Experiment with it.

You're probably asking, "But what if I need to use a quote inside a quote?" No problem. I said you had four sets of punctuation, and this is the fourth. But to tell the shell that the quote you're about to use is not part of the open/close quote sequence, you escape it by preceding it with a backslash (\). In fact, the backslash can be used to escape any character the shell can interpret, such as $, *, and so on. So, `echo \$HOME` produces $HOME.

SHELL PROGRAMMING (SCRIPTS)

When you're comfortable with the command-line interface, you'll find yourself performing some tasks repeatedly. Personally, if I have to do something more than twice, I'll write a quick script to handle it for me. When you learn how to do this, you have a really powerful ally at your side.

However, writing scripts also necessarily entails a few more steps. For one thing, because you'll save them (probably in a `scripts` directory), you'll want to be able to reuse them. You might also find that you'll want to have cron run them late at night, or when the system is idle, or just daily so that you don't have to remember to do it yourself. But when you get to this level of sophistication, you'll need to ensure that your scripts are written to compensate for certain conditions, including the shell to use and the proper environment.

The previous discussions and examples all revolved around one shell, bash, but you know that other shells exist: csh, pdksh, and so on. Scripts written and tested on one shell might very well not work on another. Additionally, when cron runs a script for you, it really doesn't know about your specific login environment. So, again, the script might fail—but it doesn't need to.

SOLVING THE SCRIPT COMMAND DILEMMA

Solve the first problem, that of the correct shell, at first. On Linux, all files have a "magic number" as determined by the contents of the first two bytes of the file. The file program reads these two bytes and determines what type of file you have. If you expect file to return the fact that the file is a shell script and executable, two things must happen. The first (in Chapter 11, see "File Permissions" section) is to ensure that when it is saved, the execute bit is set, such as chmod a+x *scriptname*. The second is to begin every script the same way:

```
#!/bin/bash
```

Using the combination #! (sometimes called a *shebang*) as the first two characters in a file ensures that the file is seen by the system as a shell script. The rest of the line is the full path to the program needed to execute the statements in the script. This can be /usr/bin/perl, /usr/bin/awk, /usr/bin/_sed -f, and so on. Now, whether run from a C shell or from cron, the system always uses the correct program to execute the code.

ADDRESSING THE SCRIPT ENVIRONMENT QUANDARY

The second problem you need to overcome is the shell environment. We've discussed the environment as it applies to a logged-in user, and any script or program run by a logged-in user inherits all exported environment variables in the parent shell. But if cron runs the script, how will the environment look? If you start with the assumption that any environment that cron or any other user might have either doesn't exist or is wrong, your scripts will work correctly. That means explicitly declaring any environment variables that you want your script to know about. This also prevents manipulation of your script by unethical users.

There are two rules you should always use when writing scripts:

- If you need an environment variable, declare it.
- If you call a program, call the full path to the executable (to ensure that the script can find it and to prevent cron from running a trojan horse). As an added precaution, you'll want to write temporary files that you will subsequently read from to a protected directory, and not /tmp, for security reasons.

Earlier you learned how to get the contents of a variable. You did this by prefacing the variable with a $. Suppose that you have the variable KLUDGE='this ', and another variable BAR='that', and you want to combine these two and add a word in between. If you type echo $KLUDGEAND$BAR, you see "that" printed on the screen. This is not what you wanted. The shell thought the first variable was KLUDGEAND, not KLUDGE. To get around this problem, use {} to surround the variable:

```
echo ${KLUDGE}AND${BAR}
```

This time you get the correct output:

```
this AND that
```

Another sticky issue that you run into with scripts, and particularly with those that you run non-interactively, is how to handle output. For this, you have *redirectors*. Normally, the system takes commands and input from stdin (the standard input), or the keyboard. This is device 0. You then see output on the screen, also known as stdout (the standard output, or device 1). But you also have a third channel. This is known as stderr (standard error, device 2). It would be nice if you never needed stderr—but no such luck.

REDIRECTION

The system ordinarily shows stderr on the screen when you are working interactively. However, with a script that runs when no one is around, and with stdout—if any—that goes to a file, you need to deal with stderr or the system administrator will wonder why the console has error messages when he looks at it in the morning. But first, let's cover how you're going to deal with getting just stdin and stdout redirected.

To have the normal output from the script redirected to a file so that you can see the results later, use a redirector (>) . If you enter `ls > direct`, you create a file called direct in the current directory, and in that file are the results of the ls command. If you then enter `ls -l > direct`, you overwrite the previous file direct with a new file direct that contains a long listing of the directory. But that's not what you wanted. You wanted to append the results of the second command to the file. For that, you use >>. So entering `ls -l >> direct` leaves what's already in the file intact and adds this new listing to the bottom.

I want to point out that `ls > direct` is the same as entering `ls 1> direct` because you are redirecting stdout (device 1) to the file. To include stderr (device 2) in the file so that it has somewhere to go, you can do the following:

`ls > filename 2>&1`

What this says is that you want to send a directory listing to filename and, by the way, any error messages are to be included with the listing. You also can send them their own separate ways, as in the following example:

`ls > filename 2> /dev/null`

This sends the listing to filename but dumps any error messages on the floor.

Similarly, you can redirect input, such as cat < filename. Input and output redirection can also be combined:

cat < filename 2>&1 nextfile

Those of you who are keeping score on this have probably noticed that you have >, >>, and <, but you don't have <<. The doubled input redirector does have a legitimate role. Assume that you want to get a file every morning from an FTP site. Because this is repetitious, you'll write a script. The Linux ftp client will automatically log you in if you create a .netrc file, but you need to send input to the FTP prompt to cd into a new directory (pub), to ensure you are in binary mode, to get the file, and to terminate FTP. That part of the script looks like this:

```
ftp ftp.server.com <<EOF
cd pub \n
binary \n
get file \n
bye \n
EOF
```

What you are going to do is read from the file as input to the command until you reach the EOF. The \n is a new line. So you can see that you have some very powerful allies with scripts.

DEBUGGING

If you have trouble with your script, the best way to debug it is to enter the line set -x at the top. When the shell encounters the set -x, it will print out all the commands and their arguments until a set +x is encountered. You can surround problem areas in your script or exclude loops this way.

CASE STUDY: SCRIPTING SUGGESTIONS

As part of furthering your knowledge in shell scripts, look at the scripts in /etc/rc.d/init.d. They will show you how a script can give a usage statement if it requires an argument (the case statements), how to test for conditions ([` equals test, but also requires a closing] to terminate the test—enter man test for details), and proper use of variables. Other scripts you'll find on your Linux system will show you how to loop through a (sometimes previously undetermined) number of items using a for ..do .. done syntax (as in /etc/rc.d/rc. modules). Scripts can be a powerful ally. While you're learning, feel free to borrow from scripts on your system. Also look into sed and s, which work with lines and paragraphs of text.

To give your scripts a professional touch, the following tips are offered. Just following the first line, but before you begin declaring your environment and executing code, it's a good idea to include a few commented lines about the script. Lines that begin with a # are not treated as commands by the script, but are ignored as comments. Here, near the top of the file, add a few things such as the name, date, and purpose of the script. Many times I've looked at a script and wondered who did this kludgy hack, and there at the top was my own name. I had no one to blame for this except myself, (and perhaps insufficient quantities of coffee or a lack of sleep).

I also recommend that you insert comments throughout the script. This will help you troubleshoot it later (or just figure out what you did in the first place). Script changes need to be noted and dated as well, both at the top and in the body. There's no such thing as a script with too many comments. Finally, use variables. If you use a path or filename, for example, more than once in a script, assign it to a variable near the top of the script. That way, when you need to change something, you can change the variable, and all references will be changed—and you won't miss one.

## CHAPTER 15

Understanding PAM

In this chapter

ENCRYPTION AND AUTHENTICATION

Originally, all Linux (and UNIX) systems used /etc/passwd to hold the username/password pair needed to authenticate a user and permit access. The password was saved as a DES (Data Encryption Standard) hash to prevent anyone from reading the actual password. DES uses a 13-character field, the first two characters acting as a salt for the DES algorithm.

The salt acts as a random number passed to the encrypting algorithm. Each salt will produce a different encryption for a particular password, so even if 100 users choose the same (obviously bad) password, examining the encrypted field would not make this apparent as long as each had a different salt. (Microsoft does not use this approach, so examining the encrypted password database for Microsoft NT immediately reveals whether two or more users have the same password.)

The hashed password field permits a password of up to eight characters. The hashed field is like a scrambled egg. It can't be unscrambled, but using the salt, a plaintext password can be scrambled in the same way and compared with the hashed field, with a match successfully authenticating the user.

Note
A new encryption scheme based on MD5 is slowly being introduced. This encryption scheme allows a 4-character salt and up to a 25-character password. However, weak passwords based on dictionary words can still be easily broken.

In the early days of computing, DES encryption was strong enough that the passwords were considered unbreakable, so allowing anyone to see the hash posed no problem. As time went by and computers became more powerful, a cracker permitted access to the hashed password could break into accounts with weak passwords. To prevent just anyone from gaining access to the hashed password and thereby improve the systems' security posture, shadow passwords came about.

The shadow password system used a file readable only by root to be used as the storage place for the hashed password. This proved to be a formidable defense against crackers gaining access to the hashed passwords to run dictionary attacks against them.

However, changing to a shadowed system caused problems. For a restricted service, a service that requires username/password pair authentication, to make use of shadowed passwords, it had to be compiled to understand how to use this authentication scheme. Proprietary UNIX systems, as they changed over to shadow passwords, also included modified binaries for restricted services for their users. But Linux users suffered problems as a result of piecemeal upgrades.

At about the same time the Shadow system started becoming popular, Sun Microsystems began working on a way to permit restricted services to make use of alternative authentication systems such as biometric devices, smart cards, and other authentication schemes. They recognized the problem that restricted services would encounter having to be recompiled to include support for each different authentication method. Therefore, they came up with a solution: Build a library with pluggable modules, whose modules can be built as needed, and just build the restricted services to pass all authentication requests to this library, called `libpam`.

Linux developers, seeing a good idea, built their own implementation of this PAM library. Today, you can switch between a shadowed system and an unshadowed system, or include biometric or other authentication methods, as long as you have a module that can communicate with the authentication scheme. The restricted service just asks PAM to pass back to it whether authentication is confirmed or denied.

USING PAM

To use *PAM (Pluggable Authentication Modules)*, you need to understand how it works. PAM uses a number of files to help determine whether authentication is approved or denied. The first set of files you need to understand are the files in `/etc/pam.d/`. Listing 15.1 shows the contents of `/etc/pam.d`. (Your directory might not look like this listing.) Each restricted service you install or uninstall should add or delete its own corresponding service file.

LISTING 15.1 SAMPLE `/etc/pam.d` LISTING

```
README   chsh   imap   login   passwd   rexec    rsh     su
chfn     ftp    kde    other   pop      rlogin   samba
```

Every restricted service has a corresponding file. If one is not installed, you can create one. If the installed file does not suit your purposes, you can modify it (more on this later). If a file does not exist for a service, the file `other` handles authentication for that restricted service.

Caution

The first iteration of PAM used an `/etc/pam.conf` file. If you have a `pam.conf` file on your system and no `/etc/pam.d`, convert to the individual service files in `pam.d` and delete `pam.conf`. If you already have `pam.d`, `pam.conf` is not used. The `pam.conf` file is deprecated. If you are using `pam.conf`, the first package you install that creates `pam.d` can cause you no end of problems with login authentication failures.

READING THE `/etc/pam.d` FILES

Each file in `/etc/pam.d` contains the authentication methods required to authenticate a service. Listing 15.2 shows the contents of the default `rlogin` file provided with OpenLinux.

LISTING 15.2 DEFAULT `rlogin` FILE

```
#%PAM-1.0
auth       required     /lib/security/pam_securetty.so
auth       sufficient   /lib/security/pam_rhosts_auth.so
auth       required     /lib/security/pam_pwdb.so shadow nullok
auth       required     /lib/security/pam_nologin.so
account    required     /lib/security/pam_pwdb.so
```

LISTING 15.2   CONTINUED

```
#password   required    /lib/security/pam_cracklib.so
password    required    /lib/security/pam_pwdb.so shadow nullok use_authtok
session     required    /lib/security/pam_pwdb.so
```

Each file contains four columns. The first column is the type column, which is one of the following:

- **auth**—Short for authentication. This type deals with verifying that a user is who he claims to be. This is normally done via a username/password pair, but it can also be done through a biometric device or a smartcard. You need modules to interact with the biometric device or smart card.

- **account**—Verifies access privileges and status of a particular account (active, expired, inactive, or disabled).

- **password**—Used to update authentication tokens. If a password has expired, it forces a password update.

- **session**—Prepares the environment for the user. Can perform logging actions and run programs at login and logout (such as mounting directories, performing a chroot, and more).

The second column is the control field and indicates how the value returned by the module is used. Modules return SUCCESS, FAILURE, or IGNORE as a value to the PAM library. SUCCESS and FAILURE are self-explanatory. IGNORE means that the module could not determine a success or failure. This might have happened because the mechanism for determining success or failure was not present or was inaccessible. The control field has one of the following values:

- **requisite**—This means that a FAILURE determination from this module is final. If this module is first and a logging module is included later, a FAILURE here passes FAILURE back to the restricted service immediately and the logging module does not run. You probably don't want to use this control.

- **required**—The required control is combined with all other lines. That is, regardless of the determination from this module, all successive modules are evaluated as well (unless a requisite is encountered and it returns FAILURE— see the preceding text—or a sufficient is encountered and it returns SUCCESS—see the following text).

- **sufficient**—The sufficient control immediately passes a SUCCESS back to the calling restricted service as long as no prior required control holds a value of FAILURE. If a sufficient control holds a value of IGNORE or FAILURE, it is treated as an optional control with the same value.

- **optional**—An optional control field is ignored unless it is the only module for its type. If an optional control is the only one for its type, it is treated as a required control.

> **Caution**
>
> The order of lines is important where `requisite` and `sufficient` controls are concerned; otherwise, order is unimportant. Always test authentication scenarios when making changes to the `pam` authentication files.

The third column specifies the particular module to use. Modules are installed by default in `/lib/security`. To properly use modules, you'll need to understand them. This text discusses some of the more common modules in the next section. These modules change from upgrade to upgrade, normally with more being added, so this text cannot be the authoritative source for the modules. That must be left to the READMEs installed in `/usr/doc/libpam-<version>/`.

The fourth column contains any options you want to assign to the module. The READMEs for the modules contain a list of the valid options available for each module. These options can also change from upgrade to upgrade, so the READMEs should be consulted.

UNDERSTANDING THE MODULES

The following is a list of modules installed in earlier versions of OpenLinux (2.4 and earlier):

pam_access.so	pam_cracklib.so	pam_deny.so
pam_dialup.so	pam_env.so	pam_ftp.so
pam_group.so	pam_lastlog.so	pam_ldap.so*
pam_limits.so	pam_listfile.so	pam_mail.so
pam_nologin.so	pam_permit.so	pam_pwdb.so
pam_radius.so	pam_rhosts_auth.so	pam_rootok.so
pam_securetty.so	pam_shells.so	pam_stress.so
pam_tally.so	pam_time.so	pam_unix_acct.so
pam_unix_auth.so	pam_unix_passwd.so	pam_unix_session.so
pam_warn.so	pam_wheel.so	

Some of the modules are only applicable for one type; others are applicable for all types (auth, account, password, session). All modules can take any control value (`requisite`, `required`, `sufficient`, `optional`). Table 15.1 lists these types and options.

Lines of modules are read line by line from the beginning of the file to the end unless a `requisite` or `sufficient` causes PAM to exit early.

> **Note**
>
> Table 15.1 is not meant to be an exhaustive or even authoritative list of available PAM modules. If it were, it would be notable only for the modules not included or changed. Different distributions might even have different modules (ones written or modified by distribution-employed programmers, but not yet in general use). For more up-to-date information, see the documentation in `/usr/doc/libpam-{$version}/`.

TABLE 15.1 **SOME PAM MODULES** (pam_ **PREFIX REMOVED FROM MODULE NAME**)

Module	Type(s)	Options	About
access.so	auth	none	Uses file /etc/security/access.conf to determine authorization eligibility.
cracklib.so	password	type= retry= debug	Checks new password against dictionary.
deny.so	all	none	Returns FAILURE.
dialup.so	auth	none	Checks /etc/security/ttys.dialup to see whether a dialup password is required. If so, the password is taken from /etc/security/passwd.dialup.
env.so	session	none	Reads user's environment from /etc/security/env.conf—these would be special env variables.
ftp	auth	none	Always returns IGNORE and logs the service. Is a diagnostic tool only.
group	session	none	Provides additional groups based on /etc/security/groups.conf if all pre-conditions in the file exist.
lastlog	session	none	Creates a lastlog entry.
limits	session	debug conf=	Imposes limits based on /etc/limits entries or a file defined by the conf= option.
listfile	session	item= sense= file= onerr= apply=	Checks the file listed in the file= option and takes action (succeed/fail) based on that.
nologin	auth	none	If /etc/nologin exists, returns FAILURE.
permit	all	none	Always returns SUCCESS.
pwdb	all	debug audit use_first_pass try_first_pass use_authtok not_set_pass shadow unix md5 bigcrypt nodelay	This is the UNIX module for password authentication. It understands the old /etc/passwd file with the password stored inside or the shadowed passwords or the new MD5 passwords.
radius	session	debug "verbose logging"	Provides session service for users authenticated by a RADIUS server. Does not yet start PPP for the user.

TABLE 15.1   CONTINUED

rhosts_auth	auth	no_hosts_equiv no_rhosts Debug nowarn suppress promiscuous	Permits use of .rhosts/hosts.equiv files. README contains detailed instructions for setting up these files.
rootok	auth	debug	If UID 0 user is requesting authentication, this module returns SUCCESS. Used in su so root can become any other user without knowing the password.
securetty	auth	none	Requires root to be on a secure tty as listed in /etc/securetty before allowing login.
shells	auth	none	Verifies user's shell is listed in /etc/shells, or login is denied. If shell field in /etc/passwd is blank, /bin/sh is assumed.
stress	all	debug no_warn use_first_pass try_first_pass rootok expired fail_1 fail_2 prelim required	Used for changing password. Module has different behaviors depending on the type field. For full details, see the README and Developers' Guide.
tally	auth account	onerr= file= auth: no_magic_root acct: deny= no_magic_root even_deny_root account reset no_reset	Tracks login attempts and can deny access to an account after a predetermined number of failed login attempts. Can reset counter or not after successful login.
time	auth	none	Permits/denies login based on time/port of login as listed in /etc/security/time.conf.
unix	all	debug audit use_first_pass try_first_pass use_authtok not_set_pass shadow md5 bigcrypt	Previously had four implementations, one for each type (auth, account, password, session). Specifies login authentication type.

TABLE 15.1   CONTINUED

		nodelay nis remember=X	
user_db	auth	debug db=[path] icase dump	Uses a .db database file to authenticate users.
warn	all	none	Always returns IGNORE. Makes an entry in syslog. Is a diagnostic tool.
wheel	auth	debug user_uid trust deny group=	Allows only root authentication to members of wheel group. This group is used on some systems as the administration group (but is not used as such in most Linux distributions).

STACKING MODULES

When required, more than one module can be used for any given type. This is often the case with auth. If you look at Listing 15.2 again, you'll see that four different modules are checked for the auth type. If root is trying to log in, he must first be on a secure terminal, but he is still going to pass through the other tests. Anyone listed in an .rhosts or hosts.equiv file and permitted access stops at the second module; otherwise, all further modules are run.

This provides a great deal of flexibility and a "layered defense" so that one weak link doesn't cause a breach. Be careful. You should thoroughly test several scenarios after changing the pam authentication file for a service because you can easily defeat any security you had through a misconfiguration. Be sure you understand the module and its use before trying to install it.

MODIFYING YOUR PAM CONFIGURATION

Three files that you might think should be somewhat similar are the three "r" command PAM files. The r commands are considered extremely unsecure (and rightly so); therefore, the PAM files should be fairly strict.

Examining the default rlogin file from Caldera OpenLinux in Listing 15.3, you can see that it is fairly strict.

LISTING 15.3   DEFAULT rlogin LISTING

```
#%PAM-1.0
auth       required     /lib/security/pam_securetty.so
auth       sufficient   /lib/security/pam_rhosts_auth.so
auth       required     /lib/security/pam_pwdb.so shadow nullok
auth       required     /lib/security/pam_nologin.so
account    required     /lib/security/pam_pwdb.so
#password  required     /lib/security/pam_cracklib.so
password   required     /lib/security/pam_pwdb.so shadow nullok use_authtok
session    required     /lib/security/pam_pwdb.so
```

The first line prohibits root from using `rlogin` except from a secure terminal as listed in `/etc/securetty`. The second line will permit a login without going further if an `rhosts` file exists. If you believe that `rhosts` files are not a good idea, you might want to remove this line.

The rest of the file looks much like the login file, but it might be a good idea to copy the `pam_lastlog.so` line just to make sure the session is logged. However, remember that this last log entry must appear before the `pam_rhosts.so` line or the session will not be logged if access is permitted using the `rhosts` file.

Examining Listing 15.4, the default Caldera OpenLinux `rexec`, though, is a little on the thin side.

LISTING 15.4   THE DEFAULT `rexec` FILE

```
#%PAM-1.0
auth        required        /lib/security/pam_pwdb.so shadow nullok
auth        required        /lib/security/pam_nologin.so
auth        required        /lib/security/pam_listfile.so file=/etc/ftpusers item=user
➥sense=deny onerr=succeed
account     required        /lib/security/pam_pwdb.so
```

This file completely prevents root from using `rexec`, and does not make use of the `rhosts` files at all (if you consider that desirable). No logging takes place with this `rexec` file. A great security improvement here (if there is such a thing as security with `rexec`) would be to use the `rlogin` file from listing 15.3 with the improvements mentioned above.

Examining Listing 15.5, the default Caldera OpenLinux `rsh` file is in the same shape as `rexec`.

LISTING 15.5   THE DEFAULT `rsh` FILE

```
#%PAM-1.0
auth        required        /lib/security/pam_rhosts_auth.so
auth        required        /lib/security/pam_nologin.so
account     required        /lib/security/pam_pwdb.so
session     required        /lib/security/pam_pwdb.so
```

This file requires `rhosts`; you can't use `rsh` without it. Beyond that, root is permitted along with everyone else. This prevents the passing of passwords in the clear, a problem with older restricted services. This file shows another way to provide an r command. You might want to at least add the `pam_lastlog` line and `pam_securetty` lines to improve security and add a log event. This file, with these modifications, would also suffice for both the `rlogin` and `rexec` files. The choices are yours.

TROUBLESHOOTING

I tried to log in using telnet as root, but received a `login incorrect`, and I know I used the correct password for root.

The problem is not the password, but the line in /etc/pam.d/login that calls pam_securetty.so. This line enables root to only login from those terminals listed in /etc/securetty. If you want to enable root to log using telnet (a uniformly bad idea), you'll need to comment out or remove that line. One way around this restriction is to telnet in as an ordinary user and then use the su command to become root. This is just as bad as enabling a root login using telnet. A better way would be to install and use openssh, which encrypts the entire session, including the login.

I need to upload some files as root, but I can't log in.

This is a very similar problem to the previous telnet problem. Again, this is not a good idea, but if you insist on doing it, you'll need to do one of two things: Remove the pam_list-file.so line in /etc/pam.d/ftp, or remove root from the file /etc/ftpusers. A better idea would be to use scp to transfer the files using an encrypted channel where your root password is safe from prying eyes running tcpdump. You can transfer files to any server running sshd using the following command:

```
scp xferfile [user@]remotehost:/path/to/save/xferfile
```

CHAPTER 16

SOFTWARE PACKAGE MANAGEMENT

In this chapter

INTRODUCTION TO PACKAGE MANAGEMENT

This section will introduce you to the basic concepts of package management, which is the fundamental means for you to install and manage software on your OpenLinux system.

WHAT IS PACKAGE MANAGEMENT?

The *package management system* is the part of your Linux system that enables you to install, uninstall, and manage the software on your machine. If you are familiar with Microsoft Windows 95, this is similar to the Add/Remove Programs option in the Windows Control Panel, though in Linux, it is generally much more flexible and easier to query.

Almost all distributions of Linux include some kind of package management system. The most popular of these is the *Red Hat package manager* (*RPM*), and this is the system discussed in this chapter. RPM enables you to perform the basic tasks of installing and uninstalling packages. You can also use it to perform other important package management tasks, such as analyzing the disk space used by certain software or verifying that a particular package's files have not been deleted or corrupted.

Debian uses another package manager called dpkg. In many ways, dpkg is superior to RPM, particularly in maintaining package dependencies. With its front-end, dselect, dpkg is quite easy to use (assuming you know the answers to the numerous configuration questions Debian packages tend to ask). For more information on dselect, see http://www.debian.org/releases/stable/i386/dselect-beginner.

MORE THAN JUST AN INSTALL PROGRAM

Although RPM is the primary installation program for your Linux system, it is much more than that. Most of the things you will install on your system are available in package format, which means that you will use RPM to install virtually all the software you use. (Exceptions to this are discussed in the section "Working with TAR Files" in Chapter 17, "Building/Rebuilding a Package.") Under some other operating environments, such as Microsoft Windows, each component you add to the system comes with its own installation program. Sometimes an uninstall program is provided as well, but sometimes it is not. In contrast to this, RPM provides a single uniform installation and uninstallation mechanism for all the software for your system. RPM keeps track of all kinds of information about the packages installed on your system in a special package database. RPM uses the information in the database to uninstall a package so that it can remove all traces of the package cleanly from your system. However, the information in the package database also can be used for many other management tasks, which are described in the following section.

THINGS YOU CAN DO WITH A PACKAGE MANAGER

Following is a list of some of the tasks you can perform to manage the software on your OpenLinux system:

- Examine the contents of a package before you install it to see how much space it will take up on your hard drive, what files it contains, and where they will be placed in your filesystem.

- Check to see whether you have the necessary libraries or other files that are required for a new software package to run.

- Check to make sure that a new package won't conflict with one already installed on your system.

- Examine the procedure used to install a package, and verify that it doesn't do anything to corrupt your system or defeat your system security.

- Verify that a package comes from a reliable, trusted source.

- Verify that a package's files have not been corrupted or deleted.

- Find out other information about a package, such as where the software in it originally came from, or what restrictions exist on using or redistributing it.

- Upgrade to a newer version of software while preserving all your customizations to the software's configuration files.

- Determine what package a particular file comes from.

- Surprisingly, there is much more that you can do with RPM.

PART

III

CH

16

Note

RPM is the name of the package management system, but several different programs exist that can be used to manage your packages. A program called rpm is used to manage packages from the shell command line. This same program is used to create a package. Unfortunately, a package file itself is often referred to as an RPM because its filename ends in the extension `.rpm`. This overloaded use of the acronym can (and does) cause a lot of confusion. In this book, the package management system is referred to as RPM (all caps), the command-line utility as rpm, and an `.rpm` file as a package.

WHAT IS A PACKAGE?

A *package* is a special file that contains the directories and files that are part of a particular piece of software or system component. It also contains additional information about the software that is used by the package manager. Two different kinds of packages exist: binary and source. A *binary* package contains software components that have already been built for a particular architecture and are ready to use. This is the kind you normally install on your system. A *source* package contains the source code and other items used to build the corresponding binary package. Source packages are provided in the event that you want to modify—and recompile—a program yourself.

Binary package filenames end in the suffix `.rpm`, whereas source package filenames end in the suffix `.src.rpm`. The use and manipulation of source packages is covered in Chapter 17, "Building/Rebuilding a Package," so it is not covered here. From now on in this chapter, wherever there is an unqualified reference to a package, it is a reference to a binary package.

WHAT'S IN A NAME?

A binary package has a filename that looks similar to the one shown in Figure 16.1.

Figure 16.1
Anatomy of a
package filename.

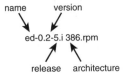

The first part of the filename is a short string that identifies the package. After the name is the version number (in this case 0.2), which identifies the version of the *software* contained in the package. This is followed by the package release number (5). It is important to distinguish between the software *version*, and the package *release*: The version number is the version of the software that is provided by the package. In the example in Figure 16.1, it is ed, version 0.2. This number is set by the original author of the software, who is often different from the person who created the package for the software. The version number reflects the status of the software. The release number refers to the version of *this package* of the software. Sometimes, even if the original software inside the package has not changed, it is necessary to repackage it. The release number indicates which instance of the package this is.

After the release number is a short string that indicates the architecture for the package. Most packages contain software that has been compiled for a particular processor or machine architecture. For example, packages with programs compiled for Intel x86 or compatible processors usually include the architecture string i386, although they can be compiled specifically for Pentium or Pentium II processors, in which case they will include the string i586 or i686, respectively. In some cases, the contents of a package are independent of any machine architecture (for example, a package that only contains icons and not executable programs). In these cases, the architecture string noarch is used. Table 16.1 shows some common architecture strings.

TABLE 16.1 ARCHITECTURE STRINGS IN RPM FILENAMES

String	Processor
noarch	Any
i386, i586, i686	Intel x86, Pentium, and compatibles
alpha	DEC Alpha
sparc	Sun Sparc
mips	MIPS
ppc	PowerPC
m68k	Motorola 68000 family

Often, the files required for a piece of software are bundled into a single package. Sometimes, however, the files are provided in multiple separate packages. This is done to give you additional flexibility in installing only those parts of a program that you are actually going to use. When the software's files are separated in this manner, you can often tell from the package name what kinds of files are contained in the package. Table 16.2 shows a few naming conventions that will help you to identify packages that have files for particular uses.

TABLE 16.2   NAMING CONVENTIONS FOR PACKAGE FILENAMES

String	Package Contains	Example
static	Programs that have been statically linked with certain libraries	nwutils-static
devel	Files required for developing new programs with this system	slang-devel
devel-static static	Files required for developing statically linked programs with this system	slang-devel
doc	Regular text documentation	lilo-doc
doc-html	Documentation in HTML format	povray-doc-html
doc-<format>	Documentation in the specified format	povray-doc-ps

Often, software that provides a library to be used by other programs comes as three separate packages:

- The main package provides the shared library program binaries use to run.

- A development package provides the header files and programming documentation necessary to develop new programs that use the library.

- A static development package provides a version of the library that is ready to be statically linked to a new program.

Unless you plan to create or alter programs that use a particular library, you do not need to install the devel packages for that library.

PACKAGE CONTENTS

To understand how the package manager can support all the tasks listed previously, it is important to know what a package contains.

A binary package contains the following items:

- Name and description of the software
- Version information
- Information about the RPM provider
- URL for product home page
- Licensing and copyright information
- Product classification
- Operating system and architecture information
- Files and directory information for each file, including names, sizes, permissions, MD5 checksums, symbolic links, file classification (regular, configuration, or documentation), and other information

- Relocation information so the package can be installed in different directories
- Requirements on and conflicts with other packages, operating systems, and architectures
- Packages made obsolete by this package
- Scripts to run during installation and uninstallation
- Scripts to run when related packages are installed and uninstalled
- Information on how to verify that the package has not been corrupted, both before and after installation
- Change logs

The Name, Summary, Version, Size, and Description fields of the package provide information about the software or component that the package contains.

The Packager, Build Date, Build Host, Release, and Source RPM fields provide information that is helpful in tracking down problems with a package. The Distribution and Vendor show what product and company produced the package. The URL helps you find the original sources and documentation for this package. Finally, the License and Copyright fields let you know how you can redistribute this package.

The Group field indicates the general category of software. Packages are categorized by the type of software they contain into a hierarchy of groups and subgroups. This is done to enable you to view related packages more easily in the graphic management tools.

The Operating System and Architecture fields ensure that this binary package was built for your target system.

The core of a package is the files and directories that are the actual software or component in the package. The files in a package are divided into three different types: *configuration*, *documentation*, and *regular* files. The reason for this distinction is to enable more intelligent handling of these different types of files by RPM. For example, you can choose whether to install the documentation files for a package. Often, documentation takes up a lot of disk space, and if you are familiar enough with how to use a piece of software, it might not be necessary to have the documentation installed. In a pinch, you can always go back and install the extra files if necessary.

Configuration files receive special handling during remove and upgrade operations. This is discussed more in later sections of this chapter, but the basic idea is to preserve configuration files when upgrading the package.

For each file in a package, other attributes are stored in the package and recorded in the package database upon installation. These attributes include the file owner and group, the permissions on the file, and a special checksum called the MD5SUM. The MD5SUM can be used to determine whether the contents of a file have changed, even if the time, date, and size are the same.

The Relocation field lets you know what parts of this package have been designed to be relocated. For instance, if this field lists /usr, you can run rpm with the --relocate /usr=/opt option to move all the /usr/bin files to /opt/bin, /usr/lib files to /opt/lib, and so on.

Even if no `Relocation` fields are listed, you can force this kind of relocation using the `--badreloc` option; however, the package might not work in this configuration.

The `Dependency` information in a package is there to help you make sure that the software on your system has all the other libraries and components that are necessary for the package to run.

Although it comes in separate packages, the software on your system is interrelated—sometimes in not so obvious ways. Dependencies help keep track of the relationships between packages. For example, many packages include software that relies on shared libraries or interpreters (for example, Perl) to run. If you remove the package that provides this required component, the dependent software stops working. The most dramatic example of this is the main system shared library, libc. In a default installation of OpenLinux for instance, more than 2,000 of the installed programs contain software that stops working if libc is removed.

PART

III

CH

16

Packages that rely on other pieces of software, or that provide components on which other pieces of software rely, contain dependency information. Each package that relies on another component includes a *requires* entry for that component. A package that provides a required component includes a *provides* entry for that component. By matching up the requires and provides entries of the packages, the package manager can determine whether it is safe to install or remove a package.

Packages can also conflict with other packages. For example, qmail and sendmail don't work well together. By indicating this conflict in their packages, the package manager can prevent you from trying to install both at the same time.

Sometimes packages are made obsolete by new packages. For example, TrueType fonts used to be handled by a package called xtt. This functionality has now be added to XFree86-xfs, which obsoletes xtt. So, if you have xtt installed and try to install XFree86-xfs, the package manager can detect this and automatically remove xtt.

For example, when you try to install a package, RPM examines your system to see whether all the items required by the new package are present on your system. If not, you are warned about the missing items and the installation is aborted. This gives you an opportunity to install all the necessary components to ensure that all your software runs smoothly.

Something similar happens when you try to remove a package. RPM determines whether other packages are dependent on that package and warns you about the problem. By default, it does not proceed with the removal. If you determine that it is okay to proceed, you can override the dependency check and force the removal to occur.

Finally, a package might also include installation and trigger scripts. A pre-installation script is run before the package is installed and a post-installation script is run after the package is installed. Likewise, a pre-uninstallation script and a post-uninstallation script exist. Trigger scripts enable a package to watch for other packages' installation and uninstallation. This enables a package to reconfigure itself if related packages are installed or uninstalled. Most of these scripts are very short and involve steps such as updating the shared library cache for newly installed (or removed) libraries.

Packages include information used to determine whether the package has been corrupted before or since its installation. Most packages are "signed" by the packager before being sent out. By verifying this signature, you can be certain that the package you are installing is the package the vendor produced. For more information on verifying signatures, see the section "Security Concerns" later in this chapter.

After the package has been installed, RPM can use the information stored in its database to verify that the installation has not been corrupted. See the section "Verifying Packages" later in this chapter for more information on verifying an installed package.

WHERE TO FIND PACKAGES

If you are using an RPM-base distribution, your installation media or download site will have appropriate packages. Package files are also available from a variety of sites on the Internet, generally including your distribution's FTP site and many other sites that provide Linux software.

Increasingly, in addition to the Linux distribution vendors, the original authors of the software provide their software in package format. If you see a piece of Linux software you want on the Internet, check the download area of the site that provides it. Frequently, you will find package files you can install directly on your system using RPM. As with all software, of course, you should be sure you know your source before installing anything you find on the Internet.

WORKING WITH rpm

Just to get acquainted with the rpm command, try using it to examine the contents of a package right now. The arguments to the rpm command fall into several major categories. The entire man page isn't reproduced here, but Table 16.3 shows a basic summary of the important options for rpm. Notice that some option letters have different meanings when combined with another main option.

TABLE 16.3 THE MOST FREQUENTLY USED OPTIONS FOR rpm

Option	Sub-Option	Meaning
-q		Query
	-i	Show detailed package information
	-l	List all files
	-d	List only documentation files
	-c	List only configuration files
	-f	Find which package owns a file
	-p	Operate on a package file (as opposed to an installed package)
	--scripts	View install/uninstall scripts
-i		Install
-e		Erase (uninstall)

TABLE 16.3   CONTINUED

Option	Sub-Option	Meaning
-U		Upgrade, or install if the package is not already installed
-F		Freshen (upgrades a package only if it is already installed)
-V		Verify a package installation
-b		Build a package (covered in Chapter 17, "Building/Rebuilding a Package")

We'll use OpenLinux as an example for demonstration purposes. Other RPM-based distributions will be very similar. Be sure that the OpenLinux Installation CD-ROM is in the CD-ROM drive and that it is mounted. If not, as superuser, mount it using the following command:

```
mount /mnt/cdrom
```

Now, cd to the directory /mnt/cdrom/Packages/RPMS, and list the files in this directory. You see more than 600 packages listed for OpenLinux eDesktop. To examine the information about a package, use the following command:

```
rpm -qpi ed-0.2-5.i386.rpm
```

This shows a listing similar to the following:

```
Name         : ed                    Relocations: (not relocateable)
Version      : 0.2                         Vendor: Caldera Systems, Inc.
Release      : 5                       Build Date: Thu Jan 13 18:30:32 2000
Install date: (not installed)         Build Host: bm.calderalabs.com
Group        : Textprocessing/Editor  Source RPM: ed-0.2-5.src.rpm
Size         : 89238                      License: GPL
Packager     : rwp@lst.de (Roger Pook)
Summary      : GNU Line Editor
Description :
ed is a line-oriented text editor.  It is used to create,
display, modify and otherwise manipulate text files.  red
is a restricted ed: it can only edit files in the current
directory and cannot execute shell commands.
```

To see a listing of the files in this package, type the following:

```
rpm -qpl ed-0.2-5.i386.rpm
```

This prints a listing similar to Listing 16.1.

LISTING 16.1   FILES IN ed-0.2-5.i386.rpm

```
/bin/ed
/bin/red
/usr/doc/ed-0.2
/usr/doc/ed-0.2/NEWS
/usr/doc/ed-0.2/POSIX
/usr/doc/ed-0.2/README
/usr/doc/ed-0.2/THANKS
```

LISTING 16.1   CONTINUED

```
/usr/info/ed.info.gz
/usr/man/man1/ed.1.gz
/usr/man/man1/red.1.gz
```

The ed package should already be installed on your system. You can find out whether it is by querying the RPM database, instead of the package. Omit the p option and use just the package name (not the whole filename), as follows:

```
rpm -qi ed
```

In this case, the Install date will be set, indicating when the package was installed. If the package is not installed, rpm reports this to you:

```
$ $ rpm -qi edsel
package edsel is not installed
```

Note

Sometimes it's tricky to remember when you need to specify the whole filename of the package versus just the name of the package (that is, *ed-0.2-5.i386.rpm* versus *ed*). For software that is not installed, you refer to the package file itself (by full filename) to query it for information or to install it. For operations on packages currently installed on your system (operations such as query, verify, or remove), use just the package name.

INSTALLING NEW SOFTWARE

Now that you understand the basics of package management, you probably want to install some software. The first step is to figure out which package provides the software you need.

FINDING THE PACKAGE YOU WANT TO INSTALL

Unfortunately (or fortunately!), so much software is available for Linux that even if you know exactly what you want, you might have a hard time finding it.

USE THE PACKAGE NAME

Sometimes, the package that contains your software is easily identifiable from its filename. So if you are looking for GIMP (a powerful image manipulation program), you can find the packages for GIMP by simply listing the contents of your distribution's RPMS directory. Use wildcards or pipe the output of ls through more, or else you will be overwhelmed, because as many as 600 packages can be in some versions of OpenLinux. Also, use the naming conventions shown in Table 16.2 to help you identify the packages you need. When using wildcards, remember that sometimes the name you're looking for is in the middle of the filename. For example, the package that provides cron is called vixie-cron.

INTERNET RESOURCES FOR FINDING A PACKAGE

If you are trying to find a particular software package on the Internet, you might want to visit one of the package indexing sites. One good site is http://rpmfind.net.

By following the instructions at this site (or at one of its many mirrors), you can see the contents of several thousand different package files located at various sites on the Internet.

The Freshmeat Web site is another online resource for tracking recent updates to software. You can access it at http://www.freshmeat.net/. Freshmeat is a fairly definitive guide to current releases of software available for Linux. Much of the software referred to on Freshmeat is provided as tar files. Often, however, when a new release of software is mentioned on Freshmeat, the software is made available as a package soon after.

> **Caution**
>
> When downloading RPM packages from the Internet, be sure to check which distribution of Linux they are intended to run with. Although many packages built for one vendor's distribution of Linux run perfectly fine on another, it is wise to check the package information, file lists, and dependencies to ensure that the package will operate correctly with your system.
>
> The section "Library Compatibility" in Chapter 17, "Building/Rebuilding a Package," discusses how to resolve some issues with programs that have been compiled for a Linux system with different shared libraries.
>
> If you can find the software you need in a package specifically built for your distribution, use it. However, you also can use packages built for other distributions of Linux. When in doubt, try to find out by searching or participating in mailing lists or newsgroups related to that software; alternatively, you can check to see whether others have already tried the package with OpenLinux and find out what success they have had with it.

DECIDING WHICH UTILITY TO USE

As with many operations in Linux, more than one way exists to manage packages. The three preferred utilities are rpm for command-line use and kpackage for graphical use under KDE and GnoRPM for graphical use under GNOME. rpm offers the capability to perform more complex operations, whereas kpackage and GnoRPM are easier to use. The descriptions in this chapter focus on the rpm command.

SECURITY CONCERNS

With the large amount of software available for your Linux system, and with it coming from a variety of sources, you might wonder if all of it is harmless. When you add any piece of software to your system, you want to be sure that it will do what you expect it to, and no more. You can be quite certain that the software packages directly from a commercial vendor or other major distributor can be trusted because they were built and signed by developers who have their reputation to protect. If the site you downloaded your package from is public and widely used, you also have some degree of assurance that the package is safe. However, if you are ever unsure of the software in a package, RPM includes two features that enable to you protect yourself.

First, you can verify that the installation itself will not do funny things to your system: You can use RPM to examine the exact scripts that will be executed to install the software. Because you install a package as the root user on your system, it is crucial that the scripts used during installation don't do strange things (such as installing trapdoors or Trojan Horses).

Second, you can use RPM to verify the source of a package in two ways. If a package is signed, and you have PGP installed, you can verify the package signature with a special rpm option. This enables you to validate that the package comes from where it says it comes from. Also, each package includes a whole-package checksum that can be verified against some public list to ensure that the package has not been tampered with. Most distributions provide a file listing the checksum (MD5SUM) for all the packages they provide. See the section "Verifying Package Signatures" later in this chapter.

STEPS PERFORMED DURING AN INSTALLATION

The package manager completely automates the process of installing software on your system. In most cases, you can type a single command and everything is done for you. Behind the scenes, however, quite a few steps make up the installation process:

1. Verify that RPM is being run as root.
2. Verify the package is not already present.
3. Verify the package does not conflict with one already present.
4. Verify other files or components required by this package are present.
5. Verify that there is sufficient disk space to install the package.
6. Run the pre-install script.
7. Relocate the package if requested.
8. Copy the files and directories to the filesystem.
9. Correctly set the ownership and permissions on the files and directories.
10. Record the package information in the RPM database (usually in the files in /var/lib/rpm).
11. Run the post-install script.
12. Run triggers that other packages have set for the installation of this package.
13. Run triggers that this package has set for the installation of other packages.

Note that all the verification steps are performed for all the packages to be installed before any other steps are performed. For example, if you list three packages on the command line, the package manager will ensure that all three packages can be installed before any of them are installed. Furthermore, if packages listed on the command line depend on other packages listed on the command line, the package manager will automatically reorder the installation to resolve these dependencies.

THE ACTUAL INSTALL

After all that explanation, the actual installation of the package is somewhat anti-climactic. Just be sure that you are root, and use the rpm command with the -i option and the filename of the package you want to install:

```
# rpm -i /mnt/cdrom/Packages/RPMS/ytalk-3.1-1.i386.rpm
#
```

That's it. There are no questions and no output (when the installation is successful). This is as easy as software installation gets. If you do want to see the installation as it progresses, add the option vh as follows:

```
# rpm -ivh /mnt/cdrom/Packages/RPMS/ytalk-3.1-1.i386.rpm
ytalk                        #################################################
#
```

If you want to see full details about the installation, add the option vvh:

```
# rpm -ivvh /mnt/cdrom/Packages/RPMS/ytalk-3.1-1.i386.rpm
D: counting packages to install
D: found 1 packages
D: looking for packages to download
D: retrieved 0 packages
D: New Header signature
[...]
D: running preinstall script (if any)
ytalk                        #################################################
D: running postinstall scripts (if any)
```

PART

III

CH

16

REMOVING A PACKAGE

Removing a package from your system is also very simple. For example, you could try to remove perl-cgi, a package that simplifies writing CGIs in Perl, and type the following:

```
# rpm -e perl-cgi
error: removing these packages would break dependencies:
    perl-cgi is needed by kquery-0.9-2
```

Only Root Can Perform Package Modifications on Your System

As with installation, you must be logged in as root to perform the remove operation. In general, this is true of any package operation that actually modifies the contents of your system, such as installing, removing, or upgrading packages. Regular users can perform other operations that are purely informational, such as querying or verifying packages. If you are logged in as a regular user and try to perform an operation with rpm that requires root privileges, you see an error message similar to the following:

```
failed to open //var/lib/rpm/packages.rpm
error: cannot open //var/lib/rpm/packages.rpm
```

In this example, RPM aborts the remove operation and informs you that there is a problem with removing perl-cgi because of dependencies.

DEALING WITH A DEPENDENCY PROBLEM

Apparently, another piece of software on the system needs perl-cgi in order to run. With RPM, you can't blindly mess up the software on your system.

One way to deal with this problem is to remove the packages that are dependent on the one you are trying to remove. In this case, query your packages through KDE or the Web. These scripts require a particular Perl module and are useless without it installed. If you are not planning to use this functionality, both the Perl module and the scripts can be removed.

The other way to deal with this situation is to force the package to be removed despite the dependency problem. Perhaps you do plan to install a different cgi module, or the same module at some later date. The option can be used during install, upgrade, or remove operations to continue despite dependency problems. The `--force` option will override other types of problems, such as `package already installed` errors.

This example demonstrates how the dependency information helps you do the right thing with regard to your software. Whether you decide to remove the dependent package, force the removal of the original package, or just leave things as they are, RPM enables you to make an informed decision so you won't run into problems later.

OTHER TYPES OF REMOVAL PROBLEMS

Because of the interrelated nature of the various system components, when you remove a package, RPM might not be capable of removing the directories owned by that package.

For instance, if you modify the file `/home/httpd/conf/access.conf` and then try to remove the apache package, you get a list of messages similar to the following:

```
cannot remove /var/log/httpd/apache - directory not empty
cannot remove /home/httpd/html - directory not empty
cannot remove /home/httpd/cgi-bin - directory not empty
cannot remove /home/httpd - directory not empty
cannot remove /etc/httpd/conf - directory not empty
cannot remove /etc/httpd/apache - directory not empty
```

Three different causes exist for these messages. The directory `/var/log/httpd/apache` can't be removed because it contains `perl-cgi` log files. These log files are new and are not part of the `perl-cgi` package, even though apache created them. This is an important distinction to make. RPM tracks only files that it installed, and not ones that were created later, even if it is obvious (to a human, anyway) that the files belong to a specific package. This is actually the right and safe thing to do; RPM does not remove any files it can't restore by reinstalling the package.

The `/home/httpd` directory (and some of its subdirectories) can't be removed because other packages have files placed there. Specifically, the apache package provides a default home page for the Web browser placed in these directories. Once again, it is appropriate for RPM to leave these files alone. You probably want to preserve any Web content you have created, even though you are removing the Web server.

Finally, the `/etc/httpd/apache/conf` directory (and its parent) is preserved because the file `access.conf` was modified. If you look in that directory, you can see that the modified file was saved with the filename access.conf.rpmsave.

Any configuration files that have been modified are saved by RPM with the extension `.rpmsave`. This is a valuable feature because it saves you from inadvertently removing a file you have worked very hard to customize for your system. By saving the file with a special name, it is possible to restore the configuration later if you decide to re-install the package. If, however, you are really, really, *really* sure that you won't need this customized configuration file in the future, you can remove it manually.

Periodically—and especially after performing much package management—it is worthwhile to check your system for configuration files that have been saved in this way. Use one of the following commands to locate saved configuration files on your system:

```
locate rpmsave
find / -name "*.rpmsave"
```

You need to know the reason each file is there, and be sure you keep the ones you might need in the future.

Caution

Do not run `find /` on a multiuser system or on a system that mounts filesystems from other machines. This is an incredibly resource-intensive process. In general, it's better to wait until the locate database is updated at night and then just use locate to find these files. If you want to force an update of the locate database, use updatedb, but avoid running this on a multiuser system when other people are working, because it is also a very intensive process.

UPGRADING A PACKAGE

You can use RPM to upgrade a package on your system, to get a later release of the package, or to get a newer version of software on your system. Upgrading a package is logically the same as removing the currently installed package and installing a new one. However, using the upgrade feature makes these steps a single operation. This enables you to avoid dependency and other file conflict problems that might arise if you perform the steps separately. Use the `-U` (uppercase U) option with rpm to upgrade a package on your system. For example, if you had already installed perl-5.00503 on your system and wanted to upgrade to perl-5.6.0, you would download the new perl package and upgrade using the following as root:

```
# rpm -U perl-5.6.0-1.i386.rpm
```

HOW ARE CONFIGURATION FILES DEALT WITH?

You might recall that a package's files are categorized into three different types: configuration, documentation, and regular files. During a package upgrade, the configuration files receive special handling.

It is impossible for RPM to know whether the configuration files used for the new version of software are the same—in location and format—as those used by the old version. Therefore, to be especially safe during an upgrade, RPM renames your old configuration files with the extension .rpmsave before installing new configuration files. You must manually restore these files after an upgrade. If a change has occurred in the configuration file, you can now deal with it. Although this seems like a tedious process, it is the safest policy for RPM because it ensures that the software installed on your system is using configuration files it can read and utilize.

Tip

It is a good habit to look for `.rpmsave` files after you have upgraded packages on your system, and to make sure that any customized configuration files that were saved are replaced into their proper files.

VERIFYING PACKAGES

If you suspect that a package has become corrupt, perhaps because of removing one of its files, you can have RPM verify the package to ensure that everything is as it should be. At the very least, RPM verifies that the files it installed are still installed and have not been changed (unless they're configuration files), and that all the package's dependencies are installed. Depending on the package, it can also verify that package or system configuration files are correct, or anything else a package needs done.

To verify a package, use the -V option of rpm:

```
$ rpm -V apache
S.5....T c /etc/httpd/conf/httpd.conf
missing     /etc/rc.d/rc0.d/K15httpd
missing     /etc/rc.d/rc1.d/K15httpd
missing     /etc/rc.d/rc2.d/K15httpd
missing     /etc/rc.d/rc3.d/S85httpd
missing     /etc/rc.d/rc5.d/S85httpd
missing     /etc/rc.d/rc6.d/K15httpd
```

The first line of the output indicates that httpd.conf has a different file size, MD5 checksum, and timestamp from when it was installed. The c indicates that this is a configuration file, though, so it is probably OK. The next six lines indicate that there are files missing that should be installed. This might be because of the user manually deleting these files (as it is in this case).

Table 16.4 describes the various columns in the first field.

TABLE 16.4   RPM VERIFY COLUMNS

Column	Meaning
5	MD5 sum
S	File size
L	Symlink
T	Mtime
D	Device
U	User
G	Group
M	Mode (includes permissions and file type)

VERIFYING PACKAGE SIGNATURES

Most packages are signed by their packagers using a cryptographic key. This is to ensure that the package has not been modified between the time it was packaged and the time you received it. It also ensures that the package was created by the person who claims to have created it. GNU Privacy Guard (GPG) is used to sign the packages. For more detailed information on GPG, see Chapter 25, "Email Clients and Servers."

A distribution's public keys are generally available on the CD in a file called pgp-keys or something similar. To install these keys into your keyring, type the following on an OpenLinux system:

```
$ for file in /mnt/cdrom/col/pgp-keys/PGP-*; do gpg --import $file; done
```

Then, to check packages that claim they are from your distributor (or any other packagers whose public keys you have installed), type the following:

```
$ rpm -K coas-1.1-12.i386.rpm
Pretty Good Privacy(tm) Version 6.5.1i
 1999 Network Associates Inc.

Export of this software may be restricted by the U.S. government.

coas-1.1-12.i386.rpm: md5 gpg OK
```

PART

III

CH

16

Notice that both md5 (checksum) and gpg (cryptographic signature) are verified. If the package were not signed, then only md5 would have been checked. If you see NOT OK anywhere, you should re-run the check with the -Kv option to output more information. This should give you a better idea as to whether you simply have not installed the proper public keys, or if there is really a problem.

TROUBLESHOOTING

When I query for a package I know I installed, RPM says it isn't installed.

A few possible solutions to this exist. First, make sure you are querying based on the package name, not the package's filename. For example, if you have installed coas-1.1-12.i386.rpm, you should query it with the following:

```
$ rpm -q coas
```

If you try typing rpm -q coas-1.1-12.i386.rpm, it won't find that, because that is the name of a file, not a package.

Another possibility is that you have forgotten the name of the package. For example, /usr/bin/crontab is in a package called vixie-cron, not cron as you might expect. It also can be easy to capitalize incorrectly. A couple of ways to figure out the proper name for a package are available. First, you can look it up based on a file you know is in the package:

```
$ rpm -qf /usr/bin/crontab
vixie-cron-3.0.1-19
```

Another solution is to search for it in the list of all packages:

```
$ rpm -qa | grep -i cron
crontabs-1.12-1
vixie-cron-3.0.1-19
```

One final reason that you might not be able to find a package is that the RPM database might be corrupt. If this is the case, you can try to recover it using rpm --rebuilddb.

I receive a `failed to open` *message when running rpm.*

If you receive a message such as `failed to open //var/lib/rpm/packages.rpm`, you are almost certainly running a system-modifying operation such as install or remove as a non-root user. These operations must be run as root.

If you are running as root, the problem might be that your database is missing or corrupt. If so, you can try rebuilding it with `rpm --rebuilddb`.

I've downloaded several packages that depend on each other.

If you have several packages in a directory to install and they have dependencies on each other, it is usually best to just run `rpm-i *.rpm`. The package manager is smart enough to order the installation, so the packages that depend on others are installed after their dependencies. Note that this is new in RPM version 3 and is a big change from RPM version 2 if you ever used that. You don't need to run `rpm -i *` repeatedly anymore.

It is possible for a packager to create circular dependencies. This is an error on the packager's part, but occasionally it happens. If you encounter this, you can instruct the package manager to ignore dependency problems by adding the `--nodeps` flag during the install. You should also send a bug report to the packager (not the developer of the software).

I've accidentally removed a file that belonged to a package.

If you just try to reinstall the package, you will get an error complaining that the package is already installed. You can overcome this error by using the `--oldpackage` flag when installing.

Alternately, you can use rpm2cpio to extract the one file you need and put it where it needs to go. See "Extracting the Contents of an rpm" (Chapter 17, "Building/Rebuilding a Package") for more information on rpm2cpio.

CHAPTER **17**

BUILDING/REBUILDING A PACKAGE

In this chapter

WORKING WITH TAR FILES

When software is not available in package format, the next most common form is a TAR file. *TAR* stands for Tape Archive and refers to the original use of these files, which was to archive information on magnetic tapes. The term is now used for any bundle of files created with the tar command. In terms of package management, this section refers only to TAR files that contain software that you plan to use on your system.

A TAR file is similar to a package file in that it contains files and directories, along with their ownership, permission, size, and date information. However, because a TAR file doesn't include the additional information that a package does, you don't get nearly the same management benefits. They are often harder to install and more difficult to keep track of after they are installed. Therefore, try to find the software that you are looking for in package format first, and only rely on TAR files if you can't find what you want.

Often a TAR file contains binaries that can run directly on your system, but sometimes the TAR file contains the actual source code for the software, which you are expected to compile yourself.

Regular TAR files end in the extension .tar; however, it is more common to find compressed TAR files, which end in .tar.gz, .tgz, or .tar.Z. The tar command is capable of dealing with either compressed or uncompressed TAR files.

> **Note**
>
> .tar.gz and .tgz files are compressed using GNU's gzip utility, whereas .Z files are compressed using the older compress utility. tar automatically understands both types of compression.

The files and directories in a TAR file all share a common root directory. Therefore, after a TAR file is installed it is often necessary to perform additional steps to move some of the files from the common directory tree to their proper installation locations.

INSTALLATION STEPS

The first thing to decide when installing a TAR file is where to put it. Chapter 10, "Understanding the Linux Filesystem," describes the various parts of the Linux filesystem and where things need to go. Generally, software that is provided as part of your distribution is placed in the / (slash) and /usr main directory hierarchies. It is highly recommended that you place other software that you install into the /usr/local directory hierarchy. This keeps the software from TAR files separate from the software provided by your distribution, which makes it easier to keep track of and remove or update later. If you are dealing with a TAR file that contains source code, place it under /usr/local/src. For any other file, you might want to place it in its own directory under /usr/local.

A TAR file can be arranged in three different ways, which generally require different handling. Look at the TAR file using one of the following commands:

```
$ tar tf tarfile.tar
$ tar tfz tarfile.tar.gz
```

> **Note**
>
> Note that you should include the z option only for compressed tar files (`.tar.gz` or `.tgz`). Also notice that the `tar` command does not use a - before its option parameters. Because of the unusual format of `tar`'s parameters (otherwise known as "historical reasons"), it is traditional not to include the leading `-`. Doing so, though legal in most modern versions of `tar`, subtly changes how the parameters are interpreted and is not recommended.
>
> The t option requests a table of contents, and the f option indicates that the following parameter is the file to be used (instead of the default source, which is the tape drive.)

When you examine the table of contents, you will likely see one of the following formats:

- **Top level, relative directory**—A TAR file like `ppp-2.3.tar` might have a top-level directory like `ppp-2.3/` or `ppp/`. If so, copy this file to `/usr/local` and extract it there.

- **Relative, but no top level directory**—Again using a TAR file like `ppp-2.3.tar`, you might find that the files have no leading directory. Before extracting this file, create a directory in `/usr/local` with the same name as the tar file (without the extensions). Move the tar file into this directory before extracting it.

- **Absolute directories**—Some tar files (extremely rare today), store absolute directory paths. For example, if the creator of the archive intended you to install the file `pppd` in `/usr/bin/pppd`, that full path will be listed in the archive. This is very inconvenient because it makes it difficult to look at the archive without installing it. It is so inconvenient that most modern versions of `tar` will not allow you to even create these kinds of archives without using special parameters. Even if the packager did create it this way, most modern versions of `tar` will by default ignore the absolute path and extract the archive as though the current directory were `/`. Given the preceding example (`/usr/bin/pppd`), if you ran `tar` in `/usr/local/pppd`, this file would be extracted to `/usr/local/pppd/usr/bin/pppd`. This is generally the best way to extract these archives. After you have checked them over, you can always move the files to where they need to be.

After you have looked over the contents of the tar file, you can extract the files using one of the following commands:

```
$ tar xvf tarfile.tar
```

```
$ tar xvfz tarfile.tar.gz
```

Note again that the z option should only be used for compressed archives (`.tar.gz`, `.tgz`, or `.tar.Z`).

Common Installation Aids

Because TAR files can include any conceivable arrangement of files, or require any sequence of installation steps, it is impossible to cover all the possible TAR installation issues. However, there are a few common conventions for dealing with TAR files.

Almost every TAR file contains a set of instructions in a README or INSTALL file at the root of its directory tree. It is best to read these instructions carefully and to follow them precisely.

Sometimes, TAR files that contain binaries have an installation program, which usually has a name that is easy to identify such as install or setup.

TAR files that contain source files often include a configure script (made by the GNU autoconf system). This is a script that tries to detect information about your system, and to automatically configure the build environment for the source code so that you can compile it for your system. You can identify these kinds of systems by looking for a file called configure. If you find this file, you should still look at the INSTALL and README files, but almost universally, the install steps will be as follows:

```
$ ./configure
$ make all install
```

The configure utility takes many customization options that you can list by using configure --help.

Basically, RPM and deb packages are generally much easier to install than TAR archives, and packages developed specifically for your distribution will generally install much more easily and consistently. Even so, given that the vast majority of TAR distributions now use a very consistent autoconf interface like the one listed earlier, compiling and installing them is generally very easy.

> **Note**
>
> If you have the disk space, it is handy to save the source tree for autoconf-generated tar distributions. By going to the source directory and entering make uninstall, you can generally remove the package from your system very cleanly. To save the tree but clean up a lot of the disk space, you can run make clean. This will delete the files from the tree that you installed other places in your system and will also delete various derived files.

LIBRARY COMPATIBILITY

This section describes how to overcome the problem of incompatibility between the programs and shared libraries installed on your system.

Most of the software that you install onto your system uses shared libraries. Shared libraries are files of shared subroutines and functions that programs use to perform their operations. When a program is compiled to use shared libraries, as most are, the linker records information about the version number of the shared library with which the program needs to be run.

Sometimes as you manage your software you will run into software that was compiled for different versions of shared libraries than what you have on your system. Luckily, there are straightforward ways of dealing with this problem.

HOW SHARED LIBRARIES ARE VERSIONED

First, you need to know how the versions of shared libraries are determined, and how they are expressed in the filesystem.

Library version numbers provide at least two, and sometimes three, levels of versioning. For example, one instance of the libc shared library has version number 5.4.38. The major version of the software is the one that counts the most with regard to software compatibility. If you look in the /lib/gnulibc1 and /lib directories, you should see that libc.so.5 is a symbolic link (a reference) to libc.so.5.4.46, and that libc.so.6 is a symbolic link to libc-2.1.1.so, which is the primary C shared library on your system. This is the single most important and widely used library in the system.

The shared library system is maintained with ldconfig. Whenever a new shared library is installed on the system, ldconfig is run and a new entry is made in the file /etc/ld.so.cache. Then a symbolic link is created with the name of the library and its major version number, which references the actual shared library file with the full version in its name. This all happens automatically when packages are installed using RPM because packages that install shared libraries generally have a post-install script that runs ldconfig for you. If you have installed shared libraries from TAR files, you might need to run this command yourself so that the libraries are registered with the system.

PART
III

CH
17

USING ldd TO DISCOVER REQUIRED SHARED LIBRARIES

When a program is created, the linker records the versions of the shared libraries that it requires in the program file. You can examine which shared libraries an executable program needs by using ldd. For example, you can find out what shared library is used by man by typing ldd /usr/bin/man, which should result in something similar to the following output:

```
libc.so.6 => /lib/libc.so.6 (0x2aac6000)
/lib/ld-linux.so. => /lib/ld-linux.so.2 (0x2aaab000)
```

man is a fairly simple program. For a more interesting listing, try ldd /usr/bin/emacs.

If you determine that you have a shared library incompatibility problem, there are several ways to handle it.

If the library that is missing has a different major version number than the one your program needs, just find the package that provides the version of the library that you need and install it. If the major version numbers are different, the other software on your system will be unaffected by the addition of another library, even one of the same name.

Another solution is to create a symlink for the shared library name you need. Link it to an existing shared library on your system and hope that the library is compatible. This might work in some circumstances, depending on how extensively the library is used and what subroutines are referenced by the program. This is, however, a stopgap measure and should be used only when you know (that is, have it on good authority) that the library versions in question are compatible for the purposes of the target program.

The recommended solution is to actually install the correct version of the shared library that you need and use the environment variable LD_LIBRARY_PATH to alter the shared libraries that are used by your program.

Programs are loaded in Linux as follows: The runtime loader examines /etc/ld.so.cache to determine the correct shared libraries to load with the program. However, if LD_LIBRARY_PATH is set in the user's environment, the loader uses any libraries found in the specified directories first.

> **Note**
>
> This is actually a simplification of the load process. There are other environment variables that can be used, such as LD_PRELOAD, to influence library loading. LD_LIBRARY_PATH is by far the most commonly used, however. For more information about these variables and the rest of the load sequence, see the ld.so man page.

The steps to set this up for a specific program are somewhat involved but not complicated. You want to run the one program you need with the special version of the shared library without affecting any other program running on the system. This is done by creating a wrapper script that sets up the shared library environment, and then executes the original program.

Following are the steps for setting this up, for the hypothetical program /usr/bin/prog1, which requires libgoo.so.2.1.18. Your system has the incompatible libgoo.so.2.1.23:

1. Obtain a copy of libgoo.so.2.1.18. The easiest way to do this is to search the Internet for old packages or TAR files. Often, when incompatibilities such as this are discussed in online forums, pointers to libraries are mentioned. If you can only find an old package, you can use rpm2cpio to extract the files you need. See the section "Extracting the Contents of an rpm (rpm2cpio)," later in this chapter.

2. Make a new directory to hold this compatibility library, separate from the library where libgoo.so.2 normally resides. For example, create the directory /usr/lib/compat, and copy libgoo.so.2.1.18 to it.

3. Make a symlink for the shared library with the major version number included. For example:

   ```
   ln  s libgoo.so.2.1.18 /usr/lib/compat/libgoo.so.2.
   ```

4. Rename the prog1 program to something else:

   ```
   mv /usr/bin/prog1/usr/bin/prog1.real
   ```

5. Create a wrapper script called prog1, which refers to the shared library. The script might look similar to the following:

   ```
   #/bin/sh
   export LD_LIBRARY_PATH=/usr/lib/compat
   exec /usr/bin/prog1.real
   ```

6. Don't forget to mark the script as executable:

   ```
   chmod a+x /usr/bin/prog1
   ```

When you have done all this, you can run prog1 and have it use /usr/lib/compat/libgoo.so.2.1.18 instead of /usr/lib/libgoo.so.1.23.

ADVANCED RPM PACKAGE QUERYING

RPM provides many ways to query packages and the RPM database. This is very helpful when troubleshooting packages and your Linux system.

EXTRACTING THE CONTENTS OF AN rpm (rpm2cpio)

Sometimes it is useful to extract the contents of an RPM package without installing it. This is especially useful if you want to examine particular files before installing them or if you need to recover a configuration file. The tool rpm2cpio allows you to do this. To extract all files from an rpm, go to a temporary directory and enter

```
$ rpm2cpio rpmfile.rpm | cpio -ivd
```

This will extract all files from the package. If you want only particular files, you can use wildcards as follows:

```
$ rpm2cpio rpmfile.rpm | cpio -ivd 'etc*'
```

FINDING OUT WHICH RPM PACKAGE OWNS A FILE

Use the rpm -qf command to find out which package owns a file. This can be very useful when you find problems with the software on your system and need to find other related files. You must specify the full pathname to the file for rpm to find the matching package in the package database, for example:

```
$ rpm  -qf /usr/bin/emacs
Xemacs-emacs-link-21.1.8-3
```

CUSTOMIZING THE FORMAT OF RPM PACKAGE QUERIES

rpm enables you to customize the format of the output of your queries. You can create custom reports or use the output of rpm with other programs by specially formatting the query output. Use the -queryformat option to specify the format string for the query output. If you want each item listed on a separate line, be sure to include a newline character (\n) at the end of the line. Special tags in the format string are used to output a particular piece of information about a package or file.

For example, the following command shows a list of all the packages on your system, along with their size in the format shown:

```
rpm -qa --queryformat="Package: %-25{NAME}  Size: $10{SIZE}\n"
```

The format of the fields is as follows:

```
%[-][width]{[=]field[:typetag]}
```

The fields options are as follows:

- A leading - indicates that the field should be left justified instead of right justified.
- *width* is the field width.
- An = before the field name indicates that the first element of an array field should be used for all lines. See "Array Fields" for more information.

- *field* is the field name. Use rpm --querytags for a list of all the available fields.

- *typetag* is one of octal, date, shescape, perms, fflags, or depflags. See "Typetags" for more information.

 Tip

> rpm --qf is the same as rpm --queryformat.

ARRAY FIELDS

Several package fields contain lists of values rather than a single value. For example, the FILENAMES field lists all the files that are in the package. It's easy to tell array fields from normal fields, because array field names are plural. For example, FILENAMES is an array field, but NAME is a normal field.

In a queryformat string, you can have rpm iterate over arrays by enclosing the format in square brackets ([]). This will iterate once for every element in the first field. Because normal fields are really just array fields with only one entry, you need a way to let rpm know that it should keep iterating even when it runs out of entries in a normal field. You can do this by prefacing the field name with =. For example, this very popular format lists all the files in all packages:

```
$ rpm -qa --queryformat="[%25{=NAME} %{FILENAMES}\n]"
```

This format is so popular that it is actually built into rpm:

```
$ rpm -qa --filesbypkg
```

Tip

> filesbypkg is an alias defined in /usr/lib/rpm/rpmpopt (by default). You can find many other aliases in this file as well. If you want to create your own aliases, you can put them in /etc/popt or $HOME/.popt. See the "Option Aliasing" section of the popt man page (man popt) for more information on using aliases with RPM and other Linux tools that use popt.

TYPETAGS

When rpm uses a queryformat, it doesn't know what kind of data is held in each field. It assumes that you want to display all numbers as decimal integers and all strings exactly as they appear in the database. Usually this is the correct thing to do, but some data is better suited to other formats. For example, time and date information is stored in the database as the number of seconds since the *epoch* (1970-Jan-1 00:00:00 UTC). If you use the INSTALLTIME field without any modifiers, it will output in a very human-unfriendly way:

```
$ rpm -q --queryformat="%{NAME}: %{INSTALLTIME}\n" rpm
rpm: 950061266
```

To display this in a human-readable way, you can use a field modifier called a *typetag*. In this example, we want to display this number as a date:

```
$ rpm -q --queryformat="%{NAME}: %{INSTALLTIME:date}\n" rpm
rpm: Tue 08 Feb 2000 08:54:26 PM EST
```

Table 17.1 lists the available typetags.

TABLE 17.1   TYPETAG MODIFIERS

Typetag	Description
octal	Output numeric values in octal rather than decimal. This is often used for file permissions.
date	Output date and time values as a human-readable date and time string.
shescape	Output a string that can be passed directly to the command shell.
perms	Output numeric values as a human-readable string representing file permissions. This is the same string that ls -l uses.
fflags	Output numeric values as a human-readable string representing file flags. These flags are
c	Configuration file
d	Document file
s	Spec file
m	Don't worry if file is missing
n	Don't replace existing version when installing
g	Ghost. A ghost includes file ownership and permission, but the file itself is not included. This is generally used for log files.
depflags	Output numeric values as a human-readable string representing comparison operators (<, =, >).

PART
III

CH
17

ANALYZING DISK SPACE USED BY PACKAGES

When your disk space starts to get low, you can use rpm to find the packages that are using up all your disk space. For example, use the following commands to list how much space each package on your system is consuming:

```
rpm -qa --queryformat "%-30{NAME} %{SIZE}\n" | sort
```

It can also be used to get the top ten packages:

```
rpm -qa-queryformat "%10{SIZE} %{NAME}\n" | sort -rn | head
```

For a real shock, look at the xemacs packages and see how much room they take. If you don't use xemacs, now is a good time to remove these packages and save yourself that disk space.

BUILDING FROM SOURCE RPMs

The tool used to rebuild RPM packages is the same command-line tool used to manage them: rpm. This section gives an overview of the build process, starting with a little history to explain why the packaging system works the way it does. (For an introduction to RPM, see Chapter 16.)

WHY WOULD YOU WANT TO REBUILD AN RPM PACKAGE?

There are many good reasons for rebuilding RPM packages. You might not be able to find a binary RPM that works well with your distribution. *Source RPMs* (also called *SRPMs*) are often much more adaptable to different distributions and architectures than binary RPMs. You might also want to change the options that the software was compiled with, or even change the software itself. Finally, using SRPMs can help protect you from malicious packages because you can look at all the source code.

PHILOSOPHY OF RPM

Before diving into the details of rebuilding packages, it helps to learn some of the philosophy behind the package manager as well as something about the development methods commonly used with open source software.

In the UNIX and UNIX-like world, open source software has historically been distributed in the form of TAR files that contain the source code necessary to build the software on your machine. Sometimes these bundles of files include readily executable binaries. Often, however, you are expected to compile the software and install it yourself using the source files in the TAR. Because there are various versions of UNIX-like operating systems from different vendors, the software has to be written so that it can compile for many different OS versions and platforms (processors).

RPM is derived from this heritage of starting with source code from TAR files and, from that, producing working software. What differentiates RPM from other packaging systems is that it tries to automate the steps required to go from the author's original source code to a very easy-to-install package. This was done to make it easier to maintain a distribution of Linux, which might include hundreds or even thousands of packages. Therefore, although the automation provided by the package-building system is essential to a distribution vendor, it also provides some important benefits to the end users of the software—they can use the same automated steps to rebuild the software on their own machines.

WORKING WITH ORIGINAL SOURCES

One overriding philosophy of RPM is that it can be used to rebuild—from original sources obtained from the Internet—software that runs effectively.

Getting software to run on a particular machine or version of OS often requires that changes be made to the software. To help others who might want to use the software on similar machines, a developer makes changes and then submits the modifications back to the original author of the software in the form of patches. The original author often includes the changes in the next release of the software. Sometimes, however, the author doesn't have the time or inclination to include new patches; therefore, subsequent releases of the software need to have the same set of patches applied in order to get them to compile again on the target platform.

The philosophy behind RPM is to provide clean sources plus patches. "Clean sources" means that an SRPM is expected to be shipped with an exact copy of the sources that the original author provided. Because these sources might not meet the needs of the packager's audience, the packager can also include *patches* to be applied to the clean sources. Patches are short files that instruct a tool called patch how to change one source tree into another. For instance, the patch may include instructions to delete several lines of code, add a new file, and modify the documentation. Any text file can be manipulated using patch, and RPM also provides mechanisms for distributing new versions of binaries if these are required.

Many advantages exist to providing the clean sources plus patches rather than just providing the patched sources. By providing clean sources, the user can more easily verify that the program they have received is what it claims to be. It also makes it much easier to rebuild the package when a new version of the software becomes available.

STEPS IN THE BUILD PROCESS

The RPM build process includes four basic steps based on what a human might do to produce working binaries from a software base. These are referred to as stages of the build process:

1. **Prep Stage**—Extract the source files from a TAR file and apply patches that are relevant for the target platform.

2. **Build Stage**—Build the software by compiling the programs and (possibly) formatting the documentation.

3. **Install Stage**—Install the software on your system.

4. **Packaging Stage**—Bundle the files and directories for the software into a package.

This last step is unique to package management. Although automating the first three steps is great, it is the final step—creating a working package—that results in all the benefits of packages mentioned in Chapter 16, "Software Package Management."

DIRECTORIES INVOLVED IN THE BUILD PROCESS

The directories used by the RPM build process are underneath the directory /usr/src/ *distribution*, where *distribution* is something like redhat, OpenLinux, or sometimes even just RPM. The following directories are used during the build process:

- **SOURCES**—This directory contains the source TAR files, patches, and icon files for the software to be packaged.

- **SPECS**—This directory contains the spec files for building packages. A spec file for a package contains information about the package as well as scripts that are used to automatically build the package from the files in the SOURCES directory.

- **BUILD**—The BUILD directory holds the source code for the software while it is being compiled and constructed (during the build process). Source files are extracted to subdirectories of the BUILD directory during the prep stage. Compiled program binaries and configuration and documentation files are moved from this directory into the main filesystem during the install stage.

PART

III

CH

17

■ **RPMS**—The resulting binary package is placed in a subdirectory underneath the RPMS directory when the package is finally assembled (during the packaging stage). Subdirectories beneath RPMS hold the packages for particular platforms. These subdirectories have the same name as the architecture string used in the package filename. (See Table 12.1 for a list of architecture strings.) Packages compiled for Intel-based Linux distributions are generally placed in the i386 subdirectory, though they can be in the i586 or i686 directory depending on your particular processor and the distribution.

■ **SRPMS**—This directory holds the source RPM package that results from a build. This is a snapshot of all the materials required to produce the corresponding binary RPM. The location of this directory tree can be overridden by setting the value of %_topdir in either /usr/lib/rpm/macros or ${HOME}/.rpmmacros.

To perform the examples in this chapter, you need to access the directories listed in the preceding section. Normally, this means you need to log in as the root user (or use the su command to become root).

LOCATING AND INSTALLING SOURCE RPMs

Web and FTP sites that provide binary RPMs generally also provide source RPMs, also called SRPMs. You can identify an SRPM by the .src.rpm extension.

SRPMs are installed using rpm with the same parameters as binary RPMs. For example, to install ed-0.2-5.src.rpm, type

```
# rpm -i ed-0.2-5.src.rpm.
```

> **Tip**
> You can install directly from FTP and Web sites by using the URL as the package name.

The files ed-0.2.tar.gz and ed.gif are placed in the SOURCES directory, and the file ed-0.2.spec is placed in the SPECS directory.

REBUILDING THE PACKAGE

With the ed sources installed on your system, you can proceed directly to building the binary package. First, cd to the packaging area at /usr/src/*distribution*, and then type the following:

```
rpm -ba SPECS/ed-0.2.spec
```

Watch as the various stages of the build take place. First, the files in ed-0.2.tar.gz are extracted into the BUILD directory. Then the ed program is compiled and installed in a temporary place on your system. Finally, a new ed 0.2-5.i386.rpm file is created from the installed files and placed in the RPMS/i386 directory, and a new ed-0.2-5.src.rpm is placed in the SRPM directory.

If your goal was simply to create an RPM compatible with your distribution, you should be done now. Simply install the package from the RPMS/i386 directory:

```
# rpm -i RPMS/i386/ed-0.2-5.rpm
```

THE spec FILE

When you build packages, you use spec files to provide the information and scripts which automate the package-building process itself, and the information and scripts that are bundled as part of the package. This second set of scripts is used on the user's system when the package is installed.

These two sets of information are intermingled in the spec file, without any distinction between them other than their names. However, it is important to remember which items are used on your system during the package build process, and which items are used on the end user's system during package usage.

The spec file for a package is located in the SPECS directory and needs to have a filename consisting of the name of the package, the version number, and the extension .spec. For example, the name of the spec file for ed is ed-0.2.spec. For spec files that are used to produce multiple packages (such as -devel or -static packages), the base package name needs to be used for the filename.

A spec file includes two different kinds of entries: one-line fields and multiline sections. The one-line fields are placed at the top of the file in the header, and the sections follow. Most sections in the spec file contain Bourne shell scripts that run either during the package building process or on the end user's system during package installation or removal. However, the %Description section is just a series of text lines that describe the package. Listing 17.1 shows the spec file for the ed package, which is used for the examples in this chapter. This spec file has been simplified to shorten it for inclusion in this book. If you have installed the ed source RPM, you can look at the unedited version at /usr/src/*distribution*/SPECS/ed-0.2.spec.

PART

III

CH

17

LISTING 17.1   THE spec FILE FOR ed (SIMPLIFIED)

```
Summary: GNU Line Editor
Name: ed
Version: 0.2
Release: 5
Group: Textprocessing/Editor
Copyright: GPL
Packager: rwp@lst.de (Roger Pook)
Icon: ed.gif
# URL: No WWW site found
Source0: ftp://prep.ai.mit.edu/pub/gnu/ed-0.2.tar.gz
# Patch: - optional -
# Provides: - optional -
# Requires: - optional -
# Conflicts: - optional -
BuildRoot: /tmp/ed-0.2
%Description
ed is a line-oriented text editor.  It is used to create,
display, modify and otherwise manipulate text files.  red
is a restricted ed: it can only edit files in the current
directory and cannot execute shell commands.

%Prep
%setup
```

LISTING 17.1   CONTINUED

```
%Build
./configure-prefix=/usr-exec-prefix=/
make CFLAGS="$RPM_OPT_FLAGS" LDFLAGS=-s

%Install
DESTDIR=$RPM_BUILD_ROOT; export DESTDIR
make CFLAGS="$RPM_OPT_FLAGS" LDFLAGS=-s install \
prefix=$DESTDIR/usr exec_prefix=$DESTDIR/
gzip -9fn $DESTDIR/usr/info/ed.info
%Post
lisa-info install ed-section "Miscellaneous:"-entry \
"* ed:(ed).                    The GNU line-oriented text editor."
%PreUn
lisa-info remove ed $1

%Files
%doc NEWS POSIX README THANKS
/bin/ed
/bin/red
/usr/info/ed.info.gz
/usr/man/man1/ed.1.gz
/usr/man/man1/red.1.gz
```

FIELDS IN THE spec FILE

Fields are indicated with the field name followed by a colon. A pound sign (#) indicates a comment in the spec file, either in the header or in any of the sections.

Most of the fields are pieces of information that are just put into the package when it is built. However, some are used during the actual build process.

INFORMATIONAL FIELDS   Following are descriptions of the informational fields most commonly used in a spec file:

- **Summary**—A one-line description of the package.
- **Name**—The name of the package.
- **Version**—The version of the software in the package.
- **Release**—The release number of the package. This is what you modify if you make changes to the package (that is, when the original version of the software has not changed).
- **Group**—The group is a multipart (usually two-part) string used by package management utilities to organize the packages into a hierarchy. The parts of the group are separated by a slash. For example, the ed package is in the Textprocessing/Editor group. A list of all the groups is available in the GROUPS file with your RPM documentation (usually /usr/doc/rpm-3.0.5 if you have it installed.)
- **Copyright**—This indicates the copyright holder and/or the license that the software uses. Common values for the license are BSD, distributable, GPL, artistic, public domain, MIT, freeware, and shareware.

- **Packager**—This provides the name and email address of the person who built this package. In the case of packages that come with your distribution, this field is often used to track who internally maintains the package. Please don't contact this person to get support for the software in the package. If you have questions about the software provided by a package, visit the site at which the software originated, or use other normal support channels.

- **Provides**—This lists the items that the package provides. The package automatically provides its own name and all the files that it contains (including shared libraries and interpreters), so these do not need to be explicitly listed.

- **Requires**—This lists the items that the package requires. If programs in the package require shared libraries or interpreters, rpm detects this automatically, and these items do not need to be explicitly listed.

- **Conflicts**—This lists conflicts that the package has. For instance, if this were a mail engine, it might conflict with sendmail because there can usually only be one mail engine on a machine. This information is used by RPM to prevent two conflicting packages from being installed on the same machine.

- **Obsoletes**—This lists packages which are obsoleted by this package. This is a more specific version of Conflicts.

- **BuildRoot**—This option instructs RPM to place files in a temporary directory during the install step. This is very useful when building packages for a distribution (which is why Caldera uses it heavily). For more information, see the section "BuildRoot" later in this chapter.

- **%Description**—This is a multiline description of the package. Actually, this is a section and not a field, but it fits better here because it is purely informational and is not used during package building.

PART

III

CH

17

FIELDS USED DURING PACKAGE BUILDING

The following fields are used during the build process:

- **Icon**—The graphics file (often GIF) that contains an icon for this package (used by graphical package management tools).

- **Source#**—This is an URL for the source files for the software. The filename part is used by the build process, and the rest of the URL is for informational purposes. Note that Source is the same as Source0 (the 0 is optional).

- **Patch#**—These entries denote the filenames of the patch files used during the build process. Patch is the same as Patch0.

SECTIONS IN THE SPEC FILE

Sections in the spec file begin with a section identifier and continue until the next section identifier. The section identifiers start with a percent sign.

Unfortunately, rpm uses a percent sign to indicate both section identifiers and directives in the %Prep and %Files sections, which can be confusing. Some packagers capitalize the first letter of section identifiers and leave directive names in all lowercase to distinguish the two in their spec files, but this is not universal.

Most sections in the spec file contain shell scripts that perform the actions required for that stage of the build process. If you are not familiar with shell scripting, you might want to refer to the "Shell Programming" section in Chapter 14, "Customizing Your Shell Environment."

SECTIONS USED DURING THE BUILD PROCESS   The following sections are used during the build process:

- **%Prep**—This section contains a shell script to extract the source files and apply the patches. It is used during the prep stage.
- **%Build**—This contains a shell script to build (compile) the software. It is used during the build stage.
- **%Install**—This contains a shell script to install the software. This is used during the Install stage. (You can probably see a pattern emerging here!)
- **%Files**—This section contains a listing of the files and directories in the package.
- **%Clean**—This optional section contains a shell script to clean up after a package build.
- **%Changelog**—This contains changelog information about the SPEC file itself.

SECTIONS FOR PACKAGE SCRIPTS   The following scripts are not used at build time; they are inserted into the package and used by the package manager on the end user's system when the package is installed, removed, or verified.

- **%Pre/%Post**—Scripts to run on the end user's system before and after installing the package files
- **%Preun/%Postun**—Scripts to run on the end user's system before and after removing the package files
- **%Triggerin/%Triggerun**—Scripts to run when a specific package is installed and uninstalled. For example, these could be used by a mail client to add sendmail support whenever sendmail is installed.
- **%Triggerpostun**—Script to run after a specific package is uninstalled (versus before the package is uninstalled in the case of %Triggerun).
- **%Verify**—Contains a script run on the end user's system to verify the package files. If empty, the default verification mechanism of RPM is used.

HELPER PACKAGES

It is common to have helper packages defined in a spec file. For example, if a package mypackage also has a mypackage-devel package, both will be described in the same spec file.

Generally, the only thing that differs in the helper packages is the list of files and the information fields. To define the information fields for a helper package, the spec file uses the %package directive followed by the fields. After that, sections use the package's name to differentiate—for example,

```
%package devel
Summary: Development files for applications which will manipulate RPM packages.
Group: Development/Libraries
%ifos linux
Requires: python >= 1.5.1
%endif
%description devel
This package contains the RPM C library and header files.  These development files
will simplify the process of writing programs which manipulate RPM packages and
databases and are intended to make it easier to create graphical package managers
or any other tools that need an intimate knowledge of RPM packages in order to
function.
```

BUILDING A PACKAGE

Use the -b option with rpm to build packages. You can use other options with this command to perform only certain stages of the build process. This is useful for debugging the build process for a package. Table 17.2 lists the build options and the stages that they refer to.

TABLE 17.2   RPM BUILD OPTIONS

Option	Stage, or Action
p	Prep
c	Build (compile)
i	Install
b	Packaging (create a binary package)
a	All (build binary and source packages)
l	Check file list
--short-circuit	Only execute this stage (not preceding ones)

THE PREP STAGE

During the prep stage of the package build, the script in the %Prep section of the spec file is run. This script will extract the source files from the TAR file and apply patches in preparation for the actual compilation of the software.

During this stage, a directory is created under /usr/src/*distribution*/BUILD. This is where the files are placed and where other stages will operate.

You can use any commands you need to prepare the source files in the BUILD directory. However, two special directives handle most of the actions that need to be performed. The %setup directive is used to extract the source files listed in the Source lines. The %patch directive is used to apply the patches listed in the Patch lines.

THE BUILD STAGE

The build stage is where rpm actually compiles the software for your system, using the script in the %Build section. Often this script includes running programs such as configure to set up the software build environment, and make to actually compile the software.

No special directives are available for this section of the spec file. However, rpm sets several shell variables that have values that might be useful for this script.

The following shell variables are available for your use throughout the scripts in the spec file:

- **RPM_SOURCE_DIR**—Location of RPM SOURCES directory. This is /usr/src/*distribution*/ SOURCES by default, but can be overridden by configuration values in /etc/rpmrc or ~/.rpmrc.

- **RPM_BUILD_DIR**—Location of RPM BUILD directory. This is /usr/src/*distribution*/BUILD by default. This can also be overridden.

- **RPM_DOC_DIR**—Location at which the document directory for this package is placed. The default value is /usr/doc.

- **RPM_OPT_FLAGS**—String of compiler options for producing optimized code for the target architecture (i386). This is often used with make during the compilation of the software.

- **RPM_OS**—String indicating the OS (not just Linux!) used during the build process.

- **RPM_ARCH**—String indicating the architecture during the build process.

- **RPM_ROOT_DIR**—Root directory used during all steps of the build process.

- **RPM_BUILD_ROOT**—Root directory used for the install and packaging stages of the build process.

- **RPM_PACKAGE_NAME**—The name of the package.

- **RPM_PACKAGE_VERSION**—The version of the software in the package.

- **RPM_PACKAGE_RELEASE**—The release of the package.

THE INSTALL STAGE

During the install stage, the commands are run to actually install the software onto your system. At the end of this stage, the software will be installed on your system, compiled, formatted, and ready to run, exactly as it needs to be on an end user's system. The shell script to perform this is found in the %Install section of the spec file.

The files put in a package during the packaging state (described in the next section) are taken from their regular positions in the working filesystem. Their placement, ownership, and permissions are recorded in the package so that they will have those same attributes on the user's system when the package is installed. Thus, it is critical that the install stage sets up the files completely and properly.

THE PACKAGING STAGE

During this stage, the package files (binary and source RPMs) are actually created. The files that were placed into your filesystem during the install stage are collected and placed into the binary package file, along with information from the spec file. Then all the materials used to produce the package are collected and bundled together into a source RPM package, which can be used (with a similar set of tools and libraries) to reproduce the package at a later date.

The %Files section of the spec file lists the files and directories on your filesystem that will be put into the package. This will correspond with the files that were placed on your filesystem during the install stage of the build process.

The %Files section supports the following directives and options:

- **%doc**—Marks documentation files. These go in a directory under /usr/doc on the end user's system. Don't use this for man pages or other documents that have to reside in specific locations on the end user's system. Note that the paths listed with this directive are relative to the BUILD directory, not the regular filesystem. For example, in Listing 17.1, the NEWS file listed with the %doc directive refers to /usr/src/*distribution*/BUILD/ed 0.2/NEWS, which will be placed on the user's system as /usr/doc/ed-0.2/NEWS when this package is installed.

- **%config**—Marks configuration files. These files get special handling during remove and upgrade operations on the user's machine.

- **%dir**—Indicates a directory. This causes rpm to package all the files in the indicated directory and all its subdirectories.

- **-f filename**—The -f option used with the %Files section indicates to read the file list from a separate file. For example, the following line:

```
%File -f edlist
```

reads the file list from the file /usr/src/*distribution*/BUILD/ed 0.2/edlist, instead of from the spec file.

PART

III

CH

17

> **Caution**
>
> Be careful with listing directories in the file list. If an item in the file list is a directory, rpm interprets it as a %dir item and reads all the files in it. This can end up placing a huge number of files (and not the right ones) in the package, if the directory is not correct.

At the end of this stage, a binary package file is in the RPMS/i386 directory and a source package file in SRPMS.

PACKAGING MISCELLANY

This section has a few miscellaneous tips to help you debug the package building process. Also, some of the conventions used by major distributions for their packages are described. You might want to use similar techniques when you build packages.

DEBUGGING THE BUILD PROCESS

rpm executes the shell commands and scripts that it processes with the shell `set -x` option set. This means that in the output of rpm, the commands that it executes are displayed with a plus sign in front of them. Output from these commands appears unmodified. You can use the output of rpm to determine what commands RPM is executing at each stage of the build process, for debugging purposes.

BuildRoot

Virtually all packages produced by major distributions use the BuildRoot feature of RPM. The BuildRoot directive instructs RPM to place files in a temporary location during the install stage. This prevents the act of building a SRPM from modifying your system.

This means you can't just install the source RPM for a package, modify a few things, and rebuild it to get the software in the package installed on your system. For example, to make a quick patch, some people are accustomed to installing a source RPM on their system, running the prep stage of the build process, and then applying the patches and manually running the steps in the install stage. Because the packages use BuildRoot, the software doesn't end up in the live part of the filesystem. With these packages, you actually have to build the binary package and install it.

PROJECT: MODIFYING A PACKAGE

In this project, you'll actually modify an existing package. The modifications will be trivial (and not very useful), but this will take you through the steps required to make minor modifications. The examples are given for an OpenLinux system so that specific directories can be listed, but other RPM-based distributions are very similar.

1. Install the sources for ed:

   ```
   # rpm -i /mnt/cdrom/Packages/RPMS/ed-0.2-5.src.rpm
   ```

2. Extract the sources so you can work on them:

   ```
   # cd /usr/src/OpenLinux; rpm -bp SPECS/ed.spec
   ```

3. Make a copy to work on (you don't want to work on the sources in the BUILD directory):

   ```
   # cd BUILD; cp -a ed-0.2 /usr/local/src
   ```

4. Make main.c writable:

   ```
   # cd /usr/local/src/ed-0.2; chmod u+w main.c; vi main.c
   ```

5. Add a line to say `Hey, I modified ed!` to the `usage()` routine, (see Listing 17.2):

LISTING 17.2 THE FIRST PART OF THE `usage()` ROUTINE IN `ed-0.2/main.c`

```
void
usage (status)
int status;
{
```

LISTING 17.2   CONTINUED

```
if (status != 0)
fprintf (stderr, "Try `%s-help' for more information.\n", program_name);
else
    {
printf ("Hey, I modified ed!\n");
printf ("Usage: %s [OPTION]... [FILE]\n", program_name);
```

---

6. Test your changes:

```
# ./configure && make && ./ed-help
[...]
Hey, I modified ed!
Usage: ./ed [OPTION]... [FILE]
[...]
```

7. Clean up the tree and make a patch file:

```
# make distclean; rm stamp-h
# diff -cr /usr/src/OpenLinux/BUILD/ed-0.2 . > /usr/src/OpenLinux/SOURCES/
ed-mypatch.patch
```

8. Update the spec file to update the release number and include your new patch (see Listing 17.3). To prevent confusion, you should add your initials to the release number.

LISTING 17.3   PORTION OF ed.spec

```
Summary: GNU Line Editor
Name: ed
Version: 0.2
Release: 5ran
Group: Textprocessing/Editor
[...]
Source0: ftp://prep.ai.mit.edu/pub/gnu/ed-0.2.tar.gz
Patch0: ed-mypatch.patch
[...]
%Prep
%setup
%patch
```

---

9. Build the package to the installation stage:

```
# rpm -bi SPECS/ed.spec
```

10. Test the package:

```
# /tmp/ed-0.2/bin/ed-help
Hey, I modified ed!
Usage: /tmp/ed-0.2/bin/ed [OPTION]... [FILE]
[...]
```

11. Build the whole package, install, and enjoy:

```
# rpm -ba SPECS/ed.spec
# rpm -i RPMS/i386/ed-0.2-5ran.i386.rpm
```

I wouldn't recommend actually installing this package, because it's a rather silly patch, but that's how it would be done. Notice the 5ran in the name of the package, which comes from the Release line we put in the spec file.

You can use these same techniques to make new packages. Generally the best way to do that is to use the spec files from your distribution as a guide. Copy what you need and change what is different for your program. Congratulations! You are now a software packager.

CHAPTER **18**

BUILDING A CUSTOM KERNEL

In this chapter

THE LINUX KERNEL

The Linux kernel is one of the largest and most complex portions of your Linux system, and you wouldn't have a Linux system without it. However, as long as you have all the proper tools installed, building a new kernel is one of the easier tasks you'll have. It is guaranteed to build if you follow the instructions in this chapter. If you configure it incorrectly, it might not boot, but you'll be prepared for that eventuality before the end of the chapter.

The Linux kernel is similar to the engine for your car: Without the kernel, you're not going to get anywhere. It is the central nervous system behind the software that controls your computer. It's easy to take for granted how an operating system works, but it really is quite complex. Every aspect of the interaction between you and your computer is controlled, in some fashion, by the operating system. In everything from typing at the keyboard or moving your mouse to printing a file or accessing data across the network, the kernel plays a part.

The Linux kernel has two very distinct versions available at any given time: the *stable* version and the unstable, or *developmental*, version. These can be differentiated by the numbering system. The first number is the kernel major number. At this time, the version is 2. The minor number is the one to pay attention to. If the minor number is even (0 is considered even), the kernel is one of the stable versions. Current stable versions, then, are 2.0.x, 2.2.x, and 2.4.x. The developmental kernels have an odd minor number, with current developmental kernels being 2.5.x. The final number is the revision number. Although it is not necessary to run the most current revision number, if the revision was because of a security bug fix and you are susceptible to the particular exploit that was fixed, or if the revision added or fixed support for your software, you'll want to upgrade. Unless you are an experienced kernel builder, you'll want to build only stable kernels. The developmental kernels are often problematic.

BUILDING A NEW KERNEL

One distinct advantage of Linux is the capability to truly recompile the complete operating system, rather than just reconfigure some of the system parameters. Because Linux comes complete with the source code, you can optimize the code for a specific hardware configuration as well as design the kernel. The steps to building a new kernel are as follows:

1. Obtain the kernel source.
2. Prepare the source tree.
3. Configure the source.
4. Build the source and install the modules.
5. Move the kernel.
6. Configure and run LILO or GRUB.
7. Verify module support.
8. Reboot the system and try out your new kernel.

It is important that all the necessary steps be performed in the correct order.

If you've already performed these steps at one point, you might want to obtain and install a patch to the kernel instead of starting over with a new source. Patching a kernel is not as difficult as it sounds and is explained later in this chapter. Using a patch will save you a significant amount of time and bandwidth.

OBTAINING THE KERNEL SOURCE (STEP 1)

Your distribution comes with the kernel source. However, this source might not be the most current. By the time you're comfortable with your new Linux installation, a newer kernel is probably out. Kernel sources are released when there are significant new drivers to add, old drivers with important updates, or security updates.

The best way to get the kernel sources is not from the RPMs on your distribution's CD-ROM, unless you know you need something special that Caldera, Red Hat or your distribution producer has added that is not yet in the stable kernels. You can get pristine sources from `ftp://ftp.us.kernel.org` (a number of mirror sites are also available) in the subdirectory `pub/linux/kernel/v2.4`. Look for the latest source and download it. Put the file in `/usr/src`.

> **Note**
>
> If you want to keep the graphical Caldera bootup screen, you'll need to use the Caldera-supplied SRPMs to do so because they have been modified to support the graphical boot process. The latest kernels in SRPM format should be available on the Caldera FTP site. See Chapter 17, "Building/Rebuilding a Package," section "Advanced Package Management," for details as well as instructions on the Caldera Web site.

Create a directory for the kernel source. Normally, you'll want it to be something like `linux-2.4.10`, where the 2.4.10 is the kernel version you just downloaded (`mkdir linux-2.4.10`). Then create a link to this directory called `linux` (`ln -s linux-2.4.10 linux`).

If the `linux-2.4.10` already exists because you've installed the RPM, remove it first. You can do this either by removing the RPMs (recommended) or by simply removing the `linux-2.4.10` directory before you begin.

PREPARING THE SOURCE TREE (STEP 2)

When you've successfully completed step 1, you're going to prepare the source tree. The source tree is all the source code opened into its own portion of the directory tree and ready for use.

The command to open the file you downloaded depends on which file you grabbed. The source file is either `linux-2.4.10.tar.gz` or `linux-2.4.10.tar.bz2`. Each uses a slightly different set of commands to open.

For `linux-2.4.10.tar.gz`, use the following command:

```
tar xzvf linux-2.4.10.tar.gz
```

For `linux-2.4.10.tar.bz2`, use the following command:

```
bzcat linux-2.4.10.tar.bz2 | tar xv.
```

Both expand the contents into the directory pointed to by your `linux` link.

Now `cd` into the `linux` directory (`cd linux`). This directory is called the top-level directory for the source tree. This directory contains a number of subdirectories. The most important one for learning more about the kernel is the `Documentation` directory. This should be your first stop if you want to learn more about your `linux` kernel.

To begin the process of compiling a new kernel, run the following command:

```
make mrproper
```

This particular command is very special. It sets up the kernel environment. If you recompile this kernel, you will not have to run this command again unless you change the kernel type from SMP to Uniprocessor or vice versa. If you only patch this kernel to a new level, you will not have to run this command again. This command is only needed the very first time you install the kernel sources (and when switching kernel types as noted above), so you can now forget this command successfully.

Note

The `make mrproper` command deletes the `.config` file created during the configuration process. If you want to save your configuration from a previous build, either do not run this command or save your `.config` file to a directory outside the kernel build tree.

CONFIGURING THE SOURCE (STEP 3)

This is the step in which you must select all the options that you want in the new kernel. Don't be intimidated by all the selections. The key to completing this step is to trust the default settings. If you come across a parameter that you don't understand, keep the default selection. There are actually three methods for creating the configuration file that is used in building a new kernel:

- `make config`
- `make menuconfig`
- `make xconfig`

Each of these methods provides a system for configuring the desired parameters in building a kernel and all do the same thing in the end—create a `.config` file; however, they differ greatly in ease of use. Of course, this is all a matter of personal preference. The first option is a simple, text-based, sequential script. It looks somewhat similar to the following:

```
# make config
rm -f include/asm
( cd include ; ln -sf asm-i386 asm)
/bin/sh scripts/Configure arch/i386/config.in
#
# Using defaults found in arch/i386/defconfig
```

```
#
*
* Code maturity level options
*
Prompt for development and/or incomplete code/drivers (CONFIG_
EXPERIMENTAL) [Y/n/?] y
*
* Loadable module support
*
Enable loadable module support (CONFIG_MODULES) [Y/n/?] y
Set version information on all symbols for modules (CONFIG_MODVERSIONS)
[Y/n/?]
```

Because of the large number of options and the dependence of one option on others, this method is difficult for all but the most experienced kernel builders. You cannot back up; you must go sequentially from beginning to end.

The second option, like the first, is not dependent on an X Window environment, but it's not a sequential script either. In other words, you have the capability to select options and make changes in any desired order. The main screen for make menuconfig looks somewhat similar to the following::

```
Linux Kernel v2.4.0-test7 Configuration
-----------------------------------------------------------------------------
|------------------------------- Main Menu -----------------------------------|
|  Arrow keys navigate the menu.  <Enter> selects submenus --->.              |
|  Highlighted letters are hotkeys.  Pressing <Y> includes, <N> excludes,     |
|  <M> modularizes features.  Press <Esc><Esc> to exit, <?> for Help.         |
|  Legend: [*] built-in  [ ] excluded  <M> module  < > module capable         |
|  -------------------------------------------------------------------------  |
| |            Code maturity level options  --->                          | | |
| |            Loadable module support  --->                              | | |
| |            Processor type and features  --->                          | | |
| |            General setup  --->                                        | | |
| |            Memory Technology Devices (MTD)  --->                      | | |
| |            Parallel port support  --->                                | | |
| |            Plug and Play configuration  --->                          | | |
| |            Block devices  --->                                        | | |
| |            Networking options  --->                                   | | |
| |            Telephony Support  --->                                    | | |
| |-------------(+)-------------------------------------------------------| | |
|-----------------------------------------------------------------------------|
|                    <Select>    < Exit >    < Help >                         |
-----------------------------------------------------------------------------
```

This particular type of screen is referred to as an *ncurses* (or just *curses*) screen because it requires the ncurses libraries. If these are not installed, you won't be able to use this method.

The last method is by far the easiest to use, but you must be in the X Window environment to use it. The initial screen is displayed by running the following from a shell prompt:

```
# make xconfig
```

Initially, some necessary pieces are compiled, and then a dialog box is displayed (see Figure 18.1).

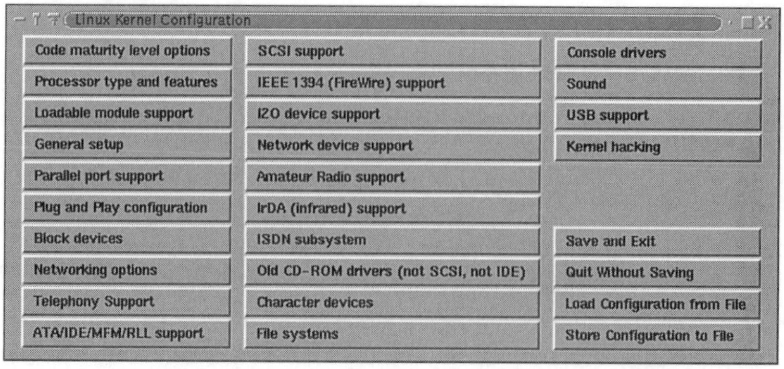

Figure 18.1
The X Window-based
kernel configuration
screen.

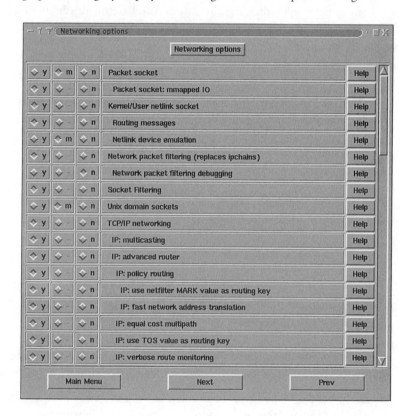

Click the desired category for a complete list of configurable options. For example, selecting the Networking options category displays the dialog box that is depicted in Figure 18.2.

Figure 18.2
The Networking
options dialog box.

Each listed option (regardless of the method used above) has two or three configurable settings: y, m, or n. The definition of these settings is described in Table 18.1.

TABLE 18.1   KERNEL CONFIGURATION SETTINGS

Settings	Value	Description
y	yes	Select this setting to include support for the corresponding option and build it directly into the kernel.
m	module	Select this setting to create a loadable module for the corresponding option. A module can be loaded or removed dynamically. Rebooting the system is not required.
n	no	Select this setting to disable any support for the corresponding option.

You'll find that some options are not available as modules, so the module option is not offered. Also, some options are dependent on other options being enabled. If the setting choices are grayed out, the option on which it is dependent has been set to No. Simply enabling the master option enables you to then select support for the dependent option.

Remember that many choices are available in a wide range of categories. If you're not familiar with what a particular option does, click the Help button for further information. If it's still not clear what a particular option does, leave the default setting.

The X Window-based kernel configuration program provides the capability to save and load previously saved configuration files. This can be quite handy when you're first learning to set kernel options.

Besides being in an X environment to use this method, you'll also need the TCL/TK libraries installed.

SUMMARY OF CRITICAL KERNEL CONFIGURATION OPTIONS

Each of the preceding three options creates a file in the /usr/src/linux directory named .config. This file contains the parameter selections that are defined by the previous steps. In fact, if you really want to, you can hand-edit this file and make any desired changes, although that is not the recommended method of making changes.

> **Note**
>
> There is no .config file until after you complete the make config, make menuconfig, or make xconfig step for the first time. You might want to make a backup copy of this file before configuring subsequent kernel configurations.

As you can see from the category options that are listed in Figure 18.1, there is a wide range of selections. You must take care with a few selections. Because every possible situation cannot be foreseen, some guidelines are provided here.

Some options you must set properly for your system to boot include the following:

■ **Processor type and features (Processor Family)**—Do not select a processor beyond that installed in your system. A 386 processor kernel boots on any system. A K6/II/III kernel does not boot on a 386.

- **General configuration**—This is as follows:
  - **PCI support**—This is a must for a system with PCI (Pentium and above, and some 486s).
  - **Sysctl support**—This must be enabled. (Disabling is only for embedded systems, which you almost certainly do not have.)
  - **Kernel core**—This must be ELF. (Do not change to A.OUT, or your system will not boot.)
  - **Kernel support for ELF binaries**—This must be compiled in; do not make this a module.
- **Block devices**—Any device you will boot the kernel from and mount as a root partition must be compiled in and cannot be compiled as a module. For example, if you boot from /dev/hda1 and mount it as the root partition, at least the following two options must be compiled in and cannot be modules:
  - Enhanced IDE/MFM/RLL disk/CD-ROM/tape/floppy support
  - Include IDE/ATA-2 DISK support
- **SCSI support**—In the same way as the block devices, if you have a SCSI drive you will boot from, this must be compiled in and cannot be a module. Here, you must select at least the following three options:
  - SCSI support
  - SCSI disk
  - SCSI low-level drivers (Select the specific SCSI controller you have installed.)

Note

It is possible to boot SCSI devices without compiling in SCSI support by using an initial initrd ramdisk. OpenLinux and Red Hat do this on their boot disks and CD-ROM. If you are interested in doing this, read /usr/src/linux/Documentation/initrd.txt; the use of initrd is beyond the scope of this book. You must include initial ramdisk support for this option to work.

- **Character devices**—You will also want as a minimum the following three devices::
  - Virtual terminal
  - Support for console on virtual terminal
  - UNIX98 PTY support
- **Mouse devices**—If you have a PS/2 or bus mouse, you will also need to select the mouse option you need support for, but this can be compiled as a module.
- **Filesystems**—Filesystem support is also mandatory and must be compiled in (not a module) for the root filesystem. Linux uses ext2 as its native filesystem, but this might change in the future. Also include support for the /proc filesystem and /dev/pts:
  - /proc filesystem support
  - /dev/pts filesystem for Unix98 PTYs
  - Second extended fs support

■ **Console drivers**—In the console drivers, you'll need two items compiled in:

- VGA text console
- Video mode selection support (needed by Caldera's LIZARD for the graphical startup screen)

The preceding are only the required settings for a usable system to boot properly. You will also want to compile in other options. Read the help that comes with each item. If you don't understand the option, in most cases the default or help text recommendation is the safe bet. Expect to spend a great deal of time reading the first few times you configure a kernel.

BUILDING THE SOURCE AND INSTALLING THE MODULES (STEP 4)

This particular step is actually composed of a number of substeps, most of which are not important to understand, only to do. The steps that are important will be detailed in this section, and then a shortcut to completing the entire build without interruption will be demonstrated.

The following are the substeps to building a kernel:

- `make dep`
- `make clean`
- `make bzImage|bzdisk|bzlilo`
- `make modules`
- `make modules_install`

The first two substeps—`make dep` and `make clean`—are preparatory. The `make dep` step creates the dependencies files (`.depend`) that you'll find in each of the build subdirectories. Unless something is drastically wrong within the source tree, this will not cause any problems; it will just write the `.depend` files. The `make clean` file is the other preparatory step to clean out the remnants of previous builds that might interfere with the current build.

Following these two preparatory commands come the commands that actually build the kernel. Here, you have a choice among three commands: `make bzImage`, `make bzdisk`, and `make bzlilo`. Each accomplishes the same thing, the latter two performing one additional step.

make bzImage

This is the standard step that does nothing more than compile a new kernel. If all components compile correctly, a new kernel can be found in the `/usr/src/linux/arch/i386/boot` directory. The new kernel is aptly named `bzImage`. Of course, this is nothing more than a compiled kernel. You must configure the boot loader, that is LILO (or GRUB, see following Caution), to find the new kernel and boot. This is normally done by copying the `bzImage` file to its new home and running `lilo` to reinstall the boot loader. Moving the kernel (and the associated kernel map file) is discussed in the following section.

Caution

> Caldera has converted to GRUB, and although LILO is available, it has not been configured in a new installation of OpenLinux. You can tell whether your system is using GRUB because you will see the following
>
> `stage 1 stage 2`
>
> flash on the screen just before the graphical boot screen comes up. If you want to continue using GRUB, do not use the `make bzlilo` command. Also, do not run lilo, but follow the steps for using GRUB in Chapter 12, "Boot Loaders."

`make bzdisk`

This method performs exactly the same task as the `make bzImage` method, but after the compilation is complete, it automatically copies the newly built kernel to a floppy disk. This new disk can then be used to boot the system; the new kernel will then be active. This method is typically used to test a kernel with the system on which it was built, or it is used in testing the kernel on other hardware.

Note

> This method can be used to create an emergency boot disk. However, it might not be usable for a different system. The kernel image contains a pointer to the root filesystem from the system it was created on. This pointer must be changed if used on a system whose root filesystem is on a different partition than that of the system where the kernel was built.

`make bzlilo`

This is the recommended method of building and installing a new kernel, but you must have `lilo` prepared ahead of time. This method does not move the associated kernel map file, can overwrite a good kernel, and is wrought with pitfalls, so it not recommended. However, if after several kernel builds you decide to try this method, it can save you one extra step. This method is exactly like the `make bzImage` method except that it automatically performs an additional step. After the compilation completes, the newly built kernel is copied to the / directory as `vmlinuz` (a backup copy is made of the original `vmlinuz`), and `lilo` is run to reinstall the boot loader (to recognize the new kernel).

`make modules` **AND** `make modules_install`

The last two commands that complete the actual build process are `make modules` and `make modules_install`. The `make modules` does exactly what it says: It builds the modules that correspond to the kernel you built in the previous step. The `make modules_install` command moves those modules from within the kernel source tree to `/lib/modules/` `<kernel-version>/kernel/<module-type>`, the module-type being a category that modules are assigned to, such as `block`, `fs`, `ipv4`, `ipv6`, `misc`, `net`, `pcmcia`, and so on.

As promised, a simple, one-line command to accomplish the entire process is provided:

```
make dep;make clean;make bzImage && make modules && make
➥modules_install
```

The semicolons run the commands one after the other as if they were on subsequent command lines. The && means if the previous command finished without error, run this command. This prevents make modules from running if there was an error in the make bzImage portion of the build. You want to do this so that you see the error message. The use of the semicolons and doubled and signs works for any command. The make command also recognizes the following as a string of anded makes:

```
make dep clean bzImage modules modules_install
```

MOVING THE KERNEL (STEP 5)

After the kernel is built, you need to install it and the kernel map where they can be found. Most distributions are getting away from the kernel in the directory root. Most kernels are now being installed in /boot, a directory created just to hold the kernel and kernel map files, and this is where you'll put your kernel.

Copy (or move) the file system.map to the /boot directory, appending the kernel version to the end:

```
cp System.map /boot/System.map-2.4.10
```

Then copy (move) the kernel in the same way:

```
cp arch/i386/boot/bzImage /boot/bzImage-2.4.10
```

When the system map and kernel have been moved, you only have two more quick steps, and you can reboot into your new kernel (or your old one should that kernel fail to boot).

CONFIGURING AND RUNNING LILO (STEP 6)

The LILO boot loader enables you to specify several boot images. An additional boot image can be added by inserting another image section in the /etc/lilo.conf file. See Chapter 12 for further information on LILO or for configuring GRUB. The following is an example of a simple, single-image LILO configuration:

```
#
# /etc/lilo.conf - generated by Lizard
#

# target

boot = /dev/hda
install = /boot/boot.b

# options

prompt
delay = 50
timeout = 50
message = /boot/message
```

```
default = linux

image = /boot/vmlinuz-pc97-2.2.14-modular
        label  = linux
        root   = /dev/hda1
        vga    = 274
        read-only
        append = "debug=2 noapic nosmp"
```

The six lines in the `default` entry section must be duplicated and modified for the second boot image to be available at boot time. The `image` line and the `label` entry must be changed to accomplish this correctly. The `image` entry must match the kernel name that was copied in the previous step: `/boot/bzImage-2.4.10`. The `label` entry must be unique. This `label` is the unique identifier that enables you to select between the choices that are configured in the `/etc/lilo.conf` file. The complete `/etc/lilo.conf` is changed to look as follows:

```
#
# /etc/lilo.conf - generated by Lizard
#

# target

boot = /dev/hda
install = /boot/boot.b

# options

prompt
delay = 50
timeout = 50
message = /boot/message

default = linux

image = /boot/bzImage-2.4.10
        label  = linux
        root   = /dev/hda1
        vga    = 274
        read-only
        append = "debug=2 noapic nosmp"
image = /boot/vmlinuz-pc97-2.2.14-modular
        label  = linux.orig
        root   = /dev/hda1
        vga    = 274
        read-only
        append = "debug=2 noapic nosmp"
```

After the `/etc/lilo.conf` file is configured to include the additional boot image and the old image is renamed, you must reinstall the boot loader for it to be an option at boot time. Use the following command:

```
# lilo
Added linux *
Added linux.orig
```

Note

The preceding steps apply if LILO is used as the boot manager. If another boot loader, such System Commander, is used, the documentation for the loader needs to be referenced for setup instructions. For instructions on GRUB, refer to Chapter 12.

After this step is complete, you can reboot; both selection options are available at the LILO boot prompt. You can now boot to the original kernel even if the new kernel fails to boot the system. You must enter the label name of the desired boot image in order for it to boot. Display the available boot options (labels) by pressing the Tab key.

Tip

You can use the install floppy (or install CD-ROM) to boot to an existing Linux partition by supplying the parameter `boot root=/dev/<device_name>`. Just replace `<device_name>` with the actual partition name (such as hda1, hda2, sda1, sda2, and so on). If you create a boot disk by copying a kernel to floppy, you can make it boot and use your system's root with the following command, substituting your root device for `/dev/hda1`:

`rdev /dev/fd0 /dev/hda1`

Before you reboot, you need to perform just one more step.

PART

III

CH

18

VERIFYING MODULE SUPPORT (STEP 7)

Here, you'll verify that your module file (if applicable) has the modules listed you want to load automatically at bootup.

Verify that the file `/etc/modules/default` (Caldera OpenLinux) contains those modules you want loaded automatically. (Debian maintains the list in /etc/modules.) If you have more advanced requirements (needing to boot different kernels with different configurations), review Chapter 15, "Understanding PAM," which details how `/etc/rc.d/rc.modules` searches for files to load modules from.

Note

It is no longer necessary to create the `modules.dep` file. This file is now created as part of the make `modules_install` step when building a new kernel.

REBOOTING THE SYSTEM (STEP 8)

This is the easy step in this process. Sometimes it takes a little faith that what you've configured will work, but if you've followed the preceding steps, you can always recover if your newly built kernel fails to cooperate.

PATCHING A KERNEL

If a new kernel version comes out and you have reason to upgrade, you can save yourself a lot of time and trouble by patching it. In some cases, such as if you've applied another patch or built the FreeS/WAN as outlined in Chapter 20, "Building a VPN (FreeS/WAN)," you'll need to make some preparations first. These will be covered in the following text; for now, don't worry about them.

Download the kernel patch. If your current kernel is 2.4.10, the patch file is `patch-2.4.11.bz2`. You can only patch one level up. To patch up two levels, you need to apply two patches.

Put the patch in the `/usr/src` directory. If you have a `symlink` to `linux-2.4.10` called `linux` (or if you just put your kernel source in a directory called `linux`), proceed by issuing the following command:

```
bzcat patch-2.4.11.bz2 | patch -p0 --dry-run
```

As long as the preceding command does not result in any lines with `FAILED`, you can remove the `--dry-run` and apply the patch for real.

If you don't have a `symlink` called `linux` (or a directory), `cd` into the `linux` kernel tree and issue the command this way:

```
bzcat ../patch-2.4.11.bz2 | patch -p1 --dry-run
```

If necessary, you can append the previous commands with the following:

```
> error.log ; grep FAIL error.log
```

As long as you get no output from `grep` for `FAIL`, the patch will work correctly.

One advantage of applying a patch this way is that you can skip the steps `make mrproper` and `make [x|menu]config` and go straight to the kernel build (assuming the patch did not introduce a functionality you want to include. If it did, you'll need to run the `config` again, make just that one change, and save the configuration).

If you find that the patch failed to properly patch a file, this is because the source tree was changed, either by another patch or by something such as the FreeS/WAN package.

If you've applied a patch, such as for an ethernet card, you might need to back that patch out before applying the kernel patch. Just perform exactly the same steps you did when you patched it, but use `-R` to indicate reverse. Normally, this is something like the following:

```
patch -p1 -R < ethernet.patch
```

For the FreeS/WAN package, you need to replace the current files with the `preipsec` file where they exist. All files the FreeS/WAN package altered were saved. For example, in the `drivers/net/` subdirectory, the file `Space.c` was modified, but the original was saved as `Space.c.preipsec`. Move the `preipsec` file back (remove the `preipsec` extension). When you rebuild with the FreeS/WAN package, it reapplies the patch.

TROUBLESHOOTING

I followed the steps, but when I rebooted, I got `kernel panic`.

One of several things occurred. Most probably, you forgot to run `lilo` to install the new boot image. If you did run `lilo`, did you ensure it terminated with no errors? (You saw the list of kernel images by name.)

To fix this, you'll need to boot from your boot disk or CD-ROM, and at the `LILO:` prompt, press Shift+Tab and enter the following:

```
boot root=/dev/hda1
```

Remember to change `/dev/hda1` for the correct device to mount your root filesystem. Now `cd` into `/etc`, review your `lilo.conf` file, and rerun `lilo`.

I'm getting an error when the kernel boots about VFS: `cannot mount root partition`.

Whenever you get an error regarding the VFS (virtual filesystem) for a Linux partition, it usually means that you didn't compile in support for that partition type. Linux uses `ext2` as its native filesystem type. This cannot be compiled as a module, but it must be compiled in. The same holds true if you don't have support for the disk or controller (particularly in the case of a SCSI controller).

It could also mean you aren't pointing to the correct root partition—you're pointing to the wrong partition (particularly one of a different partition type, like a DOS partition). If you are booting from a floppy, use `rdev` to make sure the kernel image contains a reference to the correct root partition.

Reboot from the old image (`linux.orig`) and review your kernel configuration. Make any changes, rebuild, reinstall, run `lilo`, and reboot.

I'm getting an error `L` *or* `LI`, *and the kernel isn't loading.*

Here, again, you have one of several problems. This is more a LILO problem, and you should refer to Chapter 15. However, either you didn't run `lilo`, your `lilo.conf` needs `append="linear"` (which can be added to the other options). If you just upgraded, you can also have a stale copy of lilo in the MBR. Review Chapter 12 to fix this problem.

During the kernel compile, it stops at the end and complains it can't find `as86`.

If you've gotten this far, you have most of the packages installed that are required to build the kernel (`gcc`, `make`, and the libraries), but you've forgotten one important package: `bin86`. Find and install this RPM, and you should have no more problems.

During the kernel compile, I'm getting a Signal 11, and the kernel compile fails.

This is almost (99.44%) always a hardware problem. Most often, the problem is bad RAM, but it can also be bad cache. The commercial RAM testers do not stress RAM as severely as a kernel compile does. GCC makes use of all available RAM. You might also have a bad compiler (which is unlikely, but not unheard of).

Go into setup and turn off your cache. Reinstall your GCC package (which might be called `egcs`). Then run your kernel compile again. If it fails, run it again. If the failures happen in different places, you have bad RAM. Replace it. If the failures happen in the same place, suspect a problem with the kernel sources (improbably with the stable kernel, very probable with the unstable kernels). Review the file `Documentation/Changes` in the kernel source tree and ensure you have the software version number or higher listed in this file.

## CHAPTER 19

KERNEL MODULES

In this chapter

THE LINUX KERNEL, MODULES, AND DRIVERS

Anyone who has added a driver to another operating system (such as one that runs Windows) will undoubtedly appreciate the virtues of modular kernels. Although hardware is not "hot-swappable" with Linux (yet), drivers are, and the capability to remove, recompile, and reload drivers in Linux systems without completely restarting the system is one of Linux's strongest features.

This is especially useful when running in a multiuser environment. Restarting a multiuser system to load a new driver results in all the users being kicked off; however, the capability to unload and reload modules on-the-fly without restarting the system enables users to stay logged on. Also, when debugging problems with hardware drivers, it is quicker to unload a module and reload it with different settings than it is to change a setting in a startup file (such as CONFIG.SYS in the DOS operating system) and restart the system. Minutes turn into seconds when you remove the system restart step, enabling you to solve driver problems in a fraction of the time.

In operating systems such as DOS (and in operating environments such as the many flavors of Windows), a kernel is incorporated to handle most of the low-level tasks that are expected of an operating system, such as interaction with the CPU, memory management, and so on. These kernels are supplemented with smaller chunks of code for those items that can not be compiled into the kernels themselves for whatever reason.

A good example of this is a driver for a piece of hardware. How could the operating system manufacturer know you were going to be using that particular piece of hardware on your system? Obviously, there is no conceivable way to know this information ahead of time, so mechanisms are put in place that allow these items to be loaded after the operating system is shipped and installed.

In DOS and Windows systems, these drivers and other loadable chunks of operating system code can be installed by adding lines to the CONFIG.SYS, AUTOEXEC.BAT, or other files. In environments such as the various Windows offerings, .INI files often accomplish this task. Other systems have their own methods, but in the end it all boils down to the same thing: Features and drivers can be added to the operating system after it has been shipped and installed.

Linux is no exception. As indicated in Chapter 18, "Building a Custom Kernel," recompiling the kernel is a viable option when adding hardware or enabling new features. In fact, if the items that are being added are (for lack of a better term) permanent, compiling support into the kernel is probably the best all-around option.

Kernel compilation is rarely required, however, because of the loadable module facilities that are included with modern Linux distributions. With modules, you can simply plug in the features or drivers that you want to include and leave out the rest. This saves on memory and enables you to add or remove features and drivers without recompiling the kernel. Another added benefit of the modularity of Linux kernels is that these items can be added or removed without even rebooting your Linux system (see Figure 19.1).

Figure 19.1
Modular Linux kernel.

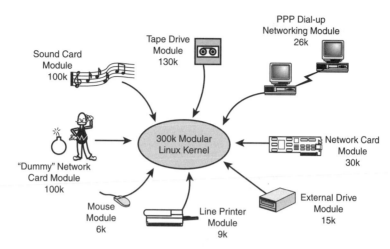

When a Linux kernel is compiled to include modular support for various optional drivers, the modules themselves are stored in a directory under /lib/modules, which matches the version number of the kernel with which they are associated. So if a version 2.2.1 kernel is compiled to use modules for some of its supported drivers, the modules are stored under the /lib/modules/ 2.4.0 directory. This way, if more than one version of the Linux kernel is compiled to include optionally loaded modules, the different kernels' modules are not mixed.

The classifications of modules are further broken down under /lib/modules/`uname -r` to group the modules into logical sets (see Listing 19.1). These sets are described fairly clearly by the names of the subdirectories in which they are contained.

PART

III

CH

19

LISTING 19.1 SUBDIRECTORIES UNDER /lib/modules/2.4.##

```
/lib/modules/2.4.0/
   build@@
   kernel/
        arch/
               i386/kernel/
        drivers/
               acorn/
                      block/
                      char/
                      net/
                      scsi/
               acpi/
               atm/
               block/
                      paride/
               cdrom/
               char/
                      agp/
                      drm/
                      ftape/
                      ip2/
                      joystick/
```

LISTING 19.1   CONTINUED

```
                        pcmcia/
                        rio/
            dio/
            fc4/
            i2c/
            i2o/
            ide/
            ieee1394/
            input/
            isdn/
            macintosh/
            media/
            misc/
            mtd/
            net/
                        appletalk/
                        arcnet/
                        fc/
                        hamradio/
                        irda/
                        pcmcia/
                        tokenring/
                        tulip
                        wan/
            nubus/
            parport/
            pci/
            pcmcia/
            pnp/
            s390/
            sbus/
            scsi/
                        pcmcia/
            sgi/
                        char/
            sound/
            tc/
            telephony/
            usb/
                        serial/
                        storage/
            video/
            zorro/
    fs/
            adfs/
            affs/
            autofs/
            autofs4/
            bfs/
            coda/
            cramfs/
            efs/
            ext2/
            fat/
            hfs/
            hpfs/
```

LISTING 19.1   CONTINUED

```
                isofs/
                jffs/
                lockd/
                minix/
                ncpfs/
                nfs/
                nfsd/
                nls/
                msdos/
                ntfs/
                openpromfs/
                qnx4/
                ramfs/
                romfs/
                smbfs/
                sysv/
                udf/
                ufs/
                umsdos/
                vfat/

        net/
                802/
                appletalk/
                atm/
                ax25/
                bridge/
                decnet/
                econet/
                ethernet/
                ipv4/
                        netfilter/
                ipv6/
                        netfilter/
                ipx/
                irda/
                        ircomm/
                        irlan/
                khttpd/
                lapb/
                netlink/
                netrom/
                packet/
                rose/
                sched/
                sunrpc/
                unix/
                wanrouter/
                x25/

        pcmcia/
```

PART

III

CH

19

The preceding list is not an exhaustive list of subdirectories within `/lib/modules/2.4.x/`
directory. What you see when you look here will depend specifically on what modules you

built and installed. The build entry is a symlink to /usr/src/linux. The kernel directory contains all the modules below it. The pcmcia directory contains symlinks, which point to modules located below ../kernel in various locations.

Below the kernel subdirectory are four major subdirectories: arch, drivers, fs, and net.

The arch directory will contain architecture-specific modules below their particular architecture. Modules like cpuid and apm will be found here in i386/kernel/.

The driver directory contains numerous subdirectories, but all modules located here are related to physical hardware. If you can touch it and you built a module for it, it's located somewhere here below drivers.

The fs directory contains filesystem-specific drivers. These drivers handle any filesystems you compiled support for as modules. Often this would be modules such as vfat, msdos, and others.

The net directory contains all network-related modules that are not hardware based. Here you'll find the ipv6 module, all the netfilter modules, the kernel httpd module (khttpd) and much more.

You can get a good idea of what modules are installed on your system by perusing the /lib/modules/`uname -r`/modules.dep file created by the kernel build.

MODULE VERSIONS

By default, when recompiling a Linux kernel, all the modules that are to be loaded with the new kernel must be recompiled as well. This can become a tedious process, especially if the system on which the kernel is being compiled uses legacy hardware. Compilation of the kernel can take a long time on slow hardware, so cutting down on the time required to do a compilation is desirable.

However, an option by which modules can be reused without recompiling them is available during the kernel configuration process. If you activate the following option, version information is set on all modules that will allow non-kernel modules to be loaded with any kernel that matches the version of the kernel symbols against which the modules were compiled:

```
Set version information on all symbols and modules
```

In other words, a Linux kernel that is at version 2.4.1 loads modules compiled for 2.4.1 kernels as long as the symbols within the module are set at version 2.4.1 as well. In most cases, this will be fine because you will use modules built with your kernel. But if you don't have the sources to compile kernel modules against your kernel, such as from a hardware manufacturer that only includes a binary module with their hardware, you might need to set version information so that it will load.

Note

Kernel modules essentially have two version numbers: one *internal* (referencing symbols within the module) and one *external* (referencing the version that the driver author assigned to the driver and reflected in the symbols). It is the internal version number that is set to match the Linux kernel with which the module was compiled. This sets up the kernel/module association that prevents the module from loading on different versions of the Linux kernel (this is a simplified explanation).

This is a very useful feature, especially if the modules that are being used did not ship with the kernel sources, (for example, OSS Sound). Modules that are external to the kernel sources can be reused as long as the overall kernel version against which the module was compiled remains the same. Moving from a 2.4.1 kernel to a 2.2.18 kernel causes a 2.4.1 compiled module load to fail because the overall version of the kernel does not match the symbols within the module. In a case like this, the following error message is displayed:

```
Error: The module was compiled on kernel version 2.4.1.
       This kernel is version 2.2.18. They don't match!
       Check that the module is usable with the current kernel,
       recompile the module and try again.
```

Another error message that you might receive looks like the following:

```
Loading failed! The module symbols (from linux-2.4.1) don't match your_ålinux-2.2.18
```

Either way, the errors are descriptive enough to tell you what the problem is. Recompile the modules for the kernel (being sure to set versions on all the module symbols), and the modules load.

MODULE MANAGEMENT

Kernel modules can be loaded manually as well as automatically. Typically, a system administrator starts off manually loading modules until he becomes familiar with the process (and with which modules he really wants to load on a regular basis); he then moves on to loading modules automatically.

Familiarity is not the only reason to do this, however. Many modules require that special behavior-altering parameters be passed to them before they can load successfully. Without experimenting with these parameters and figuring out exactly which ones are needed, a few things might happen.

Sometimes the module might load with incorrect settings, such as those for the interrupt and I/O port. These two settings have not prohibited the older 3c509 Ethernet card driver from loading, which gives the appearance of successfully adding support for the card while actually just acting as a red herring.

Also, the autoprobing process might dramatically extend the time that is required to boot the system. A good example of this is the driver for SoundBlaster CD (sbpcd.o), which probes a rather long list of drives before giving up, thus adding a solid five to ten minutes to the time that is required to boot your system.

In some cases (and only for ISA hardware), without module parameters being passed, modules do not load at all. An example of this is the Sony CDU-31a driver (cdu31a.o), which does absolutely no autoprobing for hardware; therefore, it does not load unless it is told explicitly where your hardware can be found.

Caution	It is very important to make a distinction between boot parameters and module parameters. Module parameters are passed to a kernel module when the module is loaded, and they only apply to kernel drivers that are compiled as modules. Boot parameters are parameters that are passed to the kernel itself to alter the behavior of drivers that are compiled directly into the kernel. Boot parameters are passed at the LILO boot prompt (or through LILO itself using the append= tag in /etc/lilo.conf), or can be added to the GRUB boot line (or in /boot/grub/menu.lst). For more information regarding passing boot parameters with LILO or GRUB, see Chapter 12, "Boot Loaders."

Unfortunately, there is little or no consistency in the optional parameters from one module to the next, with the possible exception being module parameters for Ethernet cards—but even there, some of the options differ from one module to the next. Therefore, getting to know the appropriate parameters for the modules that you are loading before automatically loading them can save you much grief.

MANUAL LOADING

Four utilities are commonly used for manual module loading, unloading, and listing:

- **modprobe**—Loads, or inserts, modules into the currently located/running kernel after checking dependencies in /lib/modules/<kernel-version>/modules.dep and loading those modules first. Modprobe uses insmod to accomplish the actual loading.

- **insmod**—Loads, or inserts, modules into the currently loaded/running kernel. insmod knows nothing about module dependencies.

- **rmmod**—Removes modules that are currently loaded.

- **lsmod**—Lists the modules that are currently loaded.

The syntax is fairly simple for each utility. To insert a module (for example, the bttv driver for BT848-based video capture cards), execute something like the following:

```
modprobe bttv
```

To remove the module after loading it, run the following:

```
rmmod bttv
```

To get a verbose listing of what is going on while the module is being loaded, add the -v option:

```
modprobe -v bttv
```

Using the verbose mode shows you which dependent modules, if any, are loaded. Listing 19.2 shows the output from modprobe -v.

LISTING 19.2   SAMPLE OUTPUT FROM modprobe -v

```
/sbin/insmod /lib/modules/2.3.45/misc/videodev.o
/sbin/insmod /lib/modules/2.3.45/misc/i2c.o
/sbin/insmod /lib/modules/2.3.45/misc/bttv.o
```

To get extremely detailed information about a particular module as it loads (probably only of value to developers), you'll need to use insmod with the -m option, which will provide a long, detailed memory map of the module as it loads.

Both modprobe and insmod contain a list of options. For the most part, these options will not be of general use. If you have a problem loading a module or want information about a module, you can use these options. See the man pages for more details. Most options' explanations will not mean much to the average user, and the output from these options will mean even less.

AUTOMATIC LOADING

Module loading at boot time is handled slightly differently among the three different distributions. Each method will be described, but details of common files such as the /etc/modules.conf or /etc/conf.modules will only be described once in the Caldera OpenLinux section.

Note that all distributions should be moving to /etc/modules.conf. The /etc/conf.modules is deprecated and will not be used if /etc/modules.conf is encountered first. If your distribution does not use /etc/modules.conf, you should create a link, because in the future, support for /etc/conf.modules will be dropped. If you have the /etc/conf.modules file but not the /etc/modules.conf file, do the following:

```
ln /etc/conf.modules /etc/modules.conf
```

This will update your system and you won't need to worry about which one is used.

CALDERA OPENLINUX

Three module autoloading methods are available on OpenLinux systems:

- The modules are loaded by command lines that are added to the end of /etc/rc.d/rc.local.
- The kmod method loads modules on demand, although it doesn't automatically unload them when finished.
- The modules are loaded from a list in /etc/modules/ by a script.

By default, OpenLinux uses the third method, which is covered in this chapter.

In this method, a file residing in /etc/modules/ contains a list of modules to load. Each module in this list is loaded by a script called /etc/rc.d/rc.modules. This script runs the modprobe utility against each of the modules in the list. All this happens when the OpenLinux system is booted. (For more information on rc.modules, see Chapter 13, "System Initialization.")

Note

> The filename used to contain a list of modules to load during boot is called `default`. Note that using this name will make the file kernel version independent. (In other words, if your module list is named `default`, an attempt will be made by your OpenLinux system to load all the modules in that list regardless of the version of the Linux kernel you are booting.) If you tend to compile and boot multiple different Linux kernels and want to have different sets of modules load with each one, follow the `uname` method detailed that follows.

To use the `uname` method, first create a directory in `/etc/modules` based on the name of the kernel version you are running:

```
mkdir /etc/modules/`uname -r`
```

This command produces a directory based on the current kernel you are running—for example, `/etc/modules/2.4.10`. Alternatively, you can create this by hand if you are not currently running the kernel version for which you want to create the specialized modules file.

The `rc.modules` loads the file named `default` in this directory (if it exists) and skips loading the modules in the `/etc/modules/default` file.

To boot into different kernels with the same release number (for example, you built two different 2.4.10 kernels) that will load different modules based on the kernel version, you need to go one step further. You need to create files based on the kernel operating system version within the `/etc/modules/`uname -`r` directory. To do this, you need to know the specific version of the kernel you are running or want to run.

On a currently running kernel, use the following command:

```
uname -v
```

This command produces a timestamp string on the currently loaded or running Linux kernel. A `.default` extension is added to the timestamp to complete the filename. For instance, consider whether the output of running `uname -v` on the current kernel produced the following timestamp:

```
#1 Wed Mar 25 15:23:05 MST 1998
```

The resulting module list in `/etc/modules/2.#.##` is named the following:

```
#1 Wed Mar 25 15:23:05 MST 1998.default
```

Note

> This is just an example; your output from `uname -v` will be different.

If the filename `/etc/modules/`uname -r`/`uname -v.default` exists, it will be loaded and the other default files will be skipped. The `uname -v` only works on a running kernel. If you need to determine what `uname -v` will return on a particular kernel image before it loads, you need to use the following command. This command assumes that the kernel image you want to know about is called `bzImage-2.3.45` and that it is located in the current directory:

```
strings bzImage-2.3.45 | grep 2000
```

The output from this command will look like this:

```
2.3.45 (root@volcan.pananix.com) #1 Wed Mar 12 10:33:42 EST 2000
```

The information that will be returned by uname -v is the first line starting with the #. You just need to use this information to create your filename:

```
touch "/etc/modules/2.3.45/#1 Wed Mar 12 10:33:42 EST 2000.default"
```

You can then add your list of modules to the empty file.

Because of the way the rc.modules script works with this file, there is no way any other kernel can load modules from this list except for the kernel that matches the timestamp after which the file is named. This way, different sets of modules can be loaded with different kernels. This is especially handy for people who enjoy experimenting with booting back and forth between different kernels (for instance, one stable kernel and one bleeding-edge ALPHA grade kernel); each kernel has its own personal module autoload list that is never shared with the other versions of the kernel.

Whenever a kernel is compiled on an OpenLinux system, the module autoload list needs to be copied over (or renamed) to a file that matches the timestamp of the new kernel. With that done, when the computer is rebooted for the first time with the new kernel, the modules load just like they did with the former kernel.

The following is an example of a short module autoload list:

```
sb
bttv
```

Because the rc.modules script uses modprobe, you no longer have to determine module dependencies. Similarly, the bttv module has two dependencies, but you don't need to worry about that here, they are handled automatically. What are not handled automatically are additional modules that are not dependencies, but are needed to make the loaded driver completely functional. In the case of bttv (which will automatically load i2c and videodev), the non-dependent but complimentary modules are tuner, msp3400, and saa5249. In this case, you can modify the /etc/modules.conf file as follows:

```
post-install bttv modprobe tuner; modprobe msp3400 ; modprobe saa5249
```

What if parameters must be passed to the modules? In the case of the sb module, parameters are absolutely required, at least to indicate an I/O port for the installed SoundBlaster card.

If parameters are required for any of the modules that are being loaded, they are added to the /etc/modules.conf file.

Using the sb driver as an example, say that there is a SoundBlaster card at I/O port 0x220, IRQ 5, DMA=1, DMA16=5, and MPU_IO=0x330. To pass these parameters to an automatically loaded sb module, add two lines to the /etc/modules.conf file, which contains the following information:

```
alias sound sb
options sb io=0x220 irq=5 dma=1 dma16=5 mpu_io=0x330
```

PART

III

CH

19

This file is read by modprobe and the parameters on the options sb line are passed to the sb module when it is loaded.

Settings within each parameter can be stacked and separated by commas for cases where more than one device is being controlled by a module. For example, if there are two NE2000 cards in the system, one at I/O port 0x300 and IRQ 10, and a second one at I/O port 0x240 and IRQ 11, the following lines can be used:

```
alias eth0 ne
alias eth1 ne
options ne io=0x300,0x240 irq=10,11
```

In this case, the NE2000 at I/O port 0x300 and IRQ 10 will be used as eth0 and the second parameter for each argument in the options line will be used for eth1. The order of the parameters is important and should not be mixed between arguments.

DEBIAN

Debian uses a simplified system for automated module loading at bootup. The list of modules to load is contained in /etc/modules. This has the advantage of added simplicity, but can be awkward if you boot to kernels requiring different modules.

Debian also uses the /etc/modules.conf file in the same manner as described in the preceding Caldera OpenLinux section.

One set of files that Debian users might like to be aware of can be found under the /etc/modutils/ directory. This directory contains files used to build and customize the /etc/modules.conf file. These files are used by the update-modules script to (re)build the /etc/modules.conf file.

RED HAT

Red Hat doesn't use a list of modules to load unless the file /etc/rc.d/rc.modules is present. This file isn't installed by RH, but is used if present. This file will determine where any list of bootup modules is kept.

Red Hat depends on the kernel module loader and the information in /etc/conf.modules to handle loading required modules as described in the preceding Caldera section.

MODULES AVAILABLE OUTSIDE THE KERNEL SOURCES

Not all the modules that are considered part of a standard Linux system are included with the kernel source code. Some items are shipped external to the kernel sources but are included with almost every Linux distribution that is in existence today. Sometimes, updates (or new drivers) are available between kernel version releases in separate packages.

Under normal circumstances, there is no real reason to download, compile, and install an updated version of any of these packages. Occasionally, however, the need to do so arises. For PCMCIA hardware, occasionally a new card is supported only in a newer version of the pcmcia-cs package, so an upgrade is understandable.

It is always recommended that the package set that ships with the distribution be adhered to as long as is humanly possible. The assembly of packages on the CD is tested as a set, proven to work as a set, and is to be used as a set unless a serious need arises to break away and download updates. So be forewarned that although little risk is involved in performing an upgrade of any of these packages if you follow the directions, you are altering a tested, proven system; when you do so, you run the risk of having something not work exactly as it did before.

UPGRADING pcmcia-cs

The pcmcia-cs (PCMCIA Card Services) package is very special. If you upgrade your kernel, the pcmcia-cs modules installed with your distribution might not work. The modules that compose this package need to be compiled against the kernel sources for the kernel you are running. You can wait for your distribution to release a new kernel binary package and the pcmcia-cs package that goes with it, or you can do the upgrade to both the kernel and pcmcia-cs package yourself.

With the new 2.4.x series kernel, many pcmcia modules are being built into the kernel, but not all are available. It is anticipated that this will change during the life of the 2.4.x kernels, but until it does, these instructions are necessary for those drivers not supported directly in the kernel.

The pcmcia-cs package offers drivers for PCMCIA chipsets and hardware (Ethernet cards, SCSI controllers, and modems), mostly for laptop systems. It also offers support for CardBus if it is compiled to do so.

One primary source of confusion with this package is the fact that it is composed entirely of modules, and therefore is not affected by the use of special boot parameters. So entering

```
ether=11,0x340,0,0,eth0
```

as a parameter when booting Linux does not pass any behavior altering information to the modules in the pcmcia-cs package (details on boot parameters and LILO are offered in Chapter 12, "Boot Loaders."

In fact, regular module parameters that are passed in the manner that was detailed earlier in this chapter do not work either. The pcmcia-cs package uses its own set of configuration files for its modules, so in essence it is an island among the sets of modules. However, adjusting how the modules load and passing parameters to those modules are not overly complex tasks after you know where to look and what to edit.

The main distribution site for the pcmcia-cs package is located at
```
ftp://sourceforge.org/pcmcia.
```

There you can find the most recent version of pcmcia-cs, pointers to configuration information for hardware that is not included in the default configuration files, and developer versions of the package. (These are not for production systems—they are for testing purposes only.) Extensive documentation also is included at that site in the form of the PCMCIA-HOWTO and the PCMCIA-PROG documents. (The latter is intended for programmers.)

PART

III

CH

19

The main Web site for Linux PCMCIA information is http://pcmcia.sourceforge.org/.

To build pcmcia-cs yourself, follow these instructions (pcmcia-cs-3.1.19.tar.gz is used in this example):

1. Download the pcmcia-cs package and extract it into /usr/src:

```
cd /usr/src
tar zxvf pcmcia-cs-3.1.19.tar.gz
```

2. Configure the pcmcia-cs package in preparation for the actual compilation:

```
./Configure
```

This step runs a configuration script called Configure in the top-level pcmcia-cs source code directory. It is generally safe to accept the defaults offered by the script. (Items such as the kernel source code directory and the compiler/linker names are okay as they are.) But a few options for new and experimental features are offered, which you might or might not want to take advantage of.

Listing 19.3 is sample output from Configure.

LISTING 19.3   SAMPLE Configure SESSION FOR pcmcia-cs

```
-------- Linux PCMCIA Configuration Script --------

The default responses for each question are correct for most users.
Consult the PCMCIA-HOWTO for additional info about each option.

Linux source directory [/usr/src/linux]:

The kernel source tree is version 2.4.0.
The current kernel build date is Thu Aug 10 16:21:03 2000.

Alternate target install directory []:
  Module install directory [/lib/modules/2.4.0:
Build 'trusting' versions of card utilities (y/n) [y]:
Include 32-bit (CardBus) card support (y/n) [y]:
Include PnP BIOS resource checking (y/n) [n]:

Kernel configuration options:
    Symmetric multiprocessing support is disabled.
    PCI BIOS support is enabled.
    Advanced Power Management (APM) support is enabled.
    SCSI support is disabled.
    Networking support is enabled.
     Radio network interface support is disabled.
     Token Ring device support is disabled.
     Fast switching is disabled.
    Module version checking is disabled.
    /proc filesystem support is enabled.
    Maximum physical memory: 1GB

It looks like you have a System V init file setup.

X Windows include files found.
/usr/X11R6/lib/libforms.so and /usr/X11R6/include/forms.h found.

Configuration successful.
```

The kernel version and timestamp that are reported in the preceding capture might be different, but the rest of the script will closely resemble what you see.

In Listing 19.3, the `trusting` version of the card utilities was selected, and `32-bit Cardbus support` was selected. `PnP BIOS resource checking` was disabled. The package then gave a rundown of what it found in the kernel source tree. SCSI PCMCIA modules will not be built because SCSI support is disabled. If you want SCSI `pcmcia` modules, you'll need to rebuild the kernel with SCSI support. The same is true for any other options listed that show as disabled.

3. Compile the binaries and modules that make up the `pcmcia-cs` package:
   ```
   make all
   ```

4. Install all the binaries and modules in their proper places:
   ```
   make install
   ```

If an alternative directory was specified for installation during the `make config` step, the alternative directory becomes the equivalent of the root (/) directory during this installation step. Each subdirectory off the root directory that might have been affected (for example, `/lib` and some subdirectories off `/etc`) is duplicated off the alternative directory. (That is, if a file was supposed to go in `/etc/rc.d`, it goes in `/alternate-directory/etc/rc.d` instead.) This helps if the compiled binaries and modules are going to be packaged and moved to another system, or if there is no desire to overwrite an existing `pcmcia-cs` installation with a new version.

The configuration files for the `pcmcia-cs` package all reside in `/etc/pcmcia` (see Table 19.1).

TABLE 19.1 CONFIGURATION FILES FOR THE `pcmcia-cs` PACKAGE

Filename	Purpose
cdrom	Initialization script for PCMCIA CD-ROM device.
cdrom.opts	Contains configuration information for CD-ROM devices.
cis/	Directory containing CIS (Card Information Structure) information for various PCMCIA cards.
config	Main database of supported hardware and the modules associated with each device. Global, packagewide configuration information is stored here.
config.opts	Holds general configuration data for the `pcmcia-cs` package. Local configuration information is adjusted in this file, not the `config` file.
ftl	Initialization script for FTL flash memory cards (the only flash cards that are supported by `pcmcia-cs`).
ftl.opts	Contains configuration information for FTL flash memory cards.
ide	Initialization script for IDE adapters.
ide.opts	Holds general configuration data for IDE adapters.
memory	Initialization script for memory devices.
memory.opts	Contains configuration information for memory devices.

PART

III

CH

19

TABLE 19.1 CONTINUED	
network	Initialization script for PCMCIA network hardware.
network.opts	Holds the networking (IP, IPX) information for PCMCIA network interfaces.
parport	Initialization scripts for parallel port PCMCIA devices.
parport.opts	Holds the parameters for parallel port PCMCIA devices, such as the link for the printer.
scsi	Initialization script for SCSI adapters.
scsi.opts	Contains configuration information for SCSI adapters.
serial	Initialization script for serial devices (such as modems).
serial.opts	Holds configuration data for serial devices.
shared	Some scripting shared among all classes of supported PCMCIA devices.

Of all the files that are listed, only the .opts files need to be altered. Probably the main two files that will be worked with are the config.opts and network.opts files. The rest are typically fine in their default states.

The config.opts file is the one that is most often frequented. By default it is rather short, but it is the top-level configuration file for the entire pcmcia-cs package (see Listing 19.4).

LISTING 19.4   DEFAULT /etc/pcmcia/config.opts FILE

```
# Local PCMCIA Configuration File
#
# System resources available for PCMCIA devices
#
include port 0x100-0x4ff, port 0x1000-0x17ff
include memory 0xc0000-0xfffff
include memory 0xa0000000-0xa0ffffff, memory 0x60000000-0x60ffffff
#
# Extra port range for IBM Token Ring
#
include port 0xa00-0xaff
#
# Resources we should not use, even if they appear to be available
#
# First built-in serial port
exclude irq 4
# Second built-in serial port
#exclude irq 3
# First built-in parallel port
exclude irq 7
#
# Examples of options for loadable modules
#
# To fix sluggish network with IBM ethernet adapter...
#module "pcnet_cs" opts "mem_speed=600"
#
# Options for Xircom Netwave driver...
```

LISTING 19.4   CONTINUED

```
#module "netwave_cs" opts "domain=0x100 scramble_key=0x0"
#
# Options for IBM Token Ring adapters
#module "ibmtr_cs" opts "mmiobase=0xd0000 srambase=0xd4000"
```

In this file you can set such items as memory address ranges (`include memory`), I/O port ranges (`include port`), excluded IRQs (`exclude irq`), and special parameters to be passed to the various modules (`module opts`), if necessary.

The best all-around resource to have handy when working with settings down to the `Options for loadable modules` line is the manual for the machine containing the _PCMCIA hardware (which is, more often than not, a laptop). Memory address ranges, for instance, might have to be adjusted slightly if there is overlap with the machine's VGA address range. Likewise, if other devices within the machine are using certain IRQs for other, non-PCMCIA hardware, exclude those IRQs from the list of choices.

Options for loadable modules differ with each module. The best resources to have around for PCMCIA module parameters are the man pages for each module. All the information that is necessary to compile module option lines (like those in Listing 19.4) can be found there.

The `network.opts` file contains much of the same information as the files in the `/etc/sysconfig` hierarchy, as well as the information that is typically contained within `/etc/resolv.conf`. Network fundamentals are addressed in Chapter 22, "Networking," so it is best to defer descriptions of the IP addressing to that chapter. Just keep in mind that the network configuration information for PCMCIA Ethernet cards is referenced from `/etc/pcmcia/network.opts` in case anything needs to be changed.

One final note: The HOWTO document for PCMCIA acts as the documentation for the package; few—if any—other HOWTO documents act as official documentation for their associated subjects. This document comes with all `pcmcia-cs` source code archives and is available on Linux HOWTO Web sites that are mirrored all over the Internet. When in doubt, the PCMCIA-HOWTO has much more comprehensive information on topics related to this package and is the single document to fall back on when PCMCIA questions that are not answered here arise.

PART
III

CH
19

TROUBLESHOOTING

I am experiencing an IRQ conflict. The IRQ that PCMCIA wants to use is already taken by something else.

If an IRQ conflict exists between an initialized piece of hardware and a PCMCIA card that is preventing the card's driver from loading, and if there is an open IRQ, you should be able to get the card working. First, reserve the IRQ in the `config.opts` file:

```
reserve irq 5
```

Then force the use of that IRQ on the module that supports the card. If the card is an NE2000 card that uses pcnet_cs.o (look in the config file for the module name associated with the card), add a line to the bottom of config.opts that looks like this:

```
module "pcnet_cs" opts "irq_list=5"
```

That will force the use of the free IRQ on the pcnet_cs module when it loads.

(If the PCMCIA chipset is having problems, you can force an IRQ on that as well. Instead of passing an IRQ list in config.opts, you pass it in the PCIC_OPTS= line in /etc/sysconfig/pcmcia:

```
PCIC_OPTS="irq_list=11"
```

There is no need to "reserve" an IRQ in config.opts because this line will be processed before config.opts is even seen.

I have been trying to insert a module using modprobe, but I get unresolved symbol errors. How do I correct it?

A module that depends on another module being loaded causes this particular error.

First, make sure you have a current file /lib/modules/`uname -r`/modules.dep. This file lists file dependencies. You can create it with

```
depmod -a
```

After you have verified that you have a dependencies file, use modprobe to insert the driver. The modprobe utility will load any prerequisite modules. This should eliminate the unresolved symbols error you're getting.

CHAPTER 20

BUILDING A VPN (FREES/WAN)

In this chapter

GETTING STARTED

Setting up a secure WAN is like setting up any other WAN, but it provides better security for confidential data. The only difference between setting up a secure WAN with FreeS/WAN and setting one up with routing tables is that you need to build a modified kernel and then configure the software. The additional work pays off with added security.

The FreeS/WAN (Free Secure/Wide Area Network) package allows you to build encrypted tunnels between any two or more LANs (or between any two systems or between a system and a LAN)to create a secure WAN.

> **Note**
>
> The FreeS/WAN package is evolving rapidly. This text is based on 1.3, which has additional features beyond 1.1. If you use a higher revision (you might need to for your kernel) the instructions below might not be 100% in line with the release. Use them as a guide and look at the sample files and documentation provided.

To build a Virtual Private Network (VPN) using FreeS/WAN, you need to first build a custom kernel and install it. Then you need to learn how to configure FreeS/WAN to put the VPN into operation. Some "gotchas" exist that you will be made aware of later in the chapter.

To start, you want to configure a kernel and then run the `make dep` and `make clean` steps. These steps propagate the dependency information throughout the kernel tree and are necessary for the FreeS/WAN package.

Download the FreeS/WAN package (get the latest version) and move it to `/usr/src`. Open the following package:

```
tar xzvf freeswan-1.1.3.tar.gz
```

Then `cd` into the `freeswan` directory created in this step.

BUILDING THE FREES/WAN KERNEL

Building the kernel is actually quite simple. If you've already configured the kernel, you won't need to make any changes when the kernel configuration screen comes up again.

You need to choose a `make` command to build the FreeS/WAN package. The following choices are available:

- `make menugo`
- `make xgo`
- `make ogo`
- `make oldgo`

Each calls `make menuconfig (menugo)`, `make xconfig (xgo)`, `make config (ogo)`, or `make oldconfig (oldgo)`. When one of these is run, the FreeS/WAN package first patches the kernel and then runs the appropriate `make` in the kernel source directory.

When the kernel compilation begins, it starts with the `make config` you chose previously. You'll want to select Networking Options and look at the bottom of the list. Several selections (approximately 10) will have been added during the kernel patching process. These will appear at the very bottom below the QOS and/or fair queuing selection. Consider carefully before changing the default configuration as installed by FreeS/WAN. After you're satisfied with the selections, you must save this new kernel configuration or it will not compile the FreeS/WAN patches in.

The FreeS/WAN `make` will run through the kernel compile for you, starting with `make dep` and going through `make modules`. But FreeS/WAN will not install the modules or the kernel. These are left for you to do as discussed in Chapter 18, "Building a Custom Kernel."

After the kernel compile finishes, `cd` to `../linux`, return to Chapter 18 and complete all the steps beginning with `make modules_install`. After you've rebooted into the new kernel, you're ready to start configuring your VPN.

VPN PLANNING

To properly configure FreeS/WAN, you must understand a little about how it works. FreeS/WAN creates a virtual network by binding a virtual device `ipsec0-ipsec999` to a real device such as `eth0`, `tr0`, `ppp0`, or any other real communications device attached to your system. Entries are made in the system routing table. Routes going from one encrypted system to another will be more specific than the general default route, so the `ipsec` device will be chosen to send the message. Messages sent through the `ipsec` device are encrypted when they are transmitted.

This explanation glosses over a few things. The most important point it glosses over is which packets (from which sources) will be encrypted. Later in the configuration you will choose specifically the sources of the packets to be encrypted when transmitting to another system. The system you will set up to send encrypted messages to another system that accepts encrypted messages will be either a gateway, which will encrypt traffic for a LAN behind it, or an individual system, which will transmit encrypted messages for itself.

The distinction between a gateway and an individual system is important. A gateway, talking to another gateway or individual system, will not encrypt its own traffic, only traffic coming from the LAN behind it. A gateway is said to use *tunnel mode*. An individual system will encrypt its own traffic, but if the individual system is also acting as a gateway, it will not encrypt traffic coming from the LAN behind it. An individual system is said to be in *transport mode*.

A system that acts as a gateway that needs to send encrypted traffic originating with itself must be set up as both an encrypted gateway and an individual station sending encrypted traffic. In other words, you will set up two tunnels from the one system.

Before you begin, you must decide which systems or networks need to communicate securely. If you have two gateways to the Internet, known as California and NewYork respectively, and behind those are various hosts, as shown in Table 20.1, you need to decide which hosts need to talk with which other hosts securely.

TABLE 20.1 HOSTS ON TWO SAMPLE LANs	
LAN Site 1	**LAN Site 2**
California: (192.168.1.1) (Internet connection: 123.123.123.1)	NewYork: (192.168.2.1) (Internet connection: 200.200.200.1)
Encino (192.168.1.2)	Albany (192.168.2.2)
SantaB (192.168.1.3)	Erie (192.168.2.3)
SanF (192.168.1.4)	NYC (192.168.2.4)
LAX (192.168.1.5)	Buffalo (192.168.2.5)
Bakersfield (192.168.1.6)	Rochester 192.168.2.6)

If you set up California and NewYork as encrypted gateways, all traffic behind the gateways will be encrypted when communicating from California to NewYork. So all traffic from SantaB to NYC will be encrypted before leaving California and decrypted before leaving NewYork. However, traffic between hosts Encino and LAX, for example, will not be encrypted. Likewise, traffic that originates on California and goes to any other host (including NewYork or any host behind it) will not be encrypted.

So any host behind California will be able to read any traffic originating or terminating (or both) with any other host behind California. The same holds true for hosts behind NewYork. And traffic originating on either gateway is sent unencrypted.

If SanF and Albany belong to the president and vice president of the company and they need to set up private communications that no other host will be able to read, including on their own subnet, they will need individual host setups that also build an encrypted tunnel directly between SanF and Albany. If the gateway tunnels are active, the encrypted tunnel between SanF and Albany will travel through it. There is no problem having an encrypted tunnel through another encrypted tunnel apart from the slight lag each end might notice because of the dual encryption (depending on the speed of the systems doing the encrypting/decrypting). The same concept applies if NYC needs to communicate with Albany securely. These two will need to set up individual tunnels between each other.

VPN CONFIGURATION

The `ipsec` configuration files consist of two separate files. The first is `/etc/ipsec.secrets`. Within the `ipsec.secrets` file is either a preshared secret key (PSK) or an RSA key (RSA). This text will deal only with the preshared secret. This shared secret will be identical between two systems and allows these two systems to authenticate each other through this shared secret. This method is secure as long as the shared secret remains secret.

Caution

The shared secret in `ipsec.secrets` must never be transmitted in the clear. Maintain the secret by ensuring that only root can read the file (`chmod 600`), and transfer the secret to the other system only by a secure means (put the `ipsec.secrets` file on a floppy and use the sneaker net—hand carry it—or transfer it through openssh, or secure shell).

The `ipsec.secrets` file will contain pairs of IP addresses with a shared secret. The lines will look like this:

```
192.168.0.2 192.168.0.1: PSK "0xb9e67371_74116d27_bd83734a_4e247ec9_221a9826_d78475ec"
```

Each system, in this case 192.168.0.1 and 192.168.0.2, must have this line in its individual `ipsec.secrets` file. Now these two systems will be able to authenticate each other and set up an encrypted tunnel. You can add as many lines as you need encrypted tunnels. Let's assume you have three gateways that will tunnel traffic: California (192.168.1.1), NewYork (192.168.2.1), and Florida (192.168.3.1). You will need lines like this:

```
192.168.1.1 192.168.2.1: PSK "0xb0ad0fef_feccead4_cb19d474_2386a7fe_4a4f3106_6346855a"
192.168.1.1 192.168.3.1: PSK "0x23070fdf_7b54495e_dce22177_ed7f7a4b_aacf5fa3_94a6b4a0"
192.168.2.1 192.168.3.1: PSK "0x0fde3304_20722fc5_c62c68c1_c9502b5a_47952a0d_6d422387"
```

California should have the two lines containing 192.168.1.1 in its `ipsec.secrets` file; New York, the two lines containing 192.168.2.1; and Florida, the two lines containing 192.168.3.1. Although it won't hurt for California to have the line that does not pertain to it (the shared secret between NewYork and Florida), one reason for not including it is increased security. Should the California host be compromised, the attacker will also be able to read traffic between NewYork and Florida because she has the key.

> **Note**
>
> Fully qualified domain names can be used, but a DNS outage would prevent a connection. For this reason, IP addresses are preferred.

If you want to simplify things just a little, you could have all three share the same secret. You can do this with the following lines:

```
192.168.1.1 192.168.2.1 192.168.3.1: PSK
    "0x22d7faed_6357520f_a870f87f_926f6526_7efa4ff9_239d6a8e"
```

You can split the single line after any particular element in the parameter, but you must indent successive lines. The tradeoff with using one key for multiple tunnels is that one broken host exposes all encrypted tunnels.

As for where to get the key, you use the `/usr/local/sbin/ipsec ranbits <bits>` command to generate the shared secret. The preceding secrets were generated with a bits value of 192. You can make this value anything you want. But remember, the number of bits is directly related to the time it takes to encrypt or decrypt the message and also to the security of the message. That is, more bits take more time but are more secure (will take longer to "break").

ipsec.conf

The `ipsec.conf` file is the heart of the `ipsec` configuration and is broken down into two major parts: the `config` section and the `conn` section.

The `config` section contains general settings for the `ipsec` implementation on the system. The only valid `config` as of this writing is `setup`. Listing 20.1 shows a sample `config` section from an `ipsec.conf` file.

LISTING 20.1   SAMPLE `config` SETUP SECTION

```
config setup
    interfaces="ipsec0=tr0 ipsec1=ppp0"
    klipsdebug=all
    plutodebug=all
    manualstart=
    forwardcontrol=yes
    syslog=local5.warning
    plutoload=%search
    plutostart=%search
```

This section of the `ipsec.conf` file is the general section, providing FreeS/WAN its default configuration.

Note   The indentations in each section are important. The `config setup` line must start in the first column. The lines that compose the section must be indented. The amount of indent isn't important, but the lines cannot start in the first column.

Some of the more important and less self-explanatory settings found in this section are explained here:

- **`interfaces`**—Map `ipsec` devices to communications devices. You can also use the special value `%defaultroute`. Its effects are detailed in the section "Connection Specifications."

- **`forwardcontrol`**—Specifies whether to write a 1 to `/proc/sys/net/ipv4/ip_forward`.

- **`syslog`**—Specifies the facility and priority for `ipsec` system logging (see Chapter 21, "System Auditing and System Logging," for more information).

- **`plutoload/plutostart`**—Specifies whether to load or start `ipsec` connections at `ipsec` startup. The special value `%search` tells `ipsec` to look for `auto=add` or `auto=start` for load or start respectively.

CONNECTION SPECIFICATIONS

All `ipsec`-related files have some shortcuts that you can use to group information and keep it in separate small files rather than one large one. One shortcut is the `include` statement. When `ipsec` reads the keyword `include`, it looks for a parameter that is either a fully pathed filename or the name of a file in the current directory. When `ipsec` grabs the file, it includes the entire contents of that file and merges it into the calling file at that point, so included files must have the correct format. If you want to include multiple files, `ipsec` uses standard shell globbing, so you can include multiple files all at once.

This chapter does not demonstrate the use of `include`, but if you have multiple sites to set up, the FreeS/WAN documentation covers it very well.

The most important part of the `ipsec.conf` file is the connection-specification section. This is the part that tells `ipsec` what encrypted connections to set up.

Each conn section must have a unique name associated with it. Each tunnel will have a left and right end. A large number of parameters are available for use in the connection section. Some are general in nature, some are specific to the tunnel, and some are encryption/key specific. A look at many (but not all) is included here:

- **type**—Type of connection. This will be either tunnel or transport. transport is only host-host, whereas tunnel is host-host, subnet-subnet, or host-subnet. Default: tunnel.

- **auto**—Actions that you want performed automatically at ipsec startup. Your choices are add, start, or ignore. add prepares everything, but doesn't build the tunnel. start builds the tunnel. ignore does nothing. Default: ignore.

- **left**—Only mandatory parameter. One of left or right (but not both) may be %defaultroute. Default: none.

- **leftsubnet**—Subnet behind the left host. Will be in the form network/netmask. Default: left/32.

- **leftnexthop**—Next public IP leaving left. If left=%defaultroute, this parameter must be omitted. Default: right.

- **leftfirewall**—Indicates whether the left host is a firewall (or masquerading host). One of yes or no. Default: no.

- **pfs**—Indicates whether Perfect Forward Secrecy is desired. One of yes or no. Default: yes.

- **keyingtries**—An integer that expresses the number of unsuccessful negotiation attempts before giving up. The value 0 means never. Default: 3.

Listing 20.2 shows a sample setup based on the California/NewYork WAN from Table 20.1. Also included is the configsetup section.

LISTING 20.2   SAMPLE ipsec.conf SHOWING A SECURE WAN CREATED OVER THE INTERNET BETWEEN TWO PRIVATE LANS

```
config setup
    interfaces=%defaultroute
    forwardcontrol=yes
    syslog=local5.warning
    plutostart=%search

conn califnet-nynet
    type=tunnel
    auto=start
    left=123.123.123.1
    leftsubnet=192.168.1.0/24
    leftfirewall=yes
    right=200.200.200.1
    rightsubnet=192.168.2.0/24
    rightfirewall=yes
    keyingtries=0
```

PART

III

CH

20

The same caveat that held true for the config setup section—that the config had to start in the first column and the parameters had to be preceded by whitespace—holds true for the connection (conn) section. Proper indentation is essential. After this part is complete, you can test the tunnel simply by pinging from a California subnet host (say LAX) to a NewYork subnet host (such as Erie). Because the private IPs in the 192.168 range won't route over the Internet and there's no other way for LAX to talk to Erie, you know the traffic is tunneling.

FINISHING UP

Listing 20.2 shows the connection specifications for the secure tunnel connecting the subnet behind California with the subnet behind NewYork. But you also know that traffic originating or terminating on either the California or NewYork host will be unencrypted.

To ensure the security of the data originating or terminating at either of the gateways, you'll need to construct three more tunnels. Notice the name of the subnet tunnel above: califnet-nynet. The name was chosen deliberately as a hint that this tunnel was meant to connect the two subnets. A second hint is in the form of the type on the first line: tunnel. Now you need a tunnel to connect each gateway to the opposite subnet and a gateway-to-gateway tunnel to complete it all. The connection names used should help you understand what the connecting tunnel is for. Listing 20.3 uses the name of the gateway appending the designation net or gate to indicate the tunnel termination. Listing 20.3 shows the additions necessary.

LISTING 20.3   SAMPLE CONNECTION CONFIGURATION

```
conn califnet-nygate
    type=tunnel
    left=      auto=start
    left=123.123.123.1
    leftsubnet=192.168.1.0/24
    leftfirewall=yes
    right=200.200.200.1
    keyingtries=0

conn califgate-nynet
    type=tunnel
    auto=start
    left=123.123.123.1
    right=200.200.200.1
    rightsubnet=192.168.2.0/24
    rightfirewall=yes
    keyingtries=0

conn califgate-nygate
    type=transport
    auto=start
    left=123.123.123.1
    right=200.200.200.1
    keyingtries=0
```

TROUBLESHOOTING

I'm using the kernel source supplied by Caldera (or Red Hat, and so forth), but building the FreeS/WAN package fails.

The Caldera kernel sources are already modified from the original pristine sources. Depending on what Caldera has modified, it might not be possible to use their kernel sources. If you find that building the FreeS/WAN package fails, try getting the sources from `ftp.kernel.org/pub/linux/kernel/v2.4` and compiling from that.

The FreeS/WAN package seems to be building okay, but I'm getting what looks like lots of pointer errors. Are these normal?

Yes, the initial portion of the build will contain what look like lots of errors. All messages are captured to `kbuild.out`. If you have any true errors, the build will stop and you will be able to see the errors in `kbuild.out`.

I had to use the pristine kernel sources, and now when I boot up Caldera, instead of the nice graphical screen, I get a graphical mess. How can I fix it?

You have two choices. If you really want the Caldera graphical boot, you'll need to find kernel patches that fix the graphical boot. If the graphical boot isn't important to you, in either `/etc/lilo.conf` or `/boot/grub/menu.lst` (depending on which you are using), comment out the `message=` line (put a "#" in front of it) and change the `vga=274` line to `vga=normal`. If you're using LILO, don't forget to run `lilo`.

I've set up the two gateways and subnets, and I can send traffic between the gateways, but I can't seem to send traffic between the subnets. I've tried pinging from 192.168.0.4 (on one subnet) to 192.168.0.20 on the other subnet, and it just times out. I'm using a netmask of 255.255.255.0 on each.

The two subnets are overlapping. You cannot have two overlapping subnets. You can do two things: Change one subnet to 192.168.1.x (changing the IPs of all the systems) or change the netmask to 255.255.255.128 on each subnet, and make sure each subnet contains non-overlapping Ips. (Subnet A would have IPs from 1–126, and subnet B would have IPs from 129–154).

## CHAPTER 21

SYSTEM AUDITING AND SYSTEM LOGGING

In this chapter

SYSLOG

System logging is taken care of using syslogd, the system-logging daemon. This daemon listens for programs to send it information, which it writes to logs (or ignores) based on the contents of its configuration file. The configuration file also tells syslog where to write the log file.

Every Linux distribution comes with logging turned on. Although you can turn system logging off with no adverse affects on how the system runs, this is not prudent for several reasons, not the least of which is you'll have no records if something does go wrong with your system. All important messages are sent to the system logger.

Because the system logger is so important, it is also very flexible. One system logger can watch not only its own system, but also many other systems. If you have several systems, you might want to designate one as the central system logger. You might want to do this for convenience, or to keep logs on a less-sensitive system. For example, you might want to send the logs from your firewall to a different machine. That way, if your firewall is compromised, the intruder will have to access a different system to modify the logs. This gives you more time to detect a break-in before the intruder can get to the other system and modify the logs.

Not all programs write to syslog, and those that do will often have a mechanism to enable or disable logging partially or completely. For example, the ppp daemon will only write debugging to syslog if debug is specified. Otherwise, only standard logging messages are sent to syslog. Just enter the word *debug* on a line in the /etc/ppp/options file.

SYSLOGD

The syslog daemon starts during system initialization. It is one of the first daemons to start. The only time syslog is not running is when the system is in runlevel 1 (single user or maintenance mode). The reason for not enabling syslog in runlevel 1 is that nothing is running to talk to syslog (except the kernel, but it has a buffer where messages are saved until syslog is ready).

When syslogd starts up, it listens for programs to send it messages using a UNIX socket: /dev/log. This socket is like an open-ended pipe that programs can send messages to, and syslogd will receive them on the other end. Then syslogd will process the message and either write it to a log file or send it to /dev/null (the trash bin).

The syslogd program has several option switches that alter its behavior. None of the switches are enabled by default. Most will not be of general interest. Those few that are of interest are explained in the following table. You can enable these switches under Caldera OpenLinux by putting them in /etc/sysconfig/daemons/syslog. They should be added to OPTIONS_SYSLOGD just as they would appear on the command line. (The OPTIONS_KLOGD entry will be discussed under klogd later in this chapter.) Neither Red Hat nor Debian have a convenient mechanism for adding options during startup except to modify the syslog startup script (in Red Hat located in /etc/rc.d/init.d/syslog, and in Debian in /etc/init.d/sysklogd). In Red Hat you need to directly modify the line that calls syslogd. In Debian, a convenient SYSLOGD="" line is provided, and just above it is an example of adding the -r option.

Option	Use
`-a <socket>`	If you run any daemons in a chroot jail, you can specify the log socket location. Up to 19 additional log sockets can be added. (A chroot jail consists of a subdirectory a particular user cannot climb up out of and so becomes his system root, and because it's not the real system root, limits the damage that can be done by someone subverting the daemon running as that user.)
`-h`	This option forwards syslog messages received from other hosts to a central logging host (requires `-r`).
`-l <hostlist>`	Normally, syslog will record the fully qualified domain name of remote systems it is logging for. The `-l` switch turns off long names for those hosts listed. `hostlist` is a colon-separated list of hostnames (see also `-s` that follows).
`-m <interval>`	This option specifies the interval between `--MARK--` entries in the log. By default, this is 20 minutes. A zero turns off `--MARK--` logging.
`-r`	This option tells syslog it can receive messages (binds syslog to port 514 as defined in `/etc/services`; without the entry in `/etc/services`, syslog will fail to start).
`-s <domainlist>`	This option tells syslog to strip off the listed domain names. `list` is a colon-separated list of domain names. Uses first name encountered that matches, not best match, so longer matches must appear first; that is, `acctng.bar.org` should precede `bar.org` or the `acctng` part will not strip.

Other options are available, but are principally for debugging purposes and of little use under normal circumstances.

syslog.conf

The `/etc/syslog.conf` is composed of two columns. The columns specify what to log and where to log it. The Caldera OpenLinux default `syslog.conf` with all comments (lines beginning with #) and blank lines removed looks like Listing 21.1.

LISTING 21.1   DEFAULT `/etc/syslog.conf` ACTIVE ENTRIES

```
*.*;cron.none                                   /dev/console
*.info;news,mail,authpriv,auth.none             -/var/log/messages
authpriv.*;auth.*                               /var/log/secure
mail.*                                          /var/log/mail
news.*                                          /var/log/news.all
uucp,news.err                                   /var/log/spooler
*.emerg                                         *
```

On the left side are the messages to log. This field consists of an entry with a left and right side separated by a dot. The left side is the facility, and the right side is the priority.

Note

Although this text uses Caldera as an example, all `syslog.conf` files will look similar (thought not exactly the same). The entries are subject to change from distribution to distribution, and even from version to version for any given distribution. For that reason you should always review a newly installed `syslog.conf` file.

The facility is one of `auth`, `authpriv`, `cron`, `daemon`, `kern`, `lpr`, `mail`, `mark`, `news`, `syslog`, `user`, `uucp`, and `local0-local7`. Most of these facilities are self-explanatory. For example, send-mail and other privileged mail programs log using the `mail` facility. All restricted services have provisions to send messages to syslog. Sometimes the specific facility that they use can be altered on the command line either when they start or when they are compiled.

Note   A restricted service is one that enables access to system resources or uses system resources to provide a service.

The right side of the dot contains the priority. Unless otherwise modified, the priority will always be the stated priority and any messages of higher priority. Priorities are (from lowest to highest), `debug`, `info`, `notice`, `warning` (warn), `err` (error), `crit`, `alert`, `emerg` (panic). The terms in parenthesis are obsolete and should not be used. The increasing priorities correspond to increasing severity.

Both facility and priority understand * as meaning all. Additionally, the priority recognizes `none`, which will prevent logging. If you want to specify multiple facilities at the same priority, you can use a comma-separated list:

```
auth,authpriv.info
```

This line will log any messages that come in as either `auth` or `authpriv` at `info` priority or higher.

If you want to specify multiple selections at different priorities, you can use a semicolon-separated list:

```
authpriv.*;auth.info
```

One last rule for combining the above—all lines are read from left to right, with later specifications modifying earlier ones:

```
*.info;authpriv,auth.none
```

This tells syslog to log everything it sees at `info` priority or higher; however, don't log anything that is either `authpriv` or `auth` facilities. This allows for extremely powerful, simple rules.

Finally, syslog has some extensions for the priorities. The first is the = sign. When used, it means only this priority, nothing higher. You can use ! to mean not. This reverses the meaning. You can also use them both together to exclude just one priority level, but when used together, the ! must come first (!=). So you can do the following:

- **`mail.=info`**—This will log only `info` priority.
- **`mail.!=info`**—This will log all priorities except `info`.
- **`mail.!notice`**—This will log all priorities below `notice` (`debug`, `info`).

The second column of `/etc/syslog.conf` is the file to which the selections are to be written. This entry will normally be one file or hostname. All filenames must be fully pathed and start with a /. All hostnames must start with an @. This entry can also be a named pipe, the name of which must start with a |. Messages can also be sent to users (if they are logged in). A comma-separated list of usernames is a valid target. This entry can also be * which means everywhere—quite literally. Every user, every log file, and every pipe syslog knows about will receive this message. This is normally reserved for kernel errors or above because these conditions mean the system is unstable and will probably crash in short order.

One modifier that can be used with the logging action (location) is a minus sign (–) if a file-name is the target. If the minus sign precedes the action, syslog will not flush the buffer to disk immediately, but will wait for the normal system sync. If the system crashes, the last messages sent to syslog cannot be written to disk. This is probably fine for recouping some performance with messages to non-critical logs, but messages from the kernel should not be so buffered or the reason for a kernel oops might not be known.

Note Messages sent to remote hosts are sent using UDP/IP. This means that although efficient, not all messages are guaranteed to make it to the central logging host.

Referring to Listing 21.1, the default /etc/syslog.conf logs the following:

```
*.*;cron.none                                    /dev/console
```

This line sends everything except cron messages to the console.

With the following, all messages of info priority and above are sent to /var/log/messages, except news, mail, authpriv, and auth, which are all dumped:

```
*.info;news,mail,authpriv,auth.none              -/var/log/messages
```

syslog will not immediately flush the write buffer to disk, but will allow the write at the next system sync. Here, all auth and authpriv messages are written to /var/log/secure:

```
authpriv.*;auth.*                                /var/log/secure
```

This could also be rewritten as authpriv,auth.*. The following writes all mail messages to /var/log/mail:

```
mail.*                                           /var/log/mail
```

On a mailhost that receives many messages, you might want to change the target to -/var/log/mail. With the following, all news is written to /var/log/news.all:

```
news.*                                           /var/log/news.all
```

This is another entry you might want to precede the target with -. In the following, the /var/log/spooler file gets all uucp and news messages of priority error or above:

```
uucp,news.err                                    /var/log/spooler
```

Here, emergency messages are written everywhere:

```
*.emerg                                          *
```

KLOGD

The kernel-logging daemon is a special daemon that passes messages from the kernel to the syslog daemon. The kernel daemon normally reads from /proc/kmsg to get kernel messages and passes them to syslog.

The klogd daemon under OpenLinux is run with one command-line option as entered in /etc/sysconfig/daemons/syslog. This command-line option tests for a System.map file that matches the version of the running kernel and uses that map file. Other options will not be discussed in this text because they are not of general interest.

Debian, by default, uses no options for klogd, but has an example in /etc/init.d/sysklogd of an options entry of the type used by Caldera that reads from the appropriate System.map file.

Red Hat has no convenient method of specifying any options for klogd other than by modifying /etc/rc.d/init.d/syslog and adding an option on the line that calls klogd.

What types of messages are passed to syslog from klogd? You can see these messages by running dmesg. Syslog then adds a time and hostname before logging it.

TRIPWIRE

Tripwire is an application that watches your system for changes. The program has been available for some time, first under a GPL-like license, and then as a commercial product, and it is again being made freely available to the Linux community (thanks to companies such as Caldera Systems, Red Hat, and others).

Tripwire, after it is ready, will be offered by Caldera and Red Hat, and possibly even by Debian. It might not be immediately available, but it will be worth installing when it is available.

Tripwire allows you to specify which files and directories you want to watch for change. You might think that RPM offers this facility in its verify function, and in a way it does, but Tripwire does things that RPM cannot.

For example, RPM can tell you any binary or configuration file that has changed since installation. This is fine for restricted services like /bin/login, but many other files need watching. For example, RPM will always tell you /etc/passwd has changed. Unfortunately, you can't update the RPM database. Tripwire's database can be updated, and you will know whether /etc/passwd has changed since the last database update, rather than since installation.

RPM also cannot monitor what it doesn't install. RPM doesn't install log files for those files below the /home directory. Tripwire can keep an eye on the /home directory for modification of ownership on directories and watch log files to make sure they continue to grow. (A log file that suddenly becomes smaller is an indication someone has deleted entries—not a good sign.)

As of this writing, it is unclear exactly what the new version of Tripwire will look like, and more detail is not possible. Keep an eye out. With Caldera and Red Hat backing the project, ease of configuration and ease of use will be high on the list of priorities.

TOUBLESHOOTING

I've set up syslog and it seems to be sending entries to /var/log/messages, but how do I read them?

In general, syslog entries will be different depending on the facility sending the message. However, some parts will always look the same. Syslog itself prepends the system date and time the message was received by syslog, the name of the system (in case it is acting as a central logging host), and the particular facility that sent the message (usually with the PID of the daemon in square brackets). After that it just logs whatever it was sent to log from that facility, so you'll have to refer to the particular daemon's documentation for interpretation.

I want to send the same messages to several logs. How can I do this?

This depends on the first entry. If the first entry contains many different facilities or priorities you don't want, you need another entry for that particular facility. Choose the priority you do want and point it to the second location. Otherwise, if the first entry contains exactly what you want, the target can be a comma-separated list of files or users.

I see this annoying --MARK-- recurring throughout my /var/log/messages file. How do I stop it?

This mark is made by syslog and by default is written at twenty- minute intervals (this is turned off in Red Hat). This security feature will allow you to see if the syslog daemon has been stop-ped and restarted (and the restart message erased), or if a mass deletion of log entries spanning more than this time has occurred. You can change the interval by calling syslogd with -m <interval> in minutes, where 0 turns this feature off. Modify the Caldera /etc/sysconfig/daemons/syslog and add -m 0 between the parenthesis in the SYSLOGD_OPTIONS="" line, or in Debian, add the option to /etc/init.d/sysklogd to the SYSLOG="" line.

I want to put the PPP messages in their own file. How do I do this?

All you have to do to put any particular daemon's messages in its own file is to determine the facility a daemon uses. Sometimes this is easy (mail uses the mail facility), and sometimes it's not (PPP usually uses the local2 facility). You might have to refer to the documentation to determine which facility a daemon uses. Sometimes this can be controlled either during compile-time or at runtime. After you know which facility is used, the rest is just a matter of entering a line for it in /etc/syslog.conf.

PART IV

NETWORKING WITH LINUX

CHAPTER 22

NETWORKING

In this chapter

IP

The *Internet Protocol*, or *IP*, is a very basic form of message addressing. At its heart, IP is nothing more than an envelope in which another packet (normally a TCP or UDP packet) travels to arrive at its destination.

Think of the IP as the envelope that you use when sending a letter. A letter has a recipient address and a sender or return address. IP packets contain this same information and a little more. The IP packet is basically just a header stuck on another (usually TCP) packet with a destination and source address. It also contains a checksum, an option field, and a few other fields. The exact format and contents can be found in RFC 791, available from `http://www.rfc-editor.org/rfc.html`.

When you want to send a letter to Barney at Barney's Hardware, Software, and Computer Peripherals Emporium, you might not know the address. So you look it up in the phone book and get the street address. Your computer system uses DNS to look up `www.calderasystems.com` in the same way to get an IP number. This IP number is like the street address for Barney's Hardware Shop. Now, your system can use IP and put the destination IP address in the IP header and send the packet on its way. Routers along the way read the header and pass it off to the next router in line. To understand how they know how to do this, let's look at IP network addresses quickly.

IP ADDRESSING

Every computer on the Internet has a unique IP address assigned to it. These IP addresses come in a very distinct format. When you look at an IP address, you will see four numbers ranging from 0–255 separated by three dots in a format known as *dotted decimal notation*. An IP address looks to humans like this: 209.127.112.153.

Computers use binary numbers as a base. This is many zeroes and ones. Each zero or one is called a *bit*. When eight of these zeroes and ones (bits) are strung together to form a larger number, the number is called a *byte*. Today's computers work with bytes, and normally now with multiple bytes at one time. If you have a Pentium system, that system works with 4 bytes (32 bits) at a time. Because eight bits are used to form each of the dotted decimal numbers, the numbers are sometimes referred to as *octets*.

It just so happens that 8 bits or 1 byte, although going from 0–255 in the decimal number system humans use, has a convenient equivalent for computers in hexadecimal. The numbers in hexadecimal are as follows: 0, 1, 2, 3, 4, 5, 6, 7, 8, 9, a, b, c, d, e, f. The numbers 0–255 in decimal have an equivalent of 00–ff in hexadecimal.

You don't really need to understand hexadecimal to understand networking because you will always work in decimal (0–9). But realize that some output can contain numbers that start with "0x" and then contain numbers and letters. The 0x tells you the rest of the number is hexadecimal.

Just because an IP address looks like 209.127.112.153 doesn't mean that's the only form of the address. If you change 209.127.112.153 into hexadecimal, you get the number 0xd17f7099 (remember, you always precede a hexadecimal number with 0x). If you convert that back into decimal, you get the decimal number 3514790041. The easiest way to do this is actually to change the 209.127.112.153 into binary and then into decimal again. But changing it into hexadecimal also works.

So the IP address 209.127.112.153 corresponds to computer number 3,514,790,041 (commas added for readability). This number, though, is too easy for humans to get jumbled. Besides, using a number like 209.127.112.153 is more convenient when discussing routing.

IP NETWORKS AND CIDR

Now that you know how an IP number works, let's look at an IP network. An IP network is composed of multiple systems. These systems find each other by means of their IP addresses. They package up a bundle of information into a packet, find out the IP address of the system the packet is going to, and put that packet on the wire. Or do they? Simplistically, yes. In actuality, the packet is passed to the Ethernet card where the packet is framed. Now you have an electrical packet to go on a wire. But Ethernet cards talk to each other by means of a burned-in address called a *MAC address*. The host helps the Ethernet card by creating a table that maps Ethernet MAC addresses to IP addresses for a local network, where the systems are electrically attached to the same wire. Packets for systems not on the local network are passed to the gateway system (router) to be passed to another network until reaching the network the destination system is on. So the local system's Ethernet card talks to the gateway's Ethernet card for systems not on the local network.

Note

> Routers and gateways are systems that pass traffic from one network (and sometimes one protocol) to another. Although not synonymous, routers and gateways perform the same function for purposes of this text.

But how does a system decide whether an IP is local? It does this by looking at a table that tells it that IP addresses from x to y are on the local network; otherwise, they are not. This table maps the network using a range of IP addresses bounded on the bottom by the network address and on the top by the broadcast address. You'll see how this works shortly.

Historically, IP addresses were broken down into classes—A, B, C, and D—these roughly corresponded to each of the numbers in the four octets used in IP addressing. That is, a Class A address used just the first octet to describe itself: 127.x.x.x. A Class B address used the first two octets: 172.16.x.x. And a Class C used the first three octets to describe itself: 192.168.1.x. (In Class D were experimental networks from 224.x.x.x through 255.255.255.x.) But when the Internet started experiencing real growth in 1992, it became obvious this scheme was wasteful of precious IP addresses. After all, only 4 billion addresses are available, and many of those can't or won't be used for any number of reasons. So of the 2 billion or so usable addresses, the available number was dwindling rapidly.

In 1993, to provide more IP addresses to more people, *Classless Interdomain Routing* (CIDR) was introduced. This allowed the former Class A–C addresses, which were available for 254, 65534, or 16,777,214 hosts, to be cut up some more.

Imagine you have a network and needed your own set of IPs. If you had only 5 computers, you'd still get 253 addresses. If you had no use for the other 248 addresses, they'd be wasted. With CIDR, you could be given a subnet that would just fit your needs and waste a minimum amount of addresses.

VLSM

Under the Classful system, netmasks were set. Networks were divided on the octet boundaries only. Under Classless addressing, a new concept called *Variable Length Subnet Masks* (*VLSM*) was introduced. This is how CIDR is implemented.

> **Note**
>
> CIDR and the RFCs allow for subnet masks that don't translate to VLSM netmasks. However, these netmasks are really only good as a mental exercise and should never actually be implemented. These netmasks are fodder for advanced networking and will not be discussed in this text.

Before proceeding further, you'll need four definitions. These are not the technical definitions of the terms, but are provided in layman's terms:

- **Host Address**—A unique IP given to each separate communications device in a host. No two devices or systems on a network may have the same number. A host with two or more devices will have at least that number of unique IPs, but can have more (devices can have more than one IP each if required).

- **Network Address**—The lower boundary of a network that helps define the limits of the network. No host can be assigned the network address. This address will always be an even binary multiple.

- **Broadcast Address**—The upper boundary of a network that helps define the limits of the network. Although no host will ever be assigned the broadcast address, all hosts on the network that have IP stacks conformant to Internet standards will respond to queries to this address. This address will always be an even binary multiple minus 1.

- **Netmask**—The netmask defines the division between network and hosts. The netmask will be a binary number whereby all numbers to the left (network portion) are ones, and to the right (host portion) all zeroes.

> **Note**
>
> All operating systems (some 104+) conform to the standard of the use of the broadcast address except Microsoft operating systems. This non-conformance on Microsoft's part breaks some network utilities where Microsoft hosts are present on the network. This nuisance should be kept in mind when troubleshooting network problems.

When networks and subnets are discussed, the concept of a netmask comes up. Under the old Classful system, netmasks would be one of 255.255.255.0, 255.255.0.0, or 255.0.0.0. Note that this is equivalent to all ones in the first 24, 16, or 8 bits and zeroes in the last 8,

16, or 24 bits respectively. It is possible to have a netmask of 255.255.255.255, but this is a very special case and used for point-to-point routing only.

Under Classless addressing, the netmask will always start with 255, but will change depending on how many ones until the first zero. Table 22.1 shows the various values possible for any of the three subsequent octets in binary, decimal, and hexadecimal.

TABLE 22.1   POSSIBLE OCTET VALUES FOR NETMASKS

Binary	Decimal	Hexadecimal
00000000	0	00
10000000	128	80
11000000	192	c0
11100000	224	e0
11110000	240	f0
11111000	248	f8
11111100	252	fc
11111110	254	fe
11111111	255	ff

A netmask, then, will consist of anywhere from 8–32 ones (except 31) which defines the network portion of the netmask. Using our Classful addresses, the following netmasks provide you with the appropriate VLSM as follows:

```
255.255.255.0      = /24
255.255.0.0        = /16
255.0.0.0          = /8
255.255.255.255    = /32
```

Using this same arrangement, you can substitute any number from 8 –32 (except 31) as the variable length subnet mask. That's the second time in 2 paragraphs that /31 has been excluded. That's because a /31 VLSM defines 31 ones and one zero. That one zero position can take on a value of 0 or 1, or two possible values. But remember, the low (0) value is reserved as the network address and the high (1) value as the broadcast address, so no host IPs are possible—probably not what you want.

Looking at an abbreviated table of host availability, Table 22.2 will give you an idea of how you can split up your network.

TABLE 22.2   HOW NETMASKS DEFINE AVAILABLE HOSTS

Binary Netmask	Decimal Netmask	VLSM	Number of Hosts
11111111111111111111111111111000	255.255.255.248	/29	6
11111111111111111111111111110000	255.255.255.240	/28	14

TABLE 22.2 CONTINUED

Binary Netmask	Decimal Netmask	VLSM	Number of Hosts
11111111111111111111111100000	255.255.255.224	/27	30
11111111111111111111111000000	255.255.255.192	/26	62
11111111111111111111110000000	255.255.255.128	/25	126
11111111111111111111100000000	255.255.255.0	/24	254
11111111111111111111000000000	255.255.254.0	/23	510
11111111111111111110000000000	255.255.252.0	/22	1022
11111111111111111100000000000	255.255.248.0	/21	2046

The number of hosts is derived by finding the binary multiple and subtracting two (remember, you can't use the network or broadcast addresses).

If you follow the preceding explanations, you can see that by taking an IP address and a net-mask, you can define the network. You will have to specify the broadcast address because there are (old) networks that use the lower address as their broadcast address, but this text assumes you don't have that kind of network or you already know how to handle the situation if you do.

Caution

You cannot allow subnets to overlap. That is, you cannot have a system with a /25 and one with a /24 netmask, one contained within the other. For example, if you have one system defined by IP 192.168.0.2/24 and one defined by 192.168.0.3/25, both attached to the same wire, they will not be able to communicate because each thinks it is on a different network as defined by their respective netmasks. This can cause erratic network behavior.

PORTS

Now that you have the basics of IPs and how they work, one more concept must be under-stood to complete the picture, and that is how and where ports fit in.

When dealing with information passing from one computer system to another, information passes between a server application and a client application. Each server program will have a default port that it binds to (listens on) for requests coming from a client. The client is built to send requests to the default server port.

Imagine you have a company and that company's goal is to provide clients information. You have clients that come to the company, some who speak German and some who speak Spanish. So you hire two individuals, one who speaks only German and one who speaks only Spanish. When German speakers come, they knock on the door twice, and when Spanish speakers come they knock three times. This keeps each of your employees from answering the door when it's not for them.

Ports work the same way. The *Internet Assigned Numbers Authority* (*IANA*) designates ports for certain services to bind to. Some of these include the following:

Port	Service
21	FTP
23	Telnet
25	mail (SMTP)
80	http (WWW)
110	pop3

You can find a complete listing in your /etc/services file. The services file's format is as follows:

```
service    port_number/protocol    #optional comments
```

There is almost never any reason to delete entries from the services file, but sometimes there is reason to add to it. For example, you might want to add mysql 3306/tcp. This will add the standard mysql port. Check to ensure you don't already have an entry for 3306/tcp, because the first occurrence of port/protocol is the one that will be used.

The above port number (3306) brings up another point. Ports 0–1023 are reserved. Only root (UID 0) can bind to these lower ports, known as privileged ports. The remaining ports 1024–65535 anyone (including root) can bind. These ports are used as outgoing ports by your client software. They double as incoming ports from the server as well. You'll look at this in the TCP section that follows. For more information on IP, refer to RFC 791. Also see RFC 1918 for information on Private IP allocations (available from http://www.rfc-editor.org/).

TCP

The *Transmission Control Protocol* (*TCP*) is one of the protocols carried by IP. TCP accounts for over 90% of the traffic on the average LAN. TCP creates a connection between the client and server through a 3-way handshake.

First, the client, an FTP client, sends a TCP/IP packet from a randomly chosen high-numbered port to the server on port 21. In the header of this packet requesting to connect to the FTP server, the SYN bit is set and the others are clear (other bits include ACK, RST, FIN, URG, PSH, but most are not important to this discussion). The packet also contains a random sequence starting number.

When the server, sitting on the wait queue listening for an incoming connection request, sees this packet with the SYN bit set, it sets the ACK bit (now both SYN and ACK are set), increments the sequence number, and sends the packet back.

When the client receives the SYN-ACK packet (short for the packet with the SYN and ACK bits set), it increments the sequence number and clears the SYN bit (leaving only the ACK bit set).

When the server receives the ACK packet, it moves off the wait queue and the connection is established.

This is important for several reasons. First, you need this to understand how your firewall software knows about new connections versus established connections and also how the various packets are related (IP:Port:Sequence #). You'll use this information to write firewall rules later in the book. Second, you can begin to see ways around certain network setups, such as blocked ICMP echo-request (ping) packets (initiate a connection with a SYN-ACK packet and a live system will send you a RST rather than no response). Third, you will understand better how attacks such as the TCP-SYN denial of service attack works (request connections, but never reply to the SYN-ACK which fills up the wait queue waiting for a reply that will never come).

Because TCP establishes a connection, as long as the network remains up, packet integrity is guaranteed. This is important for many types of exchanges, from file transfers to transfers of Web pages, email transfers, and much more. TCP is also used where large amounts of data that might have gone through UDP are sent through TCP because of their size; DNS transfers come in this category.

For a tutorial on TCP, see RFC-1180 (available from http://www.rfc-editor.org/).

UDP

The *User Datagram Protocol* (*UDP*) is a connectionless protocol. This protocol is used where data integrity is not as important. Whereas TCP used a strict set of rules to ensure data arrived unmangled and assembled in the correct order and error free, UDP does just the opposite. UDP/IP is normally used for small, discreet packages with order or correctness a secondary concern to network efficiency.

Sending a UDP packet is like putting a note in a bottle and throwing it into the sea and then turning your back and walking away. Maybe it will get where it's going and maybe not. UDP is used for DNS queries, where all the information will fit in one packet. If the packet doesn't arrive, DNS will just ask again until it does. UDP is also used for voice over IP, where a lost packet or two, or one that arrives slightly out of order, isn't important to the message overall and makes for a smoother voice than would a TCP connection, which would be very jerky and hard to follow. UDP is also used for trace routes in Linux.

If you look at the /etc/services file, almost all TCP entries have a corresponding UDP entry. Not all these entries are used. SNMP uses UDP, as do a few others. But only about 2%–3% of an average LAN is UDP traffic.

ICMP

ICMP is the *Internet Control Message Protocol*. This particular packet is best known for the ping packet. But this is just one of many functions ICMP serves on the Internet. ICMP doesn't use ports. Instead it talks to the Ethernet card at a low level. But ICMP does have types to identify itself.

ICMP type 0 is a common echo-request packet. You can use this to test network connectivity between two points. Its complement is the type 8 echo-reply. Many folks, for supposed security reasons, want to block ICMP. Although blocking type 0 is fine if you're paranoid, the fact is that unless you're talking about a flood ping, and at that from a system on an Internet backbone, it probably won't affect your bandwidth adversely at all.

However, blocking ICMP can have some very deleterious effects. For example, Linux uses ICMP to perform MTU discovery. It does this by sending out large (1500 bit) packets marked with the Do Not Fragment (DNF) bit set. If any router along the way needs to fragment the packet it can't, so it drops it and sends back an ICMP packet (type 3) saying the packet was too big but the DNF bit was set. Linux then sends another, smaller packet and continues this exercise until the packets get through.

You also don't want to block all the other type-3 packets that signal you that a host is unreachable (code 1) or a port is unreachable (code 3), and so forth, or communications can become unbearably slow. To get more detailed information on ICMP, see RFC 792 (available from `http://www.rfc-editor.org/`).

NETWORK STARTUP UNDER OPENLINUX

With the more esoteric information of networking basics behind, you're ready to look at how OpenLinux handles starting the network. You'll also see how you can use several utilities to view, troubleshoot, and manage your network connection.

When OpenLinux starts up, the `rc` scripts are run as described in Chapter 13, "System Initialization." First, any modules to activate your Ethernet or other interface device is inserted by `/etc/rc.d/rc.modules`. Then, one script, `S01network`, which resides in `/etc/rc.d/rc3.d`, `rc4.d`, and `rc5.d` and is a symlink to `/etc/rc.d/init.d/network`, runs when any of runlevels 3–5 are entered.

The gory details of the network script are not necessary to your understanding of how the network starts, because many tests and checks are performed by this script. But the basics of the script are described here.

First, the network script reads the `/etc/sysconfig/network` file. This file tells the network script if it is supposed to run and passes the hostname and a list of interface (communications) devices to try to start.

Assuming the network script was told to continue, it then looks in `/etc/sysconfig/network-scripts` and runs all the interface configuration scripts (`ifcfg-*`) it finds. The configuration scripts were built during installation and can be reconfigured at any time using COAS. These scripts provide parameters for the network script. Specifically, each `ifcfg-*` file contains the following:

- The device name to start
  - eth0: The first Ethernet card
  - lo: The localhost device

- tr0: The first token ring device
- ppp0: The first point-to-point device
- plip0: The first parallel port device
- fddi0: The first fiber distributed device
- ippp0: The first ISDN point-to-point device

(Subsequent devices carry sequential numbers, i.e., eth1, etc.)

- The device's IP address
- The netmask
- The network address
- The broadcast address
- The gateway address
- Whether the interface is to be initialized at bootup
- Whether to use DHCP (Dynamic Host Control Protocol) to get any of addressing information

With the information obtained from the `ifcfg-*` script, if the `ONBOOT` parameter is `yes`, then the network script will either initialize the device with DHCP if it is told to, or use the addressing information with the two utilities ifconfig and route to set up the network.

NETWORK STARTUP UNDER DEBIAN

When Debian starts up, init runs a script called `/etc/init.d/rcS`. This script runs all the commands in the `/etc/rcS.d/` directory. Among the scripts run are (in order of execution), `/etc/init.d/modutils`, which loads all modules, and `/etc/init.d/networking`.

After modutils loads the modules, the NIC should be ready for use by the networking script. Then the networking script runs. This script (linked from `/etc/rcS.d/`) reads `/etc/network/interfaces` to determine how to initialize the NIC. This is similar to Caldera's `/etc/sysconfig/network-scripts/ifcfg-eth0` file, but with a different syntax.

Debian, unlike Caldera and Red Hat, initializes networking almost immediately on bootup, and doesn't shut down networking until the very end at system halt or reboot. This is something to keep in mind while doing system maintenance.

NETWORK STARTUP UNDER RED HAT

When Red Hat starts up, it does not load all the modules necessary, instead depending on the kernel module loader to load the required moduels on demand—at least those for the Network.

Instead, starting from runlevel 2–5, a link from the `/etc/rc.d/rc<$runlevel>.d/` directory to `/etc/rc.d/init.d/network` script forces loading of the NIC module when the network starts.

Red Hat, like Caldera, uses information saved in the `/etc/sysconfig/` directory, specifically the networking file and `network-scripts/ifcfg-<$device>` files to determine what to start and how to configure it. Although these files look like the Caldera files, they are slightly different, but the information is the same. The difference comes mainly from the location of the common information such as the default route, which is stored in the networking file rather than in the `ifcfg-<$device>` files.

Red Hat also starts networking sooner than Caldera, but later than Debian. Of course, modifying any of the three poses no great problem. For Caldera and Red Hat it comes down to changing (adding or removing) symlinks to call the network script in `/etc/rc.d/init.d` sooner or later. For Debian it is a little more involved because if networking is not desired in runlevel 1, the `/etc/init.d/rcS` script must be modified to remove the call for networking and then the appropriate start/kill symlinks must be added to the various `/etc/rc<$runlevel>.d/` directories as desired.

IFCONFIG

The ifconfig utility is used by the network scripts to start, stop, and configure your interface device, and that's where its name comes from: configure network interface, ifconfig (*if* is short for interface).

This utility can be used to configure or reconfigure any interface device you have. Normally, this will be either an Ethernet card (eth0, eth1) or a Token Ring card (tr0, tr1). If called with no parameters, ifconfig will show you currently running interfaces. If called with the -a option, all devices that have been configured since the last reboot even if they have been turned off (status down) will be shown. As an example, Listing 22.1 shows a configured Ethernet card.

LISTING 22.1   AN IFCONFIG LISTING OF AN ETHERNET CARD

```
eth0      Link encap:Ethernet  HWaddr 00:10:5A:8B:0C:FA
          inet addr:192.168.0.2  Bcast:192.168.0.255  Mask:255.255.255.0
          UP BROADCAST RUNNING MULTICAST  MTU:1500  Metric:1
          RX packets:32509 errors:0 dropped:0 overruns:0 frame:0
          TX packets:24754 errors:0 dropped:0 overruns:0 carrier:22
          collisions:149 txqueuelen:100
          Interrupt:3 Base address:0x300
```

Using ifconfig, you can start, stop, and configure this Ethernet card. Almost every entry can be modified, though the card must support changing that parameter. Fields that cannot be changed by ifconfig are the Link encapsulation field, which is determined by the type device; the two lines containing card statistics (the TX and RX lines); the number of collisions; and the name of the device itself. All others can be manipulated.

Typically, you'll have no reason to change the HWaddr, MTU, Metric, transmit queue length, or interrupt or base I/O address. If you do, you'll need a more advanced discussion of networking than this text will provide.

The typical use for ifconfig is to start an interface device like this:

```
ifconfig eth0 192.168.0.2 netmask 255.255.255.0 broadcast 192.168.0.255
```

The preceding line says to configure the interface eth0 and give it the IP address 192.168.0.2. This will be on a network defined by 192.168.0.0-192.168.0.255 and will use the broadcast address of 192.168.0.255. You can omit the broadcast address and the word BROADCAST will disappear from the third line in Listing 22.1. This is not recommended because systems are expected to reply to network broadcasts. If you are concerned with someone outside trying to cause havoc by pinging your broadcast address, you don't need to worry, because most routers are designed to drop external traffic sent to broadcast addresses.

You can turn off the interface by using the following command:

```
ifconfig eth0 down
```

If you have built a kernel to support the ethertap device, feel free to experiment by configuring tap0. This makes an excellent way to test features on a host with no Ethernet device. The ethertap device can be configured almost any way you'd like. Before you start using the ethertap device, read /usr/src/linux/Documentation/networking/ethertap.txt.

ROUTE

The second utility you'll need to be able to network beyond the local systems is route. The route utility will enable you to specify a default gateway to the Internet. If your system is connected directly to the Internet through a modem, your system should have been automatically configured by your Internet provider. Otherwise, you'll have to tell your system where the system (gateway) is that's connected to the Internet.

Assuming your host has IP 192.168.0.2 and the system 192.168.0.1 is connected to the Internet, you'll need to tell your host to use 192.168.0.1 as its gateway to the Internet. You can do this as follows:

```
route add default gateway 192.168.0.1
```

This command tells route to add 192.168.0.1 as the default to reach the Internet. Any packets that don't have any other route to take to reach their destination will be passed to 192.168.0.1. If you look at the output of route with no options, you'll see where all packets will route. Listing 22.2 shows the routes on the local system.

LISTING 22.2   OUTPUT FROM ROUTE

```
Kernel IP routing table
Destination     Gateway         Genmask         Flags Metric Ref    Use Iface
192.168.0.0     0.0.0.0         255.255.255.0   U     0      0        0 eth0
127.0.0.0       0.0.0.0         255.0.0.0       U     0      0        0 lo
0.0.0.0         192.168.0.1     0.0.0.0         UG    1      0        0 eth0
```

This listing shows that anything destined for a system on the network 192.168.0.0 (from 192.168.0.1 to 192-192.168.0.255) will be put on the local wire. Anything for 127.0.0.1–127.255.255.255 will go to localhost. Anything else (designated by 0.0.0.0) will go to 192.168.0.1 for further routing.

If you don't want a system to be able to communicate with Internet hosts, you can delete the default route:

```
route del default
```

CHECKING YOUR NETWORK

If everything is working as it should, congratulations. If not, you'll need to try to find out what is wrong. You have several utilities you can use to look over the network. This text will take a quick look at each of the following network utilities: ping, traceroute, netstat, and fuser. You'll also become familiar with the files /etc/hosts, /etc/resolv.conf, and /etc/nsswitch.conf in the "Name Resolution" section at the end of the chapter.

Anytime you think you have a network problem, it is always easiest to take a methodical approach to the problem. Saying "I can't surf to http://www.calderasystems.com/" covers a lot of territory. So starting with the local system and working out is preferred.

The first step is to use the ifconfig utility to see whether your device is configured. If it's not configured, try to configure it. You can use the /etc/rc.d/init.d/network script, but configuring it by hand will provide you any error messages on the screen. If configuring it by hand fails, you might need to insert the proper driver using modprobe. You'll also want to make sure you have your default route set up as shown previously.

PING

After ifconfig says the device is configured, you can try to ping it, which sends an ICMP echo-request to the device. If the device has been enabled, it will respond with an ICMP echo-reply.

When you ping something, always try first by using the IP address:

```
ping 192.168.0.2
```

You can stop the ping by using Ctrl+c. If the ping fails, your card is not active. If the ping responds, stop it and try again by using your hostname, both the short name and the fully qualified name.

If you don't receive replies when using the hostnames, you might want to skip to the section that discusses the host resolution after you verify that the host you're pinging does in fact return pings (systems can be configured not to respond to ICMP ping packets by firewall software).

If everything works to this point, try to ping another host on your network by IP address:

```
ping 192.168.0.3
```

If that works and you can determine a good IP address on the Internet for a system you are sure is up and running, you can ping that. If that works, your basic networking is okay, and you'll want to skip ahead to host resolution.

TRACEROUTE

If you were able to ping hosts on your local network, but are unable to determine whether you've selected a good host on the Internet, you can switch to traceroute. The traceroute utility will show you the path packets take to reach a particular destination. The nice thing about traceroute is that even if the remote host is down, you'll see the systems the packets will travel through between your system and where the network finally stops.

Again, you'll want to choose a remote system so you can see where the packets are trying to go, and you'll want to start with an IP address:

```
traceroute -n 209.127.112.153
```

If you see packets stop at your gateway, you know you have a problem with your gateway. If the packets travel beyond your gateway, the part of the network you have sway over is working, and you'll just have to wait for other administrators to work on the rest.

The traceroute utility has a number of options that are beyond the scope of this book, but can enable you to determine what might be wrong. One option you will want to use is the -n option, which tells traceroute to use the numeric designation of hosts rather than trying to resolve the names. This is just in case the problem lies in hostname resolution.

NETSTAT

The netstat utility is also a multifaceted utility. Originally, if you wanted anything from routing information to open connections to servers bound to ports, you needed to use netstat. You still need to use netstat for most of those things, but routing information can now be obtained from route.

The netstat utility is more of a "now that things are running, what's going on" kind of tool. It will show you what ports are connected to from where, and what ports are ready to accept connections. It will show you the state of connections. Many of the things it will show will probably be confusing, but many are also extraneous. Executing netstat with no options will show you the state of active network connections. By default, netstat resolves both hostnames and service names. If you don't want names resolved but want to see numbers, use the -n option.

If you want to see all bound services, not just active connections, use the -a option. Adding the -v switch to netstat with or without the -a will show you which network protocols are not supported. The -r option will show you routing, and when combined with -e or -ee will provide some slightly different parameters. This text will not cover the routing support for netstat because route already provides that information.

Running netstat -avn will give you something like the output shown in Listing 22.3.

LISTING 22.3   netstat -avn

```
Active Internet connections (servers and established)
Proto Recv-Q Send-Q Local Address           Foreign Address         State
tcp        0      0 0.0.0.0:1024            0.0.0.0:*               LISTEN
tcp        0      0 0.0.0.0:512             0.0.0.0:*               LISTEN
tcp        0      0 0.0.0.0:2049            0.0.0.0:*               LISTEN
```

LISTING 22.3 CONTINUED

```
tcp        0        0 0.0.0.0:513          0.0.0.0:*            LISTEN
tcp        0        0 0.0.0.0:674          0.0.0.0:*            LISTEN
tcp        0        0 0.0.0.0:514          0.0.0.0:*            LISTEN
tcp        0        0 0.0.0.0:515          0.0.0.0:*            LISTEN
tcp        0        0 0.0.0.0:901          0.0.0.0:*            LISTEN
tcp        0        0 0.0.0.0:37           0.0.0.0:*            LISTEN
tcp        0        0 127.0.0.1:8007       0.0.0.0:*            LISTEN
tcp        0        0 0.0.0.0:9            0.0.0.0:*            LISTEN
tcp        0        0 0.0.0.0:3306         0.0.0.0:*            LISTEN
tcp        0        0 0.0.0.0:587          0.0.0.0:*            LISTEN
tcp        0        0 0.0.0.0:13           0.0.0.0:*            LISTEN
tcp        0        0 0.0.0.0:110          0.0.0.0:*            LISTEN
tcp        0        0 0.0.0.0:79           0.0.0.0:*            LISTEN
tcp        0        0 0.0.0.0:143          0.0.0.0:*            LISTEN
tcp        0        0 0.0.0.0:111          0.0.0.0:*            LISTEN
tcp        0        0 0.0.0.0:10000        0.0.0.0:*            LISTEN
tcp        0        0 0.0.0.0:6000         0.0.0.0:*            LISTEN
tcp        0        0 0.0.0.0:8080         0.0.0.0:*            LISTEN
tcp        0        0 0.0.0.0:80           0.0.0.0:*            LISTEN
tcp        0        0 0.0.0.0:721          0.0.0.0:*            LISTEN
tcp        0        0 0.0.0.0:722          0.0.0.0:*            LISTEN
tcp        0        0 192.168.0.2:53       0.0.0.0:*            LISTEN
tcp        0        0 0.0.0.0:21           0.0.0.0:*            LISTEN
tcp        0        0 127.0.0.1:53         0.0.0.0:*            LISTEN
tcp        0        0 0.0.0.0:23           0.0.0.0:*            LISTEN
tcp        0        0 0.0.0.0:25           0.0.0.0:*            LISTEN
tcp        0        0 0.0.0.0:7100         0.0.0.0:*            LISTEN
tcp        0        0 192.168.0.2:1430     192.168.0.2:7100     ESTABLISHED
tcp        0        0 192.168.0.2:1431     192.168.0.2:7100     ESTABLISHED
tcp        0        0 192.168.0.2:1429     192.168.0.2:7100     ESTABLISHED
tcp        0        0 192.168.0.2:7100     192.168.0.2:1431     ESTABLISHED
tcp        0        0 192.168.0.2:7100     192.168.0.2:1430     ESTABLISHED
tcp        0        0 192.168.0.2:7100     192.168.0.2:1429     ESTABLISHED
udp        0        0 0.0.0.0:1024         0.0.0.0:*
udp        0        0 0.0.0.0:2049         0.0.0.0:*
udp        0        0 0.0.0.0:517          0.0.0.0:*
udp        0        0 0.0.0.0:518          0.0.0.0:*
udp        0        0 0.0.0.0:9            0.0.0.0:*
udp        0        0 0.0.0.0:13           0.0.0.0:*
udp        0        0 0.0.0.0:671          0.0.0.0:*
udp        0        0 0.0.0.0:37           0.0.0.0:*
udp        0        0 0.0.0.0:177          0.0.0.0:*
udp        0        0 192.168.0.2:53       0.0.0.0:*
udp        0        0 127.0.0.1:53         0.0.0.0:*
udp        0        0 0.0.0.0:111          0.0.0.0:*
udp        0        0 127.0.0.1:123        0.0.0.0:*
udp        0        0 0.0.0.0:123          0.0.0.0:*
Active UNIX domain sockets (servers and established)
Proto RefCnt Flags         Type     State       I-Node Path
unix  2      [ ACC ]       STREAM   LISTENING   302    /var/run/ndc
unix  2      [ ACC ]       STREAM   LISTENING   338    /var/run/.ppp_socket
unix  2      [ ACC ]       STREAM   LISTENING   575    /tmp/.X11-unix/X0
unix  11     [ ]           DGRAM                283    /dev/log
unix  2      [ ACC ]       STREAM   LISTENING   446    /dev/gpmctl
unix  2      [ ACC ]       STREAM   LISTENING   78380  /tmp/.axsc2
unix  2      [ ACC ]       STREAM   LISTENING   666    /tmp/mysql.sock
```

Listing 22.3   Continued

```
unix  2       [ ACC ]      STREAM    LISTENING    118740  /tmp/.axsc5
unix  2       [ ACC ]      STREAM    LISTENING    78364   /tmp/.axnetipc
unix  3       [ ]          STREAM    CONNECTED    129400  /tmp/.X11-unix/X0
unix  111     [ ]          STREAM    CONNECTED    129399
unix  3       [ ]          STREAM    CONNECTED    118746  /tmp/.X11-unix/X0
unix  3       [ ]          STREAM    CONNECTED    118745
unix  3       [ ]          STREAM    CONNECTED    118588  /tmp/.X11-unix/X0
unix  3       [ ]          STREAM    CONNECTED    118587
unix  3       [ ]          STREAM    CONNECTED    118468  /tmp/.X11-unix/X0
unix  3       [ ]          STREAM    CONNECTED    118467
unix  3       [ ]          STREAM    CONNECTED    118451  /tmp/.X11-unix/X0
unix  3       [ ]          STREAM    CONNECTED    118450
unix  4       [ ]          STREAM    CONNECTED    118443  /tmp/.X11-unix/X0
unix  3       [ ]          STREAM    CONNECTED    118442
unix  3       [ ]          STREAM    CONNECTED    118428  /tmp/.X11-unix/X0
unix  3       [ ]          STREAM    CONNECTED    118427
unix  3       [ ]          STREAM    CONNECTED    116711  /tmp/.X11-unix/X0
unix  3       [ ]          STREAM    CONNECTED    116710
unix  3       [ ]          STREAM    CONNECTED    116706  /tmp/.X11-unix/X0
unix  3       [ ]          STREAM    CONNECTED    116705
unix  5       [ ]          STREAM    CONNECTED    116694  /tmp/.X11-unix/X0
unix  3       [ ]          STREAM    CONNECTED    116684
unix  3       [ ]          STREAM    CONNECTED    100030  /tmp/mysql.sock
unix  3       [ ]          STREAM    CONNECTED    100028
unix  2       [ ]          DGRAM                  16481
unix  2       [ ]          DGRAM                  421
unix  2       [ ]          DGRAM                  397
unix  2       [ ]          DGRAM                  379
unix  2       [ ]          DGRAM                  375
unix  2       [ ]          DGRAM                  354
unix  2       [ ]          DGRAM                  300
unix  2       [ ]          DGRAM                  292
unix  2       [ ]          DGRAM                  286
netstat: no support for `AF IPX' on this system.
netstat: no support for `AF AX25' on this system.
netstat: no support for `AF NETROM' on this system.
```

The netstat output is clearly labeled at the top of each section. The first section shows that it consists of established connections as well as bound servers. The first column shows the protocol, tcp, udp, or raw, the second and third columns show how many bytes are in the send and receive queues. The byte column will normally be 0, but can be 1 if the state is LAST_ACK.

The next two columns show the local address and port, and the foreign address and port. For established TCP connections, you will have two lines, one in each direction. So in Listing 22.3, you have three connections to port 7100 and three from port 7100 (client to server, server to client). Asterisks show listening servers and the port and address to which they are listening. The 0.0.0.0 means all addresses.

The State column shows you the state of the connection and can be any one of the following:

- **ESTABLISHED**—An active connection is made.

- **SYN_SENT**—A new connection is being initiated with a foreign host.

- **SYN_RECVED**—A new connection is being initiated from a foreign host.
- **FIN_WAIT1**—Socket closed, connection shutting down.
- **FIN_WAIT2**—Connection closed, waiting for shutdown from remote host.
- **TIME_WAIT**—Connection closed, socket is waiting to handle packets still on the network.
- **CLOSED**—Socket is not in use.
- **CLOSE_WAIT**—Remote host is shut down, waiting for the socket to close.
- **LAST_ACK**—The remote host is shut down, socket is closed, waiting for remote acknowledgement (no acknowledgement should be possible).
- **LISTEN**—Socket is bound by a server and waiting for a connection.
- **CLOSING**—Both sockets are shut down, but packets remain to be sent.
- **UNKNOWN**—You should never see this.

Most of these states occur rapidly, so you might not see them. Others occur most of the time and are quite common.

The second part of the table shows you UNIX sockets. Sockets are connections to files. The syslog daemon opens a socket to the log files. If your system crashes, these sockets are what you see being cleaned up by fsck if you had no other files open.

Finally, netstat tells us you what protocols are not supported on this system.

fuser

If you want to find out which process is binding a port, as root you can issue the `fuser` command. The `fuser` command can work with any one of three name spaces: `tcp`, `udp`, or `file`. The name space file is the default. So if you want to see which process is binding a TCP port (this example will look at port 8080), you run the following:

```
fuser -n tcp 8080
```

Your answer might look like the following:

```
8080/tcp:            564   611   621   622   623   624   625  7892
```

Comparing the numbers 564, 611, 621, 622, 623, 624, 625, 7892, against a list of running processes (`ps ax`), you have this:

```
 564 ?        S       0:01 /usr/sbin/httpd
 611 ?        S       0:00 /usr/sbin/httpd
 621 ?        S       0:00 /usr/sbin/httpd
 622 ?        S       0:00 /usr/sbin/httpd
 623 ?        S       0:00 /usr/sbin/httpd
 624 ?        S       0:00 /usr/sbin/httpd
 625 ?        S       0:00 /usr/sbin/httpd
7892 ?        S       0:00 /usr/sbin/httpd
```

This clearly shows that the `httpd` process is binding port 8080.

NAME RESOLUTION

If any of the preceding exercises, particularly the ping or traceroute, failed to work properly with a name but worked with an IP number, name resolution has failed.

Three files interact to provide name resolution for hosts on your system. The first of these is the /etc/hosts file. This file contains a list of any local host you might want to reference by name. The file format is as follows:

```
IP_address   fully_qualified_domain_name           alias(es)
```

Your host's file should always contain an entry for localhost and the local hostname:

```
127.0.0.1          localhost
192.168.0.2                  chiriqui.pananix.com    chiriqui        www
```

The entries are separated by whitespace (either tabs or spaces). Any other IP address to system name mapping can be entered, but putting hosts not under your direct control in here can cause problems if the hostname or IP address change.

The entries can be put in by hand or using COAS on OpenLinux, Linuxconf on Red Hat, or Debian. Multiple entries of the same hostname or IP address will be ignored. If you have many entries, you might be better off running DNS.

If, after putting the correct entries into the /etc/hosts file you still cannot "ping localhost", you should look at the /etc/nsswitch.conf file. This file tells the system where it should look to resolve names. Listing 22.4 shows a default /etc/nsswitch.conf file.

LISTING 22.4   DEFAULT /etc/nsswitch.conf FILE

```
# /etc/nsswitch.conf
#
# Name Service Switch configuration file.
#

passwd:         compat
shadow:         compat
group:          compat

hosts:          files nis dns
networks:       nis files dns

ethers:         nis files
protocols:      nis files
rpc:            nis files
services:       nis files
```

The hosts line tells the system where to look to resolve hostnames. In this case, files is the /etc/hosts file. If the name resolves there, the lookup stops. If the name doesn't resolve, the system queries NIS. If you don't have NIS, this is skipped and goes on to DNS. If DNS fails to resolve the name, failure is returned to the requesting application.

With an entry for localhost in the /etc/hosts file, and ifconfig showing localhost is set up, pinging localhost should work. The same is true for your local Ethernet card or any other system on your network.

Leaving the local network, if you have a your gateway properly listed in the routing table and the gateway is forwarding to the Internet by IP address, names will be resolved using DNS.

This brings you to the last file, /etc/resolv.conf. The resolv.conf file contains two things: either a domain or a search line (but not both—they are mutually exclusive), and a list of nameservers.

In most cases, a domain name, which contains the domain name of the system, is appropriate. Any unqualified (short) name will have this domain name appended. If you want (or need) to have a name searched with different domain names appended, you'll want to use the search line instead of the domain line. The search line can contain up to six space-separated domain names.

The file also contains up to three nameserver lines, with the IP address of nameservers. Verify that the IPs are actual nameservers or the lookups will fail.

TROUBLESHOOTING

I just installed/changed Ethernet cards and now I can't get this one to run.

This is a fairly common problem, but thankfully there are several solutions. The first one you should try is to run COAS or Linuxconf and select Kernel Modules. This will probe for new hardware and allow for the module immediately and at bootup. After the module has been loaded, stop and then start the network manually:

```
/etc/rc.d/init.d/network stop
/etc/rc.d/init.d/network start
```

This should start the card. If it doesn't, you should get an error. If you don't get an error, try pinging a host on the network.

Note the Ethernet module that was loaded and make sure it is listed in /etc/modules/default. If not, add it.

On a Debian system you can try modprobe -t net * and let the system attempt to guess which driver it should load. Then note any new drivers (you might have a few that are extraneous that loaded) and add it to /etc/modules.

If the network still doesn't work, stop the network, unload the Ethernet module, and try loading it again. If you get an error, it is probably the wrong module. Try a different one. For example, a tulip module will load and activate a tulip card, and the link light on the card or hub will turn on. If, when you start the network the link light goes off, you're using the wrong module—try the old_tulip module instead. There are so many cards and so many drivers that getting them properly matched is difficult. Even LIZARD, COAS, and Linuxconf or any other automated program will be fooled from time to time. And remember, some cards are not supported. Visit the manufacturer's Web site to determine whether a Linux driver is available. You might have to compile one for your system following the manufacturer's instructions if the card is very new.

I was using my system on the network, but suddenly it doesn't seem to be able to see the other hosts.

This problem is common with 10base2 networks (coaxial wire, or cheapernet networks). Try reseating the connections, particularly the terminators. If they aren't making good contact, your network will suddenly seem to be down. When you get a chance, switch to 10baseT. Small 4-port hubs are cheap and will alleviate this problem. Additionally, the link light on the hub will help you see whether your Ethernet card is active.

I use a PCMCIA Ethernet card for network connectivity, and allthough everything seems to be working all right, during bootup I see many error messages that are network related.

The reason you are seeing these errors is because you've told the system to start networking, but you don't have an internal Ethernet card. The PCMCIA card is started later and has its own startup scripts, so you can eject and insert it at any time. The error messages are harmless, but if you want to eliminate them, just change the `ONBOOT=yes` to `ONBOOT=no` in `/etc/sysconfig/network-script/ifcfg-eth0` either manually or via COAS.

## CHAPTER 23

USING DHCP

In this chapter

BACKGROUND

This chapter is about setting up servers to provide other systems on the local network with an address when they boot. In today's networking environment, it's often a better idea to configure user workstations to obtain an address as they enter and leave the network, rather than going through the trouble of setting up every machine with a permanent IP address. You might want to do this for various reasons:

■ Networks tend to be fairly dynamic.

■ Hosts come and go.

■ Network addresses change along with service providers.

■ Your internal requirements are constantly changing.

Any number of things influence address changes on your network. Changing a handful of servers is no big task. Changing several hundred workstations, though, can be a daunting task. Then there are the laptops that are on the road during the changeover: Tracking them down can take days or even weeks.

Or perhaps you need dynamic address resolution because you have diskless clients. One common diskless client you might encounter is the HP JetDirect Print spooler. The external print spoolers can only be configured dynamically. For this, several tools are at your disposal: address resolution protocol (ARP), bootstrap protocol (BOOTP), and dynamic host configuration protocol (DHCP). In the next few sections you'll find out about each of these protocols, what they offer, and their drawbacks.

ARP

The address resolution protocol was the first protocol to handle client requests for address information. This is the oldest and least secure method of handling address resolution. It was designed to provide address resolution for diskless clients. It also provided the mechanism for booting over the network. ARP can still be used, but it has fallen out of favor. When booting a diskless client through ARP (when the ARP daemon provides the address), the job of transferring the file system from the server to the client becomes the job of tftpd, the trivial file transfer daemon—unless you are using the Linux kernel, RARP, and NFS solution. If you know anything about tftp, you'll remember that it is the one service in /etc/inetd.conf that is almost universally disabled. The tftp daemon is considered a security risk, and is extremely difficult to control. Very few sites will use it, and those that do generally do so because they are using old hardware that cannot be updated to newer protocols. tftp is not secure because it does not use authentication, and therefore must rely on other programs (such as TCP Wrappers) to provide a modicum of security. This text will not address tftpd further.

But all this doesn't mean that ARP is not usable. One of the more common tasks for ARP is to configure the new equipment that is entering the network. Several network spoolers can use ARP resolution when they enter a network. The HP JetDirect print spoolers, among others, can be configured with ARP. All you need is the hardware address of the spooler's

Ethernet card. This is in the form of six pairs of hex numbers, and is provided with the spooler's documentation. When these numbers are entered into the ARP table using `arp`, the spooler is configured.

First plug in the spooler. After it is connected to the network, you can enter the following command into your Linux system at the command line:

```
arp -s hostname hwaddress temp
```

The hostname is resolved normally; that is, a lookup is performed in `/etc/hosts` or DNS for the corresponding IP address (the IP address can be used, but it is better to use the hostname). The hardware address is then supplied. This address is in the form 00:00:FF:FF:FF:00 and will have been supplied with the spooler. The final argument, `temp`, tells ARP to put the address in the kernel's ARP cache temporarily instead of permanently. Temporary entries time out and are refreshed or replaced each time the host talks to the hosts on the network (see Listing 23.1).

LISTING 23.1   OUTPUT OF THE arp COMMAND (WITH NO OPTIONS AND WITH THE -a Option Option)

```
# arp
Address               HWtype  HWaddress          Flags Mask       Iface
bar.void.org          ether   00:00:C0:34:BF:D0  C                eth0
baz.void.org          ether   00:00:A0:01:02:3D  C                eth0

# arp -a
bar.void.org (192.168.0.3) at 00:00:C0:34:BF:D0 [ether] on eth0
baz.void.org (192.168.0.2) at 00:00:A0:01:02:3D [ether] on eth0
```

Note that the two outputs are different, but because you're only looking at Ethernet interfaces, the same information is presented. As you ping or otherwise access other hosts from your system, the system (in this case the host `foo.void.org`) learns the accessed machine's hostname/hardware address combination and uses them for communication. Because these other hosts are subject to being down, the entries in the ARP cache time out; however, they are refreshed with each communication. You'll only have ARP entries for hosts on your local network.

Note   ARP plays a much greater role in network communications, but that's the subject of a networking text.

BOOTP

Following ARP, BOOTP offers a slightly more advanced way to handle requests for address resolution from clients. Sun Microsystems machines can use BOOTP to find out who they are. To implement BOOTP, you need to run the BOOTP daemon, bootpd. The configuration file for this daemon is found in `/etc`, and is called `bootptab`. The `/etc/bootptab` is highly configurable and offers more choices (as well as better security) than ARP. Also, with

BOOTP, gateway servers can be set up so that gateways don't become obstacles to address resolution, as is the case with ARP.

Linux also allows a native client-side implementation of BOOTP from within the kernel—as it does with ARP—that allows the use of NFS instead of tftp for mounting a filesystem. The advantage of using NFS over tftp is security.

DHCP

DHCP is a client/server service in the true form of the term. It requires a server, which is the DHCP daemon (dhcpd), to run from one or more hosts on the network that provide addresses to systems as they enter and leave the network. It also requires a DHCP client daemon (dhcpcd), running on machines that are requesting an IP address. Be aware that although you might have several servers running dhcpd, they cannot be offering the same or an overlapping range of addresses; the address range offering must be unique to each DHCP server.

The DHCP daemon, as implemented by Linux, is capable of handling both requests for BOOTP and DHCP configuration. Use of the new DHCP server is recommended in lieu of bootpd. Given its flexibility, there is little reason to run bootpd, and in fact, it is not included in the Caldera distribution, and might be dropped from the Red Hat distribution. Debian will probably continue to offer it as long as it is supported.

> **Note**
>
> A couple of DHCP client utilities are available. These include the standard DHCP client daemon (dhcpcd), dhclient, and dhcpxd. You might want to try the others, particularly if you have a problem getting an address from the DHCP server.

The configuration file for dhcpd is /etc/dhcpd.conf. This file is referred to as the configuration file for dhcpd for the remainder of the chapter. As of the writing of this chapter, several versions of dhcpd are available. They are all similar in many regards. The differences that are present do not matter for the purposes of this chapter, but those of you who are making extensive use of DHCP probably want to read the documentation pertaining to the DHCP server that you are running.

When you have the DHCP server running, it, of course, doles out addresses as established in its configuration file. It records the addresses that are assigned in a file called dhcpd.leases. This file is normally found in /var/dhcpd, but it can be configured to appear almost anywhere on the system. This file contains data on all the leased addresses so that DHCP doesn't duplicate addresses (see Listing 23.9 and the discussion in the "New DHCP Clients" section that follows for details). As leases are provided or renewed, entries are made in the file. When the file grows to a predetermined size (based on the server's configuration), a copy is made as dhcpd.leases~, and a new dhcpd.leases file is created with the expired entries removed. This copy is made before the alteration is done so that if the server crashes during the process, it has all the information that is necessary for it to start up again.

The DHCP server isn't difficult to set up, and it affords administrators the ability to provide dynamic address resolution for hosts on the network. As with many services, more than one DHCP daemon can be run on a network, but the range of addresses that each offers cannot overlap with another DHCP server. So a network with up to 30 hosts can be subnetted to accommodate up to 62 hosts, and two DHCP servers can each serve one half of the network, in case one server goes down. For many networks that don't have hosts entering and leaving often, this backup might not be necessary. If addresses are provided in a network environment for a week or longer at a time, an outage of several hours might not matter. On the other hand, networks that require a short renewal time because hosts are entering and leaving the network often (for example, in a production environment that works on hosts and performs operations for fewer than 30 minutes at a time, and then unplugs and connects the next one), and where an hour's down time might adversely affect operations, a backup might be necessary.

PART

IV

CH

23

Although a simple configuration for DHCP is easy to do, many complex setups can also be handled by DHCP. Because the range of situations is very large in scope, this text restricts itself to more mundane configurations and leaves it to administrators with more complex needs to research the man pages and documentation pertaining to the particular DHCP server that they have installed.

CONFIGURING DHCPD

The dhcpd.conf file can be considered to be composed of several different sections. These sections might apply to all the sections that follow them, or just to the section in question. Often this is obvious. The global parameters section, of course, applies globally (although global parameters can be overridden within a section, if necessary). Other sections are more difficult to figure out. The trick comes in understanding that this file is constructed in a fashion similar to a C program. That is, it makes extensive use of braces ({}) to enclose parameters. These braces can be nested so that subsections are enclosed within a section. The way these braces are paired is important to the section as a whole. It is important to understand that sets of braces cannot overlap—one set must be contained completely within another.

Throughout the configuration file, whitespace—in the form of new lines, or tabs—can be used for readability. The DHCPD parser ignores these. Whitespace in the form of spaces must separate parameter names, but comma-separated lists do not require spaces (although the practice is common for ease of reading).

Unlike most services, when a change is made to dhcpd.conf, the DHCP daemon must be stopped and restarted for the changes to take effect. Sending a SIGHUP to the server might not be enough for it to re-read the file. A simple call to `/etc/rc.d/init.d/dhcpd stop` and a corresponding call with the start argument is sufficient.

Within the dhcpd.conf file, lines within sections might begin with the word option, or they might just begin with a declaration, followed by its arguments. Options describe various services or network configurations for clients. Declarations provide specific information about how the DHCP server works or what it provides. This distinction will become clearer as you see examples of declarations and options.

GLOBAL PARAMETERS

The parameters that are common to all the hosts that are to be served are included within this section. This section usually contains most of the options statements for the network. Some 62 total options exist; however, a few of them are not specified in the configuration file, even though they are used by the DHCP server. That leaves more than 48 configurable options, not counting vendor-specific extensions. For most, the order does not matter—but for a few it does. For example, `netmask` must come before `routers`.

The options are normally given in the configuration file by name, but the configuration numbers can also be used, if they are known. Options that specify IP addresses might also specify hostnames, if those hostnames resolve to one and only one IP address. For strings, the string data must be quoted with double quotes (see Listing 23.2).

LISTING 23.2   SAMPLE GLOBAL PARAMETERS FOR `dhcpd.conf` FILE

```
server-identifier foo.void.org;
option domain-name "void"void.org"org";
option domain-name-servers foo.void.org;
option subnet-mask 255.255.255.0;
option broadcast-address 192.168.10.255;
option routers 192.168.10.90;
option ntp-servers foo.void.org, sol.void.org;
default-lease-time 604800;
max-lease-time 2419200;
```

Looking at Listing 23.2, the first global parameter specifies the DHCP server. The name must resolve to one and only one IP address, as was mentioned earlier. The first option specifies the domain name, and because this is a string value, it requires double quotes. Most of the options are self-explanatory. Options and declarations that accept more than one value have the values listed in order of priority from highest to lowest.

The semicolons that terminate each option or declaration are required. Remember, a new line and tabs can be used to make the configuration file more readable, so the DHCP parser needs to know where a line ends.

SUBNET STATEMENT

Every DHCP server must have a subnet statement. This statement tells the server which subnet it is serving. Inside is the range of addresses that are available, as are any options or declarations that are different from the global section. The subnet statement displays all the options and declarations that pertain to it in braces (see Listing 23.3).

LISTING 23.3   A SAMPLE SUBNET STATEMENT

```
subnet 192.168.10.0 netmask 255.255.255.0 {
  range 192.168.10.65 192.168.10.91;
  range 192.168.10.191 192.168.10.250;
  range 192.168.0.253;
```

LISTING 23.3   CONTINUED

```
    option netbios-name-servers 192.168.10.30;
    default-lease-time 1209600;
}
```

In Listing 23.3, the subnet statement specifies the network address and netmask of the net-work with which you are working. Then, in braces, options and declarations define param-eters that are specific to this subnet. Global options apply, except where they are explicitly overridden. For example, the `default-lease-time` that is shown here overrides the `default-lease-time` that is given in the global section. The time is given in seconds; therefore, the time 1,209,600 is equal to two weeks.

One of the most important declarations within the subnet statement is the range declara-tion. This tells the DHCP server the range of addresses that are in the pool, ready to be assigned to clients. The numbers are inclusive, so this DHCP server can assign the numbers ending 65–91, 191 up to and including 250, and 253.

The option for `netbios-name-server` is the address that corresponds to the Microsoft NT WINS server, indicating that the clients that are being served include Microsoft Windows desktops.

SHARED NETWORK STATEMENT

A shared network statement is used to group two or more subnets. If each department is assigned a subnet of 30 hosts, but a department grows too large and requires two subnets, these two subnets might be grouped together and served by the same DHCP server (see Listing 23.4).

LISTING 23.4   A SAMPLE SHARED NETWORK STATEMENT

```
shared-network MARKET-NET {
    option domain-name  market.void.org ;
    option routers 192.168.1.1;
    subnet 192.168.1.0 netmask 255.255.255.224 {
        range 192.168.1.3 192.168.1.30;

        option routers 192.168.1.2
    }
    subnet 192.168.1.32 netmask 255.255.255.224 {
        range 192.168.1.35 192.168.1.62;
        option routers 192.168.1.33;
    }
}
```

In Listing 23.4, the shared network has its own domain name below `void.org` of `market.void.org`. This domain name only applies to the two subnets that are grouped within the shared network statement. Likewise, the router `192.168.1.1` is probably the gateway to the Internet, or at least to anything beyond the two subnets here.

Each subnet has a range declaration as required, and also a router which looks as though it provides connectivity between the two subnets (that is, `192.168.1.2` and `192.168.1.33` are two interfaces in the same host).

GROUP STATEMENT

Sometimes it becomes necessary to group hosts together for some reason. Perhaps the hosts group shares something in common (for instance, maybe the same server holds the filesystem for nfs root mounting). Each group statement contains group-specific declarations and options, plus two or more other statements. These other statements are typically host statements that identify specific hosts and contain host-specific parameters (see Listing 23.5).

LISTING 23.5   SAMPLE GROUP STATEMENT

```
group {
    filename   zImage.nfs.boot ;
    next-server foo.void.org;
        host bar {hardware ethernet 00:00:3c:b2:08:15; }
        host baz {hardware ethernet 00:00:4f:ef:12:a5; }
}
```

In Listing 26.5 you can see that the group statement requires no parameters—because groups are only meant for the DHCP server internally, no reference outside the group statement is ever needed. You can have as many group statements as you want. You can have other groups that use other filename declarations or next-server declarations, and so on. The filename declaration tells the DHCP server to point to the hosts that are listed below to the file that is named in quotes for booting. The next-server tells the DHCP client where to look for the root filesystem. Finally, the host, which takes the hostname as an argument, includes the required declarations for the host. These are the hardware type (Ethernet) and the hardware address.

To get the hardware address from a NIC, you can boot from a modular kernel image such as the one that is provided with Linux. Look for a line similar to the following:

```
Jan 15 18:18:00 foo kernel: eth0: Digital DC21041 Tulip at 0xb800,
 21041 mode, 00 00 c0 83 c0 d0, IRQ 10
```

The part of the line that reads `00 00 c0 83 c0 d0` is the hardware address for the NIC. All that's required is that this set of six octets (six bytes) have colons substituted for the spaces. (If the host is already running Linux, you can also get this information from `ifconfig -a`— it is listed as the `HWAddr` on the first line and is colon separated rather than space separated.)

Because setup is more detailed—that is, you must also have the NIC address—these statements are not used except where they are required. If a NIC is changed in any of these hosts, you must remember to change the hardware address in the configuration file.

Although group statements are normally used for hosts, as in the previous example, the group statement can be used to group nearly anything: shared networks, subnets, even other groups. Its use is determined by your specific requirements.

CONFIGURING DHCPD FOR BOOTP

The final configuration step involves configuring hosts that make BOOTP queries rather than DHCP queries. Just as with the preceding host declaration in the group statement, you'll need to know the hardware address of the NIC that is requesting configuration information. In fact, the declaration for BOOTP hosts is almost identical to the host declaration in the previous group statement (compare Listing 23.5 to Listing 23.6).

PART

IV

CH

23

| LISTING 23.6   SAMPLE BOOTP ENTRY |

```
host tazfoo {
  hardware ethernet 08:00:09:ed:8e:0d;
  fixed-address tazfoo.void.org;
}
```

In Listing 23.6, the host statement is the same as the preceding host statement for groups, but it requires a resolvable hostname or IP address. If a hostname is used, it must resolve to one and only one IP address.

One major difference between BOOTP and DHCP is that DHCP has lease times. When a BOOTP client receives an address, that address is assumed by default to have a duration of infinity. That is, the BOOTP host will use that address for as long as it is running. Two ways to avoid this problem will be discussed later in the chapter.

Two methods can be used to prevent BOOTP clients from retaining their addresses until the next shutdown. The availability of these methods depends on the DHCP server you are using. Check the documentation. The first method is with a declaration that might be used in the global section: `dynamic-bootp-lease-length time_in_seconds`. This declaration forces BOOTP hosts to re-acquire their addresses during the period that is specified in this declaration. The second method is with the following declaration: `dynamic-bootp-lease-cutoff date`. The date is in the following form:

`W YYYY/MM/DD HH:MM:SS`

It can be read as follows: `W` is the day of the week from 0–6 (Sunday to Saturday); the `YYYY/MM/DD` and `HH:MM:SS` are self-explanatory as to their parameters. Note, however, that the time expressed is interpreted as Greenwich Mean Time (GMT), also referred to as Universal Coordinated Time (UTC)—not local time. This declaration might appear as part of the global section or as a declaration under individual host statements.

Despite the use of these parameters, BOOTP clients do not renew their leases. The clients require a reboot or a shutdown and restart of their networking subsystems to regain the lease. The DHCP server just refuses to recognize the lease. Some clients might stop using the lease, but you should not depend on this.

DNS AND DHCP

Throughout the text, examples using DNS or other types of resolution have been used for many parameters. However, for pure DHCP clients, DNS resolution becomes a problem.

Because the addresses that can be given to any one client cannot be foreseen, they cannot be entered into the DNS table. Several solutions to this problem are being worked on. Some commercial DNS packages that can merge information from the dhcp.leases file into the database are available. But the DNS package that is currently offered in Linux and the DHCP server do not presently talk to each other.

The solution for the moment, at least with the packages that are provided, is to use the DHCP server to assign specific addresses. The DHCP server can provide static addresses by including host statements within subnets. These host statements are identical to those that are used in the host statements in the BOOTP example. This method is a trade-off between configuring hosts individually and allowing full, dynamic, address assignment. It permits the use of DHCP for systems that don't speak BOOTP, while permitting the micro-management of IP addresses a la BOOTP. Then, when address changes need to take place, they can be done once in the DNS files; as leases expire (or the hosts are restarted), the addresses update. This method is often used with several DSL and cable-modem providers to provide a static address without having to configure it at the client site. You will need to have a DNS entry for each host listed in the dhcpd.conf file or you will get error messages for each dhcpd.conf entry that doesn't have a corresponding DNS entry.

You can also provide each host with its hostname by specifying get-lease-hostnames true within the global section or the range statement. If you use get-lease-hostnames true;, you must have a DNS entry for each IP within the range statement, or you will get many errors. Caldera's DHCP client takes advantage of the get-lease-hostnames statement if it can.

CONFIGURING DHCP CLIENTS

The dhcpcd daemon reconfigures any interface that it is called against. Ensure that dhcpcd is configured to run against only those interfaces you want a dynamic address given to.

Looking in /etc/sysconfig/network-scripts, the file that is of interest to you is ifcfg-eth0 (or ifcfg-tr#, if your system is so configured). Within this file is a parameter called IPADDR. This parameter is one of the IP address or DYNAMIC. Naturally, the dhcpcd package must be installed for DHCPC to work.

After dhcpcd is started, Caldera's dhcpcd scripts write the information about the lease IP and related data to /var/run/dhcpcd-eth0 (or substituting eth1, tr0, or tr1, and so forth, for eth0). This information will be used by dhcpcd in future messages to the server to try to obtain the same IP address each time the system is restarted on the network. New /etc/resolv.conf and /etc/nis.conf files (with .dhcp extensions) are created and used in lieu of the original files of the same name. Debian and Red Hat do similar things to save the state of the system, though it can be saved in /var/state/dhcpcd or /etc/dhcpc, depending on the particular version of the dhcpcd server included and the scripts in the package. These scripts can be easily tailored, so if you prefer putting them in other locations or using names such as hostinfo-eth0, the changes can be made at any time.

The DHCP client, after obtaining a lease, will count down to the end of the lease. When it hits 50% of the time, it will attempt to release the IP address. If successful, the counter resets. If unsuccessful, the DHCP client will continue with business as usual until reaching the 75% time mark. Again it will try to release. If unsuccessful, it will try one last time at the 87.5% mark. If unsuccessful, it will then start looking for another DHCP server to lease an IP from. If no DHCP server can be found, the DHCP client will keep trying until the lease time expires. At that time, if no DHCP server has been found, the DHCP client will release the IP address and the system will drop off the network.

DHCP MESSAGES AND OVERVIEW OF THE DHCP PROCESS

The following paragraphs attempt to describe the process that DHCP clients and servers go through when negotiating DHCP leases. This is a summary of RFC 2131, which is authoritative and is subject to becoming obsolete if a new RFC that pertains to DHCP is released in the future.

NEW DHCP CLIENTS

When a new DHCP client enters a network, it sends out a DHCPDISCOVER message. This broadcast message is an attempt to locate DHCP servers on the subnet, or to locate a DHCP relay that is connected to the subnet.

All DHCP servers respond to DHCPDISCOVER messages with DHCPOFFER. The DHCP client looks at the DHCPOFFER messages in the order in which they arrive. The first response is examined. The client has two options: Send a DHCPREQUEST message or send a DHCPDECLINE message.

If a client believes that a parameter it received in a DHCPOFFER is incorrect (the network address is on the wrong subnet, for example), it sends a DHCPDECLINE and continues to the next DHCPOFFER. If all DHCPOFFERs are declined, it rebroadcasts a DHCPDISCOVER message.

After a client is satisfied with a DHCPOFFER, it sends a DHCPREQUEST to the appropriate server (implicitly declining offers from all other servers), requesting that the DHCPOFFER be accepted by the server.

When the DHCP server receives the DHCPREQUEST, it has two options. The server can send a DHCPACK with configuration parameters and commit this information to the dhcpd.leases database, or it can send a DHCPNAK, indicating the reason for refusal (address already in use, and so on).

A DHCPNAK back to a client results in the client restarting the process from DHCPDISCOVER. A DHCPACK that is received by the client results in the client committing the configuration and communicating on the network through its newly received address.

Listing 26.7 shows what the DHCP server commits to its dhcpd.leases file after the client sends a DHCPOFFER that is accepted by the server. This entry takes place just prior to the DHCPACK message being sent to the client.

LISTING 26.7   SAMPLE dhcpd.leases ENTRY

```
lease 192.168.10.224 {
        starts 0 1999/01/17 19:34:02;
        ends 0 1999/01/24 19:34:02;
        hardware ethernet 00:00:c0:83:c0:d0;
        uid 01:00:00:c0:83:c0:d0;
        client-hostname ÒTMTÓ"TMT";
}
```

Based on previous text, this file is simple to read. The lease statement line contains the IP address as a parameter. The declarations inside the statement contain detailed information about the lease. The start time (this date and time are read the same as the dynamic-lease-bootp-cutoff date) indicates that the lease started (or was renewed) on Sunday, 17 Jan 1999, at 19:34:02 GMT. The lease ends on Sunday, 24 Jan 1999, at 19:34:02 GMT. The hardware address is self-explanatory. The uid is a string that the client sent and that it will use to identify itself in future communications (DHCPREQUEST or DHCPRELEASE messages). Clients are now supposed to send their hardware addresses preceded by a number. Some older clients do not do this, instead sending an arbitrary string. The final declaration is optional and might not be sent by all DHCP clients. Some clients send a client-host declaration, and others send a hostname declaration. If a declaration is sent, it is duly recorded.

CONTINUING LEASES

Three things might occur during the course of a lease: A client might remain connected to the network, the client might be gracefully shut down, or the client might crash. Each of these carries with it different consequences. The two disconnection scenarios, a graceful shutdown and a crash, might each also carry with them two possibilities when the client reconnects.

In the case of a graceful shutdown, many clients send a DHCPRELEASE message to the DHCP server. This is not required, so it is not universally employed. If such a message is sent, the IP address is immediately returned to the pool. If the client does not send this message, the results are the same as a crash—the lease remains until expiration, until it is removed by the server, or until it is released by the same client.

Some clients record the information that they receive in the DHCPACK from the server and make use of this information again as if they never left the network. In the case of a graceful shutdown (regardless of whether a DHCPRELEASE message was sent), or in a crash with a client that remembers the information from the previous connection, things work as they do with a client that remains connected.

For clients that remain connected, at a predetermined time in the lease (generally the halfway point), the client will attempt to renegotiate the lease with the server from which it obtained the lease. If that fails, it uses the time to the end of the lease to recompute a value using the same algorithm to try again. This process continues until the lease expires, at which time the client must release the address and start the discovery process over again.

But for those clients that either remain on the network or remember previous information, the process explained previously for new clients is short-circuited. In this case, clients skip the discovery process and begin with the DHCPREQUEST message. If the client has moved to another subnet, it receives a DHCPNAK from the server and starts over with the discovery process. Otherwise, the server uses the uid information that it receives in the DHCPREQUEST message, along with the IP address that the client is requesting to verify that this client was the last one to have the requested address. If so, the lease might be released to that client through a DHCPACK.

TROUBLESHOOTING

I configured the DHCP server (/etc/dhcpd.conf), and told the system to start it, but it doesn't start. Any ideas on what to do now?

The most likely problem is an error (typo or other error) in your /etc/dhcpd.conf file. During bootup, error messages are suppressed, so you won't see them. What you need to do is start dhcpd from a command line. The error message will tell you where the DHCP server software (dhcpd) thinks the problem is. But remember, if you forgot a trailing semicolon, the error will show up in the next line. Also, you must have a subnet statement (even if the body is completely blank) for each interface's subnet.

I have DHCPD running, and most of my systems can get an IP address from the server, but a few cannot (those on the other side of the firewall).

If you are running a DHCP server, remember that it can only serve addresses to the local subnet unless you have a dhcrelay running on your gateway and have properly configured your DHCP server to configure that subnet. These details are beyond the scope of this chapter, but the documentation explains this setup adequately.

I am running a Microsoft's DHCP server and I can't get an address from it.

Unfortunately, Microsoft's DHCP server implementation isn't compliant with the RFCs, and dhcpcd is sensitive to this. Try getting and using either dhclient or dhcpxd, either of which will overlook Microsoft's shortcomings.

Our network has expanded to more than 250 hosts, so we've added another network. I want the DHCP server to provide addresses for that network as well. Can I do this?

Yes. You're looking for the shared-network parameter, and the dhcpd.conf(5) man page has that information. Try the following for more information:

```
man 5 dhcpd.conf
```

I have some SUN SparcStations that are older models and don't understand DHCP, only BOOTP. However, I don't want to assign them static addresses.

You're looking for the dynamic-bootp option used in the range statement. Check the man page given above for more information of its usage.

I'm running a network of Windows 95 systems and a router that uses proxy ARP. The Win95 systems can't find the router.

In this situation, you'll want to use the use-lease-addr-for-default-route, which forces Win95 to ARP for all IP addresses. This should fix the problem.

## CHAPTER 24

CONNECTING TO AN ISP

In this chapter

ISP CONNECTIONS

With the ever-increasing popularity of the Internet, the Internet service provider (ISP) is an area that is evolving quickly. Connecting to the Internet has become quite commonplace for the home user. The pervasiveness of the Internet has made a connection to it basically a necessity, even for people who are somewhat new to personal computing. A Linux system can be used as a personal workstation connected to the Internet or, perhaps more often, used as a gateway connection for a small to medium-sized local area network. See Chapter 35, "IP Masquerading," for more details on how a Linux system can masquerade for an entire local area network.

Connecting to an ISP can take several different forms. In the not too distant past, direct connections were only available to educational institutions or large corporations. However, much has evolved over the past several years. In fact, no longer do individual users and small businesses have to rely only on dial-up connections; many direct connections are now available—and very affordable. Still, dial-up connections remain the most common method for individuals and small businesses to connect to the Internet. However, with the many dedicated connection options now available at a very affordable cost, look for a dramatic shift to more and more dedicated connections over the next few years. Some of the most common methods for connecting to an ISP are listed in Table 24.1.

TABLE 24.1   COMMON METHODS OF CONNECTING TO THE INTERNET

	Hardware Method	Type	Provider	Requirements
ISP	Local or Analog Phone Line	Modem-PPP	Dial-up	National
Frame-relay card	CSU/DSU-Frame Relay	Local Phone Company	Separate digital phone	Direct connection
Local Phone	ISDN	Direct	Company	ISDN modem
Local Phone	Special Modem DSL	Direct	Company	Analog phone line
Cable	Local Cable Cable modem	Modem	Direct	TV provider
Dial-up ISP	Satellite dish Modem-PC	Direct Dish	Satellite	Analog phone line

Note

A *direct connection* to your ISP is one that is constantly attached. In other words, the need to dial an access number is not required.

The methods for connecting to the Internet go well beyond those that are listed in Table 24.1. However, this gives you a good idea of what is available at the low end, that is, reasonable *bandwidth* (connection speed) and low-cost alternatives. The connection costs for the options that are listed here range from $0.00 to approximately $200.00 a month. You are now probably asking yourself, was that a typo or did he really mean *zero*? Only time can tell if this will last, but as of this writing there were several Internet services offering access free.

The only catch that I've seen is that you have to tolerate some advertising; advertising is what enables these ISPs to offer their services to individuals free. Some offer email only; others email and Web access.

As was mentioned previously, the most common method for connecting to an ISP is through a dial-up connection using PPP. However, with the cost of direct connections decreasing, the feasibility of switching to a non–dial-up method of connecting to the Internet is becoming much more within the realm of possibility for anyone, not just the Fortune (or fortunate) 500 corporations. Following is a closer look at what it takes to get a dial-up PPP connection going, as well as a look at the requirements for making a direct connection to the Internet.

> **Tip**
>
> If you'd rather not understand the underlying concepts of how PPP works and what it takes to get a PPP connection established, skip to the later section titled "Using ksaferppp."

DIAL-UP CONNECTIONS WITH PPP

The most common method of connecting to the Internet, by far, is through a dial-up modem connection using the Point-to-Point Protocol. This is true for any operating system; PPP is the de facto standard for dial-up connections. Setting up PPP on Linux is slightly more involved than on some other operating systems, but when you understand the basics, it's really quite easy to configure. Also, an understanding of PPP setup at the level of configuration files gives you much more insight into how it works. After a connection is established, you are, for all intents and purposes, a node on the Internet. All other applications that are dependent upon an Internet connection, such as Web browsers, are then operational.

> **Caution**
>
> Be aware that after a connection to the Internet is established, you can not only access anything on the Internet, but others can see your machine as well. Take the necessary precautions to safeguard your system.

GETTING STARTED WITH PPP

PPP (Point-to-Point Protocol) is simply a means of establishing a network connection that allows normal IP (Internet Protocol) traffic. It actually supports many different protocols, but for the purposes of this book, you'll just look at it in the context of establishing an Internet connection using IP Control Protocol (IPCP). PPP connections in Linux are established using the Point-to-Point Protocol daemon, pppd. It consists of the following three components:

- **Data link layer**—Provides a method for encapsulating datagrams (packets) over serial links.
- **LCP (Link Control Protocol)**—Provides link control information over a serial link.
- **NCP (Network Control Protocol)**—Provides a method for establishing and configuring different network-layer protocols.

PPP SETUP STEPS

The setup steps for PPP are quite simple. The things that complicate the setup of PPP are usually the modem itself and the information required from your ISP. If you've ever worked with a modem before, you know that when they work they're great, but when they don't they can be most difficult to debug. Often it's just a matter of sending the appropriate setup string to the modem. If all goes well, you can skip the last step.

Following are the steps to take in the setup:

1. Gather prerequisite information.
2. Configure the chat script.
3. Configure the PPP options file.
4. Configure authentication files.
5. Configure other required network components.
6. Run /usr/sbin/pppd.
7. Troubleshoot the connection.

GATHERING PREREQUISITE INFORMATION

The most important prerequisite is to gather information about your Internet service provider. Having this information handy before you begin any configurations can save you much time and frustration. The pieces of information you need from your ISP are as follows:

- The local phone number to dial
- How your ISP assigns IP addresses (dynamic or static)
- The Name Server IP address (DNS)
- The authentication method used (manual, PAP, CHAP)

The most difficult item to identify is the authentication method that is used; this is because many Internet service providers are accustomed to Windows users, and the software that they provide handles the authentication method transparently. Don't be surprised if the person you talk to at your ISP doesn't know what authentication method is used, especially if you're dealing with a large ISP that has a big customer service staff. The good news, though, is that many of these large ISPs document this kind of information on their Web site, and some even have the scripts and configuration files for Linux. The different authentication methods are listed in Table 24.2.

TABLE 24.2 PPP AUTHENTICATION METHODS

Authentication Method	Description
Manual	This method is just logging on to a system where a user ID and password are required. The trick here is building a script of expected strings and associated responses.

TABLE 24.2 CONTINUED	
Authentication Method	**Description**
PAP	This stands for *Password Authentication Protocol.* Although it is a better method of password security than manual authentication is, it is still vulnerable to the same kind of attacks that plague any reusable password system.
CHAP	This stands for *Challenge Handshake Authentication Protocol.* This is the most sophisticated, and the most secure, method of authenticating PPP users. It does not use reusable passwords and it repeatedly reauthenticates PPP users.

Aside from the information gathered from your ISP, it's a good idea to double-check the configuration of your system. Support for PPP is built into Linux by default. However, if you've rebuilt your kernel or made other system adjustments, it's a good idea to double check that the module for PPP is loaded. You might have to manually modify the module list to have modules load automatically. See Chapter 19, "Kernel Modules," for further details on how this is done. Examining the loaded module list can be done as follows:

```
# lsmod
Module:                 #pages:  Used by:
bsd_comp                  4244   0  (unused)
ppp_deflate              41036   0  (unused)
ppp_async                 7500   0  (unused)
ppp_generic              11596   0  [bsd_comp ppp_deflate ppp_async]
```

With the new 2.4.x kernels, things changed a little. Under 2.2.x, you only had a ppp module to contend with. Now, you have a few others. The minimum required module for PPP connections is ppp_generic. However, unless you are doing PPP over Ethernet (PPPOE), you'll need at least one more. If you are using ISDN or another connection with a synchronous modem, you'll need ppp_synctty. If you are using an analog modem, you'll need to load ppp_async. If you're not sure, you can load both and then rmmod the one that's not used after the connection is established. You might also want to load ppp_deflate and bsd_comp. These two modules attempt to perform compression if the other end provides it. This provides you some speed improvement, particularly for large downloads.

CONFIGURING THE CHAT SCRIPT

The *chat script* is an automated method of talking with the modem. It is used to establish the connection with your ISP, in conjunction with your PPP settings. The chat script can be placed anywhere on the system, but it is recommended that you place it with the other PPP files in the /etc/ppp directory. Each line of the chat script is a simple combination of expected strings and strings to send, although there are a few exceptions. A sample chat script follows:

```
ABORT    BUSY
" "      ATDT5551386
CONNECT  " "
```

Each line of the chat script represents an expect/send combination (except the pppd modifiers such as ABORT, TIMEOUT). Each pair of strings in the chat script must be separated by one or more spaces or tabs. It's a good idea to use white space in such a manner that the items line up in two columns.

> **Note**
>
> Enclose all strings that contain spaces in quotes to ensure the correct parsing of what is an expected string and what is a string to be sent to the modem. For example, to send the string AT &S1 &C1 to the modem, it must be enclosed in quotes.

The expected string is placed in the left column and the string to be sent is placed in the right column. The first line of the preceding chat script is an exception. The string ABORT is not expected. It is used to identify cases in which the script is to be aborted. In this case, if the modem returns the string BUSY, the chat script aborts. This allows the script to terminate without waiting indefinitely for a string that might never come.

Line two of the script just sends a dial string to the modem without waiting because there is no expected string. The third line causes the script to pause until the string CONNECT is received from the modem, and then continues with any remaining portion of the script; in this case, pppd completes the PPP connection. A more involved chat script might look similar to the following:

```
ABORT       BUSY
ABORT       "NO CARRIER"
ABORT       "NO DIALTONE"
ABORT VOICE
ABORT "NO ANSWER"
" "         ATZ
OK          "AT S0=0"
OK          ATDT5551234
CONNECT     " "
```

See the online man page for chat for further details and options.

CONFIGURING THE PPP OPTIONS FILE

The options for pppd are stored in the /etc/ppp/options file. When pppd runs, it looks in this file for the runtime parameters, including the method by which it interacts with the modem. The options that are used most frequently with pppd are listed in Table 24.3.

TABLE 24.3   LIST OF FREQUENTLY USED OPTIONS WITH PPPD

Option	Description
tty device	Specifies which tty device the modem is connected to. The full pathname to the device that is used is typically specified. For example, the first COM port is /dev/ttyS0.
modem speed	Specifies the baud rate that is to be used.
asyncmap <map>	Sets the asynchronous character map. This map specifies which control characters cannot be successfully received over the serial line.
auth	Requires the peer to authenticate itself before allowing network packets to be sent or received. A noauth performs the opposite function.
call <name>	This parameter reads options from the file /etc/ppp/peers/<name>.

TABLE 24.3   CONTINUED

Option	Description
connect <*script*>	This parameter specifies how a connection is made via the serial port. This is typically a chat script called by the chat command.
crtscts	Sets the flow control on the serial port to use hardware handshaking (RTS/CTS).
cdtrcts	A nonstandard flow control for serial ports needed for some modems. Precludes use of DTR (data terminal ready) as a modem control line.
defaultroute	Sets the default route to the PPP interface. The route is removed when the connection is dropped.
debug	Enables debug facilities. This tells pppd to send all control packets to syslog in a human-readable form.
demand	Initiates a link "on demand." This option implies persist—that is, pppd will not exit after disconnection, but will wait for another demand and (try to) connect again.
disconnect <*script*>	Runs a script or executable after the connection has been terminated. For example, a script can be run to reset the modem after the connection is dropped.
escape *xx, yy...*	Specifies a list of characters that are to be escaped when transmitted. The list is specified as a set of hex numbers separated by commas.
file <*f*>	Reads options from the file specified here. The default file is /etc/ppp/options.
holdoff <*n*>	After terminating a link, waits *n* seconds before reinitiating the link. Only used with persist or demand.
idle <*n*>	If the link is idle (no traffic sent or received) for *n* seconds, terminates the link.
local_ip:remote_ip	The actual IPs for local_ip and remote_ip are replaced with IP addresses. This is used when static IPs are assigned or when using the demand option. In some cases, only one of the arguments will be present, but the colon must be included either before or after the lone IP as appropriate.
lock	Specifies that pppd is to create a lock file when initiated to ensure exclusive access to the serial device.
mru	Sets the maximum receive unit (MRU) in bytes. The default value is 1500. A value of 296 is recommended for slow links.
mtu	Sets the maximum transmit unit (MTU) in bytes. The maximum value is typically set by the peer with the MRU setting, but can be controlled from the transmit end as well.
netmask <*netmask*>	Sets the interface netmask in decimal-dotted notation, for example, 255.255.255.0.
noipdefault	Used for dynamic IP allocations, usually with defaultroute.
passive	Sets pppd to wait passively for a valid LCP packet response. By default, if no valid LCP packet is returned on initial request, pppd just exits.

PART

IV

CH

24

TABLE 24.3 CONTINUED

Option	Description
persist	Does not exit after connection termination, but tries to reestablish the link. Designed to provide a continuous connection.
silent	Sets pppd to not transmit any LCP packets until a valid LCP packet is received.

The preceding options are only a few of the many options available for pppd. For the complete list of options, see the man page for pppd. An example of a working /etc/ppp/options file follows:

```
connect "/usr/sbin/chat -f /etc/ppp/chat-script"
/dev/modem 38400
crtscts
defaultroute
noipdefault
```

In the preceding options file, the first two lines are the most important. The first line indicates how pppd is to access the modem line. In this example, a chat script is called through the chat utility, the script discussed in the preceding section. The second line defines what device to use. In this example, the device /dev/modem is used, but it might just as easily have been /dev/ttyS0 or /dev/ttyS1, depending on which serial port the modem is connected to.

Note

You must either use the actual device name in the /etc/ppp/options file or create a symbolic link to it and use the symbolic link name. A symbolic link is recommended for use in the options files. This enables changes to modem port without necessary changes to the options file. It's just a matter of changing the symbolic link.

The /dev/modem device is not created by default. It is only a symbolic link to the actual serial device to which the modem is connected. It can be created as follows:

```
# ln -s /dev/ttyS0 /dev/modem
```

The first COM port is usually /dev/ttyS0 and the second COM port is usually /dev/ttyS1.

CONFIGURING AUTHENTICATION FILES

Authentication to the PPP server takes place in one of several ways, the most common being manual, PAP, and CHAP (refer to Table 24.2). Manual authentication takes place by simply supplying a user ID and password to the PPP server. PAP and CHAP authentication require special files.

Note

Your Internet service provider will only offer one method of authentication. You only need to configure your system according to the authentication method used by your provider.

MANUAL AUTHENTICATION   Manual authentication of a PPP client to a PPP server is done by logging on to the PPP server and starting pppd. This method is completely dependent on the chat script written to handle the interaction between the client and the server. No other configuration files are required. It works much like the normal process of logging on: The system presents a login prompt, you enter your user ID, the system responds with a password prompt, and you enter your password. The trick is to automate this process by configuring a chat script of expect and send strings. An example of this type of script follows:

```
ABORT      BUSY
ABORT      "NO CARRIER"
ABORT      "NO DIALTONE"
""         ATZ
OK         "AT S0=0"
OK         ATDT5551386
CONNECT    ""
ogin: \d\q'mylogin'
ssword: \qmypassword
"" \d\c
```

The first part of the chat script remains the same. The last three lines represent the automated login steps. This is how it works: The chat script waits for the ogin: string, which is the expect string. When this is detected, the string mylogin (of course this is changed to the actual User ID) is sent back to the PPP Server. The same holds true with the password prompt and actual password. Notice that the expect string does not have to be a complete string. To avoid issues of whether or not the prompt is capitalized and so on, you can just place a unique portion of the string in the chat script. The final line provides a delay just in case it takes your ISP a few seconds to respond. The \d specifies a one second delay. The \q tells chat not to send the following string to syslog, send *?????* instead. The \c in the last line says not to send a carriage return. See the chat man page for a list of all the escape codes chat understands.

PAP AUTHENTICATION   PAP authentication is done by including the necessary information in the /etc/ppp/pap-secrets file. This means that you do not have to create the chat script to look for a login prompt and send the user ID and password information; this is all handled by the pap-secrets authentication protocol. Simply add the user ID and password to this file as follows:

```
# Client       Server       Secret
  mylogin        *         mypassword
```

Of course, mylogin and mypassword are changed to your user ID and password.

> **Note**
>
> With both PAP and CHAP authentication methods, you must add an entry to the /etc/ppp/options files as follows:
>
> name mylogin
>
> mylogin is your actual user ID.

CHAP AUTHENTICATION   CHAP authentication works in much the same way as PAP authentication. The information to enable CHAP authentication is stored in the `/etc/ppp/chap-secrets` file. The format of the `chap-secrets` file is described in the comment files included at the beginning of this chapter as follows:

```
# Secrets for authentication using CHAP
# client          server  secret                  IP addresses
```

According to the AT&T WorldNet Users Reference Desk Web site (http://204.127.237.208/wurd/software/dialers/linux.html), the `chap-secrets` file needs to be set as follows for authenticating to an AT&T WorldNet account:

```
# Secrets for authentication using CHAP
# client                    server  secret      IP addresses
999999999@worldnet.att.net    *    "password"    *
```

The previous setting, however, is only for AT&T Worldnet. The actual chap implementation requires two lines with 3–4 entries per line for each client server connection. Each line has a client name, a server name, a secret for authentication, and optionally, an IP address to which the server must correspond.

The first of the two lines lists the name of the local system, the name of the remote system, and then a secret. The second line is similar, but the local and remote hosts are swapped. The secret is usually also different. The IPs, if present, are used to enhance the security of this mode, because the IP must correspond to the server. When the hosts send the secret, it is first encrypted. When a challenge arrives from the remote host, the local host encrypts the secret and compares it to what it received. If your secret is a phrase containing whitespace, it must be quoted.

CONFIGURING OTHER REQUIRED NETWORK COMPONENTS

In addition to the necessary PPP configuration files that you need to make operational, you'll need to configure a couple of other files to have your Internet connection work correctly. First, the `/etc/hosts` file needs to contain an entry identifying your host name and IP address. If this machine is a standalone system (not connected to a network), add a line to your `/etc/hosts` file as follows:

```
0.0.0.0    yourmachine.yourdomain.com yourmachine
```

The IP address is set dynamically when you connect to your ISP using PPP. Of course, you'll want to set your machine name and domain to something more creative than `yourmachine.yourdomain.com`.

Also, a key piece of information gathered from your ISP is the IP address of the Domain Name Server (DNS). Set this value in the `/etc/resolv.conf` file as follows:

```
# possible entries are:
#
#      domain <domain>              Local domain name. If not present, the
#                                   gethostbyname syscall is used to
#                                   determine the local domain name.
#
```

```
#       search <list_of_domains>      Search list for hostname lookup.
#                                      The search list is normally determined
#                                      from the local domain name but it
#                                      can be set to a list of domains.
#
#       nameserver <ip_addr>          Define which server to contact
#                                      for DNS lookups. If there are
#                                      multiple nameserver lines (Max=3),
#                                      they are queried in the listed order.
#
#
domain mydomain.com
nameserver 207.179.18.1
```

RUNNING /usr/sbin/pppd

After everything is configured, you can try a PPP connection by simply running the pppd utility as follows:

```
# /usr/sbin/pppd
```

PART
IV

CH
24

The pppd utility offers several options, each of which is described in the man page for pppd. A common option is the detach option. This option starts pppd in the foreground (a nonbackground job), which allows terminating the PPP session with a keyboard sequence (Ctrl+C). Starting pppd with this option can be done as follows:

```
# /usr/sbin/pppd -detach
```

To terminate the PPP process without using the detach option, you must know the process ID. However, the process ID is stored in the /var/run directory, or you can find it by examining the process table. You can check the status of a successful PPP connection by checking the available network interfaces with the ifconfig utility.

When you want to kill this pppd process, you can use this command line:

```
kill `pidof pppd`
```

TROUBLESHOOTING THE CONNECTION

You can troubleshoot the PPP connection process by adding a couple of options in the /etc/ppp/options file. First of all, the chat utility produces more verbose output if you add the -v option as shown in the following options file:

```
connect "/usr/sbin/chat -v -f /etc/ppp/chat-script"
/dev/modem 38400
crtscts
defaultroute
noipdefault
```

The second method of capturing more information about the PPP connection is to add debug statements to the /etc/ppp/options file as follows:

```
connect "/usr/sbin/chat -v -f /etc/ppp/chat-script"
/dev/modem 38400
crtscts
defaultroute
```

```
noipdefault
debug
```

By adding the `debug` statement to this file, the contents of all control packets are logged, in readable form, in the `/var/log/messages` file.

If all else fails, you can add `kdebug #`, where # is the sum of any one or more of the following:

- **1**—General debug messages
- **2**—Print-received packets
- **4**—Print-sent packets

If you want to see the general messages plus the received packets, you would use `kdebug 3` (1 plus 2). Likewise, if you only want to see the received packets and the sent packets, you would use `kdebug 6` (2 plus 4).

USING KSAFERPPP

Older versions of KDE included a utility to connect to an ISP called kppp. Unfortunately, for this utility to work for an ordinary user, kppp had to be `suid root` with permissions for the world to run it. This was a very poor security practice. So the KDE developers came up with ksaferppp, a safer way for users to be able to use ppp.

To configure ksaferppp, the root user must first configure the modem and Internet provider. If this was done during the initial install, it is not necessary to repeat the steps. Otherwise, the following paragraphs will walk you through setting up your modem and Internet provider.

KSAFERPPP SETUP

To configure ksaferppp for the first time (or to reconfigure it), open kcontrol and then select COAS. By clicking the box with the plus key (+) in it, you can expand the selections seen (see Figure 24.1).

First, double-click Peripherals, Modem to open the Modem Setup screen. If you are not root, you will be prompted for root's password.

The Modem Setup dialog box will display information about your modem if known. You can change the model if it's not correct. If your model is not listed, the Generic Modem selections are usually sufficient; select the one that corresponds to the speed your modem is capable of. Then select the device. Devices corresponding to the DOS COM1 and COM2 will be shown, and will have COM1 and COM2 in parenthesis if you are not sure which Linux device to choose.

The speed setting is normally set automatically based on the model you chose, but you can override the setting if you so desire, although your modem's performance can suffer if you do so. The flow control will also be chosen automatically, but hardware flow control is normal and should be chosen unless you are sure your modem does not support it. The hardware setting is required for modems to achieve any decent speed. If your modem manual contains information regarding any commands or initstrings required, you can enter them here. The default initstring will normally suffice. Before you make changes to these boxes, consult your modem operator's manual.

After your modem is properly configured, you'll need to set up the Internet provider information. This can be reached under COAS, Network, Internet Provider as shown in Figure 24.1. Selecting this option also prompts you for root's password if you are not currently logged in as root.

Figure 24.1
KDE control center (kcontrol).

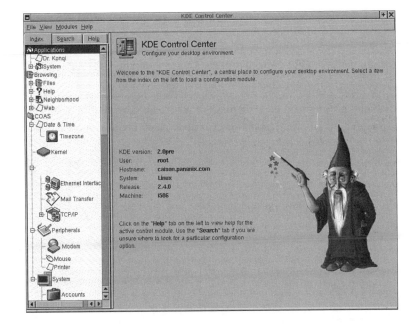

When the Setup Internet Provider box pops up, you will see a Use Dial-Up Networking check box near the top. Under most circumstances, this box should be checked. It will make your dial-up connection your default route to the Internet (which is probably what you want). If in doubt, make sure this box is selected.

The Provider box contains selections for various (principally European) countries and the United States. Under each country are subselections that consist of major cities or, for the United States, states with the major cities listed by state. Under these major cities are some of the known ISPs for the area. If you use one of the listed providers, you only need to select the provider; all information related to that provider is automatically supplied. If your provider is not listed, you'll need to select User Defined, and then select Details, which will open a dialog box requesting the required information. This information includes the name of the Provider (connection name), phone number the modem dials to connect to that provider, and two DNS servers (your provider should have supplied these).

The last box, Speaks PPP Natively should be checked for providers that immediately begin PPP negotiation. Most providers today do this, although a few might not. Those that don't often first provide a menu or some other way to tell the remote end that you want them to use PPP. If you have a choice between using PPP and SLIP or any other protocol, use PPP.

Finally, in the bottom portion of the Setup Internet Provider box is a Save Authentication Information check box. If you fill in the login and password information, you will not be prompted for it, and any user will be able to connect to the ISP using that information.

After the ISP information has been saved, you can launch ksaferppp and initiate a connection. This is a very simple, convenient, manual method for connecting to the Internet. If you want a more automated way to accomplish this, see the following section.

SETTING UP AUTOMATIC DEMAND DIALING

When you're comfortable that you can connect to your ISP, you might want to set up a system to act as an automatic gateway that connects to the Internet whenever someone on that system or another system on the network tries to access an external site. Doing so is rather easy, and the scripts to accomplish this are shown in the following text.

The first script is the System V init script. This script needs to be in /etc/rc.d/init.d. Make sure the script is owned by root (chown root:root ppp) and is executable (chmod 750 ppp).

Ensure you have a link to this script in the runlevel directory for each runlevel you want ppp active:

```
ln -s /etc/rc.d/init.d/ppp /etc/rc.d/rc5.d/S80ppp
```

You can add K (kill) scripts to the other directories, but this is not really necessary. The ppp script is shown here:

```
#!/bin/sh
# /etc/rc.d/init.d/ppp
# This script will start/stop/restart/reload pppd
test -x /usr/sbin/pppd -a -f /etc/ppp/ppp_on_boot || exit 0
case "$1" in
  start)
      echo -n "Starting PPP"
      start-stop-daemon --start --quiet --exec /usr/sbin/pppd -- call isp
      echo "."
    ;;
  stop)
      echo -n "Stopping PPP"
      start-stop-daemon --stop --quiet --exec /usr/sbin/pppd
      echo "."
    ;;
  restart|reload)
      $0 stop
      $0 start
    ;;
  *)
      echo "Usage: /etc/init.d/ppp {start|stop|restart|reload}"
      exit 1
    ;;
esac
exit 0
```

The fourth line looks for pppd, and also for a file /etc/ppp/ppp_on_boot. The ppp_on_boot is a zero-length file that you can remove if you don't want ppp to start up during bootup. If you want to put it back, simply touch /etc/ppp/ppp_on_boot and pppd starts up. The rest of the script is straightforward.

When pppd is called, it is called as pppd -- call isp. The ppp daemon looks in /etc/ppp/peers for a script called isp. This file is shown here:

```
#This script (isp) will connect you to your provider
noauth
connect '/usr/sbin/chat -v -f /etc/ppp/chatscripts/isp'
/dev/modem
115200
defaultroute
noipdefault
debug
user 'davidb'
demand
idle 300
holdoff 15
ipcp-accept-local
ipcp-accept-remote
192.168.10.10:192.168.10.11
```

PART

IV

CH

24

What's in this file is specific to only this connection. You can set up other connections and even activate them (as long as you have sufficient data ports). Global configuration items are shown in the /etc/ppp/options file:

```
asyncmap 0
modem
crtscts
```

Most of the options in the /etc/ppp/options files are (or should be) familiar by now. The final file is the /etc/ppp/chatscripts/isp file. This is the chat script used to connect to your Internet provider:

```
ABORT BUSY
ABORT "NO CARRIER"
ABORT VOICE
ABORT "NO DIALTONE"
ABORT "NO ANSWER"
"" ATZ
OK ATM0
OK ATDT7756575
#OK ATDT2651155
#OK ATDT2271155
#ATDT2130400
CONNECT ''
ogin: \d\q'davidb'
ssword: \qmypasswd
"" \d\c
```

The previous scripts have successfully connected a number of systems to the Internet. While pppd is connecting, it can be insightful to keep an eye on the logs. There, you will see the connection as it occurs and the local and remote IPs assigned during the connection.

DISTRIBUTION-SPECIFIC INFORMATION

Caldera, Red Hat, and Debian will each have ksaferppp as long as the KDE packages have been installed. If not, GNOME has a similar tool called gpppon (GNOME PPP on). This utility will be available in any system that includes GNOME and has this utility installed. Debian also includes several other PPP tools, including pppconfig, quickppp, and ppxp (which also has a Tk and X interface). The pppconfig script automates much of what was previously discussed regarding setting up automatic demand dialing (Debian just uses a different chatscript's directory location).

TROUBLESHOOTING

I set up my automatic dialing just like the example in the book, but I can't seem to get connected. I can hear it talking to another modem, but then nothing happens.

Your ISP is probably looking for something other than what you're sending or is sending something you're not looking for. Use a program like cu or another program where you can watch what the ISP is sending (you should also see this in /var/log/messages with debug). Remember that the expect/send sequence is case sensitive. Add any required sequences. At least one ISP uses username instead of login.

I did the previous step, and I'm sure the expect/send sequence is correct and in the correct case, but then suddenly the PPP daemon dies.

The expect chat sequence might be replying too quickly. Try adding a one-second delay in between the expect and the send. Also try using ' '\d\c as the last line.

I can't seem to get the modem to dial out. I put in debug and now I see something about tcesetattr being incorrect.

Most likely, you haven't chosen the correct modem. If you are using /dev/modem, make sure this is a symlink pointing to the correct ttyS device, or the modem is not present. Also make sure the serial module is loaded.

I'm getting an error when I start pppd about the kernel not supporting PPP.

You probably haven't installed the ppp module. You might also want to install the ppp_deflate and bsd_comp modules as well. Also install either ppp_async or ppp_synctty.

When I try to use demand dialing, pppd fails.

When using s with demand dialing, make sure you've built the kernel with slip support or modprobe slip. The demand dialing requires two things: the slip module to set up a psuedo-slip connection to watch for a connection attempt, and a line such as 192.168.10.10:192.168.10.11 in your /etc/ppp/peers/provider (or /etc/ppp/options) file. This provides a temporary target for packets to go to which will trip the automatic dialing.

## CHAPTER 25

EMAIL CLIENTS AND SERVERS

In this chapter

EMAIL—WHAT IS IT?

Setting up electronic mail (email) services on a Linux system is really quite simple. Depending on your objectives, email can be operational upon completing the Linux installation. However, that is not to say that email configuration and operation are simple by any means. The internals of email configuration and the process by which it works are quite complex.

Email, in simple terms, is merely an automated way of delivering conventional mail. In fact, thinking of it in terms of the conventional mail that is delivered by the postal service can actually help you understand what email is and how it works. Conventional mail delivery can be thought of in three distinct parts: sending mail, receiving mail, and transporting mail between one or more intermediate stations en route to its final destination. As a postal service customer, you are typically only involved in either sending mail or receiving it. The steps in between are, for the most part, transparent to you as a customer of the postal service. The postal service handles the intermediate steps of determining how your letter is to be handled and where it is to be delivered. After it is delivered, the recipient retrieves the letter from the mailbox.

Note The topic of email can fill a book. This chapter contains only very basic information. Although slightly Caldera-centric, the text also examines differences in default Debian and Red Hat installations and distribution-specific implementations. Underneath, it all works the same.

HOW DOES EMAIL WORK?

Email works in much the same way as conventional mail. Three distinct agents are involved in this process: the email client (sender), the mail transport agent, and the mail delivery agent (recipient). The email client is often referred to as the *Mail User Agent* (*MUA*) and the transport agent is often referred to as the *Mail Transport Agent* (*MTA*). Each of these agents and their respective tasks are listed in Table 25.1.

TABLE 25.1   ELECTRONIC MAIL COMPONENTS

Agent	Component	Description
User Agent (MUA)	Sender	Formats the message, addresses the message, and delivers the message to the Mail Transport Agent.
Transport Agent (MTA)	Message Handler	Accepts messages from User Agents and other Transport Agents. Routes the message over appropriate network. Resolves aliases and forwarding.
Delivery Agent (DA)	Recipient	Delivers messages to destination accessible by recipient.

The sender of an email constructs a message, using an email client, and addresses it to a recipient. After the email client sends the message, the Mail Transport Agent (MTA) takes over the process. This is equivalent to dropping off a letter at the post office. Of course, the MTA for email is nothing more than a sophisticated program, unlike the postal service, which has a host of employees and sorting machines and a fleet of vehicles. Caldera, Debian, and Red Hat all use a program called *sendmail* as the default Mail Transport Agent, and although this could change in the future, sendmail will likely always be included. Debian also offers Postfix and Zmailer, and Red Hat packages are available for Smail and others, but sendmail is still the one that is most commonly used.

> **Note**   sendmail was written by Eric Allman at the University of California, Berkeley, and is the most popular email Transport Agent on Linux and UNIX platforms.

The Transport Agent accepts the mail from a user agent, determines the address of the recipient, and delivers the message to the Transport Agent that services email for the recipient. The Delivery Agent is really nothing more than an email client or user agent. However, depending on the setup of incoming email for a given client, an additional component might be necessary. You can be logged in directly to the machine that acts as the email server and read your email on that system, or you can read your email on your desktop system using either Internet Message Access Protocol (IMAP) or Post Office Protocol (POP). You can find more information about these two protocols in the section "Delivery Agents."

USER AGENTS

The User Agent is that aspect of email that involves you, individually, as either the sender of a message or the recipient of a message. This is typically the email client that is used to read incoming messages or to compose outgoing messages. The job of the User Agent is really quite simple. In the case of outgoing messages, it's a matter of providing a method for you to compose a message, address the message to the desired recipient or recipients, and then send the message on its way. Many email clients are available with Linux—both character-based clients and graphical, X Window–based clients. Outbound mail is operational by default after the Linux installation is complete. The only setup that is required is the configuration of an account for each individual user. With a user account configured, you can log in and send email. Of course, you'll need to access an email client in order to complete that task. Choosing an email client is just a matter of preference, and although there is no default email client, there are several from which to choose. Table 25.2 lists some of the many email clients that are available with Linux.

TABLE 25.2   LIST OF EMAIL CLIENTS AVAILABLE WITH LINUX

Email Client	User Interface	Description
/bin/mail	Character	mail is an intelligent mail processing system that has a command syntax reminiscent of ed, with lines replaced by messages.
/usr/bin/elm	Character	elm is an interactive screen-oriented mailer program that supersedes mail and mailx.

TABLE 25.2 CONTINUED

Email Client	User Interface	Description
/usr/bin/pine	Character	pine is a screen-oriented message-handling tool. In its default configuration, pine offers an intentionally limited set of functions geared toward the novice user, but it also has a growing list of optional power-user and personal-preference features. pinef is a variant of pine that uses function keys rather than mnemonic single-letter commands.
/usr/bin/mutt	Character	mutt is a small but very powerful text-based program for reading electronic mail under Linux or UNIX operating systems, including support for color terminals, MIME, and a threaded sorting mode.
/usr/X11R6/ bin/xfmail	X Window	xfmail is an application for sending and receiving email under X. It's partially compatible with MH-style mailboxes but it does not require that any MH tools be installed on the system. xfmail supports POP and SMTP mail protocols and it has full MIME support.
Netscape Messenger	X Window	This is an email handler that is part of Netscape Communicator.

CHARACTER-BASED EMAIL CLIENTS

A character-based email client is one that is not graphical in nature. In other words, it's not pretty but it is very functional for those who like to keep their hands on the keyboard rather than on a mouse. Character-based email clients are typically ones that are used when a user is logged in directly to the system that hosts the email server.

Note

Some character-based email clients, such as mutt, have or are adding capabilities to use such protocols as IMAP, which enable the email client to retrieve messages from the email server without being directly logged in to it.

NETSCAPE MESSENGER

Many graphical email clients are available with Linux. Of course, user preferences and opinions vary, but the email client that is part of Netscape Messenger might be the easiest to configure and use. Two basic components must be configured to set up email with Netscape Messenger. To configure the necessary components of email, click on the Edit menu within the Netscape Navigator browser and then select Preferences. When the initial dialog box appears, select Mail & Newsgroups.

Be sure to click the arrow next to the heading Mail & Newsgroups in order to see the complete list of options within this category.

A list of the following options is displayed:

- Identity
- Mail Servers
- Newsgroups Servers
- Addressing
- Messages
- Copies and Folders
- Formatting
- Return Receipts
- Disk Space

Selecting Identity produces a screen similar to the one that is depicted in Figure 25.1.

Figure 25.1
Identity setup for
Netscape Messenger
Mail Handling.

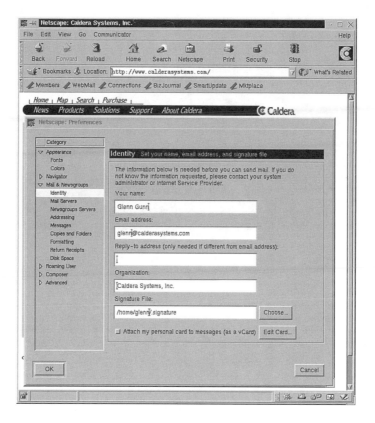

Enter the pertinent information in the appropriate fields and click OK. You are now ready to send email. You can send email by simply selecting Messenger from the Communicator menu on the Web browser and clicking the New Message icon.

The second component that must be configured is the Mail Server. Configuring this component enables the capability to receive email. Clicking Mail Servers in the Mail & Newsgroups category presents a screen that enables you to add or modify mail servers. Click Add to display the screen that is depicted in Figure 25.2.

Figure 25.2
Mail Server setup for Netscape Messenger Mail Handling.

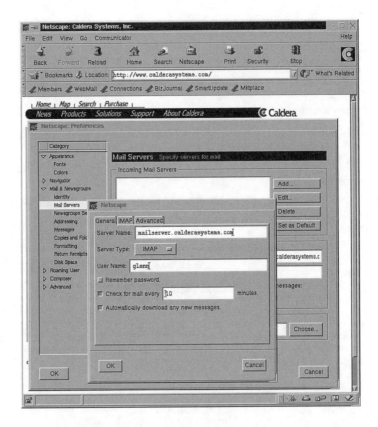

Add the hostname, complete with the domain name, as the server name; also add your username. Your username is the same as the user ID that was created as your account name on the Linux server.

Note

The mail server must be set up to support IMAP Movemail, or POP in order for the mail handler in Netscape Communicator to receive email. See the "Delivery Agents" section later in this chapter for details on how to set up IMAP or POP. Use of the internal Netscape Movemail will not be covered by this text.

KMAIL

The KMail utility is included with KDE and is a very friendly, easy-to-use agent. Before you can use it though, you will need to configure it.

KMail configuration is performed by selecting File→Settings. This will bring up a Settings dialog box with several tabs. The appropriate setting for most users will be covered in the next few paragraphs.

The Identity tab contains the settings used to put the appropriate headers on your outgoing mail. Although none are mandatory, customary practice is to include your name as you would like others to know you, your email address, and your reply-to address if different from your email address. In some cases you might want to include your organization or company and signature file (standard is .signature).

The Network tab sets up outgoing and incoming mail. This tab's fields are mandatory. In the Sending Mail section, most readers will select SMTP and put their ISP's outgoing mail server address. Unless you've been instructed otherwise, do not change the port to other than 25. You won't use sendmail as your MTA unless your system has a legitimate DNS MX RR pointing to it. If the previous sentence was unintelligible then you almost certainly are not a valid Internet mail host. In the bottom half of the Network box you need to configure your Incoming Mail. Again, this will usually point to your ISP's mail (usually a POP3 host). If you are using a utility like fetchmail to spool mail or if your system is an Internet mail host, you will point to your local mailbox for mail.

The Composer tab has one setting that, although not mandatory, is polite and should be selected: Word wrap at column. The number here is normally set at 72, but can go to 80 (not recommended). Turning this feature off can result in some mail users who don't have incoming word wrap turned on sending you an often impolite reminder to wrap your outgoing mail.

One default setting on the Misc tab should be explained. This setting is "Automatically send receive and read confirmation." Although you might want to leave this checked, be advised that spammers love this because it confirms to them that you are a valid email address. It will prompt them to keep you in their list of valid email addresses. So unless you enjoy receiving megabytes of spam, you might want to turn this feature off.

MAIL TRANSPORT AGENT CONFIGURATION

Although email clients are becoming more and more sophisticated and user-friendly, they remain the simplest part of the whole email process. The email client handles the step that is the equivalent of someone dropping off their letter at the post office or retrieving it from the mailbox in their front yard. In other words, it's the easy part. The mail transport agent, on the other hand, handles the most complicated aspects of email. In the conventional mail scenario, the MTA is the equivalent of the postal service. The postal service receives the letter, determines how it is to be routed, delivers it to the appropriate local office, and gets it on the correct mail truck to be delivered. The transport agent for email works in a similar fashion. The MTA receives the email from an email client, determines how to route it, transports it to the appropriate MTA for the given recipient, and places it in a retrievable location for the addressee. The configuration of the MTA is complicated by the fact that it needs to be prepared to handle a number of system and network configurations. This is enough of the theory, however—here's a look at what is required.

> **Note**
>
> In most cases, your MTA should be turned off unless you are a legitimate Internet mail receiver or are using fetchmail to get mail from your ISP. Also, you won't be able to specify your local host's MTA to send messages on the Internet unless you have a registered domain name and have DNS MX records pointing to your system as a legitimate Internet Mail Exchanger. Most MTAs today won't accept mail from an unregistered host, thanks to the incredible problems surrounding unsolicited commercial email (UCE), aka SPAM.

SENDMAIL CONFIGURATION FILES

The primary configuration file for sendmail operation is the /etc/mail/sendmail.cf (or sometimes the /etc/sendmail.cf) file. This file is very complex and should only be modified if you are certain of the changes that you are making.

> **Note**
>
> Starting with sendmail v 8.10.0, all configuration files have been relocated to /etc/mail/ for uniformity, although the different distributions may elect to put them elsewhere.

> **Tip**
>
> As with all system administration, it is a good practice to make a back-up copy of this file before making any modifications.

The sendmail.cf file can be modified in one of two ways: by editing it directly or by modifying the m4 configuration file and regenerating a new sendmail.cf file. The m4 utility is a macro processor. Rather than having to know all the aspects of the sendmail.cf file, the m4 configuration file offers a method of identifying and configuring the desired components (in somewhat simpler terms), and then processing them with the m4 utility to create a new sendmail.cf file.

> **Tip**
>
> For more information on the m4 utility, type info m4 at a shell prompt. A comprehensive README document can also be found in the /usr/share/sendmail/cf directory.

M4 CONFIGURATION FILES

The m4 configuration file that is used to generate the default /etc/mail/sendmail.cf is stored in the /usr/share/sendmail/cf/cf directory. The m4 configuration file used for Caldera's OpenLinux sendmail setup is generic-col2.2.mc. The file for Debian is debproto.m4, and the file for Red Hat is /usr/lib/sendmail-cf/cf/redhat.mc.

A new sendmail configuration file can be generated using this file as follows (note that on Caldera and Red Hat systems, the package sendmail-cf must be installed):

Caldera:

```
# cd /usr/share/sendmail/cf/cf
# m4 ../m4/cf.m4 generic-col2.2.mc > /etc/sendmail.cf
```

Debian:

```
# cd /usr/share/sendmail/cf/cf/
# m4 ../m4/cf.m4 debproto.m4 > /etc/sendmail.cf
```

Red Hat:

```
# cd /usr/lib/sendmail-cf/cf
# m4 ../m4/cf.m4 redhat.mc > /etc/sendmail.cf
```

EMAIL MASQUERADING

The MTA can be configured to masquerade for other domain names. This can be accomplished easily by modifying the m4 configuration file with the needed features and regenerating the `/etc/mail/sendmail.cf` file as follows:

```
# cd /usr/share/sendmail/cf/cf
# cp generic-col1.2.mc tempfile.mc
```

Add the following two lines to the end of this file:

```
MASQUERADE_AS(domain-name.com)dnl
FEATURE(masquerade_envelope)dnl
```

Then regenerate the file as follows:

```
# m4 ../m4/cf.m4 tempfile.mc > /etc/mail/sendmail.cf
```

Of course, you'll want to replace the name `domain-name.com` with the hostname for which you want to masquerade, and use the appropriate file and pathname from above.

The `masquerade as` option changes the name on the email header. sendmail is not just about moving mail; it's more about rewriting email headers. Normally, sendmail will write the current, fully qualified domain name as part of the from address, but because most people send mail from a domain and not from a specific host, `masquerade as` allows the name to be changed.

You also saw `masquerade envelope`. The envelope is the portion of the message at the very top, not normally seen, that is passed from one MTA to the other. Masquerading the envelope extends the masquerade to this outer wrapper portion of the message as well.

Some other sendmail features you might want to know about are shown in Table 25.3.

PART

IV

CH

25

TABLE 25.3   SENDMAIL FEATURES

Feature	Effect
accept_unresolvable_domains	Prevents bouncing mail for domains that can't be resolved.
access_db	One of the features used for spam control.
bestmx_is_local	Accepts mail if DNS says we are the mailhost.
blacklist_recipients	Another spam control feature (requires access_db).
dnsbl	Formerly rbl, consults the sendmail maintained blacklist.
domaintable	Used to provide domain-name mapping.

TABLE 25.3   CONTINUED

Feature	Effect
genericstable	Used to change sender address on outgoing mail. This feature is resource-intensive and should not be enabled unless needed.
ldap_routing	Implements LDAP-based email recipient routing.
local_procmail	Uses procmail as the local mailer.
mailertable	Used to override routing for particular domains.
masquerade_entire_domain	Used with masquerade_as and masquerade_domain to hide all domains behind the masquerade.
masquerade_envelope	Masquerades the received from line passed between MTAs.
nouucp	Rules for handling UUCP addresses (bang paths) will not be added.
nullclient	A special case with an argument of the mail hub. The .m4 file specifying nullclient should have no other features except nocanonify.
redirect	Rejects mail addressed to address.REDIRECT and returns a please try <address> message.
relay_based_on_MX	Permits relaying, but only from hosts with valid MX entries.
relay_entire_domain	Permits all hosts in your domain (as defined by Dm) to relay.
relay_hosts_only	Changes default behavior for access_db from relaying entire domains listed for relay, to relaying only specific hosts listed in access_db for relay.
relay_mail_from	Allows relay if the mail sender is listed as RELAY in the access_db. Caution: sender addresses can be forged.
smrsh	Uses the sendmail restricted shell.
use_ct_file	Consults sendmail.ct for a list of trusted users.
use_cw_file	Consults sendmail.cw for a list of local host names.
virtusertable	Used to map a recipient address on incoming mail to a local username.

For many features in Table 25.3, you can specify a filename and map type. The filename and map type specifications are meant to override the defaults.

Other specifications, such as those for PrivacyOptions, can be changed as well. You can change the PrivacyOptions in the sendmail.cf itself or, if you prefer and expect to build several sendmail.cf files and want consistency (and don't want to forget to change it), the default is found in the /usr/share/sendmail/cf/m4/proto.m4 file. Be careful making changes to this file, though. Table 25.4 lists the privacy options.

TABLE 25.4 PRIVACY OPTIONS FOR SENDMAIL

Privacy Option	Action
public	Allows open access.
needmailhelo	Insists on HELO or EHLO commands before honoring MAIL command.
needexpnhelo	Insists on HELO or EHLO before honoring EXPN command.
noexpn	Disallows EXPN.
needvrfyhelo	Insists on HELO or EHLO before honoring VRFY command.
novrfy	Disallows VRFY.
noetrn	Disallows ETRN.
noverb	Disallows VERB.
restrictmailq	Restricts the mailq command.
restrictqrun	Restricts -q command-line flag.
noreceipts	Doesn't return success DSN (Delivery Status Notification).
nobodyreturn	Doesn't return the body of a message with DSNs.
authwarnings	Puts X Authentication Warning headers in messages.
goaway	Disallows most SMTP queries. goaway sets all above flags except noreceipts, restrictmailq, restrictqrun, noetrn, and nobodyreturn.

PART

IV

CH

25

You can have several of the above options on one line by separating them with a comma:

```
O PrivacyOptions=goaway,noreceipts,restrictmailq,restrictqrun,noetrn
```

These restrictions are designed to prevent remote human interaction with the sendmail daemon. The VERBose, EXPN (expand), and sometimes VRFY (verify) commands were meant to be used for debugging purposes, but are now often used by spammers to obtain or verify lists of victims. ETRN allows someone to externally run the mailq.

The previous discussion only touches briefly on all the possibilities. If you need to do much sendmail administration, you'll need a good sendmail reference as provided with the sendmail source.

THE sendmail.cw FILE

The sendmail.cw file must be modified to contain all the names by which your host can be recognized. For example, if your fully qualified domain hostname was main.calderasystems.com, you'd want to add the following to the /etc/mail/sendmail.cw file:

```
# sendmail.cw - include all aliases for your machine here.
calderasystems.com
```

This enables incoming mail to be correctly handled by sendmail. Otherwise, sendmail doesn't know what to do with email that is addressed to me@calderasystems.com. Email that is sent to me@main.calderasystems.com is handled by sendmail just fine by default.

THE /etc/rc.d/init.d/mta FILE

This file contains the script for initiating the startup of sendmail or any other MTA. To manually start or stop sendmail, do the following:

```
# /etc/rc.d.init.d/mta start
# /etc/rc.d.init.d/mta stop
```

To have sendmail start automatically at system boot, modify the ONBOOT line in the /etc/sysconfig/daemons/mta file as follows:

```
# /etc/sysconfig/daemons/mta
IDENT=MTA
DESCRIPTIVE="Mail Transfer Agent"
ONBOOT="yes"
VARIANT="sendmail"
```

THE /etc/mta/options/sendmail FILE

The /etc/mta/options/sendmail file defines the actual binary that is used as the Mail Transfer agent and the options that are used when it is started up initially. The default settings are as follows:

```
# /etc/mta/sendmail/options
ONBOOT=yes
DAEMON=/usr/sbin/sendmail
OPTIONS="-bd -q5m"
```

The -bd option tells sendmail to run as a daemon in the background, and the -q5m tells sendmail to flush its queue (/var/spool/mqueue) every 5 minutes. A large number of other options are available, but these are the most commonly used.

Note   The Mail Transfer Agent must be enabled to receive incoming mail with OpenLinux. This is done by modifying the /etc/sysconfig/daemons/mta file.

ALIASES

Aliases can be used in a number of ways. One of the most common uses of an alias is to handle different spellings or the complete name of a given person. An alias can also be used to set up generic names that don't necessarily point to a specific person. For example, an alias for a Webmaster can be set up to have all incoming mail directed to Glenn. The aliases file looks similar to the following:

```
#  This file lists the default mail aliases for Caldera OpenLinux.
#
#  Aliases in this file will NOT be expanded in the header from
#  Mail, but WILL be visible over networks or from /bin/mail.
#
#                       IMPORTANT NOTE:
#
#  After you make any changes to this file, you have to run
#
```

```
#        /usr/sbin/mta-switch newconfig
#
# or the program `newaliases' (works for smail and sendmail).
# Otherwise, the changes won't be visible to your MTA.
#

# Basic system aliases -- these MUST be present.
MAILER-DAEMON:  postmaster
postmaster:     root

# General redirections for pseudo accounts.
bin:            root
games:          root
ingres:         root
system:         root
toor:           root
news:           root
uucp:           root
operator:       root
ftp:            root
nobody:         root

# Well-known aliases.
manager:        root
dumper:         root
newsadm:        news
newsadmin:      news
usenet:         news
netnews:        news
gnats:          root
ftpadm:         ftp
ftpadmin:       ftp
ftp-adm:        ftp
# trap decode to catch security attacks
decode:         root

# Person who is to get root's mail
#root:          col
```

Adding an entry to the `/etc/mail/aliases` file as follows directs all mail that is coming to webmaster@calderasystems.com to be sent to glenn@calderasystems.com:

```
webmaster:      glenn
```

An alias can also be used to set up small (usually internal) mailing lists. For larger, departmental lists, you can use Include statements to include file lists. Large mailing lists should be handled with a mailing list program such as majordomo. To create a small mailing list, put the name of the mailing list in `/etc/mail/aliases` followed by a comma-separated list of users:

```
maillistname:   john,sally,mike,andrew
```

Run newaliases, and any mail sent to maillistname will be forwarded to john, sally, mike, and andrew.

> **Note**
> For changes to this file to take effect, you must run the newaliases utility.

NOTES ON DEBIAN SYSTEMS

Although sendmail is sendmail regardless of the system you're running on (any of the various Linux distributions, or even other UNIX systems), some distribution-specific quirks exist of which you must be aware.

The information in the preceding section will work on Debian, but you need to do a few things in addition to just changing some pathnames and filenames.

Debian has a sendmailconfig script that can be used to do basic sendmail system setup. This script will work for most sendmail installations. Only special or advanced configurations need be added.

When sendmailconfig runs, one of the things it does is create a /etc/mail/sendmail.mc from the debproto.mc file previously mentioned. If this sendmail.mc file does not exist, sendmail will not start at bootup. You might find it easier to use sendmailconfig first, and then if the resulting configuration doesn't fit your needs, modify the sendmail.mc file and use it to create subsequent sendmail.cf files.

You can do this by making modifications by hand to the /etc/mail/sendmail.mc file and invoking sendmailconfig again. Changes added to the bottom of the file will not be touched.

Debian also uses a differently named file as its SysV boot file. This file is /etc/init.d/ sendmail, and takes any of the following arguments: start, stop, restart, reload, force-reload, or debug.

NOTES ON RED HAT SYSTEMS

Red Hat maintains a sendmail.mc file in /etc as well as /usr/lib/sendmail-cf/cf. The redhat.mc file in the sendmail-cf directory and the /etc/sendmail.cf file are basically copies of each other. Decide which you want to use, modify it, and create the new sendmail.cf from it. A fairly generic sendmail.cf is provided during installation.

For bootup, Red Hat's init script looks in a file /etc/sysconfig/sendmail to determine whether to run. If you want sendmail to run, just make sure that /etc/sysconfig/sendmail contains a line DAEMON=yes. Change to no to stop running sendmail at bootup.

In the /etc/sysconfig/sendmail file you can also modify the queue setting. By default, Red Hat runs the queue once an hour. Just change the 1h to 15m or 30m to run the queue more often (every 15 or 30 minutes).

DELIVERY AGENTS

The Delivery Agent is very similar to the user agent; it is merely a method of getting the actual message into the recipient's hands. For example, with conventional mail the recipient can walk out to the mailbox in his front yard or drive to the location of a post office box. Similarly, the recipient of email can use different methods of collecting his or her messages.

A POP Server

Post Office Protocol (POP) provides a way for end users to retrieve their mail. It's similar to you walking out to your mailbox, collecting the mail, walking back into your house, and sitting down and reading it. Using POP, email is delivered to the email client on your desktop when you indicate that you want to retrieve it. Often, the client desktop is configured to do this each time a dial-up connection is made or at a predetermined time interval. The mail is literally moved from the server to the client.

POP3 requires very little in the way of setup and runs by default in a standard Linux install. POP3 runs from /etc/inetd.conf, so access can be controlled with TCP Wrappers if desired. As long as the pop3 entry is listed in /etc/services and the pop3 line shows up in /etc/inetd.conf (and hasn't been commented out), you're already running POP3. You can verify this by inspecting the output of netstat -an for a local port 110 that is listening.

An IMAP Server

An IMAP server behaves much like a POP server, but with one major difference—the IMAP server does not literally transfer the email from the server to the client desktop. It basically creates a "map" for a given user that enables him to read the mail directly on the email server system. The advantages and disadvantages of IMAP versus POP are very similar to the advantages and disadvantages of central versus distributed processing.

IMAP, although a different program from POP3, runs out of /etc/inetd.conf in exactly the same way as POP3—it just uses port 143 instead of 110. Because IMAP is slightly more powerful, it is also slightly more vulnerable to exploits. If you use IMAP, you will want to use TCP Wrappers to limit access.

Enabling POP and IMAP Services

If not already running, enabling either POP or IMAP service is a very simple task. Each of these protocols is predefined in the /etc/services file. The only real requirement is to install the IMAP RPM.

After the RPM is installed, the appropriate daemon is called when requests are detected for either POP or IMAP services on the respective ports, as defined in the /etc/services file. That's all there is to setting up both POP and IMAP services. After they are enabled, email clients can be configured to receive email through this server.

FETCHMAIL

fetchmail is a specialized type of delivery agent that can download mailbags from an ISP or grab mail from different POP and IMAP servers and deposit it locally.

PART

IV

CH

25

fetchmail requires that sendmail be running on the receiving system. This is the one exception to a non-email system not needing to run sendmail. This is because fetchmail hands off all mail through port 25 to the email server.

The fetchmail documentation is very clearly written and contains examples of how to set up fetchmail to run as a daemon and startup after specified intervals and download mail, which makes it perfect for companies with only dial-up access. But fetchmail comes with an X utility, fetchmailconf, which can be used to easily configure and test fetchmail to ensure proper operation. This utility requires python in order to run.

MBOX

Mail on the local system is saved in what is known as the UNIX mbox (mailbox) format. This is a file with mail messages appended to the bottom as they come in. Messages received locally by your sendmail server will be deposited in /var/spool/mail/$USER by the deliver or procmail program. These can be accessed by any of the methods mentioned previously or directly accessed by the mail program.

ENCRYPTION AND PRETTY GOOD PRIVACY (PGP)

Picture sending out a private letter to someone through the U.S. Postal Service, written on a postcard. Everyone who comes across that post card can see it, right? Therefore, it does not require a major stretch of the imagination to understand why private letters are typically sent to their destinations sealed in envelopes. If the letter is delivered incorrectly, or if some other problem with delivery develops, the letter is sent back still sealed in the envelope. At no point was the privacy of that letter compromised (unless someone decided to rip the letter open and read it).

Now, picture email over the Internet, or even within a small network. At least one machine other than the sending machine receives that message; if you are talking about passing it to someone out on the Internet, numerous different machines are in the email's path. At each stopping point—and at a few points in between—it is entirely possible that someone can read that message. It is in plain text, after all, and is not sealed in anything. If a problem comes up in the delivery and it ends up in another destination, odds are that the message was read before it was returned.

Put simply, email, by default, is not secure at all. Nor are file attachments that are sent using email. Even sensitive files sitting on a local machine that will never be passed through any network pipe are insecure if the machine is left unattended for any period of time.

Electronic documents, binary files, and anything else that can sit on a hard drive—and that need to be kept confidential—require some sort of envelope that can be sealed around them. Short of packing the computer in a large box and sealing it every time it is unattended, only one technology seems to provide a valid solution: encryption.

Not just any encryption will work, though. An encryption scheme known as *public key encryption* has almost become the de facto method for encrypting sensitive information.

This scheme incorporates two keys: one private key, which you keep to yourself; and one public key, which you pass out to others. The public key—belonging to you or to someone to whom you want to send an encrypted file—is used to encrypt a file, and only the holder of the associated private key can decrypt it. A third key—the session key—is generated automatically and is used for encryption and decryption. Because it is handled automatically in the background, however, it is rarely credited for its involvement in the process.

The biggest problem with public key encryption systems is that they are resource intensive. The mathematics involved in decrypting an encrypted message are tremendous—heads and shoulders above the single-key method (in which each party has the exact same private key and no public key—the private key is used to encrypt and decrypt files), and significantly slower to process. The mathematics are not as intense with single-key methods because there are no mathematical relationships to establish between any public and private keys. The single keys on both ends of the exchange match, so the extra math is not required.

Two encryption packages that incorporate public key encryption are Pretty Good Privacy (PGP)—slowly being replaced by GPG, the GNU Privacy Guard, an open source implementation of PGP—and OpenSSH (an open source secure shell). See Chapter 37, "Remote Administration," for more information on OpenSSH. Both are available for UNIX variants such as Linux, as well as for other platforms (Windows and Mac versions of each are available). Although nothing short of disconnecting a computer and sticking it in a locked closet can keep your data safe from attack, using encryption in your everyday operations drastically reduces the possibility of your data being compromised.

This text will discuss the GNU Privacy Guard, because the distributions included with this text now ship with GPG. If you've used PGP (particularly version 2.6) and are accustomed to it syntax, the GnuPG RPM includes a compatibility program called pgpgpg, which will enable you to continue to use pgp syntax, but will translate to gpg.

The primary use of GnuPG (GPG) is file encryption. It does not set up secure channels between local and remote systems, nor does it use a server/client topology. It simply encrypts data to be shared with specific individuals, and sets up criteria for determining data integrity on the receiving end of the file exchange. Although a number of interfaces exist for the various platforms to which GPG is available, GPG itself is command-line driven. The list of parameters that can be passed to GPG is rather extensive, and not all will be covered here, only the more common functions. Consult the man pages for a complete list of commands and options.

SETTING UP GPG FOR USE

With GPG installed, your first task is to create a legitimate public/private key pair for yourself. Do this while you are logged in as the user that you plan to be logged in as the most, or while you are logged in as the user who you plan to be whenever you encrypt things with GPG. Make sure that a .gnupg subdirectory is created off your home directory (if none exists, create one using mkdir). If you don't create a directory first, GPG will do so the first time it is run, but will abort and you'll have to run the command again.

Following is the command that is used to generate key pairs:

gpg --gen-key

Listing 25.1 is a sample key generation session for the fake user Sherman T. Potter, whose machine is rumble.fish.net.

LISTING 25.1   GENERATING A KEY PAIR

```
[stp@rumble stp]$ gpg --gen-key
gpg (GnuPG) 1.0.1; Copyright (C) 1999 Free Software Foundation, Inc.
This program comes with ABSOLUTELY NO WARRANTY.
This is free software, and you are welcome to redistribute it
under certain conditions. See the file COPYING for details.

gpg: /home/stp/.gnupg: directory created
gpg: /home/stp/.gnupg/options: new options file created
gpg: you have to start GnuPG again, so it can read the new options file
[stp@rumble stp]$ gpg --gen-key
gpg (GnuPG) 1.0.1; Copyright (C) 1999 Free Software Foundation, Inc.
This program comes with ABSOLUTELY NO WARRANTY.
This is free software, and you are welcome to redistribute it
under certain conditions. See the file COPYING for details.

gpg: /home/stp/.gnupg/secring.gpg: keyring created
gpg: /home/stp/.gnupg/pubring.gpg: keyring created
Please select what kind of key you want:
   (1) DSA and ElGamal (default)
   (2) DSA (sign only)
   (4) ElGamal (sign and encrypt)
Your selection?
DSA keypair will have 1024 bits.
About to generate a new ELG-E keypair.
              minimum keysize is   768 bits
              default keysize is  1024 bits
    highest suggested keysize is 2048 bits
What keysize do you want? (1024)
Requested keysize is 1024 bits
Please specify how long the key should be valid.
        0 = key does not expire
      <n>  = key expires in n days
      <n>w = key expires in n weeks
      <n>m = key expires in n months
      <n>y = key expires in n years
Key is valid for? (0)
Key does not expire at all
Is this correct (y/n)? y

You need a User-ID to identify your key; the software constructs the user id
from Real Name, Comment and Email Address in this form:
    "Heinrich Heine (Der Dichter) <heinrichh@duesseldorf.de>"

Real name: Sherman T. Potter
Email address: stp@fish.net
Comment:
You selected this USER-ID:
    "Sherman T. Potter <stp@fish.net>"
```

LISTING 25.1   CONTINUED

```
Change (N)ame, (C)omment, (E)mail or (O)kay/(Q)uit? O
You need a Passphrase to protect your secret key.

Enter passphrase:
Change (N)ame, (C)omment, (E)mail or (O)kay/(Q)uit? O
You need a Passphrase to protect your secret key.
Enter passphrase:
Reenter passphrase:

We need to generate a lot of random bytes. It is a good idea to perform
some other action (type on the keyboard, move the mouse, utilize the
disks) during the prime generation; this gives the random number
generator a better chance to gain enough entropy.
+++++..+++++++++++++++++++++..++++++++++.++++++++++.+++++.++++++++++++++++++++++++++
++.+++++++++++++++++++++++++.++++++++++++++++++++++++.+++++>..+++++++++++>+++++.
...........................................+++++

Not enough random bytes available.  Please do some other work to give
the OS a chance to collect more entropy! (Need 12 more bytes)
;laksjdfWe need to generate a lot of random bytes. It is a good idea to perform
some other action (type on the keyboard, move the mouse, utilize the
disks) during the prime generation; this gives the random number
generator a better chance to gain enough entropy.
+++++++++++++++.+++++.++++++++++++++++++++++.++++++++++++++++++++++.+++++++++++++++.
++++++++++++++++++++++++++++++++.+++++++++++++++.+++++.........+++++^^^^^^^^
^^^^^^^^^^^^^^^^^^^^^^^^
public and secret key created and signed.
```

At this point, the private/public key pair is ready to use. Both files—pubring.gpg, the public key ring, and secring.gpg, the secret key ring—are stored in binary form in your $HOME/.gnupg directory. Leave all these files intact and in the $HOME/.gnupg directory.

MANIPULATING PUBLIC/PRIVATE KEY RINGS

None of this does anyone much good if no one is encrypting anything for you. To allow this to happen, you must share your public key.

You need to consider sending your public key to some public key servers on the Internet if you end up using GPG a lot; that way, people can send you encrypted files without pestering you for your public key. Otherwise, you can simply have a copy of your public key handy in case someone asks for it.

The public key can take two forms: binary and plain text. By default, your pubring.gpg file is binary, so all the keys within are binary as well. The default extraction process extracts a binary version of your public key. You'll probably want an ASCII armored version, since even allowing the binary to be written to the screen can garble your terminal setting. The following command does it:

```
gpg -a --export youruserid > youruserid.pub.key.asc
```

The youruserID portion can be fudged a bit to contain enough characters to identify the key that you want to extract. For example, if Sherman T. Potter decides that he wants to extract his public key to give to someone else, he might use the following command to extract his key in binary form:

```
gpg -a --export sherman > potter.pub.key.asc
```

The `> potter.pub.key.asc` redirects the output (which would otherwise be sent to the screen) to the file called `potter.pub.key.asc`. The name of the file makes no difference at all; it could be called `foo`, but it should be something that you can easily associate with its contents, in this case Potter's public key in ASCII armor.

> **Note**
>
> An ASCII armored version of a key is a version in which all non-printing characters have been converted to a printable version. This process also makes the file approximately 30% larger. Should you accidentally export a binary key to your terminal, try typing `reset` to get back to a sane terminal.

Listing 25.2 shows what an extracted key looks like.

LISTING 25.2 A PUBLIC KEY

```
-----BEGIN PGP PUBLIC KEY BLOCK-----
Version: GnuPG v1.0.1 (GNU/Linux)
Comment: For info see http://www.gnupg.org

mQGiBDlK4UsRBACqGUwz8bzWncjnWaizpA3ak9SoNpEvBqraJucRpTHva085y7qV
ebROX1pxS98g7bI0JUZ4mdz0vgqt4hApEc6XQiDfEJ8GqERnabRpHp5uJnpzwitG
ft4aUiAzqD+AnKdUbh+dRHtDaUk1CtIgnns5D+yxq29t2FopH2YDpaVhuwCgj2i6
JDftWCn91aDL9BX1kwVBl4MD/RZvvBMWzGyUnaSfpH27jh2pJDhW4PXt1+VoHWb/
135qYBQI2hyn89g4xk3zFMr23PnkEAfKI/PhYd3f0plUFdklQLBsseqGC/eut6Nt
vJkQ74BGE8fDDeh8vAkt4+csnf54pMiSFwl7lLnCUGacG++NCfuLa4sinR1vthI0
sz3DBACEi7oSn/YY4LoTnjJdA78Gd0e/vB9DlrIgW+KUVnxL7nawepWErMR39sM/
iJ11WfZLzYvg39m+0jsf55C01Kwxlk9tuIwErnD8mPBKn1zXQ0JsVRVjY9N13gfP
FJlhCn5QCRRYNTPw6Zk/92/gN4/InB9aDWN18jrAaS5Ls0jjvLQjRGF2aWQgQS4g
QmFuZGVsDxkYXZpZEBwYW5hbml4LmNvbT6IVgQTEQIAFgUCOUrhSwQLCgQDAxUD
AgMWAgECF4AACgkQ60cOBBLqho1TZQCdFH9LdX+dpK5IhXEq4W8YeDhK32QAnRrJ
9314YY6LEM5Tk/4lcU0G5RptuQENBDlK4V0QBACDjyZDXyi7/7hiB6hYsKxM4IH9
JKXPZdKSmNIG0TZjCsAzJzUqj+dkKegxTmgOfWYpBjFMkg1e6nAac6B/zIFGaJo7
J2Zf7+tEiLMX8hSqf8XQRf/yHIMr/otddjWPQZfi6iS5uB7FaqphMf8ZESrZjbKC
T8xy595nR60FTEd7twADBwQAgTGGjSZQpRkllOHGu+BgIINAv3ynsmUGJunVrNV9
uYa7ve/uGcBbPqQF2CWuE/gyotuzMr6P0KSFKorlABVI+0uHqTgi9x4mst8uyK3x
gy7mPD8JfAmiczKKBiwYByjY/G3smHrgU75velJaPkvdru9KH+5IAjPY9SBsk4iv
gy+IRgQYEQIABgUCOUrhXQAKCRDrRw4EEuqGjZHhAJsHf4JOdyEq3mE+Exknva+a
frVaIwCfSHBG2PVOZgXYrcOg01gvSQO9r+s=
=uHvY
-----END PGP PUBLIC KEY BLOCK-----
```

To see the ID for a key, Sherman can optionally run a key verification and get a listing of the keys in `pubring.gpg` using the following command:

```
gpg --list-keys
```

Listing 25.3 shows how the verification looks.

LISTING 25.3   VERIFYING KEYS IN pubring.gpg

```
[stp@rumble stp]$ gpg --list-keys
/home/stp/.gnupg/pubring.gpg
----------------------------
pub   1024D/BACD540A 2000-04-27 Hawkeye Pierce <hawkeye@mash4077.army.mil>
sub   1024g/CD8D9B14 2000-04-27

pub   1024D/12EA868D 2000-06-17 Sherman T. Potter <stp@fish.net>
sub   1024g/727C0E64 2000-06-17
```

What needs to be done about other peoples' keys? Does anything need to be done before using them?

The answer is that you must add the keys to your public key ring first. You can add public keys to a sample key ring using the following command:

```
gpg --import hawkeye.pub.key.gpg.asc
```

Replace ../keys.asc with the filename (path included, unless it is in the current directory) for the public key that is being added.

Note that if someone sends you a public key, you can also simply run gpg against the file that contains the public key to add it to your key ring. GPG can see that the file contains a public key and ask what you want to do with it.

USING GPG

It is now time to start putting GPG to work. In the following section, you learn how to set up files so that their integrity can be checked and, if necessary, so that you can be warned when they are not received by their intended audiences. This section also discusses how to use public keys to encrypt files that are to be sent to others.

SIGNING FILES

Encrypting files is only one way of maintaining file authenticity and integrity. Another method is signing files. This method takes into account characteristics of the file, and then creates a unique signature using your—or a specified ID's—secret key. If the file is not changed between the time it is signed and the time it reaches its destination, when the file is decrypted or checked with GPG on the recipient's end, a message similar to the following appears:

```
[stp@rumble stp]$ gpg --verify foo.txt.asc foo.txt
gpg: Signature made Sun Jun 18 21:48:50 2000 EST using DSA key ID 12EA868D
gpg: Good signature from "Sherman T. Potter <stp@fish.net>"
```

If the file was changed, however, the message looks more like the following:

```
[stp@rumble stp]$ gpg --verify foo.txt.asc foo.txt
gpg: Signature made Sun Jun 18 21:48:50 2000 EST using DSA key ID 12EA868D
gpg: BAD signature from "Sherman T. Potter <stp@fish.net>"
```

Continuing from this point constitutes an informal agreement that the file's contents are acceptable even if the integrity has been compromised.

Different ways to sign files are available. For example, if Sherman just wants to sign the encryptme file and send it to John, he can use the following command:

```
gpg -b signme
```

This says to sign the `signme` file (specifies the ID that is doing the signing) and make the resulting file binary (the default). Of course, the file is not readable in this state because it is not ASCII. To make it a signed ASCII armored file instead, use the following command:

```
pgp -ba signme
```

The resulting file looks similar to Listing 25.4.

LISTING 25.4   GPG SIGNED FILE WITH ASCII ARMORING (ENCODED)

```
-----BEGIN PGP SIGNATURE-----
Version: GnuPG v1.0.1 (GNU/Linux)
Comment: For info see http://www.gnupg.org

iEYEABECAAYFAjlNktMACgkQ60cOBBLqho2/fACfWAD+14OhZH02emtCA2cJgf9o
g8IAniFn/yl2XY0m2QnmdEx85rlmgY1z
=/c0p
-----END PGP SIGNATURE-----
```

The `-b` option creates a detached signature file. The signature file carries the same name as the file signed, but with either a `.gpg` suffix, or an `.asc` suffix, depending on whether simple (binary) or ASCII armored signing was specified.

ENCRYPTING FILES

Imagine that you have a public key from someone else and you want to encrypt something for that person. The key has been added to the public key ring, a file is ready to be encrypted, and all that is needed is a command to encrypt it.

The following command does the trick:

```
gpg -r recipient -e filename
```

The recipient parameter (`-r`) needs to be enough of an identifier to allow GPG to locate the ID in its public key ring. For instance, use Sherman's `signme` file as an example again:

```
John,

Something fishy is going on here...
Can you come over and check it out?

Thanks...

Sherman
```

The following command can be executed by Sherman to encrypt the `signme` file in such a way that only John can read it:

```
pgp -r john -e signme
```

As you can see, a file called `signme.gpg` has been created and is ready to be sent to John. This is a binary file because Sherman did not specify that he wanted ASCII armoring. If the command is changed to

```
pgp -r john -ea signme
```

the resulting file is `signme.asc`; it looks similar to Listing 25.5.

LISTING 25.5 ENCRYPTED FILE WITH ASCII ARMORING

```
-----BEGIN PGP MESSAGE-----
Version: GnuPG v1.0.1 (GNU/Linux)
Comment: For info see http://www.gnupg.org

hQEOA3XveGfNjZsUEAQAstJC1WqPBt1ZGsLMlbkjYbgSiI2/IjTP/B2QS58/0EmD
M0vJwYwxKXJ4y0nGTl/DkKzx9P3RcMUprwdP4cejq94s0ABxmbUMKkWcwQueOQTG
2oAfK3u1/VrTgcSOYnO9h0YYSRChUCX1b2nQA3mzmtky+aDoMecDtWcICi0QrEgE
AKvDp76yKaEmaAvrpnypYkVyVEvys+HuEwfp7U8hBUiP5JBjqcDsprRHH4wuamOp
9llv/izrvO15gNgi4eyXHGOrzY/sE2UHRhpiHMTVoICvMuPVikB2Z8nSgyb61eKh
WJ85M+T5wJaQIn3yUz8oGMsIloAh+USG6hi7CposclWMycB56ypt6uVaKpGppk1U
hc1wnTcuw2uHqpYNWeHhV78xksrW3NxvSft+Va5lufST3LNwmgcjwGRP6i7ZQ+oE
/NDkZicDSCZd0BTKkF3HQFGv3/wEv0d+7bfdbuRYxqUjJVTuQGt0zWjP4KMDYwqN
6MSCwt6MWm5aOFP4WyyVF9ld5mluA6rga77o8Wwwn1irYlNlsv+ysDGzy+8fRlDP
5YHf63rJ0WQa1Sygm9hvGXEij+joAN1/xGEMxDZfNbNE3g17UD/1F/C7aihPRSEJ
2v7RuPgSPv63Hlm8CGhWac9OAthaipDTJ32dONNJV+vz4/4JgkEa+1Kl5ksHbEiB
ocwokVgfuQQszV5pzn/pFAuAISJ6c2HUvI7wu4SjYqg+lQlahQuXEPwaqMgkRxkc
vvW5bXTC2cnrBE6WEw==
=OA4T
-----END PGP MESSAGE-----
```

This is a much more suitable method if Sherman plans to send John the encrypted file through email.

When John receives this file, he somehow needs to decrypt it before he reads it. The file was encrypted with his public key, and he has the associated secret key, so all he needs to do is run pgp against the encrypted file—it knows what to do from there.

After giving a password for his secret key, the file is decrypted using the following syntax:

```
gpg -d signme.asc
```

Because the file was ASCII armored, it was first decoded back into binary form and then decrypted. If the file that is being decrypted is already binary, this step can be eliminated, but the rest of the decryption process is identical.

If the file is meant for John's eyes only, and Sherman is worried about it being tampered with before John gets it, he can sign the file when he encrypts it. This gives an extra layer of insurance that is not there with plain encryption. If the file is tampered with, the signature does not match and a warning is presented (as discussed in the preceding section).

The command to perform these actions resembles a combination of the encryption commands and the signing and ASCII armoring commands:

```
gpg -r john -bea signme
```

The resulting file looks similar to a typical ASCII armored encrypted file, but when the file is decrypted, the extra steps that were taken to sign it pay off. Signing encrypted files or binary files is a good way to ensure they have not been tampered with since you encrypted them. Many software packages, especially security-related software packages, are signed. This process has prevented the sabotage of at least one security program offered using anonymous FTP on the Internet.

TROUBLESHOOTING

I've set up my email client, but I seem to be having trouble sending mail. It keeps bouncing with a message about sender domain must resolve.

You've probably configured your email client to use your localhost's sendmail instead of your ISP. This will no longer work, thanks to spammers' abuse of the email systems. Most MTAs don't accept mail from systems if they don't have a valid MX record. Change your email client to point to your ISP's outgoing mail host.

I set up my email at home to run through the sendmail server at my work rather than at my ISP, but I keep getting an error message 550 relaying denied and the messages won't go out.

By default, sendmail will not permit any messages to come from an external system with another external system as its destination. This is called relaying, and is prohibited. You'll need to ask your administrator to open up your ISP's network, your IP, or your range of IPs (if you have a dialup with dynamic IP allocation). Alternately, you'll need to dial in to your place of work to send mail through your work mail server.

But I am the administrator of my work system. How do I accomplish the above?

Unfortunately, in the past, Caldera has elected not to build in the access_db into their sendmail configuration. If this is still the case, you'll need to add access_db in a line like this in your sendmail.mc file:

```
FEATURE(access_db, hash `/etc/mail/access.db')
```

After you've rebuilt your sendmail config file, you can start this and do the following:

As root, cd to /etc/mail. Create a file called access. In this file put the appropriate entry to allow yourself access, for example:

```
192.168.0        RELAY
```

The first column can be a full or partial IP address (partial assumes the entire range of IPs in that block) or a domain name. You can also specify an email address in some cases. Legitimate values that can replace RELAY include OK, REJECT, DISCARD, or certain error codes and text.

You then need to issue the following command to create the access.db file:

```
makemap hash access.db <access
```

If you feel uncertain about how to do this, you might want to consider using Webmin, which uses drop down boxes in many places and performs sanity checking.

See the sendmail documentation for more information on the use of `access_db`.

I run a mail server. A local company asked if we could swap services, us as a secondary email server for them and they for us in case one of our mail systems goes down. Do I need to do anything special?

Short answer: no. The only thing that needs to happen is each of you will need a second MX entry in your DNS records specifying the other sendmail system, and with a higher priority. You should not just arbitrarily add someone else's mail server as a secondary without asking first, however.

I'm using GnuPG and I occasionally use it when someone needs to send me confidential information. But I forgot what my pass phrase is. Can I recover it?

Unfortunately, no. What you'll need to do is immediately create a new private and public key pair using the method discussed in this chapter and contact anyone who has your old key and give them your new one. Don't forget to do this if you've put your public key on a key server.

CHAPTER **26**

DNS AND BIND

In this chapter

ABOUT DNS

You might not be familiar with DNS, but if you've ever surfed the Internet, you've made extensive use of it. Computers know how to find each other by means of their addresses, and specifically by an IP address, just as you can (usually) find the book store after looking up its address in the phone book. DNS is to computers what the phone book is to you. You don't remember Internet sites by their IP addresses, but by their names. But you don't know where the FOOBAZ bookstore is if you've never been there (or seen it in passing), so you need to look up the address. Similarly, when you want your Web browser to find www.calderasystems.com, your system uses DNS to look up the IP address.

On your Linux system you have resolver libraries that know how to resolve names into IP addresses. In your /etc/nsswitch.conf (name service switch configuration) file you have a line that looks like the following:

```
hosts:          files dns
```

This line tells the resolver routines that when they are looking for hosts, they need to first consult the system's files, and if they don't find what they're looking for there, they need to perform a DNS lookup.

> **Note**
>
> The nsswitch.conf file replaced the /etc/host.conf file when Linux moved from libc5-based systems to the new glibc (libc6). The nsswitch.conf file follows Sun Microsystems's lead and acts as a single reference for system database files for applications requiring this information.

The system files start with /etc/hosts, where commonly accessed local network hosts might be listed. This lookup is faster than a DNS lookup. But if names that might change are included, you might wonder why the lookup failed to find what you were looking for. Therefore, refrain from putting any entries over which you have no control into /etc/hosts.

The resolver libraries, failing to find the address they seek in /etc/hosts, consult /etc/resolv.conf to find the IP addresses of machines known as *Domain Name Servers*, or *name servers* for short. Up to three, but not fewer than two, need to be entered in this file. Why two? In case one is down. But no more than three are consulted, so all name server entries beyond the first three are ignored.

> **Note**
>
> If you run your own name server, you'll want to make sure all your hosts point to your name server first. The host the name server is running on should point to 127.0.0.1 for name resolution.

WHAT IS BIND?

Several different DNS servers are available under different names. The most common, and the one you'll find on your Linux system, is the Berkeley Internet Nameserver Daemon (BIND). As of this writing, the current major version number is 8.

ABOUT DOMAINS

Before you go further, it is helpful to understand a little about domains. You've seen domain names before. They are in the form of `bar.org`, and contain at least two parts. Reading from the right, the `org` part is called a *top-level domain*. A number of top-level domains exist. In the United States, currently, are the following top-level domains:

- `.com`—Commercial entities (businesses)
- `.org`—Non-commercial organizations
- `.net`—Network affiliated organizations
- `.mil`—U.S. military branches
- `.gov`—U.S. government agencies
- `.edu`—Educational institutions
- `.int`—International organizations
- `.us`—The U.S. domain, which has each state as lower-level divisions

Additional top-level domains have been proposed, but have not yet been implemented.

In other countries, top-level domains are administered by the Internet authorities of those countries and include a two-letter country suffix. Some examples are as follows:

- `.uk`—United Kingdom
- `.ca`—Canada
- `.mx`—Mexico
- `.za`—Zud Africa (South Africa)

Within each of the countries, a top-level domain structure, which is decided by the country's Internet authority, exists. These might or might not correspond to the top-level domains found in the U.S.

Below the top-level domain is the name of the institution or organization that constitutes the actual domain name. For example, `ibm.com`, or `ibm.co.uk`. These examples are IBM's domain names in the United States and the United Kingdom, respectively.

Some large domains also have *subdomains*. Very large institutions might have subdomains. For example, the `army.mil` domain, which has military bases all over the world and which has very large units on those bases, might be further broken down into subdomains. Therefore, a large base such as Fort Bragg, North Carolina, will have a subdomain `ftbragg.army.mil`. Because

Ft. Bragg is so large, this might be further divided based on units; for example the Corps Support Command at Ft. Bragg might have its own subdomain, coscom.ftbragg.army.mil, under the ftbragg subdomain. Finally, individual host computers have their own hostnames added to the domain name. So the hostname eagle1 becomes eagle1.coscom.ftbragg.army.mil. If this host exists, you can learn the IP address for this host using DNS (assuming that the host has a record in the DNS database).

For current information on domains, visit the Internet Assigned Numbers Authority domains page at http://www.iana.org/top-level-domains.html.

ROOT NAME SERVERS

The existence of these top-level domains suggests a structure for DNS lookups. Each top-level domain is the top of a tree (an upside-down tree, that is). So when you do a lookup of calderasystems.com, a name server looks to the top-level domain name server for .com and is directed to a name server down the branches for calderasystems. The name server for Caldera listed in the top-level domain is one of the servers that is authoritative for the calderasystems.com domain; it can give the answer to the DNS server that is making the query.

Fortunately for all involved, this lookup at the top level doesn't have to happen often. Because this kind of activity can generate significant traffic, it causes delays in querying for domain name resolution. Each DNS server that queries a DNS server for a domain gets several pieces of information. In addition to the address resolution that is requested, each original query also returns a time to live (TTL) value. This TTL tells the querying DNS server how long to cache the records it received from the authoritative source. It saves the answers and uses them to respond to further queries until the TTL drops to zero, at which time it queries the authoritative source once again. These values are often as long as a week. You'll see this again later.

TYPES OF DNS SERVERS

Despite anything you might read here or elsewhere, only two types of name servers are defined by the DNS specs—primary masters and secondary masters. The top-level DNS servers, called *Root Name Servers*, are just primary or secondary masters for the top-level domain; they only point queries to other primary or secondary masters that are authoritative for the second-level domain, the domain that you are looking up. You'll often see text that discusses primary and secondary name servers (but not necessarily masters), forwarding name servers, stub servers, caching name servers, and so on. These terms are related to the use or type of setup rather than to the role they play in the DNS hierarchy.

Note

> The difference between primary masters and secondary masters is that the primary master has the master list for the domain, and the secondary masters perform a zone transfer to get the information to answer queries authoritatively. This design is to reduce administrative tasks to maintaining only one DNS server. You might see secondary masters referred to as slaves, and primary masters as only masters.

DNS servers can be set up to perform different roles. If you register a domain name with Internic.net, you are asked to provide at least two DNS servers, a primary and a secondary master. You might have chosen to administer these yourself, or you might have asked your Internet provider to do the honors. You must supply two, and it's better if these two are not on the same network.

If your provider is handling DNS resolution for your domain, all you need to do is provide them with the names of those hosts that you want to have registered. Not all hosts need to be registered, just those that you want to be available from outside—these are most likely your Web server, your FTP server, and your mail server. You can give your provider something like a hosts file, with hostnames and aliases. That is, you might give them something such as

```
192.168.100.2    foo.bar.org    www.bar.org
192.168.100.3    baz.bar.org    ftp.bar.org
```

and a note that `192.168.100.3` receives mail for `bar.org`.

Your provider, in return, gives you the addresses of the primary and secondary masters for DNS resolution for your host's `/etc/resolv.conf` files. This is true whether you or they host your DNS. However, if you host your own DNS, your internal hosts look at your DNS servers rather than your providers.

If you host your own DNS, either primary or primary and secondary masters, you need to learn more about DNS than this chapter can tell you. The same is also true if you're going to run a private network with full DNS because this requires the same level of knowledge. But if you only want to run a caching DNS server, you can do so under most Linux distributions "straight out of the box." That is, most distributions already have the default files necessary for you to do this without knowing more. The system with the caching DNS server only needs to have `/etc/resolv.conf` pointing to your provider's DNS, and your other hosts pointing to your caching DNS servers.

BIND FILES

Each distribution tends to go their own way to some extent with the BIND files. All will have a `named.conf` in `/etc`, and they will also have startup scripts.

CALDERA OPENLINUX

The BIND v8 that comes on OpenLinux installs a number of files. First, a file called `named` is installed in `/etc/sysconfig/daemons`; COAS uses this to configure `named` for startup at boot. A `named` script is installed in `/etc/rc.d/init.d`, which has links for startup from run-levels 3–5.

Finally, in `/usr/sbin`, four files—`named`, `named-boot`, `named-xfer`, and `ndc`—are installed. These are the name server daemon, a Perl script to convert `named.boot` to `named.conf`, an external zone file transfer program, and a name server daemon control program, respectively.

DEBIAN

The bind package installs all the files required and implements a caching name server that can be expanded simply by adding the zone files and entries to `named.conf`.

Debian installs the bind files in a different place than either Caldera or Red Hat, choosing to locate all bind files in `/etc/bind/`. You'll want to keep this in mind when reading the rest of the chapter. Debian also calls the initialization script bind rather than named as do Caldera and Red Hat.

RED HAT

When you install the Red Hat bind package, you will still not be able to start named until you have created an `/etc/named.conf` file. This is not included in the bind package. The `/etc/named.conf` file is included in a caching-name server package. After you install the caching-name server package or create the proper files, named will start at bootup, or when you issue the `/etc/rc.d/init.d/named start` command.

The Red Hat bind package installs basically the same files as the Caldera package. After the files are installed, overall administration of the DNS system is the same.

NDC: NAME SERVER DAEMON CONTROL

The program ndc helps an administrator control the name server daemon. After running, named caches hits until they expire. The ndc program provides a way to interface with the running name server daemon. With ndc, you can do things such as dump the cached database to a file. This does not clear the cache—it just allows you to look at the contents. It also enables you to trace queries and start a query log. The ndc interface can show you the status of the daemon or dump a statistics file. It can start, stop, or restart the daemon.

The ndc program itself is a shell script. The script works by sending different signals to named. These signals tell the daemon what to do. But remembering the different signals and what they mean is difficult, so the script gives you a simple means of controlling the daemon, with easy-to-remember terms. If you feel so inclined, take a look at the script. It isn't very long, and it can be educational.

CONFIGURATION FILES AND DNS TERMS

The name server daemon uses a number of files. Some are read to provide an initial configuration and tell it where to find other needed files; others are read at startup and retained in memory for use in answering queries. The first of these files is `/etc/named.conf` (see Listing 26.1).

LISTING 26.1   A SAMPLE `/etc/named.conf` FILE

```
// generated by named-bootconf.pl

options {
        directory "/var/named";
     allow-query { any; };
```

LISTING 26.1   CONTINUED

```
    allow-transfer { 192.168.0.2; !0.0.0.0; };
        /*
         * If there is a firewall between you and nameservers you want
         * to talk to, you might need to uncomment the query-source
         * directive below.  Previous versions of BIND always asked
         * questions using port 53, but BIND 8.1 uses an unprivileged
         * port by default.
         */
        // query-source address * port 53;
};

//
// Boot file for name server
//
// type        domain                    source        file
zone "." {
        type hint;
        file "named.root";
};

// Zone boot information and daemon options are kept in other files
// (autoincluded from boot.zones)
//
// Name server zone boot file
// See named(8) for syntax and further information
//
// type        domain                    source        file
// (autoincluded from boot.options)
//
// Options for name server
// Use `bindconfig' to automatically configure this file
//
// type        domain                    source        file
zone "localhost" {
        type master;
        file "localhost.hosts";
};

zone "127.in-addr.arpa" {
        type master;
        file "127.0.0.hosts";
};
// Custom configurations below (will be preserved)
```

The comments (followed by // to the end of the line) are fairly self-explanatory. The sections themselves each start with a statement and are surrounded by {} and terminated by ;. Each sub-statement within a statement also ends with a ;. The first statement in the options section tells named where zone files are located. Other startup options, such as query-source, listen-on port, and more might also be included. In all, some 43 separate sub-statements within the options statement are possible, many of which only pertain to large sites with multiple zones and specific requirements.

PART

IV

CH

26

> **Note**
>
> *Zone files* are databases that hold a table of hostnames/IP addresses for which the name server is authoritative, with one exception. This exception is the hints zone file (.), which is a list of root name servers.

The next three statements in Listing 26.1 list zone files. These three zone files are all that are required for a caching. Sites that are authoritative for a zone have no fewer than two zone entries. All name servers, including caching-only name servers, are masters of their own domain, the domain defined by localhost. The applicable files (zone `localhost` and zone `127.in-addr.arpa`) are needed when installing the bind package. Contents of the zone files are explained in the following sections.

> **Note**
>
> Zone files are made up of resource records (RRs). These resource records are named to IP mappings, one RR per mapping.

The newer BIND v8 has a number of other configuration statements. Many of these are new to v8. The various statements include acl (access control list), include (include files), logging, key (for authentication and authorization), and server (sets per-server options). The options and logging statements might occur only once. Other statements might occur multiple times.

ZONE DATABASE FILES

A set of zone files containing RRs is found by default in the directory named in `named.conf`, often `/var/named`, although any location can be chosen. Each zone file is listed as a statement in the `named.conf` file as shown in Listing 26.1.

A number of different RR types make up the zone files. Several that are of note are discussed later. A complete list of RRs in database (`db`) files includes the following:

- **SOA record**—Admin data and info about this data's authority
- **NS record**—Name servers for this domain
- **A record**—Name to address mapping
- **PTR record**—Pointer for address to name mapping
- **CNAME record**—Canonical (alias) name
- **MX record**—Mail exchange record
- **TXT**—Textual information
- **WKS**—Well-known services
- **HINFO**—Host information

START OF AUTHORITY HEADER

The Start of Authority Header (SOA) is the first entry in the db file. The SOA indicates that this name server is the best (authoritative) source for information in this domain. There can be only one SOA entry per db file. A sample SOA looks like the following:

```
bar.org. IN SOA  foo.bar.org.  dab.bar.org.  (
                1998122300  ; Serial
                10800       ; Refresh time -- 3 hours
                3600        ; Retry -- 1 hour
                604800      ; Expire -- 1 week
                86400  )    ; TTL - 1 day
```

The first part of the entry, bar.org. (note the trailing .), indicates the domain to which this db file refers. The IN indicates Internet. The SOA indicates that this is the SOA record entry for this file. The entry foo.bar.org. is the host on which you created the file, and the entry dab.bar.org is the email address of the db file's contact. The address is converted from dab.bar.org to dab@bar.org.

> **Tip**
>
> One of the most common misconfiguration problems with name servers has to do with the use of terminating periods (.) on entries. The rule is, if you don't want to have the domain name (bar.org) appended to the entry, remember to include the trailing period.

The parentheses permit the data that follows to span multiple lines. The opening parenthesis must be on the first line. Within the parentheses are various values that the name server passes to querying name servers. The first is the serial number. Serial numbers are for secondary masters. They compare the current serial number with the one that they had when they downloaded the data. If the two are different, they download the new data. If the two are the same, they do not. This serial number can be any number which increments. One method is shown: the eight-digit date plus a two-digit trailing sequence number (it is unlikely you'll make more than 99 changes to the db file in one day). Note that a ; begins a comment and continues to the end of the line.

> **Tip**
>
> Remember to change the serial number and restart the name server (ndc reload) or your changes will not take effect.

The refresh time, retry time, and expire time are also for secondary masters. These tell the secondary that it needs to refresh its data (check the serial number and, if it is different, reload) at this interval in seconds. If the primary master is not available, it needs to retry every hour. If it cannot make contact for a week, the zone expires and the domain data needs to be flushed.

The TTL tells how long a name server that is not a secondary master is to cache the data. If your zone is static, longer times decrease the load on your name server. If you need to change the file often, you'll want to decrease this time; however, this will cause a significant increase in queries because after this amount of time, name servers must re-query.

These four times—refresh, retry, expire, and TTL—give you a good indicator of how long it will take a DNS change to propagate through the Internet. Remember that in the instant before you did a restart, a secondary might have refreshed. If, just before the secondary came back to the primary to refresh (3 hours later), a foreign DNS query returned the old value with the TTL, it might be more than 27 hours from the change before the change propagates out. This is assuming, too, that the secondary had no problems connecting to the primary at its first refresh.

> **Tip**
>
> The entire SOA entry (minus comments and parentheses) can be put on one line, but it is best to follow the preceding template because the order of the values is important.

db FILE ENTRIES

Each `db` file has entries that correspond to hosts in the domain. The first entries look like the following:

```
bar.org.    IN NS foo.bar.org.
bar.org.    IN NS baz.bar.org.
```

These entries are the name servers for this domain. Again, note the trailing . on each entry.

The next RR that is found in the `db` file is the A or address record. These appear as follows:

```
foo.bar.org.        IN A 192.168.0.1
;
baz.bar.org.        IN A 192.168.0.2
baz.bar.org.        IN A 192.168.10.90
;
baz2.bar.org.      IN A 192.168.0.2
baz90.bar.org.     IN A 192.168.10.90
```

Nothing is special about the first entry. The host `baz` either has two Ethernet cards, each on a different network, or one card with two addresses on different networks. This host is what's known as a *multihomed host*. You can use comments with blank lines to separate parts of the file. A good recommendation is to separate multihomed hosts from those with only one address. The same separation can be used for other sections. This just makes it easier to read and troubleshoot.

The last two entries are additional names that each map specifically to only one interface of the multihomed host. These entries are here because a lookup on `baz.bar.org` returns both addresses—you can't pick out the one that you want to ping specifically for debugging. Therefore, additional entries exist for each interface that are particular to only one interface. This is especially useful for routers that might have several NICs.

The next RR of interest is the `CNAME`. This is used to map aliases to A records as follows:

```
www.bar.org.    IN CNAME foo.bar.org.
ftp.bar.org.       IN CNAME baz.bar.org.
```

Note that, because host `baz` has more than one address, you'll want to either make sure that FTP is binding all addresses or have `ftp.bar.org` point to a specific interface. Using the same name for multiple IP addresses can cause problems. For example, some services do not bind two addresses. They bind only one address. But which one? Normally, it will be the first one encountered. Likewise, clients looking to connect to that service sometimes connect and sometimes do not, depending on which IP address they get first in reference to their query. Such confusion needs to be avoided; you can only do so by assigning multihomed hosts unique names to each IP address.

The final RR you'll look at in this section is the MX, or mail exchange address. This RR takes a little more explanation. A sample MX record looks like the following:

```
bar.org.    IN    MX    50     foo.bar.org.
bar.org.    IN    MX    100    baz.bar.org.
```

The records read as follows: For mail being sent to user@bar.org, foo.bar.org is the primary mail host, and baz is the secondary mail host. The numbers 50 and 100 indicate the priority for the mail hosts. The lower the number, the higher the priority. The numbers can range from 0–65535, but in practice, the most common numbers tend to be 5, 10, 50, and 100 for simplicity's sake. This allows MX hosts to be inserted before or after any existing entries without rewriting all the entries.

So if the primary mailhost is foo, but for whatever reason foo can't receive an email message, baz receives it. But because our mail host is foo and that's where folks receive their mail, what happens to mail delivered to baz? Well, baz checks the MX records too and sees that foo is the primary mail host, so baz tries to send to foo. If more MX records are found, baz looks at the hostname and priority. The host baz does not re-send mail to itself or an MX host with a higher or equal number; it only sends to those with a lower number. Eventually, though, foo comes back up and accepts the messages that baz has queued up (at least, we hope so).

The other RR types, HINFO, TXT, and WKS, are of little value to most sites, so they are not covered here. The important RRs for forward resolution have now been reviewed.

PART

IV

CH

26

REVERSE RESOLUTION DATABASES

Up to this point, you've looked at RRs for forward resolution db files. But sometimes a lookup is needed on a reverse resolution. That is, you have an IP address, but don't know the host to which it belongs. Look at Listing 26.1, near the bottom of the listing, at the last two statements; the first refers to a zone localhost, and the substatements point to localhost.hosts. This is your forward resolution database. The next one, with a statement zone 127.in-addr.arpa, tells named that this is a reverse lookup statement and to use this on any lookup for an IP address beginning 127.x.x.x. If you are master for bar.org and have a zone bar.org with filename bar.org.hosts and the IP network is 192.168.0.0/24, your zone statement for the reverse resolution database is 192.168.0.in-addr.arpa. Your filename can be anything you want to call it—but 192.168.0.hosts is nice and descriptive.

The reverse resolution db file is slightly different from the forward resolution database, but only in the RRs used within. The SOA is very similar and might look like the following:

```
0.168.192.in-addr.arpa.    IN SOA foo.bar.org.  dab.bar.org. (
1998122301 10800 3600 604800 86400 )
```

The only difference here is the use of the backward network portion of the IP address corresponding to the domain, and the use of the `in-addr.arpa.` suffix. This special suffix is required on all RRs in the reverse resolution database.

The rest of the RRs in the database are of the following form:

```
1.0.168.192.in-addr.arpa.    IN PTR foo.bar.org.
2.0.168.192.in-addr.arpa.    IN PTR baz.bar.org.
```

These two entries are PTR records and point from the reversed IP address annotation with the `in-addr.arpa.` suffix to the host name. This file also carries the NS records in reverse form as follows:

```
0.168.192.in-addr.arpa.    IN NS foo.bar.org.
0.168.192.in-addr.arpa.    IN NS baz.bar.org.
```

Again, nothing unusual. The reverse address is that of the domain, just as the forward NS addresses were for the domain.

named.root DATABASE

The `named.root` database is a special database. This `db` file contains hints to the name server as to where to look for the root name servers on the Internet. Because these servers do change from time to time, this file also needs to be updated. A good rule of thumb for updating this is once a month. A script in the "dig" section that follows can be run to perform the update automatically.

NAME SERVER TOOLS

A number of tools that are useful for debugging DNS are available in Linux under the `bind-utils` and `whois` packages. These tools are invaluable to administrators. Although some overlap exists between the tools, each has its advantages and disadvantages. The best way to compare them is to take a look at some of them. This will also give you the opportunity to check your name server setup.

NSLOOKUP

The nslookup program performs name server lookups. The program has two modes, interactive and non-interactive. Two ways are available to enter interactive mode. The first way is to run nslookup with no arguments. The second way is to run nslookup with a hyphen (signifying input from the keyboard) and a name server. If nslookup is not given a name server to use, it consults the `/etc/resolv.conf` file and uses the first one listed. If you are running a name server on your system, the first name-server line in `/etc/resolv.conf` should point to the localhost (`127.0.0.1`).

The nslookup program has eleven possible commands; two are the lookup name itself and the lookup name with a name server to use to perform the lookup. Other commands provide specific types of lookups or set options. The `set` command has 14 options that can be set. After they are set, these options remain in use until `set` is invoked to change them again.

The most common of the set arguments is to set the querytype. Querytypes can be any of the valid RR types plus a few extras (A, ANY, CNAME, HINFO, MX, PX, NS, PTR, SOA, TXT, WKS, SRV, NAPTR). The PX option provides information regarding zone creation, zone contact, serial number, and TTL information—just slightly less information than the SOA option. The ANY option provides PX information plus name servers, plus SOA. The SRV and NAPTR options provide information similar to the PX option, but specify the forward or reverse lookup databases respectively. The default is A.

When nslookup starts, it reports the DNS server that it will use for lookups and presents you with a prompt as follows:

```
bash-2.01$ nslookup
Default Server:  localhost
Address:  127.0.0.1
>
```

Each subsequent use reports the server again, so this information is omitted in subsequent examples.

Now, you'll take a look at some output. First, look at the default output (querytype=A) for the domain calderasystems.com. The following is the non-authoritative answer:

```
Name: - calderasystems.com
Address:  207.179.18.130
```

Note that the first line tells you that the answer you've obtained is non-authoritative. This means that the information was provided from information that the current DNS server cached.

Now look at the output after setting the querytype to ANY. Following is the non-authoritative answer:

```
calderasystems.com        nameserver = gw.caldera.com
calderasystems.com        nameserver = ns.calderasystems.com
calderasystems.com        internet address = 207.179.18.130

Authoritative answers can be found from:
calderasystems.com        nameserver = gw.caldera.com
calderasystems.com        nameserver = ns.calderasystems.com
gw.caldera.com  internet address = 207.179.18.252
ns.calderasystems.com    internet address = 207.179.18.7
```

Here again you see that the answer is non-authoritative. Following that, you see the name servers for the caldera.com domain listed. Then is the information from the SOA. Looking at the serial number, you can see that this is update 1 on 30 Jan 2000. Because this domain is maintained by someone other than the author of this chapter, you can see that the serial numbering convention I suggested earlier is a sound one from more than my point of view. Looking through the rest of this data, about the only information you don't have is the MX data.

Setting the querytype each time by typing it out can be annoying at best, especially if your typing skills are not the greatest. But the querytype can be set by just using q, as in `set q=MX`.

Here's a look at that:

```
calderasystems.com        preference = 10, mail exchanger = mail.calderasystems.com
calderasystems.com        preference = 50, mail exchanger = caldera.caldera.com
calderasystems.com        nameserver = ns.calderasystems.com
calderasystems.com        nameserver = gw.caldera.com
caldera.caldera.com       internet address = 207.179.18.1
ns.calderasystems.com     internet address = 207.179.18.7
gw.caldera.com  internet address = 207.179.18.252
```

Here you see the mail exchange with a preference of 10 and the backup with a preference of 50, which is where mail will go if the primary is down.

Normally, nslookup uses the search list specified in /etc/resolv.conf when trying to resolve names. Sometimes, this can return undesired results. Put a period (.) at the end of domain queries, as in `nslookup calderasystems.com`, to avoid this.

DIG

The next program that is useful for debugging—and some other purposes—is dig. dig returns more information than nslookup does, and in a different form. The easiest way to show what dig can do for you is to give you a sample script used to update the named.root hint file, and then look at the output (see Listing 26.2). Remember to make the appropriate changes to the script depending on your particular configuration.

LISTING 26.2   A NAME SERVER UPDATE SCRIPT, hintupdt.sh

```
#!/bin/bash
# Original script author unknown -- modified
#
# Update the nameserver cache information file once per month.
# This is run automatically by the following cron entry.
# 0 0 1 * * /usr/local/sbin/hintupdt.sh
(
echo "To: sysadmin <root@localhost>"
echo "From: system <root>"
echo "Subject: Root servers hint file update"
echo

export PATH=/usr/local/sbin:/sbin:/usr/sbin:/bin:/usr/bin:/usr/local/bin
cd /var/named

dig > named.root.new

echo "The hint file (named.root) has been updated to contain"
echo "the following information:"
echo
cat named.root.new
```

LISTING 26.2   CONTINUED

```
chown root.root named.root.new
chmod 444 named.root.new
mv named.root named.root.old
mv named.root.new named.root
ndc restart
echo
echo "The nameserver has been restarted to ensure that the update is complete."
echo "The previous named.root file is now called /var/named/named.root.old."
) 2>&1 | /usr/lib/sendmail -t
exit 0
```

The line that is of interest to you is the following:

```
dig
```

This returns the output that is shown in Listing 26.3.

LISTING 26.3   DIG LOOKUP OF ROOT SERVERS FROM internic.net

```
; <<>> DiG 8.1 <<>> . @rs.internic.net
; (1 server found)
;; res options: init recurs defnam dnsrch
;; got answer:
;; ->>HEADER<<-opcode: QUERY, status: NOERROR, id: 10
;; flags: qr rd; QUERY: 1, ANSWER: 0, AUTHORITY: 13, ADDITIONAL: 13
;; QUERY SECTION:
;;      ., type = A, class = IN

;; AUTHORITY SECTION:
.               5d6h47m12s IN NS  D.ROOT-SERVERS.NET.
.               5d6h47m12s IN NS  C.ROOT-SERVERS.NET.
.               5d6h47m12s IN NS  B.ROOT-SERVERS.NET.
.               5d6h47m12s IN NS  H.ROOT-SERVERS.NET.
.               5d6h47m12s IN NS  A.ROOT-SERVERS.NET.
.               5d6h47m12s IN NS  M.ROOT-SERVERS.NET.
.               5d6h47m12s IN NS  L.ROOT-SERVERS.NET.
.               5d6h47m12s IN NS  K.ROOT-SERVERS.NET.
.               5d6h47m12s IN NS  J.ROOT-SERVERS.NET.
.               5d6h47m12s IN NS  G.ROOT-SERVERS.NET.
.               5d6h47m12s IN NS  F.ROOT-SERVERS.NET.
.               5d6h47m12s IN NS  I.ROOT-SERVERS.NET.
.               5d6h47m12s IN NS  E.ROOT-SERVERS.NET.

;; ADDITIONAL SECTION:
D.ROOT-SERVERS.NET.     5w6d16h IN A    128.8.10.90
C.ROOT-SERVERS.NET.     5w6d16h IN A    192.33.4.12
B.ROOT-SERVERS.NET.     5w6d16h IN A    128.9.0.107
H.ROOT-SERVERS.NET.     5w6d16h IN A    128.63.2.53
A.ROOT-SERVERS.NET.     5w6d16h IN A    198.41.0.4
M.ROOT-SERVERS.NET.     5w6d16h IN A    202.12.27.33
L.ROOT-SERVERS.NET.     5w6d16h IN A    198.32.64.12
K.ROOT-SERVERS.NET.     5w6d16h IN A    193.0.14.129
J.ROOT-SERVERS.NET.     5w6d16h IN A    198.41.0.10
G.ROOT-SERVERS.NET.     5w6d16h IN A    192.112.36.4
F.ROOT-SERVERS.NET.     5w6d16h IN A    192.5.5.241
```

PART

IV

CH

26

LISTING 26.3   CONTINUED

```
I.ROOT-SERVERS.NET.     5w6d16h IN A    192.36.148.17
E.ROOT-SERVERS.NET.     5w6d16h IN A    192.203.230.10

;; Total query time: 360 msec
;; FROM: foo to SERVER: rs.internic.net   198.41.0.6
;; WHEN: Fri Jan  1 06:43:30 1999
;; MSG SIZE  sent: 17  rcvd: 436
```

The dig program returns data in a format that is usable directly by the DNS server, making updates like this easy. Remarks are marked with ;; by dig. The header section shows you the options that are set for this dig query, but not necessarily those that are used. The HEADER tells you that this was a query that returned no errors. The authority section provides a simplified (translated from seconds) readout of the expire time, the time after which the DNS server that obtained these results needs to stop using them. The internic expires its root servers at six weeks (604,800 seconds).

Compare the following dig output for calderasystems.com to the output in the previous nslookup section. The dig lookup also defaults to querytype A (see Listing 26.4).

LISTING 26.4   OUTPUT FROM A DIG QUERY

```
; <<>> DiG 8.2 <<>> calderasystems.com
;; res options: init recurs defnam dnsrch
;; got answer:
;; ->>HEADER<<- opcode: QUERY, status: NOERROR, id: 4
;; flags: qr rd ra; QUERY: 1, ANSWER: 1, AUTHORITY: 2, ADDITIONAL: 2
;; QUERY SECTION:
;;      calderasystems.com, type = A, class = IN

;; ANSWER SECTION:
calderasystems.com.     53m3s IN A      207.179.18.130

;; AUTHORITY SECTION:
calderasystems.com.     25m17s IN NS    gw.caldera.com.
calderasystems.com.     25m17s IN NS    ns.calderasystems.com.

;; ADDITIONAL SECTION:
gw.caldera.com.         5h53m7s IN A     207.179.18.252
ns.calderasystems.com.  1d23h26m54s IN A  207.179.18.7

;; Total query time: 3 msec
;; FROM: chiriqui.pananix.com to SERVER: default -- 127.0.0.1
;; WHEN: Wed Mar 22 09:37:43 2000
;; MSG SIZE  sent: 36  rcvd: 129
```

This provides the same basic information, just more of it and in a slightly different format. Whether you use dig or nslookup is a personal choice, but nslookup is less cluttered.

The dig utility also enables you to easily perform reverse lookups. If you know an IP, you can use the -x option with dig and you don't need to write the IP address backward using the in-addr.arpa notation:

```
dig -x 207.179.18.252
; <<>> DiG 8.2 <<>> -x
;; res options: init recurs defnam dnsrch
;; got answer:
;; ->>HEADER<<- opcode: QUERY, status: NOERROR, id: 4
;; flags: qr aa rd ra; QUERY: 1, ANSWER: 1, AUTHORITY: 2, ADDITIONAL: 2
;; QUERY SECTION:
;;      252.18.179.207.in-addr.arpa, type = ANY, class = IN

;; ANSWER SECTION:
252.18.179.207.in-addr.arpa.  1H IN PTR  gw.calderasystems.com.

;; AUTHORITY SECTION:
18.179.207.in-addr.arpa.  1H IN NS  caldera.com.
18.179.207.in-addr.arpa.  1H IN NS  gw.caldera.com.

;; ADDITIONAL SECTION:
caldera.com.            6H IN A      207.179.18.1
gw.caldera.com.         6H IN A      207.179.18.252

;; Total query time: 1766 msec
;; FROM: chiriqui.pananix.com to SERVER: default -- 127.0.0.1
;; WHEN: Wed Mar 22 10:13:46 2000
;; MSG SIZE  sent: 45  rcvd: 174
```

DNSQUERY

The dnsquery program is similar to dig, shown in Listing 26.4, but returns the data in a slightly different format. It also returns a little more information than dig, but not as verbosely. Because it provides more information from the start, it has fewer options; therefore, it is, in some ways, less intimidating than dig and as easy as or easier than nslookup. Two sample outputs, one from the Caldera domain and one from the Caldera host at caldera.com, are shown in Listing 26.5.

LISTING 26.5   TWO DNSQUERY RETURNS

```
[david@chiriqui new]$ dnsquery calderasystems.com
;; ->>HEADER<<- opcode: QUERY, status: NOERROR, id: 41158
;; flags: qr rd ra; QUERY: 1, ANSWER: 5, AUTHORITY: 2, ADDITIONAL: 2
;;      calderasystems.com, type = ANY, class = IN
calderasystems.com.     22m47s IN NS    gw.caldera.com.
calderasystems.com.     22m47s IN NS    ns.calderasystems.com.
calderasystems.com.     51m45s IN A     207.179.18.130
calderasystems.com.     54m49s IN MX    10 mail.calderasystems.com.
calderasystems.com.     54m49s IN MX    50 caldera.caldera.com.
calderasystems.com.     22m47s IN NS    gw.caldera.com.
calderasystems.com.     22m47s IN NS    ns.calderasystems.com.
gw.caldera.com.         5h51m49s IN A   207.179.18.252
ns.calderasystems.com.  1d23h25m36s IN A  207.179.18.7

[david@chiriqui new]$ dnsquery gw.calderasystems.com
;; ->>HEADER<<- opcode: QUERY, status: NOERROR, id: 31478
;; flags: qr aa rd ra; QUERY: 1, ANSWER: 1, AUTHORITY: 2, ADDITIONAL: 2
;;      gw.calderasystems.com, type = ANY, class = IN
gw.calderasystems.com.  1H IN A         207.179.18.252
calderasystems.com.     1H IN NS        ns.calderasystems.com.
```

LISTING 26.5 CONTINUED

```
calderasystems.com.        1H IN NS    gw.caldera.com.
ns.calderasystems.com.     1H IN A     207.179.18.7
gw.caldera.com.            3h26m31s IN A  207.179.18.252
```

Notice that the first query returns all information, including NS, MX, and all A entries that are applicable. The second query returns all the entries it found about the host gw, including the host ns. If you can't see why, the host gw has an RR that corresponds to calderasystems.com. Likewise, calderasystems.com corresponds to both host gw and ns. Also note that gw has two domain names, the old caldera.com as well as the newer calderasystems.com.

HOST

If all you want to know is the IP address for a particular hostname, the host program provides it in a clean format that is easily redirected to a file or run through awk for direct inclusion into a file such as /etc/hosts. Sample output of host caldera.caldera.com returns the following:

```
caldera.calderasystems.com        A       207.179.18.1
```

To change this, simply do something like the following:

```
host caldera.calderasystems.com | awk "{print $3 "\t" $1 }' -
```

The awk print command reverses the order of the output and inserts a Tab character (\t) between them. This can be redirected and appended to /etc/hosts via >>.

> **Caution**
>
> The preceding example is only to be used for hosts over which you have control, or which you know will not change. Putting Caldera's hosts in your /etc/hosts file if you are not the domain administrator for Caldera is a bad idea.

WHOIS

The last program you'll look at in this chapter is whois. Although it is not one of the BIND utilities, this program provides DNS-related information. Specifically, it provides information from the internic.net database regarding domain registration information. It is advisable to direct your query to the appropriate whois server. As of this writing, whois servers include the following:

- **whois.internic.net**—International InterNet NIC
- **whois.nic.gov**—U.S. Government NIC
- **whois.nic.mil**—U.S. Military NIC
- **whois.ripe.net**—RIPE European Network Coordination Centre
- **whois.apnic.net**—Asia Pacific NIC
- **whois.arin.net**—American Registry for Internet Numbers
- **whois.funet.fi**—Finland NIC

- `whois.nic.af`—Afghanistan NIC
- `whois.nic.as`—American Samoa NIC
- `whois.nic.br`—Brazil NIC
- `whois.nic.bt`—Bhutan NIC
- `whois.nic.ch`—Swiss NIC
- `whois.nic.cx`—Christmas Islands NIC
- `whois.nic.fr`—France NIC
- `whois.nic.hm`—Heard and MC Donald Islands NIC
- `whois.nic.it`—Italy NIC
- `whois.nic.li`—Liechtenstein NIC
- `whois.nic.lk`—Sri Lanka NIC
- `whois.nic.mx`—Mexican NIC
- `whois.nic.nu`—Nuie Islands NIC
- `whois.nic.pw`—Palau NIC
- `whois.nic.sh`—ST. Helena NIC
- `whois.nic.tj`—Tajikistan NIC
- `whois.nic.tm`—Turkmenistan NIC
- `whois.nic.uk`—United Kingdom NIC
- `www.nic.at`—Austria NIC
- `whois.dns.pt`—Portugal NIC
- `whois.nic-se.se`—Swedish NIC
- `whois.nic.ad.jp`—Japanese NIC
- `whois.aunic.net`—Australian NIC
- `domain-registry.nl`—Netherland NIC
- `whois.jpl.nasa.gov`—NASA Jet Propulsion Laboratory NIC
- `whois.berkeley.edu`—Berkeley University NIC

A whois query on the caldera.com domain returns the following:

```
# whois -h whois.internic.net calderasystems.com

   Domain Name: CALDERASYSTEMS.COM
   Registrar: NETWORK SOLUTIONS, INC.
   Whois Server: whois.networksolutions.com
   Referral URL: www.networksolutions.com
   Name Server: NS2.CALDERA.COM
   Name Server: NS.CALDERASYSTEMS.COM
   Updated Date: 12-apr-1999


>>> Last update of whois database: Wed, 22 Mar 00 03:32:04 EST <<<

The Registry database contains ONLY .COM, .NET, .ORG, .EDU domains and Registrars.
```

TROUBLESHOOTING

When I use nslookup interactively, I get the following error:

```
*** Can't find server name for address 127.0.0.1: Non-existent host/domain
```

Your DNS server is running, but you haven't correctly configured your localhost reverse lookup file. Remember that within the reverse file, your line citing 127.0.0.1 should look like this:

```
1.0.0.127.in-addr.arpa.          IN      PTR      localhost.
```

Note that the IP address is written backwards.

How can I tell if I'm using my caching name server?

First, make sure your /etc/hosts file has the following as the first name server line:

```
nameserver 127.0.0.1
```

Then, start nslookup with no arguments. Your default server should be localhost with address 127.0.0.1. If it's not, you're not using your local name server.

When I use nslookup with the localhost, I get the following error:

```
*** localhost can't find pancall.com: Non-existent host/domain
```

This occurs for all lookups (except localhost). If you change the name server to an external name server, the lookups come back successfully.

This also can occur if your hints file is empty. The script in Listing 26.2 should mail you a copy of the new hints file after it runs. If you don't receive it, most likely the hints file didn't properly update. Run the script again.

## CHAPTER 27

SHARING FILES WITH NFS

In this chapter

WHY SHARE?

As soon as you have more than one computer on a network, certain conveniences become apparent. It is nice to sit down at any system on the network and have access to the same mail, the same files, and the same programs. It is even better if instead of having to put every single file on all the computers, the files can be shared. This saves disk space as well.

The original implementation for the capability to share files and directories over the network was developed by Sun Microsystems. Called the *Network Filesystem* (NFS), it enabled directories to be mounted from one computer to hosts across the network. This system also enabled any computer that understood NFS to mount or share its filesystem seamlessly with other hosts, whether they were other UNIX flavors, or even Macintosh or PC systems. From this was born the concept of "the network is the computer."

PREPARATION FOR NFS

The Linux kernel can be configured to permit or deny the use of NFS. In order for NFS operations to be permitted, they must be configured into the kernel. In the 2.4.x kernels, two parameters must be considered, and a third is optional. In the kernel configuration menu, select Filesystems, Network File Systems, and then you can select either or both of "NFS filesystem support" and "NFS server support." Both are available as modules or can be built in to the kernel. If you select server support, you also have the choice of selecting "Emulate SUN NFS server."

The Linux kernels since 2.2.x can support only mounting NFS directories from other systems, can support only making directories on the local machine available to other machines (called *exporting*), or can do both. The third parameter, the Emulate SUN filesystems, has to do with exporting a local filesystem for mounting locally. Sun supports this on Solaris, so the option is available to allow Linux to export a filesystem, such as /export/home, and mount it on /home.

The new 2.4.x kernel provides similar flexibility. Under Filesystems, Network File Systems you'll initially see two choices: NFS filesystem support, and NFS server support. Each of these can be included in the kernel or compiled as modules. When selected, each also provides for NFSv3 support to be included in the driver (but the option for Emulating SUN no longer shows up). You'll only need to compile NFS file system support into the kernel if you will be NFS mounting the root filesystem.

PLANNING NFS MOUNTS

The time to think about NFS directories is prior to installing your first system. You might not think that you will need it, but as soon as you add a second host to the local network, you'll be glad you did. Rearranging everything after the fact makes it much more difficult because you might have files scattered across several machines in "common" directories.

So which directories make sense to share with NFS and which do not? Looking at the file structure, some are obvious. You probably want to share /home because this is where users keep not only their files, but also their personal configurations. If they have their $HOME directory following them from machine to machine, when they log in, every machine looks and feels the same, making them more comfortable and productive.

This applies to mail as well. Depending on how you're handling mail, it might also make sense to export the mailhub's /var/spool/mail directory to each machine.

Often, in larger installations where it is important to maintain a consistency of applications across a network, the /usr directory is exported. But this poses some interesting problems, which are addressed in the next few paragraphs.

PREPARING THE FILESYSTEMS

In the previous paragraphs you looked at those filesystems that you want to share—but what about those you don't want to share? In fact, this constitutes a large number of directories. You need to have all the files necessary to boot a system on that system (excluding network computers that NFS-mount their entire root directory structure). That means that /bin, /boot, /dev, /etc, /lib, /sbin, /tmp, and /var are not to be exported—at least not in their entirety.

Caution

Never export the /proc filesystem. Doing so puts your entire system at risk from anyone with malicious intent that might gain access to your network. Additionally, only the local machine needs any information contained within.

Also notice that in the preceding example you considered /usr in its entirety as an NFS. But within /usr, you have /usr/local. Normally, /usr/local is where files specific to a local host's installation are maintained. So how do you deal with that? The best recommendation here is to move the local directory from /usr to another location (such as the root directory or under /var) and put a symlink in /usr that points to it.

Another problem that you might encounter in exporting a filesystem such as /usr is that it includes /usr/X11R6. This becomes a problem only if you are running X servers on different machines. It is very likely that these different machines have different hardware (video cards and monitors). Therefore, any symlink in /usr/X11R6 from X to a specific X server needed for one machine might be pointing to the wrong X server executable for another machine. The previous paragraph points out this problem and suggests a solution. Because you are not NFS exporting /etc, it is safe (and indeed prudent) to make the symlink /usr/X11R6/X point somewhere such as /etc/X11/X first, with /etc/X11/X then pointing to the correct X server binary for that particular host. This entails ensuring that the needed binaries for the different hardware exist in the exported directory.

The final problem that might need to be addressed concerns those software packages that use the flexlm licensing scheme. When these packages are installed, a license file is installed in a subdirectory of /etc called flexlm/licenses. Although copying these licenses to each machine is an obvious solution, it allows more copies of the software to run than the number of licenses that are owned. So within /etc, you might want to export flexlm so that only that number of copies of the software that you own can be run at any given time.

PART

IV

CH

27

Note that below /var, you might have other subdirectories that it makes sense to share. Consider a number of factors, including whether or not the directories (or any subdirectories) contain dynamic information that is applicable only to the local host—particularly information that might confuse other hosts, such as lock files, temporary files, and so on. Fonts, for example, although they can be exported, need to be shared by other, more appropriate methods, such as via a font server.

REQUIRED CONFIGURATION FILES AND PROGRAMS

Simply wanting to start using NFS and exporting the filesystem will not give you the results you want. The way NFS is shared across a network is slightly more complicated. Several different configuration files and programs are involved. You'll see in the following sections which programs are involved and which configuration files are needed.

PROGRAMS FOR NFS

Before looking at the specific programs involved in NFS, a few words regarding how NFS is implemented are in order. NFS uses *RPC*, *remote procedure calls*, in order to work. This is because different systems that might use NFS might have different system calls. RPC levels the field, making calls across the network and allowing each system to interpret the calls and translate them into local system calls.

In order to use RPC, the first program run must be /sbin/portmap. This program maps each port that is used by an RPC program to the specific daemon. So as each RPC daemon is started, it contacts the portmapper to register itself. If the portmap daemon dies or crashes, it is necessary to stop and restart all RPC daemons. Generally, RPC daemons use UDP over IP for communications because UDP is more efficient than TCP on a local network and results in less traffic. However, NFS on Linux can work via TCP if necessary.

One program that is useful for examining what the portmapper knows about is rpcinfo. This program provides you (or anyone else who can query your hosts, for that matter) with information regarding your hosts (see Listing 27.1).

LISTING 27.1   OUTPUT OF rpcinfo -p foo

```
program vers proto   port
    100000    2   tcp    111  portmapper
    100000    2   udp    111  portmapper
    100003    2   udp   2049  nfs
    100003    2   tcp   2049  nfs
    100005    1   udp    869  mountd
    100005    2   udp    869  mountd
    100005    1   tcp    872  mountd
    100005    2   tcp    872  mountd
```

Hosts that do not support NFS over TCP do not have the corresponding tcp entries.

Most Linux distributions today have opted to use the naming convention that that has become common in recent years, renaming daemons such as nfsd and mountd that use RPC as rpc.nfsd and rpc.mountd, respectively.

This brings up two more programs with which you need to be concerned: rpc.nfsd, which is the NFS daemon, and rpc.mountd, which is the mount daemon for NFS. As was stated earlier, these must be started after the portmapper in order to register themselves. These two programs are the two that actually do all the work in serving the exported directories to clients.

The nfsd program has a number of arguments that can be passed to it. Some of the more notable ones include -d call and -f, which are usually used together to debug nfsd in the foreground. The -l option enables nfsd to log transfers, and is particularly useful when used with the -R, or public root option, and -p, for promiscuous mode, which permits any host access. These enable you to provide a public NFS server at which you can log transactions, just like FTP. The public root option requires a corresponding entry in the /etc/exports file (see the example under "Restricting Mount Access," which follows). The port number that NFS uses (2049 by default) can be changed by using the -P # option. Finally, you can allow clients that mount your directories to re-export them by specifying the -r option. Other options are available, but are of limited value.

> **Caution**
>
> When allowing re-export of a directory, be sure that you do not permit re-entry into the exported directory, or NFS will lock up. That is, if host foo is exporting /usr and host bar has a directory /usr/X11R6, do not export /usr/X11R6 to mount under /usr on host foo, and then mount /usr on host bar. Because this is a circular reference, it cannot be resolved and results in a "cat chasing its tail" situation.

The mountd program, like the nfsd program, enables you to troubleshoot using the -d and -f options to put the program that is in the foreground in debug mode. It also has a corresponding -r option to re-export imported mounts. The program can also be put into promiscuous mode with -p, or have its port number specified with -P #. Normally, mountd uses a random port below 1024 (one not already reserved). This can be changed by specifying the port on the command line or in the /etc/services file.

> **Note**
>
> If you are using modules, although the daemons might be started, you cannot share directories if the nfsd.o module is not loaded. Furthermore, if the nfs.o module is not loaded, you cannot mount directories. This can result in an RPC error on the client that the program is not registered, the same as if the portmapper were started after the RPC daemons on the server.

One final program that is of interest is the showmount program, which shows you what it believes are filesystems mounted on other hosts. This program does little more than read the /etc/rmtab file, which is a table of remotely mounted directories. However, the information contained in this file, and therefore the information returned by showmount, might be totally inaccurate. Although entries are made in /etc/rmtab, they are often not removed, giving a false sense of what is exported.

CONFIGURATION FILES

A number of configuration files affect the NFS programs. The first is `/etc/hosts.allow`. Earlier, you saw that rpcinfo enables anyone with access to your network to find out which RPC programs you are running and on which ports. To prevent this, you can disallow hosts that will not be using your RPC services from accessing the portmapper. The following line in `/etc/hosts.allow` restricts clients:

```
portmap: ALL EXCEPT .bar.org : DENY
```

This line permits all the hosts in the domain `bar.org` to connect, and it denies all others access.

Similar lines can be used to restrict access to `rpc.mountd` and `rpc.nfsd`. (See Chapter 34, "TCP Wrappers," for more information.)

The next file to look at is the `/etc/fstab` file. This file is used on the client machines to determine which NFS directories from which NFS servers to mount where. Lines in `/etc/fstab` look like the following:

```
server:/exported/directory   /mount/point   nfs   options,rsize=8192,etc
```

You'll note that this format is different from standard mounts in that the two final arguments are not included. Also note that whitespace separates the various arguments, so no whitespace can appear in the options, or else mount stops reading the options at that point. The options that are available to the `mount` command for NFS mounts are different from the standard options. The options for NFS mounts are principally concerned with network behavior, and therefore modify the defaults. Two values that are of interest are the read and write size (`rsize=` and `wsize=`). By default, the value is `1024` bytes. This can be changed in the kernel source, but it is easier to do using these variables. Increasing the size to `8192` improves performance.

Another option that is of interest is `intr`. This option is only valid with the default hard mount, and permits operations on NFS files to be interrupted. Without this, a program would continue trying forever to access the filesystem. This option needs to always be used with hard mounts, which are the best. If the network is unreliable, a better option might be to specify `soft` as an option. With a soft mount, NFS operations time out, rather than try forever, if a `server not responding` message is received.

More options that are of interest are `port=`, `mountport=`, `mountprog=`, `nfsprog=`, and `tcp`. These options can be used to change the default port number, which is `0`, telling mount to query the `portmapper`; they can also change the `mountport` from its default of `2049`; the `mountprog` from its default of `100005`; the `nfsprog` from its default of `100003`; and, finally, they can change an argument to use TCP instead of UDP.

Each program has a program number to help identify it. You'll usually not want to change this number, or clients might not be able to identify the server. However, if you find a primitive firewall between the client and server that blocks most ports below 1024, you might need to move the server ports up to accommodate. Obviously, if you move the portmapper port, you'll need to tell the client where to find the new port. After the client finds the portmapper, it will find all the other programs through it.

Although these are not all the options that are available, the rest are fairly specialized and of little interest. For more information, see the NFS man page. Naturally, all these are available from a command line to the mount command because the /etc/fstab file is little more than default arguments when none are given.

DEFINING THE METHOD OF SHARING

Now that you've looked at a large part of the NFS process, you're going to look at the /etc/exports file. Other files and programs, even the programs that provide NFS services, pale in comparison. You've seen how to deny access to NFS. You've seen how to mount NFS. But the /etc/exports is the heart and soul of the NFS process. This is, without a doubt, the most important file because it defines the method of sharing, whether clients can read and write or read only, how to respond when the user root is the filesystem user on the client, and so on. This file does far more than just list those directories that other hosts can mount—it controls what they are permitted to do to the filesystem while it is remotely mounted.

When thinking about a directory that is listed in /etc/exports, it helps to remember that that directory and all the files in it belong to the kernel that is running on the server where the filesystem actually resides. What you are doing is permitting an extended kind of FTP access to the client that is requesting to mount the filesystem. This client is being provided with a listing of all the files and subdirectories that it is permitted to see, and that it can read from and possibly write to, in this filesystem. But it still belongs to the server that is exporting it. So the NFS server (and the kernel controlling the disk) permits or doesn't permit operations based on the permissions granted, implicitly or explicitly, in /etc/exports.

As a very simple example, you might see something similar to the following:

```
/home   (rw,no_root_squash)
/cdrom  (ro)
```

This particular server is giving all the hosts that can access it the capability to mount the /home directory read-write; furthermore, if the user is root, root has all the privileges of the root user on the NFS server itself, that is, root is not to be "squashed." Never use something as simple as the preceding in any environment other than perhaps a private home network of two computers used only by family members.

RESTRICTING MOUNT ACCESS

Most probably, one of the first things you'll want to explore is how to keep those unwanted or unknown hosts from mounting your directories. Expanding on the example in the preceding paragraph, assume that you have the following four hosts:

- A domain called bar.org
- Two subdomains, accounting and engineering
- Four hosts: acctpay and acctrec in accounting, and CAD and CAM in engineering

The /etc/exports file enables you to specify wildcards of the form *.bar.org as follows:

```
/home         *.bar.org(rw,no_root_squash)
```

However, if you do this, none of the four hosts in your organization can mount /home because the . is not expanded by the wildcard *. So, you either have to specify something similar to

```
/home         *.accounting.bar.org(rw,no_root_squash)
/home         *.engineering.bar.org(rw,no_root_squash)
```

or, more simply

```
/home         *.*.bar.org(rw,no_root_squash)
```

Note also that if you had a host foo.bar.org, it is unable to access /home based on this example. In general, the easiest way to specify a range of hosts that are permitted access on an IP network is to substitute the network_address/netmask pairing. So if you want to allow access for hosts with addresses 192.168.0.1–192.168.0.62, you can substitute 192.168.0.0/ 255.255.255.192 for *.bar.org in the preceding examples. For more on netmasks, see Chapter 22, "Networking."

Occasionally, you'll want to export a directory, but not a subdirectory. By default, all subdirectories are exported. But if you have a subdirectory under /home called /home/private that you don't want other hosts to access, you can deny them access to that subdirectory without affecting any of the others:

```
/home         *.bar.org(rw,no_root_squash)
/home/private   *.bar.org(noaccess)
```

The noaccess option denies clients access to the files or subdirectories of /home/private. The subdirectory private still shows up, but nothing more than the . and .. are seen.

In the paragraphs that discussed nfsd and mountd, you learned that you can make a public NFS server by specifying the -R option. To fully implement this option, two separate entries are required in /etc/exports:

```
/usr/share/apache/htdocs     =public
/usr/share/apache/htdocs     (ro,root_squash)
```

Despite the fact that root_squash is the default in the preceding case, prudence dictates specifying it explicitly. Furthermore, you won't want to export a directory to the world in read-write mode. This can leave you open to numerous problems, both from a security as well as a legal standpoint.

TROUBLESHOOTING

I get a `port not registered` *or* `server denied access` *error when I try to mount a remote share.*

This problem can be very frustrating for those new to NFS. It seems that almost all errors result in a `port not registered` error. You might also see a `server denied access` error. You need to take the following steps:

1. Run `rpcinfo -p` `hostname`, substituting the server and then client name for `hostname`. All registered ports show up. If any ports don't show up (nfs or mountd), you need to restart those daemons so the `portmapper` knows which ports they have chosen.

2. Check to ensure that you have the necessary modules loaded on both the server and client. The server needs nfsd (if loaded with modprobe, nfsd should load sunrpc and lockd first—if not, you don't have a `/lib/modules/2.4.x/modules.conf` file). The client needs nfs, which also loads sunrpc and lockd first.

3. Ensure that you are exporting the directory on the server that you want to mount on the client.

4. If you still can't mount the NFS share, ensure that your `/etc/hosts.allow` and `/etc/hosts.deny` files on the server are permitting you to mount the shares. Also ensure that you haven't inadvertently blocked yourself out with `netfilter`. Your logs should note any attempts to mount the filesystem.

5. Finally, make sure your program versions are the same. This should not be an issue if you're using the same distribution and version, but it might be if one system is running Caldera OpenLinux 1.3 and the other Red Hat 6.2 or varying versions of Debian or Red Hat.

When I use one client with shares mounted from the server, all my files have the correct ownership. When I use a different client, my files either have numbers or the wrong name.

What has happened is that you have `/etc/passwd`, `/etc/shadow`, and `/etc/group` files that are dissimilar between systems. If your account name is `dab` on all three systems, two of them might have your UID as `500`, and the other as some other number (like 1000). What the operating systems and NFS use are UIDs, whereas you use a name. Always use one system as your administrative system, update those files, and have `cron` run `rsync` to update those files on the other systems. Until Linux has a workable NIS+ server and client, `rsync` is the most feasible method for keeping systems in sync. Alternatively, just copy or FTP these three files, but be careful with file permissions. The NIS implementation, while available, is notoriously unsecure and should be used only on a very secure network.

USING NETWARE

NETWARE CLIENT UTILITIES

This chapter reviews the client and administrative utilities for NetWare that are included with Linux, in particular those included with Caldera OpenLinux eDesktop 2.4. The utilities enable you to access and manage NetWare resources in a network environment where NetWare and Linux coexist. Utilities are available for both Bindery Services and Novell Directory Services (NDS).

First you will learn about the utilities that enable client access to NetWare servers and NDS. Next you will learn about the NDS administrative utilities. Finally, you will learn about the Bindery-based administrative utilities. Figure 28.1 shows the sample NDS tree that is used in the examples throughout this chapter.

Figure 28.1
Sample NDS tree used in this chapter.

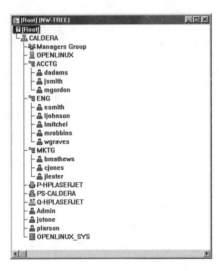

The NetWare client utilities available with Linux enable Linux users to access NetWare file and print services from the Linux environment. This section reviews the NetWare client utilities included with Caldera OpenLinux eDesktop 2.4 and provides examples of how to use them—you'll find a discussion about the ncpfs package that turns your (generic) Linux machine into a NetWare client in the "Project" section at the end of this chapter. The available NDS- and bindery-based NetWare client utilities are shown in Table 28.1.

TABLE 28.1   OVERVIEW OF NETWARE CLIENT UTILITIES

Client Utilities	Use
nwlogin	Logs in to a NetWare (NDS) tree or server (bindery); default is NDS mode
nwdelqjob	Deletes print jobs in a NetWare print queue
nwmsg	Configures client options for broadcast messages
nwmount	Mounts a NetWare volume

TABLE 28.1 CONTINUED

Client Utilities	Use
nwpasswd	Changes NetWare password
nwprint	Prints to a NetWare print queue
nwqstat	Displays NetWare print queue status
nwsend	Sends messages to a NetWare client
nwwhoami	Displays current connection information
xnwmanageq	Displays NetWare print queue status (X Window based)
xnwprint	Prints to a NetWare print queue (X Window based)
nwlogout	Logs out of a NetWare Tree (NDS) or Server (bindery)

To access and utilize NetWare resources from OpenLinux, your Kernel must have IPX support enabled and the NetWare client daemon (nwclientd) must be running. (For information on building IPX support in your kernel, see Chapter 18, "Building a Custom Kernel." For information on autostarting the nwclientd daemon, refer to Chapter 13, "System Initialization.")

CONFIGURING NETWARE CLIENT SETTINGS

Accessing NetWare resources requires that you log in to either an NDS tree or a NetWare bindery server. Set up your NetWare client preferences to facilitate easy login and use of resources. NetWare client preferences are configured through environment variables and can be set up in your Linux environment scripts (for example, .bashrc). Table 28.2 shows the environment variables that can be used to configure the NetWare client.

TABLE 28.2 NETWARE CLIENT CONFIGURATION ENVIRONMENT VARIABLES

Environment Variable	Purpose
NWCLIENT_PREFERRED_SERVER	Preferred server to use when logging in (if not set, client uses first NetWare server that replies to GET_NEAREST_SERVER NCP request).
NWCLIENT_PREFERRED_TREE	Preferred NDS tree to use when logging in (if not set, client uses NDS tree of first NetWare server that replies to GET_NEAREST_TREE NCP request).
NWCLIENT_DEFAULT_NAME_CONTEXT	Default NDS context to be used by client when logging in and accessing NDS resources (if not set, client uses [ROOT] of NDS tree to log in). Because no users exist in the [ROOT] of the NDS Tree, the client attempts to find the user in the context of the server the user is using to authenticate. After logging in, client still points to [ROOT] of NDS tree.
NWCLIENT_DEFAULT_USER	Default user to log in as (if not set, client prompts for username).

If you are using Bash as your shell, and you use the admin account in the O=CALDERA context to log in, you can set the preferences for the sample NDS tree by adding the following lines to .bashrc:

```
export NWCLIENT_PREFERRED_TREE="NW-TREE"
export NWCLIENT_DEFAULT_NAME_CONTEXT="O=CALDERA"
```

LOGGING IN TO NETWARE

nwlogin is a command-line utility used to log in or authenticate to both NDS- and bindery-based NetWare networks. The following syntax is used (Table 28.3 shows the possible command-line options for the nwlogin utility):

```
nwlogin [OPTIONS]
```

TABLE 28.3 COMMAND-LINE OPTIONS FOR nwlogin

Option	Description
-b	Forces a bindery-based login, even if the server is running NDS
-h	Displays command help
-n	Attempts NDS-based login (default)
-p <PASSWORD>	Specifies password in command line
-s <SERVER>	Specifies server to log in to or authenticate to
-t <TREE>	Specifies NDS tree to log in to
-u <USER>	Specifies user to log in as
-l <LINUX USER>	Specifies which Linux user you want to log in

If you want to log in to an NDS tree named NW-TREE as the NetWare user jsmith in the context OU=ACCTG.O=Caldera, issue the following command:

```
nwlogin -t NW-TREE -u .jsmith.acctg.caldera
```

> **Note**
>
> NetWare is not case sensitive; therefore, you can specify user information and any NetWare resources (such as print queue names) in either upper- or lowercase, or a mix. The one exception is the filesystem if non-DOS namespaces are present.

If you have set up your client properties (such as NWCLIENT_PREFERRED_TREE and NWCLIENT_DEFAULT_NAME_CONTEXT) as described previously, you do not need to specify a tree name or use a distinguished username. Instead you can simply log in by issuing one of the following two commands:

```
nwlogin -u jsmith
```

```
nwlogin
```

If you do not specify a username in the command line with the -u option and you have not set up the NWCLIENT_DEFAULT_USER environment variable, you are prompted for a username, as shown in Figure 28.2.

Figure 28.2
Sample login session for NetWare user jsmith.

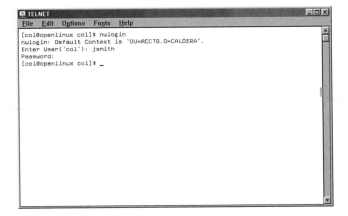

If you are logged in to Linux as root, you can use nwlogin to establish a NetWare connection for another Linux user with the -l option. If you want to log in the Linux user col to the sample tree with the NetWare account jsmith in the OU=ACCTG.O=CALDERA context, issue the following command:

```
nwlogin -l col -u .jsmith.acctg.caldera
```

> **Note**
> The client preferences used during login with the -l option are the ones for root, and not for col; however, the client preferences used when the col user is using NDS resources are those of col.

When a Linux user logs in to NDS or a bindery server, the login session is valid for any terminal that the Linux user is logged in to. If the user has multiple telnet sessions open on the OpenLinux server, all sessions for that user are considered logged in to NetWare and can use NetWare resources.

> **Caution**
> If a user logs in to NDS or a bindery server, and then logs out of Linux, the Linux server keeps the user's NDS or bindery connection open; the next time that the user logs in to Linux, the NDS or bindery connection will still be usable. This is true as long as the nwclientd daemon is not stopped or restarted. Therefore, if the Linux machine is shared by multiple users, be sure you're logged out of NetWare before logging out of Linux.

VIEWING CURRENT NETWARE CONNECTIONS

You can use the NetWare client for Linux to log in to multiple NDS trees and bindery servers simultaneously. The nwwhoami utility enables a user to view all current NetWare connections. The utility does not have any command-line parameters associated with it. To view your NetWare connections, issue the following command:

```
nwwhoami
```

LOGGING OUT

When you no longer need a NetWare connection, log out. To log out from an NDS tree or NetWare bindery server, you can use the `nwlogout` utility. The following syntax is used (Table 28.4 shows the possible command-line options for the `nwlogout` utility):

```
nwlogout [OPTIONS]
```

TABLE 28.4   COMMAND-LINE OPTIONS FOR nwlogout

Options	Use
-a	Logs out of all NDS trees and NetWare Servers
-h	Displays command help
-s <SERVER>	Logs out from server (bindery)
-t <TREE>	Logs out from tree (NDS)

Because the NetWare client enables you to log in to multiple NDS trees and bindery servers simultaneously, during logout you must specify from which server or tree you want to log out.

If you want to log out from the NW-TREE NDS tree, issue the following command:

```
nwlogout -t NW-TREE
```

By issuing this command you are logged out of the NW-TREE and all associated servers. However, you remain logged in on all other NDS trees and bindery servers.

If you want to log out from all NDS trees and bindery servers at once, you can issue the following command:

```
nwlogout -a
```

This command disconnects you from *all* connected NetWare resources (both NDS- and bindery-based).

THE NETWARE AUTOMOUNTER

The NetWare client (`nwclientd`) enables you to access both NDS and bindery-based objects through the Linux filesystem. The /NetWare/ directory is called the automount path. After you log in, you can navigate through an NDS directory tree or through NetWare server resources by using simple `cd` commands in the /NetWare/ directory.

As you can see in Figure 28.3, you can navigate through both the NDS tree contexts as well as through the NetWare filesystems by changing directories in the NetWare automount path. You can also navigate through bindery servers and volumes by changing to the /NetWare/ bindery/ directory in the NetWare automount path.

Figure 28.3
Navigating through the
NW-TREE NDS tree
using the NetWare
automount path.

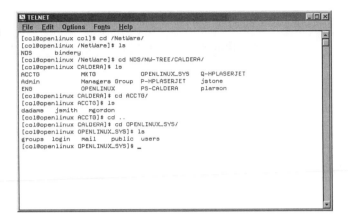

PRINTING TO NETWARE PRINT QUEUES

All printing utilities that are described in this section can use environment variables as previously explained in the "Configuring NetWare Client Settings" section. The relevant variables for printing are shown in Table 28.5.

TABLE 28.5   ENVIRONMENT VARIABLES USED BY THE PRINTING UTILITIES

Environment Variable	Function
NWCLIENT_PREFERRED_SERVER	Used by printing utilities to specify NetWare server that holds the print queue when not specified by the -s option
NWCLIENT_PREFERRED_QUEUE	Used by printing utilities to specify print queue object to be used by default when not specified by the -q option

The two utilities available for printing from OpenLinux to NetWare print queues are nwprint and xnwprint. The following syntax is used (Table 28.6 shows the possible command-line options for the nwprint and xnwprint utilities):

nwprint [*OPTIONS*]

xnwprint [*OPTIONS*]

TABLE 28.6   COMMAND-LINE OPTIONS FOR nwprint AND xnwprint

Options	Description
-q <*QUEUE NAME*>	NetWare print queue to be used
-s <*SERVER*>	NetWare server where queue resides
-b <*PATH*>	NetWare automount path of bindery queue object to print to
-n <*PATH*>	NetWare automount path of NDS queue object to print to
-p <*PRINTSERVER*>	Print Server object that will service print job
-# <*NUMBER*>	Number of copies to be printed

PART

IV

CH

28

TABLE 28.6   CONTINUED

Options	Description
-l <NUMBER>	Number of printable lines per page
-t <NUMBER>	Number of spaces to expand each tab
-w <NUMBER>	Number of printable columns on a page
-f <FORMNAME>	Name of NetWare print form to use (form must exist in NetWare container object)
-j <JOBNAME>	Name of job that appears on banner page
-u <NAME>	Name of user that appears on banner page
-c	Inserts carriage return before each line feed
-N	Suppresses banner page from printing
-h	Displays command help

Printing three copies of a file called myfile to the Q-HPLASERJET NetWare print queue in the O=CALDERA context can be accomplished with the following command:

```
nwprint -s OPENLINUX -q .Q-HPLASERJET.CALDERA -# 3 myfile
```

Note

You must specify the distinguished name of an NDS print queue. The distinguished name used can be type-full (such as .CN=Q-HPLASERJET.O=CALDERA) or type-less (such as .Q-HPLASERJET.CALDERA).

You can also print using a NetWare automounted path for the Q-HPLASERJET print queue in the sample NDS tree by issuing the following command:

```
nwprint -n /NetWare/NDS/NW-TREE/CALDERA/Q-HPLASERJET myfile
```

Note

When using the NetWare automounted path, you can specify the NDS print queue or the NDS printer object.

Note

At the time of this writing, there is no support for the Novell Distributed Printing Services (NDPS). However, you can create a print queue to be serviced by NDPS and have the Linux client print to the queue using the preceding outlined procedures.

CHECKING PRINT JOB STATUS

Checking the status of your print jobs can be accomplished with the nwqstat or xnwmanageq utilities. The following syntax is used (Table 28.7 shows the possible command-line options for the nwqstat and xmanageq utilities):

```
nwqstat [OPTIONS]
```

```
xnwmanageq [OPTIONS]
```

TABLE 28.7   COMMAND-LINE OPTIONS FOR nwqstat AND xnwmanageq

Options	Description
-q *<QUEUE>*	Name of print queue
-s *<SERVER>*	NetWare server where queue resides
-b *<PATH>*	NetWare automounted path of bindery queue object
-n *<PATH>*	NetWare automounted path of NDS printer or print queue object
-h	Displays command help

To view the status of Q-HPLASERJET in the O=CALDERA context using the NetWare auto-mount path, issue the following command:

```
nwqstat -n /NetWare/NDS/NW-TREE/CALDERA/Q-HPLASERJET
```

The previous command shows you a listing of print jobs currently in the print queue in the order in which they will be printed.

The xmanageq utility enables you to get a graphical view of the jobs in the print queue as shown in Figure 28.4. This utility also enables you to delete print jobs if you have the appropriate NDS rights.

Figure 28.4
The xmanageq utility screen.

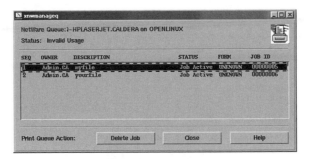

DELETING JOBS FROM A PRINT QUEUE

The nwdelqjob utility enables users to delete print jobs that they submit to a NetWare print queue. By default, users can only delete their own print jobs. If you have the appropriate NDS rights, however, you can use this utility to delete other users' print jobs. The following syntax is used (Table 28.8 shows the possible command-line options for the nwdelqjob utility):

```
nwdelqjob [OPTIONS] <JOB ID>
```

TABLE 28.8   COMMAND-LINE OPTIONS FOR nwdelqjob

Options	Description
-q *<QUEUE>*	Name of print queue
-s *<SERVER>*	NetWare server where queue resides

PART

IV

CH

28

TABLE 28.8	CONTINUED
Options	**Description**
-b *<PATH>*	NetWare automounted path of bindery queue object
-n *<PATH>*	NetWare automounted path of NDS printer or print queue object
-h	Displays command help

To delete a job, you *must* identify it using the job ID returned when you submitted the print job. If you do not know the job ID, you can find it by using the nwqstat or xnwmanageq utilities to view the jobs in the print queue.

You can also delete print jobs using the xnwmanageq utility described in the previous section.

To delete job number 012311 from the NetWare print queue Q-HPLASERJET using the NDS automounted path, for example, issue the following command:

```
nwdelqjob -n /NetWare/NDS/NW-TREE/CALDERA/Q-HPLASERJET 012311
```

CHANGING NETWARE PASSWORDS

You can change your NetWare password with the nwpasswd utility. This utility is used for both NDS and bindery services. The following syntax is used (Table 28.9 shows the possible command-line options for the nwpasswd utility):

```
nwpasswd [OPTIONS]
```

TABLE 28.9	COMMAND-LINE OPTIONS FOR nwpasswd
Options	**Description**
-h	Displays command help
-p *<PASSWORD>*	Specifies the new password in the command line (this option can only be used by a user with supervisor object rights in NetWare)
-s *<SERVER>*	Bindery server to change password in
-t *<TREE>*	NDS tree to change password in
-u *<USER>*	Specifies the user whose password is to be changed (this option can only used by a user with supervisor object rights in NetWare)

Changing your NetWare password in the sample NDS tree can be accomplished by issuing the following command:

```
nwpasswd -t NW-TREE
```

You are asked to enter your old password and then to enter your new password twice. Only users with supervisor rights in NetWare can change a user's password without knowing what the old password was.

Note Passwords in NetWare are *not* case sensitive, unlike in Linux.

NETWARE CLIENT MESSAGE OPTIONS

The NetWare client for OpenLinux enables you to specify whether you want to receive broadcast messages sent by users, administrators, or system messages (from servers). Client message options are set for each server to which you are attached. The following syntax is used (Table 28.10 shows the possible command-line options for the nwmsg utility):

```
nwmsg [OPTIONS] none|system|all
```

TABLE 28.10   COMMAND-LINE OPTIONS FOR nwmsg

Options	Description
-h	Displays command help
-a	Modifies message options for all connections
-s <SERVER>	Modifies message options for specified server only

Setting your NetWare client to receive messages from all sources can be accomplished by issuing the following command:

```
nwmsg -a all
```

To receive messages from the system administrator only for the OpenLinux NetWare server, you can issue the following command:

```
nwmsg -s OPENLINUX system
```

The previous command only modifies the message option for the OpenLinux server. All other connections remain unchanged. The nwwhoami utility displays the message options set for each server to which you are connected.

You can configure your NetWare client to not receive any messages from any system to which you are attached. If you want to do so, issue the following command:

```
nwmsg -a none
```

ADMINISTRATION UTILITIES FOR NDS

Most Linux implementations do not include any NetWare administration utilities. However, Caldera OpenLinux eDesktop 2.4 ships with several utilities that enable you to administer a NetWare NDS tree. This section reviews each of these utilities. Table 28.11 contains a brief overview of each utility.

PART
IV

CH
28

TABLE 28.11   OVERVIEW OF NDS ADMINISTRATION UTILITIES

Utility	Use
nwdsaddtrust	Gives an NDS object rights to a NetWare directory or file
nwdsattrs	Lists attributes of an NDS object class
nwdscreate	Creates an NDS object
nwdsmodify	Modifies values of an NDS object
nwdsrm	Deletes an NDS object
nwdssetspace	Sets directory size restriction for a NetWare directory
nwdsshowspace	Shows directory size restriction for a NetWare directory
nwdsshowtrust	Shows trustee assignment and rights for NetWare directories
nwdsvalues	Shows values for attributes of an NDS object
xnwdstrustees	Gives an NDS object rights to a NetWare directory or file
nwpasswd	Changes password for an NDS user

Note

At the time of this writing, Novell is working on a Linux version of their Java-based administration utility, ConsoleOne. It is expected to be available for download, free of charge, in late 2000.

MAKING FILE AND DIRECTORY TRUSTEE ASSIGNMENTS

The two utilities available to manage directories and file trustee assignments for NDS objects are nwdsaddtrust and xnwdstrustees. The following syntax is used (Table 28.12 shows the possible command-line options for nwdsaddtrust; Table 28.13 shows the possible command-line options for the xnwdstrustees utility):

nwdsaddtrust [*OPTIONS*]

xnwdstrustees [*OPTIONS*]

TABLE 28.12   COMMAND-LINE OPTIONS FOR nwdsaddtrust

Options	Description
-o <*OBJECT*>	Object being made a trustee and receiving rights.
-p <*PATH*>	Directory or file trustees assignment is being added to.
-r [RWCEMFA]	Rights to assign to new trustee. The possible rights are: R = Read W = Write C = Create (only applicable for directories) E = Erase M = Modify F = File scan A = Access control
-h	Displays command help.

To make the user jsmith in the OU=ACCTG.O=CALDERA context a trustee of the OPENLINUX_SYS: groups\acctg directory, and to assign read, write, and create rights, issue the following command:

```
nwdsaddtrust -o /NetWare/NDS/NW-TREE/CALDERA/ACCTG/jsmith -r [RWC] -p /NetWare/_
NDS/NW-TREE/CALDERA/OPENLINUX_SYS/groups/acctg
```

If jsmith is already a trustee of the acctg directory, his rights will be overridden by the new assignment.

The xnwdstrustees utility gives you a graphical interface for managing trustee assignments for NetWare files and directories.

TABLE 28.13 COMMAND-LINE OPTIONS FOR xnwdstrustees

Options	Description
-p <PATH>	Directory or file to which trustees assignment is being added
-h	Displays command help

To make the user jsmith in the OU=ACCTG.O=CALDERA context a trustee of the OPENLINUX_SYS: groups\acctg directory, and to assign read, write, and create rights, issue the following command:

```
xnwdstrustees -p /NetWare/NDS/NW-TREE/CALDERA/OPENLINUX_SYS/groups/acctg
```

The command brings up the graphical interface shown in Figure 28.5.

Figure 28.5
The xnwdstrustees
utility window.

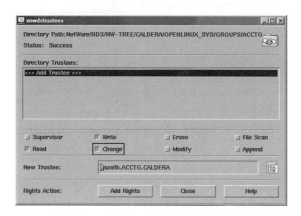

After the window opens, you need to perform the following steps to accomplish the desired results:

1. Click Add Trustee in the Directory Trustees window.
2. Click the search icon next to the New Trustee field.
3. Navigate the NDS Tree to find jsmith.
4. Click jsmith and choose OK.

PART

IV

CH

28

5. Choose the rights that you want to give jsmith by clicking the appropriate check boxes (treat the Change option as the Create Right).

6. Click the Add Rights button.

After you have performed these steps, the same command that opened the graphical interface can be used to modify or remove the rights assigned to jsmith.

Note   Trustee assignment changes take place immediately. You do not need to re-authenticate to see the changes.

VIEWING NETWARE DIRECTORY AND FILE TRUSTEE ASSIGNMENTS

The nwdsshowtrust utility can be used in one of two ways. You can use it to show directories and files on a server of which the specified object is a trustee, or it can be used to list all trustees of a specific directory or file. The following syntax is used (Table 28.14 shows the possible command-line options for the nwdsshowtrust utility):

nwdsshowtrust [OPTIONS]

TABLE 28.14   COMMAND-LINE OPTIONS FOR nwdsshowtrust

Options	Description
-o <OBJECT PATH>	Specifies the object NetWare automounted path whose rights are being checked (must be used with the -s option)
-s <SERVER>	Specifies the NetWare automounted path of the server where you want to see an object's rights (must be used with the -o option)
-p <PATH>	Specifies the path of the directory for which to list trustee assignments (used without -s or -o options)
-h	Displays command help

You can see which directories on the server OPENLINUX the user jsmith in the OU=ACCTG. O=CALDERA container is a trustee of and what his rights are by issuing the following command:

nwdsshowtrust -o /NetWare/NDS/NW-TREE/CALDERA/ACCTG/jsmith -s /NetWare/_NDS/NW_TREE/CALDERA/OPENLINUX

A list of objects that are trustees of the OPENLINUX_SYS:groups\acctg directory can be retrieved by issuing the following command:

nwdsshowtrust -p /NetWare/NDS/NW-TREE/CALDERA/OPENLINUX_SYS/groups/acctg

The xnwdstrustees utility can also be used to view the trustees of a directory. Use it as follows:

xnwdstrustees -p /NetWare/NDS/NW-TREE/CALDERA/OPENLINUX_SYS/groups/acctg

In addition, the `xnwdstrustees` utility can be used to make rights assignments changes and to add new trustees.

VIEWING ATTRIBUTES OF AN NDS OBJECT

The `nwdsattrs` utility enables you to view the NDS attributes for an object class by specifying an existing object. The following syntax is used:

```
nwdsattrs -o <PATH>
```

The `<PATH>` option is the NetWare automounted path of an NDS object.

You can view the attributes for an Organization object by pointing to the `O=CALDERA` container. To accomplish this, issue the following command:

```
nwdsattrs -o /NetWare/NDS/NW-TREE/CALDERA
```

The results of this query are shown in Figure 28.6.

Figure 28.6
NDS attributes for an
Organization object.

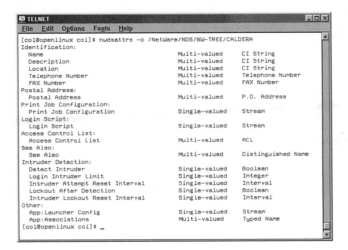

VIEWING VALUES FOR NDS OBJECT ATTRIBUTES

The `nwdsvalues` utility can be used to display the values of NDS object attributes for a specified object. The following syntax is used (Table 28.15 shows the possible command-line options for `nwdsvalues`):

```
nwdsvalues [OPTIONS]
```

TABLE 28.15   COMMAND-LINE OPTIONS FOR nwdsvalues

Options	Description
-o `<PATH>`	NetWare automounted path for NDS object being queried
-a `<ATTRIBUTE>`	Attribute of object being queried
-h	Displays command help

PART

IV

CH

28

To view the `Telephone Number` attribute value for user `jsmith` in the `OU=ACCTG.O=CALDERA` container, issue the following command:

```
nwdsvalues -o /NetWare/NDS/NW-TREE/CALDERA/ACCTG/jsmith -a "Telephone_Number"
```

> **Note**
> Remember to enclose any attribute or object name that contains spaces in double quotes. NDS treats underscores the same as spaces.

CREATING AN NDS OBJECT

The utility used to create NDS objects is `nwdscreate`. The following syntax is used (Table 28.16 shows the possible command-line options for `nwdscreate`):

```
nwdscreate [OPTIONS] [ATTRIBUTE VALUE]
```

TABLE 28.16   COMMAND-LINE OPTIONS FOR `nwdscreate`

Options	Description
-p <PATH>	NetWare automounted path of container where object will be created
-o <NAME>	Name of object that will be created
-t <CLASS>	NDS object class to be created—some of the possible classes are Computer, Directory Map, Group, Organizational Role, Organizational Unit, Print Server, Printer, Profile, Queue, User, and Volume
-H <PATH>	NetWare automounted path to HOME DIRECTORY (only applicable for user objects)
[ATTRIBUTE]	Mandatory attribute(s) for object being created—the mandatory attribute for the user object is Surname
[VALUE]	Value for the mandatory attribute
-h	Displays command help

> **Note**
> Object types that contain spaces must be enclosed in double quotes (for example, "Print Server").

You can create a user object called `john` in the `O=CALDERA` container with the following command:

```
nwdscreate -p /NetWare/NDS/NW-TREE/CALDERA -o john -t User -H /NetWare/_NDS/NW-TREE/
CALDERA/OPENLINUX_SYS/users/john Surname Doe
```

Notice that there is a specified value for the mandatory attribute `Surname` and that a home directory for the user john is being created at the same time as the account is being created. You can also specify non-mandatory values during account creation by entering them in the command line. Remember to enclose any attributes or values that contain a space in double quotes.

Tip

> If your NetWare network has a NetWare 5.1 server running eDirectory and has an LDAP server configured, you can manipulate NDS objects using LDAP utilities, such as `ldapmodify`.

MODIFYING NDS OBJECT ATTRIBUTE VALUES

You can change the values of an NDS object's attributes with the `nwdsmodify` utility. The following syntax is used (Table 28.17 shows the possible command-line options for `nwdsmodify`):

```
nwdsmodify [OPTIONS]
```

TABLE 28.17   COMMAND-LINE OPTIONS FOR `nwdsmodify`

Options	Description
`-o <PATH>`	NetWare automounted path of object to be modified
`-a <ATTRIBUTE>`	Object attribute to be modified
`-v <VALUE>`	Value for the attribute being modified
`-s <SYNTAX>`	Attribute syntax for the attribute (the attribute syntax is the field type in NDS. It can be found using the `nwdsattrs` command. Figure 28.6 shows the syntax for each container object attribute in the rightmost column.)
`-c <OPERATION>`	Defines what the command will do with the specified attribute and value— the possible values for `<OPERATION>` are as follows: a = add d = delete r = replace
`-h`	Displays command help

Note

> All options (except `-h`) are required for the `nwdsmodify` command.

You can add the telephone number property value for the user `jsmith` in the `OU=ACCTG.O=CALDERA` container with the following command:

```
nwdsmodify -o /NetWare/NDS/NW_TREE/CALDERA/ACCTG/jsmith -a "Telephone_Number" -v
"801-555-1212" -s "Telephone Number" -c a
```

Note

> Remember to enclose any single item that contains spaces, such as "Telephone Number," in double quotes.

CHANGING NDS USER PASSWORDS

A NetWare user with administrative privileges can change another user's password with the `nwpasswd` command explained previously. The following syntax is used:

```
nwpasswd -t <TREE> -u <USER>
```

PART

IV

CH

28

Note that with the nwpasswd command the NDS distinguished name for the user must be used. After the command is issued, you are asked to enter the new password twice.

Change the password for user jsmith in the OU=ACCTG.O=CALDERA container with the following command:

```
nwpasswd -t NW-TREE -u .jsmith.ACCTG.CALDERA
```

You can use type-ful or type-less distinguished names to specify the user.

DELETING NDS OBJECTS

You can delete any NDS object with the nwdsrm utility. The following syntax is used:

```
nwdsrm -o <PATH>
```

The <PATH> is a NetWare automounted path for the object being deleted. Container objects can only be deleted if no subordinate objects are in the container.

You can delete the username john in the O=CALDERA container by issuing the following command:

```
nwdsrm -o /NetWare/NDS/NW-TREE/CALDERA/john
```

Caution

The command is performed and you are returned to a command prompt. *There is no confirmation.* After an object is deleted, it cannot be undeleted. If you delete an object and you need it back, your only option is to restore that object from an NDS backup. Be careful to restore only the objects you need, and not all of NDS, because you might corrupt your tree. Most of the time it is easier, and safer, to just re-create the deleted objects.

Home directories are not deleted when a user object is deleted. You must manually delete home directories after deleting user objects.

SETTING DIRECTORY SIZE RESTRICTIONS

Directory size limits can be placed on NetWare directories with the nwdssetspace utility. The following syntax is used (Table 28.18 shows the possible command-line options for nwdssetspace):

```
nwdssetspace [OPTIONS]
```

TABLE 28.18   COMMAND-LINE OPTIONS FOR nwdssetspace

Options	Description
-d <PATH>	NetWare automounted path for directory where restriction is to be set
-b <BLOCKS>	Directory size limitation specified in number of 4K blocks
-k <KILOBYTES>	Directory size limitation specified in number of KB
-m <MEGABYTES>	Directory size limitation specified in number of MB
-h	Displays command help

To set a directory size limit of 30MB for the `OPENLINUX_SYS:groups\acctg` group directory, you can issue the following command:

```
nwdssetspace -d /NetWare/NDS/NW-TREE/CALDERA/OPENLINUX_SYS/groups/_acctg -m 30
```

VIEWING DIRECTORY SIZE RESTRICTIONS

The size restrictions placed on a NetWare directory can be viewed with the `nwdsshowspace` utility. The following syntax is used:

```
nwdsshowspace -d <PATH>
```

The `<PATH>` is specified using the NetWare automounted path of the directory being queried.

BINDERY-BASED ADMINISTRATIVE UTILITIES

As mentioned in the beginning of the previous section, most Linux implementations do not include NetWare-based utilities, but OpenLinux eDesktop 2.4 includes utilities that enable you to manage bindery-based NetWare servers. This section reviews each of these utilities in detail. Table 28.19 shows a brief description of each available utility.

TABLE 28.19	OVERVIEW OF BINDERY ADMINISTRATION UTILITIES
Utility	**Use**
nwboaddtrust	Gives a NetWare bindery object rights to a NetWare directory
nwbocreate	Creates a new NetWare bindery object
nwboprops	Lists the properties of a NetWare bindery object
nwborm	Removes an object from the NetWare bindery
nwbosetspace	Sets a disk quota for a specific NetWare bindery directory
nwboshowspace	Shows the disk quota for a specific NetWare bindery directory
nwboshowtrust	Displays NetWare bindery object's rights for NetWare directories
nwbpadd	Adds a value to a property of a NetWare bindery object
nwbpvalues	Lists all values of a property of a NetWare bindery object
xnwboadmin	Manages NetWare bindery objects
xnwbocreate	Creates NetWare bindery objects
xnwborights	Gives a NetWare bindery object rights to a NetWare directory
xnwborightsDD	Gives a NetWare bindery object rights to a specified NetWare directory
xnwbotrustees	Manages trustees of a NetWare directory
nwpasswd	Changes a NetWare bindery user's password

PART

IV

CH

28

ASSIGNING NETWARE FILESYSTEM RIGHTS TO BINDERY OBJECTS

nwboaddtrust and xnwbotrustees are the two utilities available to make NetWare bindery objects trustees of directories or files, and to make rights assignments. The following syntax is used (Table 28.20 shows the possible command-line options for nwboaddtrust; Table 28.21 shown the possible command-line options for xnwbotrustees):

nwboaddtrust [OPTIONS]

xnwbotrustees [OPTIONS]

TABLE 28.20   COMMAND-LINE OPTIONS FOR nwboaddtrust

Options	Description
-o <OBJECT>	Object being made a trustee and receiving rights
-p <PATH>	Directory or file to which trustees assignment is being added
-r [RWCEMFA]	Rights to assign to new trustee—the possible rights are as follows: R = Read W = Write C = Create (only applicable for directories) E = Erase M = Modify F = File scan A = Access control
-h	Displays command help

To make the user jsmith in the NetWare bindery for server OPENLINUX a trustee of the SYS:groups\acctg directory, and to assign read, write, and create rights, use the following command:

```
nwboaddtrust -o /NetWare/bindery/OPENLINUX/objects/jsmith -r [RWC] -p
/NetWare/bindery/OPENLINUX/volumes/SYS/groups/acctg
```

If the user jsmith is already a trustee of the acctg directory, his rights will be overridden by the new assignment.

TABLE 28.21   COMMAND-LINE OPTIONS FOR xnwbotrustees

Options	Description
-p <PATH>	Directory or file to which trustees assignment is being added
-h	Displays command help

The xnwbotrustees utility gives you a graphical interface for adding trustees and making rights assignments to files and directories.

To make the user jsmith in the OPENLINUX server NetWare bindery a trustee of the SYS:groups\acctg directory, and to assign read, write, and create rights, use the following command:

```
xnwbotrustees -p /NetWare/bindery/OPENLINUX/volumes/SYS/groups/acctg
```

The command brings up the graphical interface shown in Figure 28.7.

Figure 28.7
The `xnwbotrustees` utility window.

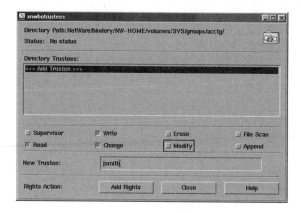

After the window opens, you need to perform the following steps to accomplish the desired results:

1. Click Add Trustee in the Directory Trustees window.
2. Type the username in the New Trustee field.
3. Choose the rights that you want to give jsmith by clicking the appropriate check boxes (treat the Change option as the Create Right).
4. Click the Add Rights button.

After you have performed these steps, the same command that brought up the graphical interface can be used to modify or remove the rights assigned to jsmith.

VIEWING NETWARE FILESYSTEM TRUSTEES ASSIGNMENTS AND RIGHTS

The `nwboshowtrust` utility can be used in one of two ways. You can use it to show directories or files on a server of which the specified object is a trustee, or you can you can use it to list all trustees of a specific directory or file. The following syntax is used (Table 28.22 shows the possible command-line options for the `nwboshowtrust` utility):

```
nwboshowtrust [OPTIONS]
```

TABLE 28.22   COMMAND-LINE OPTIONS FOR `nwboshowtrust`

Options	Description
`-o <OBJECT PATH>`	Specifies the object NetWare automounted path whose rights are being checked (cannot be used with the `-p` option)
`-p <PATH>`	Specifies the path of the directory for which to list trustee assignments (cannot be used with the `-o` option)
`-h`	Displays command help

You can see what directories on the server OPENLINUX the user jsmith is a trustee of and what his rights are with the following command:

```
nwboshowtrust -o /NetWare/bindery/OPENLINUX/objects/JSMITH
```

To see which bindery objects are trustees of the SYS:groups\acctg directory on the OpenLinux NetWare server, issue the following command:

```
nwboshowtrust -p /NetWare/bindery/OPENLINUX/volumes/SYS/groups/acctg
```

The xnwbotrustees utility can also be used to view the trustees of a directory. You can do this with the following command:

```
xnwbotrustees -p /NetWare/bindery/OPENLINUX/volumes/SYS/groups/acctg
```

In addition, the xnwbotrustees utility can be used to make rights assignments changes and to make new trustee assignments.

VIEWING NETWARE BINDERY OBJECT PROPERTIES

The nwboprops utility enables you to view the properties for a specified bindery object. The following syntax is used:

```
nwboprops -o <PATH>
```

The <PATH> is a NetWare automounted path for the bindery object you are querying.

To view the attributes for user object jsmith in the OPENLINUX NetWare server bindery, issue the following command:

```
nwboprops -o /NetWare/bindery/OPENLINUX/objects/JSMITH
```

VIEWING NETWARE BINDERY OBJECT PROPERTY VALUES

You can view a bindery object's property values with the nwbpvalues utility. The following syntax is used (Table 28.23 shows the possible command-line options for the nwbpvalues utility):

```
nwbpvalues [OPTIONS]
```

TABLE 28.23   COMMAND-LINE OPTIONS FOR nwbpvalues

Options	Description
-o <PATH>	NetWare automounted path for NetWare bindery object being queried
-p <PROPERTY>	Property of object being queried
-h	Displays command help

To view the Surname property value for user jsmith in the OPENLINUX NetWare server bindery, issue the following command:

```
nwbpvalues -o /NetWare/bindery/OPENLINUX/objects/JSMITH -p Surname
```

CREATING A NETWARE BINDERY OBJECT

Two utilities that can be used to create bindery objects are nwbocreate and xnwbocreate. The following syntax is used (Table 28.24 shows the possible command-line options for nwbocreate):

```
nwbocreate [OPTIONS]
```

```
xnwbocreate
```

TABLE 28.24   COMMAND-LINE OPTIONS FOR nwbocreate

Options	Description
-s <PATH>	NetWare automounted path of server where object will be created.
-o <NAME>	Name of object that will be created.
-t <TYPE>	NetWare bindery object type to be created—type is an integer between 1 and 3. Possible types are: 1 = User 2 = Group 3 = Print Queue
-H <PATH>	NetWare-automounted path to HOME DIRECTORY (only applicable for user objects).
-h	Displays command help.

You can create a user object called john in the OPENLINUX NetWare server bindery with the following command:

```
nwbocreate -s /NetWare/bindery/OPENLINUX -o john -t 1 -H
/NetWare/bindery/OPENLINUX/volumes/SYS/users/john
```

Notice that you are creating a home directory for the user john at the same time that the account is being created.

The xnwbocreate utility gives you a graphical interface for adding a NetWare bindery object. The following syntax is used:

```
xnwbocreate -s <SERVER> -t <TYPE>
```

The <SERVER> and <TYPE> follow the same rules as nwbocreate (see Table 28.24).

To create a user object named mary in the OPENLINUX NetWare server bindery, issue the following command:

```
xnwbocreate -s /NetWare/bindery/OPENLINUX -t 1
```

When the graphical interface appears, use the following steps to achieve the desired results:

1. Type the username in the New User Name field.
2. Type the Home Directory path in the Home Directory Path field. Note that this path is relative to the server, and not to the NetWare automounted path; therefore, a sample home directory path for mary is sys/users/mary.
3. Click the Create button.

MODIFYING BINDERY OBJECT PROPERTY VALUES

The two utilities available to modify property values of a bindery object are `nwbpadd` and `xnwboadmin`. The following syntax is used (Table 28.25 shows the possible command-line options for the `nwbpadd` utility):

```
nwbpadd [OPTIONS]
```

```
xnwboadmin -o <PATH>
```

TABLE 28.25   COMMAND-LINE OPTIONS FOR nwbpadd

Options	Description
`-o <PATH>`	NetWare automounted path of object to be modified
`-p <PROPERTY>`	Object attribute to be modified
`-v <VALUE>`	Value for the attribute being modified
`-t <TYPE>`	Option for the property being added—valid types are as follows:
	`SET` = Add value to property specified with the `-p` option (can only be used in properties of type `SET`)
	`STRING` = Is used as literally as the new value for the property specified with `-p` option (can only be used in properties of type `ITEM`)
	`SEGMENT` = Hexadecimal value to be translated and stored as a byte stream value
	You can view the property type by using the `nwboprops` command and looking at the third column
`-h`	Displays command help

Note: All options (except `-h`) are required for the `nwbpadd` command.

To modify the `Surname` property value for the user `jsmith` in `OPENLINUX` NetWare server bindery, issue the following command:

```
nwbpadd -o /NetWare/bindery/OPENLINUX/objects/JSMITH -p SURNAME -t _STRING -v Smith
```

The graphical utility `xnwboadmin` enables you to add and edit values for bindery object properties of a specified object.

To edit the properties of `jsmith` in the `OPENLINUX` NetWare server bindery, issue the following command:

```
xnwboadmin -o /NetWare/bindery/OPENLINUX/objects/JSMITH
```

When the graphical utility opens, you can select the property that you want to edit, make the changes using the Edit Property Value field, and then click the Add Value button.

CHANGING BINDERY USER PASSWORDS

A NetWare user with supervisor privileges can change another user's password with the previously explained `nwpasswd` command:

```
nwpasswd -s <SERVER> -u <USER>
```

To change the password for user jsmith in the OPENLINUX NetWare server bindery, issue the following command:

```
nwpasswd -s /NetWare/bindery/OPENLINUX -u jsmith
```

In addition to changing a user's password, you can also remove a bindery user's password with the nwnulpaswd utility with the following syntax:

```
nwnulpaswd -o <PATH>
```

The *<PATH>* is a NetWare automounted path for the bindery object.

> **Note**
>
> NetWare passwords are not case sensitive, as is the case in Linux.

DELETING BINDERY OBJECTS

The utility used to delete bindery objects is nwborm. The following syntax is used:

```
nwdsrm -o <PATH>
```

The *<PATH>* is a NetWare automounted path for the object being deleted.

You can delete a user named john from the OPENLINUX NetWare server bindery by issuing the following command:

```
nwborm -o /NetWare/bindery/OPENLINUX/objects/JOHN
```

> **Caution**
>
> The command is performed and you are returned to a command prompt. *There is no confirmation*. After an object is deleted, is cannot be undeleted. If you delete an object that you need back, your only option is to restore the entire bindery or re-create the deleted objects (which is safer because a restore can wipe out changes to the bindery since the backup).

Home directories are not deleted when a user object is deleted. You must manually delete home directories after deleting user objects.

SETTING DIRECTORY SIZE RESTRICTIONS

The nwbosetspace utility is used to set size limitations on NetWare directories. The following syntax is used (Table 28.26 shows the possible command-line options for the nwbosetspace):

```
nwbosetspace [OPTIONS]
```

PART

IV

CH

28

TABLE 28.26   COMMAND-LINE OPTIONS FOR nwbosetspace

Options	Description
-d *<PATH>*	NetWare automounted path for directory where restriction is to be set
-b *<BLOCKS>*	Directory size limitation specified in number of 4K blocks
-h	Displays command help

To set a directory size limit of 400KB for the SYS:groups\acctg directory on the OPENLINUX server, issue the following command:

```
nwbosetspace -d /NetWare/bindery/OPENLINUX/volumes/SYS/groups/acctg -b 100
```

VIEWING DIRECTORY SIZE RESTRICTIONS

The nwboshowspace utility is used to display directory size restrictions placed on a NetWare directory. The following syntax is used:

```
nwboshowspace -d <PATH>
```

The <PATH> is a NetWare automounted path to the directory being queried.

GRANTING NETWARE FILESYSTEM RIGHTS BINDERY OBJECTS

The two utilities that enable you to grant NetWare file system rights to a bindery object are xnwborights and xnwborightsDD. The following syntax is used (Table 28.27 shows the possible command-line options for the xnwborightsDD utility):

```
xnwborights -o <OBJECT PATH>

xnwborightsDD [OPTIONS]
```

TABLE 28.27   COMMAND-LINE OPTIONS FOR xnwborightsDD

Options	Description
-o <OBJECT PATH>	NetWare automounted path to which bindery object rights will be granted
-p <PATH>	NetWare automounted path of directory of file where rights will be granted
-h	Displays command help

Both utilities are graphical and allow granting filesystem rights to a specified bindery object. The xnwborights utility enables you to grant and modify rights to multiple locations on the filesystem by selecting the server and volume where rights will be granted.

The xnwborightsDD utility enables you to grant or modify rights of a specified object to a specified directory or file.

To grant or modify rights for user jsmith in the OpenLinux NetWare server bindery for multiple directories or files, issue the following command:

```
xnwborights -o /NetWare/bindery/OPENLINUX/objects/JSMITH
```

After the graphical utility comes up, you need to perform the following actions:

1. Select a server (note this must be the bindery server where the user exists).
2. Navigate the filesystem by clicking the search button next to the New Trustee Directory field.
3. Make your rights assignments and click OK.

Granting or modifying the rights that user `jsmith` has to the `SYS:groups\acctg` directory can be accomplished with the following command:

```
xnwborightsDD -o /NetWare/bindery/OPENLINUX/objects/JSMITH -p
/NetWare/bindery/OPENLINUX/volumes/SYS/groups/acctg
```

After the graphical utility comes up, you can modify the rights by clicking the appropriate radio buttons and clicking the Modify Rights button.

Note

Treat the Change option as the Create right for both of the previously listed utilities.

PROJECT: USING THE `ncpfs` PACKAGE

Of all the Linux flavors available today, Caldera's OpenLinux is the first, and only, implementation that offers a commercial and fully licensed NetWare client and server that supports the latest Novell standards, including support for NDS—it is not too surprising since Caldera was founded by Ray Noorda, the former CEO of Novell. However, what can you do to access NetWare resources if you don't have OpenLinux? The `ncpfs` package developed by Volker Lendecke is your answer! The `ncpfs` package allows Linux machines to mount volumes on network-connected NetWare file servers. `ncpfs` also include tools that allow printing to and from NetWare by Linux clients.

Note

For the latest version of `ncpfs`, you must use kernel 1.3.71 or newer; this includes the 2.0.* kernels. If you are using a kernel that is version 1.3.71 or newer, then the `ncpfs` kernel code has been included in the standard kernel distribution. You need only answer Y to the prompt:

```
Networking options  --->
    ...
    ...
    <*> The IPX protocol
    ...
Filesystems  --->
    ...
    ...
    <*> NCP filesystem support (to mount NetWare volumes)
    ...
```

and you can start at Step 5 below.

Use the following steps to use `ncpmount` to access your NetWare server:

1. Download Volker's `ncpfs` package, which is available prepackaged in most modern Linux distributions or in source form from `ftp://ftp.gwdg.de/linux/misc/ncpfs/` or from `ftp://sunsite.unc.edu` or mirror sites. The version current at the time of writing is `ncpfs-2.0.11.tgzm` or `ncpfs-2.2.0.tgz`, which adds the NDS support.

2. Ensure your IPX network interface is configured correctly (refer to Chapter 18, "Building a Custom Kernel," for more details).

3. Install the ncpfs package by first cd'ing to the directory in which you placed the downloaded file.

4. Next, untar the file:

```
# tar xvfz ncpfs-2.0.11.tgz
```

You need to cd to ncpfs since that is where the untared files are placed.

> **Note**
>
> If you intend to use kerneld to autoload the ncpfs kernel module, then you must uncomment the line in the makefile that refers to KERNELD.

5. Compile the software by executing the make command.

6. After the make has completed, you should find all of the tools you need in the ncpfs/bin directory. You can do make install to install the tools in different directories. If you are running on an ELF-based system, then you will need to rerun ldconfig -v to ensure that the shared library can be found.

> **Note**
>
> If you are compiling for a 1.2.* kernel, then you will find a file called ncpfs.o in the ncpfs/bin directory after the make has completed. This is the ncpfs kernel module. You should copy this somewhere useful. On the debian system, for example, copy it to the /lib/modules/ 1.2.13/fs directory and added ncpfs to the /etc/modules file so that it will be automatically started at boot time. If you are using some other distribution, you should find where its modules are and copy it there, or you can just copy it to your /etc directory. To load the modules manually you need to use the command:
>
> ```
> # insmod ncpfs.o
> ```

7. Before you can mount a NetWare volume, you must know your login details on the NetWare server you want to mount; this includes the user ID and password. And you need to know which volume you want to mount and what local directory you want to mount it under (for example, the mount point).

8. Assuming your NetWare server name is TEST1, your login ID is linux with a password of *novell*. If you want to mount the DATA1: volume under your /mnt/data1 directory, the ncpmount command looks like the following:

```
# ncpmount -S TEST1 /mnt/data1 -U linux -P novell -V DATA1
```

Refer to the man pages for more information about ncpmount, ncpumount, and explore other utilities, such as slist, nsend, and so on, that are included in the ncpfs package.

CHAPTER 29

SHARING RESOURCES WITH SAMBA

In this chapter

SHARING INFORMATION

Today's networking environment is normally a heterogeneous mix, consisting of various UNIX servers and workstations, the seemingly inevitable Microsoft NT server, Microsoft Windows desktops, and so on. As much as some of us want the Microsoft operating systems to completely disappear, it appears that they will continue to challenge connectivity and information sharing for some time to come. Fortunately, the Linux community is rife with programmers whose level of frustration has prompted them to write programs that overcome the obstacles that Microsoft has erected in an effort to deny users connectivity options (except on their terms). One such program is called Samba. This chapter attempts to introduce Samba in the most expeditious manner possible. Because the subject of Samba is enough for its own book, this chapter highlights a few common, basic configurations and some of the new features in version 2.0.x.

In the UNIX world, NFS, the Network File System, enables heterogeneous filesystems to be shared among hosts (see Chapter 27, "Sharing Files with NFS"). As part of its quest to dominate the industry, Microsoft decided to eschew NFS in favor of its own flavor of file sharing. This chapter explains how to cope with that decision.

SAMBA

Samba is a set of programs that allows UNIX and UNIX-like operating systems (including Linux) to communicate with Microsoft hosts. Microsoft uses a superset of the LanManager protocol—NetBIOS, which was developed by IBM and is sometimes referred to as the Common Internet File System (CIFS). The Microsoft version is called NetBEUI. The foundation for the LanManager protocol is *server message blocks* (*SMB*); this is where Samba derived its name. The Samba team, headed by Andrew Tridgell in Australia, managed to take what little public information is available (because Microsoft does not release protocol information) and reverse-engineer what NetBEUI does; they then mimicked that to allow communication with Microsoft hosts on their terms.

Note

Throughout the text, three terms appear: NT hosts (workstation, standalone, or member server; or Primary or Backup Domain Controller–PDC or BDC, respectively) running the NT OS or any of the Windows 2000 Server or Professional Operating systems, Win9x hosts, and Microsoft hosts. The first two references (NT/Win2K or Win9x hosts) are specific to the OS that is running on the host; the third (Microsoft hosts) refers to either. The distinction is required because of the way that each participates in the networked environment. (For more information, see the "Network Environments" section that follows.)

Note

The latest Microsoft offering, Windows 2000 in all its manifestations, again introduced a number of "enhancements" designed to break Linux-Microsoft networking despite Microsoft announcements that it would integrate into a UNIX environment. What Microsoft meant with the announcements is that Microsoft-specific add-on packages could be bought to allow MS hosts to talk to UNIX on Microsoft's terms. The Samba team is working on these problems and expects to solve them by the time this book is published.

SAMBA PROGRAMS

Some of Samba's suite of programs run as daemons and offer services; others are client programs that perform specific tasks. These programs include the following:

- **smbd**—The Samba daemon provides SMB services to clients.
- **nmbd**—The NetBIOS Name server daemon provides NetBIOS over IP naming services to clients to allow the UNIX host to appear in the Network Neighborhood.
- **smbclient**—A client utility that allows FTP-like access to SMB resources on the network, sends "pop-up" messages, and prints to Windows/Samba shared printers.
- **swat**—Samba Web administration tool. This tool configures the smb.conf file.
- **testparm**—A sanity checking tool for the smb.conf configuration file.

You'll look at these programs and more in this chapter. The focal point, however, is swat because proper swat configuration is not intuitively obvious. Furthermore, improper setup can result in anything from an inability to run swat to an insecure server because anyone on the network can run swat and overwrite the smb.conf file.

> **Caution**
>
> You must protect your smb.conf file (and, by extension, your swat binary). This file defines what access is permitted to individuals using the Samba services to access your Linux host. Because smbd runs as root, an improperly configured smb.conf can give any user coming in root privileges. The smbd program overrides all security settings and permissions that the user has as a standard UNIX user.

THE SAMBA WEB ADMINISTRATION TOOL

The Samba 2.0 release introduced a new program to assist in setting up and administering Samba, the Samba Web administration tool (swat). This tool is a boon to those who need Samba, but who do not have time to devote to its complexity. Samba configuration options go on for pages, and some settings conflict with others. To save you a very steep learning curve, you need to get swat properly set up.

> **Note**
>
> Throughout this chapter, some swat options are only available if you select the Advanced view.

GETTING READY TO RUN SWAT

Two ways are available to run swat on your system. The first (and preferred) method uses inetd to launch swat when your Web browser is pointed at the correct port on your Linux host. The second method requires that you run a Web server. This text will not detail running SWAT from Apache. If you need to do this, consult the Samba documentation.

RUNNING SWAT FROM INETD

To run swat from inetd, you'll need to take care to configure several things. Some of these might already be taken care of for you during installation of the Samba RPM, but just in case you want to troubleshoot a setup or install from source, the process is explained here. The first step involves `/etc/services` and `/etc/inetd.conf` files. As root, you'll need to add the following line to `/etc/services`:

```
swat      901/tcp
```

This line assigns port 901 as a TCP connection to the program swat.

> **Note**
>
> The swat setup in this section is accomplished for you if you installed the swat RPM (`rpm -qa | grep swat`). This section on running swat from inetd is for those who want to install from the `tar` file.

Then, according to the Samba documentation, you'll need to add the following to `inetd.conf`:

```
swat      stream   tcp    nowait.400    root     /path/to/swat swat
```

This line tells inetd, the Internet metadaemon, to spawn swat as a TCP stream (as root). The documentation also suggests the `nowait.400` option. This permits swat to be spawned up to 400 times per minute. Without this option, the default is `40—`, which is probably sufficient. You might want to have tcpd, the TCP Wrappers program, spawn swat. In this case, your entry might look similar to the following:

```
swat      stream   tcp    nowait        root     /usr/sbin/tcpd      /path/to/swat
```

Feel free to add a .100—or any number of your choosing—as the maximum number of instances of swat that can be spawned during a given 60 second period (the Samba documentation recommends 400).

> **Note**
>
> In the preceding examples, `/path/to/swat` needs to have the correct value substituted. This binary is most likely located in `/usr/bin`, although it might be located in `/usr/sbin`. Use the `locate` command to find swat.

If you use TCP Wrappers to limit access (as in the second second example above), check your `/etc/hosts.allow` and `/etc/hosts.deny` files to ensure you have access.

The Samba utilities are PAM aware; that is, they make use of the Pluggable Authentication Modules (PAM) that are found in `/etc/pam.d`. These control what is required to access certain programs. The particular file that you need to verify is `samba`. For more information on PAM, see Chapter 15, "Understanding PAM."

> **Caution**
>
> The inetd process requires a hangup signal following the editing of the `/etc/inetd.conf` file and before it responds to queries on the newly inserted line. Any time you see a reference to sending a SIGHUP to a process, this is what they are talking about. You can do this by using one of the two following syntaxes: `kill -1 pid` or `kill -HUP pid` (substituting the process ID number for pid).

An alternative to looking up the pid is to use `kill -HUP ` /sbin/pidof inetd` (substituting the name of the program for the name `inetd`).

You are now ready to access swat. Fire up your Web browser, enter `http://_localhost:901` in the location bar as the uniform resource locator (URL), and press Enter. You are prompted for a username and password. Enter root as username, and root's password.

If you enter any other valid username/password pair at the prompt, you get the swat screens, but some of the options are not available. The Commit Changes button does not appear because only root can make changes to `smb.conf`, and the capability to start and stop the smbd and nmbd daemons is not available.

If, when swat is started, a `smb.conf` file does not exist, swat opens with some default values.

> **Caution**
>
> If you have a hand-configured `smb.conf` file that you want to preserve, either make a copy of it or don't use swat. The swat program reads what it can (comments are not preserved) and rewrites the file in its own format; includes and copy statements are lost.

RUNNING SWAT FOR THE FIRST TIME

After you start using swat, you can quickly become spoiled. Nearly anything that you can do from a command line to configure `smb.conf`, including reloading nmbd and smbd and getting the status of Samba, can be done using this tool (see Figure 29.1). You can also access all the man pages for Samba, which open in a separate browser window.

When you start swat for the first time, you'll be prompted for a username/password pair. Use root unless you only want to view the `smb.conf` file because only root can change it. swat opens on its home page as shown in Figure 29.1. As you can see, this is principally a documentation page. The various links point to man pages, but don't actually run any of the programs. Each of the graphical links across the top of the swat page (Home, Global, Shares, Printer, Status, View, and Password) invoke a page dedicated to that purpose.

> **Note**
>
> If you leave swat but do not close your Web browser, you can reenter swat and not be prompted for a password. This is normal behavior. After you exit your Web browser, you are once again prompted for a password when you enter.

Figure 29.1
The swat home page.

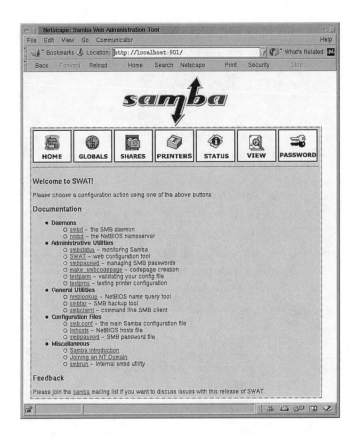

When you start Samba, if you have no `smb.conf` file, Samba starts with all defaults. If you look at the View page, you see exactly what will be written. This file is written each time you click Commit Changes, Create Share, or Create Printer. If you leave a page (Globals, Shares, or Printers) without committing the changes, they will be lost. A default `smb.conf` file with no changes looks similar to the following:

```
# Samba config file created using SWAT
# from localhost (127.0.0.1)
# Date: 1999/01/09 13:06:14

# Global parameters
```

As changes from the default are made and committed, the file is written. You still need to send a SIGHUP to the smbd and nmbd daemons for the changes to take effect.

Caution

Currently, swat does not create a backup file when it starts, so it is wise to have a copy of your current `smb.conf` file before starting swat.

NETWORK ENVIRONMENTS

You can have essentially two different network environments. The first is an NT server environment, in which one NT server acts as a Primary Domain Controller (PDC). The PDC and any Backup Domain Controllers act in a way that is similar to Network Information Services (NIS) masters and slaves; they also provide user network logons and grant permissions within the NT domain.

> **Note**
>
> An NT domain has no relation whatsoever to the IP address domain that is normally referred to when networking IP is discussed. This text makes use of the term NT Domain to describe the Microsoft idea of a domain, and just domain, to describe IP networking.

The second type of network is a peer network. No PDC exists on this type of network; all machines are standalone. Although they can share information among themselves, directory and file sharing is performed on a share by the machine and can be restricted in any manner by the user of the host.

NT SERVER AS PDC ON A LOCAL NETWORK

When you are running Samba on a network with a PDC, pay attention to certain settings. Within an NT Domain, hosts have a pecking order. Microsoft hosts all have hard-coded values for their OS level, and so on. These define the way a Microsoft host acts as it enters and leaves the NT Domain.

When a new host that uses SMB enters a network, it looks at the other hosts on the network. If no other system outranks it, it triggers a phenomenon known as a browser war. That is, it challenges the other systems that are present on the network to determine which host is to be the browse master (this can be turned off in Samba). This also happens when a host that acted as the browse master leaves the network. But because a Samba host isn't a Microsoft host, it doesn't have a hard-coded value.

> **Caution**
>
> A Samba server can be set up to outrank any machine on the network and win (hands down) all browser wars. However, this can be a very bad idea, particularly in an NT Domain. Although a Samba server is capable of wresting control of the domain from the PDC, this can cause all manner of erratic browsing behavior among Microsoft hosts.

ENTERING AN NT DOMAIN

One feature that has been introduced in the Samba 2.0.x version is the capability to enter an NT domain. The procedure is simple.

First, the hostname by which the Samba server will be known within the NT domain (which does not need to correspond to its DNS hostname) must be entered into the PDC in Server Manager for Domains. Enter this host as a standalone server or as a workstation.

The rest of the steps are performed from the Samba server. Note that for the purpose of this text, NTDomain is the NT Domain name, PDC is the NetBIOS name of the PDC, and BDC is the NetBIOS name of the Backup Domain Controllers.

Stop all Samba daemons and make the following entries in your smb.conf file (if you use swat, you must choose the Advanced View at the top of the Global page):

```
Security = Domain
Workgroup = NTDomain
Password Server = PDC BDC(s)
encrypt passwords = yes
```

You might also want to set the WINS server. This particular variable requires either the IP address or DNS name (not the NetBIOS name) of the WINS server.

Then run the following command:

```
smbpasswd -j NTDomain -r PDC
```

If it is successful, the message Joined domain NTDomain appears. This creates a file in the Samba private directory with a suffix of .mac (for Machine).

More setup needs to be done to this host, but it is now visible in the Network Neighborhood, and shares are made available on the host.

One final step remains in order for users to log in to the Samba server, and that is to create a Samba password. This is done by using the smbpasswd program, and passing the argument -a to add a user in addition to the username of the user that is being created. You'll then be prompted for a password. This addition fails if the user does not exist as a valid Linux user on the system.

> **Tip**
>
> To reduce administrative burdens, you can have new users dynamically created as they attempt to access shares on the Samba server by adding the following to the Global parameter add user script: /usr/sbin/useradd %u.

Shares still remain to be created, but the preceding procedure prepares a Samba server for use in an NT domain.

> **Tip**
>
> Another administrative timesaver comes in the form of the UNIX password sync parameter on the Global page under Advanced View. Setting this to true updates the UNIX password each time the NT password is changed.

PDC ON A DISTANT SUBNET

On some occasions you might find that your Samba server is connected to a subnet with no PDC or BDC on the local subnet. That is, traffic on the local network must pass through a gateway to reach the PDC or a BDC. If this is true, the Samba server is on a broadcast isolated network. The NetBIOS protocol is a broadcast protocol; that is, the local network browse master sends broadcast traffic to all hosts on the local net to update its browse lists, and as hosts enter the network they broadcast their presence. But NetBIOS won't pass through a gateway—broadcasts are isolated to the local network. So hosts on a broadcast isolated network have names of the local machines, but not ones on other subnets.

Enter local browse masters. These hosts act as browse masters for the local subnet and know the location of the domain master browser—normally the PDC. To allow the Samba server to act as a local browse master, you must set the Preferred Master setting to true. The Samba server also needs to know the IP address (or DNS name) of the WINS server. Upon restarting the nmbd daemon, the Samba server forces a browser election (browser war). By default, the OS level is 0, but all the parameters that are discussed in this paragraph are available on the Global page under Basic View. Set this to 65 to win all elections. You might also want to set the WINS support parameter to Yes if no other WINS server exists on the local subnet.

> **Caution**
>
> Never set the WINS support to Yes on a subnet with a Microsoft WINS server. This Samba server needs to be the only WINS server on the subnet, or erratic browsing behavior results.

PEER NETWORK WITH MICROSOFT HOSTS (NT AND WINDOWS 95/98)

This configuration is the default for Samba. If no changes are made, only shares need to be added; otherwise, Samba can be used as is. However, from this starting point it is almost certain that some changes will be made. For example, Windows NT 4 with Service Pack 3 or 4 and Windows 95 with the OSR2 updates or Win98 require the use of encrypted passwords. Some common changes of interest are discussed in the following sections.

All that is required from here is to set up shares and printers. You might also tell Samba to act as a WINS server for the Win95/98 machines and NT workstations, and for standalone servers.

LINUX AS A PDC SUBSTITUTE

The Samba team has been working to implement Samba as an NT PDC replacement. As of this writing, the code is still experimental, but it is included.

> **Caution**
>
> This setup is not to be used in a production environment yet because some users report that the Samba code has corrupted the SAM databases (the databases that are used by NT and that permit logins and grant permissions). Consider this the ALPHA code.

However, in the expectation that these bugs will be fixed, a short recipe for creating a Samba PDC and allowing hosts to enter its domain is presented. This recipe is subject to change. Think of the Samba documentation that comes with the package as authoritative.

Make the following changes in the Global section of swat (some of these parameters can be found on the Advanced View page):

- **Workgroup**—SAMBA (substitute the name of your choice for your domain)
- **Encrypted passwords**—Yes
- **Domain logon**—Yes
- **Domain master**—Yes
- **Preferred master**—Yes
- **Security**—User (if you are using another SMB server, this can be changed to server, but then you'll also need to fill in the password server = value with an IP address or DNS name)

Additionally, you might want to add the following:

- **WINS support**—Yes
- **Logon script**—%U.bat

In order to use the logon scripts, you'll also need to create a share to keep the netlogon scripts, as follows:

```
[netlogon]
path=/path/to/netlogon
writable=No
guest=No
```

The preceding can be added easily in the Shares section of swat.

Then you'll need to create machine entries in the Samba server. This is equivalent to creating entries in the Server Manager for Domains:

```
smbpasswd -m NetBIOSname
```

(This is the NetBIOS name of the machines that will enter the SAMBA domain.) You are prompted for a password. Use the word machine as the password.

You'll also need to create, if you haven't already, some logins with smbpasswd (as previously discussed). Now restart (SIGHUP) smbd.

On the Microsoft host, go to Start, /Control Panel, /Networking and change the domain to SAMBA (substitute the name from workgroup =). Do not select Create an Account. When you select OK, you see the following: Welcome to the SAMBA Domain.

Now reboot. On NT Workstations, the time that you press Ctrl+Alt+Del to the time at which you receive the login box should be less than 20 seconds (or else something is probably wrong). You see three text boxes labeled Name, Password, and Domain.

SHARING DIRECTORIES

Sharing directories is a fairly straightforward affair with Samba. The swat utility makes setting them up not much more difficult than selecting almost any name for the share and reviewing some of the parameters, such as the path. Most selections don't require any extraordinary measures, and if you want a particular option, it's just a matter of selecting it. However, one or two parameters can cause problems—these are noted later. In addition, one share name, Homes, has a special significance for Samba and is also explained. The Share section is broken down by functional areas that correspond to the sections that follow.

BASE OPTIONS

After naming a share with swat, it is created with default values and written to `smb.conf`. For all except the special Homes share, the path defaults to `/tmp` and the comment is blank. These can be changed as you desire.

> **Caution**
>
> Shares define an area below which a user cannot leave unless wide links is `Yes` (default). Within that share, the user has whatever privileges Samba is told to grant. These privileges can exceed what the user has when logging in as a Linux user.

SECURITY OPTIONS

The security section deals with the permissions that users have to read, write, create files, and so on. Guest permissions and the identity of the guest are also here. If guest only is chosen, all users are forced to be the guest account user when accessing this share.

This is also the place to allow or deny host access to the share. This option works in a fashion that is similar to the `/etc/hosts.allow` and `hosts.deny`.

The revalidate option can be used to force users to log in to the share each time they access it.

The most confusing parameter in this section deals with create mask, which is a synonym for create mode. The value to insert here is the value that you use in a `chmod` command.

LOGGING OPTIONS

The logging option serves several purposes. In addition to logging access to the share, it also enables or disables the capability to see, by use of smbstatus, whether anyone is accessing the share. Leave this parameter set to `Yes`.

TUNING OPTIONS

The default max connections `0` means unlimited connections. The number is enforced through locks.

The two sync variables, which default to `No`, require some explanation. Many Windows applications, including the Windows 98 Explorer, confuse flushing a buffer with doing a sync to disk. Under Linux, a sync to disk normally suspends the client process until the buffers are written to stable storage. Having a large number of Windows applications that are allowed to do syncs to disk when they mean to flush a buffer can seriously degrade performance; hence the No default for strict sync.

The sync always option has to do with whether a sync to disk call returns before the write is finished. The Samba server then follows the client's lead for syncs. If this is set to Yes, strict sync must be Yes; otherwise, sync always is ignored.

FILENAME HANDLING

The file handling defaults are sufficient for most environments with NT 4 and Windows 95 or better. Environments that still have DOS or Windows 3.1 might have to look into various filename handling routines to ensure that clients can read and access files properly.

This section also deals with how to map differences between the Microsoft OS files, such as hidden and system files, and UNIX files (dot files). Because a one-to-one correlation does not exist, administrators can choose how different types of files are to be handled.

BROWSE OPTIONS

The only browse option is whether a share is browsable. Windows NT has a default method for hiding shares. Any share name that ends with $ is hidden and does not show up in a browse list. With Samba, any share can be hidden just by setting the browsable option to No.

LOCKING OPTIONS

The parameters in this section, by default, protect shares that are set to read-write. The parameters are also set to enable fast operations in which they don't interfere with actual locking (blocking locks). But for some shares that are read-only, tremendous performance increases can be realized by setting fake oplocks to Yes.

Caution

Before changing locking options on shares or files, make sure that you understand what the implications are. Setting fake oplocks to Yes on read-write shares can cause file corruption, with several clients writing to the file at the same time.

Some parameters can be changed, depending on the network. For example, on a reliable network, leaving oplocks (opportunistic locks) set to Yes increases speed. However, on an unreliable network, you'll want to forego the speed so that files aren't locked by clients that become disconnected.

MISCELLANEOUS OPTIONS

The miscellaneous section deals with a myriad of problem options that affect various areas or that don't clearly belong to any of the previously mentioned areas. This can be as simple as whether the share is available or whether symlinks are to be followed.

Among the options that bear consideration is the wide links option. This controls whether areas outside the share are permitted. If wide links is Yes (default), a symlink to another part of the system outside the share is followed. This is combined with the `follow symlinks` option (default is `Yes`), which permits or denies the use of symlinks to files. The `wide symlinks` option, when set to `No`, prevents users from following a symlink if it changes directory to outside the share. But setting the `follow symlinks` option to `Yes` enables a user to read a file anywhere on the system. The difference is subtle and often confusing, especially because the two are implemented separately. Note that setting `follow symlinks` to `No` slows down filename lookups.

The other parameters that are of interest are the four exec options. These options execute programs as the user logs in or out, whether as the user or as root. Consideration needs to be given regarding the security risk or necessity of running a program either as the user or as root. For example, the `mount` (and `umount`) command might need to be run as root unless you have an entry in the `/etc/fstab` file for that mount, permitting the user to perform the action.

HOMES SHARE

The Homes share is a special share. When it is implemented, each user accessing the Samba box has his username compared to `/etc/passwd` for his home directory. That user's Linux home directory is made available as a share, but other users' home directories do not appear. This can provide users with a directory that is "safe" from the prying eyes of other Samba users. It might be prudent to give users a subdirectory to use to avoid naming convention problems between Linux and Microsoft clients. This is one share that does not default to `/tmp`; rather, it automatically defaults to the user's home directory.

SHARING PRINTERS ACROSS THE NETWORK

Printing within Linux tends to be one of the most difficult things for novice users to set up—and it is extremely difficult to understand. This text assumes that you can set up and print files from your Linux host. If printing from Linux cannot be accomplished, Samba does not help because it adds yet another layer of complexity. However, when you can print from Linux, printing from Samba is simple.

To begin, printers can be connected in one of three ways for use on the network. They can be connected directly to a port on the Linux host, in which case they use the Linux print daemon and print spool. They can be connected directly to a Microsoft host, and that host can share the printer on the network, in which case the Microsoft host is spooling jobs for the printer.

The third way of connecting has two variations. The printer is connected to the network through a print spooler. This can be an HP JetDirect card, an IBM print spooler, or another print spooler. The key is that the printer itself is identified as a host with its own IP address (and possibly a DNS entry). This third way is considered to work as one of the two preceding options: Either a Microsoft host has this printer set up as part of its print spooler, or the Linux host acts as the print spooler. So you are back to treating printers as though they are spooled by Linux or by a Microsoft host.

From a UNIX (Linux) perspective, the server that acts as the print server owns printers. This print server is in charge of formatting documents for the specific printer. The print server receives the document to print as either ASCII text or generic PostScript, formats it for the specific printer using its filter, and prints the document. Alternatively, it can receive a document that is formatted by the client for the printer and, by use of the -b binary switch, the server can pass the document untouched to the printer.

Enter Microsoft print spoolers. Despite the widespread use of the server to format the document for the specific printer to which it was spooling, Microsoft required clients to always know to which printer they were printing, and to have the spooler act like a UNIX print spooler that was always invoked with the -b switch. Although this reduced the load on the print spooler, it added complexity by forcing clients to know specifically about every printer on the network to which they might be printing. In an effort to reduce administrative burdens, Microsoft print spoolers that are shared on the network can communicate to other Microsoft hosts (but not to UNIX hosts) what kind of printer driver is needed when the client connects for the first time. In version 2.0.x, Samba also permits this kind of communication (see the section "Printing Options").

To print using Samba shares on a Linux box, you can choose one of two avenues. You can set up each client that is to connect to a printer on a Samba share to print natively to the printer (using a specific Microsoft driver for the printer), or you can set up all clients to use a generic Passthrough PostScript driver and allow them to print to any Samba client and any printer identically, regardless of the printer type.

THE PRINTERS SHARE

The Printers share is a special share that is similar to the Homes share. This share needs to be created on the Printers page and can only be removed on the Printers page. After it is created, the Printers share only appears on the Printers page.

The Printers share is created by default with path = /tmp and print ok = Yes. If the global default for load printers has not been changed from Yes to No, after the Printers share is created, all printers in /etc/printcap show up in the list of print shares. They can be identified by the * in front of the share name. If you delete the Printer shares or turn off the Global load printers option, these printer shares no longer appear. The printer shares that are identified with * cannot be deleted from Samba—they can just be made not to appear.

If changes are made to the Printers share, the changes are global for all the printers that are marked with an asterisk. If you choose one of the printcap printers (ones with an asterisk) and make a configuration change that applies to that printer only, a new section under Printers is created with the name of that printer (without the asterisk) in the smb.conf file. That printer now also appears in the Printers list in swat without the asterisk. You'll notice that in the View page this printer now has its own entry. If that share is subsequently deleted, it reverts to showing up with an asterisk and has the Printers defaults. If the Printers share is deleted, this print share without the asterisk remains. In other words, when it is created as a share by itself, it behaves as if it were created from the swat Printers page. Otherwise, it has an asterisk and is only an appendage to the special Printers share.

> **Tip**
>
> When setting up printers, the most common printing problem is that the spool directory does not have the proper permissions. These directories are world writable with the sticky bit set—that is, `chmod 1777 spool`.

Going through the functional areas that are available under printing, you'll see a few differences from the Shares functional areas. Again, some of these options are only available from the swat Advanced View page.

BASE OPTIONS

These options are no different from the Base Options in Shares: a comment field for identification and a path for the spool directory.

SECURITY OPTIONS

Only four options are available, but they are important. The first, guest account, is only of interest if Guest OK is set to `Yes`. The default guest account is nobody, and this account can be so restricted that printing isn't possible. You might want to change this to the account FTP or to another account set up for the purpose of printing.

> **Tip**
>
> Make sure that your guest account has enough privileges to print before looking elsewhere.

LOGGING OPTIONS

Read the entry under Shares called Logging Options. You'll find this in swat in the Shares section, Advanced View, between the Security Options and Tuning Options.

TUNING OPTIONS

The only option here, `min print space`, defaults to `0`, meaning that a user can always print. But this might become a problem on a system with low disk space and large print jobs.

PRINTING OPTIONS

This section is specific to printers. The first option,, `print ok`, must be `Yes` for all print shares. Many of the other options are for commands. These depend on your system. Linux uses LPRprng, so the commands for LPRprng need to be used, although the defaults in swat work.

The last two options are probably of interest to those with extensive Microsoft hosts on their network. The printer driver must be the name that the Microsoft hosts are expecting. If you don't know, don't fill it in—let one of the Microsoft machines provide you with a list, and you can copy the printer driver from that list. It must be an exact match, including case. The next option, printer driver location, must be a share that you set up called PRINTER$, where the printer drivers (copied from a Microsoft host or from the Microsoft CD-ROM) are located.

BROWSE OPTIONS

This option controls whether the printer share can be seen in the Network Neighborhood.

MISCELLANEOUS OPTIONS

The few options that are available here are the same as those that are found in the Shares section under Miscellaneous Options.

RESTRICTING ACCESS TO SERVICES

The Samba server configuration is extremely flexible. It can make use of UNIX NIS groups for access control, giving certain users read-only access, others read-write access, some users admin access, and still others no access. It can also force all users to be treated as members of the guest account (which is, by default, the UNIX user nobody) or as another special user. It can force users to belong to a certain group. All these options and more are part of the Shares page, in the Security Options section under Advanced View. Specifically, these options are Valid and Invalid Users, Admin Users, Read List, Write List (which is both Read and Write), Force User, and Force Group.

By making use of these advanced options, very tight control can be maintained over users' connections to any given share. An option is also on the Global page to set a root directory to something other than the default of /.

> **Caution**
>
> If you set the root directory, make sure that everything that is required to run the Samba server, plus binaries and all the libraries that are used by users, is copied below this new root directory. This functions the same as the FTP `chroot` command.

VARIABLES AVAILABLE TO SAMBA

If you've followed along in swat and looked at any of the default entries on the Advanced View pages, you've seen variables in the form %X, where X is one of many upper- or lower-case letters. These variables can be used to extend the flexibility of Samba. Following is a list of the variables and a short explanation of each:

- %S—The name of the current service, if any.
- %P—The root directory of the current service, if any.
- %u—Username of the current service, if any.
- %g—Primary group name of %u.
- %U—Session username (the username that the client requested, not necessarily the same as the one received).
- %G—Primary group name of %U.
- %H—The home directory of the user (%u).

- **%v**—The Samba version.

- **%h**—The Internet hostname (DNS) on which Samba is running.

- **%m**—The NetBIOS name of the client machine.

- **%L**—The NetBIOS name of the server. This enables you to change your configuration based on what the client calls you. Your server can have a dual personality.

- **%M**—The Internet name (DNS) of the client machine.

- **%N**—The name of your NIS home directory server. This is obtained from your NIS auto.map entry. (Without NIS, this is the same as **%L**).

- **%p**—The path of the service's home directory, obtained from your NIS auto.map entry. The NIS auto.map entry is split up as **%N:%p**.

- **%R**—The selected protocol level after protocol negotiation. It can be CORE, COREPLUS, LANMAN1, LANMAN2, or NT1.

- **%d**—The process ID of the current server process.

- **%a**—The architecture of the remote machine. Only some are recognized, and those might not be 100% reliable. It currently recognizes Samba, WfWg, WinNT and Win95. Anything else is UNKNOWN.

- **%I**—The IP address of the client machine.

- **%T**—The current date and time.

TROUBLESHOOTING

SWAT doesn't appear to be working for me. When I type `http://localhost:901`*, I get a* `connection refused` *error.*

Ensure you have an entry in `/etc/services` like this:

```
swat            901/tcp        # Samba Web Administration Tool
```

Also ensure you have an entry in `/etc/inetd.conf` like this:

```
swat    stream  tcp     nowait.400 root     /usr/sbin/tcpd swat
```

Stop and start inetd:

```
/etc/rc.d/init.d/inet stop && /etc/rc.d/init.d/inet start
```

Grep netstat's output for an open port 901:

```
netstat -an | grep 901
tcp       0      0 0.0.0.0:901           0.0.0.0:*            LISTEN
```

If the results of the first line above yield the second line, you should get a login prompt from swat.

I get a login prompt, but I am denied access.

Make sure you are logging in as root exactly as you would if you were logging in to the system.

Ensure you have an /etc/pam.d/swat file. For more information see Chapter 15, "Understanding PAM."

Also make sure that you're not denying yourself entry via the /etc/hosts.allow/hosts.deny files. You can check it by entering this:

```
tcpdmatch swat localhost
```

This assumes you used as an address to access swat:

```
http://localhost:901/
```

If you used something different, substitute whatever you used for localhost in the tcpdmatch statement above. You should get the following as the last line:

```
access: granted
```

I can't seem to connect to any of the Windows hosts. Every time I try to connect, I am asked for a password, and no matter what I put in, I'm denied access.

One problem you can encounter is that your usernames and passwords are different between your Windows account and your Linux account. They must be the same. If they are, ensure that in the Global Options sections you have encrypt passwords = yes.

I'm having trouble printing. Seems no matter what I try, all I get is garbage—pages of it.

Printing is one of those areas that are not well-understood by many, so let's try to make it simple:

- **Linux/UNIX**—Clients send what they want printed as text (formatted or not) or post-script. Clients know nothing about the printer. The print server knows all about the printer and how to handle either text or postscript, and performs all the formatting.

  In the Linux/UNIX world, then, if an administrator changes a printer and makes a quick change to the filter and any of the thousands of clients know no different, jobs flow as usual because they always send postscript (or ASCII text).

- **Windows**—Servers know nothing about the printers, they just queue jobs. Clients are expected to micro-manage print jobs and know all about all the printers on the network, so they must send print jobs specifically formatted for the printer to which they want to print.

  In the Windows world, every client, no matter where they are in the world, must know every detail about the printer they are sending to because the client must format the output. If an administrator changes a printer out, all clients must know about it and change their setup.

You must choose which way to do things. Obviously, if the printer is connected to the Windows system, the Linux system must send the print job formatted for that specific printer (see the information on "bounce queues" (bq) in Chapter 31, "Printing)."

If the printer is connected to the Linux system, you can either have all Windows systems send postscript format or you can set up a raw print queue on the Linux system and send preformatted output to the the raw (no print filter) queue. But you can't send preformatted output to a print filter or you'll receive garbage from the printer.

I created a HOMES share, but my users can't exchange files. How can I fix that?

You must set up another share for them pointed at a directory (/tmp works well) where they can share files. Any user connecting to the Linux box HOMES share is relegated to their own directory, and only their own directory.

I connected to my Linux (Windows) sytem from Windows (Linux). I'm trying to run programs from one on the other. I can see the program, and it's executable, so why can't I run it?

You cannot run Linux binaries on Windows and vice-versa. Each accesses the system through hooks, but the hooks are different on each system, so the binaries won't run on the other system.

## CHAPTER 30

SETTING UP A NETWORK

In this chapter

ABOUT NETWORKING

Probably one of the most exciting moments for new Linux users is when their first network is successfully implemented. Linux, as illustrated elsewhere in this book, works great as a desktop system, but to limit it to desktop use is like purchasing a Ferrari just to drive back and forth to the grocery store. Linux is a fantastic operating system for networking; you are cheating yourself if you do not at least try networking with it—even between only two machines—just to see what it is like.

One of the fastest growing uses of Linux seems to be in home networking. It is common to find more than one computer in a home, so this is somewhat understandable. The classic SneakerNet, in which data was transferred by copying it to a disk and carrying the disk to another machine, is no longer acceptable to most people with multiple computers, and it is a waste of resources. Resources such as printers, disk drives, and even Internet access can be shared across a network, and the cost of setting it all up is rather low. (An average low-end Ethernet card for a PC can cost around $25, and the cabling that connects the machines is even less expensive—you will learn about hardware shortly.)

However, the principles and concepts of setting up a small network are not unique to home use; you can take these instructions into your office and use them to set up a network server there. Furthermore, with the way that Linux is licensed, you can take your CD-ROM in and use it to set up all the other machines on the network as well without incurring any extra costs or per-seat restrictions. It is a win-win situation for everyone involved.

> **Note**
>
> If you purchase the boxed Caldera or Red Hat Linux versions, they include some commercial software that is licensed for use on only one system; you must purchase a separate license for each system you want to use the software on for these commercial programs.

HARDWARE

Network hardware covers quite a range of possible network connections. Some items cover networking over frame relay through the same cable that gives you television services, digital subscriber lines (DSL), or even satellite dishes. Router boxes and firewall boxes, and today embedded Web server machines exist, some of which even run Linux. Watchdog boxes monitor your network and make sure that the server is rebooted if it appears to have crashed. Multiport serial devices set up dial-in connections through the use of modems. As many different types of networking hardware devices exist as there are types of networks, and the list continues to grow.

Despite the many different types of hardware that are available for networks, for the sake of simplicity only the three most basic, most essential kinds are discussed here: network cards, cabling, and hubs.

NETWORK CARDS

Naturally, each computer that is going to be networked must have its own network card. Of the many different kinds of network cards, the ones most commonly used are of the Ethernet variety. The quality of these cards run the gamut from $25 NE2000 clones all the way up to major name-brand offerings that can transfer data one hundred times as fast as the low-end clones, and then some. Find out what others who have networks either at home or at work recommend.

Unless you are doing serious data transfers over your network, you will be just fine with the low-end NE2000 clones. These come in a few different varieties, the most common being 10Base-T, 10Base-2, and 10Base-T/2. As indicated by the classification of the card, it is capable of transferring ten megabits of information at any given time. The T, 2, and T/2 at the end of the classification indicate the cabling that is required by the card.

CABLING

Computers with network cards are pretty much useless unless they are connected with network cables. 10Base-T cards use what is known as Cat 5 (category 5) twisted-pair cabling. This kind of cabling has what look like telephone plugs at each end; because it does not normally permit direct card-to-card connections between computers, it is typically used in conjunction with a hub (hubs are discussed a bit later). A special kind of twisted pair cable called a *reverse pair* or *cross-connect* cable permits direct connections, though, and is commonly used to connect one hub to another or one computer directly to another computer. The use of a hub is much more common. Networks that use these cards tend to be arranged in a star topology around a central location at which the hub resides (see Figure 30.1).

Figure 30.1
A 10Base-T network scheme.

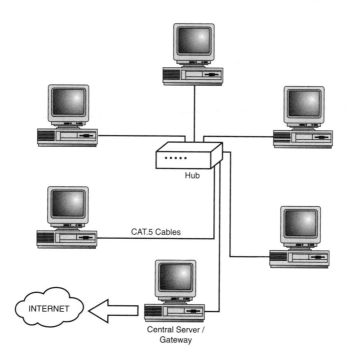

10Base-2 cards use coaxial cables similar to those used with cable TV. Instead of having what look like phone plugs at the ends, these cables have what are called terminators—little metal devices that terminate the line by looping the wiring back into the cable. The cables themselves are connected to the network cards with small tees. Networks that use these types of cables tend to be strung together in one long line, with each computer joining the connection at the tee in the back of the network card (see Figure 30.2).

Figure 30.2
A 10Base-2 network scheme.

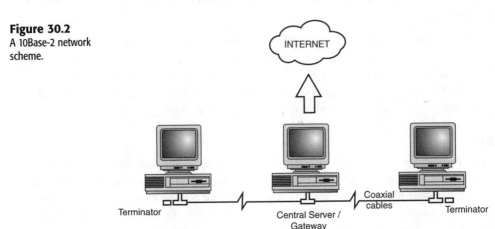

The drawback to using this kind of cabling with 10Base-2 cards is that for each cable coming into the computer's room from the previous system, another cable must go out of the room for the next system. The benefit to using twisted-pair cabling with 10Base-T cards is that only one cable is needed to connect the computer in the room.

What about 10Base-T/2 cards? They simply have jacks on the back that can handle both types of cables and generally autosense which one is to be used.

HUBS

Hubs are small boxes that can accommodate a number of different network cable connections, but they are primarily used to connect computers containing 10Base-T cards. Among their benefits, they can act as the central connection point for all systems on a network, or they can help to split the network connections into more easily manageable chunks. For instance, if multiple rooms have multiple computers in each, it makes more sense to take one cable into each room and give each its own hub than it does to have multiple cables coming out of each room going to a central hub.

Hubs can also act as traffic cops by helping monitor network traffic for packet collisions.

A typical 4- or 8-port hub can cost anywhere from $40 to more than $100, depending on the brand and the features. Again, unless you are planning on passing around bandwidth-intensive network traffic, stay inexpensive. Buying features can be fun, but if you never really use the features you are wasting your money.

Caution

Hardware is available for 100MB and 1000MB networking if you are interested. Be careful about mixing bandwidths if you are using a hub, though; if you have 10Base-T or 10Base-2 (or 10Base-T/2) cards, do not purchase a 100Mb hub to connect them. Mixing bandwidths in this manner does not work without special, expensive switching hubs. If you plan on eventually moving to a 100MB network, it might be cheaper in the long run for you to simply go 100MB right from the start.

ASSUMPTIONS

The following sample network consists of five computers: four PCs running various operating systems (including Windows NT and Linux) and one Mac. All are connected using 10BaseT/2 Ethernet cards through a small 10BaseT hub with twisted-pair cabling (see Table 30.1).

TABLE 30.1   ASSUMPTIONS FOR YOUR SAMPLE NETWORK

Computer Name	IP Address	Type	O/S Used
rumble.fish.net	192.168.1.1	PC	Linux
gefilte.fish.net	192.168.1.2	PC	Windows 95
go.fish.net	192.168.1.3	PC	Windows NT
silver.fish.net	192.168.1.4	Apple	System 7.5
tuna.fish.net	192.168.1.5	PC	Linux

fish.net *is being used as an example only. If your network is going to be connected to the Internet, please register your own domain name and do not use* fish.net. *Of course, if* fish.net *is not taken...*

All systems are connected using TCP/IP, plus various other protocols that allow the connection of networked drives. For the sake of brevity, only the TCP/IP setup is addressed here. Also for the sake of brevity, it is assumed that the names of the Linux systems were assigned when the systems were installed. For the Windows and Mac systems, the assumption is made that they already have names as well.

Each system has the equivalent of a hosts file that contains all the preceding addresses plus the localhost address. A DNS server can work on this network as well, providing not only local resolution, but also Internet resolution and saving you the trouble of putting hosts files in each system. You could also assign a static IP to rumble.fish.net, configure a DHCP server on it, and let the other systems get their IP address through DHCP. Each additional step will require more initial effort on your part, but for larger networks, it is definitely worth the trouble.

The format of the hosts file is consistent across the various platforms. Each one will resemble Listing 30.1.

LISTING 30.1   SAMPLE hosts FILE

```
127.0.0.1      localhost
192.168.1.1    rumble.fish.net    rumble
192.168.1.2    gefilte.fish.net   gefilte
192.168.1.3    go.fish.net        go
192.168.1.4    silver.fish.net    silver
192.168.1.5    tuna.fish.net      tuna
```

This file has different locations depending on the system in question:

- For Linux, it is /etc/hosts.
- On WindowsNT, the file is most likely \WINNT\SYSTEM32\DRIVERS\ETC\HOSTS.
- The file for Windows 95 is \WINDOWS\HOSTS.
- The hosts file for the Mac is in the System Folder.

rumble.fish.net—the server—is set up to dial out to the Internet. It has IP masquerading set up, so the other computers on the network can use it as an Internet gateway (see Chapter 35, "IP Masquerading," for more details).

Rumble's Linux kernel was precompiled with the necessary protocol support (TCP/IP, PPP), IP forwarding/gatewaying, and everything required for IP masquerading support (the norm for most distributions today).

Note

You must be logged in as root to perform the Linux configurations detailed in this chapter. The ownerships and permissions on the files that will be edited require superuser status; therefore, ordinary users cannot perform any edits.

THE INDIVIDUAL SYSTEMS

The tuna.fish.net system (which runs OpenLinux) is used as an example. The TCP/IP configuration for Caldera OpenLinux and Red Hat is held in the /etc/sysconfig/network-scripts directory. The configuration for each network interface is contained in its own separate file within this directory. The Ethernet configurations are held in the ifcfg-eth# files (starting with ifcfg-eth0). Assuming that tuna.fish.net only has one Ethernet interface, Listing 30.2 shows the contents of its ifcfg-eth0 file.

LISTING 30.2   SAMPLE OPENLINUX /etc/sysconfig/network-scripts/ifcfg-eth0 FILE

```
#!/bin/sh

#>>>Device type: ethernet
#>>>Variable declarations:
DEVICE=eth0
IPADDR=192.168.1.5
NETMASK=255.255.255.0
NETWORK=192.168.1.0
```

LISTING 30.2   CONTINUED

```
BROADCAST=192.168.1.255
GATEWAY=192.168.1.1
ONBOOT=yes
#>>>End of variable declarations
```

The Red Hat file contains basically the same information. In Red Hat, a `PROTO` line will be present with either `static` or `dynamic` as its argument. The `NETWORK` and `BROADCAST` entries are not included, and the `GATEWAY` entry is found in `/etc/sysconfig/network`.

Note the `GATEWAY` specification in the sample entry. It is pointing to the IP address used by `rumble.fish.net`, which is the server that will eventually be connecting to the Internet. All computers that will be given access to the Internet through rumble need to have it specified as the gateway system; otherwise, no Internet access will be possible.

You cannot have your system gating through an Ethernet card and through a modem at the same time; if you are using PPP and a modem to gate out to the Internet, do not specify an Ethernet gateway. Replace any address in the `GATEWAY=` line with `none`.

> **Note**
>
> Although all other systems list `rumble.fish.net` as their gateway, the `rumble.fish.net` system should not have any entry as a gateway in this example. If `rumble.fish.net` were connected to a router (DSL router or cable modem box) using an Ethernet cable, it would have that router or modem's IP listed as its gateway. In this network, the gateway will be set up dynamically through the modem when a connection is made to the Internet.

Also note the `netmask`, `network`, and `broadcast` addresses. These are used on all computers on the network. In fact, the only address that changes per machine on a typical network is the IP address; all the rest of the addresses are shared among all computers on the same subnetwork.

> **Caution**
>
> The netmask defines the network in use (its beginning and ending). If you assign a different netmask to any of the hosts, they will be on another network. This can adversely affect their capability to communicate with other hosts on the network.

When discussing addresses, it is important to note that some sort of name server is required for Internet use (your hosts files only cover address conversion on the local network). Because Internet navigation will be common on this network, the ISP's name servers need to be used when addresses outside the local network are requested (unless you've opted to set up your own DNS). These addresses are entered in various locations on the various systems (for instance, in the Network setup under Control Panel on Windows systems, and in the MacTCP extension on the Mac), but on Linux, they are entered in the `/etc/resolv.conf` file. Assuming the IP address for the ISP's nameservers are `192.168.100.100` and `192.168.100.101`, Listing 30.3 illustrates the Linux systems' `/etc/resolv.conf` files (including `rumble`'s):

LISTING 30.3   SAMPLE /etc/resolv.conf FILE

```
domain fish.net
nameserver 192.168.100.100
nameserver 102.168.100.101
```

The search line or domain line (only one or the other should be used) contains the domain name that you are using on your network. If you use the search line instead of the domain line, you can have up to six space-separated entries. You can have up to three nameserver lines, and if you are running your own DNS, that entry should go first, because nameservers will be used in the order listed. If you do run DNS, make sure the DNS server has as its first nameserver entry 127.0.0.1.

When networking changes are made on the Linux systems, you can use the /etc/rc.d/init.d/ network SysV initialization script to restart the networking (not necessary for changes to resolv.conf or the hosts file, but necessary for changes to the ifcfg-eth# scripts). This causes the changes to take effect without rebooting:

```
/etc/rc.d/init.d/network stop
/etc/rc.d/init.d/network start
```

DEBIAN DIFFERENCES

The Debian distribution uses a different set of scripts to automatically initialize the network. The main configuration file is found in /etc/network and is called interfaces.

The interfaces file consists of stanzas read and parsed by the if-up and if-down scripts. Each stanza begins with the word iface and defines the interface type, family, and method of configuration. This line can optionally include commands to run before and when the interface comes up, and when and after it goes down.

Interface types include eth<number[:<number>]>, tr<number>, lo, ppp<number>. Interface families can be any of inet (for IPv4), ipx, or inet6 (for IPv6). The method of configuration depends on the family and can be any of static (all families), dhcp (inet), bootp (inet), ppp (inet), dynamic (ipx), or v4tunnel (inet6). So a sample line might look like the following:

```
iface eth0 inet static
```

Depending on the family and configuration type, an indented list of arguments will follow. Assuming the preceding line in the interfaces file, arguments might look as follows:

```
    address 192.168.0.8
    netmask 255.255.255.0
    network 192.168.0.0
    broadcast 192.168.0.255
    gateway 192.168.0.2
```

The address and netmask are required; all other entries are optional.

Other families and configuration methods take other options. Consult the interfaces man page if you find you need to modify this file. After it is modified, you can implement the changes with the following command:

```
/etc/init.d/networking restart
```

THE SERVER

When all computers on the network are set up with their proper addressing, it is time to set up the IP masquerading rules on rumble. First, you'll need to load the appropriate modules before you can set up any rules:

```
modprobe ip_tables
modprobe ip_conntrack
modprobe ip_conntrack_ftp
```

These modules are a minimum; you might need (or want) more. Add the module names to /etc/modules/default (as discussed in Chapter 19, "Kernel Modules") so they'll load during system boot. Other modules you might want are discussed in Chapter 35, "IP Masquerading," and Chapter 36, "IP Firewalling."

Now for the basic rules. The sample rules in Chapter 35 are similar to what you'll see here, but more detailed.

The following line must be placed in rumble's /etc/rc.d/rc.local file or another file that you call from rc.local (something like rc.iptables would be good):

```
iptables -t nat -A POSTROUTING -o ppp0 -s 192.168.1.0/24 -j MASQUERADE
```

If you are not connected through analog modem, but perhaps have a permanent connection to the Internet (using cable modem or DSL) with a permanent IP (here assuming your ISP assigned you 209.127.112.160), you'll want to substitute the following line for the previous one:

```
iptables -t nat -A POSTROUTING -o eth0 -j SNAT --to 209.127.112.160
```

At this point, you should be able to pass packets from any host that uses rumble as a gateway. If you made changes to /etc/rc.d/rc.local and /etc/modules/default, this will happen automatically when you reboot.

Of course, this is all for naught if there is no Internet connection on rumble, so a reliable dial-up connection to an Internet provider is required. For this network, a simple PAP authenticated PPP connection (by far the most common method used today with ISPs) is assumed. Following the instructions listed in Chapter 24, "Connecting to an ISP," a pap-secrets file and an options file are created in the /etc/ppp directory. For this example, the following is assumed for the dial-up Internet account:

```
Username: myname
Password: mypass
ISP phone number: 555-1111
Address is allocated: dynamically
Modem port: /dev/ttyS1 (the same as COM2 under DOS/Windows)
```

With these assumptions, the pap-secrets and options file looks like that shown in Listing 30.4.

LISTING 30.4   /etc/ppp/pap-secrets

```
# Secrets for authenticating using PAP
# client      server        secret        IP addresses
myname          *           mypass
```

Because this file contains sensitive information such as the password required by the ISP, it should only be readable and writeable by the root user. Because the file was created by root, the only thing that is required for this security measure is a change in the permissions to the file:

```
chmod 600 /etc/ppp/pap-secrets
```

Following this change, the options file looks like Listing 30.5.

LISTING 30.5   /etc/ppp/options

```
connect "/usr/sbin/chat ?f /etc/ppp/chat-script"
/dev/ttyS1 115200
noauth
modem
crtscts
defaultroute
noipdefault
user myname
```

With this options file, PPP uses the second serial port as the modem device (locked in at 115,200 bps), does not require the ISP to authenticate back, reads modem control messages, uses hardware handshaking (crtscts), sets the modem device as the default network route when connected, negotiates a dynamically allocated IP address, and uses myname to start the authentication process after connecting.

As you can see in the first line, the chat utility is being executed and a file called chat-script, which contains the parameters that chat uses to connect to the ISP, is passed to it. With a PAP-authenticated login, all that needs to be done is to make a successful modem connection; PAP takes it from there.

Listing 30.6 shows what the chat-script file contains.

LISTING 30.6   /etc/ppp/chat-script

```
ABORT     BUSY
""        ATDT5551111
CONNECT        ""
```

That covers the basic PPP dial-up configuration.

MISCELLANY

Some odd items that are set up on a per-client basis on non-Linux systems are set up on a systemwide basis on Linux systems. For instance, things such as the address of the ISP's news server and the masquerading of outgoing mail (making it look as though it's emanating from the ISP, and not from your personal machine) are typically handled on a systemwide basis. This is not necessarily a bad thing; this way, you can set or change one setting and all the applicable client programs you use will utilize the new setting.

By far, the most popular item set in this manner is the domain used for outgoing email. Chapter 28, "Email Clients and Servers," addresses configuration issues and schemes used with sendmail; the m4 configuration system discussed in that chapter is used to accomplish masquerading a domain name.

Simply put, the following two lines are added to your system's .mc file:

```
MASQUERADE_AS(isp-domain.net)
FEATURE(masquerade_envelope)
```

Afterward, a new /etc/sendmail.cf file is created as follows:

```
cp /etc/sendmail.cf /etc/sendmail.cf.backup
m4 ../m4/cf.m4 yourmcfile.mc > /etc/sendmail.cf
```

PART

IV

CH

30

Note that you must have the sendmail-cf package installed (not applicable to Debian) to do this (see Chapter 16, "Software Package Management," for information on package management). After performing this step, sendmail needs to be stopped and started again as follows (for Caldera):

```
/etc/rc.d/init.d/mta stop
/etc/rc.d/init.d/mta start
```

Or (for Debian):

```
/etc/init.d/sendmail restart
```

Or (for Red Hat):

```
/etc/rc.d/init.d/sendmail restart
```

With that done, all outgoing email is sent as username@isp-domain.net. To change the domain name that is used, change the MASQUERADE_AS() line in the system's .mc file and recompile the /etc/sendmail.cf file.

Setting up systems to read news from a remote NNTP host is another common change to Linux systems. Luckily, it requires fewer steps than masquerading mail addresses.

The address of a remote NNTP news server is typically stored in an environment variable called NNTPSERVER. Setting this with the bash shell is fairly simple:

```
export NNTPSERVER=news.isp-domain.net
```

Using the C shell (csh), the command looks more like the following:

```
setenv NNTPSERVER news.isp-domain.net
```

The command can be placed in the appropriate rc file in a user's home directory (.profile or .cshrc, respectively) to set the variable automatically every time a shell is started, or it can be placed in one of the main shell configuration files in /etc (profile or csh.cshrc, respectively) to have the variable set systemwide when the system is started.

TROUBLESHOOTING

I have a PCI card that has the tulip *chip on it. When I* modprobe tulip, *the link light comes on, but when I start the network, the link light goes out and I can't talk to the network.*

Looks like you've run into the tulip versus old_tulip problem. Try the old_tulip first. If that doesn't work it might use the even older de4x5 module. The same is true for other chipsets, such as some of the RealTech chipsets. Some use the rtl8129 module, but others will use the ne2000 (ne) or ne2k-pci module. You might have to experiment or check with the NIC manufacturer.

I set up a network and HostX can ping HostA (the Internet gateway), but can't seem to reach the Internet even though HostA can.

Perform the following steps:

1. Ensure HostX has HostA listed as its default route by issuing the command netstat -rn on HostX. The last line of output should look like the following:

   ```
   0.0.0.0          192.168.0.1      0.0.0.0         UG       40 0       0 eth0
   ```

   You should have only one 0.0.0.0 line containing UG in the flags section.

2. On your gateway system (HostA), make sure you have a similar line to the one above that points to the remote system connected to your Internet connection.

3. Ensure forwarding is turned on in your gateway system (HostA) by issuing the command cat /proc/sys/net/ipv4/ip_forward. You should get a 1 as an answer.

4. Ensure you have a rule permitting IP masquerading if necessary as shown above (check with iptables -L). Your specific ruleset will be determined by whether you have a dynamically assigned IP (MASQUERADE) or a statically assigned IP (SNAT). For more information, see Chapter 35, "IP Masquerading."

5. If you still can't connect from HostX, ensure you can resolve domain names using nslookup or dig. If you can't, check your /etc/resolv.conf file and make sure you have at least two valid nameserver lines and the the the IPs listed are good.

I can't connect to any Internet site by name, but I seem to be able to connect by IP address. What's wrong?

Step 5 in the previous question covers the answer. You don't have valid nameservers listed in your /etc/resolv.conf file. Check with your ISP for valid IPs and put them in this file using coastool.

I bought some Ethernet cards, a hub, and some cables. The Ethernet cards look like they should be working—that is, I see blinking link lights on the Ethernet cards, but the hub link lights don't light.

You can have mixed and matched 10MB cards or hubs with 100MB cards/hubs. All system components need to be able to talk at the the same speed, so if you have 10MB cards and a 100MB hub, you won't be able to communicate. Also make sure, if you're using 100MB or faster components, that you've purchased a good category 5 straight-through cable and not category 3 or cross-connect (cross-over) cables (which would allow you to connect Ethernet card to Ethernet card). You might also want to make sure that if your hub has an uplink port that you're not using that for one of your computers.

I installed an ISA NIC and I just can't seem to get it working. What could be wrong?

First, make sure in the BIOS setup you have turned off PNP OS. Also, make sure your Ethernet card is set up manually. If it's set for PNP, you'll need to use pnpdump to create an `/etc/isapnp.conf` file, and then configure the file and run isapnp `/etc/isapnp.conf` to configure the card. Usually it's just easier to simply set the IRQ and I/O port using the jumpers on the card. Ensuring that you have your NIC set to unused values for the IRQ and I/O settings (`cat /proc/interrupts` and `cat /proc/ioports`), should help you find unused settings.

I'm having lots of problems trying to connect with my modem to my ISP.

I suggest you look at Chapter 24, "Connecting to an ISP," for help with this.

PART

IV

CH

30

SERVICES AND SPECIAL APPLICATIONS

CHAPTER **31**

PRINTING

In this chapter

PRINTING IN LINUX

Printing in Linux is similar to printing in other operating systems, with one major exception: You control the entire process from beginning to end, with the capability to customize the printing process to fit your exact needs.

Unfortunately, this usually translates into added confusion and complication—especially for people who are more used to DOS/Windows print systems, which generally allow printing as soon as a driver is loaded from a disk and the system is restarted.

In Linux (and most of the other UNIX variants), the process is totally visible. You set up a print queue and create a filter if your print jobs need to be translated from one print language to another (such as translating from PostScript to PCL so that HP LaserJet printers can process the print job). You then specify the final destination for the print job, be it remote or local (see Figure 31.1). All these steps are done in print setups on non-Linux operating systems as well; you just do not see it as openly as on a Linux system.

Figure 31.1
Path of a print job.

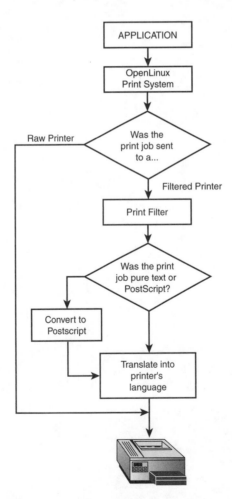

Most distributions of Linux use or have available for their printing system a package called LPRng, which is an enhanced version of the system used by Berkeley Software Distribution's version of UNIX. At the center of this system is a program called lpd that maintains the spooling of print jobs in the print queue. This program temporarily holds on to print jobs until the printer associated with the print queue is free to process the job; at that point, lpd sends the print job to the printer and clears the job from the queue.

Details on how to set up print queues are given later in this chapter.

PRINTING WITH lpr

LPRng (as well as its predecessor from BSD) uses a binary called lpr to send print jobs to print queues. This is the equivalent of DOS's print command, but it offers greatly enhanced control over such items as banner pages, the number of times the print job will be printed, special functionality for binary files, and a slew of other options that help to control the final printouts.

PART

V

CH

31

The syntax for lpr is quite extensive, but in general the following syntax is used (check the man page for lpr to see all the options offered):

```
lpr -Pprinter [-b] file-to-print
```

For example, to print out the /etc/printcap file to a printer called ps, the following command can be executed:

```
lpr -Pps /etc/printcap
```

Like most Linux utilities, lpr can be used as a filter of sorts, accepting standard output (stdout) from the command line or console just as easily as if it were being sent an actual file. For instance, the following command captures the output from cat and pipes it through lpr instead of sending the output to the console, essentially mirroring the printout from the preceding command line:

```
cat /etc/printcap | lpr -Pps
```

This functionality can also be used to print data that is not contained in files. For example, to capture a printout of the partition information on the computer, the following command works nicely:

```
fdisk -l | lpr
```

Simple redirection of files works with lpr as it does with any filter:

```
lpr -Pps < /etc/printcap
```

The utility in using this method is sometimes questionable because it is the same as the first example (given earlier) but with an extra character (<). However, the functionality is there.

As indicated in the upcoming sections of this chapter, more than one print queue can be used on one machine. This extends beyond just the hardware level; not only can more than one printer be connected to the computer, but more than one print queue can be assigned to each printer—each queue treating the print jobs that it receives differently. The -Pprinter parameter allows for the specification of an exact print queue to which to send a print job.

If no print queue specification is indicated on the lpr command line, an environment variable called PRINTER is checked. This environment variable needs to point to the printer to be used by default (see Chapter 14, "Customizing Your Shell Environment," for details on setting environment variables). What is referred to by this variable is a string that matches one of the print queue names in /etc/printcap, which is the file that houses all the print queue configurations. This file is covered in the "Setting Up Printers" section later in this chapter.

If no printer is specified on the lpr command line and no PRINTER environment variable is set, the first print queue entry in /etc/printcap is used for the print job.

When the print job is sent, a few things happen. First, a copy of lpd is started to handle the print job. The reason for this is that the instance of lpd that loads when the system is first started is really only meant to sit in system memory and wait for incoming print job requests. When a request is received, the original lpd spawns copies of itself to handle each print job, leaving itself alone to continue to watch for incoming print requests.

Next, some files are created in the selected print queue that contain control information on the print job (these files start with cf, indicating that they are control files). They contain the actual data to be printed (these files start with df, which indicates that they are data files). Other files are created during the actual spooling procedure as the print data is being collected, but in the end there will only be cf and df files created for each print job that is waiting in the print queue.

When the printer is ready to accept another print job, the next print job in line is opened, filtered (if a print filter is specified in /etc/printcap), and then sent out to the printer through the appropriate printer device in the /dev directory (or through a network device if so configured). At that point, if everything worked out well, the job will print. After the job is printed, the control and data files are removed from the queue.

On occasion you need to specify that the print job you are sending is, in fact, a binary file. Such is the case with some versions of WordPerfect for Linux; if the print job is not specified as being binary, the print job either does not print or produces erratic results. The -b parameter to lpr remedies this nicely. It is good to keep that in mind when specifying data from applications such as word processors and spreadsheets; if there are problems, specify the print output from the application as being binary and the problems might disappear.

SETTING UP PRINTERS

When you set up a printer configuration in an lpr/lpd-based print system, what you are actually setting up is a print queue. This print queue acts as a first-in/first-out holding cell for incoming print jobs (see Figure 31.2). When a job comes in, it enters at the back of the line, and as the jobs in front of it are processed and consequently dropped from the queue, the new job moves up in the line. The order of incoming print jobs is maintained until all jobs in the queue are printed and erased, or until a system administrator intervenes and moves the order of jobs around (more information on that can be found in the "Managing Print Queues" section later in this chapter).

Figure 31.2
Print spooling.

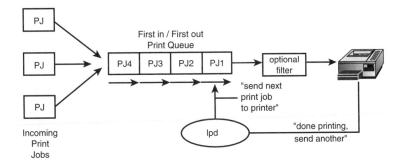

This process is known as *spooling*, and the settings assigned to a print queue in an lpr/lpd system such as LPRng determine how spooling is to be handled within each print queue.

The configuration of the print queue/spooling system is stored in a file called /etc/printcap. This file contains information such as the following:

- The location on your filesystem where you want to spool print jobs
- The name and location of your print filter (if one is used)
- The printer to which you are going to send print jobs
- Alternative printer entries that are set up to handle print jobs differently
- Various other commands that will be addressed later in this chapter

Fortunately, you only really need to know a handful of configuration items to get a solid, effective print configuration going.

Caution

You must be logged in as root to configure print services. Only an individual possessing system administrator—or superuser—status can create, modify, or delete system-level services such as print systems.

LOCAL PRINTERS

As with the Berkeley implementation of the lpd spooler, the difference between a print server and a print client is indicated by the configuration of lpd itself. In other words, the same software package used to set up a print server on your local system can be used as a client to connect to a remote print server that is also running some version of lpd. Also, after you set up a print configuration locally—regardless of whether it is for a printer on your machine or for a printer pointed to on another machine—you can serve print services from your machine to others on your network (see Figure 31.3).

Figure 31.3
A sample networked printer scenario.

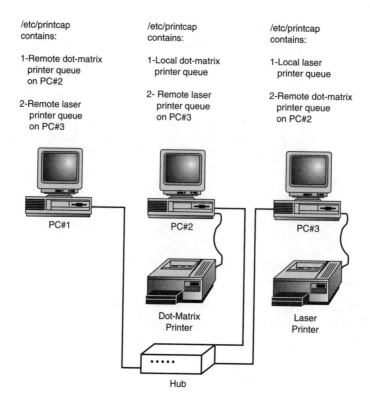

/etc/printcap
contains:

1-Remote dot-matrix
   printer queue
   on PC#2

2-Remote laser
   printer queue
   on PC#3

/etc/printcap
contains:

1-Local dot-matrix
   printer queue

2- Remote laser
   printer queue
   on PC#3

/etc/printcap
contains:

1-Local laser
   printer queue

2-Remote dot-matrix
   printer queue
   on PC#2

PC#1

PC#2

PC#3

Dot-Matrix
Printer

Laser
Printer

Hub

SETTING UP THE /etc/printcap FILE

Listing 31.1 is an example of a typical BSD printcap file (many Linux systems still use this type of print system).

LISTING 31.1   SAMPLE /etc/printcap FILE FOR LOCAL PRINTERS

```
1  lp
2       :lp=/dev/lp0
3       :sd=/var/spool/lpd/lp
4       :mx#0
5       :sh
6
7  ps
8       :lp=/dev/lp0
9       :sd=/var/spool/lpd/ps
10      :mx#0
11      :if=/var/spool/lpd/ps/filter
12      :sh
```

Note

Readers familiar with the Berkeley implementation of lpd might notice a difference in the syntax of LPRng's `/etc/printcap` file. With LPRng, you do not need to have `:\` at the end of each line. If you are more comfortable putting the characters in, go ahead; LPRng simply ignores them.

Examine the contents of this file more closely. You see that two chunks of configuration information are here. Each one is actually for a different printer queue. Each treats the print jobs it receives differently.

If you look closely, you can also see that the only real difference between the two queues is the title associated with each, and the line that starts with `:if=` in the ps queue. This is the line that specifies a print filter; therefore, the ps queue is for print jobs that require some sort of special processing before being sent to the printer. The other queue, lp, does not have this line, so print jobs that are sent there must already be in a format that the printer understands. Both `/etc/printcap` entries in Listing 31.1 have the same `:lp=` line. This line tells where to send print jobs locally; that is, to which printer port on your system the printcap entry sends print jobs.

A full breakdown of the lines in this file is in order. Because the ps entry contains everything the lp entry has and then some, ps is used as the example.

The first line in the ps entry—line 7—is where you specify all the names by which the `/etc/printcap` entry can be called. More than one name can be in this line, as long as all the names are separated by a pipe character (|). For instance, if the ps section of this `/etc/printcap` file is associated with an HP LaserJet 5L printer connected to a server called rumble, conventional procedures indicate that `ps|rumble-lj|HP LaserJet 5L` is a good set of names (general name|server-printertype|brand and model).

Line 8 indicates which device to send print jobs to on your system. The device `/dev/lp0` is a rather common device used for standard printer ports on modern PCs. Occasionally the printer port is located on `/dev/lp1`, but this is not as common. Generally speaking, one or the other is probably the one you will be using; devices numbered higher than that are quite uncommon unless multiple printers or parallel ports are installed on your system.

For printers connected to serial ports, the serial port device needs to be specified here instead of an lp# device. If this is the case, you must also specify at least a `:br` line to indicate the baud rate of the serial connection. The possible values for `:br` are 50, 75, 110, 134.5, 150, 200, 300, 600, 1200, 1800, 2400, 4800, 9600, 19200, and 38400. Indicating a speed higher than the speed at which the printer prints is considered to be a bad idea; be safe and stick with the appropriate baud rate used by the serial port. The number is specified by a pound sign (#) followed by the baud rate, such as `:br#19200`.

Line 9 indicates in what directory the print queue is located. The queue is where print jobs spool. When you send multiple print jobs one after the other (or if your printer is networked and you are spooling print jobs from others on your network), this is the directory where the print jobs are spooled before being sent to the printer. Print jobs are processed in the order they are spooled in unless an administrator moves the jobs around manually in the queue. Utilities that enable this kind of shuffling of print jobs are covered in the "Managing Print Queues" section later in this chapter.

The mx# line (line 10) specifies the maximum size of an acceptable print job. If it is set to 0, no size limit is imposed. The 0 value is usually used unless there is a serious need to limit job sizes.

As stated earlier, line 11 specifies the print filter location and filename (in this example, /var/spool/lpd/ps is the path and filter is the name of the filter file). Any special processing or translation that needs to be done to the print job before it is sent out to the printer needs to happen within this filter. The name and path to the filter is not set in stone anywhere, but the syntax used here is fairly standard and probably needs to be adhered to for consistency across systems.

A typical (simple) print filter for a Linux system might look like Listing 31.2.

LISTING 31.2 SAMPLE FILTER FILE

```
#!/bin/sh

# Specify the language ghostscript should translate#  PostScript into
# (run 'gs -h' to see device list)
DEVICE=ljet4

# The maximum resolution for the printer
RESOLUTION=600x600

# The paper size - a4 or letter
PAPERSIZE=letter

# If an EOF (end of file) character is required
#  after print jobs, put in a 1; otherwise, ignore
SENDEOF=

# Determine the correct paper size
#
if [ "$PAPERSIZE" = "a4" ]; then
  T=A4
else
  T=US
fi

# If the print job is pure text, use
#  either nenscript or enscript to
#  convert the plain text to PostScript
#
if [ -x /usr/bin/nenscript ]; then
nenscript -T$T -ZB -p-
else
if [ "$T" = "US" ]; then
T="Letter"
```

LISTING 31.2   CONTINUED

```
fi
enscript -M $T -Z -p -
fi |

# If the value of the DEVICE variable
#  is "PostScript", do nothing to the
#  print job and send it to the printer
#
if [ "$DEVICE" = "PostScript" ]; then
cat -

# Otherwise, send the data - now in
#  PostScript format - through the
#  ghostscript interpreter to be converted
#  into the language specified in DEVICE above
else
gs -q -sDEVICE=$DEVICE \
-r$RESOLUTION \
-sPAPERSIZE=$PAPERSIZE \
-dNOPAUSE \
-dSAFER \
-sOutputFile=- -
fi

if [ "$SENDEOF" != "" ]; then
printf "\004"
fi

exit 0
```

This sample filter does the following:

- If plain text is piped into the filter, it is converted into PostScript (by the nenscript text-to-PostScript converter if it is installed; otherwise, it converts it using enscript, which performs the same task). The output is piped through an interpreter called ghostscript (specified as gs in the script because that is its executable name), which takes the PostScript data and translates it into a specific printer language (specified in Listing 31.2 as ljet4 or LaserJet 4 PCL language). After that, the formatted/translated print job is sent to the print queue to be printed.

- If the data that is being piped through the filter is PostScript already, it is sent straight to the ghostscript interpreter for translation. If the printer specified at the beginning of the filter is PostScript (indicating that the printer has PostScript handling capabilities built into the hardware), the PostScript data the filter receives or creates bypasses ghostscript and is sent right back out of the filter and on to the printer (the cat - line does this).

Be sure to set a filter like this to be executable before using it (see Chapter 11, "Users, Groups, and Permissions," for details on permissions).

Note that this is just one example of a print filter. The possibilities of what can be used here are almost limitless. Simple filters such as the previous one are fine for basic use, but some

PART

V

CH

31

situations might require something a bit more sophisticated. For instance, print jobs might have to be formatted for wide carriage printers, for ledger paper, or for check printing. Covering all the options might require a complete book in itself.

The best thing to do for a filter is to start small and simple, and then work up to more complexity. Also, a number of print filter packages that might warrant an evaluation (such as LPRng's lpf and various free offerings on the Internet, such as apsfilter and magicfilter) are available.

:sh, which is a rather simple configuration item, suppresses the use of headers on print jobs. This is more of a paper saving item than anything else. Note that headers are not the same as banner pages, like those that are printed with many printers that are networked with hardware such as HP JetDirect cards. These banner pages must be disabled in the network card's hardware; they cannot be disabled from within /etc/printcap.

That should be sufficient for dealing with a basic /etc/printcap file that covers one non-filtered and one filtered local printer configuration. Note that the directories for the print queue set up by default with Linux are located in /var/spool/lpd, so all that needs to be set up after /etc/printcap is created are the specific subdirectories of /var/spool/lpd for each print queue containing an :sd= line.

CREATING THE QUEUE (FILES AND DIRECTORIES)

With Berkeley's lpd package, you had to set these items up manually, including the log files that were used for each print queue. With LPRng, however, you do not need to do this.

LPRng ships with a utility called checkpc that can build all these items for you. It takes the information entered into your /etc/printcap file and makes your print queue directories and logs automatically, right down to the ownership and permissions on the individual files. All you need to do is ensure that the information in /etc/printcap is correct for your print configuration and run the following command:

checkpc -f

What you will see is similar to the output shown in Listing 31.3.

LISTING 31.3 OUTPUT FROM checkpc -f

```
[root@trident /root]# checkpc -f
 LPRng version LPRng-3.2.3
 Get_perms: permissions entry '/etc/lpd.perms'
 Get_perms: permissions entry '/usr/etc/lpd.perms'
 Cannot open '/usr/etc/lpd.perms' - No such file or directory
 Get_perms: permissions entry '/var/spool/lpd/lpd.perms.trident'
Cannot open '/var/spool/lpd/lpd.perms.trident' -No such file or directory
 LPD lockfile '/var/spool/lpd/lpd.lock.trident'
  Checking directory: '/var/spool/lpd'
    checking file '/var/spool/lpd/lpd.lock.trident'
 Truncating LPD log file '/var/spool/lpd/lpd.log.trident'
 Checking /var/spool/lpd/lpd.log.trident file '/var/spool/lpd/lpd.log.trident'
checkpc: Warning - cannot open '/var/spool/lpd/lpd.log.trident'
 lp: Checking printer 'lp'
```

LISTING 31.3 CONTINUED

```
 lp:   Checking directory: '/var/spool/lpd/lp'
 lp: directory stat '/var/spool/lpd/lp' failed -No such file or directory
 lp: Printer 'lp' spool dir '/var/spool/lpd/lp/' needs fixing
 lp:   Checking directory: '/var/spool/lpd/lp'
checkpc: Warning - creating '/var/spool/lpd/lp'
checkpc: Warning - changing ownership '/var/spool/lpd/lp'
 lp:    checking file '/var/spool/lpd/lp/control.lp'
 lp:    checking file '/var/spool/lpd/lp/status.lp'
 lp:    checking file '/var/spool/lpd/lp/log'
checkpc: Warning - owner/group of '/var/spool/lpd/lp/control.lp' are 0/2, not 2/2
checkpc: Warning - owner/group of '/var/spool/lpd/lp/status.lp' are 0/2, not 2/2
checkpc: Warning - owner/group of '/var/spool/lpd/lp/log' are 0/2, not 2/2
 lp:   Need to fix 'lp' files, control dir '/var/spool/lpd/lp/log'
checkpc: Warning - changing ownership '/var/spool/lpd/lp/control.lp'
checkpc: Warning - changing ownership '/var/spool/lpd/lp/status.lp'
checkpc: Warning - changing ownership '/var/spool/lpd/lp/log'
 lp: Checking log file '/var/spool/lpd/lp/log'
 lp:    'log' file 0 bytes long: no truncation
[root@trident /root]#
```

The items in bold text indicate where changes are made to match the configuration in /etc/ printcap. Actions such as directory creation, log file creation, and ownership changes are performed when the checkpc program detects that an inconsistency is in your print queue setup (which is understandable here because there was no existing print queue when checkpc was executed).

REMOTE/NETWORKED PRINTERS

The syntax is quite different for *basic remote* (also known as *networked*) printer configurations, usually because you are sending generic text or PostScript output to the remote printer and letting the remote print queue worry about any special filtering requirements. The server end has a setup similar to the one described in the "Local Printers" section of this chapter.

> **Note**
>
> No special syntax is in /etc/printcap to specify whether a printer is to be served to others on a network. After a local printer is set up and operational with LPRng, anyone else on the network with lpr printing capabilities will be able to access it, unless it is otherwise configured.

Listing 31.4 is an example of what a simple remote printer entry looks like.

LISTING 31.4 SAMPLE /etc/printcap FILE FOR A REMOTE PRINTER

```
remote
:mx#0
:rm=server.domain.com
:rp=ps
```

Two lines are being introduced here: the :rm= and :rp= lines. As might be evident by the letters used to label the lines, rm stands for *remote machine* (not to be confused with the rm command, which erases files and directories) and rp stands for *remote printer*. These lines were added in place of the :lp= line because remote printers do not require the specification of local printer ports (an exception to this will be addressed later in this chapter).

Note that the printer on the remote machine needs to be set up on its own lpr/lpd print system for this to work. In other words, if server.domain.com is a machine running Windows 95 and you do not have the ps printer on that machine set up with some kind of Windows 95 port of lpd, the preceding printer entry is useless; lpd systems speak to lpd systems and nothing else.

As mentioned earlier, remote print queues are typically expected to perform any formatting/filtering that might be required to successfully print incoming jobs. For this reason there is no :if= line in the remote queue entry in Listing 31.4. Filters on the remote print server's end do not have to be any different from print filters on a local printer. Remember, the same software is used to set up print servers and print clients; after a local printer is set up on a print server, it is ready to be used by remote clients on a network. Simply use the preceding syntax to forward all printing to a remote printer.

LOCAL FILTERING FOR REMOTE PRINTERS—OPTION I (FILTER REDIRECTION)

What happens if no filter is running on the remote print server end? This is actually becoming a common occurrence with the popularity of network cards for printers. In these cases, printers simply accept print jobs and expect the format of the job to be sufficient for getting it printed, using whatever graphics language the printer uses. In other words, the printer is not connected to a server, it does not have any built-in filtering capabilities, and, basically, if you do not format or filter your print jobs before sending them on their way, you will fail to get printouts.

For these situations, you must perform some minor trickery to spool and filter your print jobs locally. Keeping in mind the logic of the print filter in Listing 31.2, some sleight of hand with the lpr command enables you to illustrate one way of accomplishing this.

Because filtering must be done locally and the print job needs to be sent to a remote queue, you must set up both a local and a remote queue to accomplish this. Listing 31.5 is a good example of how an /etc/printcap file looks.

LISTING 31.5   SAMPLE /etc/printcap FILE FOR LOCAL FILTERING OF REMOTE PRINT JOBS

```
ps
:lp=/dev/null
:sd=/var/spool/lpd/ps
:mx#0
:if=/var/spool/lpd/ps/filter
:sh

remote
```

LISTING 31.5   CONTINUED

```
:mx#0
:rm=server.domain.com
:rp=ps
```

At this point, nothing seems to be especially exciting or different. The `:lp=` line points to `/dev/null` because there is not a local printer in this case—a local queue is being used for filtering of remote print jobs. One print queue filters and one print queue sits on `server.domain.com`.

So where does the redirection happen? The trick occurs within the filter itself.

In Listing 34.2 you see a number of places where there is a hyphen (-). These are actually routes out of the filter. They sit in place of filenames, and they simply say, "Send whatever came into this filter right back out now that I have done my magic." What needs to happen at each of these portions of the filter is a redirection to the remote queue in `/etc/printcap`.

As indicated earlier, the `lpr` command offers a command-line parameter `-P`, after which you can indicate a specific queue from the `/etc/printcap` file to which to send the print job. Using this, the filter can capture the output from each one of the command lines using `-`, and then send the output to the remote queue.

Listing 31.6 is the revised version of the filter in Listing 31.2, with the necessary changes for local filtering applied.

LISTING 31.6   SAMPLE FILTER FILE ALTERED FOR LOCAL FILTERING OF REMOTE PRINT JOBS

```
#!/bin/sh

DEVICE=ljet4
RESOLUTION=600x600
PAPERSIZE=letter
SENDEOF=

if [ "$PAPERSIZE" = "a4" ]; then
  T=A4
else
  T=US
fi
Listing 34.6  Continued

if [ -x /usr/bin/nenscript ]; then
nenscript -T$T -ZB -p- | lpr -Premote
else
if [ "$T" = "US" ]; then
T="Letter"
fi
enscript -M $T -Z -p - | lpr -Premote
fi |
if [ "$DEVICE" = "PostScript" ]; then
cat - | lpr -Premote
else
```

LISTING 31.6 CONTINUED

```
gs -q -sDEVICE=$DEVICE \
-r$RESOLUTION \
-sPAPERSIZE=$PAPERSIZE \
-dNOPAUSE \
-dSAFER \
-sOutputFile=- - | lpr -Premote
fi

if [ "$SENDEOF" != "" ]; then
printf "\004"
fi

exit 0
```

Every route out of this filter now pipes to the remote queue specified in /etc/printcap. Print jobs are sent through this filter, processed based on the setting in the DEVICE line at the top of the filter, and then are sent out to the remote queue. If the remote printer is busy, the print jobs are spooled locally until the printer is ready.

LOCAL FILTERING FOR REMOTE PRINTERS—OPTION II (BOUNCE QUEUES)

Although Option I is not overly complicated, it is actually a lot of trickery to get something like this set up. However, it is the only way to get local filtering for remote printing set up on Berkeley lpd systems. As luck would have it, the LPRng package provides a slightly shorter method for accomplishing this task.

One of the nicest features offered by LPRng is the *bounce queue* setting (specified with a :bq= line in /etc/printcap). This enables the print system to filter outgoing print jobs before they are sent to the remote queue. This can be considered a shortcut to achieving the same results as the method just described.

Listing 31.7 is an example of an /etc/printcap file that uses this feature.

LISTING 31.7 SAMPLE /etc/printcap UTILIZING A BOUNCE QUEUE

```
ps
:lp=/dev/null
:sd=/var/spool/lpd/lp
:mx#0
:bq=ps@server.domain.com
:if=/var/spool/lpd/lp/filter
:sh
```

Here you see that the :bq= line is pointing to the same printer that was configured as a remote printer earlier, but the syntax used to point to it has changed slightly: remoteprinter@remotemachine is the syntax used with the :bq= line. The same :lp= line is included and is pointing to /dev/null, a spool directory is there just as there was before, no limitation is on print job size, header pages are suppressed, and a filter is specified. The main difference between this local filtering scheme is that the original print filter specified in Listing 31.2 is utilized instead of the altered one from Listing 31.6. This is because the redirection with bounce queues is specified within the `:bq=` line, and is therefore not required within the filter using `lpr` parameters.

RAW PRINTERS

A time will come when, as an administrator of a print server, you will want to have some sort of raw printing functionality. *Raw printing* means the capability to send a print job straight through the Linux print system without it being altered or processed in any way—just spooled (this is the way a Windows NT print spooler works). This functionality is important if you want certain non-Linux systems on your network to be capable of sending print jobs formatted on their systems and having them print correctly. Raw printing allows systems such as Windows to create print jobs using native Windows printer drivers, and then to send them—undamaged and unprocessed—through a Linux machine and straight out to the printer. This is important because it is quite often simpler to have a native printer driver running on one of these non-Linux machines than it is to have something general such as an Apple LaserWriter driver.

Note

The Apple LaserWriter printer was one of the first PostScript printers ever produced. Drivers written for it are guaranteed to produce quality PostScript output, so it has become somewhat of an industry standard PostScript driver for systems such as Windows and Macs. The fact that the LaserWriter printer has been around for so long has helped entrench it as an established medium for producing PostScript through print systems.

Accomplishing this task is not always the simplest thing to do with a Linux print system. Plain print queues (such as the `lp` queue in Listing 31.1) that do not do any filtering are not the same as raw print queues. Some processing is still done on the data being passed between the server and the printer, and some of that processing can render print jobs that are created with native Windows (or other) printer drivers unprintable. In this situation, a pure, raw print queue that does absolutely nothing to the print job data before it hits the printer is needed.

LPRng has the capability to do this. A few minor tweaks to the `lp` queue from the sample `/etc/printcap` file in Listing 34.1 will do the trick (see Listing 31.8).

PART

V

CH

31

LISTING 31.8   RAW `/etc/printcap` QUEUE

```
1  raw|raw printer for Windows clients
2      :rw
3      :sh
4      :lp=/dev/lp1
5      :sd=/var/spool/lpd/raw
6      :fx=flp
```

In some cases, you might need to suppress form feeds. If you do, add a line like this one:
`:sf`

Walk through the file to learn what is being said.

The `:rw` line (line 2) says to open the print device for reading and writing, rather than only for writing. Smart printers, such as modern laser printers, can send information back to the systems that are sending print jobs. Opening the device for reading as well as for writing enables this information to get back to the systems where the print jobs originated, allowing such items as print queue monitors to work from the client end. Without this item, a one-way communication would go from the client to the server, forbidding any monitoring to be done from the client end. After sending a print job, therefore, nothing short of prayer and a trip to the printer would indicate if the print job went through.

As with the queue examples in Listing 31.1, line 3 suppresses headers from printing. Line 4 points to the printer device.

As for line 5, always create a new print spool directory for each print queue. It is not essential, but it is a good practice.

The field in line 6 specifies the types of data that the printer can handle. The letter following the = sign indicates the data types:

- f indicates ordinary format, nothing special.
- l indicates binary format.
- p indicates a special format that is produced by the pr formatting program (which splits print jobs into pages).

The "raw printer for Windows clients" name is quite intentional here. The primary use for a queue like this is with Samba (covered in Chapter 29, "Sharing Resources with Samba "). The combination of the raw pass-through capabilities of this queue and the read/write functionality provides a seamless print system for Windows clients. Print Manager and other vendor-specific print queue monitors do not know the difference between a Samba printer shared through a queue like this and a printer connected to another Windows machine. The easier an administrator can make life for his Windows clients, the better—at least one queue like this needs to be set up if Samba is going to be used.

Detailed configuration of Samba is offered earlier, but the actual print configuration is addressed here (refer to Chapter 29 for the rest). When a raw print queue is set up, edit the default Samba configuration file /etc/samba.d/smb.conf and add the following line to the [printers] section of the file:

`print command = lpr -b -P%p %s`

You might have to copy the smb.conf.sample file in /etc/samba.d over to smb.conf if there is no existing smb.conf file, or you can create a new one using swat.

Following the syntax discussed earlier, the combination of this command and the information that Samba replaces for %p and %s (printer and data stream, respectively) provides the final touch to the Samba print configuration. After this edit is complete, stop and start both the lpd daemon and Samba itself:

```
/etc/rc.d/init.d/lpd stop
/etc/rc.d/init.d lpd start
/etc/rc.d/init.d/samba stop
/etc/rc.d/init.d/samba start
```

At this point, Windows clients will be able to connect to the raw print queue just like they connect to any other shared printer. Refer to Windows's documentation for details on printer connection and networking instructions.

MANAGING PRINT QUEUES

As an administrator of a Linux server, you must have the capability to enforce a certain amount of control over your print system. This control goes beyond simple settings for maximum print job sizes—it goes into actual queue management and troubleshooting, both of which are primarily administrator tasks (although some things can be done at a user level).

LPRng provides what are considered to be traditional BSD style queue administration tools: lpq, lprm, and lpc.

> **Note**
>
> Those who are more familiar with SysV print systems will note the lack of such items as lpadmin and lpstat. Odds are, however, that by using combinations of lpq, lprm, and lpc, you will find functionality similar to that of these utilities.

PEEKING INTO QUEUES WITH lpq

The lpq utility is rather simple in nature. It merely produces a printout of the latest status of a print queue. If jobs are stacked up, it shows which jobs are there and what each job's number is, as well as its position in the queue (see Listing 31.9).

LISTING 31.9 OUTPUT FROM lpq—ONLY ONE QUEUED PRINT JOB

```
1  [erat@rumble ~]$ lpq
2  Printer: lp@rumble  'PostScript'
3   Queue: 1 printable job
4   Server: pid 716 active
5   Unspooler: pid 717 active
6   Status: printed all 670 bytes at 09:24:07
7   Rank    Owner/ID              Class Job  Files              Size Time
8  active  erat@rumble+715         A  715 /etc/printcap        670 09:24:07
9  [erat@rumble ~]$
```

In line 2, you see that the information listed pertains to the lp print queue in /etc/printcap (also known as PostScript, which means that the title of the printcap entry contains at least lp|PostScript as a name). Line 3 states that only one printable job is in the queue, and lines 4 and 5 give process information on the lpd server associated with the print job. Line 6 gives a current status on the spooling of the print job; and line 8 gives detailed information on the print job itself, including the owner, the filename, the size, and the time it was sent to the printer. If more than one print job waits in the queue, numeric ranks are assigned to each job and the preceding report might more closely resemble Listing 31.10.

LISTING 31.10   OUTPUT FROM lpq—MULTIPLE QUEUED PRINT JOBS

```
[erat@rumble ~]$ lpq
Printer: lp@rumble  'PostScript'
 Queue: 14 printable jobs
 Server: pid 728 active
 Unspooler: pid 764 active
 Status: printed all 670 bytes at 09:29:40
 Rank   Owner/ID            Class Job  Files                 Size Time
active  erat@rumble+735       A   735 /etc/printcap          670 09:29:32
2       hugh@rumble+737       A   737 /home/hugh/kludge    13240 09:29:33
3       doris@rumble+739      A   739 /etc/fstab             420 09:29:33
4       bennie@rumble+741     A   741 /home/bennie/bar      1200 09:29:34
5       george@rumble+743     A   743 /home/george/notes   58663 09:29:34
```

The jobs preceding the active job on top are given a number that corresponds with their positions in the print queue. Print queues are *FIFOs* (first-in, first-out buffers), so as one job is printed the others following it are moved up to take the printed job's place. And so it goes until the print queue is empty.

Note that the previous listings only point to one print queue. If more print queues exist in /etc/printcap, a few options are available to view their contents as well. First, you can specify queue on the lpq command line using the same syntax that is used by lpr—Printer (see Listing 31.11).

LISTING 31.11   OUTPUT OF lpq -l -Praw

```
[erat@rumble ~]$ lpq -l -Praw
Printer: raw@rumble  'winprint'
 Queue: no printable jobs in queue
 Status: aborting operations on job erat@rumble+749 at 09:35:18
 Status: server finished at 09:35:18
[erat@rumble ~]$
```

The -l tells lpq to give more detail in its printout. It is similar in scope to the same parameter used by the ls command to give more information on the contents of a directory.

Likewise, if a report of all the print queues set up in /etc/printcap is desired, the -all parameter can be used; the -l parameter is assumed when specifying -all (see Listing 31.12).

LISTING 31.12   OUTPUT FROM lpq -all

```
[erat@rumble ~]$ lpq -all
Printer: lp@rumble  'PostScript'
 Queue: no printable jobs in queue
```

Listing 31.12   Continued

```
Status: printing 'root@rumble+627', closing device at 08:47:55
Status: printing 'root@rumble+627', finished  at 08:47:55
Status: subserver status 'JSUCC' for 'root@rumble+627' at 08:47:55
Status: server finished at 08:47:55

Printer: nofilter@rumble
Queue: no printable jobs in queue
Status: printing 'erat@rumble+595', closing device at 08:43:07
Status: printing 'erat@rumble+595', finished  at 08:43:07
Status: subserver status 'JSUCC' for 'erat@rumble+595' at 08:43:07
Status: server finished at 08:43:07

Printer: raw@rumble  'winprint'
Queue: no printable jobs in queue
Status: kludge: Print_job: job 'erat@rumble+595', cannot open data file
    '/var/spool/lpd/lp/dfA595rumble.fish.net' at 08:43:17
Status: subserver status 'JABORT' for 'erat@rumble+595' at 08:43:17
Status: aborting operations on job erat@rumble+595 at 08:43:17
Status: server finished at 08:43:17
[erat@rumble ~]$
```

Here you see some interesting data. It seems that the last print job sent to the raw print queue failed to be processed because of a missing data file. Errors such as this one (which aborted the print job with a JABORT status) might indicate queue directory ownership/ permission problems, or simply an abnormally aborted print job from the server end. When having problems printing to a specific queue, sometimes the output from lpq can be useful in the debugging process.

Deleting Print Jobs with lprm

As the name might indicate, lprm is a utility that removes print jobs from the print queue. This can be run by users as well as by the system administrator, as can lpq. Certain functions are still reserved for superusers, but operations on a user's print stack can be altered by the owner of the stack whether the owner is a user or not. No single user can remove other users' print jobs unless the remover is the system administrator.

> **Caution**
>
> The lprm utility is a very trusting one, and therefore does not warn you that important print jobs might be deleted by its use. Be sure of what you want to do with lprm before executing it.

When invoked without parameters, lprm deletes the last print job sent to the printer by the user who invoked lprm. This is the default behavior for both users and the system administrator. Various command-line parameters offer extended functionality to allow print job deletions to be more specific:

- lprm username

  This deletes all the print jobs sent by the user matching username. Note that this is reserved for the system administrator.

■ `lprm 157`

This removes print job number 157 from the print queue. If the print job is not owned by the user executing lprm and the user is not the system administrator, this fails. Only the user who owns print job 157 and the system administrator can delete this print job.

■ `lprm all`

This removes all the print jobs on the default print queue that were sent by the person invoking `lprm`. Another similar command for users follows:

■ `lprm -`

When executed as a user, all print jobs sent by that user are deleted from the default printer; when invoked by the system administrator, however, it deletes all the print jobs for the default queue, period.

■ `lprm all all`

This removes all print jobs on all print queues sent by the user who invoked `lprm`. When executed by the system administrator, this deletes all print jobs on all queues regardless of who sent them.

Combinations of these commands are possible, of course. For instance

`lprm username all`

deletes all print jobs sent by the user matching *username* on all print queues.

You can see that the possibilities are extensive when deleting print jobs. Clearly, care must be taken when flipping back and forth as a user and system administrator; because similar syntax performs drastically different tasks with this utility, be sure of who you are logged in as before executing any `lprm` command. If you are not careful, you might inadvertently delete a job you did not intend to delete.

TAKING CONTROL WITH `lpc`

The `lpq` and `lprm` utilities offer some administration capabilities for users, but certain tasks are absolutely reserved for system administrators. Managing the order of a print queue, the capability to kill and print daemons, the capability to enable or disable a print queue, and the capability to redirect print jobs are but a few of the things that can be done with `lpc`, the system administrator's print control utility.

Among the items just listed, a capability also exists to run `lpq` and `lprm` from within `lpc`. It is the one true control center for all print activities on your system.

When invoked, all that is shown is a command prompt that looks similar to the following:

`lpc>`

From there, the question mark (?) key can be pressed to see a screen of help items, descriptions, and syntax for each included.

Commands are entered at the `lpc>` prompt. For instance, when getting a status listing on all the print queues, the output resembles Listing 31.13.

LISTING 31.13 OUTPUT FROM THE status all DIRECTIVE WITHIN lpc

```
lpc>status all
 Printer         Printing Spooling Jobs  Server  Slave Redirect Status/Debug
 lp@rumble        enabled  enabled  0     none    none
 nofilter@rumble enabled  enabled  0     none    none
 raw@rumble       enabled  enabled  0     none    none
 lpc>
```

With a listing like this, you can see in an instant which print queues are disabled, whether any redirection is enabled, whether a server machine is involved with the queue, and how many print jobs are currently spooled for each.

Taking down a print queue is as simple as stopping the queue from processing any more jobs:

```
lpc> stop nofilter@rumble
```

Redirecting print jobs to different printers is fairly straightforward as well:

```
lpc> redirect nofilter@rumble other-ptr@other-svr
```

To hold all print jobs on a print queue that were sent by user erat, use the following command:

```
lpc> hold lp@rumble erat
```

To disable printing from a certain print queue, the following can be executed:

```
lpc> disable lp@rumble
```

To enable the queue again, use the following command:

```
lpc> enable lp@rumble
```

This is fairly simple, to say the least. The collective commands offered by lpc are quite intuitive and will not pose too many difficulties for budding system or print administrators.

The syntax for these items, as well as for others that might prove to be useful for problem resolution, are available by invoking lpc with the -h parameter. The items mentioned previously will give a general idea of the functionality of this utility.

FINAL WORDS

The underlying setup of LPRng is quite stable and rarely, if ever, needs tweaking. In fact, the RFC (*request for comment* document) that defines how BSD printing is supposed to work is adhered to more strongly by LPRng than by many commercial implementations of the BSD lpr/lpd print spooling system. However, a time might come when you want to alter a timeout value, direct print output through a different port, or change various operational parameters that affect filtering or logging. To do these things, a systemwide configuration file called /etc/lpd.conf can be altered. The need to do so is rare (to date, we have not heard of anyone having to do anything to this file beyond leaving it on the hard drive intact), but the file still needs to be mentioned.

As always (with just about any troubleshooting activity), be sure to refer to the logs for the system you are debugging when problems arise. In each print queue directory, a log file tells what the queue has been up to and what the results of each print job have been. These log files are your best friends when printing problems occur. Also, the much maligned and well-trusted /var/log/messages file is a good source of information, as are the commands listed earlier (such as lpq and lpc). Even the lpr utility can help; it offers a -Ddebuglevel parameter that can show you more of what is happening when print jobs are being sent out. A combination of all the preceding suggestions needs to be employed when tracking down anomalies in print systems.

Nobody will argue with you when you say that printing on Linux can be a trying experience. There is much more to think about than most new Linux users are accustomed to. Just try to remember that simple is better, and follow the previous examples as much as possible before delving into man pages and HOWTO documents. On probably 90% of all Linux systems, the print setup is the same; only the filter differs, and then it is mostly because the printer being used needs different parameters for ghostscript to get successful printouts.

TROUBLESHOOTING

I have a printer directly connected to my computer, but when I try to print, nothing comes out. How can I find out if I'm connecting to the printer?

Because the printer is nothing more than a device to Linux, you can check to see whether you can print to it by finding a small text file (/etc/hosts is usually a good test file) and sending it directly to the printer port:

```
cat /etc/hosts > /dev/lp0
```

If this doesn't work, try /dev/lp1. When you find the correct port, make sure lp is linked to that port.

The previous operation worked and I checked the link, but lp still doesn't print.

Run checkpc as shown in the previous text. Then send your text file to the lp with the -b option. If that prints, you might have the wrong filter specified for your printer.

My printer isn't working, and the logs are telling me "the printer is on fire" (I checked, it really isn't). What gives?

Any nonstandard error message coming from a printer will result in this particular message. Most of the time it means your printer is offline. It could also be any of a number of other errors the print daemon doesn't understand, so check your printer.

I have a print server with its own IP on the network (could also be a printer with its own Ethernet card) that won't accept print jobs from the Linux system. Any ideas?

Odds are that a file is on the remote system called hosts.lpd that houses the names of machines that are allowed to print to the server. Fully qualified domain names must be used in such files (for example, rumble.fish.net is okay, but plain rumble is not). Nine out of ten times, if a complaint is from a remote print server, it is because of something that is missing from this file.

I have a new print server box that needs to get an IP as part of its setup. How can I set up this print server under Linux?

The print server is looking for its address through ARP when it comes online. Do the following:

1. Make sure you have a DNS entry or an entry for the print server in your `/etc/hosts` file. For this example the print server will be called `rps1.fish.net`.

2. Look on the print server itself for a hardware address (also called a MAC address). This will be six hexadecimal numbers that can be separated by spaces or colons. A sample can look like this:

   ```
   00:00:C0:7B:C0:D0
   ```

3. Use the following command to send the print server its IP/hostname mapping:

   ```
   arp -s rps1.fish.net 00:00:c0:7b:c0:d0 temp
   ```

This command tells your system to communicate with the print server's Ethernet card and send it (at its MAC address of `00:00:c0:7b:c0:d0`—your address will be different) the IP that corresponds to `rps1.fish.net`. You should now be able to telnet to your print server to program it according to the instructions that came with your print server. You might have to repeat the `arp` command if the print server is powered off.

## CHAPTER 32

FILE TRANSFER PROTOCOL (FTP)

In this chapter

FTP OVERVIEW

The File Transfer Protocol (FTP) is quite simple to use but rather powerful in its capability to facilitate the transfer of files or data between two systems. With many networking protocols and file sharing systems designed and developed subsequent to FTP, it still stands as the most popular method for remotely transferring files. Several FTP servers exist. Several distributions use what is perhaps the most widely used version of FTP, wu-ftp, which was developed at Washington University in St. Louis (see www.wu-ftpd.org for more details). Caldera and Red Hat use this by default. Debian also has this available. Other FTP servers include the netkit FTP server and ProFTPd.

FTP provides the capability to transfer any type of file between two systems. It is designed (see RFC 959) so that the two systems do not have to be the same. In other words, any operating systems that support TCP/IP and offer FTP services can exchange files. One of the systems acts as the server, and the other as the client. The format of the data, whether it's a text file, a database file, or a binary program, does not matter.

FTP service is based on the Transmission Control Protocol/Internet Protocol (TCP/IP) standard. FTP uses two entirely separate TCP sessions to complete a transfer of files. One session is commonly referred to as the Control Connection or Protocol Interpreter (PI) session, and the other as the Data Connection or Data Transfer Process (DTP). Figure 32.1 depicts the basic components of an FTP session.

Figure 32.1
The Protocol Interpreter session is predefined to take place on port 21 and the Data Transfer process occurs on port 20. These ports are defined in the /etc/_services file.

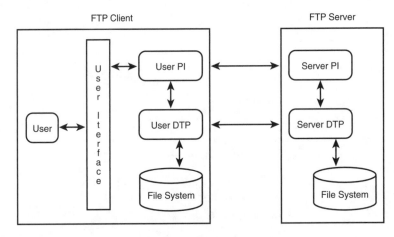

As long as the underlying TCP/IP network is in place and FTP services are configured, an FTP session can be established between two hosts. The FTP client initiates an FTP session by connecting to an FTP server. The server component must be configured and active whenever an FTP request is made from a client. By default, the FTP server is enabled with most Linux distributions (including those with this book) when an FTP server package is installed.

FTP CLIENT

Linux distributions come with a standard command-line FTP client. It's not the fanciest utility, but it gets the job done. Many other FTP clients come with Linux, including the FTP client capability that is built into the Netscape Web browser as well as several graphical drag-and-drop clients. These FTP clients can be easier to use and offer a better user interface; however, an understanding of the command-line client not only gives you a better understanding of how the FTP service works, but also adds some additional features such as unattended or batch mode transfers.

Performing a file transfer using `ftp` as the client is a simple task. It basically consists of the following two steps:

1. Establish a connection to an FTP server.
2. Specify the file to either place on the server or download from the server.

Following is a closer look at each of these steps. First, in order to establish a connection to an FTP server, you must supply the server name. Many FTP sites have configured the machine name so that the first part of the name is set to `ftp`. For example, the Caldera Systems FTP server is aptly named `ftp.calderasystems.com`. Establishing an FTP session to this FTP server can be done as follows:

```
# ftp ftp.calderasystems.com
Connected to ftp.calderasystems.com.
220 locutus4.calderasystems.com FTP server (Version wu-2.5.0(1) Tue Feb 22
08:21:59 MST 2000) ready.
ftp> (ftp.calderasystems.com:david):
```

After a connection is established, you must authenticate yourself to the FTP server. This can be done in one of two ways: as a normal user account or as an anonymous user. Unless you have an individual login account on the FTP server that you are accessing, you must authenticate yourself as an anonymous user.

Authenticating to the FTP server is done by supplying a username and password, or by giving the username `anonymous` (the name `ftp` works as well) with your email address as the password. As you might have guessed, you can enter anything you want as the password when connecting to an FTP server as an anonymous user. However, it is common courtesy to supply your email address when connecting in this way because it enables the system administrator of the FTP server to contact you if the need arises. Completing the connection to the FTP server is as follows:

```
$ ftp ftp.calderasystems.com
Connected to ftp.calderasystems.com.
220 locutus4.calderasystems.com FTP server (Version wu-2.5.0(1) Tue Feb 22
    08:21:59 MST 2000) ready.
331 Guest login ok, send your complete e-mail address as password.
230-
230-             Welcome to the Caldera Systems FTP site!
230-                    ftp.calderasystems.com
230-
230-               "Extend Your Systems to the World!"
230-
230-This site is provided as a public service by Caldera Systems, Inc.  This
230-server is located in Orem, Utah, USA; use in violation of any applicable
230-laws strictly prohibited.
230-
230-For comments on this site, please contact <ftpmaster@calderasystems.com>.
230-=======================================================================
230- ** All file transfers are logged.  If you object to this, logout now. **
230-=======================================================================
230-
230 Guest login ok, access restrictions apply.
Remote system type is UNIX.
Using binary mode to transfer files.
ftp>
```

The connection is complete when the ftp> prompt is received. It is at this point that file transfers can be initiated. This interactive method also provides the capability to perform several other tasks during an FTP session. The commands that are available within an FTP client session can be displayed by entering help (a question mark displays the same list) at the ftp> prompt as follows:

```
ftp> help
```

!	debug	mdir	sendport	site
$	dir	mget	put	size
account	disconnect	mkdir	pwd	status
append	exit	mls	quit	struct
ascii	form	mode	quote	system
bell	get	modtime	recv	sunique
binary	glob	mput	reget	tenex
bye	hash	newer	rstatus	tick
case	help	nmap	rhelp	trace
cd	idle	nlist	rename	type
cdup	image	ntrans	reset	user
chmod	lcd	open	restart	umask
close	ls	prompt	rmdir	verbose
cr	macdef	passive	runique	?
delete	mdelete	proxy	send	

A brief description of each of these commands is listed in Table 32.1.

TABLE 32.1   FTP CLIENT COMMAND LISTING

Command	Description
!	Escape to the shell
$	Execute macro
account	Send account command to remote server
append	Append to a file
ascii	Set ASCII transfer type
bell	Beep when command completed
binary	Set binary transfer type
bye	Terminate FTP session and exit
case	Toggle mget upper- and lowercase ID mapping
cd	Change remote working directory
cdup	Change remote working directory to parent directory
chmod	Change file permissions of remote file
close	Terminate FTP session
cr	Toggle carriage return stripping on ASCII gets
delete	Delete remote file
debug	Toggle/set debugging mode
dir	List contents of remote directory
disconnect	Terminate FTP session
exit	Terminate FTP session and exit
form	Set file transfer format
get	Receive file
glob	Toggle metacharacter expansion of local filenames
hash	Toggle printing # for each buffer transferred
help	Print local help information
idle	Get (set) idle timer on remote side
image	Set binary transfer type
lcd	Change local working directory
ls	List contents of remote directory
macdef	Define a macro
mdelete	Delete multiple files
mdir	List contents of multiple remote directories
mget	Get multiple files
mkdir	Make directory on the remote machine

PART

V

CH

32

TABLE 32.1   CONTINUED

Command	Description
mls	List contents of multiple remote directories
mode	Set file transfer mode
modtime	Show last modification time of remote file
mput	Send multiple files
newer	Get file if remote file is newer than local file
nmap	Set templates for default filename mapping
nlist	List contents of remote directory
ntrans	Set translation table for default filename mapping
open	Connect to remote FTP
prompt	Force interactive prompting on multiple commands
passive	Enter passive transfer mode
proxy	Issue command on alternative connection
put	Send one file
pwd	Print working directory on remote machine
quit	Terminate FTP session and exit
quote	Send arbitrary FTP command
recv	Receive file
reget	Get file restarting at end of local file
rstatus	Show status of remote machine
rhelp	Get help from remote server
rename	Rename file
reset	Clear queued command replies
restart	Restart file transfer at byte count
rmdir	Remove directory on the remote machine
runique	Toggle store unique for local files
send	Send one file
sendport	Toggle use of PORT command for each data connection
site	Send site specific command to remote server (try rhelp site or site help for more information)
size	Show size of remote file
status	Show current status
struct	Set file transfer structure
system	Show remote system type

TABLE 32.1   CONTINUED

Command	Description
sunique	Toggle store unique on remote machine
tenex	Set tenex file transfer type
tick	Toggle printing byte counter during transfers
trace	Toggle packet tracing
type	Set file transfer type
user	Send new user information
umask	Get (set) umask on remote side
verbose	Toggle verbose mode
?	Print local help information

Some commands act as toggle switches between two different FTP session parameters. For example, by default the FTP download mode is set to binary. By entering the command ascii, the transfer mode is changed from binary to ASCII. Another example of a toggle type command is prompt. The status command displays the current settings. The default settings are as follows:

```
ftp> status
Connected to localhost.
No proxy connection.
Mode: stream; Type: binary; Form: non-print; Structure: file
Verbose: on; Bell: off; Prompting: on; Globbing: on
Store unique: off; Receive unique: off
Case: off; CR stripping: on
Ntrans: off
Nmap: off
Hash mark printing: off; Use of PORT cmds: on
Tick counter printing: off
```

DOWNLOADING FILES USING AN FTP SESSION

As you saw in the previous section, it's quite simple to establish a connection with an FTP server. Use the following steps to download files using FTP services:

1. Establish an FTP session by connecting to an FTP server.

2. Authenticate yourself as an anonymous user by supplying the login anonymous and your email address as a password.

3. Navigate the FTP directories to locate the desired files.

4. Initiate the download process.

5. Close the FTP session and exit.

After a connection is established, the next step is to locate the desired files. Navigating through an FTP site is similar to navigating around a Linux filesystem at a shell prompt (see Chapter 10, "Understanding the Linux Filesystem"). The commands are the same for listing files and changing directories. After the files that are to be downloaded are located, it's just a matter of setting the download parameters and initiating the transfer. In the following sample FTP session, the complete set of QT development utilities is downloaded:

```
ftp> ls
200 PORT command successful.
150 Opening ASCII mode data connection for /bin/ls.
total 22
drwxr-xr-x  10 root      root           1024 Mar 13  1998 .
drwxr-xr-x  10 root      root           1024 Mar 13  1998 ..
d--x--x--x   9 root      root           1024 Jan  2 16:07 .private
d--x--x--x   7 root      root           1024 Dec 19 23:35 .virtual
d--x--x--x   2 root      root           1024 Oct 21 19:45 bin
d--x--x--x   2 root      root           1024 May 20  1997 etc
d-wx-wx-wt   3 root      root           1024 Dec 30 12:52 incoming
drwxr-xr-x   2 root      root           1024 Feb 15  1997 lib
drwxr-xr-x   2 root      root          12288 May 15  1997 lost+found
dr-xr-xr-x  16 root      root           1024 Dec 23 15:41 pub
-r--r--r--   1 root      root            593 Mar 13  1998 welcome.msg
226 Transfer complete.
ftp>
ftp> cd /pub/OpenLinux/contrib/RPMS
250 CWD command successful.
ftp>ls qt*
200 PORT command successful.
150 Opening ASCII mode data connection for /bin/ls.
-r--r--r-- 1 root root    643562 Dec  7 16:43 qt-1.42-1.i386.rpm
-r--r--r-- 1 root root   2646588 Dec  7 16:43 qt-1.42-1.src.rpm
-r--r--r-- 1 root root    662655 Dec  7 16:43 qt-devel-1.42-1.i386.rpm
-r--r--r-- 1 root root   1203320 Dec  7 16:44 qt-doc-html-1.42-1.i386.rpm
-r--r--r-- 1 root root    596047 Dec  7 16:44 qt-examples-1.42-1.i386.rpm
-r--r--r-- 1 root root    138712 Dec  7 16:44 qt-tutorial-1.42-1.i386.rpm

226 Transfer complete.
ftp> prompt
Interactive mode off.
ftp> mget qt*
local: qt-1.42-1.i386.rpm remote: qt-1.42-1.i386.rpm
200 PORT command successful.
150 Opening BINARY mode data connection for qt-1.42-1.i386.rpm (643562
bytes).
226 Transfer complete.
643562 bytes received in 6.71 secs (94 Kbytes/sec)
local: qt-1.42-1.src.rpm remote: qt-1.42-1.src.rpm
200 PORT command successful.
150 Opening BINARY mode data connection for qt-1.42-1.src.rpm (2646588
bytes).
226 Transfer complete.
2646588 bytes received in 27.6 secs (94 Kbytes/sec)
local: qt-devel-1.42-1.i386.rpm remote: qt-devel-1.42-1.i386.rpm
200 PORT command successful.
150 Opening BINARY mode data connection for qt-devel-1.42-1.i386.rpm
(662655 bytes).
```

```
226 Transfer complete.
662655 bytes received in 6.39 secs (1e+02 Kbytes/sec)
local: qt-doc-html-1.42-1.i386.rpm remote: qt-doc-html-1.42-1.i386.rpm
200 PORT command successful.
150 Opening BINARY mode data connection for qt-doc-html-1.42-1.i386.rpm
(1203320 bytes).
226 Transfer complete.
1203320 bytes received in 10.6 secs (1.1e+02 Kbytes/sec)
local: qt-examples-1.42-1.i386.rpm remote: qt-examples-1.42-1.i386.rpm
200 PORT command successful.
150 Opening BINARY mode data connection for qt-examples-1.42-1.i386.rpm
(596047 bytes).
226 Transfer complete.
596047 bytes received in 5.3 secs (1.1e+02 Kbytes/sec)
local: qt-tutorial-1.42-1.i386.rpm remote: qt-tutorial-1.42-1.i386.rpm
200 PORT command successful.
150 Opening BINARY mode data connection for qt-tutorial-1.42-1.i386.rpm
(138712 bytes).
226 Transfer complete.
138712 bytes received in 1.37 secs (99 Kbytes/sec)
ftp>quit
221 Goodbye.
[allan@caldera allan]$
```

Note

Commands that deal with multiple files, such as mget, mput, and mdelete, take wildcards for parameters. For example, the command mget qt* gets all the files that begin with the letters qt. If you remembered to turn prompting off (as in the preceding example), the session downloads each file it finds that starts with qt in the current directory. If prompting is on, you're asked whether you want to download each file.

PART

V

CH

32

You probably already know you can download (and upload) files with Netscape. By default, Netscape logs in as the anonymous user. Did you know you can also download (and upload) files in Netscape as a system user? You do this by specifying the user@host in the location bar:

```
ftp://david@ftp.calderasystems.com/
```

You are prompted for the user david's password, and if authenticated, you are dropped in the root directory (not david's home directory). You can also give your password as part of the location entry, but because Netscape saves this information in the history, it's a bad idea from a security standpoint. Nonetheless, you can do it this way:

```
ftp://david:password@ftp.calderasystems.com/
```

You are not prompted for a password, but you are logged in if the password is correct.

If you want to upload a file and are in a directory that you can write to (remember, write permissions depend on who you logged in as, yourself or anonymous), select from the Netscape Menu bar File, Upload. At this point a file selection box will open. Find the file you want to upload and select OK.

SERVING FILES USING FTP

As with many of the services that are available with Linux, the FTP server is configured as operational by default. This means that files can be served to anyone who has access to the system. Access to the system is only offered to users with previously set up accounts. See Chapter 11, "Users, Groups, and Permissions," for more details on user account setup.

FTP SERVER OVERVIEW

The primary purpose of an FTP server is to offer files to remote users. These users might be local to an organization, or they might be anonymous users somewhere on the Internet. Access to an FTP archive, or to any files via FTP, is controlled by a user account. For users with previously configured accounts, accessing files via FTP is allowed by default. You merely have to supply a user account and password. After a user is authenticated to the FTP server in this fashion, he can access any files on the system that he has rights to. The default directory is the user's home directory, as specified in the /etc/passwd file. The standard set of packages that is installed with OpenLinux includes one called anonftp. This package contains all the components to set up an anonymous FTP server. Red Hat also has this package as an additional install package. Under Debian, installation of an FTP server will ask you if you want to set up anonymous FTP; no separate package exists for this purpose.

ANONYMOUS FTP

Anonymous FTP is arguably the most common use of FTP services. Countless FTP archives exist all around the globe. Each of these sites offers access to unknown users to connect to the server and download files of their choice. Most software companies offer demo programs via FTP. Some FTP sites even offer the capability to place files on the FTP server system. For example, the Caldera FTP site has an incoming directory where many programmers have contributed software packages for the use and benefit of others.

If an incoming directory is set up on your FTP server, it is good practice to configure it so that the system is protected from malicious acts. For example, it is strongly recommended that the incoming directory resides on its own partition. This way, if the incoming directory becomes full—either accidentally or maliciously—it does not affect the rest of the system. Also, setting up the incoming directory as write-only (no read privileges for world) enables you to monitor the content that has been placed there. After the files have been determined to be okay, that is, there are no offensive or inappropriate files, they can be moved to a location to which all anonymous users can have access. Most FTP sites call this the *contrib area* of the FTP site.

The anonymous FTP RPM contains the following files:

```
/home/ftp
/home/ftp/bin
/home/ftp/bin/gzip
/home/ftp/bin/ls
/home/ftp/bin/tar
/home/ftp/bin/zcat
/home/ftp/etc
/home/ftp/etc/group
```

```
/home/ftp/etc/passwd
/home/ftp/pub
/usr/doc/anonftp-3.1
/usr/doc/anonftp-3.1/README
```

Installation of this package sets up everything that is required to make anonymous FTP service available. As was mentioned earlier in this chapter, in order to connect to an FTP server, you must have a user account. Even with anonymous FTP service, a user account is required. However, rather than creating a new user account for this purpose, one is already created in the /etc/passwd file. Of course it is appropriately named ftp. It's actually a special type of user account that differs from the typical user accounts found in the /etc/passwd file. The entry for the ftp account in the /etc/passwd file is as follows:

```
ftp:x:14:50:FTP User:/home/ftp:
```

It is the user account entry in the /etc/passwd file that allows a connection to the FTP server by anonymous users. Even though the user account entry is ftp, the user ID anonymous is accepted when connecting to the FTP server. In fact, many people mistakenly think that anonymous is the only user ID that works.

Controlling Access

Access to the FTP server can be controlled in one of four ways:

- Removing or commenting out the FTP user in the /etc/passwd file
- Adding a user to exclude to the /etc/ftpusers file
- Removing the class of user from the /etc/ftpaccess file
- Shutting down the FTP server via ftpshut

The /etc/ftpaccess file is used to configure access to the FTP server. Upon initial installation, the contents of the this file are as follows:

```
class   all   real,guest,anonymous   *

email root@localhost

loginfails 5

readme   README*     login
readme   README*     cwd=*

message /welcome.msg          login
message .message              cwd=*

compress      yes           all
tar           yes           all
chmod         no            guest,anonymous
delete        no            guest,anonymous
overwrite     no            guest,anonymous
rename        no            guest,anonymous

log transfers anonymous,real inbound,outbound
```

```
shutdown /etc/shutmsg

passwd-check rfc822 warn
```

Each entry defined in this file is described in detail in the man page for ftpaccess. The entries in the /etc/ftpaccess file control not only who can access the FTP server, but what they can do after a connection is made.

> **Tip**
>
> To disable access to the FTP server to all real accounts on the system, remove the entry for real in the class line of the /etc/ftpaccess file.

The /etc/ftpusers file is used to control which users do not have access to the FTP server. By default, the following entries are placed in the /etc/ftpusers file:

```
root
bin
daemon
adm
lp
sync
shutdown
halt
mail
news
uucp
operator
games
nobody
```

If a username is included in the /etc/ftpusers file, that user cannot access the FTP server. If a connection to the FTP server is attempted with one username included in this file, the following message is returned:

```
# ftp ftp.kcpartners.com
Connected to ftp.kcpartners.com
220 router.kcpartners.com FTP server (Version wu-2.4.2-academ[BETA-17](1)
Wed Aug 19 02:55:52 MST 1998) ready.
Name (kcpartners.com:col): ftp
530 User ftp access denied.
Login failed.
Remote system type is UNIX.
Using binary mode to transfer files.
ftp>
```

SHUTTING DOWN THE FTP SERVER

The ftpshut command can be used to discontinue FTP service at a given time. It provides a means of notifying users that the FTP server is temporarily shut down and that they can try again later. The ftpshut command creates a file in the /etc directory called shutmsg. When an attempt to connect to the FTP server is made, the FTP server checks for the existence of this file. If it is found, the following message is displayed:

```
# ftp router
Connected to router.kcpartners.com.
```

```
500 router.kcpartners.com FTP server shut down -- please try again later.
ftp>
```

Note You must remove the /etc/shutmsg file in order to re-establish FTP service after issuing a ftpshut command.

FILE PLACEMENT

Because the FTP server is enabled by default for anonymous user access, placing files for FTP access is a simple step. The default directory structure for anonymous FTP access is configured in such a way that simply placing files in the /home/ftp/pub directory will suffice. Note that the other two directories within the /home/ftp directory, /home/ftp/bin and /home/ftp/etc, are not accessible when connecting via FTP. Place all publicly accessible files under the /home/ftp/pub directory or a subdirectory tree structure within /home/ftp/pub.

Note Remember to set all files on the FTP server with permissions of read-only. The directory permissions for /home/ftp/pub are set this way by default.

TROUBLESHOOTING

I tried to connect to ftp *as root, but I keep getting* 530 Login incorrect. Login Failed. *I know I used the correct password.*

By default, root is denied ftp access. This is configured in PAM. The /etc/pam.d/ftp file installed by most Linux distributions contains an auth line listing pam_listfile.so and pointing to /etc/ftpusers. The sense=deny means that any user listed in this file will be denied ftp access. The root user, as well as all system accounts, are listed in the /etc/ftpuser file. You have two choices: Comment out the auth line in /etc/pam.d/ftp, or comment out the use root in /etc/ftpusers (just put a # as the first character in the line.)However, enabling root access to FTP is a very bad idea from a security standpoint. If you do this, you seriously weaken the security of your system. This is even a concern today on systems connected only occasionally using a modem.

I want to shut down the FTP server, but only temporarily, not permanently. How can I do this?

Use the ftpshut command. This command will write a file that by default is /etc/shutmsg. (You can change this in the /etc/ftpaccess, the shutdown variable specifies the file.) When you are ready to permit access again, simply remove the /etc/shutmsg file. While FTP is shut down, any user attempting to connect will have the contents of the shutmsg displayed on their screen.

I want to configure FTP so that some users cannot log in or are locked into certain directories. How can I do this?

I suggest you open Webmin in your Web browser, and look on the Servers page at the FTP Server module. This module will help you configure all aspects of your FTP server. The FTP module includes a help link on each page that is specific to the information on that page. Explore the different icons and read the help.

How can I tell who's been accessing my FTP server?

If you have logging turned on (check the Logging module under the Webmin FTP server module), logins to the FTP server will be logged to /var/log/messages. For anonymous users, this will include their "password," which should be an email address. You can enforce this by entering the Anonymous FTP module, making the FTP password check RFC822, and denying login. This will not prevent anyone from using a phony email address, but it will check that the email address provided complies with RFC822.

I have a directory full of files I want to upload. How can I do this?

The easiest way is to use your FTP client's multiple put command (mput). By using the *, you can specify all files. By default you'll be prompted for each file. If you don't want to be prompted, before you start, toggle prompting off by typing prompt. The commands you might want to use in order after logging in and changing to the upload directory are as follows:

```
binary
hash
prompt
mput *
```

## CHAPTER 33

APACHE AND KHTTPD

In this chapter

INTRODUCTION TO APACHE

One of the most basic, yet important, services available with Linux is the Web server. The Web server provides you with the ability to set up your own Web site (or multiple Web sites), where you can publish your own information, process data, or serve some community in which you are interested.

Most distributions of Linux ship with the most popular Web server available today, the Apache Web server. In this chapter, you will learn how Apache works, and you will learn about many of its configurable features. Serving Web pages is, at its core, a very simple operation; however, you can make numerous modifications and extensions to the basic Web server configuration, which you can use to customize the Web site that you create.

Apache is maintained by The Apache Software Foundation (www.apache.org), a non-profit organization devoted to the support (technical, logistical, and even legal) of various software projects. The largest project is Apache server itself, but the ASF also supports other projects such as Jakarta, focusing on Java-based solutions; and Personal Homepage (PHP), an advanced scripting language for Web pages.

OVERVIEW OF OPERATION

Before diving into the configuration of the Apache Web server, it helps to have a basic understanding of its operation on your machine. A Web server responds to requests made to it using the *Hypertext Transfer Protocol (HTTP)*. This protocol is a simple one that primarily allows clients to request documents from a server. The HTTP protocol also allows clients to provide information back to the server for interactive operations. Because the Web server uses this protocol, the actual server daemon program is called httpd.

Many distributions install Apache by default. To verify that it is installed and running on your system, start a browser (such as Netscape or konqueror) and open the following address by typing it into the location line for the browser:

```
http://localhost/
```

Note   If the above fails, it is possible that Apache is installed, but not running. See the sidebar "Restarting the Server to Experiment with Your Changes" for information on starting Apache.

If Apache is running on your machine, you will see a test page including links to the Apache Web or perhaps links provided by your distribution. Although you are accessing information on your local box, you are actually going through the network—accessing your local Web server— to see it. The basic sequence of operations performed by the browser and server is as follows:

1. The browser opens a connection to the server that is listed in the URL (in this case localhost). This involves looking up the address of the machine, based on its name, and using TCP/IP port 80 if none is specified. In the preceding example, localhost resolves to 127.0.0.1, which is your networking loop-back port.

2. The browser sends a GET request to the server with the path to the document that it wants to retrieve. In the preceding case, the path is /, which is the root directory.

3. The server translates the requested path into a path in its local filesystem. By default, Apache uses a document root of /usr/local/apache/htdocs for the Web server; therefore, the requested path / is translated into the path /usr/local/apache/htdocs/. This is just the default location. Many distributions move it to locations like /home/httpd/html.

4. The server evaluates the path to see whether any security or other restrictions apply to that path. If so, the server might request that the user enter his name and password to see the document, or it might reject the request immediately (depending on the access control settings for the document in question).

5. If the path indicates a regular file, the server returns the file to the client, indicating the file type as part of the response. The file type is returned in MIME format as part of the response header. (MIME types are discussed later in this chapter.)

6. If the path indicates a directory (as it does in the current example), the server can do one of several things. It can look for a specially named file in the directory (usually index.html) to return to the client; generate a directory listing of the directory as an HTML page and return that to the client; or return an error to the client.

7. If the path indicates a special program, called a CGI script, the server can run the program and return the output of the program to the client.

8. After the server finishes sending the data to the client, and after the client receives it, the client and server terminate their connection.

9. At this point, the server usually makes an entry in a log file about the request.

The Web server is generally started automatically when you boot your machine. The following steps describe how the Web server begins operation when it is started:

1. The Web server generally begins operation when an rc script is run by the init daemon. See Chapter 13, "System Initialization," for an explanation of the init process and the different rc scripts that run during system startup.

2. The Web server reads its configuration file and configures many of its internal settings, including its name and address, the location of the documents that it serves to requesting clients, security settings, and the location and format of log files.

3. The server generally changes its privileges from root to some less-privileged user account on the system to reduce the risk of someone using the Web server to break into your machine to access private documents.

4. The Web server *binds* to an address (or multiple addresses) on your machine. Binding is when a program registers with the operating system, requesting that any connections to that port be directed to the application.

5. The Web server starts several child processes to handle actual requests from clients and begins receiving and responding to requests.

BASIC CONFIGURATION

Although the Web server is essentially a mechanism to transfer files from your machine to another (the client) on the network, it is a surprisingly flexible piece of software.

It supports many options for changing its name, address, and performance characteristics. You can specify multiple directories from which to serve documents, and you can apply different document and directory handling options, security settings, and access rights to each. You can also control how errors are returned to the user, where and how log files are written, and how the server assigns types to files that it returns.

INTRODUCTION TO CONFIGURATION

Before presenting all the different configuration options for Apache, this section first covers some basic items, such as where the configuration files are located and the default values for some important Web server settings. It also presents an overview of the types of options that are available for configuring the Web server.

There are too many different directives, options, and modules in Apache to list them all in this chapter. Instead, the most common customizations to the Web server are presented here. Detailed online documentation has more information about each directive; furthermore, it covers the other modules and features of Apache.

Most Linux distributions provide an RPM or deb package including the Apache documentation, usually named apache-doc or something similar. Apache documentation is also available at the Apache Web site: http://www.apache.org/docs.

APACHE CONFIGURATION DIRECTORIES

Various distributions tend to place Apache's configuration files in very different locations. Since even the directory structure radically varies between distributions, we cannot even refer to a variable like ${APACHE_ROOT} as we do with ${KDEDIR} or ${HOME}. For consistency, this chapter focuses on the default locations, but Table 33.1 shows the locations of the major configuration components for various distributions. Distributions generally place configuration and log files under ServerRoot, and place all HTML documents (including documentation) under DocumentRoot.

TABLE 33.1 APACHE CONFIGURATION BY DISTRIBUTION			
Option	**Default**	**Red Hat/OpenLinux**	**Debian**
ServerRoot	/usr/local/apache	/etc/httpd	/etc/apache
DocumentRoot	/usr/local/apache/htdocs	/home/httpd/html	/var/www
executables	/usr/local/apache/bin	/usr/bin	/usr/bin

APACHE CONFIGURATION FILES

The Apache configuration files are located in the directory /usr/local/apache/conf by default, though this is often different by distribution. If you look in this directory, you see several files that control different aspects of the Web server's behavior and functionality.

The base directory for the Web server configuration files is specified in the file httpd.conf, using the ServerRoot directive. When the Web server is started by the initialization scripts, the path to httpd.conf is specified on the command line of the server (httpd), and the other configuration files are determined from there.

There are five basic configuration files in the configuration directory. These files, and their usual contents, are described in Table 33.2. The most common configuration changes for Apache are made in httpd.conf.

TABLE 33.2 WEB SERVER CONFIGURATION FILES

File	Contains
httpd.conf	General server configuration settings. This file now tends to hold all the configuration, removing the need for srm.conf and access.conf.
srm.conf	Request processing directives, including error responses, directory indexing options, and script handling. This file basically defines the document tree (name space) that is visible to the outside world, as well as how the server delivers information from that tree to remote clients. The structure of the document tree doesn't necessarily match the directory structure of your local filesystem. This file is generally no longer used (see httpd.conf).
access.conf	Per directory options, including access control and security restrictions, this file is generally no longer used (see httpd.conf).
mime.types	MIME file type definitions for different file extensions.
magic	MIME file type definitions based on file contents.

Historically, the .conf files hold the different types of information that are described in Table 33.2. However, any Web server directive can be put in any of the three .conf files, and the Web server will interpret it correctly. To reduce confusion, Apache now ships with all of the options in the main httpd.conf file. If the other .conf files do exist, they are processed in the following order: httpd.conf, srm.conf, and then access.conf. Additional configuration files (particularly those that are related to security) might be present in the actual document tree that is processed by the server. These files are described in greater detail in the sections "Defining Options Using a File in the Current Directory" and "Adding Security to Your Web Site" in this chapter.

There might be other files in the configuration directory that end in -dist or -dist-win. These files are provided as examples of the original versions of the configuration files, as distributed by the Apache organization (with settings for UNIX and Windows machines, respectively).

Modifying the names and locations of configuration files used by the server is discussed in the section "Global Server Options."

PART

V

CH

33

Note

> If you have followed some of the examples in previous chapters of this book (or if you have reinstalled or upgraded the Apache package), you might see configuration files with the extension .rpmsave. For a description of how these files are used by the package manager, see Chapter 16, "Software Package Management." Don't worry about them for now.

LOCATION OF LOG FILES

Log files are configured by default to be written in the directory /usr/local/apache/logs, though this is often changed by various distributions. Log file options are discussed later in this chapter in the section "All About Logging."

DEFAULT DOCUMENT DIRECTORY

The default document directory for Apache is /usr/local/apache/htdocs, though this varies among distributions. This means that when you put a file in this directory, or in subdirectories of this directory, remote users can see the file.

Other directories are also configured, by default, to be available through the Web server to the outside world, including the following directories:

- /usr/local/apache/cgi-bin
- /usr/local/apache/icons
- public_html under each user's home directory (for example, /home/tim/public_html)

All these directories appear at different locations in the directory structure (name space) that is visible to the outside world. This is explained in the section "Defining the Document Name Space."

TYPES OF CONFIGURATION DIRECTIVES

At this point, before a detailed presentation of server configuration directives, it is useful to categorize the different options for the server.

Table 33.2 showed the different files that are used to hold configuration information for the Web server. The configuration data falls into roughly four major categories (represented by the files mentioned in the table).

There are global server directives, which control aspects of the server such as its address, the user and group account it runs as, and log file formats and locations. Also, there are numerous options for tuning the performance and responsiveness of the server, and for setting timeouts and limits used by the server for its network connections.

Another category of directives has to do with how the server handles requests. The server provides a whole tree of documents to the outside world. Certain directives define this tree, including the location of the main document directory and other directories that the server provides. Furthermore, these directives control how the items in the tree are presented to clients (whether they are returned as files, as directory listings, or as output from programs in the document tree). You can configure many aspects of the directory listings that are provided by the server, and you can control how documents are selected and manipulated before they are returned to the user.

A third category of directives controls access to the items that are returned by the file server. There are directives to limit access to clients that are making requests from certain locations, as well as directives to limit access to users who supply specific name and password combinations to the Web server. Other options control how the access limitations are applied and what options are allowed when files and directories are processed by the server.

Finally, there is the file typing system of the server. The server uses a system called MIME typing (*MIME* stands for *Multipurpose Internet Mail Extensions*) to communicate to the client the type of data that it is returning in each of its documents. This allows the client to handle the data more intelligently. For example, if the server identifies a document as a sound file, the client can load a sound program to play the file when it is received. There is a set of directives for defining the type of each file, based on its filename extension. Also, file types can be defined based on the content of the file.

It is important to distinguish between the different types of directives for several reasons. First, it helps you keep related directives near each other, and in the correct file. Some directives, such as those for defining file types, must reside in the correct file in order for the server to process them correctly. Another reason to distinguish the directives has to do with their scope. Some directives apply to the whole server and specify either general server behavior or apply to every document returned by the server. Other directives, however, can be applied to specific directories or files in the document tree. For example, you might have a part of your Web site where only authorized users can view documents, and another part for the general public. The per-directory configuration options enable you to completely customize the different areas of your Web site to suit your individual needs.

Restarting the Server to Experiment with Your Changes

As you make modifications to the Web server configuration, you probably want to notify the server so the changes can take effect. How you notify the server depends on your distribution.

For example, with distributions using an `/etc/rc.d/init.d` directory (such as Red Hat and OpenLinux), you can generally notify the server by typing the following as root:

```
/etc/rc.d/init.d/httpd reload
```

Under Debian, it is similar, but instead of `/etc/rc.d/init.d`, the directory is `/etc/init.d`.

Another way to do this (which works for all distributions) is to send the running server a SIGHUP signal, which causes the main process of the server to terminate its children, reread the configuration files, and—if all goes well—restart child processes with the new configuration. To do this, use the following command:

```
kill -s SIGHUP <PID of httpd>
```

You can determine the PID of httpd by using ps, or by looking at `/var/run/httpd.pid` on some distributions. This is generally what `/etc/rc.d/init.d/httpd reload` actually does. The drawback of these methods is that if there is any problem with the modifications to the configuration files, the server just exits without any message. Alternately, you can force a full restart of the server, which will often provide more error messages by running

```
/etc/rc.d/init.d/httpd restart
```

or your equivalent, or by killing the process completely and restarting it.

GLOBAL SERVER OPTIONS

The global server options control how the server interacts with the network and the host machine. Also, many options are available to control the performance of the server.

The directives for these options are in the file `httpd.conf`.

CHANGING SERVER CONFIGURATION FILES

If, for one reason or another, you need to change the names or locations of the server configuration files, you can do so using the `ServerRoot`, `ResourceConfig`, `AccessConfig`, `TypesConfig`, and `MIMEMagicFile` directives.

The `ServerRoot` directive specifies a base directory for Apache. Any filenames that are specified with the other directives, and do not start with a slash, are appended to the `ServerRoot` path. This makes it possible to leave all the other filenames alone and just switch the server to use another configuration directory. The default value for `ServerRoot` is `/usr/local/apache`, but this is commonly reconfigured by distributions to `/home/httpd` (Red Hat/OpenLinux) or `/var/www` (Debian).

The most common reason to change the configuration filenames is when you are running more than one Web server. Obviously, the configuration of the servers must be different for the Web servers to respond on different addresses and serve different documents. You can decide whether you want to keep all the configuration files in one directory and change the names for each set, or whether you just want to make another directory (for example, `/usr/local/apache2/conf`), keep all the filenames the same, and change the value of `ServerRoot`.

The following list shows the default values for the other configuration file directives:

- `ResourceConfig`—`conf/srm.conf`
- `AccessConfig`—`conf/access.conf`
- `TypeConfig`—`conf/mime.types`
- `MIMEMagicFile`—`conf/magic`

If you use these directives, place them in the `httpd.conf` file. For example, to change the name of the access configuration file, edit `httpd.conf` and add a line such as the following:

```
AccessConfig conf/myaccess.conf
```

Note

Note that `srm.conf` and `access.conf` are generally no longer used, and all configuration directives are placed in `httpd.conf`. It is still legal to split the directives into these three files.

CHANGING THE ADDRESS OF THE SERVER

Three directives are used to control the address of the server. Often, your machine has only one IP address, and you use that address with the server. If you have multiple IP addresses, you might want the Web server to respond to requests on any of the machine's addresses. In these cases you can leave the configuration of the address for your server alone.

However, if your machine has multiple IP addresses, you might want to have it respond on only one of them. You can then run another instance of the Web server on a different address, to serve a different set of pages to clients. This enables you to make it appear, to the outside world, as if your machine were actually two (or more) different Web sites. This feature is called *virtual hosting*, and is a rather complex subject (which is covered in greater detail later in this chapter).

To simply change the address or port used by the server, use one of the following directives: `BindAddress`, `Listen`, or `Port`.

Use `BindAddress` when you want to specify either a single address or all addresses on your machine to which the server is to respond. You can specify any of the following:

- *—Respond on all IP addresses for the machine.
- **address**—Respond on just this IP address.
- **name**—Respond on the address that corresponds to this hostname (the name must be a fully qualified Internet domain name).

Only one `BindAddress` can be specified per server, and the directive doesn't enable you to specify the port that is to be used for service (use the `Port` directive for this). The `Listen` directive, on the other hand, can be used multiple times, and does enable you to specify the port as part of the address. This allows more precise control over the exact set of addresses on which the server will respond. Use of the `Listen` directive is discussed in greater detail in the "Virtual Hosting" section of this chapter.

To change the TCP port that is used by the server, use the `Port` directive. The default port used by Web servers is port 80. If you change the port, users are required to either type it in as part of the URL to access your site, or to follow a link which includes the port number. Changing the port number can be useful for setting up test servers, or multiple servers on a single machine. For example, if you change the port to 8093, users are required to type something such as the following in their browsers to access your site:

```
http://www.example.com:8093/somedir/somepage.html.
```

Caution

> Do not rely on a non-standard port address as a form of security, unless it is part of a larger security scheme. It is nearly trivial for an intruder to find Web servers on non-standard ports by port-scanning. Occasionally, however, system administrators like to move the Web server to another port and place an intrusion detector on port 80. Should anyone try to connect to port 80, the server might page a system administrator to warn that someone might be port-scanning the system.

For security reasons, certain ports under Linux are reserved for use only by the root account. If you choose a port lower than 1024, you cannot start the server as a user other than root. This prevents ordinary users on your machine from starting servers to handle well-known networking services (which might enable them to trick unsuspecting clients into giving them privileged information). This restriction is usually not a problem because the server is normally started as root during the startup of the machine (by the initialization

PART

V

CH

33

scripts). However, if you use a different initialization sequence, be aware of this restriction. If the default port is set to a port over 1024, it is possible for a non-root user to start a Web server (provided they have configured it to use directories the user has access to). This can be considered either a feature or a security concern, depending on your situation.

CHANGING THE ACCOUNT USED BY THE SERVER PROCESS

When the Web server first starts, it is usually running as root. This allows it to access privileged configuration information and to open the restricted networking ports (if it is configured to do so). However, after the server is all set up, it is unwise for it to continue to run as root—the root account has access to every file and directory on the system. Because the Web server provides a conduit for remote users to access files and directories on your system, it is very dangerous for the Web server to run as root.

Therefore, the Web server changes its user and group account shortly after startup. Use the User and Group directives to control the way the Web server runs (which user and group account on your system it uses) during normal operation. By default, the Web server is configured to run as user nobody and group -1 (which doesn't correspond to any real group). Note that you can specify the values for these either by name or by account number (preceded by a pound sign).

The user and group that you specify need to be accounts with limited access to the resources on your machine to prevent remote clients from accessing sensitive or private material. If you change the accounts that the server uses to run, you must make sure that the server can still access the documents it needs to serve. You might need to modify the owner, group, or permissions on files and directories in the Web document tree after changing these settings. See Chapter 11, "Users, Groups, and Permissions," for additional information on this topic.

For example, if you want the Web server to run as a special Webmaster account, perform the following steps:

1. Create a user account with the name Webmaster.
2. Edit the file `httpd.conf`, and change the user directive to read the following:
   ```
   User Webmaster
   ```

> **Note**
>
> Some distributions have default User or Group directives. If you want to use your own directives, make sure to comment out an existing settings. In particular, you may need to comment out the Group setting if you don't want to use it.

3. Make sure that all the files you want the Web server to provide to remote clients are readable (or executable, if applicable) by the Webmaster account.

MODIFYING THE SERVER PERFORMANCE CHARACTERISTICS

By default, Apache is configured for modest Web traffic. It is basically configured to serve as a LAN server, with perhaps a few hundred clients. However, Apache is capable of acting as the server for a full-blown, high-traffic Web site. Some options that are discussed in this section enable you to configure the server for higher performance, or to tune it to best match the traffic that you expect. It can also be tuned down to reduce its impact on the system if there are only a handful of users.

Note

There is no magic "make Apache go faster" switch or combination of switches. Getting optimal performance from Apache is highly dependent on what kind of data you are serving and how it is accessed. There are many things to tune, including Apache's configuration, the rest of Linux (including the kernel), hardware, network, your Web pages themselves, CGI scripts, and other factors.

A great deal of research has been put into the subject, though, and a FAQ is available at `http://www.apache.org/docs/misc/perf-tuning.html`.

Do note that Apache's primary goal is not performance. Although it is a consideration, Apache is a general-purpose Web server, focused primarily on correctness of output and configurability. For the vast majority of users, Apache's performance (even in the default configuration) is more than sufficient.

HANDLING HIGH SERVER LOADS GRACEFULLY The `StartServers`, `MinSpareServers`, and `MaxSpareServers` directives affect the way in which the Web server pre-launches child processes to handle high request traffic at startup and runtime.

`StartServers` indicates the number of child processes that the server starts when it first initializes. Because the server responds automatically to the load that is placed on it, it is rarely necessary to adjust this value.

`MinSpareServers` and `MaxSpareServers` are used to configure the number of idle child processes that are started by the server during runtime to handle *load spikes* (sudden increases in request traffic). If extra (or spare) child processes are already present when a sudden burst of requests comes in, the server can avoid the overhead of starting the child processes, which allows it to respond to the requests more quickly. This makes the server more responsive than it might otherwise be under heavy, fluctuating loads. Because these spare processes essentially do nothing until a load spike occurs, and because they take up valuable memory and add overhead to your system, be careful about setting these numbers very high.

Periodically, the main Web server process checks to see how many spare servers are present. If the number is greater than `MaxSpareServers`, some child processes are terminated. If it is less than `MinSpareServers`, some child processes are started at a rate of one per second.

By default, Apache configures these numbers as `MinSpareServers` 5 and `MaxSpareServers` 10. This is appropriate for a regularly used Web server, but is probably too high for a simple desktop machine. For very low-use machines, you might want to change the minimum and maximum to 1 and 2, respectively.

`MaxClients` indicates the maximum number of clients that the server can support simultaneously. This limits the number of child processes that the Web server creates to respond to client requests, and is mainly intended to limit the server and keep it from exhausting all the resources on your machine in case of server malfunction or outside attack.

SUPPORTING PERSISTENT CLIENT CONNECTIONS THROUGH KeepAlive   In the original HTTP protocol specification, every request that was made to a server required a separate connection to the server. The complexity of Web pages and Web sites has grown, however, and it is now very common for a single page, as viewed by the client, to consist of many different files and images. To avoid the overhead of establishing (and terminating) a connection for each individual file requested by the client, newer versions of the HTTP protocol provide for persistent (multiple request) client connections. This feature is called KeepAlive, and it is configured in Apache with the following directives: KeepAlive, MaxKeepAliveRequests, and KeepAliveTimeout.

Use of KeepAlive greatly reduces the overhead of clients accessing your site (and thus greatly increases the performance of your server). Normally, you do not need to modify these settings. However, use of the KeepAlive feature might enable malicious users to tie up your Web server with bogus connections, which can disrupt your service. The KeepAlive directives enable you to tune whether the server supports persistent connections, how many requests a client can make on a single connection, and how long a connection remains open before it is terminated automatically by the server.

KeepAlive support is on by default. To turn off support for this feature, change the setting of KeepAlive to Off in the httpd.conf file.

Set the value of MaxKeepAliveRequests to control how many requests a client can make on a single connection. After this number of requests, the server closes the connection, and the client must make a new one to continue downloading documents. Setting this to 0 will allow unlimited requests per connection.

Use KeepAliveTimeout to control how long the server keeps a connection open when the client has not made a request on it. By default, connections are left open for 15 seconds so that if the user selects another page on the same site (within a short period of time), they can continue using the same connection. Be careful about making the timeout too long because higher timeout values tend to make the server connection table fill up, and might result in other clients not being able to connect.

CHANGING THE SERVER NAME

Sometimes the server returns information about itself to the client that the client can use on subsequent requests. For example, when the server returns a directory listing to a client, it includes a self-referencing link (URL) on each column heading so that the client can sort the listing by the contents of that column. Several directives are available to control what information is used for this link, as well as other pieces of server information.

To set the name of the server, use the ServerName directive. This name needs to match the actual hostname of your machine. You can't just make up a name here because the client must use this name in a URL to access your machine.

When self-referencing links are constructed by the server, it can use either the value specified by ServerName or the value that is currently being used by the client to access your machine. The reason for using the value that is supplied by the client is that in cases in which the client provides a shortened name or an alias, it is better to continue having the client use that name. This is done to avoid confusing the user, or to avoid requiring the client to log in to your machine again (because the name is different) when you have turned on security.

The UseCanonicalName directive controls this feature. To have the server use the name that is supplied by the client, set UseCanonicalName to Off. Note that the value of the SERVER_NAME environment variable that is passed to CGI scripts is also affected by this setting.

A few other directives are used to provide information about your server to clients, on certain server generated pages (primarily error response or directory listing pages). To set the email account for the server administrator, use the ServerAdmin directive. For example, to set the email account to Webmaster, use a line such as the following:

```
ServerAdmin Webmaster@www.example.com.
```

Use the ServerSignature directive to specify an information line to be included with server-generated documents, using one of the following options:

- **Off**—Don't include server information on error pages.

- **On**—Show server name, version, and address.

- **Email**—Include an email link (for the email address specified by ServerAdmin) in the signature line.

Defining the Document Name Space

This section discusses the document name space, and the ways in which you can modify it.

PART
V
CH
33

Testing Configuration Options

When you make modifications to the options for the document name space and for request processing settings, test them out by restarting the server (see previous sidebar), loading a browser, and trying to access an item that is affected by your modification. For example, if you modify directory indexing options, try to access an affected directory using a browser right away.

One important thing that you need to do to make sure that you see the right results is to reload the document in your Web browser. When you access a URL that you have looked at before, some browsers use their local cache and display the results for the last page they retrieved from the server. This can be confusing, making you think that your changes did not take effect. In some extreme cases, you might need to clear the cache of the browser to see exactly which documents the server is responding with for your request.

Various directives in the httpd.conf configuration file define the document tree (or name space) that the Web server presents to the clients that access it. Also, they define how the items in the document tree are processed by the server. The server can perform four basic types of processing on an item requested by a client:

- If the item referenced by the client's URL is a file, the server simply returns the file to the client.

- If you have enabled the *server side includes* (*SSI*) feature, the server might do additional processing of the file. This is also referred to as *server-parsed HTML* because it makes the server read the file and process it (parse it) on each request.

- If the client's URL refers to a directory, the server does one of three things: returns a specially named file (usually `index.html`) to represent that directory, generates a listing for the directory and returns that to the client, or returns a failure message to the client.

- Finally, if the item is a special program called a CGI script, the server runs the program and returns its output to the client.

The structure of the document tree that is visible to clients is a logical structure that does not necessarily match the layout of the filesystem of your machine. The Web server takes requests from the server and translates the path in the URL of the request to a path in your local filesystem, using rules that you define. The server has a main document root (by default `/usr/local/apache/htdocs`) where the main document tree resides. This is configured using the `DocumentRoot` directive. Additional directories can be logically grafted into this tree using the `Alias` directive. If a directory contains CGI scripts, the `ScriptAlias` directive is used to make that directory accessible.

The default settings for the name space of the Web server (without comments and intervening directives) are shown in Listing 33.1.

LISTING 33.1   DEFAULT NAME SPACE FOR THE DOCUMENT TREE SERVED BY THE WEB SERVER

```
DocumentRoot "/usr/local/apache/htdocs"
UserDir public_html
Alias /icons/ "/usr/local/apache/icons/"
ScriptAlias /cgi-bin/ "/usr/local/apache/cgi-bin/"
```

With these definitions, the following URL translations (and actions) are performed by the server:

- `http://example.com/man.html`—Translated to `/usr/local/apache/htdocs/man.html`, and file is returned to the client.

- `http://example.com/icons/bomb.gif`—Translated to `/usr/local/apache/icons/bomb.gif`, and the file is returned to the client.

- `http://example.com/`—Translated to `/usr/local/apache/htdocs`, which is a directory. Because there is a file called `index.html` in this directory, it is returned to the client (see the description of the `DirectoryIndex` directive). If directory indexing is on and this file is not present, the server generates a listing of this directory and returns it to the client.

- `http://example.com/cgi-bin/rpm_query`—Translated to `/usr/local/apache/cgi-bin/rpm_query`. Because this is in a `ScriptAlias` directory, the program is run and its output is returned to the client.

- `http://example.com/~tim/page1.html`—Translated to `/home/tim/public_html/page1.html`, and the file is returned to the client (if the user tim is defined and the page is present).

Table 33.3 summarizes the different directives and their effect on the logical document tree, as seen by clients.

TABLE 33.3   NAME SPACE DIRECTIVES

Directive	Refers to
DocumentRoot	Main document tree
Alias	Other directories logically grafted into the tree
ScriptAlias	Directories containing CGI programs
UserDir	Directories for individual user pages

These directives are discussed in detail next.

To change the location of the main document tree, edit the value of DocumentRoot. By default, all files and directories under the directory that you specify are made available to remote clients. Be careful with any of these directives to make sure that private or sensitive data on your system does not reside underneath these directories. There are options available (listed later in this chapter in the section "Per Directory Options") to keep the Web server from following symbolic links to other parts of your filesystem from the document tree.

To set an Alias, you need to provide the "fake" name that the clients will use to access the directory, and the real directory name on your filesystem for the directory. The same is true of ScriptAlias values.

For example, you can use the following Alias statement to make files in the /usr/share/data/jpeg directory available from your Web site:

```
Alias /images/ /usr/share/data/jpeg/
```

So if the client accesses

```
http://www.example.com/images/alien.jpg
```

the server translates it to the following path:

```
/usr/share/data/jpeg/alien.jpg
```

ScriptAlias values are also specified using a fake name and a real directory name. However, when an item is referenced in a ScriptAlias directory, the server tries to execute the resulting filename and returns the output of the program to the user.

By default, the directory /usr/local/apache/cgi-bin is defined as a ScriptAlias directory, and is where CGI scripts are stored.

Use the UserDir directive to control whether individual users are allowed to publish pages from your machine and to control where the Web server reads their pages from.

When a user page is requested (using the ~user syntax in a request URL), the server combines the path part of the URL with the value of the UserDir directive. If a single directory name is specified with the UserDir directive, that directory is combined with the user's home directory, as specified in the /etc/passwd file. If a path is specified with UserDir and starts with a slash, the URL path is combined with the path (and username) directly.

For example, if the directory public_html is used (this the default value), the following requested URL

```
http://www.example.com/~tim/subdir/file.html
```

translates to the following filesystem path:

```
/home/tim/public_html/subdir/file.html
```

Use the disable or enable option with UserDir to allow or disallow user pages on an individual account basis. The UserDir directive can be used multiple times to establish the correct set of available directories. For example, the following directives will allow david and allan to publish pages through their public_html directories, but no other users:

```
UserDir disable
UserDir enable david allan
UserDir public_html
```

FILE PROCESSING DIRECTIVES

When a client requests a file from the server, the server transfers the document to the client. In the process, however, the server might perform additional operations on the file. For example, the server tries to indicate to the client the type of file it is transferring so that the client knows what to do with it. Also, the server can indicate an encoding and language for the document. Some browsers can automatically decode documents to make handling easier on the client side. Finally, the server can tell a client that a file has moved and indicate the new location for it. In this case, the client usually automatically loads the document from the new location, avoiding an error for the remote user.

All these operations can make the file handling between the client and server easier for the end user. The different directives to control these features are described in the sections that follow.

DEFINE FILE TYPES

The server indicates the type of file that it is returning to the client using a special header in the response. The type is expressed as a MIME type.

Basically, the server uses two files to define the file types on your system: mime.types and magic. The mime.types file assigns a MIME file type based on the extension of the file. The magic file can be used to assign a MIME type to a file based on its contents. To add a MIME type definition, add a line to the file mime.types, or use the AddType directive in the httpd.conf server configuration files. The lines in the mime.types file have the following format:

```
type/sub-type    extension [extension2 ...]
```

For example, the definitions for a few video file formats are as follows:

```
video/mpeg        mpeg mpg mpe
video/quicktime   qt mov
video/x-msvideo   avi
```

The following line adds a new file type for files with the extension .mdoc:

```
AddType text/x-mydoc mdoc
```

In situations in which you cannot use file extensions to identify the files on your system, you can use content-based file typing. This system tries to identify a file's type based on whether small strings or sequences of bytes can be found in the file at particular offsets. These matching rules are defined in a file called the magic file.

Content-based file typing is not turned on in the default Web server configuration files. Use the LoadModule directive to load the magic module:

```
LoadModule mod_mime_magic
```

To modify the magic file to support additional file types based on content, see the magic man page, which describes the syntax that is used for defining entries in this file.

DEFINING ENCODINGS AND LANGUAGES

Some browsers are capable of more intelligent handling of a file if they know the file's *encoding*. The encoding of a file is the way the file is formatted, and includes things such as whether the file is compressed and which character set is used for the file.

You can define encodings for files using the AddEncoding directive, which defines a MIME encoding based on the extension of the file. The default encodings that are specified in httpd.conf are as follows:

```
AddEncoding x-gzip gz tgz
AddEncoding x-compress Z
```

Content-based encodings can also be defined in the magic file. See the previous section for a description of this file.

Unless you have a good understanding of how encodings are interpreted by browsers, you probably need to leave these definitions alone.

The Web server can indicate the language of a file to the client, using definitions created with the AddLanguage directive. This feature can be used by add-on server modules to select the correct file to deliver to a client based on its language preference (this is called content negotiation). Use the AddLanguage directive to assign a language code to a file, based on a portion of the file's name. For example, the following lines define the file page.en.html as an English HTML file:

```
AddFileType    text/html      html
AddLanguage    en     .en
```

REDIRECTING CLIENTS TO MOVED FILES

The Web is a dynamic place. Web sites undergo constant revision and maintenance to keep up with new developments and needs. Because of this, it is very common for files to be moved around in the document tree (or even to other Web sites). The Web server is capable of notifying a client of a new location for a file by sending the client a redirect response.

This is beneficial for a few reasons. When a browser receives a redirect response from a server, it usually loads the document automatically from the new location. This makes it easier for the user to deal with the transition of documents to their new locations. Also, some automated link-following software can actually use this information to adjust the links that deal with referencing pages so that they are up-to-date.

To redirect a client to a file's new location, use the `Redirect` and `RedirectMatch` directives. With both of these directives, you specify a filename or path in the document tree that is no longer present (or that you no longer want to serve), and you specify a URL with the new location for that path. In the case of `RedirectMatch`, you can specify a wildcard expression in the filename (or path) to match. You can also specify a status with these directives, which indicates a code that is to be returned to the client in the redirect response. This code tells the client what type of problem was encountered with the original path.

The following are a few examples of redirection:

- `Redirect /images http://www.example.com/icons`
- `Redirect temporary /dir1/dir2 http://www.example.com`
- `Redirect permanent /example_org http://www.example.org/subsidiary_company_a`
- `Redirect gone /old_files`
- `RedirectMatch (.*)\.gif$ http://www.example.com$1.jpg`

Most of these examples are self-explanatory. The arguments `temporary`, `permanent`, and `gone` tell the server which type of error code to return to the client. In the last example, when the client tried to access a file with the extension `.gif`, it was automatically redirected to a file of the same name, but with the extension `.jpg` on `www.example.com`.

DIRECTORY INDEXING OPTIONS

When a directory is referenced (instead of a file), the Web server tries to return a page to represent the directory. This is called the directory index. Several settings in `httpd.conf` control which file is used for static or fixed directory indexing and how dynamic directory indexes are generated.

SPECIFYING A DIRECTORY INDEX FILE

The simplest way to respond to a directory request is with a static file. Use the `DirectoryIndex` directive to indicate to the server which file in the directory is used to represent this directory on your Web site.

For example, the default value for `DirectoryIndex` is `index.html`. With this setting, if this URL is requested

`http://example.com/dir1/`

the server looks for this file:

`/usr/local/apache/htdocs/dir1/index.html`

If the file is present, the file server returns that file to the client. If not, a dynamic directory listing can be generated, which is discussed in the next section.

GENERATING DIRECTORY INDEXES

When the server cannot find a static directory index file, it has the capability to generate a dynamic listing at the time of a client request. Many options can control the format of this dynamically generated listing.

Dynamic directory indexes are allowed or disallowed using the Options directive. The Options directive supports many different directory-handling settings, and is covered more extensively in the section on per directory options, but the Indexes setting for this directive is discussed briefly here.

To turn on dynamic index generation for the entire Web server, add the following line anywhere in httpd.conf:

```
Option +Indexes
```

You can also achieve the same effect, but in a somewhat more controlled fashion, by finding the lines in httpd.conf that define options for the document root directory, and then adding Indexes to the Options line there.

Several directives enable you to control the page that is generated by the server.

CONTROLLING THE DIRECTORY LISTING PAGE

Two basic formats for the directory listings are generated by the server: simple and fancy. The simple directory listing shows the entries in the directory as a bulleted list, with each name being a link to the file or directory it represents. The fancy directory index shows a multicolumn list of files, and is described in greater detail later in this chapter.

Several directives are available to control the listing page that is generated by the server. Among the main directives that affect both simple and fancy listings are IndexIgnore, IndexOptions, HeaderName, and ReadmeName. Other directives, which mainly control fancy indexing, are discussed later.

EXCLUDING FILES FROM THE DIRECTORY LISTING   To exclude files from the directory listing, use the IndexIgnore directive. This is useful for situations in which the directory contains superfluous—or private—files that you don't want clients to see. After the directive, place the list of files to ignore. This list is space separated, and can contain filenames and wildcard expressions. For example, to hide README files and text files, you can use the following line:

```
IndexIgnore README* *.txt
```

Multiple IndexIgnore directives can be used. Each one adds items to the list of things to ignore for the directory listings that are generated by the Web server.

PART

V

CH

33

> **Caution**
>
> Don't confuse the use of `IndexIgnore` with real security access control (discussed later in the section "Adding Security to Your Web Site"). Although this option prevents certain files from being listed in directory indexes, the files can still be retrieved if the remote user accesses them by their exact name.
>
> Some crackers are good at guessing, or can find out the filenames using some other means. For data that must be kept secure, use access control and secure Web server features—not just the `IndexIgnore` option.

ADDING A PREAMBLE OR FOOTER TO THE PAGE   To add a preamble or footer to the directory listing page, use the `HeaderName` and `ReadmeName` directives, respectively. When a filename is specified with these directives, the Web server first looks for a file with the indicated name and the extension of `.html` in the directory where the listing is being generated. If that file is found, it is included in the directory listing page as HTML. If the file is not found, the Web server looks for the filename (without an extension) and includes it as plaintext, if it is found.

For example, to add the contents of the file `list_header.html` as the preamble to the directory listing page, use the following `HeaderName` directive:

```
HeaderName list_header
```

USING FANCY INDEXING

Fancy indexing provides a much "fancier" display of the contents of a directory. For example, the fancy directory listing shows directory entries as a multicolumn list. Each row displays the name, icon, date of last modification, size, and description for a directory entry. The icons in this listing are selected according to the file type, and can be customized extensively. The description is defined using an `AddDescription` directive, or by examining the files for their HTML titles. The other pieces of information come from the filesystem itself.

This section describes these and other options that are available for customizing the format of the fancy indexes produced by the Web server.

To turn on fancy indexing, place the following line in your `httpd.conf` file:

```
IndexOptions FancyIndexing
```

SETTING FILE ICONS   One of the things that you can control about the fancy directory listing is the icon used to represent each entry in the directory. Because some browsers are not configured to support graphics, you can also set a text string to be used in place of the icon (called an alt, or alternate, string).

The icon files that are used for the directory entries can be assigned by file extension, file type, or encoding type. Use the following directives to accomplish this:

- **AddIcon**—Assign an icon by file extension. If the file's type can be determined using a MIME type, it is better to use `AddIconByType` instead so that you can place all the type-related directives in one place (in the `mime.types` file).

- **AddIconByType**—Assign an icon by MIME file type. The type is determined by the settings in the `mime.types` configuration file.

- **AddIconByEncoding**—Assign an icon by MIME encoding. File encoding types are defined by `AddEncoding` directives.

- **AddAlt**—Assign alt string by file extension.

- **AddAltByType**—Assign alt string by MIME file type.

- **AddAltByEncoding**—Assign alt string by MIME encoding.

- **DefaultIcon**—Specify the icon to use, when no other icon can be found for this entry.

The syntax for the `Add...` directives is as follows:

```
<directive> <icon> <match> [<match2> ...]
```

For any of the `AddIcon...` directives, for the icon field you can specify either just the icon filename, or a combination of alt string and icon filename. This enables you to bypass use of the `AddAlt...` directives, if you want. The icon filename is expressed as a path relative to the Web server document tree, not relative to your local filesystem. Also, an `AddIcon` directive can use the string `^^DIRECTORY^^` to match directory entries. The following example shows several different icon assignment lines. Some of these overlap in functionality, but they are shown for illustrative purposes:

```
AddIcon /icons/binary.gif .bin .exe
AddIcon /icons/text.gif .txt
AddIconByType /icons.apache/text.gif text/*
AddAltByType ""TXT"" text/*
AddIconByType (TXT,/icons/text.gif) text/*
AddIconByType (HTM,/icons/layout.gif) text/html
AddIconByEncoding (CMP,/icons/compressed.gif x-compress x-gzip
AddIcon (DIR,/icons/folder.gif) ^^DIRECTORY^^
DefaultIcon /icons/unknown.gif
```

The icon directives are processed in the order that they occur in the `httpd.conf` file. The Web server uses the first match that it finds as the icon for a file. Therefore, place more specific directives earlier in the file for the matching to work.

You can, of course, add your own icon files if you want to completely customize the look of the directory listing pages. The icons need to be in `.gif` or `.jpg` format and reside in a directory somewhere in the document tree. The default icons provided with Apache are in the directory `/usr/local/apache/icons`, and are 20×22 8-bit color GIF files. These icons use very few colors (a good idea) and a transparent background.

USING DESCRIPTIONS   The Description column in a fancy directory listing has a short description of each entry. The Web server determines the value for this field based either on `AddDescription` directives used in server configuration files, or on the title of the document, if it is an HTML file.

Use the AddDescription directive to add a description for an entry. For example, the following line adds a description for the file foo.txt at the root of the document tree:

```
AddDescription "foo text file" /foo.txt
```

The server can automatically add descriptions to the directory listing, based on the title of HTML documents in the directory. Add the ScanHTMLTitles option to the IndexOptions directive in httpd.conf to have the server do this. Note that this causes the server to read each HTML file in the directory and parse out the HTML title every time the directory is read. This takes a relatively long time, and should not be used on busy Web sites.

CONTROLLING COLUMNS AND DIRECTORY FORMATTING   The IndexOptions directive enables you to control several other aspects of the fancy directory listing. Table 33.4 shows the options you can use and their effect on the listing page.

TABLE 33.4   OPTIONS TO CONTROL FANCY DIRECTORY LISTINGS USING IndexOptions

Option	Meaning
IconHeight=pixels	The Web server includes the height of icons in the IMG tag used in the directory index page. This can speed up processing of the page by client browsers.
IconWidth=pixels	The Web server includes the width of icons in the IMG tag used for directory indexes.
IconsAreLinks	This makes the icons part of the link to the entry, so the user can click either the entry name or the icon to access it.
NameWidth=n|*	Indicates the width of the filename column. If * is used, the column is sized automatically.
ScanHTMLTitles	The server scans HTML files for their titles, to be used in the Description column.
SuppressDescription	Hide the Description column.
SuppressLastModified	Hide the Last Modified column.
SuppressSize	Hide the Size column.
SuppressColumnSorting	Do not make the column headings links that can be used to sort the listing by that column.
SuppressHTMLPreamble	Do not precede the file specified by HeaderName with the standards HTML preamble (HTML, HEAD, and so on). This allows you more flexibility in controlling the page output with the header file.

CUSTOMIZING ERROR MESSAGES

The Web server automatically generates error message responses for certain error conditions. However, you can customize the error response for your Web site to provide your own messages (and look and feel) to remote clients when things go wrong.

Use the `ErrorDocument` directive to customize the error response for a particular error condition. This directive can be used multiple times, to specify a response for each different error code that the server generates. Common error codes used by the Web server are shown in Table 33.5.

TABLE 33.5 COMMON HTTP ERROR CODES

Error Code	Summary	Meaning
400	Bad Request	The request from the client was malformed.
401	Unauthorized	Client must provide a name and password to access the item. Note that the error response for this code cannot be customized because the client automatically displays a login prompt (and not the returned page) when it receives this error from the server.
402	Payment Required	Access to the requested item requires that the client provide some kind of payment.
403	Forbidden	Client is not allowed to access the item. Providing a name and password does not help.
404	Not Found	The server did not find a document or directory matching the URL submitted by the client.
500	Fatal Error	The server encountered some unresolvable condition and could not fulfill the request.
501	Not Implemented	The server does not support the requested functionality.
502	Temporary Overload	The server cannot service the request because of high load. It can possibly service the request at a later time.

The error document can be specified in several ways. First, you can specify just a string to return to the user as the value for the `ErrorDocument`. You can also refer to a local file to return a static error page, or to a CGI script to generate one at the time of the request. Using a CGI script enables you to customize the response to exactly match your situation because the script can examine information about the client, its request, and the local filesystem at the time that the request is made. Finally, you can also specify an external document as an error response.

For each `ErrorDocument` directive, specify the error code, and then the item with which you want the server to respond for that error. Following are some examples of `ErrorDocument` lines:

```
ErrorDocument 400 "Hey, you sent invalid request."
ErrorDocument 402 http://www.example.com/pay_me.html
ErrorDocument 500 /fatal.html
ErrorDocument 404 /cgi-bin/missing.pl
```

CONFIGURING SETTINGS ON A PER DIRECTORY BASIS

When you use the configuration directives for controlling file information, directory indexing, error responses, and authorization (discussed later) in `httpd.conf`, they apply to the entire document tree that the Web server provides. However, you can also apply these directives to specific directories and files on your system.

PART
V

CH
33

There are a few different reasons that the server supports per directory customizations in this way. First, you might want to have some directories on your Web site available to the general public, whereas other files and directories are restricted to a specific set of users. In addition to security-specific directives, many other directives have important security ramifications. For instance, you usually do not want the general public to see the contents of the directories in your document tree. Therefore, it is customary to disable directory indexing for the part of your document tree that is accessible to any remote user. You might still want, however, to allow indexing for users within your organization.

Sometimes the content of a Web site is maintained by different organizations in a company. In this case, they might have different policies and conventions for controlling their part of the site. For example, one department might use server-parsed HTML files for some of their content, whereas another might not. Because server-parsed HTML files require extra processing by the server, it is wise to limit its use to only the part of the document tree that needs it.

The use of per directory settings allows for fine-grained control over the presentation, handling, and access control of the server document tree.

PER DIRECTORY OPTIONS

Some of the main options that can be configured on a per directory basis are controlled with the `Options` directive. This directive enables you to set many policies with regard to directories:

- **All**—All options except for `MultiViews`
- **ExecCGI**—Execution of CGI scripts is allowed.
- **FollowSymLinks**—The server follows symbolic links in this directory. This can be a potential security risk.
- **Includes**—Server-side includes (server-parsed HTML) are allowed.
- **IncludesNOEXEC**—Server-side includes are allowed, but certain directives are not processed (#exec and #include).
- **MultiViews**—Allows the server to select a document that best matches the client's request when the requested file does not exist. This is referred to as content-negotiation, and is covered in the online manual on at `http://www.apache.org/docs/content-negotiation.html`.
- **SymLinksIfOwnerMatch**—Allows the server to follow a symlink if the target of the link and the link have the same owner ID.

Caution

Most options in this list have important security consequences. For example, allowing any kind of execution by the Web server (for example, use of `ExecCGI` and `Includes`) might lead to situations in which unauthorized users can allow remote clients to run dangerous programs or scripts. Consult the online documentation for each of these options for information about the security ramifications before using them on a multiuser system.

In addition to the settings that are configured using the `Options` directive, many other directives can be used on a per directory basis. These include directives for the following:

- File content handling
- File indexing options
- Error response settings
- Authorization and access control (security) settings

In fact, although many of the directives that have been discussed so far have been presented in the context of the server configuration files, many are more appropriately placed in a per directory area of `httpd.conf`. If you need to determine whether a particular directive can be applied on a per directory basis, see the online documentation. For each directive, the documentation indicates the contexts in which the directive can be used.

DEFINING OPTIONS FOR A SPECIFIC PART OF THE DOCUMENT TREE

Options that apply to a specific part of the filesystem are defined by placing their directives within a section of the `httpd.conf` file or in a special file called `.htaccess`.

A section in the `httpd.conf` file is defined by an opening and closing directive. For example, to apply certain options to only the objects in the directory `/usr/local/apache/icons`, you can declare a section in `httpd.conf` such as the following:

```
<Directory /usr/local/apache/icons>
    Options Indexes
    IndexOptions FancyIndexing SuppressDescription SuppressSize
</Directory>
```

Several different section directives can indicate the set of objects to which they apply based on different criteria:

- `<Directory>`—Matches objects based on the directory where they reside.
- `<Files>`—Matches objects based on their filenames.
- `<Location>`—Matches objects based on the URL path used to access them.

Each of these directives is used by placing the target path or filename inside the angle brackets. Then the desired directives, which apply to the indicated object set, are declared, followed by a matching close-section directive (`</Directory>`, `</Files>`, and `</Location>`, respectively).

You can also use the directives `<DirectoryMatch>`, `<FilesMatch>`, and `<LocationMatch>`, which take a regular expression as their argument instead of a simple string; this results in even more flexibility in defining a target object set. A few examples follow:

- `<Directory /usr/local/apache/icons>`—Declares a section for specifying settings in the icons directory.
- `<FilesMatch "*\.txt$">`—Declares a section that applies to files that end in `.txt`.

PART

V

CH

33

- **<Location /private>**—Declares a section that applies to objects referenced using the URL prefix http://example.com/private. With the default document root, this means files and subdirectories under /usr/local/apache/htdocs/private.

- **<LocationMatch ".*www*">**—Declares a section that applies to anything with "www" as part of the path portion of the URL (including both files and directories).

DEFINING OPTIONS USING A FILE IN THE CURRENT DIRECTORY

Instead of defining per directory settings in the configuration files, you can also define the settings in a special file in the directory in which you want the settings to apply. This is useful in the event that you move directories around. Instead of having to modify the pathname in the configuration files, the configuration follows the directory to its new location automatically because the file resides in the directory.

Also, you might want to generate some directives (such as AddDescription) automatically. There are cases in which it is unwise to allow an end-user program to modify the server's general configuration files, but where modification of per directory configuration files can be allowed.

The default filename for per directory settings is .htaccess. You can modify the name that is used for this file using the AccessFileName directive. Basically, .htaccess files can contain any directive that you can place in a <Directory> section in the configuration files.

To avoid certain security problems, the Web server provides an extra facility to limit the options that are allowed in a .htaccess file. Specifically, each <Directory> section in the server configuration file needs to include an AllowOverride directive that controls which classes of directives can be used in .htaccess files. The following classes of directives can be specified (one or more of them) as arguments to the AllowOverride directive:

- **All**—.htaccess files can contain any per directory directive.
- **AuthConfig**—Allows the use of directives which control authorization (user-based security).
- **FileInfo**—Allows directives that deal with file types, encodings, languages, and error responses.
- **Indexes**—Allows directives related to directory indexing.
- **Limit**—Allows directives related to host-based security.
- **Options**—Allows use of the Options or XBitHack directives.
- **None**—Doesn't allow .htaccess files to be used to define per directory options.

For example, to allow for the use of .htaccess files under the directory /home/httpd/www but limit users to controlling directory indexing and host-based security, add the following entry to access.conf:

```
<Directory /home/httpd/www>
AllowOverride Indexes Limit
</Directory>
```

SECTION ORDERING

There might be overlaps between the sets of files that are specified by different section directives and the .htaccess file. When this happens, the options are accumulated from the sections that apply, in the order that the sections are processed. This means that the last section that is processed determines the settings.

Sections are processed in the following order:

- <Directory> and .htaccess files. Within this group, sections are ordered by directory name length from shortest to longest. .htaccess files are processed after <Directory> sections for matching directories.
- <DirectoryMatch>.
- <File> and <FileMatch>.
- <Location> and <LocationMatch>.

The result of the "shortest to longest" part of the first rule is that the options for a directory apply to that directory and all its subdirectories, until another section (with a longer, and thus more specific directory path) overrides them.

In the case of duplicate entries within each category (for example, two <Directory> sections with the same directory name), the sections are processed in the order in which they occur in the configuration files. The configuration files are read in the following order: httpd.conf, srm.conf, and access.conf.

> **Note**
>
> The srm.conf and access.conf files are only processed for historical reasons. Generally, all directives should be placed in httpd.conf to reduce complexity.

ALL ABOUT LOGGING

One nice thing about the Web server is that you can configure it to provide all kinds of information about itself and the operations that it is performing, through server log files. By default, the Web server logs each request that it fulfills and each error that it encounters in the access log and the error log, respectively. However, you can create additional logs of server activity and customize the format of each log entry.

There are five basic types of logs that the Web server can produce:

- Transfer log
- Agent log
- Referrer log
- Error log
- Script log

Each of these logs is described in detail in the sections that follow.

TRANSFER LOG

The main kind of log is referred to as a transfer log or access log. With a transfer log, an entry is made for each response that the server sends. Multiple logs of this kind can be created, using either of the `TransferLog` or `CustomLog` directives.

The simplest way to create a transfer log is to specify the log filename using the `TransferLog` directive. If no `LogFormat` directive has been used to set the format of the log entries, the log is created and formatted using the Common Log Format. This log format includes most of the basic information about a request and is used by several different Web servers. Several log analysis tools are available on the Internet, all of which work with this format to do statistical analysis of the traffic that is handled by your Web server.

CUSTOMIZING LOG FORMATS   Instead of using the Common Log Format, you can also customize the format of the log entries for transfer log files. If you configure the server to produce multiple transfer logs, you can separate the information about the requests into different logs, making it easier to write your own custom log analysis tools.

The `LogFormat` directive is used to define the format string used to output log entries. The format string can contain literal characters as well as conversion specifiers. The conversion specifiers are replaced with information about the request when the log entry is made. Table 33.6 shows the conversion specifiers that are available for use in log format strings.

TABLE 33.6   `LogFormat` **CONVERSION SPECIFIERS**

Specifier	Translates To...
%h	Client hostname or IP address.
%l	Client identity (if identd information is available from the client).
%u	Username (if user logged in).
%t	Time of day, in [day/month/year:hour:minute:second:zone] format.
%(t_format)t	Time in the specified format. See the `strftime` man page for the syntax of the format string.
%r	The client request line. This is usually put in quotes because it includes spaces.
%s	Status code for the request.
%>s	Last status code for the request. For requests that get redirected, %s specifies the status of the original request, and %>s specifies the status of the final request (after redirection).
%b	Number of bytes in the returned item.
%f	Filename.
%{VAR}e	Value of environment variable VAR.
%{Header}i	Value of request header line Header.
%{Header}o	Value of response header line Header.
%{Var}n	Value of note Var from a server module.

Specifier	Translates To...
%p	Server port.
%P	Process ID of the child that handled the request.
%T	Number of seconds it took to handle the request.
%U	The URL path requested.
%v	Server name.

TABLE 33.6   CONTINUED

The Common Log Format uses the following format string:

`"%h %l %u %t \"%r\" %s %b"`

Listing 33.2 shows sample entries from an access log using the Common Log format.

LISTING 33.2   SAMPLE ACCESS LOG USING COMMON LOG FORMAT

```
200.251.107.134 - - [24/Oct/2000:17:06:38 -0700] ""GET/ HTTP/1.1"" 200 3304
200.251.107.134 - - [24/Oct/2000:17:06:40 -0700] "GET /moro1s.jpg _HTTP/1.1" 200
➥26625
192.168.1.3 - - [24/Oct/2000:17:23:31 -0700] "GET /robots.txt _HTTP/1.0" 404 163
203.93.18.173 - - [24/Oct/2000:17:37:29 -0700] "GET / HTTP/1.0" 200 3304
203.93.18.173 - - [24/Oct/2000:17:37:33 -0700] "GET /moro1s.jpg _HTTP/1.0" 200 26625
203.93.18.173 - - [24/Oct/2000:17:37:33 -0700] "GET /blueball.gif _HTTP/1.0" 200 326
203.93.18.173 - - [24/Oct/2000:17:37:45 -0700] "GET /redball.gif _HTTP/1.0" 200 326
192.168.1.2 - - [24/Oct/2000:22:17:57 -0700] "GET /starcraft/ _HTTP/1.1" 200 3003
192.168.1.2 - - [24/Oct/2000:22:17:59 -0700] "GET /starcraft/topban1.gif _HTTP/1.1"
➥200 6780
192.168.1.3 - - [25/Oct/2000:06:56:37 -0700] "GET /david/ball.gif _HTTP/1.0" 200 1135
203.93.18.173 - - [25/Oct/2000:14:05:01 -0700] "GET/tim HTTP/1.0" 301 173
```

Many conversion specifiers can include a status indicator to conditionally show the value for that specifier. The status indicator follows the % and consists of a comma-separated list of status codes (optionally preceded by ! for negation). If the request results in the indicated status codes, the value for the specifier is included in the log entry. Otherwise, the specifier is replaced with a dash in the log entry.

Following are some example conversion specifiers with status indicators:

- **%404f**—Logs the filename that the server tried to open when it encountered error 404, Not Found.

- **%!200,304,302r**—Logs the request for anything not returning a valid status.

- **%302{UserAgent}i**—Logs the value of the UserAgent header in the request when the URL is redirected.

To specify a log format, use the directive LogFormat followed by the format string in quotes and a name for that format. If no name is provided, the format string is used as the default format for subsequent logs defined in the configuration file. The following log formats are defined in the default Web server configuration files:

PART V
CH 33

```
LogFormat "%h %l %u %t \"%r\" %>s %b \"%{Referer}i\" \"%{User-Agent}i\""_combined
LogFormat "%h %l %u %t \"%r\" %>s %b" common
LogFormat "%{Referer}i -> %U" referrer
LogFormat "%{User-agent}i" agent
```

USING CLIENT HOSTNAME LOOKUPS   By default, the server logs the address, but not the hostname, of requesting clients when the %h conversion specifier is used in a log format string. Use the HostNameLookups directive to make the server log the hostname instead of the address.

When HostNameLookups is configured to On, the logging software in the server tries to determine the hostname of the requesting client by doing a DNS lookup using the client's IP address at the time of the request. This adds a considerable amount of overhead for each request that the server processes, so the feature is defaulted to Off. For low traffic sites, it is usually all right to turn this on.

Tip

If you have HostNameLookups turned off, you can use the program logresolve, which comes with Apache to process logs and convert IP addresses to hostnames after the fact. This is usually much more efficient than adding the hostname at the time of each request because logresolve doesn't have to look up the same IP address over and over again. However, logresolve might not be able to determine some hostnames accurately because some clients might change their name or address between the time of their request and the time that logresolve is run.

To resolve the IP addresses in a log file, use logresolve with the target log file as standard input and the processed log file as standard output. For example, log in as root, switch to the directory /usr/local/apache/bin, and type the following:

```
./logresolve </usr/local/apache/logs/access_log
>/tmp/log_with_names
```

DEFINING ADDITIONAL LOGS   You can define as many transfer logs as you want. When combined with custom log formats, this enables you to divide your log information among different files, which might make it easier to process with log analysis tools.

To define additional logs, use the CustomLog directive. Each CustomLog directive needs to be followed by the name of the log file and a log format string or name (as defined by a LogFormat directive). For example, an agent log (described next) can be defined with the following directives:

```
LogFormat "%{User-agent}i" agent
CustomLog /usr/local/apache/logs/agent_log agent
```

AGENT AND REFERRER LOGS

In addition to the transfer log, you can define additional log files to record information about the requests that your server handles. Two other commonly used logs are called the agent log and the referrer log. An agent log is used to record information about the client browser (user agent) that is used to make requests of your system. This information is useful because it enables you to develop a profile of the types of users who are visiting your site. The referrer log is used to record information about what page referred the client to your site (that is, what page held the link that the client followed to get to one of your pages). This is useful for determining how users are getting to your site, which might help you advertise or promote your Web site more effectively.

These logs are defined using the `AgentLog` and `RefererLog` directives, respectively.

Caution

Note that "Referer" is a misspelling of "referrer," but because it is now part of the HTML standard, this is the correct spelling for the directive. Occasionally this can cause a lot of confusion. For instance, the default referrer log format in Apache is called "referrer," even though the directive is `RefererLog`.

You can define a log, using `LogFormat` and `CustomLog`, to record the same information that goes into either the agent log or the referrer log. In fact, use of the `AgentLog` directive is now deprecated. However, when you use the `RefererLog` directive to create a referrer log, it allows you one additional capability that the `CustomLog` method does not—you can use the `RefererIgnore` directive to eliminate a specific set of referrers from the log.

For example, if you use the following line, no record of references from example's Web site will be included in your log:

```
RefererIgnore www.example.com
```

This can help reduce the size of your log and help you pinpoint new entries in the referrer log.

ERROR LOG

The error log is a special log that records server status—usually error—events. Use the `ErrorLog` directive to set the output location for the log. This can include a filename, a pipe to another program, or the syslog daemon. The default definition of the error log is as follows:

```
ErrorLog /usr/local/apache/logs/error_log
```

To specify a pipe to another program, use a vertical bar in front of the program specification, as follows:

```
ErrorLog |/usr/local/bin/page_me_at_home.pl
```

To output the error log records to the syslog daemon, use an argument of syslog, as in the following:

```
ErrorLog syslog
```

You can use the `LogLevel` directive to control the verbosity of the error log. Table 33.7 shows the list of available log levels and their descriptions.

TABLE 33.7	ERROR LOGGING LEVELS
Level	**Description**
emerg	Emergency—system is unusable
alert	Action needs to be taken immediately
crit	Critical condition
error	Error
warn	Warning conditions
notice	Normal, but important, event
info	Information message
debug	Debugging messages

The levels in the table are shown in order of decreasing event importance. If LogLevel is not defined, the level error is used. The default value of LogLevel is warn.

SCRIPT LOG

The server supports another special log specifically to aid in debugging CGI scripts. This is the script log. A script log holds information about the parameters, input, and output to a CGI script when the script fails. Debugging CGI scripts has historically been difficult because the server silently discards the context of the request and output of the script. The script log is a fairly recent addition to the Web server, which makes debugging scripts much easier.

To define a script log, specify the log name with the ScriptLog directive. When a CGI script runs on your system and fails, the following information is logged:

- Time of the failure
- Request line from the client
- HTTP status code
- CGI script filename
- An error message, if the script failed to run
- HTTP headers received in the request
- HTTP headers produced by the CGI script
- CGI script standard output
- CGI script standard input

Using this information, you can probably track down problems with the CGI script in question. Many problems with CGI scripts come from improperly formatted response headers.

Note that a script log is intended for debugging use only. It creates overhead that is not appropriate for a Web server in production use. Also, because of the amount of information logged on each failed request, a script log can become quite large. To avoid problems caused by an over-sized script log file, the `ScriptLogLength` and `ScriptLogBuffer` directives enable you to limit the maximum size of the script log and the size of an individual request buffer, respectively.

ADDING SECURITY TO YOUR WEB SITE

One of the most common customizations that Webmasters make to their site is adding security. This is particularly important for your site if you are only serving documents for use inside your own organization. Adding security enables you to limit access to clients with specific addresses or hostnames, or to require users to authenticate themselves to the Web server by providing a user name and password.

If you are new to security, the following definitions will help you as you follow the descriptions in this chapter:

- **Authorization**—The process of determining whether a client is allowed to access your Web site.
- **Access control**—The process of allowing or preventing access to specific Web site objects, based on the authorization of a client.
- **Host-base authorization**—Controlling access to your Web site based on the location (hostname or IP address) of the client.
- **User-based authorization**—Controlling access to your Web site based on the identity of a user.
- **Authentication**—The process of determining the identity of a remote user. This involves having the user provide a name and password, which only an authorized user will know.

PART

V

CH

33

Authorized Access Versus Secure Communications

This section of the chapter deals with the authorization and access control aspects of your Web site security. Another key ingredient in the overall security of your Web site is secure communications (that is, encryption). If you have private or sensitive data on your Web server, it does little good to create strict authorization and access controls if you subsequently allow the server to send the data to the client in the clear. The section "Using Apache with SSL," later in this chapter, describes the use of Secure Sockets Layer (SSL) to provide a secure communications channel between the server and its clients, to complement the security features that are discussed here.

Adding authorization and access control to your Web site is not complicated, and the paragraphs that follow will help you set up your own security for your Web site.

In general, the directives discussed here are used as per directory options in one of the sections in the `httpd.conf` configuration file. This enables you to customize the security for your Web site by individual directory, file set, or location path.

In this section, the directives are discussed as if they were applied to the entire document tree (Web site). However, remember that these settings can be customized on a per-directory basis. As with other per-directory options, you can also place security-related directives in .htaccess files, in the directories that you want to secure.

Note

If you decide to place the security control directives in a .htaccess file, make sure that the AllowOverride settings that apply to the directory you are working with enables you to do so. It will support AuthConfig for user-based security directives and Limit for host-based security directives.

HOST-BASED AUTHORIZATION

Restricting access to your site by client host location is fairly simple. Use the allow and deny directives to indicate the hostnames or addresses of clients that are allowed or denied access to your site, respectively. You can also use the order directive to control what to do with hosts that are not covered by the allow and deny rules and to control the order in which the rules are evaluated.

For the allow and deny directives, specify the host location as a fully qualified hostname or a domain name part (starting with a .) to match every host in the domain. For example:

- **deny foo.example.net**—Denies access to the specific host that is named.
- **deny .baddudes.example.net**—Denies access to all hosts from domain baddudes.example.net.

You can also use a host location of all to allow or deny access by all hosts.

To specify an IP address, put the address after the directive. To refer to a whole network of hosts, use one of the following syntaxes to express the network address and netmask:

- *a.b.c*—Example: allow 207.179.18. This implies a 24-bit mask because of the use of three address digits. Other whole-digit mask sizes are supported.
- *a.b.c.d/masksize*—Example: allow 207.179.18.128/25. This example uses a 25-bit mask.
- *a.b.c.d/m.n.o.p*—Example: allow 207.179.18.160/255.255.255.248. This example uses an explicit mask.

After you decide which hosts to explicitly allow or deny, you need to decide how to handle the rest of the hosts in the world.

There are two different approaches that are supported by the server in defining host-based authorization. One is based on the principle of including every host that is not specifically excluded by the allow and deny directives, and the other is based on the principle of excluding every host that is not specifically included. The order directive indicates which of these approaches is used by the server. The way to remember how this directive works is as follows: The last rule wins. These approaches are defined by specifying arguments to the order directive, as follows:

- **order deny,allow**—Process the deny rules, followed by the `allow` rules. In cases where the rules conflict, the `allow` rules override the deny rules. For hosts not covered by any rule, allow access.

- **order allow,deny**—Process the `allow` rules first, followed by the deny rules. In cases where the rules conflict, the deny rules override the `allow` rules.

For hosts not covered by any rule, deny access.

The following are some examples to clarify the use of these directives. This only allows hosts in the domain `example.com` to access to your site:

```
order deny,allow
deny from all
allow from .example.com
```

This accomplishes the same thing as the previous example:

```
order allow,deny
allow from .example.com
```

This allows all hosts except those from the domains `baddudes.example.com` and `spammer.example.net` to access your site:

```
order allow,deny
allow from all
deny from .baddudes.example.com
deny from .spammer.example.net
```

USER-BASED AUTHORIZATION

The second method of authorization is based on user identification. The attractive thing about host-based authorization is its simplicity and non-intrusiveness. With host-based authorization, the process of authorizing clients does not affect the user at all. User-based authorization, on the other hand, requires that a user enter a name and password to access your Web site. This is more secure and reliable than host-based authorization, but requires more administrative work on your part and imposes some inconvenience on the users who access your site.

To establish user-based authorization, you must define user accounts for your Web server. Each user account consists of a name and password. You can also create groups and assign users to them to ease the administration burden of working with sets of users. After users and groups are created, you specify the access allowed for the different accounts to the objects on your Web site.

After the server is configured to user-based authorization, the sequence of events between the server and a client goes something like this:

1. The client requests a document.

2. The server responds that the document requires authorization, and indicates an authorization realm and type.

3. The client browser prompts the user for a name and password, including the realm name in the prompt.

4. The client requests the document again, this time sending the name and password to the server, in the format requested.

5. The server verifies the name and password and grants the access indicated by its configuration. If the verification is successful and the access is allowed, the server sends the document to the client.

6. On subsequent requests, the client includes the name and password automatically (that is, the user is not prompted for the name and password again during the session).

DEFINING USERS AND GROUPS

To define users and groups for use with user-based authorization, you need to create some new files. This section describes how to create these files, as well as how to add and remove entries from them to manipulate the accounts on your system. The files described here are flat text files. The server can use other file formats to define user and group accounts, but text files are very simple to manipulate and suffice for almost all uses.

The format of the user file is very simple. Each line of the file consists of a username, a colon, and an encrypted password string. The user account file needs to be located outside the document tree; otherwise remote clients can download the file and use the information in it to try to crack your system. In the following examples, the file /usr/local/apache/conf/htuser is used. Refer to Table 33.1 to check where your distribution keeps these files and executables.

Use the program htpasswd (located in the directory /usr/local/apache/bin by default) to create the file to hold user accounts, and to add user accounts to the file. You create the file when you add the first user account to it by using the -c parameter. For example, to create a file with the user tim in it, log in as root and cd to your configuration directory (/etc/httpd/apache/conf by default). Then type the following command:

```
htpasswd -c htuser tim
```

You are prompted for the password for tim twice. The password is encrypted and placed in the file. You can cat the file if you want to see its contents.

To add additional users, use the same command, but without the -c option. To remove a user, just edit the file with a text editor and remove the line for that user. Add a few users now to the htuser file, using the htpasswd command.

You can also define a group file to enable you to manage sets of users more easily. Each line in a group file consists of a group name, followed by a colon and a space-separated list of user names. To create and modify this file, just use a normal text editor. For example, to define a group file with one group in it, start an editor and enter the following line:

```
admin: tim ron fred
```

Of course, you need to substitute names that you entered in your user file for the accounts listed here. Save the file out as htgroup in your configuration directory (/usr/local/apache/conf by default).

The user and group files are specified to the server using the `AuthUserFile` and `AuthGroupFile` directives. If the filenames you use with these directives do not start with a slash, they are appended to the end of the `ServerRoot` value. To define the files that you just created, enter the following in an appropriate section in `httpd.conf`:

```
AuthUserFile conf/htuser
AuthGroupFile conf/htgroup
```

SETTING THE AUTHORIZATION REALM AND TYPE

The *authorization realm* is used to tell the client what authorization system they are logging in to. In some complicated systems, a Web server might use a back-end (non-local) authentication system to validate users. In this case, the server needs to tell the client what system it is using so that the user can enter the correct name and password. Also, you might define different areas of your Web site with different user accounts and access privileges. Using the authorization realm, you can tell the user which part of the site they are logging in to—again, so they can enter the correct name and password.

Set the authorization realm string for the server using the `AuthName` directive as follows:

```
AuthName "Main Document Tree"
```

The authorization type specifies the format of the items passed between the client and server during the authorization. This is specified using the `AuthType` directive. The Web server supports both `Basic` and `Digest` authorization. `Digest` is a fairly new authorization format that not all browsers support. Unless you have reasons to do otherwise, use the value `Basic`.

CONFIGURING ACCESS CONTROL

The last part of the whole user-based authorization system is actually defining the access control on a per-user or per-group basis. The `require` directive is used for this.

The `require` directive tells the server to require a particular account to grant access to the object on the server. The `require` directive can be used in three different ways: with the user, group, and valid-user options. These options are used as follows:

- **`require user username [username2 ...]`**—Allow the listed users to access the Web site.
- **`require group groupname [groupname2 ...]`**—Allow the users in the listed groups to access the Web site.
- **`require valid-user`**—Allow all users that are defined in the user account file to access the Web site.

Listing 33.3 shows an example with all the directives required to set up user-based authorization, in the context of a `/private` location.

PART

V

CH

33

LISTING 33.3   EXAMPLE OF USER-BASED AUTHORIZATION DEFINITION

```
<Directory /private>
AllowOverride None
Options Index
```

LISTING 33.3   CONTINUED

```
AuthUserFile conf/htuser
AuthGroupFile conf/htgroup
AuthName "private files"
AuthType Basic
require user tim ron
require group admin
</Directory>
```

The first two directives in Listing 33.3 (`AllowOverride` and `Options`) disable `.htaccess` usage and allow directory indexing in the private directory. They are not required parts of user-based authorization, but are presented for illustration purposes.

For this example to work, you need to use the files created earlier in this chapter (`htuser` and `htgroup`), with the user accounts `tim` and `ron` defined and the group account `admin` defined. Also, make the directory `/usr/local/apache/htdocs/private` (assuming your `ServerRoot` is `/usr/local/apache`), and put some private files there.

Try to access the directory by opening a browser and entering a URL such as the following:

```
http://localhost/private
```

You are prompted with a dialog box with the phrase private files in it, asking for a name and password. If you enter valid information for tim, ron, or any of the users in the group admin, you are allowed to see the directory.

VIRTUAL HOSTING

With the explosion of interest in the Internet and the resulting increase in the number of Web sites, it is increasingly common to see a single machine acting as the server for more than one Web site. When multiple Web sites are provided on the same machine, it is referred to as *virtual hosting*. This section describes the different virtual hosting options that are available with the Apache Web server and shows examples of some basic virtual host setups.

There are a few different ways to provide more than one Web site from a machine. One way is to run multiple copies of the Web server, one for each site. However, this can be prohibitive in terms of machine resources. Supporting 20 Web sites requires 20 instances of the Web server, which means that your machine probably runs 60–120 processes (or more) just for serving Web documents. Fortunately, Apache supports the capability to use a single server to serve multiple Web sites, using the `VirtualHost` directive.

There are two methods of supporting virtual hosts with a single server. One is based on using multiple IP addresses—one for each Web site—and the other is based on supporting multiple hostnames on (usually) one IP address. These are called *IP-based* and *name-based* virtual hosting, respectively. A minor variant of IP-based virtual hosting is port-based virtual hosting, where only the port part of the address differs between virtual hosts.

The procedures and settings that are required to set up virtual hosting using these different methods are discussed in the sections that follow. Here are a few criteria you can use to select one of the virtual hosting methods:

- **Does your machine have more than one IP address?**

  If your machine has multiple IP addresses, and particularly if it already has an IP address for each Web site you want to configure, use IP-based virtual hosting.

  If your machine doesn't have multiple IP addresses, consider whether you can add them. Although configuring multiple IP addresses on a machine is not difficult, you need to consider whether you have enough addresses for the sites you want to host.

- **How many Web sites do you plan to host?**

  If you plan to run two or three Web sites on a single machine, using two or three IP addresses for IP-based virtual hosting is probably all right. However, if you plan to set up many Web sites, you probably need to use name-based virtual hosting. This requires more effort in terms of configuring the name server, but consumes fewer IP addresses (which are quickly becoming a precious commodity).

- **Do all your sites need to use the default HTTP port (80)?**

  If you are doing multiple internal sites (or sites that are interrelated, and are not linked to from the outside), you can set up virtual hosting using the same IP address, but with multiple ports. This option is simple to set up, but requires that your Web authors use the port number that you choose as part of the links in the documents that they create; therefore, there is some extra work in that area of your site maintenance.

- **Does your system have multiple hostnames assigned to it?**

  If you have multiple names that resolve to the same IP address, you need to use name-based virtual hosting. This requires local as well as remote clients to resolve the different names for your machine successfully; furthermore, it usually requires that you have control over the DNS name server for your domain.

- **Do you want to rigidly separate the Web sites?**

  You might have a situation in which the security requirements or administration requirements of your Web sites are dramatically different. For example, if you have one Web server that runs as a privileged account (for example, to allow remote administration of the machine through a Web interface), you might want to run it separately from your main Web site server to decrease the risk that a misconfiguration of the main server might compromise your overall machine security. In this case, you probably want to set up virtual hosting with multiple separate Web servers.

RUNNING A SINGLE SERVER ON MULTIPLE IP ADDRESSES

One way to configure your machine with multiple Web sites is to use a different IP address for each site. This is called IP-based, or address-based, virtual hosting; it easy to set up after you have your machine configured with multiple IP addresses.

There are a couple of different ways to configure your box with more than one IP address. If you have multiple networking cards (for example, two Ethernet cards), each card has its own IP address. You can also assign more than one IP address to a single network card, using a feature of Linux called IP aliasing. For the rest of this section, it is assumed that you have already set up and tested the IP addresses that you plan to use for your Web sites.

To configure the Web server to listen to multiple addresses and respond differently to each one, use the <VirtualHost> directive. You use the <VirtualHost> directive to declare a section (much similar to a <Directory> section) in one of your server configuration files. As part of the <VirtualHost> directive itself, you specify an address to match. Inside the virtual host section, you specify the settings that are to be used when that address is used by clients to access the server. For clients that access the server using some other address, the main server settings (outside any <VirtualHost> section) are used.

A simple virtual host setup, for a machine with addresses 192.168.1.1 and 192.168.1.2, is shown in Listing 33.4.

LISTING 33.4 A SIMPLE EXAMPLE OF IP-BASED VIRTUAL HOSTING

```
...
BindAddress *
Port 80
DocumentRoot /usr/local/apache/htdocs
ServerName site1.example.com

<VirtualHost 192.168.1.2>
DocumentRoot /usr/local/apache/htdocs2
ServerName site2.example.com
...
</VirtualHost>
```

In this example, the server binds to address 0.0.0.0:80 (because of the BindAdress * and Port 80 directives). This means that it receives TCP requests on port 80 for all the IP addresses on the machine. When the server receives a request, it determines which address the request was received on. If the address is 192.168.1.1, the server responds with a document from the document tree under /usr/local/apache/htdocs. Otherwise (when the request is received on address 192.168.1.2), the server responds with a document from /usr/local/apache/htdocs2. In this example, clients access the two different Web sites as http://site1.example.com/ and http://site2.example.com/.

Inside a <VirtualHost> section, you place directives to control all the aspects of the server that are specific to the particular site that you are defining. This includes directives to do the following:

- Define the document name space.
- Control the document and script handling.
- Define the directory indexing options.
- Set log file options.
- Perform access and authorization control.

For example, to define per directory options for htdocs2, you add a `<Directory>` section, nested inside the `<VirtualHost>` section shown in the example in Listing 33.4.

For each virtual host you define, you need to at least define a new `DocumentRoot`. You also need to set up transfer and error logs that are specific to that site, using appropriate log directives. It is up to you to decide what other customizations to make for each Web site (that is, inside each virtual host section) that you define.

You specify the IP address for a virtual host in the `<VirtualHost>` directive itself. This can include a port number, which is separated from the IP address by a colon. The server must be listening on the address that you specify. In certain complex situations, you might need to tell the server to listen to specific address and port combinations, using some combination of `BindAddress`, `Port`, and `Listen` directives. Use of `BindAddress` and `Port` was discussed earlier in this chapter. The `Listen` directive allows more precise control over the addresses that are used by the Web server. The example in Listing 33.5 uses the `Listen` directive to specify three separate addresses to listen to, and for subsequent mapping to virtual hosts.

LISTING 33.5 AN EXAMPLE OF IP-BASED VIRTUAL HOSTING, USING COMPLEX ADDRESSING

```
Listen 192.168.1.1:80
Listen 192.168.1.1:8080
Listen 192.168.1.2:80

<VirtualHost 192.168.1.1:80>
...
</VirtualHost>
<VirtualHost 192.168.1.1:8080>
...
</VirtualHost>
<VirtualHost 192.168.1.2:80>
...
</VirtualHost>
```

By default, any client access to the machine on an address that is not matched by a virtual host directive is handled using the directives outside any virtual host statement. To make the definitions for the sites more consistent, you can use the keyword `_default_` in place of the IP address in a `<VirtualHost>` directive, and place the settings for alternative Web site access inside that virtual host section. This can be important in complex virtual hosting configurations. For example, Listing 33.6 accomplishes the same thing as Listing 33.4, when only two IP addresses are used.

LISTING 33.6 USING `_default_` WITH VIRTUAL HOSTING

```
...
BindAddress *
Port 80

<VirtualHost 192.168.1.2>
DocumentRoot /home/httpd/site2
ServerName site2.com
...
```

PART

V

CH

33

LISTING 33.6   CONTINUED

```
</VirtualHost>

<VirtualHost _default_:*>
DocumentRoot /home/httpd/html
ServerName site1.com
...
</VirtualHost>
```

RUNNING A SINGLE SERVER WITH MULTIPLE DNS NAMES

IP-based virtual hosting is fine if you have multiple IP addresses that you can configure on your machine. However, if you are hosting many sites, you might not obtain all the addresses you need. Also, you might have a machine that already has more than one name assigned to a single IP address. In these cases, you need to use name-based virtual hosting.

The principles in name-based virtual hosting are basically the same as those for IP-based virtual hosting. In this case, however, the server also uses the hostname in the client's request to determine which virtual host to use for the request. Name-based virtual hosting can be used with a single IP address or with multiple IP addresses.

To set this up, use the `NameVirtualHost` directive to indicate which addresses are being used for name-based virtual hosts. Then, inside the `<VirtualHost>` sections for that address, indicate a name (or set of names) to match using the `ServerName` and `ServerAlias` directives. When the server tries to match the incoming request to a virtual host section, it examines the hostname sent by the client and matches it against these names. Listing 33.7 shows an example of name-based virtual hosting. This example shows the server supporting two site names on address `192.168.1.1`.

LISTING 33.7   AN EXAMPLE OF NAME-BASED VIRTUAL HOSTING

```
Listen 192.168.1.1:80
NameVirtualHost 192.168.1.1:80

<VirtualHost 192.168.1.1:80>
DocumentRoot /home/httpd/html
ServerName www.example.com
ServerAlias www www.example.com
</VirtualHost>

<VirtualHost 192.168.1.1:80>
DocumentRoot /usr/local/apache/htdocs2
ServerName www2.example.com
</VirtualHost>
```

Note the use of the `ServerAlias` directive in the first virtual host definition. If a client request contains either the name `www.example.com` or just `www`, the first host definition is used. Use of `ServerAlias` is useful to allow clients on the local network to use short alias names instead of fully qualified domain names, in conjunction with name-based hosting.

Running More Than One Web Server on the Same Machine

Another way to run more than one Web site on a machine is to load multiple instances of the Web server on the machine. Instead of using `<VirtualHost>` directives, you configure each server with its own set of configuration files, making sure that the servers do not interfere with each other.

Making a Set of Configuration Files for Each Server

In this setup, each server needs to have its own set of startup and configuration files. The startup file is the initialization script `/etc/rc.d/init.d/httpd` for Red Hat, OpenLinux, and similar distributions (`/etc/init.d/httpd` for Debian). This file can be edited to add a second and subsequent invocation lines for a server when the script is run at system boot. To do this, duplicate the commands in the `start)` and `stop)` sections of the case statement in this file and edit them to reflect the additional servers that you want to start. See Chapter 13, "System Initialization," for more information about initialization scripts.

The directives for adjusting the configuration files were discussed earlier in this chapter. Basically, you want to configure each server with its own set of configuration files, using the `ServerRoot` and `ResourceConfig`, `AccessConfig`, `TypeConfig`, and `MimeMagicFile` directives to accomplish this. Note that it is likely that you will want to share the MIME typing files. If you create a new configuration directory, you might want to use filesystem links so that the files `mime.types` and `magic` are shared between the two directories.

Other settings that are specific to each server instance need to be placed in the appropriate configuration file for that server.

Binding Each Server to Its Own Address or Port

For the servers to run without interfering with each other, they need to use different addresses, or at least different ports. Use the `BindAddress`, `Port`, and `Listen` directives in each server's `httpd.conf` to establish the IP address and TCP port used by that server.

Other Per-Instance Configuration Variables

You must change a few other configuration variables for subsequent instances of the server for the different server processes not to interfere with each other. These include the values set by the `ScoreBoardFile`, `LockFile`, and `PidFile` directives, as well as log file locations (set by `TransferLog`, `ErrorLog`, `CustomLog`, and so on).

Part
V

Ch
33

Dynamic Shared Objects (DSO)

Many of Apache's features are provided using *modules*. A module is a piece of code that can or cannot be made part of the system and which provides specific features. For example, `mod_perl` provides a fast way to load Perl scripts, whereas `mod_mime_magic` allows Apache to determine a file's type by its contents.

Apache's features are provided by modules for several reasons:

- Loading unneeded features wastes resources, particularly memory.
- If you don't load a feature, bugs in it can never cause you problems.
- Breaking features into modules generally leads to better design.
- Modules can be written by groups other than Apache and then integrated by the user.

Before Apache 1.3, modules had to be chosen at compile time. They were then statically linked into Apache so that they were always available. With version 1.3, Apache added the Dynamic Shared Object (DSO) model, which allows modules to be installed at run time with LoadModule directives in the httpd.conf file.

To use DSO modules, you must install the mod_so module statically (that is, at compile time), but after that, most modules can be installed at runtime. There are some tradeoffs, however. In particular, startup will be approximately 20% slower and execution will be approximately 5% slower. For heavily loaded sites, this is generally unacceptable, but for smaller sites that can afford the overhead, you can gain the flexibility of adding and removing modules simply by updating your httpd.conf file and restarting Apache (instead of recompiling and reinstalling Apache). For more information on DSO modules, see http://www.apache.org/docs/dso.html.

USING APACHE WITH SSL

Earlier in this chapter, authorization and access control were discussed as two important aspects of your Web site security. This section deals with another aspect of security: making the communications between the clients and your Web server private. This is done by encrypting the communications between the clients and the server, using the *Secure Sockets Layer* (*SSL*) protocol.

This section gives an overview of the mechanisms that are used for secure communications, as well as providing some information about the mod_ssl modification to Apache, which allows it to function as a secure Web server. This section also discusses some of the creation and manipulation of special data files that are used for secure communications.

The availability of SSL for use with your Web server creates some interesting dilemmas for governments that want to control encryption to avoid having it fall into the hands of foreign entities that they want to spy on. This topic is discussed as well.

OVERVIEW OF SECURE COMMUNICATIONS CONCEPTS

SSL is a protocol that was originally defined by Netscape Communications Corporation to allow two machines communicating over TCP/IP to encrypt the information sent between them. After a communication session is secured in this way, the two machines can exchange private or sensitive information without worrying about eavesdroppers or other interlopers stealing or using the information. This is an essential feature for Web servers used for e-commerce because they often require the transfer of personal, confidential information, such as credit card numbers or account codes.

Public-Private Key Systems

To encrypt the packets that travel between two machines, the machines must understand a common encryption algorithm, and must exchange some information which allows one machine to decrypt (unscramble) what the other one encrypts. The parts of the security information that are used to encrypt or decrypt data are called keys.

Encryption is performed by making a modification to the information at one location, using a key. The information is then transmitted to another location, where a key is used to restore the information to its original form (decrypt it). In a simple system, the key used to encrypt the information is the same key that is used to decrypt it. This is called a *private key system* because the contents of the key must be kept secret for the information to be kept secret. However, private key systems present a problem because the key must be somehow transmitted securely to the new location. SSL uses a special kind of encryption, called a *public-private key system*, as a part of the overall system it uses to allow secure communications sessions.

A discussion of the mathematical details of public-private keys is outside the scope of this short section. However, in such a key system, two keys are used for the encryption/ decryption process, and one of them (called the *public key*) can be made freely available to anyone without damaging the security of the communications between the two machines. This solves the problem of secure key distribution, inherent to private key systems.

Certificates: Verifying Who Is at the Other End of a Secure Session

Another issue that is related to secure communications is whether to trust the Web server with which you are communicating. Although a Web server might send a client a key so that the server can communicate securely with the client, it is possible that the client might be talking to the wrong Web server (for example, the server might provide a credit card number to some fake server run by con artists). When a public-private key system is used, it is also possible to transmit some additional information, called a *certificate*, which describes the Web server and the organization behind it.

This certificate can be electronically "signed" by a trusted agency. Various agencies research both the organization that is running the Web site and the information in the certificate, and then sign the certificate—for a price. Client browsers have a list of trusted agencies that they use to verify the signature on a certificate. The use of a signed certificate allows a client to verify that it is communicating with the server that the user intends it to (that is, that the server is actually run by the organization that the user expects).

When you set up a secure Web server, you must create a public-private key pair and a certificate for use with the server. If you want to run a secure Web site for public use, you must also get your certificate signed by one of these trusted agencies.

PART

V

CH

33

USE OF SECURE HTTP: HTTPS

When communicating with a secure Web server, the client uses a different protocol, called *HTTPS* (or *Secure HTTP*), instead of HTTP. As the name implies, it is similar to HTTP, but with security added to it.

To access a secure Web server, a user must specify the URL with the HTTPS protocol identifier, as follows:

```
https://www.example.com/cgi-bin/process_credit_card
```

One of the most common mistakes that new administrators of secure Web servers make is failing to use the correct protocol type (https) in URLs that refer to the secure Web site. Whereas the default TCP port for the HTTP protocol is port 80, the default port for HTTPS is 443. When a browser tries to access a secure server at the wrong port, the browser appears to hang, and eventually times out.

This can be disconcerting to end users, so take special care to test all the URLs that you create and that link to your secure site.

CREATING A SECURE WEB SERVER USING mod_ssl

Because of governmental export restrictions in the U.S., most Linux distributions do not provide secure Web server functionality directly. Linux is sold worldwide, and the U.S. government does not allow certain kinds of encryption to be shipped outside the U.S. Unfortunately, this means that you have to do a bit of legwork to obtain, build, and install the secure Web server functionality for Apache.

There are a couple of different options for adding SSL to Apache. The one described here—which is recommended—is called mod_ssl. It consists of a set of patches and a special module for use with the Apache source code. It uses a cryptography library that provides SSL functions called OpenSSL.

> **Note**
>
> OpenSSL is based on an older library called SSLeay. mod_ssl is based on an older package called Apache-SSL (which is still being developed). The fact that one package can form the base of another, even another competing package, is one of the great strengths of Open Source. It can also be quite confusing.

OBTAINING SOURCES

To build Apache with mod_ssl, you need sources from three places. Examine the following Web sites, and follow the links to an appropriate download area, to obtain the source code you need.

If there are U.S. mirrors for the download areas listed on the respective Web sites for these software pieces, use those instead if you are in the United States.

APACHE SOURCE CODE   For the Apache source code itself, either use the source code from your distribution or obtain the latest release from the Apache organization download area.

The Apache organization Web site is at `http://www.apache.org/`.

To obtain the latest release of Apache from the Apache organization, download the source `tar` file from the following location:

`http://httpd.apache.org/dist/`

OPENSSL SOURCES   OpenSSL is an essential cryptographic library for programs using SSL, including a secure Web server. The OpenSSL Web site is at `http://www.openssl.org/`. The OpenSSL library can be obtained by downloading the latest version at this site.

mod_ssl SOURCES   mod_ssl is a set of patches for Apache that allows it to use the OpenSSL library. Also, mod_ssl provides a special module that adds additional functionality related to processing client and server security data.

The mod_ssl Web site is at `http://www.modssl.org`.

The mod_ssl TAR file can be obtained at the following URL:

`http://www.modssl.org/source/`

NOTES ON BUILDING THE SOURCE   At the mod_ssl Web page, Ralf Engelschall (the primary author of mod_ssl) provides detailed instructions for installing and building all the required components. The Web page to examine is `http://www.modssl.org/source/exp/mod_ssl/pkg.mod_ssl/INSTALL`.

Download this document, print it out, and follow it exactly. If you are in the United States, follow the U.S. instructions.

When you are finished with the instructions, the Apache software is installed in a subdirectory under the directory that you chose as the argument to `--prefix`. You can run the secure Apache from that location (highly recommended), or you can install the software over the top of your existing Apache files.

PREPARING SPECIAL FILES REQUIRED FOR SECURITY

Several special files are required by the server for it to operate in secure mode. During the course of the build, you probably made a server key file and certificate using the (patched) makefile in the Apache source directory. However, you can make these files manually at a later time, and some of them require special processing by a trusted agency (a Certificate Authority) for your Web site to be used correctly by the general public.

The following files are used for server security:

- **A server key file**—This file contains a public and private key, which are used by the server for encryption and decryption operations.

- **A certificate file**—This file specifies that the key and Web site are run by a certain organization. If this certificate is signed by a trusted agency, the user can trust that the Web site is indeed run by the indicated organization.

- **A certificate signing request**—This file contains information from the certificate, as well as information about the key. It is intended to be sent to a trusted agency (called a Certificate Authority) for signing.

All these are made when you run the command `make certificate` in the Apache source directory. Each of these files is described in greater detail in the paragraphs that follow.

THE PUBLIC/PRIVATE KEY PAIR

The public/private key pair is saved in the file `server.key` by default. This file contains the keys that are used to perform encryption by the server.

The private key of the public/private key pair needs to be protected at all times. For this reason, during the creation of the key, you are asked to enter a pass phrase to encrypt the key file. When the key file is encrypted, you are required to enter this pass phrase every time the server starts in order for the server to access the file. Although this can be annoying, it is very dangerous to leave the private key unencrypted on the disk without a pass phrase.

Use the `SSLCertificateKeyFile` directive in the server configuration file `httpd.conf` to specify the key file that is to be used for secure operations.

THE SERVER CERTIFICATE

The server certificate file contains information about the organization that runs the Web site. The server certificate file is transmitted to the client when a secure session is set up, and the client tries to use it to verify that the site is legitimate. This file is sometimes called an X.509 file because that is the name of the standard that defines the format used for this file.

For the certificate to be accepted by the client, it must be digitally signed by a *Certificate Authority (CA)*. Each major browser that supports SSL has a list of trusted certificate authorities whose signatures it accepts. When a browser sees a certificate signed by a CA that it does not know about, it usually provides the information about the CA and the certificate to the user, and asks whether it is to proceed. It is then up to the user to determine whether she can trust that the site to which she is connecting is valid.

The certificate file to use is specified in the server configuration file using the `SSLCertificateFile` directive.

THE CERTIFICATE SIGNING REQUEST

For your site to be trusted by clients, you need to have your certificate signed by a trusted agency that operates as a Certificate Authority. To have the certificate signed by a Certificate Authority, create a *certificate signing request (CSR)* and send it to the authority with some documentation and some money.

Several agencies act as Certificate Authorities, which involves verifying the information in the certificate and digitally signing it. The price that they charge for their service is in exchange for the cost of researching the information in your CSR and taking on the liability of certifying your Web site.

The following are some Certificate Authorities:

- CertiSign (Brazilian, part of VeriSign)
  `http://www.certisign.com.br/servidores`
- Entrust
  `http://www.entrust.net`
- IKS GmbH (German)
  `http://www.iks-jena.de/produkte/ca`
- Thawte (part of VeriSign)
  `http://www.thawte.com`
- VeriSign
  `http://www.verisign.com/site`

All of these companies accept certificate-signing requests generated by the `mod_ssl` package, for use with Apache with `mod_ssl`. When you make your server key file and certificate, you also make a certificate-signing request. The information required for this request must match exactly the company name, registered domain name, and other details that are required by the Certificate Authority, in order for them to process your request. Also, the file is automatically encoded in a special format. Detailed information on pricing instructions for creating the CSR and submitting it, and the required accompanying documentation to the Certificate Authority, are available on the Web sites of the respective companies.

To test your server, or to run your server internally in your organization, you can act as your own Certificate Authority and self-sign your certificate. This is also referred to as *self-certifying*. The browsers that connect to your server won't recognize your signature as one from a valid Certificate Authority, but users can manually accept the certificates on their browsers after seeing an error message.

For internal use, you can eliminate the error message on the client by adding a Certificate Authority file to the client's browser. The steps involved in doing this are beyond the scope of this section, but see the online `mod_ssl` documentation for more information.

After you receive a certificate signed by a real Certificate Authority, you substitute it for the self-signed one by copying it over the old file, or by modifying the value of the `SSLCertificateFile` directive.

SPECIAL SECURITY DIRECTIVES

The security directives to control `mod_ssl` are added to the Apache documentation that is installed when you build the secure Web server—you can examine them in-depth there. However, a few security directives are worth highlighting here, to give an overview of their use.

PART
V

CH
33

Use the SSLCipherSuite directive to control which algorithms are allowed for secure sessions. Unless you are a security expert, you probably need to leave these settings alone.

Use the SSLSessionCache directive to indicate whether to support an interprocess cache of SSL session information (and if so, what the filename for it is to be). Because secure sessions require substantial setup, and because client requests can be served by multiple server/child processes, use of a session cache to share information between child processes can speed things up considerably. Use the value none, to turn off the session cache, or dbm: followed by the path of a file to use as the session cache.

Use the SSLLog and SSLLogLevel directives to create logs to hold SSL-specific information.

Finally, SSL and X.509 certificates can also be used by the server for authenticating clients—much as the server certificate is used by the client to authenticate the server. Use the following directives to set up client authentication using client certificates: SSLCACertificatePath, SSLCACertificateFile, SSLVerifyClient, SSLVerifyDepth, and SSLRequire.

MAKING SURE YOU ARE LEGAL

In their infinite wisdom, agencies of the U.S. government have created regulations that make it a crime to export certain strong encryption software from the United States. This is ostensibly done with the intent to prevent strong encryption capabilities from falling into the hands of unfriendly governments and terrorists. The actual result of this situation, however, is that most good encryption software development is now done in other countries and imported to the U.S., rather than vice versa. Encryption software that is imported to the U.S. cannot be exported from the U.S.—even to the original author of the software!

Until recently, the company RSA Data Security, Inc. had a U.S. patent on certain public/private key encryption algorithms used in SSL. In 2000, the patent to the RSA algorithm expired, so restrictions are no longer on most of this code. However, if you have code specifically from RSA, you may still be bound by their license agreement. See www.rsa.com for more information.

If you just plan to use Apache with mod_ssl as a secure Web server at your organization, you are probably all right. If, however, you plan to distribute the Web server or a machine containing it overseas, check with an attorney to determine what the applicable U.S. export laws are and to make sure that you are in compliance with them. Luckily, recent changes in both U.S. law and governmental attitude are making the traffic in cryptography easier. Time will tell whether this trend will continue.

CASE STUDY: BOOSTING APACHE WITH KHTTPD

One enhancement added to the new 2.4 kernel is the http kernel daemon, khttpd. This daemon is a very basic Web server that handles static Web pages, copying them to the network without processing. Some of you might be thinking that this is overkill, a kernel daemon Web server. But if you think about it this way, it makes sense:

■ Many Web sites use mostly static pages.

- Static pages are just copied to the network unchanged.

- Apache, or any other Web server, has to call on the kernel to perform the actual copy to network anyway (after processing the file itself, often a lengthy process).

The kernel Web daemon just copies static pages to the network, bypassing the overhead of a large program like Apache and all the system calls Apache must make. More complicated Web pages are automatically forwarded to Apache (or another Web server). This means that khttpd can provide a performance boost without reducing the flexibility of your Web site.

To use khttpd, you must compile it into the kernel. You can check to see whether your distribution has included khttpd as a kernel module by trying to load it. If it's not included, recompile your kernel per the instructions in this book. The khttpd option can be found in the Networking options section. Include this as a module. Add the khttpd module to your list of modules to be loaded at boot time.

To provide the advanced features that khttpd lacks, you'll still need a full Web server. So it can work with khttpd, you'll want to reconfigure Apache or another Web server to run on a port other than 80, the default Web port. You can specify 8080, a common alternative Web port, 8000, or just about any other unused port on your system. If you also change Apache's `BindAddress` directive from * to 127.0.0.1, no one will be able to connect directly to Apache from the outside, only through khttpd.

To make it easy to run the khttpd daemon, you can use something like `rc.khttpd`, shown in Listing 33.8, which can be called from your `rc.local` bootup script.

LISTING 33.8 `rc.khttpd`

```
#!/bin/sh
# suggested rc.khttpd script -- called from rc.local
modprobe khttpd  # this makes sure khttpd is loaded
echo 8080 > /proc/sys/net/khttpd/clientport
echo /usr/local/apache/htdocs > /proc/sys/net/khttpd/documentroot
echo phtml > /proc/sys/net/khttpd/dynamic
echo inc > /proc/sys/net/khttpd/dynamic
echo shtml > /proc/sys/net/khttpd/dynamic
echo php3 > /proc/sys/net/khttpd/dynamic
echo php > /proc/sys/net/khttpd/dynamic
echo 1 > /proc/sys/net/khttpd/logging
echo 1 > /proc/sys/net/khttpd/threads
echo 80 > /proc/sys/net/khttpd/serverport
echo 1 > /proc/sys/net/khttpd/start
```

PART

V

CH

33

Going down the list of variables, the first, `clientport`, is the port on which you put Apache or another Web server. This tells khttpd where to send requests for advanced services. If khttpd encounters anything other than a static page, it will call on the client to process it first. By default this value is 80.

The `documentroot` variable should be changed to reflect your document root on your Web server. By default this is `/var/www`.

Next come several settings to tell khttpd that when it sees a document file with various extensions, it should send it to the client on the clientport. By default, this variable only contains cgi-bin and ... The .. setting makes khttpd more secure by disallowing the user from trying to "sneak" outside of the main tree. A more full-featured server like Apache is better suited to determine whether the .. is appropriate.

Not listed in the script above, but also configurable, is logging. You can turn on logging by adding echo 1 > /proc/sys/net/khttpd/logging to the above script. The default is to do no logging (0).

Also not listed is maxconnect, which contains the maximum simultaneous connections permitted. By default this number is 1000, which is normally more than sufficient.

The next two values you probably won't want to change. These are the perm_forbid and perm_required. Without a good understanding of how file stats are handled in Linux (man 2 stats), you probably should not change these values. The default value for perm_forbid is 16969, and for perm_required is 4. This setting of perm_required checks to see whether the file is world readable. This setting of perm_forbid looks for a number of things, including whether the file is a FIFO (a special type of system pipe), SUID/SGID, and more.

The serverport value is the port khttpd should listen on. By default, this value is 8080. You'll probably want to change this to 80 as in the previous script.

The sloppymime variable determines whether unknown mime-types should be treated as text/html or passed to the client http daemon.

The start and stop options do exactly what they say. The initial value for each is 0. After you change start to 1, khttpd will begin handling Web content. Sending a one to stop will send a corresponding 0 to start and khttpd will shut down.

To remove the khttpd module, first send a 1 to the stop variable, and then a 1 to the unload variable.

The threads variable defaults to 2. This particular variable determines how many threads you will want. You should change this to one thread per CPU if you have a small site. If you have a large Web site, you can make this two. Generally, you'll use 2 if the active files would not fit in available RAM.

That's all there is to using khttpd. You should notice a significant increase in the speed in which static pages are rendered, particularly on a small machine with many static pages.

Tip

Because khttpd runs directly in the kernel, it effectively has even greater permissions than root. This means that any security vulnerability in khttpd could be extremely serious and any instabilities could bring down the whole machine. If you want a smaller speed improvement, but don't want some of these risks, you might consider phhttpd, originally developed by Zach Brown while he was with Red Hat. phhttpd is a user-space Web server that also handles static Web content while passing dynamic content to a more full-featured Web server like Apache. Although not as fast as the in-kernel khttpd, phhttpd is still quite efficient at handling static content without some of the dangers of khttpd. For more information, see http://www.zabbo.net//phhttpd/.

## CHAPTER 34

TCP WRAPPERS

In this chapter

WHAT ARE TCP WRAPPERS?

A *wrapper* is something that is put around something else to protect it or modify its environment. TCP wrappers are put around server programs to help protect the host from exploit using that program, or to track abusers as they access the programs in an attempt to circumvent security safeguards. Although not a foolproof method of preventing intrusions, TCP wrappers do provide good early warning—via system logging—of possible intrusion attempts, and they are one more piece of the puzzle used to prevent subsequent intrusions and to track intruders back to their source.

> **Note**
>
> On the intrusion early warning and prevention side, you'll look at TCP wrappers—what they are, how they work, and how to configure this facility. Because of the nature of TCP wrappers, it is expected that the reader already has a firm grasp of `/etc/inetd.conf`, what it contains, and its file format.

Perhaps a better way to explain what the TCP wrappers program is is to explain what it isn't. TCP wrappers isn't a program that can be run around every process on the machine—it is only effective for some programs run by the `inetd` metadaemon. Processes with which TCP wrappers is only partially effective, or totally ineffective, include the r commands (for example, `rlogin`, `rsh`) and `udp`-based services. Unless the r services are absolutely vital (for most, better substitutes exist), they need to be shut off by commenting out the line that calls them in `/etc/inetd.conf`, and then sending a `SIGHUP` to `inetd`.

> **Tip**
>
> You can send a signal to a program to reread its configuration file in one of several ways. The signal is a call a hangup signal, SIGHUP, or signal 1. To send a signal like this you use a line similar to: `kill -<signal> <PID>`. A PID is a process ID number. Here are just a few of the easiest ways to send a SIGHUP to a program:
>
> ```
> kill -HUP `pidof inetd`
> kill -1 `cat /var/run/inetd.pid`
> killall -HUP inetd
> ```
>
> The program /sbin/pidof reads the pid of a program directly from the process table. The killall program performs a similar function. Feel free to substitute signal numbers for s ignal names at any time. See man 7 signal for a complete listing of kernel signals.

HOW TCP WRAPPERS WORK

The TCP wrappers program is called in place of the actual service that it is to protect. There are two different methods for implementing TCP wrappers. The first is to simply replace the actual program with `tcpd` (the TCP wrapper daemon). Because this is a rather limited usage, and because the second method is more flexible, this chapter looks exclusively at the second implementation method—to have either the `inetd` metadaemon call `tcpd` for every invocation of a daemon, or to use `tcpd` within the `/etc/hosts.allow` file for certain patterns.

Some of the functionality of TCP wrappers is based on compile-time options. If you desire or require any of this functionality that is not built by default, you'll need to recompile, and turn the features on (or off). One of the default compile-time features is PARANOID. With this turned on, TCP wrappers perform name-to-address lookups using DNS and compare them to address-to-name lookups for the client that is requesting the connection. If this check fails, TCP wrappers assume that the client is trying to fool, or *spoof*, you as to his true identity; in that case, the connection is dropped. Some sites might want to recompile to include this functionality.

The daemon provided in the Caldera OpenLinux distribution has been compiled without the PARANOID option because other rules can then run. Because PARANOID immediately drops the connection if the forward and reverse names don't match, it doesn't allow other rules to fire.

Another reason not to include PARANOID is that many hosts connected to the Internet do not have DNS listings, so the reverse lookups fail. They also fail if the primary and secondary DNS servers are offline. So unless you have a compelling reason to include PARANOID, it's probably better not to, and to handle those suspect connections in another manner.

Another related function has to do with source-routing. TCP wrappers can be compiled to disallow host address spoofing by ignoring source routing information provided by the client. (This is not effective for udp-based services.)

A final compile-time option is RFC 931 lookups. This uses the ident daemon running on the remote machine. Because few PCs run the ident daemon, turning this feature on results in response times in excess of 10 seconds (the default timeout) for those clients. This feature is also not effective for udp-based services.

Most distributions' versions of tcpd do not use most of the compile-time options. Although this is always subject to change, the package is compiled in a way that is believed most useful to the most users. Other packages (such as netfilter—see Chapter 36, "IP Firewalling") or the 2.2.x or 2.4.x kernel itself have features that can be activated to prevent IP spoofing and ignore source routing. If you still insist on having these features compiled into tcpd, however, consult Chapter 17, "Building/Rebuilding a Package."

TCP wrappers uses the syslog facility to log captured information pertaining to client:daemon connections. You'll look at the specifics of this configuration in the following sections.

IMPLEMENTING TCP WRAPPERS

PART
V

CH

34

You can begin to use the TCP wrappers daemon by finding the line in /etc/inetd.conf that looks similar to the following:

```
telnet          stream  tcp     nowait  root    /usr/sbin/in.telnetd
➡  /usr/sbin/in.telnetd
```

Change it to look like the following:

```
telnet          stream  tcp     nowait  root    /usr/sbin/tcpd
➡  /usr/sbin/in.telnetd
```

inetd starts tcpd, and when tcpd has logged the client:daemon request—and has satisfied any conditions—it starts the telnet daemon. Do not be surprised that your inetd.conf file is already using tcpd; this is standard practice in most distributions today. What will be missing are any sane limitations on connections and is covered below in the /etc/hosts.allow and (if used) the /etc/hosts.deny files.

Note

inetd needs to be signaled to re-read the /etc/inetd.conf file by sending the SIGHUP signal after each change.

At this point, you have a log of all connection attempts to the telnet port. You can do this for every service started by inetd that you are not denying in inetd.conf simply by using tcpd as the target and making the argument the service daemon (as shown previously).

Sometimes, however, this might not be the real intention. For example, say you want to log all attempts to connect to services, but don't want to provide certain services, such as telnet. You just want to use the logging facilities to provide early warning of intrusion attempts. For this, look at your /etc/hosts.allow and hosts.deny files.

Originally, tcpd required both hosts.allow and hosts.deny for full functionality. Although this option is available for those wanting to use it, you can now consolidate everything into /etc/hosts.allow and maintain only one file. This one-file-fits-all configuration (looked at later in this chapter) is enabled by ensuring that tcpd is compiled with PROCESS_OPTIONS turned on (this is the default with OpenLinux). Some syntax, specifically in the shell commands used by the two different methods (with and without hosts.deny), is different. So blindly combining the two files into one can produce unexpected results, and is not recommended.

Tip

As rules are being written, remember that the first match terminates the search, so subsequent rules are not processed.

The format for the hosts.allow file is as follows:

```
daemon(s) : client(s) : option : option ...
```

Each line is a colon-separated list. Start with any daemons that you are interested in protecting, followed by a client list, and then any number of options you need, with each option separated by a colon. If any option uses colons within the option (as in a PATH statement), the colons that are not used as column separators must be protected by a backslash (\). Also, every line, including the last line in the file, must be terminated by a newline or it will not be executed.

Start by taking a look at valid values for each of the columns.

DAEMONS AND WILDCARDS

The daemon list is a list of daemons separated by whitespace and/or commas. It is only the daemon name itself as it is on the system, that is, `in.telnetd`. In the case of multihomed hosts, the form `daemon@host` is acceptable to differentiate one bound NIC from another. Wildcards are also acceptable. Valid wildcards include the following:

- **ALL**—Universal match (all daemons/hosts)
- **LOCAL**—Matches hosts whose name do not contain a dot, as in the hosts `foo` or `baz`
- **UNKNOWN**—Matches any user whose name is unknown, or any host whose name or address is unknown
- **KNOWN**—Matches any known user, and any host whose name and address are both known
- **PARANOID**—Matches any host whose name does not match its address

Note that KNOWN and UNKNOWN are subject to the vagaries of DNS. When said service is unavailable, these wildcards might not match properly. Likewise, with PARANOID, if DNS is not available, the hostname does not match an address.

CLIENTS, PATTERNS, AND HOSTNAMES

The client list is a list of hostname(s), host IP address(es), patterns (see next paragraph), or wildcards to be matched. Patterns can be either leading or trailing dot.

If you have the following hosts table in your system (`foo`)

```
192.168.0.1   foo.void.org   foo
192.168.0.2   bar.void.org   bar
192.168.0.3   baz.void.org   baz
```

you can specify as a hostname `.void.org`, and match `foo`, `bar`, or `baz` at `.void.org`. If you omit the leading dot (`.`), only the (non-existent) host `void.org` is matched. Likewise, if you specify `192.168.0.` as a host, you match all hosts that have an address beginning with `192.168.0.`.

FORMS AND OPERATORS

You can also use a network/netmask form to match a range, as in `192.168.0.0/` `255.255.255.128`. This matches `192.168.0.0` through `192.168.0.127`. So, an individual host can be singled out by using a specific host address and a netmask of `255.255.255.255`.

The final pattern match possible is of the form @ and the netgroup name (valid for clients only). Note that this form is only available if you are running NIS. The netgroup name is case-sensitive.

One operator is possible for use in either daemon or client lists: EXCEPT. Exercise caution if EXCEPT is to be nested. An argument in the form `a EXCEPT b EXCEPT c` translates as `(a EXCEPT (b EXCEPT c))`.

Two basic options that you'll want to use are ALLOW and DENY. You will look at more advanced options later.

RULES

You now have enough information to create some basic rules:

- `ALL : LOCAL, .void.org EXCEPT dab@bar.void.org : ALLOW`

- `ALL EXCEPT in.telnetd : dab@bar.void.org : ALLOW`

- `in.ftpd : ALL : ALLOW`

- `ALL : ALL : DENY`

These rules allow any host from void.org, unless it is the user dab connecting to you from bar.void.org in an attempt to use any of the services. (Maybe he's attempted a telnet exploit from here, so you disallow him telnet using rule 2.) Everyone is allowed ftp access. Anyone else attempting to connect to any other service is denied. The order of most of the preceding rules above is unimportant because they don't overlap. However, if rule 4 is moved up, all rules following it become academic.

Additional options with any of these rules can include shell commands, network options lookup options, and miscellaneous options. Two commands enable you to run shell commands as options: spawn and twist.

The spawn command enables you to run a shell command as one of your options, and does not interfere with client/server communications because all stdin, stdout, and stderr are directed to /dev/null. A common usage for this is described in the man pages as follows:

```
spawn (/path/to/safe_finger -l @%h | /usr/bin/mail root) &
```

The preceding command mails root the results of a safe_finger on a connecting system (character expansion is explained later). The preceding can be used with DENY as an option to booby-trap services not offered to outsiders. Be careful not to use this on the in.fingerd daemon—you can finger a host that fingers you, that you then finger back, ad infinitum (or until one of you runs out of resources). In the preceding example, you might want to add a rule 3 that is similar to the following:

```
in.telnetd : dab@bar.void.org : spawn (/usr/sbin/safe_finger -l @%h \
        | /usr/bin/mail root) & : DENY
```

This tells root when dab@bar.void.org has been attempting to use telnet again. Add this just after the second line in your hosts.allow file.

> **Note**
>
> Note that long lines can be broken into two lines by making the last character of the first line a \ (as in the preceding example).

A second way to invoke a shell command is to use twist. The difference between spawn and twist is that spawn sends all communications to /dev/null, whereas twist sends all communications back to the client. This can be used to substitute a different command for the usual one:

```
in.ftpd : ... : twist /bin/echo 421 Message to client
```

`twist` must be the last option on the line. Instead of invoking the `ftp` daemon, the previous line sends a `421 Message` to client to any client matching the `in.ftpd` rule.

Other options include: `keepalive`, `linger`, `rfc931`, `banner`, `nice`, `setenv`, `umask`, and `user`. These are used as follows:

- **`keepalive`** `(no arguments)`—The server periodically sends a `keepalive` packet to the client. If the client does not respond, the server terminates. This is useful for users who turn off their machines while still connected to the server.

- **`linger`** *`<number of seconds>`*—Length of time the kernel is to continue to try to send undelivered data to the client after a connection is closed.

- **`rfc931 [`** *`timeout in seconds`* **`]`**—Perform RFC 931 username lookups. Only valid for TCP. If the client is not running IDENT or a similar RFC 931 service (as is the case with many PCs), noticeable connection delays can result. Timeout is optional; if it is not specified, compile-time default is used.

- **`banners`** *`</some/path>`*—Look in */some/path/* for a file with the same name as the daemon process (for example, in `.telnetd` for the `telnet` service), and then copy its contents to the client. This option uses character expansion within the file (explained as follows). Banners only work with TCP connections.

- **`nice [`** *`number`* **`]`**—Change the `nice` value from its default of `10`.

- **`setenv`** *`<name value>`*—Used to set environment variables for those daemons that don't reset their environment on startup. The *`value`* is subject to character expansion.

- **`umask`** *`< octal >`*—Similar to the shell `umask` variable.

- **`user`** *`<user[.group]>`*—Sets the daemon's user and, optionally, the group.

CHARACTER EXPANSION

The following character expansions can be used as noted previously:

- **`%a (%A)`**—The client (server) host address.

- **`%c`**—Returns client information depending on what's available. Can be a `user@host` or IP address, or just an IP address.

- **`%d`**—The daemon process name (for example, `in.telnetd`).

- **`%h (%H)`**—Client (server) hostname or IP address.

- **`%n (%N)`**—Client (server) hostname (or `unknown` or `paranoid` if not available).

- **`%p`**—Daemon process ID.

- **`%s`**—Server information: `daemon@host` or IP address, or just a daemon name, depending on available information.

- **`%u`**—Username (or `unknown`).

- **`%%`**—Expands to single `%`.

PART

V

CH

34

MISCELLANEOUS CONCERNS

There are, however, some problems with implementing `tcpd` for all services. As noted earlier, r commands and `udp` won't work effectively—if at all—and neither will RPC-based services (indicated by `rpc/tcp`) work. Another stopping point comes from the use of `wait` instead of `nowait` with services. A service using `wait` lingers on the queue for other connections. TCP wrappers log only the first connection request (the one that spawned the service), but not any subsequent ones while the same service is still alive. So a second connection can occur with no logging for daemons already sitting on the wait queue.

Do not use TCP wrappers with the Apache Web Server. Apache has the TCP wrappers functionality built into it. Use of `tcpd` in this case is redundant. The Apache configuration is similar to `tcpd`, so it will be understandable to anyone already familiar with `tcpd`.

tcpdchk

`tcpdchk` is a utility that enables you to see what kind of syntax errors you've made while creating your `/etc/hosts.allow` file. The utility has several options, including `-d`; this option enables you to start from a directory other than `/etc`, create your `hosts.allow` file, and then test against that file before replacing the one that you are currently using. The `-d` option reads the `hosts.allow` file in the current directory (rather than in `/etc`). Obviously, this option is somewhat limiting if you are already in `/etc`.

By using the `-v` option, you can see every line that `tcpdchk` is reading and how it operates. See Listing 34.1 for a sample output.

LISTING 34.1   SAMPLE `tcpdchk` TEST OUTPUT

```
# tcpdchk -v
Using network configuration file: /etc/inetd.conf

>>> Rule /etc/hosts.allow line 1:
daemons:  ALL
clients:  .void.org EXCEPT dab@bar.void.org
option:   ALLOW
access:   granted

>>> Rule /etc/hosts.allow line 2:
daemons:  ALL EXCEPT in.telnetd
clients:  dab@bar.void.org
option:   ALLOW
access:   granted

>>> Rule /etc/hosts.allow line 4:
daemons:  in.telnetd
clients:  dab@bar.void.org
option:   spawn (/usr/sbin/safe_finger -l @client_hostname /usr/bin/mail root) &
option:   DENY
access:   denied

>>> Rule /etc/hosts.allow line 5:
daemons:  in.ftpd
```

LISTING 34.1 CONTINUED

```
clients:  ALL
option:   ALLOW
access:   granted

>>> Rule /etc/hosts.allow line 6:
daemons:  ALL
clients:  ALL
option:   DENY
access:   denied
```

If `tcpdchk` is having trouble finding your `/etc/inetd.conf` file, `-i path/to/inetd.conf` can be used.

Finally, the `-a` option checks for any ALLOWs that aren't explicitly declared—that is, which daemons can be started by a client as a result of omitting a statement to specifically ALLOW them.

tcpdmatch

The `tcpdmatch` utility enables you to test specific examples against your configuration files. Again, `tcpdmatch` enables you to test against a `hosts.allow` file in your current directory by specifying the `-d` option. It also recognizes the `-i/path/to/inetd.conf` if `tcpdmatch` has trouble finding it.

The syntax for `tcpdmatch` is as follows:

```
tcpdmatch daemon[@server] [user@]client
```

The `server` option is for multihomed hosts, and the `user` is for specific users at a client. See Listing 34.2 for sample `tcpdmatch` output.

LISTING 34.2 FOUR SAMPLE tcpdmatch OUTPUTS

```
# tcpdmatch in.telnetd bar
warning: bar: hostname alias
warning: (official name: bar.void.org)
client:   hostname bar.void.org
client:   address  192.168.0.2
server:   process  in.telnetd
matched:  /etc/hosts.allow line 1
option:   ALLOW
access:   granted

# tcpdmatch in.telnetd dab@bar
warning: bar: hostname alias
warning: (official name: bar.void.org)
client:   hostname bar.void.org
client:   address  192.168.0.2
client:   username dab
server:   process  in.telnetd
matched:  /etc/hosts.allow line 4
option:   spawn (/usr/sbin/safe_finger -l @bar.void.org |/usr/bin/mail root) &
option:   DENY
```

LISTING 34.2   CONTINUED

```
access:    denied

# tcpdmatch in.ftpd rim.caldera.com
client:    hostname rim.caldera.com
client:    address  207.179.39.2
server:    process  in.ftpd
matched:   /etc/hosts.allow line 5
option:    ALLOW
access:    granted

# tcpdmatch in.telnetd rim.caldera.com
client:    hostname rim.caldera.com
client:    address  207.179.39.2
server:    process  in.telnetd
matched:   /etc/hosts.allow line 6
option:    DENY
access:    denied
```

CASE STUDY: SITE CONSTRUCTION

Putting together all you've learned, you can now construct a good /etc/hosts.allow for your site. Here, you'll do just that.

First, see what is enabled. Use the following command to get your listing (it might be different from the text):

```
grep -v ^# /etc/inetd.conf | grep -v ^$ | grep -v internal
```

The preceding command line searches (grep) inetd.conf and excludes lines (-v) that begin with #. The results are piped to another grep, which excludes blank lines (show as the regular expression ^$), and then excludes lines with the word internal:

```
ftp     stream  tcp     nowait  root     /usr/sbin/tcpd in.ftpd -l -a
telnet  stream  tcp     nowait  root     /usr/sbin/tcpd  in.telnetd
pop3    stream  tcp     nowait  root     /usr/sbin/tcpd ipop3d
imap    stream  tcp     nowait  root     /usr/sbin/tcpd imapd
swat    stream  tcp     nowait.400 root     /usr/sbin/tcpd swat
```

Now that you know what inetd is serving out to the world, you're going to want to put some restrictions on who can access which servers. Your local network is .void.org with the 192.168.0/24 set of IP addresses. The following restrictions apply:

- **ftp**—Anyone can access ftp. It's set up as an anonymous server. No special restrictions apply. PAM is denying access to any local users, such as root, that should not be using ftp.

- **telnet**—Only local systems can access telnet.

- **pop3**—Anyone can access from anywhere.

- **imap**—You have a local Web program to access imap but only via the local system. You don't want to permit remote access except through the local Web server.

- **swat**—You want anyone on the local network to be able to administer Samba, but no remote access is to be allowed.

Constructing your `hosts.allow` file in your local subdirectory, you decide to put the easy lines first. The first two lines enable anyone anywhere to access both `pop3` and `ftp`:

```
ipop3d: ALL: ALLOW
in.ftpd: ALL: ALLOW
```

For the `imap` daemon, you only want `localhost`. This includes `127.0.0.1`, but you're going to open that to the entire 127 IP range because only `localhost` will have an IP starting with 127. You'll also enable the local system by name, `bar.void.org`, and the corresponding IP of `192.168.0.2`. You want to deny everyone else and let root know about the connection attempt:

```
imapd: LOCALHOST, 127., bar.void.org, 192.168.0.2: ALLOW
imapd: ALL : spawn (/usr/sbin/safe_finger -l @%h | /usr/bin/mail root) & : DENY
```

For the `telnet` daemon, you've decided to open it up to the local network, but you also want a warning banner displayed when anyone opens `telnet`:

```
in.telnetd: LOCAL, 127., 192.168.0., .void.org: banners /etc/banners : ALLOW
```

Then you create a file called `/etc/banners/in.telnetd` with the following contents:

```
    WARNING: Unauthorized entry into this system for any reason is a criminal
    act and will be prosecuted to the fullest extent of the law.
```

Next, you permit local network access to swat:

```
swat: LOCAL, .void.org, 192.168.0., 127.: ALLOW
```

Finally, you deny all other services (just in case something slipped through):

```
ALL : ALL : DENY
```

To ensure the new `hosts.allow` file is good, run `tcpdchk` looking for any line with warning:

```
tcpdchk -vd

Using network configuration file: /etc/inetd.conf

>>> Rule hosts.allow line 1:
daemons:  ipop3d
clients:  ALL
option:   ALLOW
access:   granted

>>> Rule hosts.allow line 2:
daemons:  in.ftpd
clients:  ALL
option:   ALLOW
access:   granted

>>> Rule hosts.allow line 3:
daemons:  imapd
clients:  LOCALHOST bar.void.org 192.168.0.2 127.
option:   ALLOW
access:   granted

>>> Rule hosts.allow line 4:
daemons:  imapd
clients:  ALL
```

```
option:   spawn (/usr/sbin/safe_finger -l @client_hostname | /usr/bin/mail root)
 &
option:   DENY
access:   denied

>>> Rule hosts.allow line 5:
daemons:  in.telnetd
clients:  LOCAL 192.168.0. 127. .void.org
option:   banners /etc/banners
option:   ALLOW
access:   granted

>>> Rule hosts.allow line 6:
daemons:  swat
clients:  ALL except LOCAL .void.org 192.168.0. 127.
option:   DENY
access:   denied

>>> Rule hosts.allow line 7:
daemons:  ALL
clients:  ALL
option:   DENY
access:   denied
```

Testing a couple of clients with tcpdmatch, you get the hoped for responses:

```
tcpdmatch -d ipop3d locutus2.calderasystems.com

client:   hostname locutus2.calderasystems.com
client:   address  207.179.18.140
server:   process  ipop3d
matched:  hosts.allow line 1
option:   ALLOW
access:   granted
```

With similar results for in.ftpd, you look now to the imap daemon you only want the local host to access:

```
tcpdmatch -d imapd foo

warning: foo: hostname alias
warning: (official name: foo.void.org)
client:   hostname foo.void.org
client:   address  192.168.0.1
server:   process  imapd
matched:  hosts.allow line 4
option:   spawn (/usr/sbin/safe_finger -l @foo.void.org | /usr/bin/mail root) &
option:   DENY
access:   denied
```

Testing the telnet server shows you the following:

```
warning: foo: hostname alias
warning: (official name: foo.void.org)
client:   hostname foo.void.org
client:   address  192.168.0.1
server:   process  in.telnetd
matched:  hosts.allow line 5
option:   banners /etc/banners
```

```
WARNING:  Unauthorized entry into this system for any reason is
a criminal act and will be prosecuted to the fullest extent of the law.

option:   ALLOW
access:   granted
```

Testing a non-local client for `telnet` access, you receive the following:

```
client:   hostname locutus2.calderasystems.com
client:   address  207.179.18.140
server:   process  in.telnetd
matched:  hosts.allow line 7
option:   DENY
access:   denied
```

Creating a few more hypothetical matches shows that the rules you've created do what you want. Just remember that only those TCP services administered by `inetd` are protected in this way. Other services that do not run out of `inetd` or UDP services must be protected by other means, such as `netfilter`.

## CHAPTER 35

IP MASQUERADING

In this chapter

IP MASQUERADING, NETWORK ADDRESS TRANSLATION, AND PORT FORWARDING

This chapter, by its title, purports to discuss IP Masquerading. And in fact, it does. If you participate in any Linux mailing lists you'll undoubtedly see this term come up. But IP Masquerading as such has changed its status with the new Linux 2.4.x series kernels and the framework software that handles IP address rewriting and mangling.

Linux now uses the netfilter software through a userland interface called iptables to perform stateful packet filtering, which you can read about in Chapter 36, "IP Firewalling." It uses the same userland interface to perform network address translation (NAT), masquerading, and port forwarding.

If you're not familiar with the concept of NAT, it basically enables you to rewrite packet headers as they pass through the firewall. These headers can be written as they are leaving the firewall (post-routing) and involve changing the source address from the system initiating the connection to the firewall's outer address. The server on the Internet then sees a connection originating from the firewall or NAT system. Because the source address is what is being changed, netfilter calls this Source NAT (SNAT). You can use this to shield a network with public IPs. A specialized form of SNAT, IP masquerading, is commonly used to allow a network with private IPs (Internet non-routable IPs) to be able to access the Internet. Both do the same basic thing, and both can be used with private IPs. IP masquerading, though, is now generally reserved for dial-up accounts with dynamic IPs. If you don't know what IP you are assigned when you connect to your ISP, this is probably what you have, so you'll need the masquerading target rather than the SNAT target. More about this is in the following text.

The other type of NAT, or packet mangling, that netfilter allows is called Destination NAT (DNAT). This form of address mangling is performed pre-routing and is used to take an initial connection to the NAT system and redirect it to an internal system. In some circles this is called *port forwarding*, because forwarding generally occurs based on the initial connection port. This would enable you to have separate systems on your trusted network to handle HTTP, FTP, mail, DNS, and so forth, but look to the world like the NAT box is doing it all. This particular form of address mangling requires you to have a routable IP. If you must use masquerading, then you won't be able to use DNAT.

Most commonly, packet filtering firewall software is used to hide an internal public network and allow only certain traffic to enter. This type of network is depicted in Figure 35.1.

A networking scheme exists that does not follow this recipe. That is home and small business networks, most of which do not have legitimate blocks of IP addresses to work with, and most of which only have dial-up access to other TCP/IP networks, in particular the Internet (see Figure 35.2). They are assigned an IP from a pool of available IPs with each connection.

Figure 35.1
Network with a block
of IP addresses.

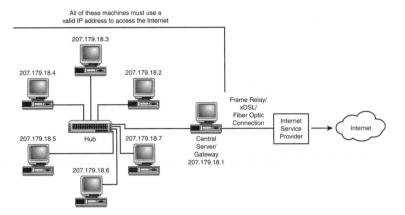

Figure 35.2
Network with one IP
public address and IP
masquerading.

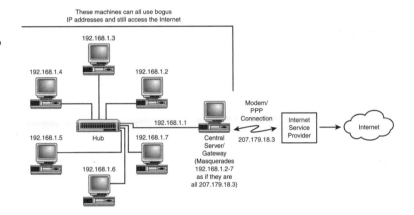

Using IP masquerading, a home or small business network can offer all connected machines access to an outside network such as the Internet using a single IP address on a single-server machine. All Internet-bound network packets are masqueraded as if they were being sent from the server that is running IP masquerading. The server maintains the information necessary to route the returning network packets back to the machines that are supposed to receive them. Those of you quick on the pickup might say, "But every connection is both SNAT and DNAT, depending on which direction the packets are flowing." But it's the initial connection packet, that is, SYN packet (a packet with only the SYN bit set), that determines which we're doing. After that, connection tracking allows return packets to get back to the originating system. Connection tracking makes netfilter *stateful*, an overused marketing buzzword that means it recognizes the state of a connection (new, established, and related). It also allows netfilter to run faster. Because related, established connections don't run the entire set of rules, netfilter remembers the rules pertaining to the connection, using those and short-circuiting the rest.

PART

V

CH

35

REQUIRED KERNEL COMPONENTS

The Linux kernel that ships with most Linux distributions is precompiled with everything you need to utilize IP masquerading. All that needs to be done to implement it is to load some kernel modules and set up some simple firewall rules.

For those who want to compile their own kernels, following is the list of items that need to be compiled into the kernel for NAT and IP masquerading to work (the names are listed as they are seen during a `make config` or `make menuconfig` procedure):

- Code maturity options:
  - Prompt for development or incomplete code or drivers
- Loadable module support:
  - Enable loadable module support
  - Kernel module loader (optional)
- Networking options:
  - Network packet filtering
  - Network packet filtering debugging (optional)
  - TCP/IP networking
  - IP Netfilter configuration:
    - Connection tracking
    - FTP protocol support
    - IP tables support
    - Full NAT
    - `MASQUERADE` target support
  - The IPv6 protocol (optional)
  - IPv6 Netfilter configuration
    - IP6 tables support
    - Packet filtering

In addition to these modules (some of which are optional), others can be chosen, depending on your needs. Consult Chapter 36 for additional information about modules that you might want to select for additional packet filtering and logging.

> **Caution**
>
> Some kernel configuration options should never be selected. Particularly, don't select Fast Switching, because it bypasses the packet filter rules. Also never select any protocols that netfilter can't handle, such as IPX, Appletalk, and so forth, or IPv6 if you don't select IP6 filter modules.

Setup

IP masquerading is accomplished though the packet-filtering firewall capabilities of modern Linux kernels. When an outgoing network packet hits the firewall machine (the server with IP masquerading set up on it), the firewall rewrites elements of each packet to make them look as if they are emanating from the firewall and not the machine behind the firewall. The return packets are modified to go back to the machine that sent the original outgoing packets. To both ends of the transaction, nothing odd seems to be going on at all.

Some services, such as FTP, require special handling, thus the module to support FTP connection tracking. This is because an active FTP connection uses two separate ports, 21 for control, and 20 for data transfer. This complicates things because the connection to port 20 comes not from the client, but from the server in response to the client. This is not required for passive downloads, which use only the control channel (port 21), the default for Netscape and Internet Explorer. But for other FTP clients, you'll need the FTP connection tracking and the nat FTP modules loaded (unless you started them in passive mode or like ncftp will automatically switch).

Chapter 19, "Kernel Modules," details how to automatically load modules every time your system boots. If you want to use any (or all) of these modules, refer to that chapter for details on how to load them. The following modules should probably be loaded for a Masquerading server:

- `ip_tables`
- `iptable_nat`
- `ip_conntrack`
- `ip_conntrack_ftp`
- `ip_nat_ftp`
- `ipt_MASQUERADE`

For the most part, the `iptables` commands you'll issue will tell you which modules should be loaded. (See Chapter 36 for a program which will load all available `iptables` modules.)

The first thing that you need to do to start masquerading is to create a network with bogus IP addresses. The blocks of IP addresses allocated for private networks as listed in RFC 1597 are shown in Table 35.1.

TABLE 35.1   PRIVATE NETWORK ADDRESS BLOCKS

Class	Address Start	Address End	Mask
A	10.0.0.0	10.255.255.255	8
B	172.16.0.0	172.31.255.255	16
C	192.168.0.0	192.168.255.255	24

Unless literally hundreds of computers are to be set up on the network, odds are that one of the Class C blocks is what you'll want to use.

The iptables utility is used to set up the forwarding rules for IP masquerading. The following syntax is used:

```
iptables -t nat -A POSTROUTING -j MASQUERADE -o ppp+ -s private_IP_network/mask -d
➥0/0
```

In this command, replace `private_IP_network` with the beginning IP address from Table 35.1 for the class of addresses you are using, and replace `mask` with the corresponding mask value. The `-o` specifies the outgoing interface. The `ppp+` means the ppp interface (usually `ppp0`, the `+` meaning any active ppp interface). You can substitute `eth0`, `tr0`, `ippp0`, and so on, for `ppp+`.

For example, if a Class C address block is being used by the computers on the network, the following command is used:

```
iptables -t nat -A POSTROUTING -j MASQUERADE -o ppp+ -s 192.168.0.0/24 -d 0/0
```

In most cases, this is all that needs to be done to set up the firewall rules. Combined with the modules listed earlier, most of the common Internet services are covered by this configuration.

> **Note**
>
> You must make sure your system has IP_forwarding enabled. You can do this in Caldera by using COAS (coastool) and selecting Network Administration, TCP/IP Network Options, IP Forwarding, Enabled from the main menu. Or you can change the `/etc/sysconfig/network` file to read `IPFORWARDING=yes`. Debian has an `ip_forward` variable in `/etc/network/options` you can change. And in Red Hat, you can change the `net.ipv4.ip_forward` variable in `/etc/sysctl.conf` from 0 to 1. As a final option, you can include a line like the following in your `/etc/rc.d/rc.local` (or equivalent) file:
>
> `echo 1 > /proc/sys/net/ipv4/ip_forward`
>
> All accomplish the same thing: changing the `/proc/sys/net/ipv4/ip_forwarding` kernel variable to 1 to permit passing packets from one interface (IP address) to another.

It is important to note that IP masquerading is, for the most part, a one-way street. You can go from the machines on your network out to the Internet, but without special packet-forwarding rules, you cannot get into the systems behind the masquerading server from the Internet. This means that a machine that has a bogus IP address and is sitting behind a masquerading server cannot serve Web pages out on the Internet, nor can it accept direct FTP connections from the outside, nor telnet, nor ssh/secure transactions, and so on without some special rules. If you have routable addresses behind the firewall/NAT system, you might want to deny forwarding so that only masqueraded addresses are passed with this rule:

```
iptables -p FORWARD DENY
```

> **Note**
>
> If you want to see the rules you've input, it is not intuitively obvious from the usage message or the man page, but remember that you're working with the NAT table. To see the rules from this chapter, you'll need to use the following:
>
> `iptables -t nat -L -n`

SNAT

Masquerading, as we have previously discussed it, is just a special case of source NAT. If you happen to have a public, static IP, you don't want masquerading—what you want is source network address translation (SNAT). You'll want to use SNAT instead of masquerading where possible for some of the features SNAT brings, including mapping your hosts to multiple IP addresses.

Looking at a few examples and their explanations might help your understanding:

```
iptables -t nat -A POSTROUTING -o eth0 -j SNAT --to 209.127.112.150
```

The preceding line says you want to use the NAT table (`-t nat`) and append to the POSTROUTING chain. You're going to use the outgoing interface `eth0` (this is the Internet-connected interface) and change the source address of the originating system (`-j SNAT`) to the public `IP 209.127.112.150` (`--to 209.127.112.150`).

This simple example performs exactly the same function as the previous MASQUERADE example, but you need to know the IP (so this won't work on a dynamically assigned address).

Now let's assume for argument's sake that you have six usable IPs, and you want to use four of them on your NAT firewall. The following example will show how to use `iptables` to make it look like you're coming from any one of four addresses:

```
iptables -t nat -A POSTROUTING -o eth0 -j SNAT --to 209.127.112.150-209.127.112.153
```

The difference between this example and the one earlier in this section is in the `--to` address. Each connection going out will pick up the next IP number. When the last IP number is reached, `iptables` will wrap the addresses back to the first IP number.

Let's also assume you have some rogue users on your network who have been connecting to non-standard ports on the outside, presumably for some unauthorized activities (like IRC chat). You want to permit them to use only standard ports. You can do this by specifying a port range as well:

```
iptables -t nat -A POSTROUTING -p tcp -o eth0 -j SNAT --to 209.127.112.150:0-1023
```

Now, outgoing TCP connections destined for ports 0–1023 will pass through. You'll want to add a UDP rule because DNS uses UDP port 53 for most queries, but large queries and zone transfers will use TCP port 53. One set of upper ports of interest includes 6000–6255 (but most commonly 6000–6010). So if you want to run X through your firewall, you'll need to add a rule that includes these ports. This text will not debate the sagacity of running X through a firewall, just remind administrators they should consider the inherent security risks.

DNAT

Complementing source NAT is destination NAT (DNAT). This particular translation works in reverse. Under the older ipchains, you had to use ipmasqadm to achieve what was called port forwarding, and is now called DNAT. DNAT enables you to use the public IP addresses for functions such as FTP server, Web server, mail server, and so forth, without putting those systems at as high a risk. Behind a firewall, they are better protected.

PART

V

CH

35

Consider the following example:

```
iptables -t nat -A PREROUTING -p tcp --dport 80 -i eth0 -j DNAT --to 192.168.0.2:80
```

This `iptables` rule will perform NAT prerouting. This allows the destination address change to be applied before the packet hits the kernel routing table. The only packets are TCP packets destined for `port 80` (our http server) and coming in on `eth0` (other interfaces are not affected by this rule). Our destination NAT (DNAT) rule says to redirect all traffic to this interface on port 80 to 192.168.0.2 on port 80 there.

The `iptables` rules can also provide some rudimentary load balancing. If a range of IPs is the target, netfilter will send the packet to the target with the fewest connections. So if you have several DNS servers behind your firewall, netfilter can help balance which DNS server is hit.

PROJECT: BUILDING A NAT SYSTEM

Let's take what you've learned and use it to build a NAT system for your network. The following are the parameters:

- You are assigned the 209.127.112.0/29 IP address block from your ISP. Your T1 router (CSU/DSU) is assigned 209.127.112.1. You will use 209.127.112.2 and 209.127.112.3 on your NAT firewall.

- Your internal network is 192.168.10.0/24, and your NAT system (gateway) is 192.168.10.1 (eth0). You have the following systems on your network:
  - 192.168.10.2 Web server
  - 192.168.10.3 mail server
  - 192.168.10.4 FTP server
  - 192.168.10.5 MySQL server on port 3306

  Each system runs Webmin w/SSL on port 10000, but you need to administer any internal system from outside.

- All incoming traffic comes in on 209.127.112.2 (eth1). You want to use 209.127.112.3 (eth2) for your outgoing connections.

- You want to allow outgoing connections to all privileged ports (0–1023) and port 3306.

- You want your road warriors to be able to POP mail from the mail server while traveling (their systems are already configured for sending and receiving mail while away from the office) .

All of this is shown graphically in Figure 35.3.

Putting the rules together you might have something like the following:

- The following two rules enable connections to privileged ports (both TCP and UDP) to be masqueraded:

```
iptables -t nat -A POSTROUTING -o eth2 -p tcp -j SNAT --to 209.127.112.3:0-1023
iptables -t nat -A POSTROUTING -o eth2 -p udp -j SNAT --to 209.127.112.3:0-1023
```

- This rule enables users to connect to a MySQL server (or any other server binding port 3306) to pass through the firewall and be masqueraded:

```
iptables -t nat -A POSTROUTING -o eth2 -p tcp -j SNAT --to 209.127.112.3:3306
```

- This rule masquerades ICMP traffic:

```
iptables -t nat -A POSTROUTING -i -p ICMP -j SNAT --to 209.127.112.3
```

- The following five rules port forward http (port 80), email (port 25), POP3 (port 110), FTP (port 21), and MySQL (port 3306) to the appropriate systems:

```
iptables -t nat -A PREROUTING -i eth1 -p tcp --dport 80 -j DNAT --to
➥192.168.10.2:80
iptables -t nat -A PREROUTING -i eth1 -p tcp --dport 25 -j DNAT --to
➥192.168.10.3:25
iptables -t nat -A PREROUTING -i eth1 -p tcp --dport 110 -j DNAT --to
➥192.168.10.3:110
iptables -t nat -A PREROUTING -i eth1 -p tcp --dport 21 -j DNAT --to
➥192.168.10.4:21
iptables -t nat -A PREROUTING -i eth1 -p tcp --dport 3306 -j DNAT --to
➥192.168.10.5:3306
```

- The next four rules use a little ingenuity to port Webmin traffic through the firewall to the appropriate system on port 10000. Note the use of matching IPs to ports:

```
iptables -t nat -A PREROUTING -i eth1 -p tcp --dport 10002 -j DNAT --to
➥192.168.10.2:10000
iptables -t nat -A PREROUTING -i eth1 -p tcp --dport 10003 -j DNAT --to
➥192.168.10.3:10000
iptables -t nat -A PREROUTING -i eth1 -p tcp --dport 10004 -j DNAT --to
➥192.168.10.4:10000
iptables -t nat -A PREROUTING -i eth1 -p tcp --dport 10005 -j DNAT --to
➥192.168.10.5:10000
```

Figure 35.3
Network configuration.

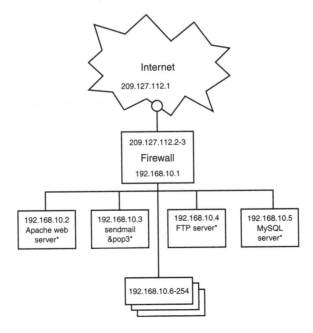

These rules should get you started and give you a good idea of how to manipulate rules and mangle IP:Port numbers. This is by no means complete. You'll want to read Chapter 36, particularly the section explaining established and related connections. Logging can also help you if you can't see where connections are refused or dropped.

CHAPTER 36

IP FIREWALLING

In this chapter

INTRODUCTION TO FIREWALLS

The term *firewall* comes from the firewall that is used in cars (and other motorized vehicles), which protects the occupants in the cabin in case of a fire in the engine compartment. A firewall on a network protects both users and the data that is behind it on the local network from the savagery of the Internet (or extranet). It can also be used to prevent users on the local network from connecting to prohibited sites, and to compartmentalize the internal network.

Some people learn too late that a firewall does not protect against insiders. Internal firewalls can be used to isolate departments so that damage is not widespread; for example, firewalls can be used to protect accounting from engineering, and engineering from sales, each of which likely has little or no business browsing through files that belong to the others.

Basically, two kinds of firewalls exist in Linux and each basic type has two subtypes. The two basic types are packet filters and proxy firewalls. The packet filter firewalls can be one of the following types:

- **Forwarding**—It is in this type of packet filter firewall that decisions are made whether to forward or not.

- **Masquerading**—These firewalls rewrite the source and destination addresses.

Proxy firewalls can be one of the following types:

- **Standard**—With this type of proxy firewall, a client connects to a special port and is redirected to go out through another. port.

- **Transparent**—With this firewall, the client doesn't use a special port, but the firewall software proxies the connection through transparently.

This chapter deals primarily with packet filtering firewalls. The information in this chapter is designed to complement and round out the information in Chapter 35, "IP Masquerading."

PACKET FILTERS

Packet filtering firewalls work on the following principle: The information that is needed to make a decision about what to do with a packet is contained in the header. The header contains information regarding the source and destination addresses, time to live (TTL), protocol, and much more. It also contains a header checksum that helps identify whether the header has been corrupted. In all, some thirteen separate fields of information are contained in an IP header, many of which contain multiple pieces of information. For complete details, refer to RFC 791 (available from `http://www.rfc-editor.org/rfc.html`).

IP does not check the payload other than to tell whether the payload is the correct size. The transport control protocol (TCP) is responsible for ensuring the integrity of the data payload. UDP packets have no inherent error checking.

Linux, starting with the new 2.4.0 kernel, uses netfilter and the iptables userland utility to provide packet filtering. To implement a packet filtering firewall, decisions must be made regarding the types of packets to address specifically, and what to do with those packets when they are encountered.

The iptables software permits a number of different criteria to be applied to packets. The criteria can be applied to incoming packets, outgoing packets, or packets that will pass through the firewall. These decisions can be based on where the packets came from by address, where they are going by address, or where they are going by port. Different rules can be applied, depending on whether these are TCP packets, UDP packets, or ICMP packets. The netfilter framework also works on packet pre- and post-routing, and can filter connections based on new, established, or related connections, as well as address packets specifically based on set flags in the packet. Netfilter can also mangle packets, changing flags, which can then be used to prioritize packet queuing. Finally, for any packets that are not specifically addressed, the overall policy determines the fate of the packets.

The netfilter ability to handle packets associated with established or related connections makes netfilter "stateful." This is an overly abused marketing term that means the software can track connections. Actually, any packet filter software (like the older ipchains from Linux kernel version 2.2.x) that permits active FTP sessions is stateful. This also applies to any software capable of tracking masqueraded connections. Netfilter allows rules to be applied specifically to established or related connections. Netfilter also tracks these connections and subsequent (established or related) packets don't traverse the entire set of rules, but only use those that applied to the initial connection, making netfilter faster.

PROXY FIREWALLS

Proxy firewalls work differently than packet filters do. All traffic is received on the firewall, whether it is incoming or outgoing. But proxies redirect permitted traffic through the firewall by rewriting the headers. To be redirected, the traffic must log in to the firewall. In fact, much of the discussion in the preceding section is applicable to a proxy. The difference is subtle; because packet filtering software is rewriting the headers when it is masquerading, it is difficult to explain that there is a difference between a transparent proxy and a masquerading (packet filter) firewall. But the main difference is that the proxy redirects (locally) the traffic that is arriving at one interface and leaving by another, and a packet filter normally does not redirect all traffic. Looking at it from a different perspective, proxies work higher up in the OSI model than packet filters.

Note

Any router, gateway, or host that transports a networking packet from one network to another rewrites the header. But this rewriting doesn't alter the source or destination addresses; it only alters the TTL and checksum, and—on occasion—the total length and fragment offset (among others), if the packet needs to be fragmented to continue. When header rewriting is discussed in this text, it refers mostly to address rewriting.

The Open Source Interconnect (OSI) model is one of the popular models that is used to explain how packets move from the Application layer to the Physical layer (it might not be completely accurate, but it's a good theoretical paradigm nevertheless). The seven layers are used to explain where certain software works. For the purposes of this text, it is only important to note that the level where each works is different, and that this is one of the distinguishing characteristics between proxies and packet filters.

But this difference is important. Proxies are more overhead intensive, but they can inspect entire packets more thoroughly. They also tend to be a little more difficult to set up initially, and can often do other things, such as cache connections to speed access.

WHICH TO USE?

Packet filtering firewalls and proxying firewalls perform similar functions. They act as shields to protect trusted network segments from untrusted ones. In this regard, each works equally well. Both require monitoring and occasional reconfiguring; both, if they are misconfigured, provide only a false sense of security; and both, when implemented in a methodical, well thought-out manner, can provide a modicum of security.

If you remember that the only secure system is the one that is not assembled and powered on (and therefore not of much use, either), you'll have a more realistic idea of what firewalls can buy you: time to react to an attack. It remains your responsibility to reconfigure the firewall to protect against this attack. I want to emphasize one point: A firewall buys you time to react to an attack. Time will be both your friend and your enemy. The warning time you get that you are under attack works for you. But the moment a breach occurs and the attacker is in, time works against you, so you do need to routinely monitor your firewall's activity.

Basically, whether you use packet filtering or proxying comes down to an individual decision, and might be based on the prior experiences of those who are involved in maintaining the firewall. If you are implementing a firewall and have worked with proxies before and are comfortable with them, by all means, continue. The use of one type doesn't preclude use of the other. Some proxies that are designed to work specifically with Web (HTTP) traffic can complement a packet filter nicely. For example, the use of junkbuster to block particular Web sites or advertising banners is often easier than writing packet filtering rules to deny or reject the banner sites. Conversely, iptables rules can be created solely for the purpose of logging traffic, and can be used in conjunction with a proxy to track specific kinds of traffic. So the best option might be to mix and match, depending on your overall objectives and level of comfort.

From a security standpoint, therefore, neither is better. The one place in which iptables might tip the balance is in situations in which you want to rewrite the Type of Service (TOS) field to optimize traffic flow.

You can use iptables to modify the TOS field to specify one of minimum delay, maximum reliability, maximum throughput, minimum cost, or normal service.

PHYSICAL CONFIGURATIONS

When discussing physical configurations, you need to look at both the hardware and the software as it applies to the firewall. Remembering that one of the reasons the firewall exists is to protect the trusted network from the untrusted network, this host must necessarily be both the funnel for network traffic that is moving between the two networks, making it a possible choke point, and the focus for those who are looking to penetrate your security. If they want to come in, they've got to pass through here first.

PART
V

CH
36

> **Note**
>
> Often overlooked, but very important, are rogue users with dial-up connections to the Internet who effectively circumvent all the security your firewall provides.

THE FIREWALL HOST

You need to consider the type of host you want to install. You can install a firewall that has only one interface, and uses that interface for both trusted and untrusted connections; but you'll want to consider whether this is wise, taking into account the cost of a second interface versus the weakened security posture that this configuration entails. It is better to have a host with two interfaces, which completely isolates one network from the other. With this configuration, bypassing the firewall becomes more difficult.

A host that isolates an untrusted network from a trusted network using two interfaces—one for each network—is termed a Bastion Host.

The question of how powerful a system needs to be depends on your decisions; if you are going to use the firewall to connect two 10Mb Ethernet cards, and if you plan to use packet filtering and no proxies, an 80486×33 processor with 16MB RAM is sufficient for low to moderate traffic loads. However, if you plan to use 100Mhz Ethernet cards in a high traffic route, this CPU will not be able to keep up with the demand and you'll experience significant packet loss.

THE FIREWALL KERNEL

Most distributions today include the firewall code in the standard kernel. Review your installation to see if that's true. If it is, you'll find the firewall modules in `/lib/modules/${kernel-version}/kernel/net/ipv[46]/`. However, this text will cover the kernel just in case you decide to reconfigure it for yourself. Several parameters must be set in the kernel to permit packet filtering. Some of these are subjective and are based on your hardware; one must be turned off; others are required. For more information on building a custom kernel, see Chapter 18, "Building a Custom Kernel." The first parameter follows:

```
Code maturity level options -> Select developmental and/or incoomplete
code/drivers
```

As of this writing, the 2.4.x kernel has not been released, so some changes to what you see here might take place. To have all the kernel parameters you will need, you'll have to select the developmental drivers. These parameters will all say "(EXPERIMENTAL)" next to them. Consider that they may be incomplete or buggy (or both).

When building a new kernel, you'll want to build a kernel with minimum modules and insert those modules during bootup. You should not build unnecessary modules, and you should have some way to ensure that the modules you're using are the ones you built (such as using Tripwire to monitor the /lib/modules/`uname -r`/ subdirectories. The reasoning behind this is that anyone can build a module. If someone manages to crack your security, they'll want access again. Rather than amateurishly adding a user with root privileges, they can drop a loadable module on your system, have it inserted, and then erase the other traces of entry. Although this is extreme and a rather sophisticated way to go about it, it has been done and will enable nearly undetectable access to your system. So kernel modules can be dangerous. On the other hand, anyone this sophisticated can, most likely, easily find other means to enter the system. Unfortunately, to enable access to some code, module support is required:

```
Loadable module support -> Enable loadable module support
```

The Set version information on all module symbols prevents modules from other kernels to be dropped on your system and used. Only disable this if you must load foreign modules (such as for an Ethernet card not supported in the kernel). You can also enable the kernel module loader, but this enables automatic loading of modules and is also a potential security risk.

In all other kernel configuration sections, give careful thought to the parameters that you select. You need to support your hardware (disk drives), the filesystem (normally ext2), Ethernet drivers, other communications drivers (modems, ISDN devices, and protocols such as PPP), and the ELF file format. But sound and other unnecessary parameters should be disabled.

If this is a home network or part of a small, low-profile business with low bandwidth dial-up connection, you might not need or want to go to the extremes detailed in this chapter. On the other hand, if you're connected through RoadRunner or @Home or are using another cable modem provider, you'll want to follow this chapter fairly closely. But only you can perform a proper risk assessment for your situation.

With the other sections appropriately set, the section that needs to be detailed is "Networking Options." Although it is not the last section in the kernel configuration, it is certainly the most important for the purposes of this chapter.

NETWORKING OPTIONS

The Linux 2.4.x kernel adds significant complexity to the networking options section from the 2.2.x kernels. The additional options can be daunting, and the help is not always very helpful. Plan to spend some time getting acquainted with this section. Items that are of interest are highlighted here; some of these items are required, others are recommended, and still others are optional.

Items that are marked as not recommended have the potential for weakening your firewall. If you know that you won't use it, don't install it.

The following parameter is required for programs such as tcpdump. However, tcpdump puts your Ethernet card in promiscuous mode, so is not recommended:

```
Packet socket                          not recommended
```

If you're going to use the packet socket, either built-in or as a module, you can use memory mapped IO, which will make it faster. Use this only if you think you need the speed:

```
Packet socket: mmapped IO              optional
```

The following parameter requires devices with major number 36 to communicate. If this option is chosen, Routing messages needs to also be chosen, as does IP firewall packet netlink device, which can be used to warn of possible attacks:

```
Kernel/User netlink socket             recommended
```

Using mknod

To create the devices mentioned in the text, you'll need to use the mknod command to create them. Consulting /usr/src/linux/Documentation/devices.txt, you see the following:

```
36 char        Netlink support

               0 = /dev/route        Routing, device updates, kernel to user

               1 = /dev/skip         enSKIP security cache control

               3 = /dec/fwmonitor    Firewall packet copies

              16 = /dev/tap0         First Ethertap device

                 ...

              31 = /dev/tap15        16th Ethertap device
```

The above citation tells you how to create the devices. Using mknod, you tell the utility the name of the device, then put c for character type device, then the major and minor numbers as follows (commands performed as root from inside the /dev directory):

```
mknod route c 36 0

mknod fwmonitor c 36 3

mknod tap0 c 36 16
```

Use of the following parameter requires /dev/route to be created with major 36 so that you can read routing information:

```
Routing messages                       optional
Netlink device emulation               optional
```

The following is required for packet filters or masquerading, but not for proxy firewalls (firewalls that don't use iptables):

```
Network packet filtering (replaces ipchains)      required
```

If you find you have problems with netfilter, you might want to turn on debugging, but be warned that this will fill your system logs very rapidly:

```
Network packet filtering debugging                optional
```

The following is only required if you also want to filter UNIX sockets (non-TCP):

```
Socket Filtering              optional
```

UNIX sockets are used for a large number of tasks on most systems. Unless you know what you are doing and are running an embedded system, you'll need this:

```
Unix domain sockets                required
```

If you're reading this chapter, the following parameter is absolutely essential:

```
TCP/IP networking                  required
```

Unless you are participating in the MBONE, you probably won't want this next parameter:

```
IP: multicasting              optional
```

The following parameter is highly recommended because one of its effects is to tell the kernel to reject packets arriving on an illogical interface (spoofing—source addresses that don't match their arrival route). Choosing this option will also prevent the use of asymmetric routing (different inbound and outbound routes or multiple inbound or outbound routes which don't use the firewall as a common route), which should not be used with netfilter:

```
IP: advanced router                recommended
```

The following parameter permits use of the source as well as destination for routing decisions, and will permit use of two subsequent parameters that can be useful for queuing and routing decisions:

```
IP: policy routing                 recommended
```

The following two parameters can be used for routing decisions where desired, including address translations:

```
IP: use netfilter MARK value as routing key     optional
IP: fast network address translation            recommended
```

The next parameter will allow the system to choose between different routes (interfaces) where possible:

```
IP: equal cost multipath           optional
```

The next two parameters are fairly self-explanatory, the first allowing for priority queuing, the second telling the kernel to be verbose in reporting what it's doing:

```
IP: use TOS value as routing key        optional
IP: verbose route monitoring            optional
```

If you have several interfaces, and large, complex routing tables, you'll need the following option. Most firewalls will not need this:

```
IP: large routing tables           optional
```

No firewall should depend on any other system for its configuration or operation, it should be 100% independent (this option has two suboptions, bootp support and rarp support, which will not be discussed):

```
IP: kernel level autoconfiguration         not recommended
```

The following parameter permits IP to tunnel (be encapsulated in) IP. Most users won't need this, but if the firewall is to act as an agent for a mobile system, you'll need this:

```
IP: tunneling                    optional
```

If you want to build an IP tunnel encapsulating GRE (that is, you have a Cisco router at the other end of the tunnel), you'll want to include this, otherwise it is not much use. Also, if you want to build a multicast WAN, the second parameter, along with multicast routing will be needed:

```
IP: GRE tunnels over IP              optional
IP: broadcast GRE over IP            optional
```

If you want to use multicast routing, you'll need to choose the first parameter below. The other two parameters act to modify how the multicast routing works:

```
IP: multicast routing               optional
IP: PIM-SM version 1 support          optional
IP: PIM-SM version 2 support          optional
```

Select the following parameter if your firewall is connected to a large, switched network (more than 256 systems):

```
IP: ARP deamon support (EXPERIMENTAL)       optional
```

The following parameter affects routing and tunneling code, permitting reporting of congestion and on which interface(s):

```
IP: TCP Explicit Congestion Notification support    optional
```

If you come under SYN denial of service attacks, you might want to include the next parameter. By default, this support is disabled in the kernel even thought the code is included, so it will not affect operations until explicitly invoked:

```
IP: TCP syncookie support (disabled per default)    optional
```

Selecting the IP Netfilter Configuration will take you to a new menu, which contains all the parameters for IP firewalling with netfilter under IPv4. You must go to this menu to choose the firewall options you want to include:

```
IP: Netfilter Configuration ->           required
```

Connection tracking allows netfilter to keep track of FTP and masqueraded connections. Choosing connection tracking will also provide the second option listed, FTP protocol support. You'll want FTP protocol support if you plan to allow active FTP connection through the firewall:

```
Connection tracking (required for masq/NAT)     recommended
FTP protocol support             recommended
```

Choosing the userspace queuing option will allow packets to be passed to the netlink device where they can be read by userspace tools:

```
Userspace queuing via NETLINK (EXPRIMENTAL)        optional
```

IP tables support is what netfilter is all about. If you don't choose this, you won't be able to run netfilter:

```
IP tables support (required for filtering/masq/NAT)    required
```

The limit option will build support that can be used to limit the number of duplicate messages logged so your logs don't overflow from hundreds of thousands of duplicate messages. If you do any logging at all, you'll want this option:

```
limit match support                        optional
```

The new netfilter allows for all kinds of ways to filter packets, including by MAC address. Obviously, this is only effective against hosts to which you are directly connected (that is, there's no router between them and you). But if someone likes to put their personal laptop on your network using their desktop system's IP, this option can prevent them from using your Internet connection:

```
MAC address match support                  optional
```

The netfilter MARK option will permit you to use netfilter to mangle packets and mark them for special routing, queuing, or logging. If you have special needs, you might want to include this:

```
netfilter MARK match support                optional
```

The multiple port match support permits a range of ports to be used in an iptables rule rather than just one port. This can reduce the number of individual rules and provide more flexibility:

```
Multiple port match support                optional
```

If you want to prioritize packets based on the TOS (which can also be set using netfilter), you'll need this option:

```
TOS match support                        recommended
```

Netfilter can recognize and work with a connection state if this option is chosen. Connection states include new, established, related, and unknown. If you want to use the stateful features of netfilter, you'll need this option:

```
Connection state match support             recommended
```

Unclean match support applies to any packet not related to an established connection that appears to be other than a new connection. This can be invalid packets, or reply packets for which netfilter knows of no related, established connection, to include ICMP echo replies for which no echo request was sent, or SYN-ACK packets for which no SYN packet was sent. You'll almost certainly want this:

```
Unclean match support (EXPERIMENTAL)          recommended
```

The owner match support permits packets generated locally (on the localhost only) to be matched for user, group, session, or process. This module is only of use if the localhost is to be used as a workstation:

```
Owner match support (EXPERIMENTAL)             optional
```

The packet filtering option is required if you want to filter packets, that is change the ACCEPT or DROP status of a packet passing through any of the iptables rules. Selecting packet filtering also provides two additional options, REJECT target support and MIRROR target support. Additional targets can be added here in the future. Although ACCEPT and DROP targets are built-in, REJECT (which sends back an ICMP message) is not. The MIRROR target can be used to swap source and destination, effectively setting up a mirror. Using this, you can reflect packets back to the sender:

```
Packet filtering                      recommended
REJECT target support                     recommended
MIRROR target support (EXPERIMENTAL)          optional
```

The full NAT support is required for any and all forms of NAT, including source NAT, destination NAT, and masquerading. Selecting this option also enables two other options, MASQUERADE target support, required for masquerading, and REDIRECT target support, required for redirecting ports within the host (used for proxying):

```
Full NAT                    recommended
MASQUERADE target support                 optional
REDIRECT target support                   optional
```

The next option, packet mangling, allows you to mangle packets apart from NAT and masquerading. Choosing packet mangling brings up two additional choices, TOS target support and MARK target support. If you want to use the TOS match (previously given) you'll first need to set the TOS with the TOS target. The same is true for the MARK target support:

```
Packet mangling             recommended
TOS target support                    recommended
MARK target support                   optional
```

The LOG target support option provides for iptables rules that allow you to select and log packets. If you choose this, you'll almost certainly want the limit match support provided above:

```
LOG target support                    recommended
```

The final two options on this menu provide for backward compatibility. Note, however, that although these provide you with the ability to load your old rulesets while you work on translating them to iptables rules, some rules simply will not work. Additionally, you can use one of iptables, ipchains, or ipmasqadm, but you cannot use more than one at any given time.

```
ipchains (2.2-style) support                    not recommended
ipfwadm (2.0-style) support                      not recommended
```

Up to this point, only IPv4 options have been selected. In returning to the main Networking options menu, the IPv6 selections are presented. If you have access to IPv6, you may enable its use here. Three options present themselves, subsequent options depend on the selection of the preceding option:

```
The IPv6 protocol (EXPERIMENTAL)            optional
IPv6: enable EUI-64 token format            optional
IPv6: disable provider based address            optional
```

If you choose any or all of the above IPv6 options, you should also choose to enter the IPv6 netfilter configuration menu:

```
IPv6: Netfilter Configuration ->              recommended
```

To filter IPv6, you'll need the IPv6 tables support:

```
IPv6 tables support (required for filtering/masq/NAT)    recommended
```

Each of the subsequent five options presented under the IPv6 netfilter configuration menu is equivalent to their QPv4 counterpart and will not be recovered here. Note that IPv6 still lacks a number of the IPv4 support options.

The two options following the IPv6 netfilter configuration menu option, kernel httpd acceleration and asynchronous transfer mode, are both acceptable options for use with netfilter. Although httpd should not run on a dedicated firewall, home users might want to run httpd and would do well to consider using the khttpd module. The ATM option is an IPv4 option and completely compatible.

The section beyond the IP protocols that starts out with IPX should not be used. Netfilter only works on IPv4 and IPv6. It does not understand any of the protocols covered beyond its scope, and in fact they can be dangerous because they can provide ways to bypass the netfilter code and the security it offers. The following options should be disabled:

```
The IPX protocol                          not recommended
Appletalk protocol support                   not recommended
DECnet Support                            not recommended
802.1d Ethernet Bridging                     not recommended
CCITT X.25 Packet Layer (EXPERIMENTAL)          not recommended
LAPB Data Link Driver (EXPERIMENTAL)              not recommended
802.2 LLC (EXPERIMENTAL)                   not recommended
Acorn Econet/AUN protocols (EXPERIMENTAL)       not recommended
```

Use of a WAN router that only uses IP protocols is acceptable:

```
WAN router                       optional
```

The fast switching option, although it works with IP, is particularly dangerous because it completely bypasses the netfilter code:

```
Fast switching (read help!)             DO NOT USE
```

Use of a slow host forwarding between two high-speed LANs can swamp a small system. If you can't upgrade, consider using this option to throttle the interfaces:

```
Forwarding between high speed interfaces       optional
```

Finally, the QoS and/or fair queuing menu is optional. If you want to use any of these options, you are welcome to, but you'll almost certainly need the iproute2 code to make use of it:

```
QoS and/or fair queuing                optional
```

The options available on the QoS and/or fair queuing menu will not be covered in this text. If you need some of the advanced options provided (such as limiting bandwidth for certain subnets, and so on), you'll want to check out the documentation for iproute2.

SOFTWARE CONSIDERATIONS

After the kernel is built, you can look over the system for software that isn't required for operation. Extraneous software should be removed. This is especially true of compilers, games, and other unnecessary software. The use of the X Window software is discouraged because this binds to ports 6000–6255 (though most commonly just 6000–6010). If you feel that it is needed, consider using iptables to deny output on the untrusted network side. This includes nfs and other services that are not used or needed. If an intruder breaches the firewall, it doesn't make sense to provide tools to use or services to activate, and most certainly not provide bridges to other systems.

The use of a secure shell (OpenSSH) program is also highly recommended. Running TCP wrappers on ports that are not forwarded and not used (normal services do not run on a firewall), as well as using Tripwire to watch files, is a good idea.

OTHER CONSIDERATIONS

A firewall should not be considered a normal network host, and it should not be treated like one. This system should not enable normal users to log in or share files or directories on the network, and should never run RPC services such as NIS or NFS. The need to use good passwords for the accounts on the firewall, along with the necessity of using of shadow passwords, goes without saying. What might need to be said is that the firewall should not have the same password as any other host on your network. The fact that the host is broken and the attacker now has the password and shadow files should not automatically provide access to other hosts on the internal network.

This host needs to also be physically separated from the rest of the hosts, and placed in a secure area where unauthorized individuals cannot gain physical access to it. Any machine to which a knowledgeable individual has access can be broken, often in minutes. The case needs to be locked, and access to the system setup password must be protected.

IPTABLES GENERAL INFORMATION

To understand how to proceed with iptables, you need to understand how iptables works. The next few sections walk you through some of the finer points. Most iptables text makes the assumption that all packets run through the tables, or list of rules. In fact, however, iptables only sees a packet if that packet is the first or only packet. Subsequent packet fragments do not traverse the rules. The reason for this is simple—a host cannot reassemble the fragments into a packet until it has the first packet. If the first packet is dropped, the others time out and are dropped. However, if you load conntrack, the connection tracking module, or are doing masquerading, the firewall will reassemble all packet fragments before doing anything with the packet.

Three default chains are built into netfilter. If you add the NAT code, two additional chains are created.

The first three chains are INPUT, FORWARD, and OUTPUT. The INPUT and OUTPUT chains work exclusively with packets with destination or source being the localhost. The FORWARD chain is used only for packets passing from one interface to another. Under the older ipchains, anything passing through the FORWARD chain first traversed the INPUT then later the OUTPUT chains. This is no longer true with iptables. This change should cut down on the confusion surrounding which chain(s) are used.

Because packets will go to one of the INPUT or FORWARD chains (but not both), any rules you want to apply equally to both will have to reside in both chains. Alternately (and also better), you can create a user-defined chain that both jump to so that you don't need to duplicate chain rules.

If you add NAT or MASQUERADING targets to any chain rules, you will use one of two additional chains: POSTROUTING and PREROUTING. The easiest way to explain these two chains (but definitely not accurate technically) is to think of these two rules as being applied outside the box. That is, if you're going to use DNAT (destination nat), which uses PREROUTING, it helps to think of the address as being changed before it hits the incoming interface. Figure 36.1 is a graphical display of how packets flow through each of the chains. You can jump to user-defined chains at any point and you will return to your departure point from there.

Figure 36.1
Packet flow through iptables.

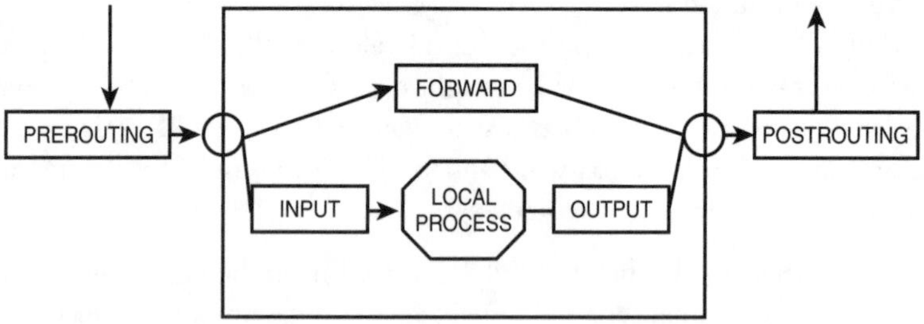

All packets flow from left to right and pass to either
the INPUT or FORWARD chains, but not both.

Remember that the PRE- and POSTROUTING don't actually happen outside the system, it's just easier to think of it that way. In explaining how the netfilter code works, this text will also conveniently talk as if the routing code is used twice, once each time a packet hits an interface (depicted by the circles), even though this is also not technically accurate.

Looking at Figure 36.1, packets flow from left to right. This is true regardless of whether the left side represents the trusted or untrusted interface—that is, the left interface represents any interface used as an incoming interface, and the right interface represents any outgoing interface. This text also conveniently ignores localhost routing decisions.

When a packet comes in to an interface, it first hits the PREROUTING chain (if it exists). Here, destination addresses are changed (DNAT) to reflect a different host. If, for example, traffic destined for the localhost's port 80 is to be sent to an internal host, the destination is changed here. The packet then hits the interface and the kernel does a routing table lookup to see where the packet needs to go (to localhost or to another interface).

The netfilter code then picks up the packet based on its destination (localhost or outgoing interface) and runs either the INPUT or FORWARD chain. If the packet went through the forward chain and was not dropped, it is again passed through the kernel routing table and sent out through the appropriate interface.

As the packet leaves the interface, netfilter once again runs the packet through the rules for POSTROUTING.

Every packet coming or going runs through the same basic process. The process also applies to packets using the localhost interface, which pass through the INPUT and OUTPUT rules.

CHAINS

When you think chain, think of a logically grouped list of rules. Each rule in a chain is a test to apply against the IP header for a match.

Chains contain rules, numbered from one. Rules can be referred to either by rule specification or by rule number.

A rule specification is the set of conditions that the packet must meet—the test. The same basic rule can exist in multiple chains, so the chain argument is normally required. If the chain target is one of ACCEPT, DROP, REJECT, or MASQUERADE, that target terminates the chain so that no more rules in that chain will be processed.

All iptables rules have a basic syntax. This syntax is

```
iptables [-t table] command chain rule-specification [options]
```

This is a generalization, and some commands modify the preceding syntax slightly. This will be discussed in the iptables commands next.

IPTABLES TABLES

The first part of the iptables syntax is the optional -t table specification. The default table is filter. Possible tables include filter, mangle, and nat. The mangle table is used when you want to modify the TOS (type of service) bits or put a mark on the packet that netfilter can use for queuing or other purposes. The nat table is used for SNAT, DNAT, and MASQUERADING and implements the PRE- or POSTROUTING chains.

To understand better how the tables work, run each of the following commands and note the output:

```
iptables -L -n
iptables -t filter -L -n
iptables -t mangle -L -n
iptables -t nat -L -n
```

The first two commands are identical. The third and fourth will return something very different from the first two and help to illustrate the chains included in each table as well as reinforce the need to declare the table.

> **Note**
>
> You even need to declare the table to use when you create or delete a user-defined chain. Only the built-in chains OUTPUT and PREROUTING can belong to more than one table.

IPTABLES COMMANDS

Six variations are possible on the iptables command line shown earlier, and they are covered in the following command descriptions.

These commands are as follows (all commands are preceded by a hyphen):

- **-A (append)**—This takes a chain name and a rule specification as mandatory arguments.
- **-D (delete)**—This takes a chain name and a rule specification or rule number as mandatory arguments.
- **-C (test/check)**—-s, -d, -p, and -i are required. This takes a chain name and a rule specification as mandatory arguments. As of this writing, this command had not been implemented, but is on the author's ToDo list.
- **-I (insert)**—An extension of append, but the rule specification is placed ahead of the rule number that is referenced. This command takes a chain name, rule number for insertion ahead of, and a rule specification as mandatory arguments
- **-R (replace)**—An Insert and Delete. This takes as mandatory arguments a chain name, a rule number, and a rule specification. The rule specification will replace the rule number in the specified chain.
- **-F (flush)**—Delete all rules in a chain, or all rules in all chains if no chain name is specified.
- **-L (list)**—List all rules in a chain or all rules in all chains if no chain name is specified.
- **-Z (zero)**—Zero counters. Zeroes counters in specified chain or all chains if no chain name is provided.
- **-N (new)**—Create a user-defined chain. This requires only a chain name as a mandatory argument.
- **-X (delete a user-defined chain)**—This requires a chain name, and the chain must be empty (flushed). Default chains cannot be deleted.
- **-P (policy)**—This takes as mandatory arguments a chain name and a target.
- **-E (rename chain)**—This takes as mandatory arguments the old chain name and the new chain name.
- **-h (help)**—This special option takes no commands, only accepts one option (-h), and optionally accepts one argument.

IPTABLES OPTIONS

A number of options are available for iptables. Where address masks are specified, the mask can be of either of the following types: /N or /N.N.N.N. Addresses can also be hostnames. Ports can be either numbers or service names.

A number of the following options require you to load a module to enable the particular option. Normally, the option to load will be obvious because it will contain the name of the option.

The ! can be used with a number of options to reverse the meaning. The options include the following:

- **-p [!] protocol**—Protocol. Can accept ! (as in -p ! icmp to match all but icmp messages); or it can accept all to match all protocols.

- **-s [!] address**—Source address. Can optionally take !, a netmask, or a port. Note that an address of 0/0 matches all addresses and is the default if -s is not specified.

- **-d [!] address**—Destination address. Same criteria as for -s.

- **-i [!] name**—Input interface name. Can accept !. Also accepts a + suffix on the interface name to signify all interfaces of that type; that is, ppp+ is all PPP interfaces (ppp0–pppN). This option can only refer to the input interface, so cannot be used in the OUTPUT or POSTROUTING chains (or chains called form those chains).

- **-o [!] name**—Output interface name. Similar to -i, but applies only to the output interface and corresponding chains.

- **-j target**—Target for rule (user-defined chain name or special value), if it matches. Special values, ACCEPT, DROP, QUEUE, or RETURN, terminate the chain.

- **-n**—Numeric output of addresses and ports. By default, iptables tries to resolve them.

- **-v**—Verbose mode. Outputs the interface address, rule options (if any), TOS masks, and packet and byte counters. Use -vv for extremely verbose reporting.

- **-x**—Expand numbers. When packet and byte counters are displayed, do not use the abbreviations K, M, or G, but display all zeros.

- **[!] -f**—Second and further fragments. Can be preceded by !.

- **--line-numbers**—Used when listing rules to show line numbers in front of rule specifications for reference.

- **--sport [!] port[:port]**—Only valid following a -p tcp or -p udp option. Specifies a source port or range (ranges are specified by using a - or : to separate the beginning and ending range). Can also be used with the multiport match option (up to 15 ports can be listed). Rule fragments can look like the following:

  ```
  -p tcp --sport 0:1023

  -m multiport -p tcp --sport 25,110
  ```

- **--dport [!] port[:port]**—Only valid following a -p tcp or -p udp option. Similar to previous --sport, but specifies the destination port(s).

- **--tcp-flags [!] flags set**—Only valid following the -p tcp option. This option looks at the listed flags and then only matches if the flags listed in set are the only flags set. Possible flags include: SYN, ACK, FIN, RST, URG, PSH, and ALL NONE. If you want to examine the SYN, ACK, RST, and FIN flags, but only accept those with both the SYN and ACK flags set (response to a new connection) the rule fragment would look like this:

```
-p tcp --tcp-flags SYN,ACK,RST,FIN SYN,ACK
```

■ **[!] --syn**—Only valid following the -p tcp option. This is equivalent to the following:

```
--tcp-flags SYN,RST,ACK SYN
```

■ **--icmp-type [!] ICMP [sub]type**—Only valid following the -p icmp option.

The following are valid ICMP types and subtypes (indented under the main type):

```
echo-reply (pong)
destination-unreachable
   network-unreachable
   host-unreachable
   protocol-unreachable
   port-unreachable
   fragmentation-needed
   source-route-failed
   network-unknown
   host-unknown
   network-prohibited
   host-prohibited
   TOS-network-unreachable
   TOS-host-unreachable
   communication-prohibited
   host-precedence-violation
   precedence-cutoff
source-quench
redirect
   network-redirect
   host-redirect
   TOS-network-redirect
   TOS-host-redirect
echo-request (ping)
router-advertisement
router-solicitation
time-exceeded (ttl-exceeded)
   ttl-zero-during-transit
   ttl-zero-during-reassembly
parameter-problem
   ip-header-bad
   required-option-missing
timestamp-request
timestamp-reply
address-mask-request
address-mask-reply
```

- **--mac-source [!] mac-address**—Only valid following the `-m mac` option. Useful in the INPUT or PREROUTING chains. Rule fragment would look like the following:

  `-m mac --mac-source 00:00:ab:c0:45:a8`

- **--limit rate**—Maximum match rate (average). Default value is 3/hour; anything beyond the match rate is dropped. If your system cannot tolerate more than one new connection per second, you can use limit with this rule fragment

  `-p tcp --syn`

  to prevent your server from overloading, although this is normally used with the LOG target to prevent logs from growing too rapidly. Rate can specify period (default is /hour) of /minute, /second, /hour, or /day. Rule fragment:

  `-m limit --limit 1/sec`

- **--limit-burst number**—Maximum initial number of matches before starting to use the preceding `--limit rate`. The burst is recharged by one each time the preceding `--limit rate` is not met. Default `--limit-burst` is 5.

- **--port [port[,port]]**—Only valid with the `-p tcp` or `-p udp` option and following the `-m multiport` option (see rule fragment that follows). Match if both source and destination ports are the same and match any optionally listed port (up to 15 comma-separated port numbers are permitted). A sample multiport rule fragment which only matches ports 25 and 110:

  `-m multiport -p tcp --port 25,110`

- **--mark value[/mask]**—Matches packets with a given mark (an unsigned value). This value must be set using the MARK target discussed in following text.

- **--uid-owner userid**—Only valid when used in the OUTPUT chain to identify packets created by a particular user, and even then only works on some locally created packets.

- **--gid-owner groupid**—Similar to `--uid-owner`, but applies to the group.

- **--pid-owner PID**—Similar to `--uid-owner`, but applies to the process ID (PID).

- **--sid-owner sessionid**—Similar to `--uid-owner`, but applies to the session.

- **--state state**—Matches TCP connection states. The state argument is a comma-separated list of values consisting of one or more of: NEW, ESTABLISHED, RELATED, INVALID. The NEW applies to new connections (similar to `--syn`, but includes the entire new connection handshake). The ESTABLISHED applies to a current, valid existing connection. The RELATED applies to packets initiating a connection because of an ESTABLISHED connection (such as the FTP data channel connection or ICMP error messages, which have no port or connection status). You will normally use ESTABLISHED and RELATED together. The INVALID state refers to any packets not covered previously—such as scans that use *TCP pings*, packets with the SYN and ACK bits set that have no corresponding SYN packet, or XMAS tree scans, with all bits set (SYN, ACK, FIN, URG, PSH, RST). A rule fragment might look like the following:

  `-m state --state ESTABLISHED,RELATED`

- **unclean**—An experimental option designed to match unusual or malformed packets:

  ```
  -m unclean
  ```

- **--tos tos**—Used to match one of the following TOS masks. The TOS value must first be set by netfilter using the TOS target discussed in the section. Rule fragments can look like this:

  ```
  -m tos --tos 16
  ```

Table 36.1 lists the values to use if you want to implement routing priorities based on the type of service (TOS).

TABLE 36.1 TOS MASKS

TOS Name	TOS Numeric	Hex Value	Sample Uses
Minimum-Delay	16	0x01 0x10	FTP, telnet, ssh
Maximum-Throughput	8	0x01 0x08	FTP-data
Maximum-Reliability	4	0x01 0x04	snmp, DNS
Minimum-Cost	2	0x01 0x02	nntp, email
Normal-Service	0	0x01 0x00	

IPTABLES TARGETS

A *target* is an action to take when the packet matches the rule specification. All built-in chains will have a default policy that, if no other rule overrides it, determines the fate of the packet. All policies default to ACCEPT.

Beyond the built-in ACCEPT, DROP, QUEUE, and RETURN targets, a number of others exist if you've loaded the modules. The number could easily increase because of the flexible framework netfilter has in place. The following list outlines currently included targets.

- **LOG**—Permits matching packets to be logged. Consider using the limit module discussed above. The LOG target can take any of the following optional arguments:
  - **--log-level level**—Permits specifying the logging level. See Chapter 21, "System Auditing and System Logging," for more information on logging levels.
  - **--log-prefix prefix**—Allows you to append up to 14 characters as the first part of the log to identify the log entry.
  - **--log-tcp-sequence**—Will log TCP sequence numbers (a possible security risk).
  - **--log-tcp-options**—Reads and logs the TCP packet header options field.
  - **--log-ip-options**—Reads and logs the IP packet header options field.
- **MARK**—Sets the firewall mark (fwmark) for use by subsequent rules. This requires the mangle table (-t mangle) and has the following mandatory argument:
  - **--set-mark mark**—The mark will be a numeric value.

- **REJECT**—Equivalent to DROP, but an error message is returned. Only valid in the INPUT, FORWARD, and OUTPUT chains (same as DROP or ACCEPT). REJECT has the following optional argument:
  - `--reject-with type`—Permits you to change the default icmp-net-unreachable message to one of icmp-host-unreachable, icmp-port-unreachable, or icmp-proto-unreachable. If the rule specifies `-p icmp`, then the reject-with argument may also take echo-reply.

- **TOS**—Permits setting the type of service field. Only valid in the PREROUTING or OUTPUT chains. Takes a mandatory argument:
  - `--set-tos tos`—Where tos can be one of the valid numeric values as listed above.

- **MIRROR**—An experimental target that attempts to mirror packets by switching the source and destination IPs. Only valid in the INPUT, OUTPUT, and FORWARD chains.

- **SNAT**—Requires the nat table (-t nat) and only valid in the POSTROUTING chain. Takes one mandatory argument:
  - `--to-source ipaddress[-ipaddress][:port-port]`—Changes the outgoing packet's source address to the one(s) specified in the argument. Will also change udp and tcp protocol ports if necessary. Normally, no port mangling will occur.

- **DNAT**—Requires the nat table (-t nat) and only valid in the PREROUTING chain. Takes one mandatory argument:
  - `--to-destination ipaddress[-ipaddress][:port-port]`—Changes the incoming packet's destination address to the one(s) specified in the argument. Will also change udp and tcp protocol ports if necessary. Normally, no port mangling will occur.

- **MASQUERADE**—Requires the nat table (-t nat) and only valid in the POSTROUTING chain. Meant for use with dial-up connections. Takes one optional argument:
  - `--to-ports port[-port]`—This overrides the default port selection heuristics. Only valid with `-p tcp` or `-p udp`.

- **REDIRECT**—Requires the nat table (-t nat) and only valid in the PREROUTING and OUTPUT chains (or user-defined chains called from those chains). Sends packets to localhost. Takes one optional argument:
  - `--to-ports port[-port]`—This overrides the default port selection heuristics. Only valid with `-p tcp` or `-p udp`.

USER-DEFINED CHAINS

User-defined chains provide a way to group rules logically. These chains are called from built-in chains as targets. At any point in the chain, you can call a user-defined chain from the same table. When a user-defined chain terminates with no matches, it returns to the next argument in the calling chain.

When creating user-defined chains, names should be lowercase because uppercase is reserved for built-in chains and targets. The name cannot be one of the built-in names or special values.

SIMPLE FIREWALL POLICIES

Now you're ready to get down to specifying what you want to filter. There are a few things to keep in mind. While you are making changes to rules, you can change `/proc/sys/net/ipv4/ip_forward` from 1 to 0 to turn off forwarding. This prevents things from slipping through while you're making changes. This is also the first place to look if nothing is passing through your firewall when you expect it to.

If you change all the built-in chain policies to DROP or REJECT, make sure that you do not specify rules that require lookups. Use IP addresses, not hostnames.

Keep in mind, also, that rules are matched in order. The first rule to match with a special value terminates that chain, so be careful about which rules come first. Take a look at the following rule: `iptables -I INPUT 1 -j REJECT` (insert, as the first rule, REJECT). Because this rule has no `-s`, it applies to all addresses. Furthermore, because it has no `-i`, it applies to all interfaces. Finally, with no `-p`, it applies to all protocols. Essentially, this rule rejects everything, even messages from localhost.

So to start, always keep your policies simple and build on them from there.

WHAT TO FILTER AND WHERE

Sometimes you need to think about not only what you want to filter, but where. Suppose you don't want to answer ping packets for any host. You can handle this in two ways—but only one makes good sense. The first way is to deny or reject echo-requests as follows:

```
iptables -A input -p icmp --icmp-type echo-request -j DROP
```

The second way is to deny or reject the echo-response before it goes out:

```
iptabless -A output -p icmp --icmp-type echo-response -j DROP
```

Although both of these work, they have very different effects. You probably want to use the first method. Normally, your first response is correct. But be aware that both of these prevent the sender from receiving a reply. If the ping packet happens to be a big ping and is being sent to a vulnerable host inside your network, the first method works. The second method might or might not work depending on whether you're using connection tracking or masquerading.

WHAT NOT TO FILTER

Some administrators believe that ICMP packets are not that important. They equate icmp with ping. Unfortunately, a number of other important network messages use ICMP. The destination-not-reachable messages travel this way, so you won't receive them. Although TCP normally times out, these ICMP messages still need to be passed. Your Linux system, for example, uses ICMP messages to set the maximum transmission unit (MTU). For Ethernet, this is normally 1500 for maximum throughput. Fragmenting causes more delays than dropping the MTU. So Linux sets the Don't Fragment (DF) bit. If a host or router needs to fragment the packets, it can't because the DF bit is set, so it drops the packet and sends an ICMP message. Linux drops the MTU and tries again until it can pass packets. If you don't accept ICMP messages, your connections with some hosts might be excruciatingly slow.

Most administrators are also aware that DNS uses UDP, and they want to block TCP on port 53 (the DNS port). But when DNS needs to do a zone transfer or other large data transfer, it switches to TCP.

The bottom line is this: If you experience network problems after implementing certain rules, back the rules out until you stop experiencing the problem, and then re-implement them one at a time, with logging turned on, until you can isolate the problem.

MONITORING

Remember to look through the logs from time to time, particularly if you put in rules that are designed to detect attacks. Furthermore, just in case someone does break in, you might want to have a trusted internal host doing your syslogging for you.

tcpd, tripwire, courtney, and all the other tools don't do any good if they are not properly used and checked. The first thing an attacker does is look for these things. Time is what your firewall is buying you. However, time works for the attacker and against you. The best time to catch an attack is before the penetration occurs, when your network is being probed. To enter, an attacker must find your weaknesses. This way, you will have warning. It might not be much, though.

UNDER ATTACK

After you've been probed or attacked, you need to have a plan to deal with the situation: Do you allow it to continue in an attempt to track it, or do you stop it cold? Do you alert the authorities? (It is a crime.) Do you have the authority to contact the police? If not, who does?

These—and many more—questions are all part of a good network security policy. But it is just as important to practice what you'll do when the time comes. Note that I said when, not if. Some Internet sites that carry tools for crackers are a constant source of new exploits, so finding out how the attacker entered, if possible, is essential to preventing a recurrence.

NETWORK SECURITY POLICY

Possibly the greatest failing of most companies is the lack of a coherent network security policy. A good policy explains clearly the network policy, penalties for violation of the policies, and enforcement guidelines (what happens to violators). This policy must apply to all—equally. A synthesis of this policy (two or three sentences) needs to be posted on Web and FTP sites to warn guests.

But the document should not focus on the prohibitive or the punitive side. Rather, a good policy needs to cover the actions that are to be taken, as well as when and by whom, when your security is at risk. Furthermore, it needs to cover a reasonable timeline for the eventuality that someone, somewhere will at least attempt to penetrate your security. When an attack is discovered, what actions are taken? This includes discovery of the attempt after the fact as well as during an ongoing attack. A number of responses are possible in each situation, but because time is often the key element, those who are involved must know their part. In many larger companies, emergency response teams have been designated. A good reference is RFC-2196, "Site Security Handbook." All current RFCs are available from `http://www.rfc-editor.org/rfc.html`.

PROJECT: A SIMPLE PACKET-FILTERING FIREWALL

This section steps you through building a very simple firewall with netfilter using iptables. This firewall is not recommended for use as-is. You'll need to determine if this is what you need. But it does give you a good idea about how to plan and implement a simple firewall, including how to write the iptables rules. In the real world, it's just not this easy; this is only a chapter, although it deserves a book. Much of this is contrived to demonstrate rules and give you an idea what you can do.

To begin, you'll need to know something about the network from which you're connecting, and about the network to which you're connecting. The following assumptions are valid for the rest of this section:

- **Internal (trusted) Network**—209.191.169.128/25
- **External (untrusted) Network**—209.191.169.0/25
- **Bastion host**—foo, with foo1/foo2 interfaces, 209.191.169.1/209.191.169.129

PLANNING

You can start from one of two general policies. The overall policy can be either "Permit everything that is not specifically prohibited" or "Prohibit everything that is not specifically permitted." Because the latter is more secure, your general firewall policy will be "Prohibit."

The network is set up internally as trusted, but all services will be run from inside. Because the company has determined the overall risk is low, all the services that the company wants to provide to the Internet will reside on the trusted network: anonymous FTP, HTTP, and so on. You might see a more elaborate setup with a third firewall NIC to a semi-trusted portion of the company's network referred to as the DMZ, the demilitarized zone, in some textbooks. This is because it is similar to the front lines in a battle; if the bad guys are going to show their faces, this is where they will be seen first. This has the advantage of better isolating your public servers from your internal network while still keeping them inside the firewall. It has the disadvantage of requiring more assets (another NIC, and isolated hub), and requiring that internal traffic route through the firewall when going from the trusted network to the mail servers on the semi-trusted network.

The following summarizes the policy you're going to implement:

- **Default policy**—Prohibit (drop)
- **Anon FTP**—Internal (port forward through the firewall to 209.191.169.135)

- **http**—Internal (port forward through the firewall to 209.191.169.136 to port 8080— https on port 443 is not offered)
- **ssh will be used**—Log and deny incoming telnet
- **smtp**—Internal (port forward through firewall to 209.191.169.137)
- **popd**—Internal (port forward through firewall to 209.191.169.137)
- **DNS**—Internal only (no external access)
- **nntp**—Do not permit access from inside
- Also drop incoming pings

Note

Dropping ICMP ping packets is illustrated here to show how it is done, but doing so gains you little, if anything. Most scan tools use SYN-ACK scans or XMAS tree scans rather than pings to test to see whether a host is connected, so dropping ping packets is only effective if you're concerned about big pings to vulnerable hosts. If you drop pings, you'll also want to drop invalid packets (SYN-ACK with no related SYN or XMAS tree packets).

LOADING THE MODULES

Until you're comfortable with which modules you need, load them all. Afterward, you can unload those that aren't used. Listing 36.1 is a small Perl program that will load all the IPv4 and IPv6 netfilter modules. If you don't have the ipv6 modules, you can remove the comma and the ipv6 from the my @dirs line in each script.

LISTING 36.1   INSERT MODULES SCRIPT

```perl
#!/usr/bin/perl -w
# Written by D. Bandel
# licensed under the GPL v2.0

use strict;
use File::Basename;

my ($file,$path,$suff,$uname,$dir);

chomp($uname=`uname -r`);

my @dirs=("ipv4","ipv6");
foreach $dir (@dirs) {
   $path="/lib/modules/$uname/kernel/net/$dir/netfilter/";
   my @list=(`ls $path`);
         foreach $file (@list) {
         ($file,$path,$suff)=fileparse($file,".o");
         `modprobe $file 2>&1 /dev/null`;
   }
}
```

To use, copy the preceding script exactly as it appears into a file called modules.pl. Then make it executable (chmod 755 modules.pl) and run it.

After you have all your rules in place, you can run the remove modules script in Listing 36.2. You'll get errors on modules in use, but those not used will be removed. If you want to remove all the modules, you'll first need to flush all the tables and remove any user-defined chains.

> **Note**
>
> The `rmmod -a` command is supposed to remove unused modules, but will look at all modules. If you only want to look at removing specific modules, you'll be better off using the script in Listing 36.2.

LISTING 36.2   REMOVE MODULES SCRIPT

```perl
#!/usr/bin/perl -w
# Written by D. Bandel
# licensed under the GPL v2.0
# crude hack to unload lots of modules quickly

use strict;
use File::Basename;

my ($file,$path,$suff,$uname,$dir,$subdir,$count);

chomp($uname=`uname -r`);
#subdirs containing the modules we want removed
my @subdirs=("ipv4","ipv6");
#a kludge to remove modules with dependencies. It's this or
#keep a list of failed modules and retry only those
my @count=("1","2","3");
foreach $count (@count) {
   foreach $subdir (@subdirs) {
           #complete path to modules
           $dir="/lib/modules/$uname/kernel/net/$subdir/netfilter/";
           my @list=(`ls $dir`);
           foreach $file (@list) {
                   ($file,$path,$suff)=fileparse($file,".o");
                   if (`lsmod | grep $file`) {
                           # the work is done here:
                           `rmmod $file 2>&1 /dev/null`;
                   }
           }
   }
}
```

The instructions for `modules.pl` above apply to this script, which should be named `rmmodules.pl`. If you run the script once after all the netfilter rules are in place, it will remove unused modules. You can then see which modules are required and which aren't (and save some memory in the process). You will want to keep the `ip_nat_ftp` module if you're using the `nat` table. The preceding script can remove this module, but you'll need it if you want to be able to do active FTP sessions from masqueraded hosts. If you want to remove all the modules, you'll need to flush all rules from all tables and delete all user-defined chains from all tables.

IMPLEMENTING THE POLICIES

Now all that's left is to implement the policies. Declare a few variables because this reduces errors. Follow these steps:

Use the following names, which are similar to the ones in the previous summary:

```
fooint=209.191.169.1/25      # this is eth0
fooext=209.191.169.129/25    # this is eth1
```

1. Start with a clean slate:

```
iptables -F
iptables -t mangle -F
iptables -t nat -F
iptables -X
iptables -t mangle -X
iptables -t nat -X
```

2. Stop pings and scans that come from outside:

```
iptables -N scans
iptables -A scans -m state --state INVALID -j DROP
iptables -A scans -m unclean -j DROP
iptables -A scans -p icmp --icmp-type echo-request -i eth1 -j DROP
iptables -A INPUT -j scans
iptables -A FORWARD -j scans
```

3. Now pass all traffic from inside out (except nntp):

```
iptables -N passthis
iptables -N blockthis
iptables -A passthis -s fooint -p icmp -i eth0 -j ACCEPT
iptables -A passthis -s fooint -p tcp --sport ! 119 -d 0/0 -i eth0 -j ACCEPT
iptables -A blockthis -s fooint -p tcp --sport 119 -j REJECT --reject-with
➥icmp-port-unreachable
iptables -A FORWARD -j passthis
iptables -A OUTPUT -j passthis
```

4. Block those pesky services that are a common security problem or that you just don't want, such as telnet and imap:

```
iptables -A blockthis -i eth1 -s 0/0 -d fooint -p tcp --sport 23 -j DROP
iptables -A blockthis -i eth1 -s 0/0 -d fooint -p tcp --sport imap -j DROP
iptables -A FORWARD -j blockthis
```

You really don't need to specify eth1 because if it came from eth0, you've already accepted it previously and, therefore, you won't get the chance to drop it. In fact, a number of the rules here have some information duplicated, but this project is intended to show examples of rules and how to put them together.

5. Be sure to accept DNS (on fooint only), ssh, and returns on most upper ports (and on both networks), but drop any requests from outside for XDM or X access:

```
iptables -I passthis 1 -m state --state ESTABLISHED,RELATED -j ACCEPT
iptables -A passthis -i eth0 -p tcp -s fooint -d 0/0 --dport domain -j ACCEPT
iptables -A passthis -i eth0 -p udp -s fooint -d 0/0 --dport domain -j ACCEPT
iptables -N passthisin
iptables -I passthisin blockthis
iptables -A passthisin -p tcp --dport 22 -j ACCEPT
```

```
iptables -A blockthis -i eth1 -p tcp --dport 6000:6010 -j DROP
iptables -A blockthis -i eth1 -p udp --dport 111 -j DROP
iptables -A passthis -p tcp -m multiport --dport 25,110 -i ! eth1 -j ACCEPT
```

6. Set the default policies on incoming to DROP:

```
iptables -P FORWARD DROP
iptables -P INPUT DROP
```

7. Forward through traffic to the appropriate servers (DNS points to our firewall for all Web, mail, and FTP traffic):

```
iptables -t nat -A PREROUTING -p tcp --dport 21 -j DNAT --to-destination
➥209.191.169.135
iptables -t nat -A PREROUTING -p tcp --dport 80 -j DNAT --to-destination
➥209.191.169.136:8080
iptables -t nat -A PREROUTING -m multiport -p tcp --dport 25,110 -j DNAT --to-
➥destination 209.191.169.137
```

8. Make some optimizations:

- Minimum delay for Web, telnet, and ssh traffic:

```
iptables -t mangle -A PREROUTING -m multiport -p tcp --dport 80,23,22 -j
➥TOS --set-tos 16
iptables -t mangle -A PREROUTING -m multiport -p tcp --sport 80,23,22 -j
➥TOS --set-tos 16
```

- Maximum throughput for FTP data:

```
iptables -t mangle -A PREROUTING -p tcp --dport ftp-data -j TOS --set-tos 8
iptables -t mangle -A PREROUTING -p tcp --dport ftp-data -j TOS --set-tos 8
```

- Maximum reliability for smtp:

```
iptables -t mangle -A REPROUTING -p tcp --dport smtp -j TOS --set-tos 4
```

- Minimum cost for pop-3:

```
iptables -t mangle -A PREROUTING -p tcp --dport 110 -j TOS --set-tos 2
```

There's just one more set of rules that you might want to stop IP spoofing (by someone from the outside who is pretending to be you). No one should connect to the external interface, claiming to be from the inside. The following rules enable you to drop them (but remember, if you have /proc/sys/net/ipv4/conf/all/rp_filter turned on, the kernel will drop the spoofed packets):

```
iptables -I FORWARD -i eth1 -s 192.168.0.0/24 -j DROP
iptables -I FORWARD -i eth1 -s 127.0.0.0/8 -j DROP
iptables -I INPUT -i ! lo -s 127.0.0.1 -j DROP
```

Don't forget:

```
echo 1 > /proc/sys/netc/ipv4/ip_forward
```

and perhaps:

```
echo 1 > /proc/sys/net/ipv4/conf/rp_filter/all
```

This should give you some idea of the flexibility of iptables. Several programs available from different sources can help you create your firewall rules. But remember to test your rules by sending traffic to it and noting the results.

## CHAPTER 37

REMOTE ADMINISTRATION

In this chapter

Encryption

You need to know about installing and configuring OpenSSH and Webmin to accomplish remote system administration securely. You will want to be able to remotely administer any system you aren't sitting in front of all the time without sending information in the clear. Although usernames are not a concern, sending passwords unencrypted over any network will allow anyone connected to that network to see your password. All that person would have to do is use a program that captures traffic as it goes by.

Recent (early 2000) rulings have lifted a number of U.S. restrictions on exporting cryptographic material, which means cryptography is now more accessible. This access is essential to e-commerce and remote systems administration. Not all the restrictions are gone, but they have been lifted sufficiently to permit users access to 128-byte (1024-bit) encryption, the minimum to permit secure transactions today.

Linux distributions made in the U.S. still cannot include some cryptography programs, so you'll have to download and install these yourself. But relax; this is easy and this chapter takes you every step of the way. You'll start with OpenSSL, the foundation for all the other secure programs and modules and proceed to OpenSSH, which permits secure telnet and file transfers. Finally, you'll learn about the Perl Net_SSLeay module, which allows you to use Netscape to securely administer your system through an encrypted Webmin session.

Caution

In many places in the world, use of cryptography is restricted or prohibited. You are responsible for adhering to the laws of your country regarding cryptography. If that puts your systems at risk, you need to discuss that with your government.

OpenSSL

Before you can begin to install either OpenSSH or the Perl Net_SSLeay.pm module, you'll need to install OpenSSL. OpenSSL provides the Secure Sockets Layer (SSL) libraries for the encryption process. Always make sure you get the latest package, and keep it up-to-date.

The OpenSSL package can be obtained from http://www.openssl.org/source/. Make sure you get the latest package, which will have [LATEST] next to its name.

In the United States, you'll need to get and compile the RSA's rsaref library. Fortunately, RSA's patent runs out in November 2000, so after that date you won't need it (unless RSA manages to have the patent extended). If you are in a position where you don't need to use it, don't install it. This library is old and contains at least one known security hole. If you determine that you do need it, RSA no longer offers it, so you'll need to search the Internet. Be careful, because some European sites have a rewritten European version of the library that you won't want if you're in the United States. Just follow the instructions carefully and you should have no problem linking it in.

To install OpenSSL, you will need to have Perl 5 installed first.

After you've downloaded the library, run the following command (assuming the latest version is openss-0.9.5):

```
tar xzvf openssl-0.9.5.tar.gz
```

The command you run should match the version of the package you downloaded.

When the package has stopped opening up, you'll have a directory named openssl-0.9.5 that you'll need to cd into.

When you're in the openssl build directory, run the following:

```
./config && make
```

This command ascertains several things about your system, and if it's successful, you should run make. After the make finishes, become root (if you're not already) and run this command :

```
make install
```

OpenSSH

The OpenSSH package allows you to run a secure shell server and connect to it with a secure shell client. All communications between the two are encrypted. Download the SSH package from http://violet.ibs.com.au/openssh/files/.

Do not get the source RPM package. The source RPM only builds if you have GNOME installed. This is a Red Hat–only RPM. The same is true for the binary RPMs; they will not work. Get the source files.

After you have the source file, open it the same way you did the OpenSSL package (assuming your OpenSSH version is 1.2.3):

```
tar xzvf openssh-1.2.3.tar.gz
```

cd into the build directory and run configure:

```
cd openssh-1.2.3 ; ./configure --with-ssl-dir=/usr/local/ssl && make
```

After the make is successful, run the following command:

```
make install
```

The install process installs the binaries, but doesn't generate a server key needed by the binaries. To install the server keys, run the following:

```
ssh-keygen
```

During key generation, you'll be asked to supply a password—do not, or you will not be able to start the server. The password should only be used if you want to generate a personal key for yourself and protect it. When the keys are generated, it will ask you where you want to write them. Tell it to write them to /usr/local/etc/ssh_host_key.

To start using the server, you'll need to make sure it's started. As root, run `sshd`. This starts the server program, which binds port 22.

You can test that the server is working by connecting to it:

```
ssh localhost
```

This should prompt you for your password. Unlike telnet, permitting root logins is safe because the entire session, including the prompt for username and password, are sent encrypted. However, the `openssh` `pam` file by default still prohibits root logins. To change this, `cd` to `/etc/pam.d` and put a # in front of the line:

```
auth          required        pam_securetty.so
```

> **Note**
>
> Depending on the version of OpenSSH and the accompanying PAM file contained with the program (which you'll need to copy to `/etc/pam.d/`), you might need to just build a correct, usable `sshd` PAM file. Your `sshd` PAM file should look like this:
>
> ```
> #%PAM-1.0
> #[For version 1.0 syntax, the above header is optional]
> #
> # The PAM configuration file for the `sshd' service
> #
> auth          required        pam_pwdb.so
> auth          required        pam_nologin.so
> auth          optional        pam_mail.so
> account       required        pam_pwdb.so
> session       required        pam_pwdb.so
> session       optional        pam_lastlog.so
> password      required        pam_pwdb.so
> ```

One advantage the OpenSSH program provides is the capability to copy files securely. You do this by using the scp (secure copy) program. This works similarly to the copy program, except you can specify a remote host to either copy from or copy to. For example, if you want to copy file `foo` from the host where you're logged in, to a remote host (to username david's home directory on the remote host), you could use the following command:

```
scp foo david@remotehost:foo
```

You would be prompted for david's password, and the file would be copied to david's home directory. You can specify a directory, but david must have write permissions to that directory. You must also be able to read any file you want to copy, but this is standard fare for Linux.

You can reverse the scp line above if you want to copy from the remote host. You don't need to include `david@` if you don't want to change identities. That is, if your username on both the remotehost and the local host is `david`, you can copy a file from the remote host with this command:

```
scp chiriqui:foo bar
```

This copies the file `foo` from `chiriqui` to the localhost as filename `bar`. You will be prompted for your password.

The OpenSSH program has a number of features, including features that allow you to generate an identity key which you keep in `$HOME/.ssh/`. The identity key will have an `identity.pub` file associated with it. By copying the contents of `identity.pub` into the `$HOME/.ssh/authorized_keys` file on the remote host, you will be logged in without having to supply a password. You might have to enable this option in the `/usr/local/etc/sshd_config` file using the RSA Authentication variable.

> **Caution**
>
> You must safeguard your `$HOME/.ssh/identity` file, because anyone who can read that file can become you. Ensure the file is `chmod 600` and belongs to you. Your `authorized_keys` file should be similarly protected, as should your `known_hosts` and `random_seed` files. (Your `identity.pub` file is unimportant and is meant to be read by others.)

OPENSSH AND X

One advantage using OpenSSH confers on users is the ability to run X applications on a remote host and display them locally. Assuming you have not otherwise blocked the X ports on either system, OpenSSH forwards the DISPLAY back to the local host. You can see this by entering the following:

```
echo $DISPLAY
```

This should return something that looks like the following:

```
chiriqui.pananix.com:10.0
```

The 10 (it might be an 11) indicates that OpenSSH set this variable and is forwarding graphical connections back to the local host. If this variable is not set, you might have to set `X11Forwarding` to yes in both the server's `sshd_config` file and the client's `ssh_config` file. Disabling this variable can actually reduce security, because if users set the DISPLAY variable manually, this connection will not go through the encrypted tunnel, defeating the purpose of using OpenSSH.

> **Note**
>
> Graphics are extremely bandwidth intensive. Forwarding graphics across slow links can take a long time. Forwarding graphics on a local Ethernet link consumes significant bandwidth, although response times are significantly faster.

If you run into problems with forwarding graphical connections, check the OpenSSH documentation. Also remember that these types of connections can be blocked by either or both hosts so they might not work. They might also not work if the server or host has been compiled without X11 support.

Net_SSLeay

To use Webmin via SSL, you need to install the `Net_SSLeay.pm` module. You can either download this module from CPAN and compile and install it manually or take the time initially to set up the CPAN module, which will allow you to automatically download and install Perl modules as you need them.

The manual method is similar to the methods used earlier to download and install both the OpenSSL and OpenSSH programs, and only minimal instructions are included here. After you have the latest Net_SSLeay tarball, open it, cd into the directory, and run the following command (as root):

```
perl Makefile.PL;make;make test;make install
```

This will take care of building, testing, and installing the Perl module. The source tarball can be obtained from the following URL:

```
http://cpan.valueclick.com/authors/id/S/SA/SAMPO/Net-SSLeay.pm-1.05.tar.gz
```

To use the CPAN module, you'll need to do some setup first, but this setup is all automated. You'll only go through the setup steps the first time and, whenever you need a Perl module, you need only invoke the CPAN module and tell it to install the Perl module you need. At the root prompt, type the following:

```
perl -MCPAN -e shell
```

The first time you do this, you walk through the configuration. If in doubt, choose the defaults. You need to decide where you want CPAN to look to download the Perl modules, but you'll be given an extensive (possibly too extensive) list. Choose three or so sane (nearby) sites and continue.

After everything is set up, CPAN downloads the latest list of modules. It does this every time you run it if the list is over 24 hours old. Finally, you will end up at a CPAN prompt:

```
cpan>
```

Just tell it the module you want to install:

```
install Net::SSLeay
```

CPAN downloads the tarball, checks its authenticity and integrity (CPAN will tell you whether you need to install other modules such as the MD5 bundle), and then runs the make, make test, and install.

If any Perl modules require other Perl modules, CPAN handles the dependency checking and installs those modules as well. The CPAN utility is friendly and tries to help you if it doesn't understand what you want. Just follow the instructions it supplies.

WEBMIN

One of the nicest and easiest local and remote administration tools to appear on the scene is Webmin. This particular utility has been around for several years, but Caldera has finally decided to adopt it for remote administration. This tool can also be used for local administration, and in its "out of the box" configuration, should be used only locally, because encryption is not included.

First, this section walks you through setting up Webmin securely. If you've installed OpenSSL and the Perl Net::SSLeay, you're ready to continue. First, ensure you've installed the Webmin RPM and that it's running. You can check that it's installed as discussed in Chapter 16, "Software Package Management." You can check that it is running either by using `grepping netstat -an` for 1000 to see if it's binding port 1000, or by looking in the process listings for a line similar to the following:

```
/usr/bin/perl /usr/libexec/webmin/miniserv.pl /etc/webmin/miniserv.conf
```

If Webmin isn't running, the following simple command takes care of running it:

```
/etc/rc.d/init.d/webmin start
```

After you have Webmin running, open Netscape (unfortunately, Lynx will no longer work with Webmin as of version 0.78, and this problem might not be rectified in the future) and go to the following URL:

```
http://localhost:1000/
```

You should be prompted for a username and password. Use your root username and root's password to access Webmin.

When Webmin opens, you'll see a screen containing several tabs across the top. The active tab should be the Webmin tab, and you should see below it several icons that include Webmin Configuration and Webmin Users.

Select the Webmin Configuration icon. This opens a page with another selection of icons. Here, you can configure a large number of options regarding how Webmin looks, feels, and runs. Change your language if you so desire, and then go into the Port and Address module.

The Port and Address module has one small configuration box inside. This box contains two text boxes, the first of which is blank, and the leading selection is All, which means Webmin will listen on all IP addresses the host has. If your situation requires, you can limit the addresses to which Webmin will listen. The default should be fine for most situations. The second box is the port. Caldera installs Webmin to run on the privileged port 1000. Unfortunately, this poses a problem when running with SSL. So change port 1000 to 10000 (just add a 0) and select Save.

When you select Save, Webmin stops the server process it has binding port 1000 and restarts on port 10000, so you will be forced to log in again. Do so.

Now you'll want to go the Webmin index and select Webmin configuration again. This time, you should see an icon for SSL Encryption. This icon will show up only if you have OpenSSL and the Perl Net:SSLeay modules installed. Select this icon.

In the SSL Encryption configuration box you will see two mutually exclusive buttons: one to enable SSL support, and one to disable SSL support. Select the Enable option and save it.

When you select Save, you will again be logged out of Webmin. This time, you'll need to ensure you change your URL to the following:

```
https://localhost:10000/
```

Note the s on `https`. The first thing you'll get is a box telling you that Netscape is unable to verify the secure certificate, and do you want to accept it? This certificate was generated and installed on your system during your install of OpenSSL. This certificate is yours. So go ahead and accept it; you might just want to accept it until it expires so you are not bothered with this query again.

Now, whenever you access Webmin, all communications are encrypted.

Note   On occasion, because of the way the RPM is built, you might have to install the latest tarball to get SSL working properly. Get the tarball from `ftp://ftp.webmin.com` and open it in `/usr/libexec`. You can remove the original Webmin directory and move the new versioned directory into the original directory's place. Then `cd` into the Webmin directory and run `./setup.sh`. If you aren't sure how to answer the questions, accept the defaults.

WEBMIN OVERVIEW

After you have time to look over Webmin, you'll find that it can perform most of your administration tasks, and you can also easily perform remote administration. Additionally, you can add third-party modules that are available from the Webmin Web site at `http://www.webmin.com/`.

It might be that not all modules are completely or correctly configured when you first start Webmin. And although it might be stating the obvious, you must have the appropriate software available on the system to administer it. Webmin will tell you when it thinks you need to install or just configure something.

Most modules, when opened, have a link in the upper-left corner for module configuration. If you have installed the correct software, you might still need to make some adjustments in this section for location of software or for your particular needs or desires. Most certainly, if you take the time to install your BIND server in a `chroot` jail, you'll have to make some changes to the BIND module configuration.

Although Webmin allows you flexibility in the configuration, it provides little help. Granted, after it is properly configured, Webmin needs little explanation. But some of the configuration options might be confusing. In that case, it might be necessary to read the documentation for that particular service.

TROUBLESHOOTING

I installed OpenSSL and am trying to build a package with SSL. I used `--with-ssl` *as an option to configure, but it says it can't find the* `ssl` *includes.*

You might need to tell configure exactly where to find the SSL libraries or includes, particularly if you installed it in a non-standard location (OpenSSL installs into `/usr/local/ssl` by default). Check the `./configure --help` options, but it is usually something like `./configure --with-ssl-dir=/usr/local/ssl`.

I enabled SSL in Webmin and now I can't get in.

You probably didn't move the port to one above 1024 first. To correct the problem, stop Webmin, then `cd` to /etc/webmin. The file `miniserv.conf` contains various configurations, and you can either change `ssl=1` to `ssl=0` or `port=1000` to `port=10000` and restart Webmin.

If you still experience a problem (no common encryption algorithms), you'll need to download and install the latest Webmin. Delete the /etc/webmin and /usr/libexec/webmin directories and install Webmin in /usr/libexec. Run the setup script and take the defaults.

I installed Webmin, but I don't remember the username or password.

You can `cd` to /etc/webmin and look at the `miniserv.users` file. This file contains lines with colon-separated entries. The first column contains the username, the second column contains an encrypted password, and last column contains the userid number. You can remove the encrypted hash so the line looks like the following:

```
root::1
```

Then you can log in with no password as root (but please do enter another password for the user in the Webmin user's module as soon as possible). If Webmin doesn't like the root user not having a password, just copy and paste the hashed password from /etc/shadow.

PART VI

APPENDIXES

COMMONLY USED COMMANDS

In this appendix

WORKING WITH COMMANDS

The majority of Linux commands perform functions in exactly the same way as their UNIX equivalents. Many commands are quite cryptic, so the typical challenge with Linux commands is matching the appropriate command with the desired function. The list of commands included in this appendix is not meant to be an all-inclusive list; rather, it is intended to provide a quick reference to commonly used commands and a brief explanation of what each command does. The commands listed here are located in one of four binary directories: /bin, /sbin, /usr/bin, and /usr/sbin.

Each command, with the exception of the cd command, has an associated online manual page. These manual pages can be referenced at any time by entering the following at a shell prompt:

```
# man <command>
```

For example, if you wanted to see the manual page for the make directory command (mkdir), you would enter the following at the shell prompt:

```
# man mkdir
```

What you should see after typing the preceding and pressing Enter is the following:

```
MKDIR(1)                                    MKDIR(1)

NAME
   mkdir ? make directories

SYNOPSIS
   mkdir  [-p]  [-m  model] [--parents] [--mode=model] [--help] [--version] dir...

(c)DESCRIPTION
   This documentation is no longer being maintained and may be inaccurate or
   incomplete. The Texinfo documentation is now the authoritative source.

   This manual page documents the GNU version of mkdir. mkdir creates a directory
   with each given name. By default, the mode of created directories is 0777
   minus the bits set in the umask.
```

OPTIONS

Some of the man pages will contain a disclaimer directing you to the info pages. The Free Software Foundation (FSF)/GNU Not UNIX (GNU) leadership have been pushing to kill man pages in favor of info pages, so much of the FSF/GNU software has inadequate man pages and a pointer to use info. I'll leave it to you to decide whether you agree with this.

The Texinfo documentation can be accessed by typing the info command at the shell prompt. A user-friendly version is the X Window-based tkinfo (not included with OpenLinux). For more detailed information on any of these commands, see the Texinfo documentation or the man pages.

The commands are categorized into one of the following four areas:

- Working with directories
- Working with files
- Networking utilities
- System utilities

Working with Directories

Command	Syntax (Example)	Description
cd	cd [*path*]	Changes directory to the specified path.
	cd ..	Changes to the parent directory of the current directory.
	cd -	Changes to the previous working directory, prior to the last cd command.
	cd	Changes to the home directory of the current login ID.
	cd ~	Changes to the home directory of the current login ID.
dir		See the ls command.
ls	ls [*path*]	Lists the contents of a directory.
	ls -l (ll)	Lists the files in long format, displaying all file attributes.
	ls -a	Lists all files (including hidden files, sometimes referred to as dot files).
mkdir	mkdir *<directory>*	Makes a new directory.
pwd		Displays present working directory.
rmdir	rmdir *<directory>*	Removes a directory.

Working with Files

Command	Syntax (Example)	Description
cat	cat *<file>*	Most commonly used to display the contents of a file. Derived from the word "concatenate," which it also does.
chattr	chattr *<option>* file	Changes the ext2 attribute of a file. Some options available only to UID 0.
cp	cp *<source>* *<dest>*	Copies a file.
dd	dd if=input of=output	Most commonly used to convert a file. Can be used to copy image files from one device to another device or file.
file	file *<file>*	Determines the type of a given file.
grep	grep *<pattern>* *<file>*	Searches a file or files for a specified pattern.

Command	Syntax (Example)	Description
gzip	gzip <name>	Compresses a file using Lempel-Ziv coding. Files compressed with this utility have a .gz suffix.
gunzip	gunzip <name>	Decompresses a gzipped file.
less	less <file>	
	cat <file> | less	Similar to the more command but it facilitates backward and forward movement through the file being examined. The name is derived from the saying "Less is more."
ln	ln <source> <dest>	Used to create hard links between files on the same partition.
	ln -s <source> <dest>	Used to create symbolic (or soft) links between files on different partitions or between directories.
lsattr	lsattr [option][file]	Lists the ext2 attribute of the file or directory.
more	more <file>	
	cat <file> | more	Used to display the contents of a file, one page at a time.
mv	mv <source> <dest>	Used to rename a file.
rm	rm <file>	Removes specified file or files.
tar	tar <archive> <files>	An archive utility. Used to archive or unarchive a set of files.
	tar -cvf a.tar /etc	Creates an archive called a.tar that includes all the files and directories in the /etc directory.
	tar -xvf a.tar	Extracts all the files in the a.tar archive.
unzip	unzip [options] file	Compression utility compatible with similar DOS compression utilities that work with ZIP archives.
vi	vi <file>	Full-screen editor.
zip	zip [options] <zipfile>	Creates a ZIP archive.

NETWORKING UTILITIES

Command	Syntax (Example)	Description
dig	dig <domain>	Domain information groper. Used to gather information from Domain Name Servers.
dnsdomainname	dnsdomainname	Displays the domain name for the given server.
host	host <host>	Looks up host or host IP address using Domain Name Server.
hostname	hostname	Displays the fully qualified domain name (FQDN) for the given server.

Command	Syntax (Example)	Description
ifconfig	ifconfig	Displays currently configured network interfaces.
	ifconfig [*interface*] [options]	Configures a network interface.
netstat	netstat	Displays the status of network connections, routing tables, and interface statistics.
ping	ping <*host*>	Sends an ECHO_REQUEST packet to the specified host. A response packet is returned by reachable hosts. Commonly used to debug network connections.
nslookup	nslookup	A name server lookup utility. Used to query Domain Name Servers.
route	route	Displays the current configuration of the routing table.
	route [*options*]	Configures the IP routing table.
traceroute	traceroute <*host*>	Displays the route of IP packets. Useful for debugging network problems.

PART

VI

CH

A

SYSTEM UTILITIES

Command	Syntax (Example)	Description
chage	chage [*option*] user	Changes password aging.
chgrp	chgrp <group> <*file*>	Changes the group to which a file belongs.
chmod	chmod <*mode*> <*file*>	Changes the access permissions of the specified file or files.
chown	chown <*owner*> <*file*>	Changes the owner of a given file or files.
coastool	coastool	Uses COAS to manage the system.
date	date	Displays the system date setting.
	date <*MMDDhhmmyy*>	Sets the date.
		MM = month
		DD = day
		hh = hour (Military)
		mm = minute
		yy = year
df	df	Displays a summary of free disk space for a given filesystem.
dmesg	dmesg	Displays the startup messages from the last system boot.

Command	Syntax (Example)	Description
du	du	Displays disk usage for the current directory and all subdirectories.
echo	echo	Displays a line of text.
	echo	
	echo $PATH	Commonly used to display the value of a given environment variable.
e2fsck	e2fsck <file system>	Filesystem check routine for ext2 filesystems.
fdisk	fdisk <hard drive> (hard drive = device)	Used to create and/or manipulate a partition table for a given hard drive.
free	free	Displays the total amount of free and used memory. Also shows swap space usage.
fsck	fsck <file system>	Front-end program that calls filesystem check routines for a specific filesystem type. Defaults to ext2.
fsck.ext2	fsck.ext2 <file system>	See e2fsck.
ftpshut	ftpshut	Shuts down ftp services at a specified time.
insmod	insmod <module>	Inserts a loadable module.
kill	kill <PID>	Kills the specified process.
killall	killall <name>	Kill all processes that are executing the specified command.
lilo	lilo	Reinstalls the boot loader.
lsmod	lsmod	Lists all currently loaded modules.
mke2fs	mke2fs <partition>	Creates an ext2 type filesystem on the specified hard drive partition.
mkfs	mkfs <partition>	Front-end program that calls make filesystem routines for a specific filesystem type. Defaults to ext2.
mkfs.ext2	mkfs.ext2 <partition>	See mke2fs.
mknod	mknod <device> type maj min	Makes device files.
modprobe	modprobe <module>	Used to load a module or a set of dependent modules.
mount	mount <device> <dirmount point>	Mounts a filesystem (device) to a specified directory (mount point).
ps	ps ps aux	Displays the process table. Process IDs (PID) for currently running jobs can be identified with this command.
pwconv	pwconv	Used to convert a traditional /etc/passwd file to use shadow passwords.

Command	Syntax (Example)	Description
pwunconv	pwunconv	Converts an existing shadow password system back to the traditional system that uses only the /etc/passwd file.
rdev	rdev [*options*]	Displays or sets values for image root device, swap device, RAM disk size, or video mode.
reboot	reboot	Reboots the system.
rpm	rpm <*options*> [*file*]	Manages RPM packages.
showmount	showmount [*options*]	Displays mount information for a given NFS server.
shutdown	shutdown <*time*>	Shuts down the system at a specific time or after a specified delay.
sync	sync	Flushes buffered data to the hard drive.
sysinfo	sysinfo	Displays system information, including kernel specifics, hardware details, and partition information.
umount	umount <*device*> umount <*mount point*>	Unmounts a previously mounted filesystem.
useradd	useradd [*option*] user	Adds a user to the system.
userdel	userdel user	Removes a user.
zcat		See gzip and gunzip.

PART

VI

CH

A

FINDING MORE INFORMATION ON LINUX

In this appendix

With the ever-increasing popularity and notoriety of Linux, the number of Web sites with specific Linux information and documentation is growing at a geometric rate. This list of URLs is by no means all-inclusive. However, it should give you a good idea of what kind of information and software is available for Linux.

OPENLINUX-SPECIFIC

The Caldera Systems Web site contains a great deal of OpenLinux-specific information. A user forum is offered in several areas, including the users list and NetWare list. If you're looking for answers to technical questions in regard to OpenLinux, the Caldera Users email list is a good resource. Many Linux experts are regular contributors to the Caldera Users email list. See the following URL for details:

```
http://www.calderasystems.com/support/forums/
```

Recently, a new support knowledge base has been added as part of the technical support services. See the following URL for details:

```
http://support.calderasystems.com/
```

Much of the OpenLinux documentation is available via the Web as well, at the following URL:

```
http://www.calderasystems.com/suuport/docs/
ftp://ftp.caldera.com/pub/mirrors/
```

DEBIAN-SPECIFIC

The Debian Web site has information on a great deal, principally concerning the Debian distributions, of which at least two exist at all times, a stable version and an unstable version. Debian developers only update the stable version when a security problem is found. Otherwise, all new packages go into unstable. At a time determined by the leadership, the unstable version is frozen, a new unstable created, and bugs in the frozen version are squashed. After they are happy that the bugs are minimal, frozen becomes stable. Recently there's been discussion of a "slushy" version that's more stable than unstable, but not good enough to be stable. This is to address complaints that Debian is always "late," that is, they are the last with whatever big change has occurred. This happened with the change to glibc, but they'd like it not to occur with the 2.4.0 kernel release and beyond.

The Debian home page is located at

```
http://www.debian.org/
```

Links from the home page include mailing list subscriptions, mailing list archives, and just about anything related to Debian you might need. In fact, unless it changes, this page is all you need to answer most questions about Debian.

RED HAT-SPECIFIC

Red Hat also has a Web site devoted to sales, support, and information about the current Red Hat distributions. Red Hat carries an assortment of commercial offerings beyond their basic distribution including support contracts. All can be accessed from their home page:

```
http://www.redhat.com/
```

Links will also take you to subscriptions to the user mailing list where you can obtain help with any Red Hat-specific problems.

LINUX GENERAL

The sites in the following list include information or news about Linux in general. Again, many more sites exist than are listed here, but these are some of the well-known sites.

LINUX STANDARD BASE

```
http://www.linuxbase.org/
```

"The goal of the Linux Standard Base (*LSB*) is to develop and promote a set of standards that will increase compatibility among Linux distributions and enable software applications to run on any compliant Linux system. In addition, the LSB will help coordinate efforts to recruit software vendors to port and write products for Linux."

LINUX INTERNATIONAL

```
http://www.li.org
```

Linux International is a non-profit association of groups, corporations, and others that work toward the promotion of and help direct the growth of the Linux operating system and the Linux community.

XFREE86

```
http://www.xfree86.org
```

The XFree86 Project, Inc. is a non-profit organization that produces XFree86. XFree86 is a freely redistributable implementation of the X Window System that runs on UNIX and UNIX-like operating systems (and OS/2).

GLIDE

```
http://glide.xxedgexx.com/
```

If you have a new graphics card that boasts 3D graphics, the Glide site has information and links for 3D software on Linux.

PART
VI
CH
B

3D GAMES

http://www.gamers.org/dEngine/xf3D/

This site includes both information and software, so you can play some games with your new 3D card.

THE K DESKTOP ENVIRONMENT

http://www.kde.org

KDE is a powerful graphical desktop environment for UNIX workstations. It combines ease of use, contemporary functionality, and outstanding graphical design with the technological superiority of the UNIX operating system.

THEMES.ORG

http://www.themes.org/

The Themes.org site has all kinds of themes for KDE. Looking for a desktop that fits your personality or makes a statement? Try here.

OPEN SOURCE ORGANIZATION

http://www.opensource.org

Open source software is an idea whose time has finally come. For twenty years it has been building momentum in the technical cultures that built the Internet and the World Wide Web. Now it's breaking out into the commercial world, and that's changing all the rules.

LINUX LAPTOP PAGE

http://www.cs.utexas.edu/users/kharker/linux-laptop/

If you have a laptop, you might want to check here before trying to install Linux on it.

LINUX PROFESSIONAL INSTITUTE (LPI)

http://www.lpi.org/

The Linux Professional Institute offers Linux certification. Although the tests cost money, LPI is non-profit and makes no money from the certifications. The tests are designed and written by the International Linux community in as open a way as possible while still protecting the integrity of the tests.

METALAB (FORMERLY SUNSITE)

http://metalab.unc.edu/

TSX-11

ftp://tsx-11.mit.edu/pub/linux/

THE LINUX KERNEL ARCHIVES

`http://www.kernel.org`

Welcome to the Linux Kernel Archives. This is the primary site for the Linux kernel source, but it has much more than just kernels—it has 20GB of disk space set aside for mirroring the largest Linux-related software archives.

KERNEL NOTES

`httpd://www.kernelnotes.org/`

Interested in what's going on with the Linux kernel? Want to know about contributing, and more? The KernelNotes site has this and links to much more to do with the kernel.

LINUX JOURNAL

`http://www.linuxjournal.com/`

The original Linux magazine, *LJ* has a paper version and an online version. The parent company, SSC (Specialized Systems Consultants) also publishes and hosts the Linux Gazette.

LINUX MAGAZINE

`http://www.linuxmagazine.com/`

A newcomer to the scene, *Linux Magazine* has both paper and online versions.

SPECIALIZED SYSTEMS CONSULTANTS

`http://www.ssc.com/`

SSC publishes the *Linux Journal* and hosts sites such as Linux Resources. They also sell handy "cheat sheets" for bash, vi, and other applications. You can find a large number of resources at this site and the next one.

LINUX RESOURCES

`http://www.linuxresources.com/`

LINUX WEEKLY NEWS

`http://www.lwn.net/`

LINUX WORLD

`http://www.linuxworld.com/`

FRESHMEAT.NET

`http://freshmeat.net/`

Freshmeat features pointers to new software as well as updates to established software. This is a good site when you are looking for something to fill a niche.

PART

VI

CH

B

LINUXBERG

http://www.linuxberg.com/

Brought to you by the TuCows folks, this site has links to thousands of software packages.

DOWNLOAD.COM

http://download.cnet.com/

A great place to find software for download. This site carries principally more mature software packages.

SOURCE FORGE

http://sourceforge.net/

The source forge is a site where aspiring developers with new software who have no Web site of their own can show off their non-commercial offerings.

SLASHDOT

http://slashdot.org/

The original geek news site, this site has caused more server crashes and network overloads than any other site. The "slashdot effect" is what happens when tens of thousands of geeks hit the link to a site within minutes of each other. Good news briefs and links, but the comment pages sometimes tend to turn into juvenile flame-fests rather quickly.

LINSIDER AND LINSIGHT

http://www.linsider.com/
http://www.linsight.com/

These two sites run by the same company contain a more balanced, mature news and Linux information site.

LINUX NEWS

http://www.linuxnews.com/

Yet another news site for Linux-specific stories. This site contains full stories that are linked to from the briefs page.

LINUX.COM

http://www.linux.com/

Linux com is a potpourri of news, information, links, and just about anything else to do with Linux. They have briefs as well as full-length articles.

SPECIFIC COMPONENTS SUPPORT

The following list of sites is more specific in nature, but a wide sampling is included. These sites are just that, a sampling. There are many, many more sites with specific Linux information—and the number of new sites is increasing.

THE LINUX KERNEL ARCHIVE

http://www.uwsg.indiana.edu/hypermail/linux/kernel/

The Linux kernel list is a majordomo mailing list hosted at vger.rutgers.edu. It exists for the discussion of kernel development issues, including new features, bug reports, and announcements of new kernel releases. This list is not for the faint of heart. It is designed for people who have some experience with the kernel and are interested in participating in the development of the kernel.

THE LINUX KERNEL

http://amelia.db.erau.edu/ldp/LDP/tlk/tlk.html

This book is for Linux enthusiasts who want to know how the Linux kernel works. It is not an internals manual. Rather, it describes the principles and mechanisms that Linux uses—how and why the Linux kernel works the way it does. Linux is a moving target; this book is based upon the current, stable, 2.0.33 sources because those are what most individuals and companies are now using.

PART

VI

CH

B

LINUX SMP

http://www.linux.org.uk/SMP/title.html

Everything you wanted to know about multiprocessor support for Linux.

LINUX USB SITE

http://www.linux-usb.org/

This site promotes itself as the central point of information on USB support under Linux.

LINUX LINKS

http://www.ai.uga.edu/~jae/linux.html

LINUX FAT32 SUPPORT

http://bmrc.berkeley.edu/people/chaffee/fat32.html

LINUX/MICROCONTROLLER HOME PAGE

http://ryeham.ee.ryerson.ca/uClinux/

LINUX AT CESDIS

http://cesdis1.gsfc.nasa.gov/linux-web/

The Center of Excellence in Space Data and Information Sciences at NASA has been a major U.S. Government supporter of Linux. The site, hosted by Donald Becker, who has written many of the Ethernet drivers for Linux, contains information about NASA's Beowulf project (Linux supercomputing clusters), network drivers, and networking technologies.

Linux in Business Settings

http://www.m-tech.ab.ca/linux-biz/

Multicast and MBONE on Linux—Overview

http://www.teksouth.com/linux/multicast/

The *MBONE* (*Multicast Backbone*) and multicast technology are an exciting branch of Internet technology that might have a major impact on how the Internet is used in the future. Where traditional IP traffic is one sender to one receiver, multicasting has the capability of allowing one sender to many receivers. Propagation can also be set to control how far traffic can go. Traffic can be restricted to a single host, site, or region—or to the whole world.

The Linux Programmer's BouncePoint

http://www.ee.mu.oz.au/linux/programming/

SSH—Products

http://www.ssh.fi/products/

This Web site contains security technology from SSH. Communications Security Ltd. forms the security backbone of several well-known products on the worldwide market. The security products are built on tested, public, cryptographic algorithms and standardized protocols. This technology provides easy access to security and the best performance available—without compromises in security.

OpenSSL

http://www.openssl.org/

Home page for the open source SSL (Secure Sockets Layer) project. This code is required for a number of applications that use SSL, including the Perl modules and OpenSSH.

OpenSSH

http://violet.ibs.com.au/openssh/

This is the site for the Linux port of OpenSSH, meant to replace the Communications Security, LTD distribution (and its non-free licensing).

FreeSSH

http://www.freessh.org/

This site serves as a central place for information, source, resources regarding free implementations of SSH.

mgetty + sendfax DOCUMENTATION CENTRE

http://www.leo.org/~doering/mgetty/

CONSISTENT BACKSPACE AND DELETE CONFIGURATION

http://www.ibbnet.nl/~anne/keyboard.html

Information on how to configure the behavior of the Backspace key and Delete key can be found at this site.

ISDN FOR LINUX

http://www.isdn4linux.de/

GHOSTSCRIPT, GHOSTVIEW, AND GSVIEW

http://www.cs.wisc.edu/~ghost/

SOUND BLASTER AWE 32/64 HOWTO

http://homepage.ruhr-uni-bochum.de/Marcus.Brinkmann/Soundblaster-AWE-HOWTO.html

This document describes how to install and configure a Sound Blaster 32 (SB AWE 32, SB AWE 64) card from Creative Labs in a Linux System using the AWE Sound Driver Extension written by Takashi Iwai. It also covers some special tools and players for the SB AWE series. Reference system is a Debian GNU/Linux System, but every other Linux Distribution also works.

ALSA PROJECT PAGE

http://www.alsa-project.org/

This site contains a wealth of information about sound cards, sound drivers, chipsets found on sound cards, and much more.

LINUX PARALLEL PORT HOME PAGE

http://www.torque.net/linux-pp.html

NSBD: NOT-SO-BAD DISTRIBUTION

http://www.bell-labs.com/project/nsbd/

LINUX PCMCIA INFORMATION

http://hyper.stanford.edu/HyperNews/get/pcmcia/home.html

BIND, DHCP, INN HOME PAGE (ISCONSORTIUM)

http://www.isc.org/

The ISC is a nonprofit corporation dedicated to production-quality software engineering for key Internet standards. Reference implementations of Internet standards often have the weight of *de facto* standards, and the ISC wants to make sure those reference implementations are properly supported. The ISC is also committed to keeping these reference implementations freely available to the Internet community.

LIN MODEMS

http://www.linmodems.org/

This site carries information about the state of support for the infamous software modems, or oft-called WinModems. They contain almost no hardware, pushing their required processing back onto the CPU.

LINUX IP MASQUERADE RESOURCE

http://ipmasq.cjb.net/

DNS TOOLS

http://www.dns.net/dnsrd/tools.html

NETATALK—ESSENTIAL FOR APPLE CONNECTIVITY

http://www.umich.edu/~rsug/netatalk/

ANDERS: NETATALK: LINUX NETATALK-HOWTO

http://thehamptons.com/anders/netatalk/

Netatalk is a package that allows a UNIX machine to supply AppleTalk print and file services on a LAN. The package supports AppleShare IP and classic AppleTalk protocols. With Netatalk, Macintosh computers can mount UNIX volumes and print to UNIX print spools as if they were standard AppleTalk network devices.

SAMBA

http://www.samba.org/

This site contains the latest Samba information and software to make MS Windows play nice with Linux by tricking Windows into thinking it's dealing with another NT server.

LINUX PLUG-INS FOR NETSCAPE

http://www.canopy.com/linuxplugins.html

XFREE86 SERVERS BY SUSE

http://www.suse.de/XSuSE/XSuSE_E.html

In cooperation with the XFree86 Project, Inc., SuSE GmbH is proud to present a small series of X servers. These servers are based on source code from XFree86-servers, but they are enhanced and extended.

THIRD-PARTY QUICKCAM SOFTWARE PAGE

http://www.cs.duke.edu/~reynolds/quickcam/

THE MESA 3D GRAPHICS LIBRARY

http://www.ssec.wisc.edu/~brianp/Mesa.html

WHIRLGIF 2.01

http://www.msg.net/utility/whirlgif/

BTTV PAGE FRAME GRABBER FOR LINUX

http://www.thp.Uni-Koeln.DE/~rjkm/linux/bttv.html

XVIDCAP—X VIDEO CAPTURE FOR LINUX

http://www.komm.hdk-berlin.de/~rasca/xvidcap/

KWINTV

http://www.mathematik.uni-kl.de/~wenk/xwintv.html

kwintv is a KDE application based on the bttv-driver by Ralph Metzler. kwintv enables you to watch TV in a window on your PC screen. It has more or less the same capabilities as xtvscreen, which is included in the bttv-driver package, but it is based on Qt, a C++ GUI application framework by Troll Tech, and integrated in the K Desktop Environment Directory of /pub/Linux/docs/linux-doc-project/module-programming-guide.

PART

VI

CH

B

INDEX

M

Other Related Titles

Practical KDE
Dennis Powell
078972216x
$29.99 US

SuSE Linux Installation and Configuration Handbook
Nazeeh Amin and Youssef A.
0789723557
$39.99 US

Linux Programming by Example
Kurt Wall
0789722151
$24.99 US

The Concise Guide to DNS and BIND
Nicolai Langfeldt
0789722739
$34.99 US

Caldera OpenLinux Installation and Configuration Handbook
Gary Wilson
0789721058
$39.99 US

C++ from Scratch
Jesse Liberty
30789720795
$29.99 US

Platinum Edition Using HTML 4, XML, and Java 1.2
Eric Ladd
078971759X
$59.99

Practical Internet
Barbara Kasser
0789722267
$24.99 US

www.quecorp.com

Red Hat Linux Installation and Configuration Handbook
Duane Hellums
0789721813
$39.99 US

Upgrading and Repairing PCs, Linux Edition
Scott Mueller
0789720752
$59.99 US

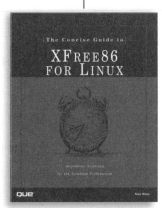

The Concise Guide to XFree86 for Linux
Aron Hsiao
0789721821
$34.99 US

All prices are subject to change.